# Government Contract Law

## The Deskbook for Procurement Professionals

# Government Contract Law

## The Deskbook for Procurement Professionals

*Based on the Contract Attorney's Course of the Judge Advocate General's School*

SECTION OF PUBLIC CONTRACT LAW
AMERICAN BAR ASSOCIATION

Printed in the United States of America.

Library of Congress Catalog Card Number 95-78269
ISBN 1-57073-175-6

Discounts are available for books ordered in bulk. Special consideration is given to state bars, CLE programs, and other bar-related organizations. Inquire at Publications Planning & Marketing, American Bar Association, 750 North Lake Shore Drive, Chicago, Illinois 60611.

00 99 98 97 96   5 4 3 2 1

# Contents

# CHAPTER 9
## *Bid Protests*

# CHAPTER 13
## *Selected Labor Standards*

## CHAPTER 14
## *Construction Contracting*

## CHAPTER 15
## *Pricing of Contract Adjustments*

## CHAPTER 16
### *Inspection, Acceptance, and Warranty*

## CHAPTER 17
### *Financing of Government Contracts*

## CHAPTER 21
### Nonappropriated Fund Contracting

## CHAPTER 22
### Minor Construction Funding

# CHAPTER 23
## *Contract Terminations for Convenience*

## CHAPTER 28
### *Contracting for Services*

# CHAPTER 29
## *Fraud: Criminal and Civil Remedies*

# Contributors

LTC John A. Krump
Chief, Contract Law Division

MAJ Douglas P. DeMoss
Senior Instructor, Contract Law Division

MAJ Andy K. Hughes
Instructor, Contract Law Division

Major Steven N. Tomanelli
Instructor and Air Force Representative

MAJ Nathanael Causey
Instructor, Contract Law Division

MAJ Timothy J. Pendolino
Instructor, Contract Law Division

MAJ Karl M. Ellcessor, III
Instructor, Contract Law Division

Mrs. Sandra M. Ralphs
Secretary, Contract Law Division

---

MAJ Patrick D. O'Hare
Instructor, Contract Law Division

---

MAJ Joseph T. Frisk
Instructor, Administrative and Civil Law Division

---

Mr. Byrd Eastham
Illustrator

Mrs. R. Chaucile Snyder
Reproduction

Our predecessors on the Faculty of the Contract Law Division

# *Preface*

One of public contract law's most important institutions has been the Judge Advocate General's School, U.S. Army, in Charlottesville, Virginia. Since its founding at the University of Michigan during World War II, the JAG School has trained military and civil service attorneys in government contract law. Its students constitute a significant percentage of the practitioners in this field and its faculty have been some of the most influential scholars in the field. This key role is best illustrated by noting that Section Officer John Kuebs and Council Member Jose Aguirre were faculty members, as were Tony Gamboa, John Jones, John Farenish, Ron Kienlin, King Culp, Gilbert Ginsberg, and Steve Schooner. Honorary faculty includes the late Gilbert Cuneo, in whose honor the Cuneo Chair at the School is named; Stanley Dees; Paul Schnitzer; Eldon Crowell; Ralph Nash; and Richard Solibakke. A host of other Section officers and members have taught at or attended JAG School, including John Miller, Don Kinlin, Karen Hastie Williams, Marshall Doke, John Pachter, David Churchill, Dan Bishop, Steve Porter, Jim Hinchman, Wendy Kirby, David Pronchick, and Les Edelman.

The centerpiece in the JAG School's government contract's curriculum is the Contract Attorneys' Course. This intensive overview to government contract law was the first introduction many of today's practitioners had. The knowledge acquired in Charlottesville gave these new government contract attorneys the confidence and skills to practice competently in this highly technical area of the law. When leaving the JAG School, a new government contract attorney would always bring home the desk book and keep it handy for future reference. As years passed, graduates often sought out recent copies of the course materials as a primary resource. Unfortunately, those who had entered the private sector were cut off from updated versions.

The Public Contract Law Section is pleased to provide practitioners in the private sector as well as the public sector, a ready source for an up-to-date version of the JAG School text. When the Section started its Fundamentals of Contract Law Course in 1994, it naturally adopted the JAG School desk book for its own text. Following on that success, the Section's Book Committee adopted the recently updated version as its second book for publication.

This single volume takes the School's two-volume course materials for the Contract Attorneys' Course and condenses it to a single volume covering the waterfront of basic government contract law. While aimed at government attorneys, this work provides a valuable resource for private sector attorneys and other contract professionals. Incorporating the changes from the Federal Acquisition Streamlining Act of 1994, this version is current, as well as complete. It represents not only the considerable efforts of the current authors, but the collective efforts of all who have preceded them

The Section of Public Contract Law believes that in making this work readily available to all public contract professionals, we contribute to the professional development of the entire public contract community. The Section hopes that our readers find it as valuable a resource as we have.

Frank B. Menaker, Jr.
Chair
Section of Public Contract Law
American Bar Association

## CHAPTER ONE

# Introduction to Government Contract Law

## I. OVERVIEW OF THE CONTRACT ATTORNEYS' COURSE (CAC).

### A. Course Goal.
Graduates of the Contract Attorneys' Course should be able to competently advise contracting officials on the propriety of proposed actions. They should be able to competently represent their agencies in contract litigation. Graduates should be able to guide contracting officials safely past pitfalls.

### B. Phase One–Contract Formation.
1. The formation phase concerns issues that arise primarily in the course of entering into a contract.
2. Major topics include:
   a. Competition.
   b. Methods of acquisition: simplified acquisition, sealed bidding, and negotiations.
   c. Contract types.
   d. Socioeconomic policies.
   e. Protests.

### C. Phase Two–Contract Performance and Special Topics.
1. The administration phase concerns the issues that arise primarily in the performance of a contract.
2. Major topics include:
   a. Contract changes.
   b. Inspection and acceptance rights of the government.
   c. Terminations for default and for the convenience of the government.
   d. Disputes.
   e. Fraud.
   f. Environmental contracting issues.
   g. Ethics in government contracting.
   h. Government information practices (FOIA).

### D. Instructional Material.
1. Instructional material includes the Government Contract Law Deskbook, Volume I (Formation Phase) and Volume II (Administration Phase).
2. Review the teaching outline in the deskbook prior to class.
3. The Deskbook is both an in-class instructional tool and a reference source after the course is over.
4. The deskbook includes two seminar problems that require the application of the general principles discussed in the conference sessions. The deskbook also includes one professional responsibility seminar problem. Review the seminar problems in advance so you may contribute meaningfully to the discussion.
5. Optional reading material:
   a. John Cibinic, Jr., and Ralph C. Nash, *Formation of Government Contracts*, published by Government Contracts Program, George Washington University, 2d edition, 1986.
   b. John Cibinic, Jr., and Ralph C. Nash, *Administration of Government Contracts*, published by Government Contracts Program, George Washington University, 3d edition, 1995.
6. A listing of some contract law terminology and common abbreviations is at Appendix A

of the Government Contract Law Deskbook, Volume I. For further information: Steve Schooner, Jr., and Ralph C. Nash, *The Government Contracts Reference Book*, published by Government Contracts Program, George Washington University, 1992.

7. A listing of some contract law research materials is at Appendix B of the Government Contract Law Deskbook, Volume I.

## II. ROLE OF THE CONTRACT ATTORNEY IN THE CONTRACTING PROCESS.

### A. Advisor to the Commander and the Contracting Officer.

1. Provide advice on how to comply with applicable laws and regulations in the award and performance of government contracts.
   a. Provide advice on Formation Phase issues.
   b. Provide advice on Administration Phase issues.
2. Provide advice on Fiscal Law issues.

### B. Litigator.

1. Litigate protests.
2. Litigate disputes.
3. Litigate collateral matters before federal bankruptcy, district, and circuit courts.

### C. Fraud Fighter.

1. Provide advice on how to prevent, detect, and correct fraud, waste, and abuse.
2. Provide litigation support for fraud cases.

### D. Business Counselor.

1. Ensure the commander and the contracting officer exercise sound business judgment.
2. Provide opinion on the exercise of sound business practices.

### E. Role of Legal Counsel in the Acquisition Process.

AR 27-1, Legal Services, Chapter 15.

1. FAR 15.805-1 indicates that legal counsel is part of the contracting officer's team.
2. Army policy provides that legal counsel participate fully in the entire acquisition process including acquisition planning through contract completion or termination and close out. AFARS 1.602-2.
   a. For negotiated or sealed bidding acquisitions in amounts of $100,000 or more, legal counsel participate as a member of the contracting officer's "team" as set forth in FAR 15.805-1, being responsible for advising as to the legal sufficiency of actions taken by the team. Each agency's regulation governing the role of the attorney in the contracting process is somewhat different. *See* AFARS 1.602-2; *compare with* NAPS Subparts 1.6 and 1.7.
   b. Legal counsel review acquisitions under $100,000 to the maximum extent consistent with the availability of legal counsel.
   c. Legal counsel shall participate in the following stages of an acquisition in addition to those areas in which existing regulations require their participation:
      (1) Review acquisition plans to ensure consistency with contract law and regulation; and
      (2) Review justifications or determinations and findings relating to actions of $100,000 or more.
3. Air Force policy provides that commanders of major commands and separate operating agencies shall issue procedures that specify a monetary threshold for obtaining legal review by the appropriate staff judge advocate on contractual documents issued by their activities. AFFARS 1.601-94.
4. Navy policy provides that contract documents shall be forwarded to the appropriate attorney or attorneys in the Office of the General Counsel for review as to form and legality and any additional pertinent comment or advice. NAPS 1.601-90.

## III. COMMERCIAL CONTRACT AND GOVERNMENT CONTRACT INTERFACE.

### A. Interrelationship of Commercial and Government Contract Law.

The government, when acting in its proprietary capacity, is bound by ordinary commercial law unless otherwise provided by statute or regulation.

> "If [the government] comes down from its position of sovereignty, and enters the domain of commerce, it submits itself to the same laws that govern individuals there." *Cooke v. United States*, 91 U.S. (1 Otto) 389, 398 (1875). *See Leadermar, Inc.*, ASBCA No. 40575, 92-2 BCA ¶ 24,919 (appellant and government traded settlement offers; each new offer effectively rejected previous offer so contractor could not revive earlier offer and accept).

**B. Federal Statutes and Regulations Preempt Commercial Law.**

Government statutes and regulations are so detailed that their unique provisions predominate over commercial law in nearly every aspect.

> "Our statute books are filled with acts authorizing the making of contracts with the government through its various officers and departments, but, in every instance, the person entering into such a contract must look to the statute under which it is made, and see for himself that this contract comes within the terms of the law." *The Floyd Acceptances*, 74 U.S. (7 Wall.) 666, 680 (1868).

**C. Role of Public Policy in Government Contract Law.**

1. The common law of federal contracts is based on public policy.
2. Contract clauses that are required by statutes or regulations are incorporated into a contract by operation of law. *G.L. Christian & Assoc. v. United States*, 160 Ct. Cl. 1, 312 F.2d 418, *cert. denied*, 375 U.S. 954 (1963) (regulations published in the *Federal Register* and issued under statutory authority have the force and effect of law).
3. Clauses that are included in a contract in violation of statutory or regulatory criteria will be read out of a contract even if physically present. *Carrier Corp.*, GSBCA No. 8516, 90-1 BCA ¶ 22,409; *Charles Breseler Co.*, ASBCA No. 22669, 78-2 BCA ¶ 13,483.
4. The government is not bound by apparent authority. *Federal Crop Ins. Corp. v. Merrill*, 332 U.S. 380 (1947).

## IV. OVERVIEW OF THE GOVERNMENT CONTRACTING PROCESS.

# THE PLAYERS

| GOVERNMENT | CONTRACTOR |
|---|---|
| Commander | Owner/CEO/Shareholders |
| Comptroller | Banker & Finance |
| Requiring Activity | Marketers |
| User | Production |
| Technical Activity | Engineering |
| Contracts Office | Contract Administration |
| Small Business Advocate | Purchasing |
| Competition Advocate | Subcontractors & Suppliers |
| Legal Office | In-house/Outside Counsel |
| Contract Administration Office | Quality Assurance |
| Defense Contract Audit Agency | Internal Auditors |

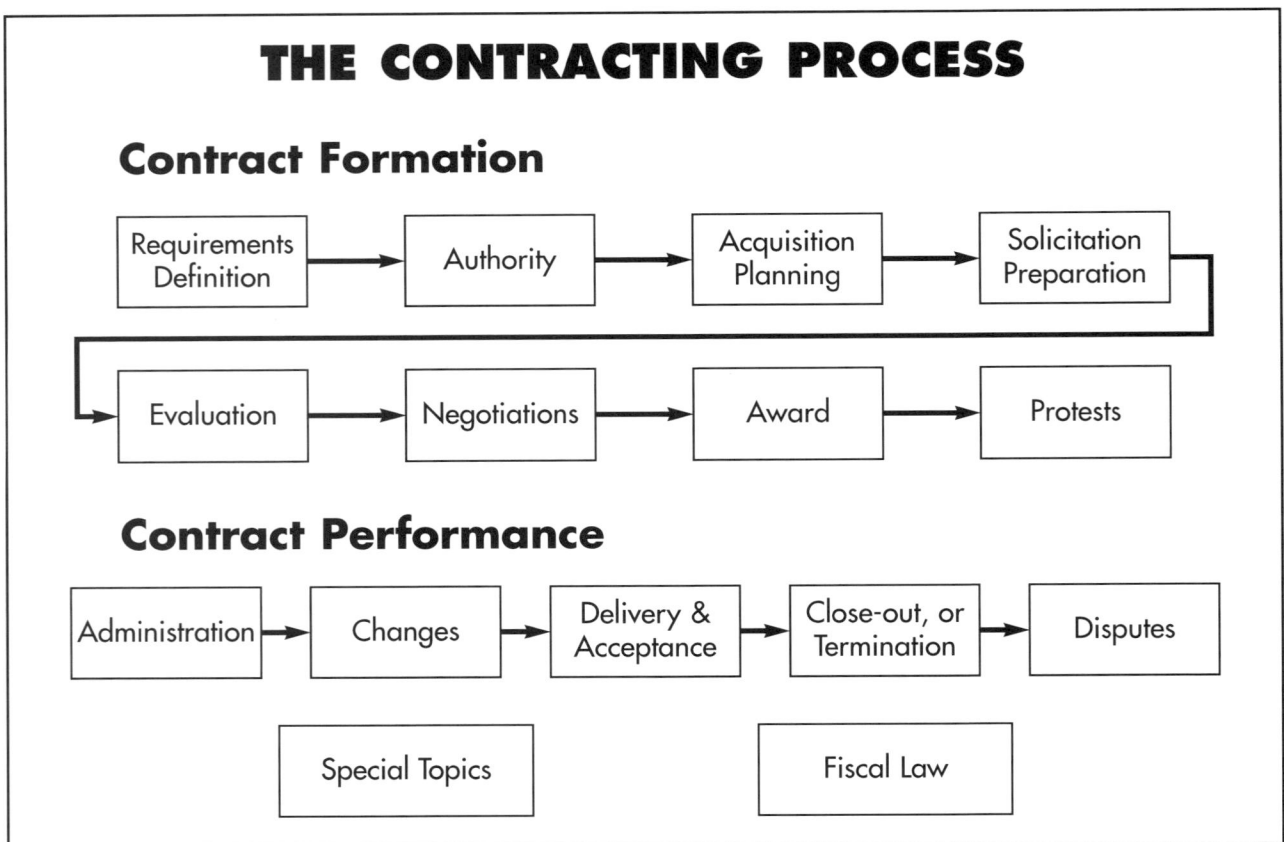

## V. CONCLUSION.

A. Contract law is a complex, challenging topic. The issues impact your agency's ability to accomplish its mission.

B. The best contract law attorneys anticipate issues and practice preventive law.

C. Preventive contract law requires insight into the objectives of the acquisition, application of complex statutory and regulatory contract and fiscal law rules, and the use of common sense and business judgement.

D. Get out of your office and meet your clients.

## CHAPTER TWO

# *Authority to Contract*

## I. INTRODUCTION.

Following this class, students should:

A. Understand the constitutional, statutory, and regulatory bases that permit federal executive agencies to contract using appropriated funds (APF).

B. Understand how individuals acquire the power to contract on behalf of the government using APFs.

C. Understand the different theories which bind the government in contract.

D. Understand the elements of a contract and the different types of government contracts.

E. Understand what constitutes an "unauthorized commitment" and be able to describe how, and by whom, unauthorized commitments may be ratified.

## II. AUTHORITY OF AGENCIES.

### A. Constitutional.

As a sovereign entity, the United States has inherent authority to contract to discharge governmental duties. *United States v. Tingey*, 30 U.S. (5 Pet.) 115 (1831). This authority to contract, however, is limited. Specifically, a government contract must:

1. not be prohibited by law; and
2. be an appropriate exercise of governmental powers and duties.

### B. Statutory.

Congress has enacted various statutes regulating the acquisition of goods and services by the government. These include the:

1. Armed Services Procurement Act of 1948 (ASPA), 10 U.S.C. §§ 2301 - 2316. The ASPA applies to the procurement of all property (except land) and services purchased with appropriated funds by the Department of Defense (DOD), Coast Guard, and National Aeronautics and Space Administration (NASA).

2. Federal Property and Administrative Services Act of 1949 (FPASA), 41 U.S.C. §§ 251-260. The FPASA governs the acquisition of all property and services, by all executive agencies *except* DOD, Coast Guard, NASA, and any agency specifically exempted by 40 U.S.C. § 474 or any other law.

3. Competition in Contracting Act of 1984 (CICA), Pub. L. No. 98-369, 98 Stat. 1175 (1984).
   a. CICA amended the ASPA and the FPASA to make them identical. Because of subsequent legislative action, they are now different in some significant respects.
   b. CICA mandates full and open competition for many, but not all, purchases of goods and services.

4. Brooks Automatic Data Processing Act, 40 U.S.C. § 759. The Brooks Automatic Data Processing Act governs the acquisition of automatic data processing equipment (ADPE) by federal agencies.

5. The Federal Acquisition Streamlining Act of 1994 (FASA), Pub. L. No. 103-355, 108 Stat. 3243 (1994). FASA amended various sections of the other statutes described above and once again eliminated some differences between ASPA and FPASA. However, FASA will not be fully effective until 1 October 1995.

6. Annual DOD Authorization and Appropriation Acts.

## C. Regulatory.

1. Federal Acquisition Regulation (FAR), codified at 48 C.F.R. chapter 1.
   a. The FAR is the principal regulation governing federal executive agencies in the use of APFs to acquire supplies and services.
   b. DOD, NASA, and the General Services Administration (GSA) issue the FAR, and changes to it, jointly.
   c. These agencies publish proposed, interim, and final changes to the FAR in the Federal Register. They issue changes to the FAR in Federal Acquisition Circulars (FAC).
2. Agency regulations. The FAR system consists of the FAR and the agency regulations that implement or supplement it. The following regulations supplement the FAR.
   a. Defense Federal Acquisition Regulation Supplement (DFARS), codified at 48 C.F.R. chapter 2. The Defense Acquisition Regulation (DAR) Council publishes DFARS changes/proposed changes in the Federal Register, and issues them as Defense Acquisition Circulars (DAC).
   b. Army Federal Acquisition Regulation Supplement (AFARS).
   c. Air Force Federal Acquisition Regulation Supplement (AFFARS).
   d. Navy Acquisition Procedures Supplement (NAPS).
   e. The AFARS, AFFARS, and NAPS are not codified in the C.F.R. The military departments do not publish changes to these regulations in the Federal Register but, instead, issue them pursuant to departmental procedures.
3. Major command and local command regulations.

## III. AUTHORITY OF PERSONNEL.

### A. Contracting Authority.

The FAR vests contracting authority in the head of the agency (e.g., Secretary of the Army). In turn, the head of the agency may establish subordinate contracting activities and delegate broad contracting authority to the heads of the subordinate activities. FAR 1.601.

1. The Heads of Contracting Activities (HCA) have overall responsibility for managing all contracting actions within their activities. There are approximately 72 DOD contracting activities, plus others who possess contracting authority delegated by the heads of the various defense agencies. DFARS 202.101.
   a. HCAs are contracting officers because of their position. *See* FAR 1.601; FAR 2.101.
   b. Agency heads or their designees select, appoint, and terminate the appointment of contracting officers below the HCA level. FAR 1.601; FAR 1.603.
2. In the Army, the Principal Assistant Responsible for Contracting (PARC) is the senior staff official responsible for oversight and administration of the contracting function for an Army contracting activity, and the HCA's alter ego for all delegated contract functions. The PARC has direct access to the HCA and should be one organizational level above the contracting office(s) within the HCA's command. AFARS 1.601-90(c). The Air Force and the Navy also permit delegation of contracting authority to certain deputies. AFFARS 5301.601-92; NAPS 5201.601.
3. Generally, only a contracting officer ("KO" or "CO") may enter into, administer, or terminate contracts, and make related determinations and findings. Different contracting officers may perform different functions. The term "contracting officer" includes certain authorized representatives of the contracting officer acting within the limits of authority delegated by the contracting officer. FAR 2.101.
   a. Only contracting officers may enter into and sign contracts on behalf of the government. FAR 1.601.
   b. Contracting officers may bind the government only within the limits of their authority. FAR 1.602-1(a).

4. Contracting officers may authorize selected individuals to administer contracts and perform other functions relating to it (e.g., contracting officer representatives (COR), inspectors). However, these individuals may not contract on behalf of the government except in very limited circumstances. FAR 42.202; AFARS 42.9001; AFARS 42.9002.

## B. Actual Authority.

Generally, the government is bound only by government agents acting within the scope of their authority to contract.

1. The acts of unauthorized government agents or agents who exceed their contracting authority do not bind the government. The government is not bound by apparent authority. *Federal Crop Ins. Corp. v. Merrill*, 332 U.S. 380 (1947) (government agent lacked authority to bind government to wheat insurance contract); *HTC Indus., Inc.*, ASBCA No. 40562, 93-1 BCA ¶ 25,560, *mot. for recon. denied*, 93-2 BCA ¶ 25,701 (recovery denied although contracting officer's technical representative ordered continued performance while he sought additional funding).

2. In contrast, contractors are bound by apparent authority. *American Anchor & Chain Corp. v. United States*, 166 Ct. Cl. 1, 331 F.2d 860 (1964) (government justified in assuming that contractor's plant manager acted with authority); *but see Woodington Corp.*, ASBCA No. 37885, 91-1 BCA ¶ 23,579 (bilateral agreements did not bind contractor because government negotiators lacked authority to contract).

3. A contracting officer may delegate actual authority to contract orally or in writing. *See Farr Bros., Inc.*, ASBCA No. 42658, 92-2 BCA ¶ 24,991 (CO delegated authority to order suspension of work).

   a. Except for "micropurchase" contracting officers (contracting officers with a maximum authority of $2,500), the FAR requires appointment of contracting officers in writing on a "Certificate of Appointment," Standard Form 1402, which must state any limitations on the contracting officer's authority. FAR 1.603-3. This form is commonly called the contracting officer's "warrant." *See* page 12.

   b. In an emergency, a person may delegate contracting authority orally. However, the delegating official should reduce to writing the scope of the contracting officer's authority as soon as practicable.

## C. Theories That Bind the Government.

Although the general rule is that the government is not bound by the unauthorized acts of its employees, courts and boards often permit contractors to recover based upon the actions of non-contracting officers.

1. Implied Actual Authority. Courts and boards may find implied authority to contract if the questionable acts, orders, or commitments of a government employee are an integral or inherent part of that person's assigned duties. *See H. Landau & Co. v. United States*, 886 F.2d 322, 324 (Fed. Cir. 1989); *Sigma Constr. Co.*, ASBCA No. 37040, 91-2 BCA ¶ 23,926 (exigent circumstance [drying cement] plus contract administrator at work site conferred authority to direct changes). *Jordan & Nobles Constr. Co.*, GSBCA No. 8349, 91-1 BCA ¶ 23,659 (contractor recovery after COR directed use of wrong color brick); *Switlik Parachute Co.*, ASBCA No. 17920, 74-2 BCA ¶ 10,970 (quality assurance representative [QAR] had implied authority to order 100% testing of inflatable rafts). *Cf. RMTC Sys.*, AGBCA No. 88-198-1, 91-2 BCA ¶ 23,873 (shipment before purchase order in response to unauthorized request created no contract).

2. Emergencies. Government employees may obligate the government if immediate action is necessary to save property or lives. *Philadelphia Suburban Corp. v. United States*, 217 Ct. Cl. 705 (1978) (Coast Guard liable for firefighting foam following collision of two ships). *Cf. City of El Centro v. United States*, 922 F.2d 816 (Fed. Cir. 1990), *cert.*

*denied*, 111 S. Ct. 2851 (1991) (government not liable for illegal aliens' medical care following high speed chase and collision).

3. Ratification.

   a. A contracting officer may ratify an unauthorized commitment, and, thereby, bind the government, by having actual or constructive knowledge of the unauthorized commitment and adopting, expressly or impliedly, the act as his own. This is known as ratification. *Reliable Disposal Co.*, ASBCA No. 40100, 91-2 BCA ¶ 23,895 (CO ratified unauthorized commitment by requesting payment of the contractor's invoice); *Tripod, Inc.*, ASBCA No. 25104, 89-1 BCA ¶ 21,305 (CO's knowledge of contractor's complaints and review of inspection reports evidenced implicit ratification).

   b. FAR 1.602-3 provides the contracting officer authority to ratify certain unauthorized commitments. *See* section V, *infra*. However, the contracting officer's failure to process a claim under the procedures of FAR 1.602-3 does not preclude ratification by implication. *Reliable Disposal Co.*, ASBCA No. 40100, 91-2 BCA ¶ 23,895; *see generally* AR 37-1, para. 20-98.

   c. Contracting officers may ratify unauthorized commitments inadvertently. *See, e.g., HFS, Inc.*, ASBCA No. 43748, 92-3 BCA ¶ 25,198 (delivery orders issued after contract complete); *T.W. Cole*, PSBCA No. 3076, 92-3 BCA ¶ 25,091 (contracting officer retained desks following unauthorized purchase); *Reliable Disposal Co.*, ASBCA No. 40100, 91-2 BCA ¶ 23,895 (request to fund garbage disposal contractor ratified unauthorized commitment); *Romac, Inc.*, ASBCA No. 41150, 91-2 BCA ¶ 23,918 (offer to pay if contractor could prove quantity of replacement materials used ratified commitment); *Mick DeWall Constr.*, PSBCA No. 2580, 91-1 BCA ¶ 23,510 (consideration of claim on the merits plus failure to rebut evidence that COR had CO's authorization to direct change ratified commitment).

4. Imputed Knowledge. When the relationship between two persons creates a presumption that one would have informed the contracting officer of certain events, the boards may impute the knowledge of the person making the unauthorized commitment to the contracting officer. *KRW, Inc.*, DOT BCA No. 2572, 94-1 BCA ¶ 26,435; *Leiden Corp.*, ASBCA No. 26136, 83-2 BCA ¶ 16,612, *mot. for recon. denied*, 84-1 BCA ¶ 16,947.

5. Estoppel. A contractor's reasonable, detrimental reliance on representations by a government employee may estop the government from denying liability for the actions of that employee. *Burnside-Ott Aviation Training Ctr., Inc. v. United States*, 985 F.2d 1574 (Fed. Cir. 1993). *See also, OAO Corp. v. United States*, 17 Cl. Ct. 91 (1989) (government liable for start-up costs for AF early warning system); *Lockheed Shipbldg. & Constr. Co.*, ASBCA No. 18460, 75-1 BCA ¶ 11,246, *aff'd on recon.*, 75-2 BCA ¶ 11,566 (government estopped by Deputy Secretary of Defense's consent to settlement agreement). *But see Office of Personnel Mgmt. v. Richmond*, 496 U.S. 414, *reh'g denied*, 497 U.S. 1046 (1990) (no pecuniary liability based on government employee's false statement if payment is barred by statute or validly promulgated regulation).

   a. To prove estoppel, a party must establish:

     (1) knowledge of the facts, by the party to be estopped;

     (2) intent, by the estoped party, that his conduct shall be acted upon, or actions such that the party asserting estoppel has a right to believe it is so intended;

     (3) ignorance of the true facts by the party asserting estoppel; and

     (4) detrimental reliance. *United States v. Georgia-Pacific Co.*, 421 F.2d 92 (9th Cir. 1970).

   b. Additionally, the contractor asserting estoppel against the government must establish that the action or inaction involved was within the scope of authority of the government representative. *State St. Mgmt. Corp. v. Gen. Servs. Admin.*, GSBCA No. 12374, 94-1 BCA ¶ 26,500; *Atlantic Gulf & Pac. Co. of Manila v. United States*, 207 Ct. Cl. 995 (1975).

6. Laches. If unreasonable and unexcused government delay prejudices a contractor's rights, the contractor may assert the defense of laches to defeat an otherwise valid government claim. *JANA, Inc. v. United States*, 936 F.2d 1265 (Fed. Cir. 1991), *cert. denied*, 112 S. Ct. 869 (1992) (no defense of laches because the government had no knowledge of claim until after audit, which was conducted in a reasonable fashion and time).

7. Waiver. If the government fails to assert its rights (e.g., to terminate for default) in a reasonable time, and the contractor relies to its detriment upon the government's actions, the courts/boards may hold that the government has waived its rights entirely. *Joseph DeVito v. United States*, 188 Ct. Cl. 979 (1969) (48-day government delay required conversion of termination for default to termination for convenience). *Cf. Twelfth & L*, GSBCA No. 10214, 90-3 BCA ¶ 23,284 (no waiver because no detrimental reliance although government failed to object to defective toilet seat cover dispensers for 14 years).

## IV. METHODS OF CONTRACT FORMATION.

### A. Definition of a Contract.
A contract is a mutually binding legal relationship obligating the seller to furnish supplies and services (including construction) and the buyer to pay for them. It includes all types of commitments obligating the government to expend appropriated funds and, except as otherwise authorized, must be in writing. Contracts include bilateral agreements; job orders or task letters issued under a Basic Ordering Agreement; letter contracts; and orders, such as pur-

chase orders, under which the contract becomes effective by written acceptance or performance. FAR 2.101; *Texas Instr., Inc. v. United States*, 922 F.2d 810 (Fed. Cir. 1990); *Robinson Contracting Co. v. United States*, 16 Cl. Ct. 676 (1989).

### B. Express Contract.
An express contract is a mutually binding written agreement. *Pacific Gas & Elec. Co. v. United States*, 3 Cl. Ct. 329 (1983), *aff'd*, 738 F.2d 452 (Fed. Cir. 1984). The elements of an express contract are:
1. mutuality of intent;
2. consideration;
3. lack of ambiguity in the offer and acceptance; and
4. conduct by an officer having the actual authority to bind the government.

### C. Implied-in-Fact Contract.
An implied-in-fact contract is a mutually binding agreement inferred from the conduct of the parties. *Baltimore and Ohio Ry. v. United States*, 261 U.S. 592, 597 (1923); *Essen Mall Properties v. United States*, 21 Cl. Ct. 430 (1990); *OAO Corp. v. United States*, supra. It has the same elements as an express contract. *Chloe-Kelly, Inc.*, ASBCA No. 43481, 94-1 BCA ¶ 26,431. *See generally* Willard L. Boyd III, *Implied-in-Fact Contract: Contractual Recovery against the Government without an Express Agreement*, 21 Pub. Cont. L. J. 84-128 (Fall 1991). However, actual mental assent is not required. *United Int'l Investigative Servs. v. United States*, 26 Cl. Ct. 892 (1992) (assent inferred from continued dealings of the parties after contract became voidable).

### D. Implied-in-Law Contract.
An implied-in-law contract is not a true agreement to contract. It requires neither mutuality of intent nor mutual assent. In an implied-in-law contract, the law imposes a duty in equity to contract to prevent unjust enrichment. *Chavez v. United States*, 18 Cl. Ct. 540 (1989) (motion to dismiss granted because government repre-

sentative lacked contracting authority); *Eaton Corp.*, ASBCA No. 38386, 91-1 BCA ¶ 23,398. The government is not bound by implied-in-law contracts because neither the Contract Disputes Act (CDA) nor the Tucker Act grants jurisdiction over implied-in-law contracts. *See Merritt v. United States*, 267 U.S. 338, 341 (1925); *Gould, Inc. v. United States*, 29 Fed. Cl. 758 (1993); 41 U.S.C. §§ 601-613; 28 U.S.C. §§ 1346 and 1491.

### E. Oral Contract.

1. The government may enter into binding, oral contracts. *Lance Dickinson & Co.*, ASBCA No. 36804, 89-3 BCA ¶ 22,198.
2. The elements of an oral contract and a mutually binding written contract are the same.
3. However, an agency must receive documentary evidence before recording an obligation of the United States. 31 U.S.C. § 1501. This requirement has been construed as a federal statute of frauds. *United States v. Am. Renaissance Lines, Inc.*, 494 F.2d 1059 (D.C. Cir. 1974), *cert. denied*, 419 U.S. 1020 (1974).

## V. UNAUTHORIZED COMMITMENTS.

### A. Definition.

An unauthorized commitment is an agreement that is nonbinding solely because the government representative who made it lacked the authority to enter into that agreement. FAR 1.602-3.

### B. Ratification.

1. Ratification is the act of approving an unauthorized commitment, by an official who has the authority to do so, for the purpose of paying for supplies or services provided to the government as a result of an unauthorized commitment. FAR 1.602-3(a).
2. Contracting officers may ratify certain unauthorized commitments. FAR 1.602-3. *See also* AFARS 1.602-3(b)(2); AR 37-1, para. 20-18; NAPS 5201.602-3; AFFARS 5301.602-3.
3. Contracting officers may ratify unauthorized commitments if—

   a. The government has received and accepted supplies or services, or the government has obtained or will obtain a benefit from the contractor's performance of an unauthorized commitment.
   b. At the time the unauthorized commitment occurred, the ratifying official could have entered into, or could have granted authority to another to enter into, a contractual commitment which the official still has authority to exercise.
   c. The resulting contract otherwise would have been proper if made by an appropriate contracting officer.
   d. The price is fair and reasonable.
   e. The contracting officer recommends payment and legal counsel concurs, unless agency procedures expressly do not require such concurrence.
   f. Funds are available and were available when the unauthorized commitment occurred.
   g. Ratification is within limitations prescribed by the agency.
4. Army HCAs may delegate the authority to approve ratification actions, without the authority to redelegate, to the following individuals.
   a. PARC (for amounts of $25,000 or less) (AFARS 1.602-3(b)(3)(i)); and
   b. Chiefs of Contracting Offices (for amounts of $2,500 or less) (AFARS 1.602-3(b)(3)(ii)).
5. The Air Force and the Navy also permit ratification of unauthorized commitments, but their limitations are different than those of the Army. *See* AFFARS 5301.602-3; NAPS 5201.602-3.

### C. Alternatives to Ratification.

1. Doubtful claims. The General Accounting Office will decide doubtful claims, upon request. 31 U.S.C. §§ 3529, 3702; AR 37-1, para. 20-19.
2. CDA claims. The United States Court of Federal Claims and the various boards of contract appeals will decide CDA claims that

have been denied by contracting officers, upon timely appeal to one of these forums. 41 U.S.C. §§ 601-613; FAR Subpart 33.2.

3. Requests for extraordinary contractual relief. Contractors may request extraordinary contractual relief in the interest of national defense. Pub. L. No. 85-804 (50 U.S.C. §§ 1431-1435); FAR Part 50; *Remington Arms Co.*, ACAB 1238, 4 ECR ¶ 59 (1991) (contract amended to allow $70.5 million for retiree health and life insurance benefit costs).

## VI. CONCLUSION.

The government, acting in its proprietary capacity, purchases goods and services costing billions of dollars annually. Although normally bound in contract only by persons possessing actual authority to contract, the government may be bound by persons without contracting authority in certain circumstances. Occasionally, the government may choose to ratify unauthorized commitments. Judge advocates, as legal advisors to commanders and contracting activities, must understand how the government enters into contracts and how it ratifies unauthorized commitments.

# CERTIFICATE OF APPOINTMENT

## Certificate of Appointment

Under authority vested in the undersigned and in conformance with Subpart 1.6 of the Federal Acquisition Regulation

DEWITTFIELD A. HENRY

is appointed

## Contracting Officer

for the

## United States of America

Subject to the limitations contained in the Federal Acquisition Regulation and to the following:

This appointment provides the authority to execute contractual documents pursuant to Part 13, Part 8, Subparts 8.4 through 8.7, and to execute delivery orders against existing contracts pursuant to Part 39 and in accordance with the provisions of requirements contracts and Federal Supply Schedules (GSA) contracts for ADPE, to include software, when and as specifically authorized in writing by the PARC.
Unless sooner terminated, this appointment is effective as long as the appointee is assigned to:

Commandant, The Judge Advocate General's School (USA), Charlottesville, Virginia

_____
(Organization)

Headquarters, U.S. Army Training & Doctrine Command

_____
(Agency/Department)

O. WAYNE DONNHOUR, COL, GS
Principal Assistant Responsible for Contracting

_____
(Signature and Title)

23 July 1993

_____
(Date)

T-562

_____
(No.)

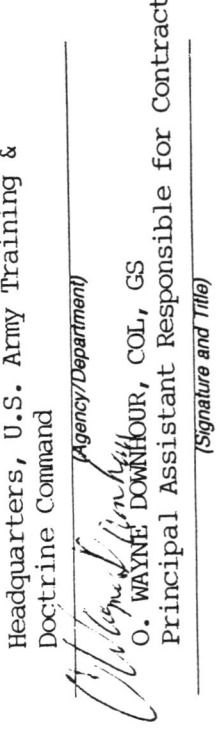

STANDARD FORM 1402 (10-83)
Prescribed by GSA
FAR (48 CFR) 53 201-1

NSN7540-01-152-5812
1402-101

## CHAPTER THREE

# *Types of Contracts*

## I. INTRODUCTION.

*[T]he determination of the type of contract the parties entered into is a question of law and is not controlled by labels or contract provision. . . . [One] must look beyond the first page of the contract to determine the legal rights for which the parties bargained, and only then characterize the contract.*

> —Court of Federal Claims,
> *Crown Laundry & Dry Cleaners, Inc. v. United States,*
> 29 Fed. Cl. 506 (1993).

Following this block of instruction, the student should:

A. Understand the fundamental differences between fixed- price and cost-reimbursement contracts.

B. Know the prerequisites that must be met before the government can use a cost-reimbursement contract.

C. Know the factors that a contracting officer must consider in selecting a contract type.

## II. CONTRACT TYPES—CATEGORIZED BY PRICE.

### A. Fixed-Price Contracts.

FAR Subpart 16.2. The contractor promises to perform at a fixed-price, and bears the responsibility for increased costs of performance. *ITT Arctic Servs., Inc. v. United States*, 207 Ct. Cl. 743 (1975); *Chevron U.S.A., Inc.*, ASBCA No. 32323, 90-1 BCA ¶ 22,602 (the risk of increased performance costs in a fixed-price contract is on the contractor absent a

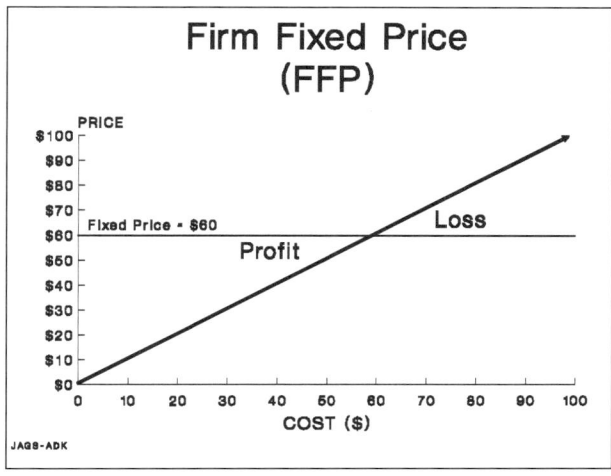

**Figure 1**

clause stating otherwise); *DK's Precision Mach. & Mfg.*, ASBCA No. 39616, 90-2 BCA ¶ 22,830.

1. Firm-Fixed-Price Contract (FFP). FAR 16.202. (Figure 1)

a. Appropriate for use when:

(1) A reasonably accurate cost estimate is available.

(2) A fair and reasonable price can be established.

(3) The specifications are reasonably clear and definite or describe a commercial item, and adequate competition is expected. *Delco Elec. Corp.*, B-244559, Oct. 29, 1991, 91-2 CPD ¶ 391 (selection of contract type committed to agency discretion and selection of FFP not unreasonable).

b. Use of firm-fixed-price contracts in research and development is limited by regulation and policy. FAR 35.006; DFARS 235.006. However, agencies may not restructure older fixed-price development

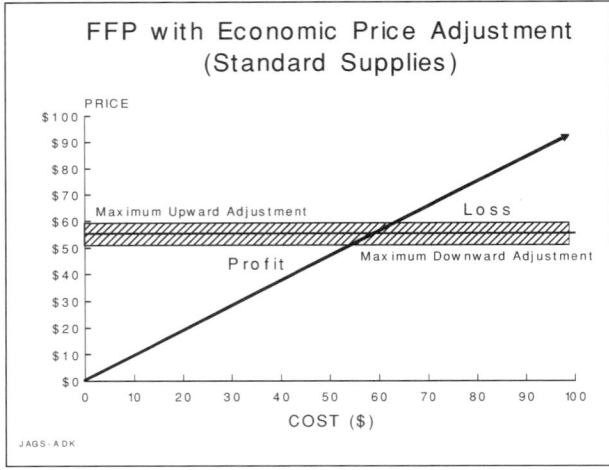

**Figure 2**

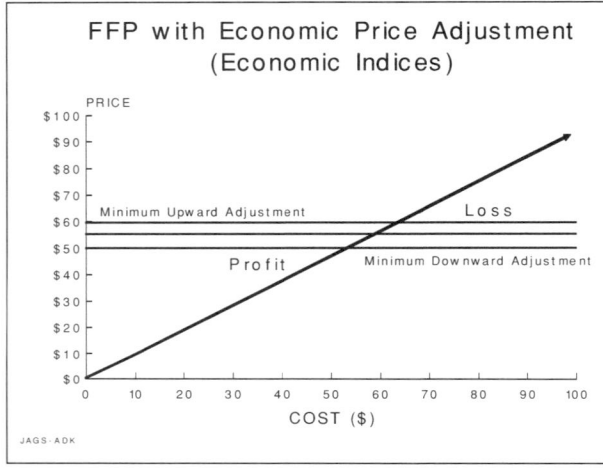

**Figure 3**

contracts without prior approval from DOD.

2. Fixed-price Contract with Economic Price Adjustment (FP w/ EPA). FAR 16.203.

a. The EPA clause, FAR 52.216-2, provides that the government assumes a portion of the cost risk of certain unforeseeable price fluctuations, such as material or wage increases. The EPA provision permits contractors to eliminate contingencies for these potential costs.

b. The contract price will be adjusted later if the contingencies occur.

c. Methods of adjustment for economic price adjustment clauses. FAR 16.203-1.

   (1) Established prices of the contractor. (Figure 2)

(2) Actual costs of the contractor. Variation in the specified costs must have at least a 3% impact on the contract price before any adjustment is required. FAR 52.216-4(c)(3).

(3) National cost indices. *See, e.g., MAPCO Alaska Petroleum v. United States*, 27 Fed. Cl. 405 (1993). (Figure 3)

(4) Moving base periods are unauthorized. *Craft Mach. Works, Inc.*, ASBCA No. 35167, 90-3 BCA ¶ 23,095 (moving base periods inconsistent with DFARS, which states that EPAs protect fluctuations from price levels at time of award).

(5) Two ceilings are authorized. *Commercial Energies, Inc.*, B-243616, Aug. 15, 1991, 91-2 CPD ¶ 152 (agency could use two ceiling in FFP w/ EPA because the ceilings protected the government against two contingencies).

d. Limitations. The contracting officer must determine use of the FP w/EPA contract is necessary. FAR 16.203-3.

e. EPA clauses are not unconscionable. *Glopak Corp. v. United States*, 851 F.2d 334 (Fed. Cir. 1988). Contractor may inadvertently waive its entitlement to an adjustment by not submitting its request within the time specified in the contract. *Betaco Indus.*, 29 Fed. Cl. 318 (1993).

3. Fixed-Price Redeterminable Contract (FP-R). FAR 16.205 and 16.206.

a. Prospective. Price is fixed for initial quantities, but is adjusted periodically for future quantities based upon the contractor's cost experience. This type is useful on initial production contracts.

b. Retroactive. Price for work already performed is subject to redetermination based upon the contractor's actual cost experience. This type is useful on small R&D contracts and other contracts where unresolved disagreements over cost accounting issues may affect price significantly.

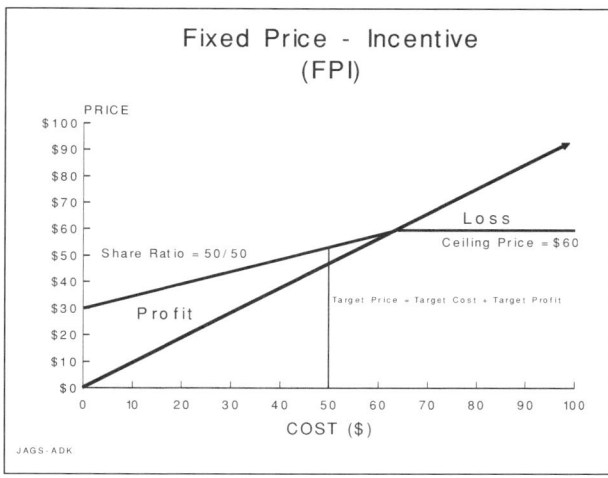

**Figure 4**

4. Fixed-Price-Incentive Contract (FPI). FAR 16.403, AFFARS 5316.403. (Figure 4)
   a. The contractor must complete a specified amount of work for a fixed-price.
   b. The government and the contractor agree in advance on a share ratio that will be used to determine how they will share cost underruns.
   c. The contractor bears all costs above the fixed-price.

**B. Cost-Reimbursement Contracts.**
FAR Subpart 16.3.
1. The contractor promises to use its "best efforts" to perform the contract within its cost estimate, but the government bears most or all of the responsibility for increased performance costs.
2. The government pays the contractor's allowable costs plus a fee (often erroneously called profit) as prescribed in the contract.
3. To be allowable, cost must be reasonable, allocable, properly accounted for, and not specifically disallowed.
4. The contracting officer is no longer required to execute a Determination and Finding (D&F) that a cost-type contract is most advantageous to the government. The statutory requirement was repealed by the Federal Acquisition Streamlining Act of 1994, Pub. L. No. 103-355, § 1021, 108 Stat. 3243, 3257 (repealing 10 U.S.C. § 2306(c)). The

FAR Council has issued an interim rule deleting this requirement from FAR 16.301-3 and 16.403. 59 Fed. Reg. 64,784 (1994).
5. The decision to use a cost-type contract is within the contracting officer's discretion. *Compare Crimson Enters.*, B-243193, June 10, 1991, 91-1 CPD ¶ 557 (decision to use cost-type contract reasonable considering uncertainty over requirements causing multiple changes), *with Delco Elec. Corp.*, B-244559, Oct. 29, 1991, 91-2 CPD ¶ 391 (selection of type committed to agency discretion and selection of firm-fixed-price found reasonable).
6. Limitations on cost-type contracts. FAR 16.301-3.
   a. Contractor must have an adequate cost accounting system. *See CrystaComm, Inc.*, ASBCA No. 37177, 90-2 BCA ¶ 22,692 (contractor failed to set up required cost accounting system).
   b. The government must be able to exercise adequate surveillance to ensure reasonable efficiency.
   c. Cost ceilings are imposed through the Limitation of Cost clause, FAR 52.232-20, or the Limitation of Funds clause, FAR 52.232-22.
      (1) Contractor must give the contracting officer advance notice of potential cost overruns.
      (2) FAR 32.704 provides that a contracting officer must, upon receipt of notice:
         (a) Fund continued performance;
         (b) Terminate the contract for convenience;
         (c) Inform the contractor that no additional funds will be allotted to the contract, direct it to submit a proposal for fee adjustment, and inform the contractor that it may request termination for convenience; or
         (d) Inform the contractor that the government is seeking additional funds, continued performance is at its own risk, and it may request a

termination for convenience of the government.

(3) The contractor may not recover costs above the ceiling unless the contracting officer authorizes the contractor to exceed the ceiling. *Hughes Aircraft Corp.*, ASBCA No. 24601, 83-1 BCA ¶ 16,396; *OAO Corp.*, DOT CAB No. 1280, 83-1 BCA ¶ 16,379; *RMI, Inc. v. United States*, 800 F.2d 246 (Fed. Cir. 1986).

(4) Exceptions to this rule include:

    (a) The overrun was unforeseeable. *General Elec. Co. v. United States*, 194 Ct. Cl. 678, 440 F.2d 420 (1971); *RMI, Inc. v. United States*, 800 F.2d 246 (Fed. Cir. 1986).

    (b) Estoppel. *American Elec. Labs., Inc. v. United States*, 774 F.2d 1110 (Fed. Cir. 1985) (successfully asserted); *Hydrothermal Energy Corp. v. United States*, 26 Cl. Ct. 7 (1992); *Southwest Marine of San Francisco, Inc.*, ASBCA No. 33404, 89-1 BCA ¶ 21,425 (unsuccessfully asserted).

d. Limitation on maximum fee. 10 U.S.C. § 2306(d); 41 U.S.C. § 254(b); FAR 15.903(d).

(1) Maximum fee limitations are based on the estimated cost at the time of award, not on the actual costs incurred.

(2) For research and development contracts, the maximum fee is a specific amount no greater than 15% of estimated costs at the time of award.

(3) For contracts other than R&D contracts, the maximum fee is a specific amount no greater than 10% of estimated costs at the time of award.

(4) In architect-engineer (A-E) contracts, the contract price (cost plus fee) for the A-E services may not exceed 6% of the estimated project cost. *Hengel Assocs., P.C.*, VABCA No. 3921, 94-3 BCA ¶ 27,080.

(5) These limitations are statutory for cost-plus-fixed-fee contracts and regulatory for other cost-type contracts.

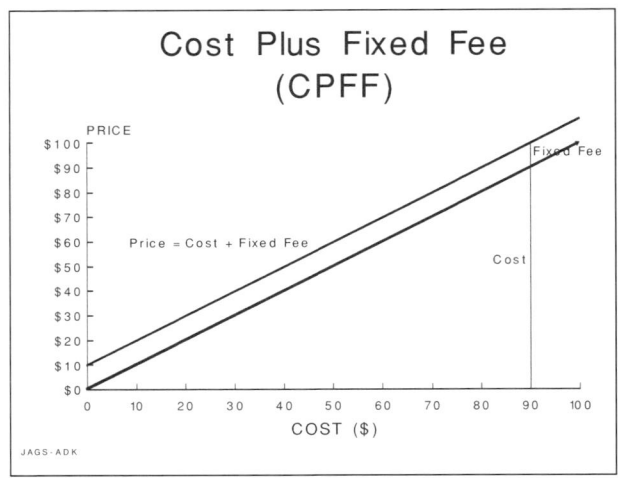

**Figure 5**

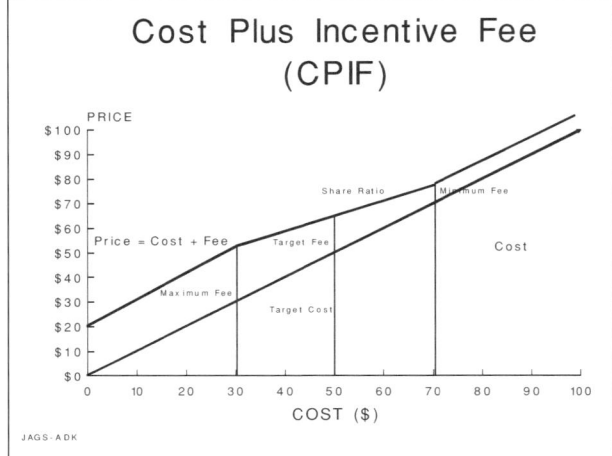

**Figure 6**

7. Cost-Plus-Fixed-Fee (CPFF) Contract. FAR 16.306. (Figure 5)

a. The contract price is the contractor's allowable costs, plus a fixed fee which is negotiated and set prior to award.

b. The fixed fee may be a loss. *See Lockheed-Georgia Co., Div. of Lockheed Corp.*, ASBCA No. 27660, 90-3 BCA ¶ 22,957 (cost plus $200 million fixed loss on initial C-5A production contract).

c. DOD agencies may not use CPFF contracts on construction contracts over $25,000 without approval of the Secretary of Defense or his delegee. Pub. L. No. 103-110, § 101, 107 Stat. 1037, 1041 (1993).

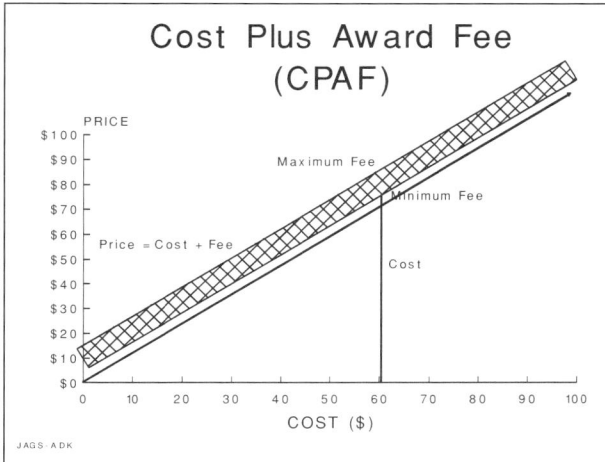

**Figure 7**

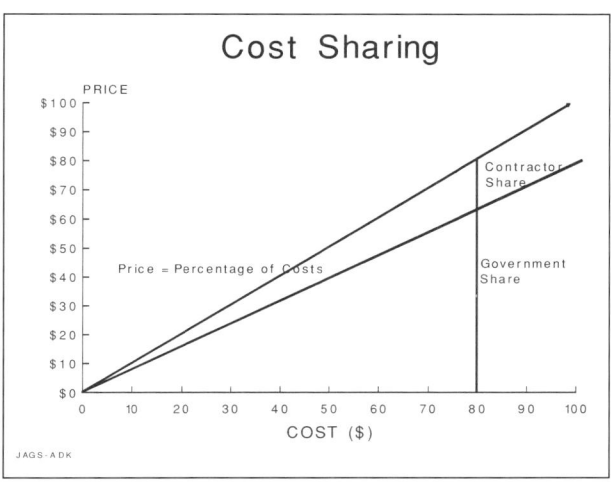

**Figure 9**

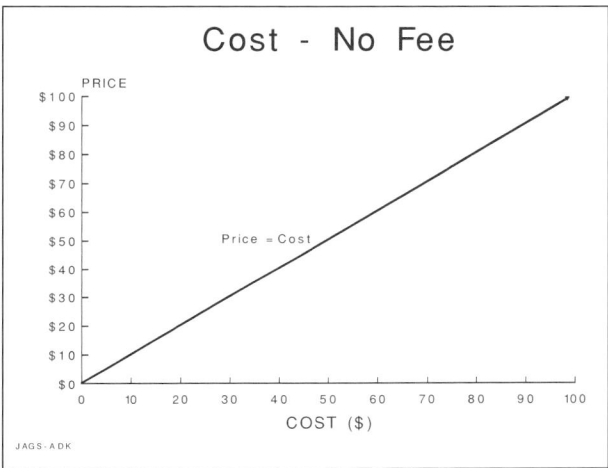

**Figure 8**

8. Cost-Plus-Incentive-Fee Contract (CPIF). FAR 16.304, FAR 16.404-1. (Figure 6)

   a. Some of the cost risk is transferred to the contractor by requiring it to share in over-runs and underruns through changes in its target fee.

   b. The government must incentivize cost. FAR 16.402-1(a).

   c. The government may combine non-cost incentives with cost incentives. FAR 16.404-1(b)(2).

9. Cost-Plus-Award-Fee (CPAF) Contract. FAR 16.305 and 16.404-2. (Figure 7)

   a. The contractor receives its costs; a base fee, that is fixed at award; and, possibly, an additional award fee based upon the quality of the contractor's performance.

b. Award fee is determined unilaterally by the contracting officer or Award Fee Determining Official.

   (1) The typical award fee clause states that the award fee decision is not subject to the Disputes Clause of the contract.

   (2) The ASBCA has decided disputes regarding award fees and similar "non-disputable" decisions. *Technical Support Servs., Inc.*, ASBCA No. 37976, 89-2 BCA ¶ 21,861 (availability of the award fee); *Burnside-Ott Aviation Training Cntr.*, ASBCA No. 43184, 94-1 BCA ¶ 26,590 (board can consider amount of award fee to determine whether contracting officer's decision was arbitrary and capricious.

   c. Limitations on base fee: For DOD con-tracts, base fees are limited to 3% of the estimated cost at the time of award. DFARS 216.404-2(c). *But see* FAR 15.901 (agencies shall not establish ceilings).

   d. Other types of contracts may include award fees, e.g., Firm-Fixed-Price. DFARS 216.470.

10. Cost Contract. FAR 16.302. (Figure 8)

   a. The contractor receives its allowable costs but no fee.

   b. Normally used where contractor will receive benefit from the contract effort and in contracts with educational institutions.

11. Cost-Sharing Contract. FAR 16.303. (Figure 9)

a. The contractor receives only a portion of its costs. Therefore, it bears some of the risk of overruns.

b. Normally used where the contractor will receive benefit from the effort.

**C. Level of Effort Contract.**

FAR 16.6.

1. Unlike the typical completion contract, the contractor need not accomplish a specific task to complete a level of effort contract. It need only devote a specific amount of labor towards the task.

2. The contract usually specifies the type of labor or professional skill required and an estimate of the number of hours of each type of "labor."

3. Time-and-Materials (T&M), FAR 16.601, and Labor-Hour (L-H) Contracts, FAR 16.602.

a. The work being acquired is defined as a specified number of hours effort by an individual of a certain skill level.

b. The contract is priced at a specified firm-fixed-price per labor hour for each skill level. In a T&M contract, materials are priced at cost plus material overhead. *JANA, Inc. v. United States*, 936 F.2d 1265 (Fed. Cir. 1991) (contractor had to repay payments on a T&M contract unsupported by labor records because it failed to maintain adequate labor records).

c. T & M contracts and Labor-Hour contracts are used when it is impossible at the outset to estimate accurately the extent or duration of work. The contracting officer must prepare a D&F indicating that no other contract type is suitable. FAR 16.601(c); *The Saxon Corp.*, B-232694, Jan. 9, 1989, 89-1 CPD ¶ 17. Approval levels are set forth in AFARS 16.601.

4. Fixed-Price Level-of-Effort Term Contract (FFP-LET). FAR 16.207; AFFARS 5316.207. Government buys a level of effort for a certain period of time, i.e., a specific number of hours to be performed in a specific period. Useful for small R&D contracts.

5. Cost-Plus-Fee-Term Contract. FAR 16.306(d).

Similar to the FFP-LET with the price equal to cost incurred plus a fee. The contractor is required to perform at a stated level of effort over a specific period of time. The contractor is not required to complete any specific work. This form of contract places all of the risk of performance and completion on the government.

## III. CONTRACT TYPES—CATEGORIZED BY QUANTITY OR TIME OF DELIVERY.

**A. Variable Quantity Contracts.**

1. Occasionally, the quantity of work the agency requires is uncertain at contract award. Because of this uncertainty, the agency may desire to retain flexibility to order only the quantity desired, and the competitors may not have sufficient information to bid adequately on the required work. In both of these instances, the agency may select a variable quantity contract, rather than a lump-sum contract. *Compare Bean Dredging Corp.*, B-239952, Oct. 12, 1990, 90-2 CPD ¶ 286 (contracting officer reasonably chose lump-sum pricing) *with Four Star Maint. Corp.*, B-240413, Nov. 2, 1990, 91-1 CPD ¶ 70 (agency wrote A-76 solicitation for lump-sum price for an indefinite amount of construction work, thereby causing contractors to assume unmeasurable risk). *See also Marine Design Technologies, Inc.*, ASBCA No. 39391, 94-1 BCA ¶ 26,355 (distinguishing requirements contract from minimum quantity contract).

2. Indefinite-Quantity/Indefinite-Delivery contract (also called Minimum Quantity). FAR 16.504.

a. The government must buy the minimum quantity, but may purchase up to the maximum quantity. The government issues delivery orders as needs arise. *Tennessee Soap Co. v. United States*, 130 Ct. Cl. 154 (1954); *Federal Elec. Corp.*, ASBCA No. 11726, 68-1 BCA ¶ 6,834; *Federal Elec. Corp.*, B-160560, Sept. 15, 1967, 1967 CPD ¶ 36.

b. FAR 16.504(a)(3)(b) no longer suggests limiting this type of contract to commercial items. *See Sletager, Inc.*, B-237676, Mar. 15, 1990, 90-1 CPD ¶ 298 (minimum quantity contract not limited to commercial items); *Astronautics Corp. of Am.*, B-242782, June 5, 1991, 70 Comp. Gen. 554, 91-1 CPD ¶ 531 (FAR does not prohibit cost plus fee indefinite quantity contract).

c. Reviewing authorities will not overturn a government estimate unless it was made in bad faith. *Crown Laundry & Dry Cleaners, Inc.*, ASBCA No. 39982, 90-3 BCA ¶ 22,993 (unlike requirements contract, reasonableness of estimates not an issue).

d. The government may not use the Termination for Convenience clause to avoid breach damages for its failure to order the minimum quantity. *PHP Healthcare Corp.*, ASBCA No. 39207, 91-1 BCA ¶ 23,647 (contracting officer may not terminate an indefinite-quantity contract for convenience after end of contract term). The proper measure of damages for the government's failure to order the minimum quantity is not the full price of the unordered IDQ work, but the amount which the contractor lost as a result of the government's failure, such as recovery of unamortized fixed costs and lost profits. *Apex Int'l Mgmt. Servs., Inc.*, ASBCA No. 38087, 94-2 BCA ¶ 26,842.

3. Requirements Contracts. FAR 15.603.

a. The government promises to order all of its requirements, if any, from the contractor. *Cleek Aviation v. United States*, 19 Cl. Ct. 552 (1990) (government breaches requirements contract when it buys requirements elsewhere; if goods or services are different, then no breach); *Systems Architects, Inc.*, ASBCA No. 28861, 90-3 BCA ¶ 23,175 (failure to order requirements is a constructive termination for convenience); *Air-Flo Cleaning Sys.*, ASBCA No. 39608, 90-3 BCA ¶ 23,071 (no termination costs for a requirements con-

tract terminated for convenience prior to first order).

b. The estimated quantity listed in the solicitation for a requirements contract must be made in good faith and based on the best information available. *Medart v. Austin*, 967 F.2d 579 (Fed. Cir 1992); *Crown Laundry and Dry Cleaners v. United States*, 29 Fed. Cl. 506 (1993); *International Technology Corp.*, B-233742.2, May 24, 1989, 89-1 CPD ¶ 497.

c. Negligent estimates entitle the contractor to additional compensation even if the government attempts to insulate itself by using a variation of quantities clause. *Chemical Technology, Inc. v. United States*, 227 Ct. Cl. 120, 645 F.2d 934 (1981).

**B. Definite-Quantity; Indefinite-Delivery.** FAR 16.502.
The quantity and price are fixed. The government issues delivery orders to specify the delivery date and location.

## IV. LETTER CONTRACTS.
FAR Subpart 16.603.

### A. Defined.
Letter contracts are used to expedite performance in exigent or emergency circumstances.

### B. Approval for Use.
Heads of Contracting Activities (HCAs) must approve letter contracts before award. DFARS 217.7404-1(a). Approved letter contracts must include a not-to-exceed (NTE) price.

### C. Definitization.
The parties must reduce the contract terms to writing within 180 days after issuance. 10 U.S.C. § 2326; FAR 16.603; DFARS Subpart 217.7404-3. Until the contract terms are definitized, the government may not pay the contractor more than 50% of the NTE price.

## V. OPTIONS.

### A. Defined.

An option is an offer that is irrevocable for a fixed period. An option gives the government the unilateral right, for a specified time, to order additional supplies or services, or to extend the term of the contract, at a specified price. FAR 17.201; *Young-Robinson Assoc., Inc.*, B-242229, Mar. 22, 1991, 91-1 CPD ¶ 319 (contractor cannot protest agency's failure to exercise an option because it is a matter of contract administration); *but see Mine Safety Appliances Co.*, B-238597.2, July 5, 1990, 69 Comp. Gen. 562, 90-2 CPD ¶ 11 (GAO will review option exercise which is, in effect, a source selection in a parallel development contract).

### B. Unpriced Options.

"Unpriced options" and other agreements to agree are enforceable if conditioned upon an obligation to bargain in good faith. *Aviation Contractor Employees, Inc. v. United States*, 945 F.2d 1568 (Fed. Cir. 1991). Otherwise, they are unenforceable. *Restatement (Second) Contracts*, § 33.

### C. Exercising Options.

1. The government must comply with applicable statutes and regulations before exercising an option. *Golden West Refining Co.*, EBCA No. C-9208134, 94-3 BCA ¶ 27,184 (option exercise invalid because statute required award to bidder under a new procurement); *New England Tank Indus. of New Hampshire, Inc.*, ASBCA No. 26474, 90-2 BCA ¶ 22,892 (option exercise invalid because of agency's failure to follow DOD regulation by improperly obligating stock funds); *see FAR 17.207*.
2. The government must exercise the option according to its terms. *The Boeing Co.*, ASBCA No. 37579, 90-3 BCA ¶ 23,202 (option exercise date was contingent on availability of funds; Navy delayed exercising because of unclear statutory language; finally,

Navy unilaterally exercised too late). *But see United Food Servs., Inc.*, ASBCA No. 43711, 93-1 BCA ¶ 25,462 (exercise of a one-year option upheld even though incrementally funded).
3. The contracting officer must prepare a Justification and Approval (J&A) for other than full and open competition if the option was not evaluated at the time of the original award. FAR 17.207(f). *See* discussion of J&A's in the Competition chapter.

### D. Total Contract Period.

1. Generally, a contract, including all options, may not exceed 5 years. FAR 17.204(e). *Delco Elec. Corp.*, B-244559, Oct. 29, 1991, 91-2 CPD ¶ 391 (use of options with delivery dates 7 1/2 years later does not violate FAR 17.204(e), because the 5 year limit applies to 5 years' requirements in a supply contract). *See also Freightliner*, ASBCA 42982, 94-1 BCA ¶ 26,538 (option valid if exercised within five years of award).
2. Military research and development contracts may extend for 10 years or more. 10 U.S.C. § 2352.

## VI. SELECTION OF CONTRACT TYPE.

### A. Cost-Plus-Percentage-of-Cost-Prohibition.

1. The cost-plus-percentage-of-cost system of contracting is prohibited. 10 U.S.C. § 2306(a); 41 U.S.C. § 254(b).
2. Identifying cost-plus-percentage-of-cost. *Urban Data Sys., Inc. v. United States*, 699 F.2d 1147 (Fed. Cir. 1983) (Problem: contractor is penalized for efficient and economical performance and rewarded for uneconomical performance); *The Dep't of Labor—Request for Advance Decision*, B-211213, Apr. 21, 1983, 62 Comp. Gen. 337, 83-1 CPD ¶ 429; *Tero Tek Int'l, Inc.*, B-228548, Feb. 10, 1988, 88-1 CPD ¶ 132.
3. Cost-Plus-Percentage-of-Cost contract. (Figure 10)
   a. Fee is paid at a predetermined rate;

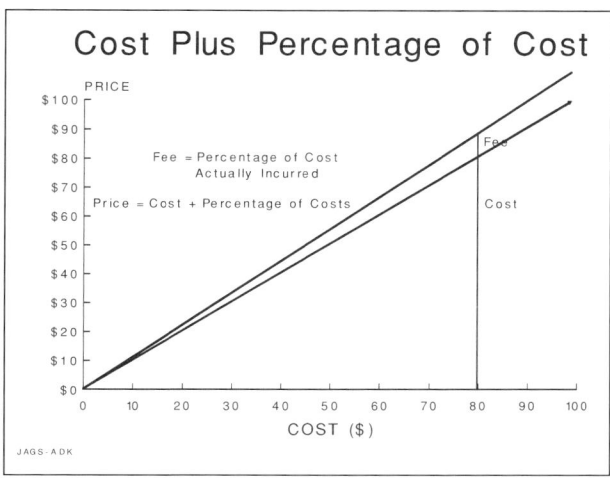

**Figure 10**

b. Rate is applied to *actual* performance cost;

c. Contractor's entitlement is uncertain at award; and

d. Entitlement to fee increases as performance costs increase.

**B. Regulatory Limitations.**

1. Sealed Bid Procedures. Only firm fixed-price contracts or fixed-price contracts with economic price adjustment may be acquired using sealed bid procedures. FAR 16.102 and 14.104. *But see Tri-Services, Inc.*, B-245698, Jan. 15, 1992, 92-1 CPD ¶ 75 (GAO upheld agency's use of an IFB to acquire cost reimbursement line items).

2. Competitive Negotiation. Any contract type or combination of types described in the FAR may be selected when using competitive negotiations. Types of contracts not described in the FAR cannot be used unless a deviation is approved. FAR 16.101 and 16.102.

**C. FAR/DFARS Guidance.**

1. The objective is to negotiate a contract type and price (or estimated cost and fee) that will result in reasonable contractor risk and provide the contractor with the greatest incentive for efficient and economical performance. FAR 16.103(a).

2. There are several factors that the contracting

officer should consider in selecting the contract type. FAR 16.104.

a. Whether price competition is available.

b. The accuracy of price or cost analysis.

c. The type and complexity of the requirement.

d. Urgency of the requirement.

e. Period of performance or length of production run.

f. Contractor's technical capability and financial responsibility.

g. Adequacy of the contractor's accounting system.

h. Concurrent contracts.

i. Extent and nature of proposed subcontracting.

j. Administrative costs to government (and contractor).

k. The "stability of design," including the subordinate considerations of adequacy and firmness of specifications, availability of relevant historical pricing data, prior production experience of the contractor, and adequacy of the contractor's estimating system.

3. Funding considerations often influence the contract type selected by the contracting officer. *See Infotec Dev., Inc.*, ASBCA No. 31809, 91-2 BCA ¶ 23,909 (government divided software development project into several requirements to allow annual funding; after accepting two years performance it unsuccessfully tried to terminate the entire contract when final product failed).

**VII. CONCLUSION.**

A. The type of contract affects the allocation of cost and performance risk between the government and the contractor.

B. Generally, a cost-reimbursement contract is appropriate if the parties cannot predict performance costs accurately, the contractor has an adequate accounting system, and the contracting officer executes a D&F that a cost-reimbursement contract is most advantageous to the government. However, FAR

## RISK ALLOCATION CONTINUUM

# ALLOCATION OF COST RISK

GOVERNMENT
RISK

COST PLUS FIXED FEE - LEVEL OF EFFORT

TIME AND MATERIALS

COST PLUS FIXED FEE

COST PLUS AWARD FEE

COST PLUS INCENTIVE FEE

COST - NO FEE CONTRACT

COST SHARING CONTRACT

FIXED PRICE INCENTIVE

FFP WITH ECONOMIC PRICE ADJUSTMENT

FIRM FIXED PRICE

CONTRACTOR
RISK

16.104 prescribes additional factors that the contracting officer must also consider.

C. Variable quantity contracts are appropriate when the government cannot accurately predict the quantity of goods or services it will need. Distinguish between indefinite-quantity contracts and requirements contracts.

D. Selection of a contract type is a discretionary governmental function requiring sound technical and business judgment. Selection of the proper contract type affects overall contractor performance, i.e., it is difficult to perform well if the government shifts unreasonable risk to the contractor.

## CHAPTER FOUR

# *Competition*

## I. INTRODUCTION.

Following this block of instruction, students will understand:

A. The levels of competition applicable to government contracts.

B. The statutory and regulatory requirements for full and open competition.

C. The exceptions to the requirement for full and open competition.

D. The impact of specifications on competition.

## II. THE COMPETITION REQUIREMENTS.

### A. Historical Perspective.

### B. Competition in Contracting Act of 1984.
Pub. L. 98-369, Title VII, § 2701, 98 Stat. 1175.

1. Congressional Intent. Congress decided to promote economy, efficiency, and effectiveness in the procurement of property and services by the executive branch of the government by requiring that federal acquisitions be conducted on the basis of full and open competition to the maximum practicable extent.

2. The Competition in Contracting Act (CICA) amended several titles of the United States Code, including:

   a. Armed Servies Procurement Act of 1947, as amended. Title 10 U.S.C. §§ 2304-2305 specifies competition requirements that are applicable to the Department of Defense, the Military Departments, the Coast Guard, and the National Aeronautics and Space Administration (NASA).

   b. Federal Property and Administrative Ser-

vices Act of 1949, as amended. Title 41 U.S.C. §§ 253, 253a-g, specify competition requirements that are applicable to executive agencies other than the Department of Defense, the Military Departments, the Coast Guard, and NASA.

   c. Office of Federal Procurement Policy Act. Title 41 U.S.C. §§ 401-424 establishes competition requirements applicable to all executive federal agencies.

   (1) 41 U.S.C. §§ 401-402 state Congressional policies regarding procurement of property and services.

   (2) 41 U.S.C. § 404 establishes the Office of Federal Procurement Policy to provide overall direction of procurement policy for all executive agencies.

   (3) 41 U.S.C. § 416 requires executive agencies to publicize notices of procurements.

   (4) 41 U.S.C. § 418 requires executive agencies to appoint competition advocates and specifies the duties and functions of such advocates.

3. Regulatory implementation of statutory competition requirements are primarily, but not exclusively, set forth in these sections of the Federal Acquisition Regulation (FAR) and in the corresponding sections of military department and civilian agency FAR supplements.

   a. Federal Acquisition Regulation (FAR), Part 6—Competition Requirements.

   b. FAR Part 7—Acquisition Planning.

   c. FAR Part 5—Publicizing Contract Actions.

   d. FAR Part 10—Specifications, Standards, and Other Purchase Descriptions: FAR

10.002, policy to promote full and open competition in developing specifications and purchase descriptions.

   e. FAR Part 13—Small Purchase and Other Simplified Purchase Procedures: FAR 13.106, competition and price reasonableness requirements.

## C. The Congressional Scheme.

The Congressional strategy has two elements:

1. The paramount principle is to achieve competition to the maximum practicable extent.

2. There are three formal types or levels of competition for all appropriated fund acquisitions, other than procurements that can be made under small purchase procedures. The above paramount principle applies to each of these levels of competition:

   a. Full and Open Competition.

   b. Full and Open Competition After Exclusion of Sources.

   c. Other Than Full and Open Competition.

## D. Full and Open Competition.

1. Policy. 10 U.S.C. § 2304(a)(1); 41 U.S.C. § 253(a)(1); FAR Subpart 6.1.

   a. With limited exceptions, contracting officers shall promote full and open competition through the use of competitive procedures in soliciting offers and awarding government contracts.

   b. Contracting officers shall use the competitive procedure or combination of competitive procedures that is best suited to the circumstances of the contract action.

2. Defined. "Full and open competition" means that all responsible sources are permitted to compete. FAR 6.003.

3. Full and open competition may not actually *achieve* competition.

4. Examples of procedures that are considered to be competitive.

   a. Sealed bidding. FAR Part 14.

   b. Competitive proposals (negotiations). FAR Part 15.

   c. Combinations, such as two-step sealed bidding. FAR Part 14.5.

5. The provisions of FAR Part 6—Competition Requirements—are inapplicable to the following types of procurements. Statutory competition requirements applicable to these acquisitions are implemented in the specific FAR provisions governing each type of procurement. FAR 6.001.

   a. Simplified acquisition procedures. FAR Part 13.

   b. Contracts awarded using contracting procedures that are expressly authorized by statute and that differ from the procedures specified in FAR Part 6 (e.g. contracts with Federal Prison Industries or set-asides for goods manufactured by the blind).

   c. Contract modifications that are *within the scope* of the contract. *See AT&T Communications, Inc. v. Wiltel, Inc.*, 1 F.3d 1201 (Fed. Cir. 1993); *Pacific Bell v. NASA*, GSBCA No. 12814-P, 94-3 BCA ¶ 27,067; *Falcon Carriers, Inc.*, B-232562.2, Jan. 30, 1989, 89-1 CPD ¶ 96 (agency may not award a contract with the intention of significantly modifying it after award).

   d. Orders placed under multiple award schedule contracts administered by GSA. 10 U.S.C. § 2302(2)(C).

   e. Orders placed under indefinite quantity contracts properly entered into under FAR Part 6.

## E. Full and Open Competition After Exclusion of Sources.

1. Policy. 10 U.S.C. § 2304(b); 41 U.S.C. § 253(b); FAR Subpart 6.2. Under certain circumstances, the contracting officer may exclude one or more sources from competition for a particular contract. Otherwise the contracting officer must seek full and open competition. FAR 6.201.

2. Circumstances that permit the exclusion of sources.

   a. Establishing or maintaining alternative sources. FAR 6.202. The contracting officer may exclude a source or sources from participation in competitive procurement procedures to establish or maintain alternative sources of supply if such an exclusion:

(1) Would increase or maintain competition and be likely to result in reduced overall costs for such property or services.

(2) Would be in the interests of national defense by making a facility, producer, manufacturer, or supplier available for furnishing supplies or services, thereby enlarging the industrial base in case of national emergency or industrial mobilization. *Martin Elecs. Inc.*, B-219803, Nov. 1, 1985, 85-2 ¶ CPD 504.

(3) Would be in the interests of national defense by establishing or maintaining an essential engineering, research, or development capability to be provided by an educational or non-profit institution or a federally funded research and development center.

(4) Section 1002 of the Federal Acquisition Streamlining Act of 1994, Pub. L. No. 103-355, 108 Stat. 3243 (1994) [hereinafter FASA], added three additional bases for limiting competition in order to establish or maintain additional sources of supply.

(a) To ensure the continuous availability of a source of supply. FASA § 1002 (amending 10 U.S.C. § 2304(b)(1)).

(b) To satisfy projected needs based on a history of high demand. *Id.*

(c) To satisfy a critical need for medical, safety, or emergency supplies. *Id.*

(5) Determination and Finding (D&F) required. Exclusions from competition on these bases must be supported by a D&F signed by the agency head or designee. FAR 6.202(b)(1); *see* FAR Subpart 1.7.

b. Set-asides for small businesses. FAR 6.203.

(1) In accordance with a statutory set-aside program, contracting officers may exclude sources other than small

business concerns (FAR 19.5) to permit only such qualifying businesses to participate in the competitive procedures of a procurement.

(2) No written justification or D&F is required by FAR Part 6 for exclusion of sources from competition pursuant to this set-aside program.

(3) FASA § 7101 repealed 15 U.S.C. § 644(e), (f) which had required agencies to set aside acquisitions for small businesses located in labor surplus areas.

**F. Other Than Full and Open Competition.**

1. Policy. 10 U.S.C. § 2304(c); 41 U.S.C. § 253(c); FAR Subpart 6.3.

a. Contracting without providing for full and open competition or full and open competition after exclusion of sources is a *violation of the CICA* unless permitted specifically by one of the statutory exceptions listed in FAR 6.302.

b. Since authority for contracting without full and open competition is statutory, it is not a discretionary agency determination. FAR 6.301.

c. Each contract awarded without full and open competition must cite the U.S. Code provision authorizing the limitation of competition. FAR 6.301(b).

d. Even though not required to provide full and open competition, the contracting officer must solicit from as many potential sources as is practicable under the circumstances. FAR 6.301(d). *See Kahn Indus., Inc.*, B-251777, May 3, 1993, 93-1 CPD ¶ 356.

e. Contracting without providing for full and open competition cannot be justified on the basis of (FAR 6.301(c)):

(1) A lack of advance planning. 10 U.S.C. § 2304(f)(5)(A); *TLC Servs., Inc.*, B-252614, June 22, 1993, 93-1 CPD ¶ 481. *Service Contractors*, B-243236, July 12, 1991, 91-2 CPD ¶ 49.

(2) Concerns regarding the availability of

funds for the acquisition, e.g., funds are about to expire.

2. There are *seven* statutory exceptions to the requirement to provide full and open competition:

a. One or few responsible sources *and* no other supplies or services can meet agency's needs.

(1) For DOD, Coast Guard, and NASA, when supplies or services are available from *only one or a limited number* of responsible sources *and* no other type of property or services will satisfy the agency's needs, full and open competition is not required. 10 U.S.C. §§ 2304(c)(1); FAR 6.302-1; *International Enters.*, B-251403, Apr. 1, 1993, 93-1 CPD ¶ 283; *Servo Corp. of Am.*, B-246734, Mar. 31, 1992, 92-1 CPD ¶ 322.

(2) For other executive agencies, when supplies or services are available from *only one* responsible source *and* no other type of property or services will satisfy the agency's needs, full and open competition is not required. 41 U.S.C. § 253(c)(1); FAR 6.302-1. *Information Ventures, Inc.*, B-246605, Mar. 23, 1992, 92-1 CPD ¶ 302.

b. Unusual and compelling urgency such that the government would be seriously injured unless the agency is permitted to limit the number of sources from which it solicits offers. 10 U.S.C. § 2304(c)(2); 41 U.S.C. § 253(c)(2); FAR 6.302-2. *Compare Magnavox, Inc.*, B-248501, Aug. 31, 1992, 92-2 BCA ¶ 143 (unusual and compelling urgency established), *with K-Whit Tools, Inc.*, B-247081, Apr. 22, 1992, 92-1 CPD ¶ 382 (unusual and compelling urgency not established).

c. Maintenance of facility or supplier for industrial mobilization or maintenance of engineering, research or development capability by an educational or non-profit institution or a federally funded research and development center. 10 U.S.C.

§ 2304(c)(3); 41 U.S.C. § 253(c)(3); FAR 6.302-3. *Greenbrier Indus.*, B-248177, Aug. 5, 1992, 92-2 CPD ¶ 74 (chemical protective suits are a critical, mission-essential item and awards to currently active production lines were justified. Agency decision will not be questioned so long as agency can demonstrate that its determinations are related to its industrial mobilization needs). *See also Magnavox Elec. Sys. Co.*; *Ferranti Techs., Inc.*, B-247316.2, May 28, 1992, 92-1 CPD ¶ 475.

—NOTE: FASA §§ 1005 and 1055 amended 10 U.S.C. § 2304(c)(3) and 41 U.S.C. § 253(c)(3), respectively, to authorize agencies to use noncompetitive procedures to procure the services of an expert for use in any litigation or dispute.

d. International agreement or treaty between the U.S. and a foreign government or international organization, written direction of foreign government reimbursing the agency. 10 U.S.C. § 2304(c)(4); 41 U.S.C. § 253(c)(4); FAR 6.302-4.

e. Purchases authorized or required by statute or purchase of a brand name commercial item for authorized resale. 10 U.S.C. § 2304(c)(5); 41 U.S.C. § 253(c)(5); FAR 6.302-5.

—For example, Federal Prison Industries purchases under 18 U.S.C. § 4124; purchases from Nonprofit Agencies for the Blind or Other Severely Handicapped, 41 U.S.C. §§ 46-48c; contracts under the Small Business Section 8(a) Program, 15 U.S.C. § 637.

f. Disclosure of agency's needs would compromise national security. 10 U.S.C. § 2304(c)(6); 41 U.S.C. § 253(c)(6); FAR 6.302-6.

—NOTE: Merely because an acquisition is classified or merely because contractors will require access to classified data to submit offers or to perform the contract does not justify limiting competition.

g. Determination by agency head that competition is not in the public interest with pre-award notification to Congress. 10 U.S.C. § 2304(c)(7); 41 U.S.C. § 253(c)(7); FAR 6.302-7.

3. *Justification and Approval* for Other Than Full and Open Competition. FAR 6.303.

  a. With few exceptions, an agency must prepare a justification and approval (J&A) document before proceeding with an acquisition using other than full and open competitive procedures.

  b. In the J&A, the contracting officer must [FAR 6.303-1(a)]:

    (1) Justify the use of other than full and open competition.

    (2) Certify the accuracy and completeness of the justification.

    (3) Obtain approval of the justification by the appropriate official (as defined in FAR 6.304) before taking any steps to negotiate or award a contract.

    (4) EXCEPTION: Unusual and compelling urgency may justify initiation of the acquisition before the J&A document is written and approved. FAR 6.303-1(e).

  c. The J&A document must contain sufficient facts and reasons to justify the use of the specific statutory authority cited. Each J&A must, at a minimum, include the following information (FAR 6.303-2):

    (1) A description of the agency's need.

    (2) Identification of the statutory provision that permits use of other than full and open competitive procedures.

    (3) A demonstration that the proposed contractor's unique qualifications or the nature of the acquisition requires use of the authority cited.

    (4) A determination that the anticipated price will be fair and reasonable.

    (5) A description of efforts made to ensure that offers are solicited from as many potential sources as is practicable, including whether a CBD notice was or will be publicized.

    (6) A description of the market survey conducted.

    (7) A listing of sources, if any, that expressed an interest in the acquisition in writing.

    (8) A statement of the actions, if any, the agency may take to remove or overcome any barriers to competition before a subsequent acquisition for the same or similar supplies or services is needed.

    (9) Evidence that technical or requirements personnel have certified that any data they provided which forms the basis for the justification and which supports the exception to full and open competition is complete and accurate.

    (10) Certification by the contracting officer that the justification is accurate and complete to the best of her knowledge and belief.

  d. The justification must be approved by the appropriate official. FAR 6.304.

## G. Reprocurement Contracts.

FAR 49.402-6(b) requires "the maximum competition practicable" for reprocurement contracts. However, if the reprocurement is for a quantity that does not exceed the undelivered quantity on the terminated contract, that FAR provision provides that the contracting officer may "use any terms and acquisition methods deemed appropriate for the repurchase."

1. The GAO will review the reasonableness of an agency's selected acquisition method against the standard specified in FAR 49.402-6(b). *International Tech. Corp.*, B-250377.5, Aug. 18, 1993, 93-2 CPD ¶ 102 (GAO "recogniz[ed], as a general rule, that the statutes and regulations governing regular procurements are not strictly applicable to reprocurements after a default.").

2. If there is a relatively short time between the original competition and the default, it is reasonable to award to the second lowest offeror of the original solicitation at its original price. *Hemet Valley Flying Serv., Inc.*, B-191922, Aug. 14, 1978, 57 Comp. Gen. 703,

78-2 CPD ¶ 117; *DCX, Inc.*, B-232672, Jan. 23, 1989, 89-1 CPD ¶ 55.

## III. IMPLEMENTATION OF COMPETITION REQUIREMENTS.

### A. Competition Advocates.

41 U.S.C. § 418; FAR 6.5; AR 715-31, Army Competition Advocacy Program; AFR 800-35, Air Force Competition Advocacy Program.

1. Policy. Congress mandated that each executive agency designate an advocate for competition for the agency itself *and* for each procuring activity of the agency. Competition advocates must:

    a. Be in positions other than that of the agency senior procurement executive.

    b. Not be assigned duties or responsibilities that are inconsistent with the obligations of a competition advocate.

    c. Be provided with staff or assistance as necessary to carry out the advocate's duties and responsibilities, such as specialists in technical operations, engineering, contract administration, financial management, supply management, and utilization of small and disadvantaged business concerns.

2. Under FAR 6.502(a), agency competition advocates must:

    a. Challenge barriers to and promote full and open competition in all of the agency's acquisitions.

    b. Review the agency's contracting operations and identify opportunities to achieve full and open competition or any condition that unnecessarily restricts competition in the agency's contract actions.

    c. Prepare and submit reports and recommendations to the agency senior procurement executive.

3. FAR 6.502(b) requires that the competition advocate for each procuring activity:

    a. Challenge barriers to full and open competition and affirmatively promote full and open competition in the activity's procurement actions.

    b. Challenge unnecessarily detailed specifications and unnecessarily restrictive statements of need.

4. Duties and responsibilities of the post or base competition advocate:

    a. Publicize competition in contracting requirements throughout the installation, command, and agency. Establish a program to meet congressional goals for maximizing full and open competition.

    b. Challenge restrictive acquisitions and seek new sources to increase competition.

    c. Establish an effective awards program to recognize employees who promote the competition program significantly.

    d. Review and approve justifications for use of other than full and open competitive procedures when designated as approval authority by statute or regulation (generally applies to contract actions between $100,000 and $1,000,000).

5. A competition advocate's "review" of an agency's procurement is not a substitute for the normal bid protest procedures. *Allied-Signal, Inc.*, B-243555, May 14, 1991, 91-1 CPD ¶ 468. *But see, Liebert Corp.*, B-232234.5, Apr. 29, 1991, 91-1 CPD ¶ 413 (reasonable reliance on a competition advocate's representations may extend the time for filing a bid protest.)

### B. Acquisition Planning.

1. Congressional policy. Agencies shall perform acquisition planning and conduct market surveys for all acquisitions to obtain full and open competition, with due regard to the nature of the supplies or services to be acquired. 10 U.S.C. § 2301(a)(5); 41 U.S.C. § 253a(a)(1).

2. Purpose. The purpose of acquisition planning is to ensure that the government meets its needs in the most effective, economical, and timely manner. FAR 7.102.

3. Definitions. FAR 7.101.

    a. "Acquisition planning" means the process by which the efforts of all personnel responsible for an acquisition are coordinated and integrated through a comprehensive plan for fulfilling the agency's need in a timely manner and at a reasonable cost. It includes the overall strategy for managing the acquisition.

    b. "Market survey" means attempts to ascertain whether sources that are capable of satisfying the government's requirements, other than those known to the agency, exist.

4. Responsibilities. FAR 7.103. The agency head or designee must prescribe procedures to:

    a. Ensure that no contract is entered into without full and open competition due to a lack of acquisition planning or because of concern regarding the amount of procurement funds available to the agency.

    b. Ensure that acquisition planners address requirements to specify minimum needs, to develop accurate specifications, and solicit offers in a manner that promotes full and open competition considering the nature of the supplies and services to be acquired.

    c. Establish criteria and thresholds at which increasingly greater detail and formality in the planning process is required based on both complexity and proposed costs, including designating when written acquisition plans must be prepared.

5. Formal acquisition plans. FAR 7.105.

    a. Formal acquisition planning applies to the more complex and costly programs, but may be adapted to acquisition of any supplies or services. Within DOD, written acquisition plans are required for (DFARS 207.103(c)(1)):

        (1) Development acquisitions with total contractual costs estimated to be $5,000,000 or more; and

        (2) Production and service acquisitions with contractual cost estimated to be $30,000,000 for all years or $15,000,000 for any fiscal year.

    b. A written acquisition plan must identify decision milestones, and should address all the technical, business, management, and other significant considerations that will

control the acquisition. The specific content of plans varies depending on the nature of the supplies or services to be acquired, on the circumstances of both the procuring activity and the business environment, and on the stage of the acquisition.

6. Market research. FASA § 8104 requires agencies to conduct market research "appropriate to the circumstances" before developing new specifications for a procurement and before soliciting bids or proposals for a contract exceeding the simplified acquisition threshold. Agencies must use the results of this market research to determine whether there are commercial items which:

    a. meet the agency's requirements;

    b. could be modified to meet the requirements; or

    c. could meet the requirements if the agency modified its requirements to a "reasonable extent."

## IV. PUBLICIZING CONTRACT ACTIONS.
41 U.S.C. § 416; FAR Part 5.

### A. Policy.
Contracting officers shall publicize contract actions to (FAR 5.002):

1. Increase competition.
2. Broaden industry participation in meeting government requirements.
3. Assist small business concerns, small disadvantaged business concerns, and labor surplus area concerns in obtaining contracts and subcontracts.

### B. Methods of Soliciting Potential Bidders.
1. Commerce Business Daily (CBD). 41 U.S.C. § 416; FAR 5.101(a)(1).
2. Posting. 41 U.S.C. § 416; FAR 5.101(a)(2).
3. Bidders List. FAR 14.204(a); FAR 14.205.
4. Handouts, announcements, and paid advertising. FAR 5.101(b).

### C. Commerce Business Daily.
41 U.S.C. § 416(a)(1)(A); FAR Subpart 5.2.
1. Basic requirements. FAR 5.101 and 5.203.

a. Currently, all contract actions expected to exceed $25,000 must be synopsized in the CBD.

b. However, when an agency implements interim FACNET capability, contract actions below the simplified acquisition threshold (which will then be $100,000) need not be synopsized. FASA § 4202 (amending 41 U.S.C. § 416(c)(1) and 15 U.S.C. § 637(g)(1)).

c. When government-wide full FACNET capability has been implemented, contract actions not exceeding $250,000 need not be synopsized. *Id.*

d. Army FAR Supplement (AFARS) 5.203. Contracting officers must verify actual date of publication. No such requirement by other services.

2. Exceptions. FAR 5.202.

a. Contracting officer determines that one or more of twelve exceptions apply (e.g., national security, urgency, authorized or required by statute, direction by foreign government).

b. Head of agency determines, after consultation with the Administrator for Federal Procurement Policy and Administrator of the SBA, that advance notice is inappropriate or unreasonable.

c. Decision not to synopsize must be proper when the Request for Proposals is issued. *American Kleaner Mfg. Co.*, B-243901.2, Sept. 10, 1991, 91-2 CPD ¶ 235.

d. If the agency fails to synopsize or synopsizes inaccurately (e.g. does not disclose full extent of the procurement) cancellation of the solicitation may be appropriate. *See generally Sunrise Int'l Grp.*, B-252892.3, Sept. 14, 1993, 93-2 CPD ¶ 160, *RII*, B-251436, Mar. 10, 1993, 93-1 CPD ¶ 223.

**D. Posting in a Public Place.**
41 U.S.C. § 416(a)(1)(B); FAR 5.101. Contract actions expected to exceed $10,000 ($5,000 for DOD) but not expected to exceed $25,000 must be posted in a public place at the contracting office issuing the solicitation.

**E. Solicitation Mailing Lists (Bidders Lists).**
FAR 14.205.

1. The contracting officer shall establish solicitation mailing lists to ensure access to adequate sources of supplies and services.

2. The contracting officer must include all contractors that request inclusion or that have received previous solicitations.

3. The contracting officer may remove from the list any contractor that fails to respond to a solicitation. If the contractor fails to respond to two solicitations, the contracting officer shall remove it from the list.

4. Rotation of lists. FAR 14.205-4. The contracting officer may use different portions of a large list for separate acquisitions. The contracting officer must solicit bids from:

a. The incumbent, *Kimber Guard & Patrol, Inc.*, B-248920, Oct. 1, 1992, 92-2 BCA ¶ 220;

b. Any contractor added to the list since the last solicitation, *Holiday Inn, Inc.*, B-249673-2, Dec. 22, 1992, 92-2 CPD ¶ 428; and

c. All contractors on the segment of the list designated by the contracting officer.

**V. SPECIFICATIONS AND COMPETITION.**

**A. Types of Specifications.**
1. Design specifications.
2. Performance specifications.
3. Purchase descriptions, including brand name or equal specifications.
4. Mixed specifications.
5. Streamlining. Programs subject to streamlining should tailor the application of specifications and standards or apply them for guidance only. FAR 10.002(c).

**B. Legal Effect of Specifications.**
1. Allocation of risk of performance.
2. Basis for competition.
   a. Agencies must specify their needs, based on market research, in a manner that permits full and open competition and includes restrictive provisions or conditions only to the extent necessary to satis-

fy the minimum needs of the agency or as authorized by law. 10 U.S.C. § 2305(a)(1); 41 U.S.C. § 253a(a); FAR 10.002.

   b. Elements of the policy. Specifications must:

     (1) Permit full and open competition.

     (2) Be restrictive only to the extent necessary.

     (3) State minimum needs or requirements authorized by law. *Integrated Sys. Grp. v. Dep't of the Navy*, GSBCA No. 12127-P, 93-2 BCA ¶ 25,637.

3. Compliance with statutory and regulatory competition policy.

   a. "The full and free competition required cannot be obtained unless the invitation and specifications are sufficiently definite to permit the preparation and evaluation of bids on a common basis. . . . There can be no legal competition unless the bidders are competing on a common basis; no intelligent bidding for a contract unless all bidders know what the contract requirements will be." 39 Comp. Gen. 570, 572 (1960).

   b. Specifications must provide a common basis for competition. Competitors must be able to price the same requirement. *See Deknatel Div., Pfizer Hosp. Prod. Grp., Inc.*, B-243408, July 29, 1991, 91-2 CPD ¶ 97.

## C. Common Preaward Problems Relating to Specifications.

1. Brand Name or Equal Purchase Descriptions.

   a. Definition: a purchase description that identifies a product by its brand name and model or part number or other appropriate nomenclature by which the product is offered for sale. FAR 10.001.

   b. Salient characteristics *must* be listed when using a brand name or equal purchase description. FAR 10.004.

     "[F]ailure of a solicitation to list the salient characteristics of the desired item improperly restricts competition by precluding potential offerors of

equal products from determining what characteristics are considered essential for its item to be accepted, and that cancellation of the solicitation is thus required." *T-L-C Sys*, B-227470, Sept. 21, 1987, 87-2 CPD ¶ 283.

   c. The failure to list salient characteristics is a significant flaw. *But see Microstar Co.*, GSBCA No. 9469-P, 89-1 BCA ¶ 21,214 (refusal to let government resolicit).

   d. All brands that meet the requirement should be listed, if feasible. DFARS 210.004(b) (3)(i)(A).

   e. Special responsiveness rules under a brand name or equal solicitation.

     (1) Bidder is required to submit data describing its product. DFARS 252.210-7000.

     (2) Failure to submit data renders the bid nonresponsive. *Interand Corp.*, B-224512.2, Dec. 31, 1986, 66 Comp. Gen. 181, 87-1 CPD ¶ 5.

     (3) Failure to conform to the salient characteristics renders a bid nonresponsive. *Elastomeric Roofing Assoc.*, B-234125, May 12, 1989, 68 Comp. Gen. 426, 89-1 CPD ¶ 451.

2. Ambiguous Specifications.

   a. Specifications or purchase descriptions that are subject to two or more reasonable interpretations are ambiguous and require cancellation or amendment of the solicitation. *RMS Indus.*, B-248678, Aug. 14, 1992, 92-2 CPD ¶ 109 (mere allegation of ambiguity does not make it so); *Flow Technology, Inc.*, B-228281, Dec. 29, 1987, 67 Comp. Gen. 161, 87-2 CPD ¶ 633 (protester's interpretation of the specifications was reasonable); *Viereck Co.*, B-227089, Aug. 14, 1987, 87-2 CPD ¶ 157 (protester's interpretation unreasonable).

   b. Issues raised by ambiguous (defective) specifications:

     (1) Adequacy of competition.

     (2) Contract interpretation and constructive change of the contract.

3. Unduly Restrictive Specifications.
    a. Specifications must promote full and open competition. Restrictive provisions may be included only to meet the agency's minimum needs. 10 USC § 2305(a)(1)(B); 41 U.S.C. § 253a(a)(2)(B); *Falcon Indus.*, B-256419, June 3, 1994, 94-1 CPD ¶ 337 (agency cannot exclude technical approach it believes would be too costly); *Dixon Pest Control, Inc.*, B-248725, Aug. 27, 1992, 92-2 CPD ¶ 132.
    b. Common examples of restrictive specifications:
        (1) Specifications written around a specific product will be scrutinized closely. *Accord Ressler Assoc.*, B-244110, Sept. 9, 1991, 91-2 CPD ¶ 230.
        (2) Geographical restrictions that result in availability only from a sole source. But specifications that impose geographical restrictions are not "unduly" restrictive if the restriction furthers a federal policy. *See, e.g., Marlen C. Robb & Son Boatyard & Marina, Inc.*, B-256316, June 6, 1994, 94-1 CPD ¶ 351; *H & F Enters.*, B-251581.2, July 13, 1993, 93-2 CPD ¶ 16.
        (3) Specifications that exceed the agency's minimum needs. *Accord Trilectron Indus.*, B-248475, Aug. 27, 1992, 92-2 CPD ¶ 130 (agency requirement for use of an air conditioner refrigerant with an ozone depletion potential of zero is reasonable, even though it prevents protestor from competing); *CardioMetrix*, B-248295, Aug. 14, 1992, 92-2 CPD ¶ 107.
        (4) An agency may not impose a restriction for approval by a testing laboratory, such as Underwriters Laboratory (UL), without recognizing equivalents. *HazStor Co.*, B-251248, Mar. 18, 1993, 93-1 CPD ¶ 242. *But see G.H. Harlow Co.*, B-254839, Jan 21, 1994 94-1 CPD ¶ 29 (requirement for approval by testing laboratory upheld for procurement of fire alarm and computer-aided dispatch system).

## CHAPTER FIVE

# *Sealed Bidding*

## I. INTRODUCTION.

Following this block of instruction, students should:

A. Understand how sealed bidding differs from other methods of procurement.

B. Understand the factors that contracting officers must consider when preparing and publishing an Invitation for Bids (IFB).

C. Understand the rules with which bidders must comply in submitting bids to the government.

D. Understand the procedures used by contracting officers to evaluate bids and award contracts.

## II. THREE CONTRACT METHODS.

### A. Simplified Acquisition Procedures.
Federal Acquisition Streamlining Act of 1994, Pub. L. No. 103-355, Title IV, 108 Stat. 3243, 3338 [hereinafter FASA]; FAR Part 13.

### B. Sealed Bidding.
FAR Part 14.

### C. Negotiations.
FAR Part 15.

## III. FRAMEWORK OF THE SEALED BIDDING PROCESS.

### A. History and Purpose.
2 Stat. 536; 6 Ops. Atty. Gen. 99; 2 Ops. Atty. Gen. 257.

### B. Current Statutes.

1. DOD, Coast Guard, and NASA - 10 U.S.C. §§ 2301-2331.

2. Other federal agencies - 41 U.S.C. §§ 251-261.

3. These parallel statutory structures provide that:

   a. The head of an agency *shall* solicit sealed bids if—

      (1) time permits the solicitation, submission, and evaluation of sealed bids;

      (2) the award will be made on the basis of price and other price-related factors [*see* FAR 14.201-8];

      (3) it is not necessary to conduct discussions with the responding sources about their bids; and

      (4) there is a reasonable expectation of receiving more than one sealed bid.

   b. The head of an agency shall request competitive proposals if sealed bids are not required. *Racal Filter Technologies, Inc.*, B-240579, Dec. 4, 1990, 70 Comp. Gen. 127, 90-2 CPD ¶ 453 (sealed bidding required when all elements enumerated in the Competition in Contracting Act (CICA) are present—agencies may not use negotiated procedures); *UBX Int'l, Inc.*, B-241028, Jan. 16, 1991, 91-1 CPD ¶ 45 (use of sealed bidding procedures for ordnance site survey was proper).

### C. Regulations.

1. FAR Part 14—Sealed Bidding.

2. DOD and agency regulations:

a. Defense FAR Supplement (DFARS), Part 214—Sealed Bidding.

b. Air Force FAR Supplement (AFFARS), Part 314— Sealed Bidding.

c. Army FAR Supplement (AFARS), Part 14—Sealed Bidding.

d. Navy Acquisition Procedures Supplement (NAPS), Part 14—Sealed Bidding.

e. Defense Logistics Acquisition Regulation (DLAR), Part 5214—Sealed Bidding.

## D. Overview of Sealed Bidding Process: The Five Phases.

FAR 14.101. *See* page 53.
1. Preparation of the Invitation for Bids (IFB).
2. Publicizing the Invitation for Bids.
3. Submission of Bids.
4. Evaluation of Bids.
5. Award of the Contract.

## IV. PHASE #1—PREPARATION OF INVITATION FOR BIDS.

### A. Format of the IFB.
1. Uniform Contract Format. FAR 14.201-1.
2. Standard Form 33 - Solicitation, Offer and Award. FAR 53.301-33. *See* page 54.
3. Standard Form 30 - Amendment of Solicitation; Modification of Contract. *See* page 55.

### B. Specifications.
1. Clear, complete, and definite.
2. Minimum needs of the government.
3. Preference for Commercial Items. *See* FASA § 8104.

### C. Definition.
"Offer" means "bid" in sealed bidding. FAR 52.214-1.

### D. Contract Type
Contracting officers may use only firm fixed-price and fixed-price with economic price adjustment contracts in sealed bidding acquisitions. FAR 14.104.

## V. PHASE #2—PUBLICIZING THE INVITATION FOR BIDS.

### A. Policy on Publicizing Contract Actions.
FAR 5.002. Contracting officers must publicize contract actions in order to increase competition, broaden industry participation, and assist small business concerns in obtaining contracts and subcontracts.

### B. Methods of Soliciting Potential Bidders.
FAR 5.101; FAR 5.102. DOD uses three primary methods to promote competition: the *Commerce Business Daily* (CBD), Bidders Mailing Lists (BML), and copies of the solicitations posted in public places.

### C. *Commerce Business Daily (CBD).*
FAR Subpart 5.2. The contracting officer may not issue a solicitation until at least 15 days after publication in the CBD. Further, when synopsis in the CBD is required, the contracting officer must give bidders a minimum of 30 days after issuance of the IFB to prepare and submit their bids. This 45-day lead time impacts the choice of contract method; i.e., whether time permits solicitation of sealed bids.

### D. Solicitation Mailing Lists (Bidders' List).
FAR 14.205. In addition, contracting activities develop sources through the use of bidders' mailing lists (BML). Such lists consist of firms known to supply particular goods or services. When a requirement arises for an item for which a BML exists, the contracting agency must send copies of the IFB to firms on the list. Failure to solicit a contractor which requests to be included on the list may require resolicitation. *Applied Constr. Technology*, B-251762, May 4, 1993, 93-1 CPD ¶ 365. If the BML is excessively long, the contracting officer may rotate portions of the list for separate acquisitions.

### E. Posting in a Public Place.
FAR 5.101. Every proposed contract action expected to exceed $5,000 ($10,000 for non-

DOD agencies) but not expected to exceed $25,000 must be posted in a public place at the contracting office issuing the solicitation not later than the date the solicitation is issued and for at least ten days.

## F. Late Receipt of Solicitations.

Failure of a potential bidder to receive an IFB in time to submit a bid, or to receive a requested solicitation at all, does not require postponement of bid opening *unless* adequate competition is not obtained. *Family Carpet Serv. Inc.*, B-243942.3, Mar. 3, 1992, 92-1 CPD ¶ 255. *See also Lewis Jamison Inc. & Assocs.*, B-252198, June 4, 1993, 93-1 CPD ¶ 433 (GAO denies protest where contractor had "last clear opportunity" to avoid being precluded from competing). *But see Applied Constr. Technology*, B-251762, May 4, 1993, 93-1 CPD ¶ 365 (although agency received 10 bids in response to IFB, GAO sustains protest where agency failed to solicit contractor it had advised would be included on its bidder's mailing list).

## G. Failure to Solicit the Incumbent Contractor.

Failure to give notice of a solicitation for supplies or services to a contractor currently providing such supplies or services may be fatal to the solicitation, unless the agency:

1. Made a diligent, good-faith effort to comply with statutory and regulatory requirements regarding notice of the acquisition and distribution of solicitation materials; and
2. Obtained reasonable prices (competition). *Transwestern Helicopters, Inc.*, B-235187, July 28, 1989, 89-2 CPD ¶ 95 (although the agency failed inadvertently to solicit incumbent contractor, the agency made reasonable efforts to publicize the solicitation, which resulted in 25 bids). *But see Professional Ambulance, Inc.*, B-248474, Sep. 1, 1992, 92-2 CPD ¶ 145 (agency failed to solicit the incumbent and received only three proposals; GAO recommended resolicitation).

## VI. PHASE #3—SUBMISSION OF BIDS.

### A. Safeguarding Bids.
FAR 14.401.
1. Bids (including bid modifications) received before the time set for bid opening generally must remain unopened in a locked box or safe. FAR 14.401.
2. Exceptions.
3. A bidder generally is not entitled to relief if the agency negligently loses its bid. *Vereinigte Gebaudereinigungsgesellschaft*, B-252546, June 11, 1993, 93-1 CPD ¶ 454.

### B. Method of Submission.
FAR 14.301; *B & T Int'l, Inc.*, B-224284, Dec. 8, 1986, 86-2 CPD ¶ 654.
1. To be considered for award, a bid must comply in all material respects with the invitation for bids, to include the method of submission, i.e., the bid must be *responsive* to the solicitation. FAR 14.301(a).
2. Transmission of bids. FAR 14.301; FAR 14.302; FAR 52.214-5.
   a. General Rule - Offerors may submit their bids by any written means permitted by the solicitation.
   b. Unless the solicitation specifically allows it, the contracting officer may not consider telegraphic bids. FAR 14.301(b); *MIMCO, Inc.*, B-210647.2, Dec. 27, 1983, 84-1 CPD ¶ 22 (telegraphic bid, which contrary to solicitation requirement makes no mention of bidder's intent to be bound by all terms and conditions is nonresponsive).
   c. The government will not consider facsimile bids unless permitted by the solicitation. FAR 14.301(c); FAR 14.202-7; *Recreonics Corp.*, B-246339, Mar. 2, 1992, 92-1 CPD ¶ 249 (bid properly rejected for bidder's use of fax machine to transmit acknowledgement of solicitation amendment); *but see International Shelter Sys.*, B-245466, Jan. 8, 1992, 71 Comp. Gen. 142, 92-1 CPD ¶ 38 (hand-delivered facsimile of bid modification is not a facsimile transmission).

**C. Time and Place of Submission.**

FAR 14.302.

1. Reasons for specific requirements.
   a. Equality of treatment of bidders.
   b. Preserve integrity of system.
   c. Convenience of the government.
2. Place of submission—as specified in the IFB. FAR 14.302(a); *CSLA, Inc.*, B-255177, Jan. 10, 1994, 94-1 CPD ¶ 63; *Carolina Archaeological Serv.*, B-224818, Dec. 9, 1986, 86-2 CPD ¶ 662.
3. Time of submission - as specified in the IFB. FAR 14.302(a).
   a. The official designated as the bid opening officer shall decide when the time set for bid opening has arrived and shall so declare to those present. FAR 14.402-1; *J. C. Kimberly Co.*, B-255018.2, Feb. 8, 1994, 94-1 CPD ¶ 79; *Chattanooga Office Supply Co.*, B-228062, Sept. 3, 1987, 87-2 CPD ¶ 221 (bid delivered 30 seconds after bid opening officer declared the arrival of the bid opening time is late).
   b. The bid opening officer's declaration of the bid opening time is determinative unless it is shown to be unreasonable. *Action Serv. Corp.*, B-254861, Jan. 24, 1994, 94-1 CPD ¶ 33. The bid opening officer may reasonably rely on the bid opening room clock when declaring bid opening time. *Gen. Eng'g Corp.*, B-245476, Jan. 9, 1992, 92-1 CPD ¶ 45.
   c. If the bid opening officer has not declared bid opening time, a bid is timely if delivered by the end of the minute specified for bid opening. *Amfel Constr., Inc.*, B-233493.2, May 18, 1989, 68 Comp. Gen. 440, 89-1 CPD ¶ 477 (bid delivered within 20-50 seconds after bid opening clock "clicked" to the bid opening time was timely where bid opening officer had not declared bid submission period ended); *Reliable Builders, Inc.*, B-249908.2, Feb. 9, 1993, 93-1 CPD ¶ 116 (bid which was time/date stamped one minute past time set for bid opening was timely since bidder relinquished control of bid at the exact time set for bid opening).
   d. Arbitrary early or late bid opening is improper. *William F. Wilke, Inc.*, B-185544, Mar. 18, 1977, 56 Comp. Gen. 419, 77-1 CPD ¶ 197.
4. Amendment of IFB.
   a. The government must display amendments in the bid room and must send, before the time for bid opening, a copy of the amendment to everyone that received a copy of the original IFB. FAR 14.208(a).
   b. If the government furnishes information to one prospective bidder concerning an invitation for bids, it must furnish that same information to all other bidders as an amendment if (1) such information is necessary for bidders to submit bids or (2) the lack of such information would be prejudicial to uninformed bidders. *Phillip Sitz Constr.*, B-245941, Jan. 22, 1992, 92-1 CPD ¶ 101; *Republic Flooring*, B-242962, June 18, 1991, 70 Comp. Gen. 567, 91-1 CPD ¶ 579 (bidder excluded from BML erroneously).
5. Postponement of bid opening. FAR 14.208; FAR 14.402-3;
   a. The government may postpone bid opening before the scheduled bid opening time by issuing an amendment to the IFB. FAR 14.208(a).
   b. The government may postpone bid opening even after the time scheduled for bid opening if:
      (1) The contracting officer has reason to believe that the bids of an important segment of bidders have been delayed in the mails for causes beyond their control and without their fault or negligence, *Ling Dynamic Sys., Inc.*, B-252091, May 24, 1993, 93-1 CPD ¶ 407; or
      (2) Emergency or unanticipated events interrupt normal governmental processes so that the conduct of bid opening as scheduled is impractical.
   c. For postponement due to the delay of an important segment of bids in the mails,

the contracting officer publicly must announce postponement of bid opening and issue an amendment.

d. In cases of postponement due to emergency or unanticipated events, the contracting officer may proceed with bid opening as soon as practical after the time scheduled without prior amendment to the invitation for bids or notice to bidders, whenever the delay incident to the amendment or notice is not in the government's interest. In such cases, the time of actual bid opening shall be deemed to be the time set for bid opening for the purpose of determining late bids. *ALM, Inc.*, B-225679, Feb. 13, 1987, 87-1 CPD ¶ 165.

## D. The Firm Bid Rule.

1. Distinguish common law rule, which allows an offeror to withdraw an offer any time prior to acceptance. *See* Restatement (Second) of Contracts § 42 (1981).

2. Firm Bid Rule:

   a. After bid opening, bidders may not withdraw their bids during the period specified in the IFB, but must hold their bids open for government acceptance during the stated period. FAR 14.407-1, 52.214-16. *Nation-Wide Reporting & Convention Coverage*, GSBCA No. 8309, 88-2 BCA ¶ 20,521 (bid irrevocable during 90-day acceptance period).

   b. If the solicitation requires a minimum bid acceptance period, a bid that offers a shorter acceptance period than the minimum is nonresponsive. *Hyman Brickle & Son, Inc.*, B-245646, Sept. 20, 1991, 91-2 CPD ¶ 264 (30-day acceptance period offered instead of the required 120 days); *Engineered Modular Structures, Inc.— Recon.*, B-236804.2, Oct. 26, 1989, 89-2 CPD ¶ 386 (120-day period required, 60-day period offered).

   c. The bid acceptance period is a material solicitation requirement. The government may not waive the bid acceptance period because it affects the bidder's price. *Valley Constr. Co.*, B-243811, Aug. 7, 1991, 91-2 CPD ¶ 138 (60 day period required, 30-day period offered).

   d. A bid that fails to offer an unequivocal minimum bid acceptance period is ambiguous and nonresponsive. *John's Janitorial Serv., Inc.*, B-219194, July 2, 1985, 85-2 CPD ¶ 20 (60-day period required, either a maximum 30 day period or an additional 30 day period offered); *John P. Ingram Jr. & Assoc.*, B-250548, Feb. 9, 1993, 93-1 CPD ¶ 117 (bid ambiguous even where bidder acknowledged amendment which changed minimum bid acceptance period).

   e. Exception - the government may accept a solitary bid that offers less than the minimum acceptance period. *Esko & Young, Inc.*, B-204053, Jan. 4, 1982, 61 Comp. Gen. 192, 82-1 CPD ¶ 5.

   f. After the bid acceptance period expires, the bidder may extend the acceptance period only where the bidder would not obtain an advantage over other bidders. FAR 14-404-1(d); *Capital Hill Reporting, Inc.*, B-254011.4, Mar. 17, 1994, 94-1 CPD ¶ 232.

## E. Treatment of Late Bids, Bid Modifications, and Bid Withdrawals.

FAR 14.304.

1. Definition: A "late" bid, bid modification, or bid withdrawal is one that is received in the office *designated* in the IFB after the *exact time* set for bid opening. FAR 14.304-1.

2. There are several exceptions to the late bid rule. These exceptions, listed in paragraph F. below, only apply if the contracting officer receives the late bid prior to contract award. FAR 14.304-1(a).

3. General rule for both mailed and hand-carried bids, bid modifications, and bid withdrawals:

   —LATE IS LATE! FAR 14.304-1; FAR 52.214-7; *Human Resources Consulting Serv.*, B-232338, Oct. 11, 1988, 88-2 CPD ¶ 340.

**F. Four Exceptions to the Late Bid Rule.**

1. The **"Five Day" Rule** - A bid sent by registered or certified mail, mailed at least 5 calendar days before the specified bid receipt date, is timely. FAR 14.304-1(a)(1); FAR 52.214-7(a)(1).

   a. The bid must be sent:

      (1) by registered or certified mail, *Diversified Computer Consultants*, B-206616, Apr. 12, 1982, 82-1 CPD ¶ 335 (government properly rejected a proposal sent by special delivery despite postal clerk error in informing protestor that certified or registered mail could not be sent to Army post office);

      (2) through the U.S. or Canadian Postal Services; and

      (3) to a contracting office in the U.S. or Canada.

   b. Count the day of mailing. Do not count the day set for bid opening. *Lo-Rencin Contracting Co.*, B-188329, Feb. 25, 1977, 77-1 CPD ¶ 144 (four calendar days).

   c. The only documentary evidence of the date of mailing which the GAO will accept is a U.S. or Canadian Postal Service postmark on *both* the envelope or wrapper and on the original receipt from the U.S. or Canadian Postal Service. FAR 14.304-1(b); FAR 52.214-7(c). *Del's Elec. Co.*, B-243123, July 1, 1991, 91-2 CPD ¶ 4; *Canadian Commercial Corp.*, B-214232, Feb. 22, 1984, 84-1 CPD ¶ 226 (Canadian mail).

2. The **"Two Day Rule"** for Express Mail bids. FAR 14.3041(a)(3); FAR 52.214-7(a)(3); *Lyttos Int'l Inc.*, B-246419, Mar. 6, 1992, 92-1 CPD ¶ 265.

   a. A bid sent by U.S. Postal Service Express Mail Next Day Service, not later than 5:00 p.m. at the place of mailing, two working days before the specified bid receipt date, is timely.

   b. The bid must be sent:

      (1) by the Express Mail Next Day Service of the U.S. Postal Service (*Austin Telecommunications Elec. Inc.*, B-254425, Aug. 19, 1993, 93-2 CPD ¶ 108 (NOT Two Day Priority Mail)); and

      (2) to a contracting office in the U.S. or Canada.

   c. The term "working days" excludes weekends and federal holidays. Count the day of mailing; do not count the day set for bid opening.

   d. The only documentary evidence of the date of mailing by U.S. Postal Service Express Mail Next Day Service which the GAO will accept is the date entered by the post office receiving clerk on the "Express Mail Next Day Service-Post Office to Addressee" label *and* the postmark on the envelope or wrapper *and* the postmark on the original receipt from the U.S. Postal Service. FAR 14.304-1(d); FAR 52.214-7(e). This is the only acceptable evidence to establish the date of mailing. FAR 14.304-1(d). *Chelsea Clock Co.*, B-251348.2, May 24, 1993, 93-1 CPD ¶ 401. *But see Lyttos Int'l Inc.*, *supra* (since agency discarded bid envelope, GAO considers "other evidence in the record").

3. The **"Government Mishandling" Rule**. FAR 14.304-1(a)(2); 52.2147-(a)(2).

   a. The government may consider a bid sent by mail or telegraph if the bid is late due "solely" to mishandling of the bid by the Government *after* the installation received the bid. *Frequency Eng'g Lab.*, B-186390, Aug. 17, 1976, 76-2 CPD ¶ 166 (government mishandling due to personnel shortage at installation); *West End Welding & Fabricating*, B-225427, Dec. 31, 1986, 86-2 CPD ¶ 724 (agency failed to follow its normal delivery procedures). *But see Data General Corp.*, B-252239, June 14, 1993, 93-1 CPD ¶ 457 (GAO rejects strict interpretation of FAR requirement that mishandling be due "solely" to mishandling by government; adopts "paramount cause" rule).

   b. The bid must be:

      (1) sent by mail (or by telegraph or facsimile, if authorized);

(2) received at the installation prior to bid opening, *Pershield, Inc.*, B-256827, July 27, 1994, 94-2 CPD ¶ 46; and

(3) in the sole custody of the government from its receipt at the installation until its actual opening. *Data General Corp., supra; but see Howard Mgmt. Group*, B-221889, July 3, 1986, 86-2 CPD ¶ 28 (Western Union exception).

c. The "Government Mishandling" Rule applies to all postal services— it is not limited to registered, certified, or next day express. Further, the government mishandling rule applies to bids submitted to any contracting office governed by the FAR, not just those located in the U.S. or Canada.

d. The offeror must not have contributed substantially to the mishandling. *PDP Analytical Servs.*, B-251776.2, Apr. 5, 1993, 93-1 CPD ¶ 294 (bidder failed to properly address bid and failed to allow a reasonable time for delivery).

e. The only documentary evidence available to prove the time of receipt at the government installation is the time/date stamp of the installation on the bid wrapper or other documentary evidence of receipt maintained by the installation. FAR 14.304-1(c); FAR 52.214-7(d). *Adscon, Inc.*, B-224209, Dec. 10, 1986, 86-2 CPD ¶ 666. *But see Data General Corp.*, B-252239, June 14, 1993, 93-1 CPD ¶ 457 (GAO will consider a "preponderance of all relevant evidence").

4. The **"Government Frustration"** Rule.

a. If timely delivery of a bid, bid modification, or bid withdrawal that is hand-carried by the bidder (or commercial carrier) is frustrated by the government such that the government is the *paramount cause* of the late delivery, then the bid is timely. *Computer Literacy World, Inc.*, GSBCA 11767-P, May 22, 1992, 92-3 BCA ¶ 25,112 (government employee gave unwise instructions, which caused the delay).

b. The bid must be:

(1) hand-carried by the bidder; and

(2) out of the bidder's control at the time of bid opening. *Fredricks Rubber Co.*, B-172974, 51 Comp. Gen. 69 (1971) (gear box case); *Select, Inc.*, B-245820.2, Jan. 3, 1992, 92-1 CPD ¶ 22 (bidder relinquished control of bid by giving it to UPS).

c. The government may consider commercial carrier records to establish time of delivery to the agency, if corroborated by relevant government evidence. *Power Connector, Inc.*, B-256362, June 15, 1994, 94-1 CPD ¶ 369 (agency properly considered Federal Express tracking sheet, agency mail log, and statements of agency personnel in determining time of receipt of bid).

d. If late delivery of the hand-carried bid is not *caused by* the government, then the general rule applies - late is late.

*To James P. Smith*, B-173392, 51 Comp. Gen. 173 (1971) (no "late kid" exception); *V.J. Gautieri, Inc.*, B-181720, Sep. 17, 1974, 74-2 CPD ¶ 173 (voting case); *Data Pathing, Inc.*, B-188234, May 5, 1977, 77-1 CPD ¶ 311 (sniper); *Work Sys. Design, Inc.*, B-223942, Nov. 26, 1986, 86-2 CPD ¶ 613 (bid left at loading dock); *National Minority Research Dev. Corp.*, B-220057, Sept. 18, 1985, 85-2 CPD ¶ 303 (car accident); *Gull's, Inc.*, B-232599, Jan. 25, 1989, 89-1 CPD ¶ 74 (building entrance locked and blocked by construction); *Fire Sec. Sys., Inc.*, B-236132, Oct. 24, 1989, 89-2 CPD ¶ 374 (manhandling of protester's agent by another bidder's agent).

e. The bidder must not have contributed substantially to the late receipt of the bid; it must act reasonably to fulfill its responsibility to deliver the bid to the proper place by the proper time. *Bergen Expo Sys., Inc.*, B-236970, Dec. 11, 1989, 89-2 CPD ¶ 540 (Federal Express courier refused access by guards, but courier departed); *Monthei Mechanical, Inc.*, B-216624, Dec. 17, 1984, 84-2 CPD ¶ 675 (bid box moved, but bidder arrived only 30 seconds before bid opening).

f. This rule has no statutory or regulatory basis; rather, the GAO fashioned the rule under its bid protest authority.

## G. Modifications and Withdrawals of Bids.

1. When may offerors modify their bids?

    a. *Before* bid opening: Bidders may modify their bids at any time before bid opening. FAR 14.303; FAR 52.214-7.

    b. *After* bid opening: Bidders may modify their bids only if one of the four exceptions to the Late Bid Rule applies to the modification. FAR 14.304; FAR 52.214-7(b).

    (1) Five Day Rule.

    (2) Two Day Rule.

    (3) Government Mishandling Rule. *CWC, Inc.*, B-204445, Dec. 15, 1981, 81-2 CPD ¶ 475 (Western Union exception); *Monaco Enter.*, B-205031, Mar. 4, 1982, 82-1 CPD ¶ 197.

    (4) Government Frustration Rule. *I & E Constr. Co.*, B-186766, Aug. 9, 1976, 76-2 CPD ¶ 139.

    c. An additional exception applies to modification of bids. The government may accept a late modification to an otherwise successful bid if it is more favorable to the government. FAR 14.304-1(e); FAR 52.214-7(f); *Environmental Tectonics Corp.*, B-225474, Feb. 17, 1987, 87-1 CPD ¶ 175.

2. When may offerors withdraw their bids?

    a. *Before* bid opening: Bidders may withdraw their bids at any time before bid opening. FAR 14.303; FAR 52.214-7.

    b. *After* bid opening. Because of the Firm Bid Rule, bidders generally may withdraw their bids *only if* one of the four exceptions to the Late Bid Rule applies. FAR 14.304-1; FAR 52.214-7(b). *See* Para. VII.G, *infra*.

3. Transmission of modifications or withdrawals of bids. FAR 14.303 and FAR 52.214-5.

    a. Offerors may modify or withdraw their bids by written or telegraphic notice, which must be received in the office designated in the invitation for bids before the exact time set for bid opening. FAR 14.303(a).

    b. The exceptions to the late bid rule apply to bid modifications and bid withdrawals only if the modification or withdrawal is received prior to contract award, unless it is a modification of the successful offeror's bid. FAR 14.304-1(a); FAR 14.304-1(e).

## VII. PHASE #4—EVALUATION OF BIDS.

### A. Evaluation of Price.

FAR 14.407-1(a).

1. Contracting officer evaluates price and price-related factors. FAR 14.201-8; *Monterey Bay Boatworks Co.*, B-255321, Feb. 24, 1994, 94-1 CPD ¶ 145 (price-related factors).

2. Award made on basis of lowest price offered.

3. The government may reject a materially unbalanced bid. A materially unbalanced bid contains inflated prices for some contract line items and below-cost prices for other line items, and gives rise to a reasonable doubt that award will result in the lowest overall cost to the government. FAR 14.404-2(g); *LBCO, Inc.*, B-254995, Feb. 1, 1994, 94-1 CPD ¶ 57 (inflated first article prices); *Custom Envtl. Serv., Inc.*, B-252538, July 7, 1993, 93-2 CPD ¶ 7.

### B. Evaluation of Responsiveness of Bids.

10 U.S.C. § 2305; 41 U.S.C. § 253b.

1. General rule: The government must reject, as nonresponsive, any bid that fails to conform to the essential requirements of the IFB. FAR 14.301(a); FAR 14.404-2.

2. A bid is responsive if it unequivocally offers to provide the requested supplies or services at a firm, fixed price. Unless something on the face of the bid either limits, reduces, or modifies the obligation to perform in accordance with the terms of the invitation, the bid is responsive. *Metric Sys. Corp.*, B-256343, June 10, 1994, 94-1 CPD ¶ 360 (bidder's exception to IFB indemnification

requirements changed legal relationship between parties); *Toyo Menka Kaisha, LTD*, 597 F.2d 1371 (Ct. Cl. 1979); *Ibex Ltd.*, B-230218, Mar. 11, 1988, 88-1 CPD ¶ 257.

3. The government may not accept a nonresponsive bid even though it would result in monetary savings to the government since acceptance would compromise the integrity of the bidding system. *MIBO Constr. Co.*, B-224744, Dec. 17, 1986, 86-2 CPD ¶ 678; *Perkin-Elmer*, B-214040, Aug. 8, 1984, 63 Comp. Gen. 529, 84-2 CPD ¶ 158.

4. When is responsiveness determined? The contracting officer determines the responsiveness of each bid at the time of bid opening by ascertaining whether the bid meets all of the IFB's essential requirements. *Gelco Payment Sys., Inc.*, B-234957, July 10, 1989, 89-2 CPD ¶ 27.

5. Essential requirements of responsiveness. FAR 14.301; FAR 14.404-2; FAR 14.405; *Tektronix, Inc.; Hewlett Packard Co.*, B-227800, Sep. 29, 1987, 66 Comp. Gen. 704, 87-2 CPD ¶ 315.

    a. *Price*. FAR 14.404-2(d); *United States Coast Guard—Advance Decision*, B-252396, Mar. 31, 1993, 93-1 CPD ¶ 286 (bid nonresponsive where price included fee of $1,000 per hour for "additional unscheduled testing" by government); *J & W Welding & Fabrication*, B-209430, Jan. 25, 1983, 83-1 CPD ¶ 92 ("plus 5% sales tax if applicable—"nonresponsive); *Grosfeld Enter.*, B-208654, Jan. 31, 1983, 83-1 CPD ¶ 106 ("plus expenses"—nonresponsive);

    b. *Quantity. Inscom Elec. Corp.*, B-225221, Feb. 4, 1987, 87-1 CPD ¶ 116 (bid limited government's right to reduce quantity under the IFB); *Pluribus Prod., Inc.*, B-224435, Nov. 7, 1986, 86-2 CPD ¶ 536.

    c. *Quality*. FAR 14.404-2(b); *Wyoming Weavers, Inc.*, B-229669.3, June 2, 1988, 88-1 CPD ¶ 519; *DeVac, Inc.*, B-224348.2, Sept. 3, 1986, 86-2 CPD ¶ 254;

    d. *Delivery*. FAR 14.404-2(c); *Viereck Co.*, B-256175, May 16, 1994, 94-1 CPD ¶ 310

(bid nonresponsive where bidder agreed to 60-day delivery date only if the cover page of the contract were faxed on the day of contract award); *HoseCo, Inc.*, B-226420, Mar. 12, 1987, 87-1 CPD ¶ 282; *but see Image Contracting*, B-253038, Aug. 11, 1993, 93-2 CPD ¶ 95 (bidder's failure to designate which of two locations it intended to deliver did not render bid nonresponsive where IFB permitted delivery to either location).

6. Other bases for rejection of bids for being nonresponsive.

    a. Ambiguous, indefinite, or uncertain bids. FAR 14.404-2(d); *Reid & Gary Strickland Co.*, B-239700, Sept. 17, 1990, 90-2 CPD ¶ 222 (notation in bid ambiguous); *Sunrise Int'l Group, Inc.; Eagle III Knoxville, Inc.*, B-252735.2, July 27, 1993, 93-2 CPD ¶ 58 (uncertainty as to identity of bidder).

    b. Variation of acceptance period. *John's Janitorial Serv.*, B-219194, July 2, 1985, 85-2 CPD ¶ 20.

    c. Placing a "confidential" stamp on bid. *Concept Automation, Inc. v. General Accounting Office*, GSBCA No. 11688-P, Mar. 31, 1992, 92-2 BCA ¶ 24,937. *But see North Am. Resource Recovery Corp.*, B-254485, Dec. 17, 1993, 93-2 CPD ¶ 327 ("proprietary data" notation on cover of bid did not restrict public disclosure of the bid where no pages of the bid were marked as proprietary).

    d. Bid conditioned on receipt of local license. *National Ambulance Co., Inc.*, B-184439, Dec. 29, 1975, 55 Comp. Gen. 597, 75-2 CPD ¶ 413.

    e. Requiring government to make progress payments. *Vertiflite, Inc.*, B-256366, May 12, 1994, 94-1 CPD ¶ 304.

    f. Failure to furnish required or adequate bid guarantee. *Quantum Constr., Inc.*, B-255049, Dec. 1, 1993, 93-2 CPD ¶ 304 (defective power of attorney submitted with bid bond); *Kinetic Builders, Inc.*, B-223594, Sept. 24, 1986, 65 Comp. Gen. 871, 86-2 CPD ¶ 342 (bond referenced another solicitation number); *Clyde McHen-ry, Inc.*, B-224169, Sept. 25, 1986, 86-2 CPD ¶ 352 (surety's obligation under bond unclear); *Design for Health, Inc.*, B-239730, Sept. 14, 1990, 69 Comp. Gen. 712, 90-2 CPD ¶ 213 (inconsistent bid bonds).

g. Exception to liquidated damages. *Dubie-Clark Co.*, B-186918, Aug. 26, 1976, 76-2 CPD ¶ 194.

h. Solicitation requires F.O.B. destination, bid states F.O.B. origin. *Taylor-Forge Eng'd Sys., Inc.*, B-236408, Nov. 3, 1989, 69 Comp. Gen. 54, 89-2 CPD ¶ 421.

i. Bid by large business on small business set-aside procurement. *Teletronics, Inc.*, B-224474, Sep. 25, 1986, 86-2 CPD ¶ 355.

j. Failure to submit Procurement Integrity Certification. *Gammon Technical Prods.*, B-257497, June 15, 1994, 94-1 CPD ¶ 370.

k. Failure to include sufficient descriptive literature (when required by IFB) to demonstrate offered product's compliance with specifications. FAR 52.214-21; *Adrian Supply Co.*, B-250767, Feb. 12, 1993, 93-1 CPD ¶ 131.

**NOTE**: The contracting officer generally should disregard *unsolicited* descriptive literature. However, if the unsolicited literature reasonably raises questions as to whether the offered product complies with a material requirement of the IFB, the bid should be rejected as nonresponsive. FAR 14.202-5(f); FAR 14.202-4(g); *Delta Chem. Corp.*, B-255543, Mar. 4, 1994, 94-1 CPD ¶ 175; *Amjay Chems.*, B-252502, May 28, 1993, 93-1 CPD ¶ 426.

## C. Responsiveness Distinguished from Responsibility.

*Data Express, Inc.*, B-234685, July 11, 1989, 89-2 CPD ¶ 28.

1. Bid responsiveness concerns whether a bidder has offered *unequivocally* in its bid documents to provide supplies in conformity with all material terms and conditions of a solicitation for sealed bids, and it is determined as of the time of bid opening.

2. Responsibility refers to a bidder's apparent *ability* and *capacity* to perform, and it is determined any time prior to award. *Triton Marine Constr. Corp.*, B-255373, Oct. 20, 1993, 93-2 CPD ¶ 255 (bidder's failure to submit with its bid preaward information to determine the bidder's ability to perform the work solicited does not render bid nonresponsive).

3. The issue of responsiveness is relevant only to the sealed bidding method of contracting.

## D. Informalities or Irregularities in Bids.
FAR 14.405.

1. Minor irregularities.
   a. Definition: A minor informality or irregularity is merely a matter of form, not of substance. The defect or variation is immaterial when the effect on price, quantity, quality, or delivery is negligible when contrasted with the total cost or scope of supplies or services acquired.
   b. Examples of minor irregularities.
      (1) Failure to return the number of copies of signed bids required by the IFB. FAR 14.405(a).
      (2) Failure to submit employer identification number. *Dyneteria, Inc.*, B-186823, Oct. 18, 1976, 76-2 CPD ¶ 338.
      (3) Use of abbreviated corporate name if the bid otherwise establishes the identity of the party to be bound by contract award. *Americorp*, B-232688, Nov. 23, 1988, 88-2 CPD ¶ 515 (bid also gave Federal Employee Identification Number).
      (4) Failure to certify as a small business on a small business set-aside. *Willis B. Simmons, Inc. & Assocs.*, B-226477, Mar. 17, 1987, 87-1 CPD ¶ 299.
      (5) Failure to submit construction progress schedule with bid. *James E. McFadden, Inc.*, B-186180, June 17, 1976, 76-1 CPD ¶ 393.
      (6) Failure to initial bid correction. *Durden & Fulton, Inc.*, B-192203, Sept. 5,

1978, 78-2 CPD ¶ 172.

(7) Failure to price individually each line item on a contract to be awarded on an "all or none" basis. *Seaward Corp.*, B-237107.2, June 13, 1990, 90-1 CPD ¶ 552; *see also Vista Contracting, Inc.*, B-255267, Jan. 7, 1994, 94-1 CPD ¶ 61 (failure to indicate cumulative bid price).

(8) Negligible variation in quantity. *Alco Envtl. Servs., Inc.*, ASBCA No. 43183, 94-1 BCA ¶ 26,261 (variation in IFB quantity of .27 percent).

(9) Failure to acknowledge amendment of the solicitation if the amendment is nonessential, its impact on the cost of contract performance is *de minimis*, or the bid received is clearly based on the IFB requirements as amended. *See* VI.E, *infra*.

c. Discretionary decision—the contracting officer shall give the bidder an opportunity to cure any deficiency resulting from a minor informality or irregularity in a bid or waive the deficiency, whichever is to the government's advantage. *Excavation Constr. Inc. v. United States*, 494 F.2d 1289 (Ct. Cl. 1974).

2. Normally, a bidder's failure to sign the bid is not a minor irregularity, and the government must reject the unsigned bid.

a. "Blank" signature block. *Valencia Technical Serv., Inc.*, B-223288, July 7, 1986, 86-2 CPD ¶ 40.

b. Typewritten name. *Power Master Elec. Co.*, B-223995, Nov. 26, 1986, 86-2 CPD ¶ 615.

c. *Exception*. If the bidder has manifested an intent to be bound by the bid, the failure to sign is a minor irregularity.

(1) Adopted alternative. *A & E Indus.*, B-239846, May 31, 1990, 90-1 CPD ¶ 527 (bid signed with a rubber stamp signature must be accompanied by evidence authorizing use of the rubber stamp signature).

(2) Other signed materials. *Cable Consul-*

*tants, Inc.*, B-215138, 63 Comp. Gen. 521 (1984); *Tilley Constructors & Eng'rs, Inc.*, B-251335.2, Apr. 2, 1993, 93-1 CPD ¶ 289; *Johnny F. Smith Truck & Dragline Serv., Inc.*, B-252136, June 3, 1993, 93-1 CPD ¶ 427 (signed certificate of procurement integrity).

(3) Hand-printed signatures. *Manheim Pattern Works*, B-186837, July 30, 1976, 76-2 CPD ¶ 103.

## E. Failure to Acknowledge Amendment of Solicitations.

1. General rule: Failure to acknowledge a material amendment renders the bid nonresponsive. *Logistics & Computer Consultants Inc.*, B-253949, Oct. 26, 1993, 93-2 CPD ¶ 250 (amendment placing additional obligations on contractor under a management contract); *Safe-T-Play, Inc.*, B-250682.2, Apr. 5, 1993, 93-1 CPD ¶ 292 (amendment classifying workers under Davis-Bacon Act); *Martech USA, Inc.*, B-245957, Feb. 11, 1992, 92-1 CPD ¶ 173; *Arboreal, Inc.*, B-231941, Oct. 17, 1988, 88-2 CPD ¶ 358; *Schell Elec., Inc.*, B-224696, Sept. 24, 1986, 86-2 CPD ¶ 348 (bidder never received amendment, but agency said it mailed one and did not consciously and deliberately intend to exclude bidder).

2. Even if an amendment has no clear effect on the contract price, it is material if it changes the legal relationship of the parties. *Anacomp, Inc.*, B-256788, July 27, 1994, 94-2 CPD ¶ 44 (amendment requiring contractor to pickup computer tapes on "next business day" when regular pickup day was a federal holiday); *Favino Mechanical Constr., Ltd.*, B-237511, Feb. 9, 1990, 90-1 CPD ¶ 174 (amendment incorporating Order of Precedence clause).

3. Exceptions:

a. The amendment was nonessential or trivial, i.e., not material. FAR 14.405(d)(2); *L&R Rail Serv.*, B-256341, June 10, 1994, 94-1 CPD ¶ 356 (amendment decreasing cost of performance not material); *Day & Night Janitorial and Maid Serv., Inc.*, B-240881, Jan. 2, 1991, 91-1 CPD ¶ 1 (negligible effect on price, quantity, quality, or delivery).

b. The bid received clearly indicates that the amendment was received by bidder. *C Constr. Co.*, B-228038, Dec. 2, 1987, 67 Comp. Gen. 107, 87-2 CPD ¶ 534.

4. How does a bidder acknowledge an amendment?

a. In writing only. Oral acknowledgement of an amendment is insufficient. *Alcon, Inc.*, B-228409, Feb. 5, 1988, 88-1 CPD ¶ 114.

b. Methods of acknowledgement.

(1) Sign and return a copy of the amendment to the contracting officer.

(2) Clearly acknowledge, within the bid submitted, receipt of any amendments. *See* Appendix 5-B, Standard Form 33, Block 14.

(3) Notify the government by letter or by telegram of receipt of the amendment.

**F. Rejection of All Bids—Cancellation of the IFB.**

1. *Prior* to bid opening, almost any reason will justify cancellation of an invitation for bids if the cancellation is "in the public interest." FAR 14.209; *Ramsey Canyon Enters.*, B-204576, Mar. 15, 1982, 82-1 CPD ¶ 237.

2. *After* bid opening, the government may not cancel an IFB unless there is a compelling reason to reject all bids and cancel the invitation. FAR 14.404-1(a)(1); *Canadian Commercial Corp./ Ballard Battery Sys. Corp.*, B-255642, Mar. 18, 1994, 94-1 CPD ¶ 202 (no compelling reason to cancel simply because some terms of IFB are somehow deficient); *Flintstone Crushing & Constr. Co.*, B-241803, Feb. 26, 1991, 91-1 CPD ¶ 216; *US Rentals*, B-238090, Apr. 5, 1990, 69 Comp. Gen. 395, 90-1 CPD ¶ 367 (contracting agency lacked compelling reason to cancel IFB for rental construction equipment; contracting officer cannot deliberately let bid acceptance period expire as a vehicle for cancellation).

a. Examples of compelling reasons to cancel.

(1) Insufficient funds. *Armed Forces Sports Officials, Inc.*, B-251409, Mar. 23, 1993, 93-1 CPD ¶ 261 (no requirement for agency to seek increase in funds); *Ignacio Sanchez Constr.*, B-238492, May 11, 1990, 90-1 CPD ¶ 467.

(2) Requirement disappeared. *Zwick Energy Research Org., Inc.*, B-237520.3, Jan. 25, 1991, 91-1 CPD ¶ 72 (specification required engines driven by gasoline; agency directive required diesel).

(3) Specifications are defective and fail to state the government's minimum needs, or unreasonably exclude potential bidders. *McGhee Constr., Inc.*, B-250073.3, May 13, 1993, 93-1 CPD ¶ 379; *Control Corp.; Control Data Sys., Inc.—Protest and Entitlement to Costs*, B-251224.2, May 3, 1993, 93-1 CPD ¶ 353; *Digitize, Inc.*, B-235206.3, Oct. 5, 1989, 90-1 CPD ¶ 403.

(4) Agency can obtain an item faster and cheaper by building it in-house. *Bush-Herrick, Inc.*, B-209683, June 20, 1983, 83-1 CPD ¶ 669.

(5) Time delay of litigation. *P. Francini & Co. v. United States*, 2 Cl. Ct. 7 (1983).

(6) All bids unreasonable in price. *California Shorthand Reporting*, B-250302.2, Mar. 4, 1993, 93-1 CPD ¶ 202.

(7) Eliminate appearance of unfair competitive advantage. *P&C Constr.*, B-251793, Apr. 30, 1993, 93-1 CPD ¶ 361.

(8) Incorporate wage rate determination. *JC&N Maint., Inc.*, B-253876, Nov. 1, 1993, 93-2 CPD ¶ 253.

(9) Failure to set aside a procurement for small businesses or small disadvantaged businesses when required. *Ryon, Inc.*, B-256752.2, Oct. 27, 1994, 94-2 CPD ¶ 163; *Baker Support Servs., Inc.; Mgmt. Technical Servs., Inc.*, B-256192.3, Sept. 2, 1994, 94-2 CPD ¶ ___.

b. Before cancelling the IFB, the contracting

officer must consider any prejudice to bidders. If cancellation will affect bidders' competitive standing, such prejudicial effect on competition may offset the compelling reason for cancellation. *Canadian Commercial Corp.*, *supra*; *Safemasters Co.*, B-192941, Jan. 22, 1979, 58 Comp. Gen. 225, 79-1 CPD ¶ 38.

   c. If an agency relies on an improper basis to cancel a solicitation, the cancellation may be upheld if another proper basis for the cancellation exists. *Shields Enters. v. United States*, 28 Fed. Cl. 615 (1993).

   d. Cancellation of the IFB may be post-award. *Control Corp.*, B-251224.2, May 3, 1993, 93-1 CPD ¶ 353.

**G. Mistakes in Bids Asserted Before Award.** FAR 14.406.

1. General rule. A bidder bears the consequences of a mistake in its bid unless the contracting officer has actual or constructive notice of the mistake prior to award. *Advanced Images, Inc.*, B-209438.2, May 10, 1983, 83-1 CPD ¶ 495.

2. The government may permit the bidder to remedy substantive mistakes affecting price and price-related factors by correction or withdrawal of the bid. Thus, a clerical or arithmetical error normally is correctable or is a basis for withdrawal. *United Digital Networks, Inc.*, B-222422, July 17, 1986, 86-2 CPD ¶ 79 (multiplication error); *but see Virginia Beach Air Conditioning Corp.*, B-237172, Jan. 19, 1990, 69 Comp. Gen. 178; 90-1 CPD ¶ 78 (bid susceptible to two interpretations).

3. Mistakes in bid which are not correctable.

   a. Errors in judgment. *American Dredging Co.*, B-229991.2, Sept. 15, 1988, 88-2 CPD ¶ 248 (incorrect assumption regarding the capacity of the scows used to tow away dredged materials).

   b. Omission of items from the bid. *McGhee Constr., Inc.*, B-255863, Apr. 13, 1994, 94-1 CPD ¶ 254; *J. W. Creech Inc.*, B-191177, Mar. 8, 1978, 78-1 CPD ¶ 186. *But see*

*Pacific Components, Inc.*, B-252585, June 21, 1993, 93-1 CPD ¶ 478 (bid correction permitted for mistake due to omissions from subcontractor quotation).

   c. Nonresponsive bid. *National Office World, Inc.*, B-224120, Sep. 5, 1986, 86-2 CPD ¶ 270; *Meyer Tool and Mfg., Inc.*, B-222595, June 9, 1986, 86-1 CPD ¶ 537 (clerical error on bidder's delivery schedule not correctable).

4. Only the government and the bidder responsible for the alleged mistake have standing to raise the issue of a mistake. *Engineering Research, Inc.*, B-187067, Aug. 6, 1976, 76-2 CPD ¶ 134.

5. Contracting Officer's responsibilities.

   a. The contracting officer must examine each bid for mistakes. FAR 14.406-1; *Andy Elec. Co.—Recon.*, B-194610.2, Aug. 10, 1981, 81-2 CPD ¶ 111.

     (1) Actual notice of mistake in a bid.

     (2) Constructive notice of mistake in a bid, e.g., price disparity among bids or comparison with government estimate. *R.J. Sanders, Inc. v. U.S.*, 24 Cl. Ct. 288 (1991) (bid 32% below government estimate insufficient to place contracting officer on notice of mistake in bid); *Central Mechanical, Inc.*, B-206250, Dec. 20, 1982, 82-2 CPD ¶ 547 (allocation of price out of proportion to other bidders).

   b. Bid verification. The contracting officer must seek verification of each bid that he has reason to believe contains a mistake. FAR 14.406-3(g).

     (1) To ensure that the bidder is put on notice of the suspected mistake, the contracting officer must advise the bidder of all disclosable information that leads the contracting officer to believe that there is a mistake in the bid. *Liebherr Crane Corp.*, ASBCA No. 24707, 85-3 BCA ¶ 18,353, *aff'd* 810 F.2d 1153 (Fed. Cir. 1987) (procedure inadequate); *Williams & Co.*, B-189926, Dec. 27, 1977, 57 Comp. Gen. 159, 77-2

CPD ¶ 506 (discrepancy must be noted specifically); *but see DWS, Inc.*, ASBCA No. 29743, Sep. 2, 1992, 93-1 BCA ¶ 25,404 (particular price need not be mentioned in bid verification notice).

(2) Effect of bidder verification. Verification generally binds the contractor unless the discrepancy is so great that acceptance of the bid would be unfair to the submitter or to other bidders. *Trataros Constr., Inc.*, B-254600, Jan. 4, 1994, 94-1 CPD ¶ 1 (contracting officer properly rejected verified bid that was far out of line with other bids and the government estimate); *VA— Advance Decision*, B-225815.2, Oct. 15, 1987, 87-2 CPD ¶ 362. *But see Aztech Elec., Inc. and Rod's Elec., Inc.*, B-223630, Sept. 30, 1986, 86-2 CPD ¶ 368 (below-cost bid is a matter of business judgment, not an obvious error requiring rejection).

(3) Effect of inadequate verification. If the contracting officer fails to obtain adequate verification of a bid for which the government has actual or constructive notice of a mistake, the contractor may seek additional compensation or recission of the contract. *See, e.g., Solar Foam Insulation*, ASBCA No. 46921, 94-2 BCA ¶ 26,901.

c. The contracting officer may not award a contract to a bidder when the contracting officer has actual or constructive notice of a mistake in the bid, unless the mistake is waived or the bid is properly corrected in accordance with agency procedures. *Ouchinikov Bros.*, B-205186, May 25, 1982, 82-1 CPD ¶ 496; *Sealtite Corp.*, ASBCA No. 25805, 83-1 BCA ¶ 16,243;

6. Correction of mistakes prior to award—standard of proof and allowable evidence.

a. The bidder alleging the mistake has the burden of proof. *VA—Advance Decision*, B-225815.2, Oct. 15, 1987, 87-2 CPD ¶ 362;

b. Apparent clerical mistakes. FAR 14.406-2;

*Action Serv. Corp.*, B-254861, Jan. 24, 1994, 94-1 CPD ¶ 33 (additional zero); *Sovran Constr. Co.*, B-242104, Mar. 18, 1991, 91-1 CPD ¶ 295 (cumulative pricing); *Engle Acoustic & Tile, Inc.*, B-190467, Jan. 27, 1978, 78-1 CPD ¶ 72 (misplaced decimal point); *Dependable Janitorial Serv. & Supply Co.*, B-188812, July 13, 1977, 77-2 CPD ¶ 20 (discrepancy between unit and total prices); *B&P Printing, Inc.*, B-188511, June 2, 1977, 77-1 CPD ¶ 387 (comma rather than period— correct bid not approved).

(1) Contracting officer may correct, before award, any clerical mistake apparent on the face of the bid.

(2) The contracting officer must first obtain verification of the bid from the bidder.

c. Unapparent mistakes disclosed before award. FAR 14.406-3.

(1) Correction by low bidder. *Shoemaker & Alexander, Inc.*, B-241066, Jan. 15, 1991, 91-1 CPD ¶ 41.

(a) The low bidder must show by clear and convincing evidence: (i) the existence of a mistake in its bid; and (ii) the bid actually intended or that the intended bid would fall within a narrow range of uncertainty and remain low. *See Three O Constr., S.E.*, B-255749, Mar. 28, 1994, 94-1 CPD ¶ 216 (no clear and convincing evidence where bidder gave conflicting explanations for mistake).

(b) Bidder can refer to such things as: (i) bidder's file copy of the bid; (ii) original workpapers; (iii) a subcontractor's or supplier's quotes; or (iv) published price lists.

(2) Correction of a bid that *displaces a lower bidder. J & J Maint., Inc.*, B-251355, Mar. 1, 1993, 93-1 CPD ¶ 187; *Virginia Beach Air Conditioning Corp.*, B-237172, Jan. 19, 1990, 69 Comp. Gen. 132, 90-1 CPD ¶ 78; *Eagle*

*Elec.*, B-228500, Feb. 5, 1988, 88-1 CPD ¶ 116.

    (a) Bidder must show by clear and convincing evidence: (a) the existence of a mistake; and (b) the bid actually intended.

    (b) Limitation on proof - the bidder can prove a mistake only from the solicitation (IFB) and the bid submitted, not from any other sources.

d. Action permitted when a bidder presents clear and convincing evidence of a mistake, or evidence that reasonably supports the existence of a mistake, but does not establish what bid was intended. *Advanced Images, Inc.*, B-209438.2, May 10, 1983, 83-1 CPD ¶ 495.

    (1) The bidder may withdraw the bid. FAR 14.406-3(c).

    (2) The bidder may correct the bid where it is clear the intended bid would fall within a narrow range of uncertainty and remain the low bid. *Conner Bros. Constr. Co.*, B-228232.2, Feb. 3, 1988, 88-1 CPD ¶ 103; *Department of the Interior—Mistake in Bid Claim*, B-222681, July 23, 1986, 86-2 CPD ¶ 98.

    (3) The bidder may waive the bid mistake if it is clear that the intended bid would remain low. *William G. Tadlock Constr.*, B-251996, May 13, 1993, 93-1 CPD ¶ 382 (waiver not permitted); *LABCO Constr., Inc.*, B-219437, Aug. 28, 1985, 85-2 CPD ¶ 240; *Hercules Demolition Corp. of Virginia*, B-223583, Sep. 12, 1986, 86-2 CPD ¶ 292.

e. Once a bidder asserts a mistake, the agency head or designee may disallow withdrawal or correction of the bid if the bidder fails to prove the mistake. FAR 14.406-3(d); *Duro Paper Bag Mfg. Co.*, B-217227, Jan. 3, 1986, 65 Comp. Gen. 186, 86-1 CPD ¶ 6.

f. Approval levels for corrections or withdrawals of bids. FAR 14.406-2; FAR 14.406-3.

    (1) Apparent clerical errors: The contract-ing officer. FAR 14.406-2.

    (2) Withdrawal of a bid on clear and convincing evidence of a mistake, but not of the intended bid: An official above the contracting officer. FAR 14.406-3(c).

    (3) Correction of a bid on clear and convincing evidence both of the mistake and of the bid intended: The agency head or delegee. FAR 14.406-3(a). Caveat: If correction would displace a lower bid, government shall not permit the correction unless the mistake and the intended bid are both ascertainable substantially from the IFB and the bid submitted.

    (4) Correction rather than withdrawal of a low bidder's bid: If (a) a bidder requests permission to withdraw a bid rather than correct it, (b) the evidence is clear and convincing both as to the mistake in the bid and the bid intended, and (c) the bid, both as uncorrected and as corrected, is the lowest received, the agency head or designee may determine to correct the bid and not permit its withdrawal. FAR 14.406-3(b).

    (5) Neither correction nor withdrawal. If the evidence does not warrant correction or withdrawal, the agency head may refuse to permit either withdrawal or correction. FAR 14.406-3(d).

    (6) Heads of agencies may delegate their authority to correct or permit withdrawal of bids without power of redelegation. FAR 14.406-3(e). This authority has been delegated to specified authorities within Defense Departments and Agencies. DFARS 214.406-3.

## VIII. PHASE #5—AWARD OF THE CONTRACT.

### A. Evaluation of the Responsibility of the Successful Bidder.

10 U.S.C. § 2305; 41 U.S.C. § 253b.

1. Government acquisition policy requires that the contracting officer make an affirmative

determination of responsibility prior to award. FAR 9.103.

2. General rule. The contracting officer may award only to a responsible bidder. FAR 9.103(a); *Theodor Arndt GmbH & Co.*, B-237180, Jan. 17, 1990, 90-1 CPD ¶ 64 (responsibility requirement implied); *Atlantic Maint., Inc.*, B-239621.2, June 1, 1990, 90-1 CPD ¶ 523 (an unreasonably low price may render bidder nonresponsible); *but see The Galveston Aviation Weather Partnership*, B-252014.2, May 5, 1993, 93-1 CPD ¶ 370 (below-cost bid not legally objectionable, even when offering labor rates lower than those required by the Service Contract Act).

3. Responsibility defined. Responsibility refers to an offeror's apparent *ability* and *capacity* to perform. To be responsible, a prospective contractor must meet the standards of responsibility set forth at FAR 9.104. FAR 9.101; *Kings Point Indus.*, B-223824, Oct. 29, 1986, 66 Comp. Gen. 74, 86-2 CPD ¶ 488.

4. Responsibility is determined at any time prior to award. Therefore, the bidder may provide responsibility information to the contracting officer at any time before award. FAR 9.103; FAR 9.105-1; *ADC Ltd.*, B-254495, Dec. 23, 1993, 93-2 CPD ¶ 337 (bidder's failure to submit security clearance documentation with its bid is not a basis for rejection of bid); *Cam Indus.*, B-230597, May 6, 1988, 88-1 CPD ¶ 443.

## B. Minimum Standards of Responsibility— Contractor Qualification Standards.

1. General standards of responsibility. FAR 9.104-1.

   a. *Financial resources*. The contractor must demonstrate that it has adequate financial resources to perform the contract or that it has the ability to obtain such resources. FAR 9.104-1(a); *Excavators, Inc.*, B-232066, Nov. 1, 1988, 88-2 CPD ¶ 421 (a contractor is nonresponsible if it cannot or does not provide acceptable individual sureties).

      (1) *Bankruptcy*. Nonresponsibility determinations based solely on a bankruptcy petition violate 11 U.S.C. § 525. This statute prohibits a governmental unit from denying, revoking, suspending, or refusing to renew a license, permit, charter, franchise, or other similar grant to, or deny employment to, terminate employment of, or discriminate with respect to employment against, a person that is or has been a debtor under 11 U.S.C. § 525, solely because such person has been a debtor under this title.

      (2) The courts have applied the bankruptcy anti-discrimination provisions to government determinations of eligibility for award. *In re Son-Shine Grading*, 27 Bankr. 693 (Bankr. E.D.N.C. 1983); *In re Coleman American Moving Serv., Inc.*, 8 Bankr. 379 (Bankr. D. Kan. 1980).

      (3) A determination of responsibility should not be negative *solely* because of a prospective contractor's bankruptcy. The contracting officer should focus on the contractor's ability to perform the contract, and justify a nonresponsibility determination of a bankrupt contractor accordingly. *Harvard Interiors Mfg. Co.*, B-247400, May 1, 1992, 92-1 CPD ¶ 413 (Chapter 11 firm found nonresponsible based on lack of financial ability); *Sam Gonzales, Inc.—Recon.*, B-225542.2, Mar. 18, 1987, 87-1 CPD ¶ 306;

   b. *Delivery or performance schedule*: The contractor must establish its ability to comply with the delivery or performance schedule. FAR 9.104-1(b); *System Dev. Corp.*, B-212624, Dec. 5, 1983, 83-2 CPD ¶ 644.

   c. *Performance record*: The contractor must have an acceptable performance record. FAR 9.104-1(c). *Schenker Panamericana (Panama) S.A.*, B-253029, Aug. 2, 1993, 93-2 CPD ¶ 67 (agency justified in nonresponsiblity determination where moving contractor had previously failed to conduct premove surveys, failed to provide adequate packing materials, failed to keep appointments or complete work on time, dumped household goods into large containers, stacked unprotected furniture onto trucks, dragged unprotected furniture through hallways, and wrapped fragile goods in a single sheet of paper; termination for default on prior contract not required).

d. *Management/technical capability*: The contractor must display adequate management and technical capability to perform the contract satisfactorily. FAR 9.104-1(e); *TAAS-Israel Indus.*, B-251789.3, Jan. 14, 1994, 94-1 CPD ¶ 197 (contractor lacked design skills and knowledge to produce advanced missile launcher power supply).

e. *Equipment/facilities/production capacity*: The contractor must maintain or have access to sufficient equipment, facilities, and production capacity to accomplish the work required by the contract. FAR 9.104-1(f); *BMY, Div. of Harsco Corp.*, B-233081, Jan. 24, 1989, 89-1 CPD ¶ 67.

f. *Business ethics*: The contractor must have a satisfactory record of business ethics. FAR 9.104-1(d); FAR 9.407-2; FAR 14.404-2(h); *Interstate Equip. Sales*, B-225701, Apr. 20, 1987, 87-1 CPD ¶ 427.

2. Special or definitive standards of responsibility: Definitive responsibility criteria are specific, objective standards established by an agency to measure an offeror's ability to perform a given contract. FAR 9.104-2(a); *D.H. Kim Enters.*, B-255124, Feb. 8, 1994, 94-1 CPD ¶ 86.

a. An example is to require that a prospective contractor have a specified number of years of experience performing the same or similar work. *BBC Brown Boveri, Inc.*, B-227903, Sept. 28, 1987, 87-2 CPD ¶ 309 (IFB required five years of experience in transformer design, manufacture, and service - GAO held that this definitive respon-

sibility criterion was satisfied by a subcontractor); *Hardie-Tynes Mfg. Co.*, B-237938, Apr. 2, 1990, 69 Comp. Gen. 359, 90-1 CPD ¶ 587 (agency properly considered manufacturing experience of parent corporation in finding bidder met the definitive responsibility criterion of five years manufacturing experience).

b. Although the GAO will not readily review affirmative responsibility determinations based on general responsibility criteria, it will review affirmative responsibility determinations where the solicitation contains definitive responsibility requirements. 4 C.F.R. § 21.3(m)(5).

c. Evaluations using definitive responsibility criteria are subject to review by the Small Business Administration (SBA) through its Certificate of Competency process. FAR 19.602-4.

d. Statutory/Regulatory Compliance.
   (1) Licenses and permits.
       (a) When a solicitation contains a *general* condition that the contractor comply with state and local licensing requirements, the contracting officer need not inquire into what those requirements may be or whether the bidder will comply. *James C. Bateman Petroleum Serv., Inc.*, B-232325, Aug. 22, 1988, 67 Comp. Gen. 591, 88-2 CPD ¶ 170; *but cf. International Serv. Assocs.*, B-253050, Aug. 4, 1993, 93-2 CPD ¶ 82 (where agency determines that small business will not meet licensing requirement, referral to SBA required).
       (b) On the other hand, when a solicitation requires *specific* compliance with regulations and licensing requirements, the contracting officer may inquire into the offeror's ability to comply with the regulations in determining the offeror's responsibility. *Intera Technologies,*

*Inc.*, B-228467, Feb. 3, 1988, 88-1 CPD ¶ 104.

(2) *Statutory certification requirements.*

    (a) Small business concerns. The contractor must certify its status as a small business to be eligible for award as a small business. FAR 19.301.

    (b) Equal opportunity compliance. Contractors must certify that they will comply with "equal opportunity" statutory requirements. In addition, contracting officers must obtain pre-award clearances from the Department of Labor for equal opportunity compliance before awarding any contract exceeding $1 million. FAR Subpart 22.8. Solicitations may require the contractor to develop and file an affirmative action plan. FAR 52.222-22 and FAR 52.222-25; *General Elec. Co.; Westinghouse Elec. Corp.*, B-228140, Jan. 6, 1988, 67 Comp. Gen. 178, 88-1 CPD ¶ 6.

    (c) Drug-free workplace certification. The contractor must certify that it will provide a drug-free workplace by publishing certain notices to its employees, establishing a drug-awareness program, etc. FAR § 23.500; *Universal Hydraulics, Inc.*, B-235006, June 21, 1989, 89-1 CPD ¶ 585.

    (d) Submission of lobby certification. *Tennier Indus.*, B-239025, July 16, 1990, 90-2 CPD ¶ 25.

(3) Organizational conflicts of interest. FAR Subpart 9.5. Government policy precludes award of a contract, without some restriction on future activities, if the contractor would have an actual or potential unfair competitive advantage, or if the contractor would be biased in making judgments in performance of the work.

—Necessary restrictions on future activities of a contractor are incorporated in the contract in one or more organizational conflict of interest clauses. FAR 9.501; *The Analytic Sciences Corp.*, B-218074, Apr. 23, 1985, 85-1 CPD ¶ 464.

**C. Responsibility Determination Procedures.**

1. Sources of information. The contracting officer must obtain sufficient information to determine responsibility. FAR 9.105.

    a. Contracting officers may use pre-award surveys. FAR 9.105-1(b); FAR 9.106; DFARS 209.106; *Accurate Indus.*, B-232962, Jan. 23, 1989, 89-1 CPD ¶ 56.

    b. List entitled *Parties Excluded from Procurement Programs.* FAR 9.105-1(c)(1); *see also* AFARS 9.4 and FAR Subpart 9.4. *But see R.J. Crowley, Inc.*, B-253783, Oct. 22, 1993, 93-2 CPD ¶ 257 (agency improperly relied on non-current list of ineligible contractors as basis for rejecting bid; agency should have consulted electronic update).

    c. Contracting and audit agency records and data pertaining to a contractor's prior contracts are valuable sources of information. FAR 9.105-1(c)(2).

    d. Contracting officers also may use contractor-furnished information. FAR 9.105-1(c)(3).

2. Standards of review of contracting officer determinations of responsibility.

    a. The GAO will not review affirmative responsibility determinations absent a showing of bad faith or fraud. 4 CFR § 21.3(m)(5); *Hard Bottom Inflatables, Inc.*, B-245961.2, Jan. 22, 1992, 92-1 CPD ¶ 103.

    b. The GAO will review nonresponsibility determinations for reasonableness. *Schwender/Riteway Joint Venture*, B-250865.2, Mar. 4, 1993, 93-1 CPD ¶ 203 (determination of nonresponsibility unreasonable when based on inaccurate or incomplete information).

c. The GSBCA reviews affirmative determinations *de novo*. *Technology Advancement Group, Inc. v. Dep't of the Navy*, GSBCA No. 12709-P, 94-2 BCA ¶ 26,714 (board defers to the contracting officer in recognition of the highly discretionary nature of the decision).

3. Subcontractor responsibility issues.

   a. The agency may review subcontractor responsibility. FAR 9.104-4(a).

   b. Subcontractor responsibility is determined in the same fashion as is the responsibility of the prime contractor. FAR 9.104-4(b).

## D. Award of the Contract.

1. Statutory standard. The contracting officer shall award with reasonable promptness to the responsible bidder whose bid conforms to the solicitation and is most advantageous, considering price and other price-related factors. 10 U.S.C. § 2305(b)(4)(B); 41 U.S.C. § 253b; FAR 14.407-1(a).

2. Multiple awards. If the IFB does not prohibit partial bids, the government must make multiple awards when they will result in the lowest cost to the government. FAR 52.214-10; FAR 52.214-22; *WeatherExperts, Inc.*, B-255103, Feb. 9, 1994, 94-1 CPD ¶ 93.

3. An agency may not award a contract to an entity other than that which submitted a bid. *Gravely & Rodriguez*, B-256506, Mar. 28, 1994, 94-1 CPD ¶ 234 (sole proprietorship submitted bid, partnership sought award).

4. Communication of acceptance of the offer and award of the contract. The contracting officer makes award by giving written notice within the specified time for acceptance. FAR 14.407-1(a).

5. The "mail box" rule applies to award of federal contracts. Award is effective upon mailing (or otherwise furnishing the award document) to the successful offeror. FAR 14.407-1(c)(1). *Kleen-Rite Corp.*, B-190160, July 3, 1978, 78-2 CPD ¶ 2; *Singleton Contracting Corp.*, IBCA 1770-1-84, 86-2 BCA ¶ 18,800 (notice of award and request to withdraw bid mailed on same day).

## E. Mistakes in Bids Asserted After Award.
FAR 14.406-4; FAR Subpart 33.2 (Disputes and Appeals).

1. The contracting officer may correct a mistake by contract modification if correction would be favorable to the government and would not change the essential requirements of the specifications.

2. The government may:

   a. Rescind the contract;

   b. Reform the contract (i) to delete items involved in the mistake or (ii) to increase the contract price if the price as increased does not exceed that of the next lowest acceptable bid; or

   c. Make no change in the contract, if the evidence does not warrant rescission or reformation.

3. Rescission or reformation may be made only on the basis of clear and convincing evidence that a mistake in bid was made, and only if the mistake was (i) mutual or (ii) if unilaterally made by the contractor, was so apparent that the contracting officer should be charged with having had notice of the mistake. *Government Micro Resources, Inc. v. Dep't of Treasury*, GSBCA no. 12364-TD, 94-2 BCA ¶ 26,680 (government on constructive notice of mistake where contractor's price exceeded government estimate by 62% and comparison quote by 33%); *Kitco, Inc.*, ASBCA No. 45347, 93-3 BCA ¶ 26,153 (mistake must be clear cut clerical or arithmetical error, or misreading of specifications, not mistake of judgment); *Liebherr Crane Corp.*, 810 F.2d 1153 (Fed. Cir. 1987) (no relief for unilateral errors in business judgment).

4. Reformation is not available for contract formation mistakes. *Gould, Inc. v. United States*, 19 Cl. Ct. 257 (1990).

   a. Reformation is a form of equitable relief that applies to mistakes made in reducing the parties' intentions to writing, but not to mistakes that the parties made in forming the agreement. To show entitlement to reformation, the contractor must prove (i) a clear agreement between the parties and

(ii) an error in reducing the agreement to writing.

b. The contractor must prove four elements in a claim for reformation based on mutual mistake. *Management & Training Corp. v. Gen. Servs. Admin.*, GSBCA No. 11182, 93-2 BCA ¶ 25,814. These elements are:

(1) The parties to the contract were mistaken in their belief regarding a fact, *see Dairyland Power Co-op v. United States*, 16 F.3d 1197 (1994) (mistake must relate to an existing fact, not future events);

(2) The mistake involved a basic assumption of the contract;

(3) The mistake affected contract performance materially; and

(4) The party seeking reformation did not agree to bear the risk of a mistake.

5. Proof requirements. Mistakes alleged or disclosed after award are processed in accordance with FAR 14.406-4(e) and FAR Subpart 33.2. The contracting officer shall request the contractor to support the alleged mistake by submission of written statements and pertinent evidence. *See Government Micro Resources, Inc. v. Dep't of Treasury*, GSBCA No. 12364-TD, 94-2 BCA ¶ 26,680 (board awards contractor recovery on quantum valebant basis).

6. Mistakes alleged after award are subject to the Contract Disputes Act of 1978 and the Disputes and Appeals provisions of the FAR. FAR Subpart 33.2; *ABJ Servs.*, B-254155, July 23, 1993, 93-2 CPD ¶ 53 (the GAO will not review a mistake in bid claim alleged by the contractor after award).

7. Extraordinary contractual relief under Public Law No. 85-804. National Defense Contracts Act, 72 Stat. 972, 50 U.S.C. § 1431-1435; DFARS Subpart 250.7001.

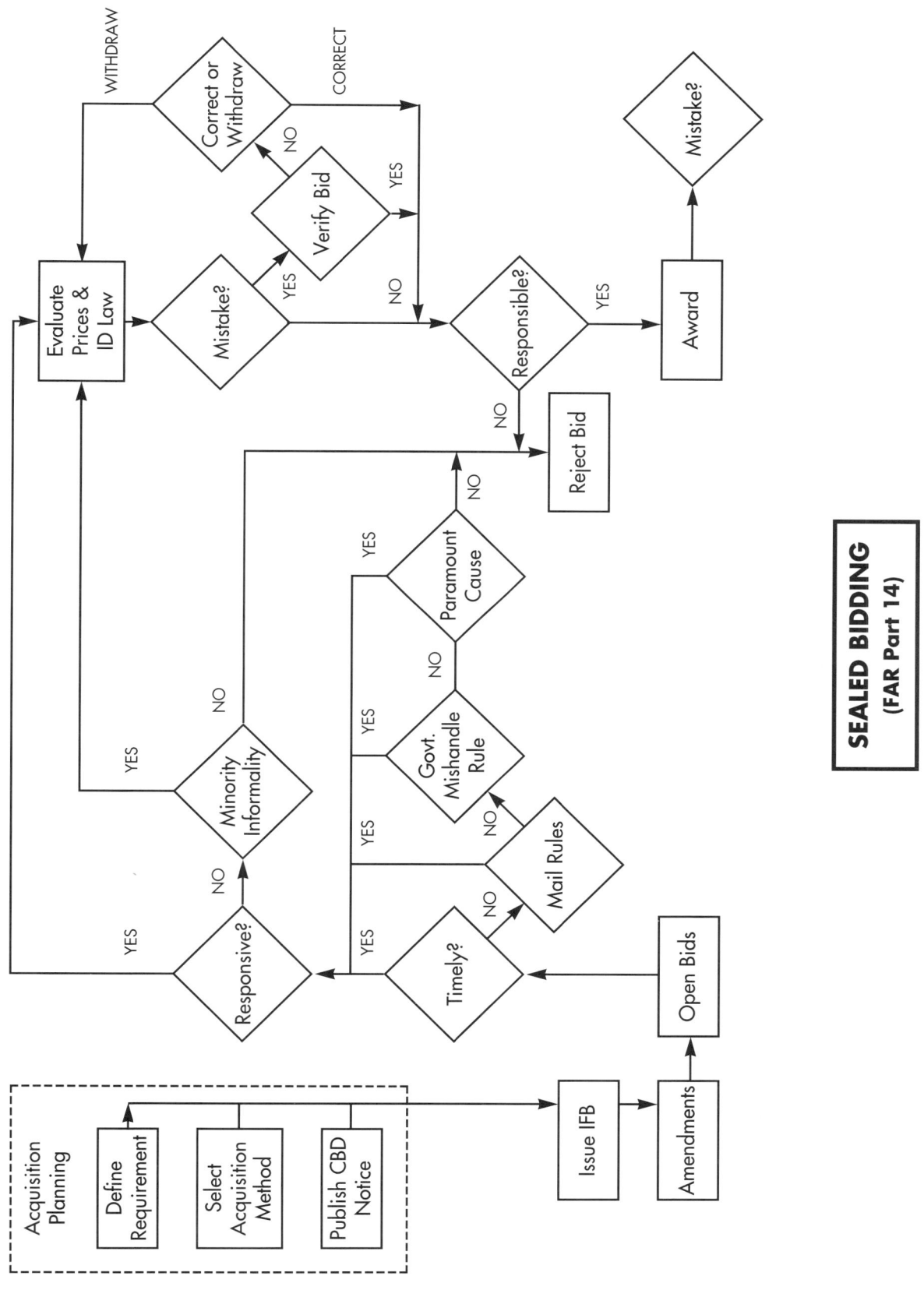

**SEALED BIDDING**
(FAR Part 14)

# STANDARD FORM 33

| SOLICITATION, OFFER AND AWARD | 1. THIS CONTRACT IS A RATED ORDER UNDER DPAS 915 CFR 350) | RATING | OMB Approved No. 9000-0008 |
|---|---|---|---|
| | | | PAGE OF PAGES |

| 2. CONTRACT NO. | 3. SOLICITATION NO. | 4. TYPE OF SOLICITATION | 5. DATE ISSUED | 6. REQUISITION/PURCHASE NO. |
|---|---|---|---|---|
| | | ☐ SEALED BID (IFB) ☐ NEGOTIATED (RFP) | | |

| 7. ISSUED BY | CODE | 8. ADDRESS OFFER TO (If other than Item 7) |
|---|---|---|
| | | |

NOTE: In sealed bid solicitations "offer" and "offeror" mean "bid" and "bidder".

## SOLICITATION

9. Sealed offers in original and _____ copies for furnishing the supplies or services in the Schedule will be received at the place specified in Item 8, or if handcarried, in the

depository located in _____ until _____ local time _____
(Hour) (Date)

CAUTION—LATE Submissions, Modifications, and Withdrawals: See Section L, Provision No. 52.214-7 or 52.215-10. All offers are subject to all terms and conditions contained in this solicitation.

| 10. FOR INFORMATION CALL: | A. NAME | B. TELEPHONE NO. (Include area code) (NO COLLECT CALLS) |
|---|---|---|
| | | |

### 11. TABLE OF CONTENTS

| (✓) | SEC. | DESCRIPTION | PAGE(S) | (✓) | SEC. | DESCRIPTION | PAGE(S) |
|---|---|---|---|---|---|---|---|
| | | PART I – THE SCHEDULE | | | | PART II – CONTRACT CLAUSES | |
| | A | SOLICITATION/CONTRACT FORM | | | I | CONTRACT CLAUSES | |
| | B | SUPPLIES OR SERVICES AND PRICES/COSTS | | | | PART III – LIST OF DOCUMENTS, EXHIBITS AND OTHER ATTACH. | |
| | C | DESCRIPTION/SPECS./WORK STATEMENT | | | J | LIST OF ATTACHMENTS | |
| | D | PACKAGING AND MARKING | | | | PART IV – REPRESENTATIONS AND INSTRUCTIONS | |
| | E | INSPECTION AND ACCEPTANCE | | | K | REPRESENTATIONS, CERTIFICATIONS AND OTHER STATEMENTS OF OFFERORS | |
| | F | DELIVERIES OR PERFORMANCE | | | | | |
| | G | CONTRACT ADMINISTRATION DATA | | | L | INSTR., CONDS., AND NOTICES TO OFFERORS | |
| | H | SPECIAL CONTRACT REQUIREMENTS | | | M | EVALUATION FACTORS FOR AWARD | |

## OFFER (Must be fully completed by offeror)

NOTE: Item 12 does not apply if the solicitation includes the provisions at 52.214-16, Minimum Bid Acceptance Period.

12. In compliance with the above, the undersigned agrees, if this offer is accepted within _____ calendar days (60 calendar days unless a different period is inserted by the offeror) from the date for receipt of offers specified above, to furnish any or all items upon which prices are offered at the price set opposite each item, delivered at the designated point(s), within the time specified in the schedule.

| 13. DISCOUNT FOR PROMPT PAYMENT (See Section I, Clause No. 52-232-8) | 10 CALENDAR DAYS | 20 CALENDAR DAYS | 30 CALENDAR DAYS | CALENDAR DAYS |
|---|---|---|---|---|
| | % | % | % | % |

| 14. ACKNOWLEDGMENT OF AMENDMENTS The offeror acknowledges receipt of amendments to the SOLICITATION for offerors and related documents numbered and dated: | AMENDMENT NO. | DATE | AMENDMENT NO. | DATE |
|---|---|---|---|---|
| | | | | |

| 15A. NAME AND ADDRESS OF OFFEROR | CODE | FACILITY | 16. NAME AND TITLE OF PERSON AUTHORIZED TO SIGN OFFER (Type or print) |
|---|---|---|---|
| 15B. TELEPHONE NO. (Include area code) | 15C. CHECK IF REMITTANCE ADDRESS IS DIFFERENT FROM ABOVE. ENTER SUCH ADDRESS IN SCHEDULE | 17. SIGNATURE | 18. OFFER DATE |

## AWARD (To be completed by Government)

| 19. ACCEPTED AS TO ITEMS NUMBERED | 20. AMOUNT | 21. ACCOUNTING AND APPROPRIATION |
|---|---|---|
| | | |

| 22. AUTHORITY FOR USING OTHER THAN FULL AND OPEN COMPETITION: | |
|---|---|
| ☐ 10 U.S.C. 2304(c)( ) ☐ 41 U.S.C. 253(c)( ) | 23. SUBMIT INVOICES TO ADDRESS SHOWN IN ▶ (4 copies unless otherwise specified) | ITEM |

| 24. ADMINISTERED BY (If other than Item 7) | CODE | 25. PAYMENT WILL BE MADE BY | CODE |
|---|---|---|---|
| | | | |

| 26. NAME OF CONTRACTING OFFICER (Type or print) | 27. UNITED STATES OF AMERICA (Signature of Contracting Officer) | 28. AWARD DATE |
|---|---|---|
| | | |

IMPORTANT – Award will be made on this Form, or on Standard Form 26, or by other authorized official written notice.

NSN 7540-01-152-8064
PREVIOUS EDITION NOT USABLE

33-134
Prescribed by GSA
FAR (48 CFR) 53.214(c)

STANDARD FORM 33 (REV. 4-85)

# STANDARD FORM 30

| AMENDMENT OF SOLICITATION/MODIFICATION OF CONTRACT | 1. CONTRACT ID CODE | PAGE OF PAGES |
|---|---|---|

| 2. AMENDMENT/MODIFICATION NO. | 3. EFFECTIVE DATE | 4. REQUISITION/PURCHASE REQ. NO. | 5. PROJECT NO. (If applicable) |
|---|---|---|---|

| 6. ISSUED BY | CODE | 7. ADMINISTERED BY (If other than Item 6) | CODE |
|---|---|---|---|

8. NAME AND ADDRESS OF CONTRACTOR (No., street, county, state and ZIP code)

| (✓) | 9A. AMENDMENT OF SOLICITATION NO. |
|---|---|
| | 9B. DATED (SEE ITEM 11) |
| | 10A. MODIFICATION OF CONTRACT/ORDER NO. |
| | 10B. DATED (SEE ITEM 13) |

CODE       FACILITY CODE

## 11. THIS ITEM ONLY APPLIES TO AMENDMENTS OF SOLICITATIONS

☐ The above numbered solicitation is amended as set forth in Item 14. The hour and date specified for receipt of Offers ☐ is extended, ☐ is not extended.

Offers must acknowledge receipt of this amendment prior to the hour and date specified in the solicitation or as amended, by one of the following methods:

(a) By completing Items 8 and 15, and returning _____ copies of the amendment; (b) By acknowledging receipt of this amendment on each copy of the offer submitted; or (c) By separate letter or telegram which includes a reference to the solicitation and amendment numbers. FAILURE OF YOUR ACKNOWLEDGMENT TO BE RECEIVED AT THE PLACE DESIGNATED FOR THE RECEIPT OF OFFERS PRIOR TO THE HOUR AND DATE SPECIFIED MAY RESULT IN REJECTION OF YOUR OFFER. If by virtue of this amendment you desire to change an offer already submitted, such change may be made by telegram or letter, provided each telegram or letter makes reference to the solicitation and this amendment, and is received prior to the opening hour and date specified.

12. ACCOUNTING AND APPROPRIATION DATA (If required)

## 13. THIS ITEM APPLIES ONLY TO MODIFICATIONS OF CONTRACTS/ORDERS, IT MODIFIES THE CONTRACT/ORDER NO. AS DESCRIBED IN ITEM 14.

| (✓) | |
|---|---|
| | A. THIS CHANGE ORDER IS ISSUED PURSUANT TO: (Specifiy authority) THE CHANGES SET FORTH IN ITEM 14 ARE MADE IN THE CONTRACT ORDER NO. IN ITEM 10A. |
| | B. THE ABOVE NUMBERED CONTRACT/ORDER IS MODIFIED TO REFLECT THE ADMINISTRATIVE CHANGES (such as changes in paying office, appropriation date, etc.) SET FORTH IN ITEM 14, PURSUANT TO THE AUTHORITY OF FAR 43.103(b). |
| | C. THIS SUPPLEMENTAL AGREEMENT IS ENTERED INTO PURSUANT TO AUTHORITY OF: |
| | D. OTHER (Specify type of modification and authority) |

E. IMPORTANT: Contractor ☐ is not, ☐ is required to sign this document and return _____ copies to the issuing office.

14. DESCRIPTION OF AMENDMENT/MODIFICATION (Organized by UCF section headings, including solicitation/contract subject matter where feasible.)

Except as provided herein, all terms and conditions of the document referenced in Item 9A or 10A, as heretofore changed, remains unchanged and in full force and effect.

| 15A. NAME AND TITLE OF SIGNER (Type or print) | 16A. NAME AND TITLE OF CONTRACTING OFFICER (Type or print) | |
|---|---|---|
| 15B. CONTRACTOR/OFFEROR | 15C. DATE SIGNED | 16B. UNITED STATES OF AMERICA | 16C. DATE SIGNED |
| _____ (Signature of person authorized to sign) | | BY _____ (Signature of Contracting Officer) | |

NSN 7540-01-152-8070
PREVIOUS EDITION UNUSABLE

30-105-02

STANDARD FORM 30 (Rev. 10-83)
Prescribed by GSA
FAR (48 CFR) 53.243

55

## CHAPTER SIX

# *Negotiations*

## I. INTRODUCTION.

### A. Objectives. Following this instruction, students will understand:

1. The extensive planning required to conduct a competitively negotiated procurement.
2. The procedures used to conduct negotiated acquisitions.
3. Some of the common problem areas to avoid to award negotiated contracts successfully.

### B. Types of Negotiated Acquisitions. *See* page 85.

1. Competitively Negotiated Acquisitions.
2. Four-Step Negotiated Acquisitions.
3. Broad Agency Announcements.
4. Architect-Engineer Contracting.
5. Sole or Limited Source Acquisitions.
6. Unsolicited Proposals.

### C. Background.

Negotiated procurements formerly were known as "open market purchases." These procurements were authorized only in emergencies. The Army Air Corps began using negotiated procurements in the 1930s to develop and acquire aircraft, despite statutory provisions to the contrary. Negotiations procedures became universal during World War II. The Armed Services Procurement Act of 1947 authorized negotiated procurements for peacetime use, if one of seventeen exceptions to formal advertising (now sealed bidding) applied. In 1962 Congress codified agency regulations requiring submission of cost or pricing data in certain procurements, to aid in the negotiations process. The Competition in Contracting Act (CICA) of 1984 expanded the use of negotiated procurements by eliminating the traditional preference for formal advertising. In 1990 and in 1994, Congress modified the procedures for award on initial proposals, expanded debriefings, and made other minor changes in negotiations procedures.

## II. CHOOSING NEGOTIATIONS.

### A. Sealed Bidding or Competitive Negotiations.

The CICA eliminated the historical preference for sealed bidding (formerly formal advertising). Now statutory criteria determine which procedures are used.

### B. Criteria for Selecting.

The CICA, at 10 U.S.C. § 2304(a)(2) and 41 U.S.C. § 253(a)(2), provides that, in determining the appropriate competitive procedure, agencies:
  (A) Shall solicit sealed bids if—
   (i) time permits the solicitation, submission, and evaluation of sealed bids;
   (ii) the award will be made on the basis of price and other price-related factors [only] [see FAR 14.201-8];
   (iii) it is unnecessary to conduct discussions with the responding sources about their bids; and,
   (iv) there is a reasonable expectation of receiving more than one sealed bid.
  (B) Shall request competitive proposals if sealed bids are not appropriate under clause (A).

### C. Contracting Officer Discretion.

1. The decision to negotiate involves a contracting officer's business judgment, which will

not be upset unless shown to be unreasonable. However, the contracting officer must demonstrate that one or more of the criteria for sealed bidding is not present. *Specialized Contract Serv., Inc.*, B-257321, Sept. 2, 1994, 94-2 CPD ¶ 90 (Army reasonably decided that it needed to evaluate more than just price in procuring lodging services). *Compare Racal Corp.*, B-240579, Dec. 4, 1990, 70 Comp. Gen. 127, 90-2 CPD ¶ 453 (possibility of discussions to assess offerors' understanding not sufficient when no technical proposal required), *with Claude E. Atkins Enters.*, B-241047, Jan. 15, 1991, 91-1 CPD ¶ 42 (procurement history and complex requirement supported reasonable expectation that discussions would be needed).

2. An RFP by any other name is still an RFP. *Balimoy Mfg. Co. of Venice, Inc.*, B-253287.2, Oct. 5, 1993, 93-2 CPD ¶ 207 (IFB that calls for evaluation of other than price in not an IFB).

D. Comparing the Two Methods.

## III. CONDUCTING COMPETITIVE NEGOTIATIONS.

*See* page 84.

### A. Developing a Request for Proposals (RFP).

Three interrelated elements of an RFP are Specifications (Section C), Instructions to Offerors (Section L), and Evaluation Criteria (Section M). Develop these three critical elements simultaneously so they are tightly integrated.

1. The specifications and statement of work (RFP, Section C) describe the required work.
2. The instructions to offerors (RFP, Section L) describe what information offerors should provide in their proposals, and prescribe a format. Instructions reduce the need for discussions merely to understand the proposals. Instructions also make the evaluation process more efficient by stating page limitations, paper sizes, and any suggested organization or content. An offeror ignores such

|  | *Sealed Bidding* | *Negotiations* |
|---|---|---|
| Evaluation Criteria | Price and price-related factors | Technical, management, probable cost, RAM, MANPRINT, environment, etc. |
| Responsiveness | At bid opening | N/A; evaluate based on factors in solicitation[1] |
| Responsibility | Pre-award survey; SBA may issue COC to small business | May evaluate comparatively based on disclosed factors |
| Contract Type | Firm-fixed-price or FFP w/ EPA | All types |
| Discussions | Prohibited | Required (unless award on initial proposals) |
| Right to Withdraw | Firm bid after bid opening until it expires | May withdraw at anytime before award |
| Public Bid Opening | Yes | No; identity of offerors and proposal contents protected |
| Flexibility to Use Judgment | None | Much |
| Late Offer/Modifications | Narrow exceptions | Slightly wider exceptions |

limitations at its peril. *U.S. Envtl. & Indus., Inc.*, B-257349, July 28, 1994, 94-2 CPD ¶ 51 (agency adjusted proposal length for type size smaller than the minimum allowed, did not consider "excess" pages, and properly excluded protester from competitive range).

3. The evaluation criteria (RFP, Section M) describe how the government will evaluate proposals. The criteria must be detailed enough to address all aspects of the required work, yet not so detailed as to mask differences in proposals.

4. Solicitations must provide offerors enough information to compete intelligently and on an equal basis, but they need not give precise details of the government's evaluation process. *QualMed, Inc.*, B-254397.13, July 20, 1994, 94-2 CPD ¶ 33.

## B. Drafting Evaluation Criteria.

1. Statutory requirement to disclose significant factors and subfactors. *See also* FAR 15.605(e).

   a. 10 U.S.C. § 2305(a)(2)(A) and 41 U.S.C. § 253a(b)(1)[2] provide that each solicitation for competitive proposals shall at a minimum include a statement of —

      (i) all significant factors and significant subfactors which the head of the agency reasonably expects to consider in evaluating . . . competitive proposals (including cost or price, cost- or price-related factors, and noncost- or non-price-related factors); and

      (ii) the relative importance assigned to each of those factors and subfactors;

   b. Further, 10 U.S.C. § 2305(a)(3) (no civilian equivalent)[3] provides:

      In prescribing the evaluation factors to be included in each solicitation for competitive proposals, the head of an agency shall clearly establish the relative importance assigned to the evaluation factors and subfactors, including the quality of the product or services to be provided (including technical capa-

bility, management capability, and prior experience of the offeror).

c. Agencies occasionally omit either significant evaluation factors and subfactors, or their relative importance, or both. *See Stone & Webster Eng'g Corp.*, B-255286.2, Apr. 12, 1994, 94-1 CPD ¶ 306 (evaluation committee applied different weights to evaluation factors without disclosure of any weights; no prejudice found, because relative merit of proposals unchanged with equal weights used); *cf. Danville-Findorff, Ltd*, B-241748, Mar. 1, 1991, 91-1 CPD ¶ 232 (agency listed relative importance of a factor as 60 in RFP, used 40 as weight in evaluation, and used the "extra" 20 points for an unannounced evaluation factor; but no prejudice to protester).

d. Must agencies disclose that they will evaluate risk in their proposal evaluations? *Compare H.J. Group Ventures, Inc.*, B-246139, Feb. 19, 1992, 92-1 CPD ¶ 203 (agency used "performance risk" (present and past performance) as a "general assessment criteria" instead of specifying it as an evaluation factor and giving its relative importance; failure to disclose this factor was improper), *with US Sprint Communications Co. v. Dep't of Defense*, GSBCA No. 11769-P, 93-1 BCA ¶ 25,255 (risk is an inherent part of every technical evaluation, if it relates to disclosed criteria), *and 4th Dimension Software, Inc.*, B-251936, May 13, 1993, 93-1 CPD ¶ 420 (agency may consider proposal risk intrinsic to stated evaluation factors).

e. The GAO generally excuses an agency's failure to identify specifically some subfactors, if the subfactors are reasonably related to the stated criteria, and are of relatively equal importance. *AWD Technologies, Inc.*, B-250081.2, Feb. 1, 1993, 93-1 CPD ¶ 83 (agency properly considered successful clean up of a similar superfund site, even though not a listed subfactor). The GAO also held, however, that agencies must disclose reasonably related subfactors if they are of significant weight. *Devres, Inc.*, B-224017, Dec. 8, 1986, 66 Comp. Gen. 121, 86-2 CPD ¶ 652 (agency should disclose subfactors of greater weight than many of the factors).

f. The GSBCA tests for prejudice in its consideration of bid protests; an agency's failure to follow evaluation criteria or apply relative weights precisely as required in an RFP *may* not be the basis for a successful protest, *if* the protester is not prejudiced. *See DPSC Software, Inc. v. Dep't of the Treasury*, GSBCA No. 12353-P, 93-3 BCA ¶ 26,144; *see also HFS, Inc.*, GSBCA No. 12010-P, 93-2 BCA ¶ 25,812 (minor deviation during evaluation from strict descending order of importance of subfactors disclosed in RFP provided no basis for relief).

g. Agencies need not disclose relative weights of elements below the subfactor level, even if the elements are listed in the RFP. *Integrated Sys. Group, Inc. v. Dep't of the Army*, GSBCA No. 12417-P, 93-3 BCA ¶ 26,225 (agency disclosed "hardware" as one of three subfactors under the technical factor, with thirty-seven elements listed below the "hardware" subfactor; held, no requirement to disclose relative importance of multiple elements listed below "hardware" or other subfactors).

2. Evaluation of cost or price.

a. Failure to consider cost or price violates statute, 10 U.S.C. § 2305(a); regulation, FAR 15.605(b); and GAO decision, *Spectron, Inc.*, B-172261, 51 Comp. Gen. 153 (1971).

b. Firm-fixed-price contracts. The offeror's proposed price is its probable price. *Ball Technical Prods. Group*, B-224394, Oct. 17, 1986, 86-2 CPD ¶ 465. Adjustments to the fixed price should be based on other identifiable costs to the government, e.g., in-house costs or life-cycle costs.

c. Cost reimbursement contracts. The agency should evaluate the offeror's probable cost of accomplishing the solicited work, not its proposed costs. FAR 15.605(d); *Kinton, Inc.*, B-228260.2, Feb. 5, 1988, 67 Comp. Gen. 226, 88-1 CPD ¶ 112. This difference results from the payment under cost contracts of costs actually incurred, not contractors' estimated costs. This rule minimizes the tendency of offerors to engage in lying contests.

3. Evaluation of technical and management factors (quality).

a. The government must address quality in every source selection. FAR 15.605(b); DFARS 215.605(e). Quality in both the FAR and in 10 U.S.C. § 2305(a)(3) means evaluation factors other than price or cost, i.e., technical, management, past performance, etc.

b. May quality have no importance? Prior to 1990, quality could have no importance. In *Kilgore Corp.*, B-235813.2, Nov. 7, 1989, 69 Comp. Gen. 59, 89-2 CPD ¶ 434, *aff'g* 89-1 CPD ¶ 576, the GAO interpreted the previous language in 10 U.S.C. § 2305(a)(3) and FAR 15.605(b) as *not* requiring "quality" to be an evaluation factor in every negotiated procurement. The GAO held that the statute and regulation merely require disclosure of the relative importance, if any, attached to quality factors. The 1990 amendments to 10 U.S.C. § 2305(a)(2)(A)(i) apparently reverse the GAO's decision in *Kilgore Corp.*

c. Agency supplements and other regulations provide guidance on particular non-cost evaluation factors.

(1) For example, AFARS app. AA and AFARS Manual 1 provide additional guidance to Army personnel. *See also* NAPS 15.605; AFFARS app. AA, *Formal Source Selection for Major Acquisitions*; AMC Pam 715-3, *Source Selection*.

(2) FAR 15.605(a) recommends limiting evaluation factors to those which will impact source selection. The evalua-

tion factors, however, should address all portions of the work being acquired. *Julie Research Lab., Inc.*, GSBCA No. 8919-P, 87-2 BCA ¶ 19,919.

    (3) An example of evaluation factors is set forth on page 82.

4. The agency must disclose the *relative importance* of all evaluation factors and subfactors, e.g., technical, management, and cost factors.

    a. Agencies disclose relative importance by:

        (1) Providing percentages or numerical weights in the RFP. If an agency evaluation plan uses numerical weights, it need not necessarily disclose those weights in the RFP. FAR 15.605(e); *Contract Servs, Inc.*, B-251761.4, July 20, 1993, 93-2 CPD ¶ 40;

        (2) Providing an algebraic paragraph;

        (3) Listing factors/subfactors in descending order of importance. *But see Health Servs. Int'l, Inc.*, B-247433, June 5, 1992, 92-1 CPD ¶ 493 (agency misleadingly set forth *equal* factors in "descending order of importance"); or,

        (4) Using a narrative statement.

    b. The GAO presumes all factors equal if RFP does not state order of importance. *North-East Imaging, Inc.*, B-256281, June 1, 1994, 94-1 CPD ¶ 332; *cf. Isratex, Inc. v. United States*, 25 Cl. Ct. 223 (1992) (relative importance of bid sample tests not disclosed; one test more important than other factors).

    c. The better practice is to state expressly the relative importance intended. Rely on the "presumed equal" line of cases only when an RFP inadvertently fails to state the relative importance. *See High-Point Schaer*, B-242616, May 28, 1991, 70 Comp. Gen. 525, 91-1 CPD ¶ 509 (GAO applied its "equal" presumption).

5. The cost/technical tradeoff.

    a. An RFP's statement of relative importance should include disclosure of how cost and technical merit will weigh in the selection for award. Generally the basis for award is:

        (1) Lowest priced, technically acceptable offer, or

        (2) An acceptable offer, the price of which is not the lowest, but which is sufficiently more advantageous than the lower priced offers to justify the payment of the additional price.[4]

    b. Following the suggested language is not a panacea. *See Jack Faucett Assoc.*, B-236396, Nov. 9, 1989, 89-2 CPD ¶ 449 (low priced, technically acceptable language ambiguous when combined with other provisions in the RFP); *National Test Pilot School*, B-237503, Feb. 27, 1990, 90-1 CPD ¶ 238 (award to the low-cost, technically acceptable offeror inconsistent with statement that technical criteria were more important than cost).

    c. More than an oblique reference to best value in a solicitation is required to permit an agency to do a cost/technical tradeoff as part of its source selection decision. *Systems Resources, Inc. v. Dep't of the Navy*, GSBCA No. 12536-P, 94-1 BCA ¶ 26,388 (citing *Lockheed Missiles & Space Co. v. Bentsen*, 4 F.3d 955 (Fed. Cir. 1993) for good cost/technical tradeoff language).

6. Problem evaluation factors.

    a. Options.

        (1) The evaluation factors should clearly address all evaluated options. A solicitation which fails to state whether options will be evaluated is defective. *Golden North Van Lines, Inc.*, B-238874, 69 Comp. Gen. 610, July 17, 1990, 90-2 CPD ¶ 44 (applying rule to an IFB). *See* FAR Subpart 17.2 for guidance on options. *N-K Constr. Co.*, B-224534, Feb. 19, 1987, 87-1 CPD ¶ 188 (solicitation stated that option price would not be evaluated).

        (2) Agencies must evaluate options at the time of award to exercise them without a Justification and Approval (J&A). FAR 17.207(f).

    b. Key personnel. In service contracts, a contractor's personnel are very important. Therefore, evaluation criteria should address evaluation of proposed personnel, including: education, training, and experience; amount of time they actually will perform under the contract; the likelihood that a proposed new hire will agree to work; impact on other contracts; etc. *See OAO Corp. v. Gen. Servs. Admin.*, GSBCA No. 12484-P, 94-1 BCA ¶ 26,392 (availability of key personnel critical to award decision); *Biospherics, Inc.*, B-253891.2, Nov. 24, 1993, 93-2 CPD ¶ 333 (offeror double bid personnel on two proposals); *cf. Man-Tech Advanced Sys. Int'l, Inc.*, B-255719.2, May 11, 1994, 94-1 CPD ¶ 326 (misrepresentation in a proposal of availability of key personnel who were material in agency's award decision is a basis for overturning the award). The RFP should request resumes, hiring or employment agreements, and proposed responsibilities.

c. Past performance. Office of Federal Procurement Policy (OFPP) Letter 92-5, 58 Fed. Reg. 3573 (1993).

(1) In all contracts, prior performance, or lack thereof, is an important predictor of successful completion of the required work. Evaluations should consider past conformance to specifications, customer satisfaction, timely performance, good workmanship, cost overrun history, compliance with administrative requirements, reasonable and cooperative behavior, business-like behavior, etc.

(2) OFPP's priorities include making past performance evaluation a major factor in all future source selections. 58 Fed. Reg. 66039 (1993).

(3) The government should specify sources of information it will use when evaluating past performance. *See NASCO Aircraft Brake, Inc.*, B-237860, Mar. 26, 1990, 90-1 CPD ¶ 330 (protest that "Blue Ribbon Program" would be used to evaluate past performance

denied because filed after closing); *ROSCO Int'l Corp.*, B-242879, June 12, 1991, 91-1 CPD ¶ 564 (quality vendor list gave 10% preference based on past performance).

(4) Past performance and price alone are adequate evaluation factors in a best value procurement. *Aqua-Chem, Inc.*, B-249516.2, May 18, 1993, 93-1 CPD ¶ 389. Payment of a 13.4% premium to a contractor with better past experience is acceptable even if price is weighted higher than past performance. *Chem-Servs. of Ind., Inc.*, B-253905, Oct. 28, 1993, 93-2 CPD ¶ 262. *Accord Corvac, Inc.*, B-254222, Dec. 2, 1993, 93-2 CPD ¶ 294 (3.5% price premium permissible for better past performance, despite lower weight); *Corvac, Inc.*, B-254757, Jan. 11, 1994, 94-1 CPD ¶ 14 (8% premium for better past performance was reasonable).

## C. Notice of Intent to Hold Discussions.

1. 10 U.S.C. § 2305(a)(2)(B)(ii)(I) provides that a request for competitive proposals shall contain:

   [A] statement that the proposals are intended to be evaluated with, and award made after, discussions with the offerors, *or* a statement that the proposals are intended to be evaluated, and award made, without discussions with the offerors (other than . . . minor clarification[s]), unless discussions are determined to be necessary.

2. Previous statutory language[5] required different notice regarding award on initial proposals, and only permitted award on initial offers based on the lowest cost, technically acceptable proposal.

3. Statutes and regulations provide no guidance on whether an agency should award with or without discussions. Contracting officers should consider factors indicating discussions may be necessary, such as procurement

history, competition, contract type, specification clarity, etc. Discussions may be as short or as long as required, but offerors must be given an opportunity to revise proposals after discussions end. FAR 15.610(c)(5).

4. A protest challenging failure to include the correct notice in the solicitation is untimely if filed after the date for receipt of initial proposals. *Warren Pumps, Inc.*, B-248145.2, Sept. 18, 1992, 92-2 CPD ¶ 187.

**D. Draft Request for Proposals.**
AFARS 15.405-90. A draft RFP is a useful method of obtaining industry comments on acquisition documents (e.g., contract provisions, specifications) and getting industry prepared to turn around quickly in providing its proposals. It is mandatory for certain acquisitions.

**E. Submission of Initial Proposals.**
1. Proposal preparation time.
   a. The deadline for submission of initial proposals for contracts over the simplified acquisition threshold shall not be earlier than 30 days after issuance of the RFP. 41 U.S.C. § 416; 15 U.S.C. § 637(d)(3); FAR 5.203.
   b. Amendments.
      (1) If an agency changes its requirements significantly, it must amend the RFP and allow all offerors to propose on the revised requirements. *United Tel. Co. of the Northwest*, B-246977, Apr. 20, 1992, 92-1 CPD ¶ 374; FAR 15.606.
      (2) After amending an RFP, the government must give prospective offerors a reasonable time to modify a proposal, considering complexity, agency needs, and other factors. FAR 15.410; *Federal Sys. Group, Inc.*, GSBCA No. 10518-P, 90-2 BCA ¶ 22,925.
2. Late proposals.
   a. A proposal is late if not received by the time and date specified in the RFP. FAR 15.412(b). If no time is stated, 4:30 p.m., local time is presumed. FAR 15.412(b). FAR 52.215-10, Late Submissions, Modifi-

cations,[6] and Withdrawal of Proposals, sets forth instances when an agency may consider late proposals. Rules are the same as for sealed bidding, except the government may consider a single proposal if no more are submitted.[7]
   b. Both technical and price proposals are due before the closing time. *Inland Serv. Corp.*, B-252947.4, Nov. 4, 1993, 93-2 CPD ¶ 266.
   c. Late proposals are retained unopened in the contracting office. FAR 15.412(f).
3. No "Firm Bid Rule." An offeror may withdraw its proposal at any time. There is no firm bid rule. *See* FAR 52.215-10(h). The agency, however, has only a reasonable time in which to accept the proposal. *Western Roofing Serv.*, B-232666.4, Mar. 5, 1991, 70 Comp. Gen. 324, 91-1 CPD ¶ 242, (if offer specifies no minimum acceptance period, agency must accept within a reasonable time; 13 months was too long).
4. Offerors may presents oral presentations as part of the proposal process. *NW Ayer, Inc.*, B-248654, 92-2 CPD ¶ 154.
5. Proposals are kept secret. FAR 15.413-1(a). Prospective offerors may restrict the use and disclosure of information contained in their proposals by marking the proposal with an authorized restrictive legend. FAR 52.215-12.

**F. Evaluation of the Proposals Received.**
1. General.
   a. Evaluators must be reasonable and follow the evaluation criteria in the RFP. *Sprint Communications Co. v. Defense Info. Sys. Agency*, GSBCA No. 12692-P, 94-3 BCA ¶ 26,966 (evaluators improperly applied different definition of "minor modification" than specified in the RFP); *Foundation Health Fed. Servs., Inc.*, B-254397.4, Dec. 20, 1993, 94-1 CPD ¶ 3, (evaluation of potential CHAMPUS health managers based on trend line analysis of past cost containment efforts was improper, despite difficulty in assessing the feasibility of utilization management plans required by the

RFP). Failure to follow criteria or apply relative weights precisely as required in the RFP *may* not be the basis for protest relief, however, *if* the protester is not prejudiced. *See DPSC Software, Inc. v. Dep't of the Treasury*, GSBCA No. 12353-P, 93-3 BCA ¶ 26,144.

b. Be consistent; if one offeror is downgraded for deficiencies, downgrade others for the same deficiencies. *Park Sys. Maint. Co.*, B-252453, June 16, 1993, 93-1 CPD ¶ 466.

c. Avoid double-scoring or otherwise exaggerating the importance of any single criteria beyond the weight accorded it in the solicitation. *J.A. Jones Mgmt. Servs., Inc.*, B-254941.2, Mar. 16, 1994, 94-1 CPD ¶ 244.

d. Evaluate compliance with the stated requirement. If an offeror proposes a better but noncompliant solution, amend the RFP and solicit new proposals *if* this can be done without disclosing proprietary data. FAR 15.606(c); *see Labat-Anderson Inc.*, B-246071, Feb. 18, 1992, 71 Comp. Gen. 252, 92-1 CPD ¶ 193 (agency must amend RFP to allow all offerors an opportunity to propose on actual requirements); *United Tel. Co. of the Northwest*, B-246977, Apr. 20, 1992, 92-1 CPD ¶ 374 (a substantial change in requirements requires cancellation and reissuance of RFP).

e. Notify offerors of changes to evaluation criteria in accordance with FAR 15.606, and provide them an opportunity to revise their proposals. *See TMC, Inc.*, B-230078, May 24, 1988, 88-1 CPD ¶ 492 (changing evaluation factors after Best and Final Offers (BAFOs) requires reopening negotiations).

f. Matters outside offerors' proposals may be considered in the evaluation so long as their consideration is not unreasonable or contrary to the stated evaluation criteria. *Intermagnetics Gen. Corp.—Recon.*, B-255741.4, Sept. 27, 1994, 94-2 CPD ¶ 119.

g. The composition of evaluation teams is left to agencies' discretion. The GAO will not review it absent a showing of conflict of interest or bias. *University Research Corp.*, B-253725.4, Oct. 26, 1993, 93-2 CPD ¶ 259.

h. *Read* the entire proposal. *Data Gen. Servs.*, GSBCA No. 9236-P, 88-1 BCA ¶ 20,458.

2. Scoring technical and management factors.

a. Agencies possess considerable discretion in evaluating proposals, and particularly in making scoring decisions. *PRC, Inc. v. Dep't of Justice*, GSBCA No. 12053-P, 93-2 BCA ¶ 25,772 (protest relief only appropriate if board finds an abuse of discretion).

b. Scoring methods. The government may adopt any evaluation method it desires, if the method is not arbitrary or in violation of procurement statutes and regulations. *BMY, A Div. of Harsco Corp. v. United States*, 693 F. Supp. 1232 (D.D.C. 1988). As a minimum, give higher scores to better proposals. *See Trijicon, Inc.*, B-244546, Oct., 25, 1991, 71 Comp. Gen. 41, 91-2 CPD ¶ 375 (agency adopted color scoring scheme with acceptable (green), marginal (yellow), and unacceptable (red) ratings; scheme improperly failed to score proposals exceeding the minimum requirements higher than those offering the minimum). Giving higher scores to proposals that exceed minimum requirements is permissible, even if RFP does not disclose how much extra credit will be given under each subfactor. *PCB Piezotronics, Inc.*, B-254046, Nov. 17, 1993, 93-2 CPD ¶ 286.

(1) Points. Agencies may rate individual factors on a numerical scale with relative importance stated in terms of numerical weights. *Modern Technologies Corp.*, B-236961.4, Mar. 19, 1990, 90-1 CPD ¶ 301 (use of arithmetic mean of point scores to determine acceptability questionable). Point scoring systems are harder to use correctly.

*See Centel Fed. Sys., Inc. v. Dep't of the Navy*, GSBCA No. 12011-P, 93-2 BCA ¶ 25,648.

(2) Adjectives. Agencies may rate factors using adjectives (e.g., exceptional, acceptable, marginal, unacceptable). *Dynamics Research Corp.*, B-240089, Dec. 10, 1990, 90-2 CPD ¶ 471 (adjectival scoring valid if it gives a clear understanding of the relative merits of the proposals). Normally state relative importance using relative standing only, because evaluators cannot multiply an integer times an adjective.

(3) Colors. Colors may replace the adjectives, and the size of the box colored may symbolize the relative importance of the represented factor.

(4) Narrative. Each factor may receive a narrative rating only. A summation of all the narratives should reflect the relative importance of the criteria.

(5) GO/NO GO. A pure pass/fail system is not prohibited, but the GAO disfavors pure pass/fail evaluation criteria in negotiated procurements. *CompuChem Lab., Inc.*, B-242889, June 19, 1991, 91-1 CPD ¶ 572. Because pass/fail criteria imply a minimum acceptable level, these levels should appear in the RFP. *See National Test Pilot School*, B-237503, Feb. 27, 1990, 90-1 CPD ¶ 238 (award to the low cost, technically acceptable proposal inconsistent with statement that technical criteria were more important than cost).

(6) Dollars. This system translates the technical evaluation into dollars which are added or subtracted from the evaluated price to get a final dollar price adjusted for technical quality. *See DynCorp*, B-245289.3, July 30, 1992, 93-1 CPD ¶ 69.

c. Evaluating past performance or experience.

(1) Using the experience of others. Evaluation of the past experience or performance of parents, subsidiaries, officers, and team members is difficult. *See Technical Resources, Inc.*, B-253506, Sept. 16, 1993, 93-2 CPD ¶ 176 (may evaluate past performance of relatively new company based on experience of management team); *FMC Corp.*, B-252941, July 29, 1993, 93-2 CPD ¶ 71 (may consider subcontractors' experience unless RFP states otherwise); *cf. Aid Maint. Co.*, B-255552, Mar. 9, 1994, 94-1 CPD ¶ 188 (may downgrade proposal that offers to meet experience requirement through subcontractor rather than as prime); *Pathology Assocs., Inc.*, B-237208.2, Feb. 20, 1990, 90-1 CPD ¶ 292 (in contract for "animal colony management" for 7,000 rats, past experience of employees did not directly translate into past experience of organization); *Barnes & Reinecke, Inc.*, B-236622, Dec. 20, 1989, 89-2 CPD ¶ 572 (may evaluate proposal which does not clearly commit the resources of the parent based on subsidiary only).

(2) Comparative evaluations of small business past performance. If an agency comparatively evaluates offerors' past performance, small businesses may not use Certificate of Competency (COC) procedures to review the evaluation. *Pearl Properties*, B-253614.6, May 23, 1994, 94-1 CPD ¶ 357. If the agency did not state it would consider responsibility-type factors, then a small business may use COC procedures. *Envirosol, Inc.*, B-254223, Dec. 2, 1993, 93-2 CPD ¶ 295 (improper to find price unreasonably low without SBA referral when RFP did not disclose agency would evaluate offerors' understanding of requirements); *Flight Int'l Group, Inc.*, B-238953.4, Sept. 28, 1990, 90-2 CPD ¶ 257 (financial capaci-

ty not a disclosed factor; therefore, SBA referral required). Pass/fail scoring of a responsibility-type factor also permits a small business to seek a COC. *Clegg Indus., Inc.*, B-242204, Aug. 14, 1991, 70 Comp. Gen. 680, 91-2 CPD ¶ 145.

(3) Evidence of past performance.

    (a) Agencies may consider their own past unsatisfactory experience with an offeror rather than relying just on references furnished. *George A. and Peter A. Palivos*, B-245878.2, Mar. 16, 1992, 92-1 CPD ¶ 286.

    (b) In *KMS Fusion, Inc.*, B-242529, May 8, 1991, 91-1 CPD ¶ 447, an agency properly considered extrinsic past performance evidence when past performance was a disclosed evaluation factor. Ignoring extrinsic evidence may be improper. *Cf. Aviation Constructors, Inc.*, B-244794, Nov. 12, 1991, 91-2 CPD ¶ 448 (experience with commercial airports different from government construction experience).

(4) Agencies should make rational, not mechanical, comparative evaluations of past performance. In *Retrac*, B-241916, Mar. 1, 1991, 91-1 CPD ¶ 239, the agency sought to acquire spare parts at a $31,000 higher price because a paperwork problem on a prior $112 order caused the low-price offeror to miss quality vendor program cutoff score. The GAO found this evaluation unreasonable. *See also American Dev. Corp.*, B-251876.4, July 12, 1993, 93-2 CPD ¶ 49 (unreasonable to give preference to offeror with a prior contract for similar work regardless of quality of work under the contract).

(5) Lack of past performance history should not bar new firms from competing for government requirements. *Espey Mfg. & Elecs. Corp.*, B-254738, Mar. 8, 1994, 94-1 CPD ¶ 180 (past performance not considered in evalua-

tion of first-time offerors); *cf. Laidlaw Envtl. Servs., Inc.*, B-256346, June 14, 1994, 94-1 CPD ¶ 365 (giving credit for commercial past performance reasonable, if equivalent to comparable prior government experience).

    d. A responsibility determination is not strictly part of the technical evaluation, but the evaluation process may include consideration of responsibility matters. *Executone Information Sys., Inc. v. Dep't of Health & Human Servs.*, GSBCA No. 12409-P, 94-1 BCA 26,274. However, if responsibility matters are considered without a comparative evaluation of offers, a small business found technically unacceptable may appeal to the SBA for a COC. *Docusort, Inc.*, B-254852, Jan. 25, 1994, 94-1 CPD ¶ 38 (management experience found inadequate).

3. Scoring methods for cost or price. Score cost or price in dollars. Avoid schemes that mathematically relate cost to technical point scores, or assign a point score to cost. *See* AFARS 15.608(a).

    a. Firm-fixed-price contracts. If a firm-fixed-price contract is offered, evaluate using proposed price, adjusted for price-related factors. Do not consider cost-realism in the *price* evaluation. *PHP Healthcare Corp.*, B-251933, May 13, 1993, 93-1 CPD ¶ 381. *Cf. Oshkosh Truck Corp.*, B-252708.2, Aug. 24, 1993, 93-2 CPD ¶ 115 (cost realism may be evaluated under fixed price proposals, and considered in the *technical* evaluation, if the risk of poor performance is a legitimate concern, such as when a contractor proposes to work for little or no profit, or with an underestimated workforce; the depth of that analysis is within the agency's discretion).

    b. Cost-Reimbursement Contracts.

    (1) If a cost type contract is offered, evaluate based on probable cost to the government. Probable cost is proposed cost adjusted for cost realism. *See*

*MR&S/AME, An MSC Joint Venture*, B-250313.2, Mar. 19, 1993, 93-1 CPD ¶ 245 (Navy properly adjusted proposed overhead rate that appeared artificially low to equal offeror's prior year rate); *see also Sabre Sys., Inc.*, B-255311, Feb. 22, 1994, 94-1 CPD ¶ 129 (agency generally may rely on DCAA advice in performing cost realism analysis).

(a) Evaluate cost realism consistently from one proposal to the next.

(b) When offerors use different assumptions in developing cost estimates, and agency does not challenge them or revise costs to reflect common assumptions, evaluation is unreasonable. *Lockheed Aeronautical Sys. Co.*, B-252235.2, Aug. 4, 1993, 93-2 CPD ¶ 80, *recon. denied, Lockheed Aeronautical Sys. Co.*, B-252235.4, Jan 21, 1994, 94-1 CPD ¶ 45 (life-cycle costs).

(2) An agency may not mechanically apply an estimated adjustment factor to evaluated costs. Proper cost realism adjustments require independent analysis of each offeror's proposal based on its particular circumstances, approach, personnel, and other unique factors. *The Jonathan Corp.*, B-251698.3, May 17, 1993, 93-2 CPD ¶ 174 (splitting the difference between offeror's estimated costs and government estimate was unreasonable, despite determination that the offeror's estimate was equally likely as government's to be correct); *United Int'l Eng'g, Inc.*, B-245448.3, Jan. 29, 1992, 71 Comp. Gen. 177, 92-1 CPD ¶ 122 (agency raised every labor rate below historical range to midpoint of range and left other rates within range alone; action was arbitrary); *Bendix Field Eng'g Corp.*, B-246236, Feb. 25, 1992, 92-1 CPD ¶ 227 (although offeror was the incumbent with a union collective bargaining

agreement for proposed labor rates, agency raised them to the level of government estimate).

(3) Cost realism evaluation involves business judgment; it will not be upset merely because a protester suggests another reasonable approach. *CompuAdd Corp. v. Dep't of the Air Force*, GSBCA No. 12021-P, 93-2 BCA ¶ 25,811.

(4) It is improper for an agency to award based on probable costs without a detailed cost analysis *or* discussions with the offeror. *Kinton, Inc.*, B-228260.2, Feb. 5, 1988, 67 Comp. Gen. 226, 88-1 CPD ¶ 112.

(5) The contracting agency must perform cost realism analysis in a public-private competition; DCAA certification that public offeror's prices are adequate for evaluation is not enough—the cost realism analysis still must be done. *Sargent Controls & Aerospace*, B-254976, Feb. 2, 1994, 94-1 CPD ¶ 66.

(6) Offeror may cap labor rates in proposal at amount it expects to bargain for with union, and agree to be bound by those rates even if it fails to reach a union agreement. If an agency adjusts upward proposed rates above the level at which an offeror proposes to cap them, the agency errs in its probable cost evaluation. *BNF Technologies, Inc.*, B-254953.3, Mar. 14, 1994, 94-1 CPD ¶ 274; *see Halifax Technical Servs., Inc.*, B-246236.6, Jan. 24, 1994, 94-1 CPD ¶ 30 (agency properly evaluated probable cost based on capped rates).

(7) An agency's cost realism evaluation is improper if it favorably credits an awardee with a subcontractor's proposed uncompensated overtime, when the subcontractor was not bound to furnish it. *Versar, Inc.*, B-254464.3, Feb 16, 1994, 94-1 CPD ¶ 230.

c. Cost realism may be used as input for evaluation of the non-cost factors.

(1) In a firm-fixed-price contract, the technical evaluation may reflect the performance risk associated with an offeror who bids little or no profit. *Systems & Processes Eng'g Corp.*, B-234142, May 10, 1989, 89-1 CPD ¶ 441.

(2) An unreasonably low cost may indicate poor understanding of the requirement. *Forensic Medical Advisory Servs., Inc.*, B-248551.2, Oct. 28, 1992, 92-2 CPD ¶ 316 (agency may use cost realism to evaluate understanding of requirement).

(3) An unexplained price reduction may suggest increased performance risk. *American Contract Health, Inc.*, B-236544.2, Jan. 17, 1990, 90-1 CPD ¶ 59 (government properly downgraded proposal for low wage rates in light of the problem attracting and retaining qualified dentists).

(4) Agencies should consider uncompensated overtime. *See* DFARS 215.608(a) (conduct risk assessment in evaluating offers proposing uncompensated overtime); NASA FAR Supp. 1815.608-72 (same); *Quantum Research, Inc.*, B-242020, Mar. 21, 1991, 91-1 CPD ¶ 310 (offeror proposed based on 2600 hours of work per year; agency properly downgraded technical proposal for likely personnel turnover and lower quality reports these hours suggested).

(5) Mechanically applying a government estimate during evaluation, however, to downgrade a fixed-price proposal's technical rating for deviation from government's estimated number of hours to do the work is unreasonable. *KCA Corp.*, B-255115, Feb. 9, 1994, 94-1 CPD ¶ 94.

d. Normalizing is the process of assigning the high point score to the low cost proposal and assigning a proportionally lower score to higher priced proposals; do not do it! *Government Technology Servs.,*

*Inc.*, GSBCA No. 10389-P, 90-2 BCA ¶ 22,673 (normalizing point scores may distort relative importance).

4. Scoring disparities are not objectionable or unusual. *Dragon Servs., Inc.*, B-255354, Feb. 25, 1994, 94-1 CPD ¶ 151 (individual evaluators' rating may differ from consensus evaluation); *Stat-a Matrix*, B-234141, May 17, 1989, 89-1 ¶ 472 (evaluation involves objective and subjective factors, so a spread of scores from different evaluators for one proposal is not invalid). However, consistency from one proposal to the next is essential. *Secure Servs. Technology, Inc.*, B-238059, Apr. 25, 1990, 90-1 CPD ¶ 421.

5. Products of the evaluation process.

a. Evaluation report.

(1) The evaluators should prepare a report of their evaluation. *See Amtec Corp.*, B-240647, Dec. 12, 1990, 90-2 CPD ¶ 482 (evaluation report did not adequately justify a marginal rating for a proposal; offeror provided lengthy explanations, while agency said very little); *accord Son's Quality Food Co.*, B-244528.2, Nov. 4, 1991, 91-2 CPD ¶ 424 (worksheets contained few substantive comments, yet proposal significantly downgraded in very important areas).

(2) The contracting officer should retain all evaluation records. *Hydraudyne Sys. & Eng'g B.V.*, B-241236, Jan. 30, 1991, 91-1 CPD ¶ 88 (record of evaluation adequate if scores are accompanied by contemporaneous comments prepared as part of summary evaluation, even though individual evaluators' notes were discarded in violation of FAR 4.801(b) and 15.608(a)(2)); *accord KMS Fusion, Inc.*, B-242529, May 8, 1991, 91-1 CPD ¶ 447; *see also* FAR 4.801(b); FAR 15.608(a)(2); *cf. American President Lines, Ltd.*, B-236834.3, July 20, 1990, 90-2 CPD ¶ 53 (protest sustained for not keeping records); *United Int'l Eng'g, Inc.*, B-

245448.3, Jan. 29, 1992, 71 Comp. Gen. 177, 92-1 CPD ¶ 122 (GAO gives greater weight to contemporaneous source selection materials than to post-protest testimony).

(3) If evaluators use numerical scoring, explain the scores. *DNL Properties, Inc.*, B-253614.2, Oct. 12, 1993, 93-2 CPD ¶ 301 (scores lacking contemporaneous narrative explanations were unreasonable); *TFA, Inc.*, B-243875, Sept. 11, 1991, 91-2 CPD ¶ 239 (evaluation record failed to explain why proposals with the same defects received different evaluation scores); *S-Cubed*, B-242871, June 17, 1991, 91-1 CPD ¶ 571 (record included no explanation of why agency considered a lowball proposal on cost contract acceptable after it initially evaluated the proposal as very unrealistic).

(4) Ensure evaluations are reasonable. *DNL Properties, Inc.*, B-253614.2, Oct. 12, 1993, 93-2 CPD ¶ 301 (same preprinted, generic narrative for each proposal is unreasonable).

b. Deficiencies. The initial evaluation must identify all parts of the proposals which fail to meet the government's minimum requirements. FAR 15.601.

c. Advantages and disadvantages (strengths and weaknesses). The initial evaluation should identify the positive and negative aspects of acceptable proposals.

d. Questions and items for negotiation. The initial evaluation should identify areas where discussions are necessary/desireable.

e. Competitive range recommendation. The evaluation report should recommend the proposals to include in a competitive range.

## G. Award Without Discussions.

1. Recent history of award without discussions.
   a. Before 1990, agencies could award on initial proposals only if the most favorable initial proposal also would result in the lowest overall cost to the government. In November 1990, Congress revised this provision for defense agencies. National Defense Authorization Act for 1991, Pub. L. No. 101-510, § 802, 104 Stat. 1589 (1990).
   b. A defense agency may not award on initial proposals if it failed to provide notice of its intent to do so in the solicitation. 10 U.S.C. § 2305(b)(4)(A)(ii). Similarly, a defense agency may not award on initial proposals if it stated in the RFP that it intended to hold discussions. A proper award on initial proposals need not result in the lowest overall cost to the government.
   c. Civilian agencies may not use this authority.[8] *Schreiner, Legg & Co.*, B-244680, Nov. 6, 1991, 91-2 CPD ¶ 432.

2. To award without discussions, a defense agency must:
   a. Give notice in the solicitation that it intends to award without discussions.
   b. Select a proposal for award which complies with all material requirements of the solicitation.
   c. Properly evaluate the selected proposal in accordance with the evaluation factors and subfactors set forth in the solicitation.
   d. *Not* have a contracting officer determination that discussions are necessary.
   e. *Not* conduct discussions with any offeror, other than for the purpose of minor clarifications.

   *See TRI-COR Indus.*, B-252366.3, Aug. 25, 1993, 93-2 CPD ¶ 137 (Army properly selected higher-priced, technically superior offeror after a reasonable cost/technical tradeoff based on initial proposals); *Federal Sys. Group*, GSBCA No. 11461-P, 92-1 BCA ¶ 24,591 (low-cost proposal included list of "Exceptions and Clarifications"; the next low, technically acceptable proposal was only $9,000 higher and properly received award).

3. Discussions v. clarifications.

a. Award without discussions means no discussions.

b. Award may not be made on initial proposals after discussions with one or more offerors. *To the Sec'y of the Navy*, B-170751, 50 Comp. Gen. 202 (1970).

c. Discussions (*see* FAR 15.601) are defined as:

> [A]ny oral or written communication . . . [other than clarifications] . . . that (a) involves information essential for determining the acceptability of a proposal, or (b) provides the offeror an opportunity to revise or modify its proposal.

*See also Crestmont Cleaning Serv. & Supply Co.*, B-252490, July 1, 1993, 93-2 CPD ¶ 2.

d. "Clarifications" are permitted. FAR 15.601. Clarifications are defined as:

> [C]ommunication with an offeror for the sole purpose of eliminating minor irregularities, informalities, or apparent clerical mistakes in the proposal. It is achieved by explanation or substantiation, either in response to Government inquiry or as initiated by the offeror. . . . [C]larification does not give the offeror an opportunity to revise or modify its proposal, except to the extent that correction of apparent clerical mistakes results in a revision.

e. Examples.

(1) Audits are not discussions. *Data Mgmt. Servs., Inc.*, B-237009, Jan. 12, 1990, 69 Comp. Gen. 112, 90-1 CPD ¶ 51 (if an auditor convinces an offeror to lower its price, the agency may still award on initial proposals).

(2) Substitution of resumes is discussions. *Telos Field Eng'g*, GSBCA No. 9735-P, 89-1 BCA ¶ 21,415; *University of S.C.*, B-240208, Sept. 21, 1990, 90-2 CPD ¶ 249. Substitution permits an offeror to submit additional information necessary to determine acceptability of its offer. *Allied Mgmt. of Texas, Inc.*, B-232736.2, May 22, 1989, 89-1 CPD ¶ 485. *But see Booz, Allen & Hamilton, Inc.*, B-236476, Dec. 4, 1989, 89-2 CPD ¶ 513 (need not reopen discussions when key person quits, and offeror informs agency and provides replacement resume).

(3) Explaining inconsistency between unit and total prices caused by rounding and transposition is not discussions. *Pauli & Griffin*, B-234191, May 17, 1989, 89-1 CPD ¶ 473 (explanation did not change offered price, and it was unnecessary to determine acceptability); *E.D.S. Fed. Corp.*, GSBCA No. 9600-P, 89-1 BCA ¶ 21,261, (request to justify price reduction was not discussions).

(4) Allowing an offeror to explain a warranty provision is discussions. *Cylink Corp.*, B-242304, Apr. 18, 1991, 91-1 CPD ¶ 384 (questions on warranty terms were not "clarifications" because answers modified the initial proposal).

(5) A request to extend proposal acceptance period is not discussions. *CompuAdd Corp. v. Dep't of Air Force*, GSBCA No. 12301-P, 93-3 BCA ¶ 26,123 (request for extension did not provide opportunity to furnish information essential to evaluation of proposal).

(6) Extensive questioning to "clarify" proposal in areas of noncompliance and unacceptability was discussions, requiring a request for BAFOs. *Telos Field Eng'g*, B-253492.2, Nov. 16, 1993, 93-2 CPD ¶ 275.

(7) An agency may be able to negotiate additional clauses with low offeror after selection and before award on initial proposals. *Planning Research Corp.*, B-237201, Jan. 30, 1990, 90-1 CPD ¶ 131 (no competitive advantage).

f. The best rule of thumb is that if you need the question answered before award, then it likely rises to the level of discussions.

**H. Determination to Conduct Discussions.**

1. If the contracting officer wishes to conduct

discussions with one or more offerors after stating an intent to award without discussions, he or she must find that discussions are necessary. 10 U.S.C. § 2305(b). The contracting officer should document this conclusion with a determination and findings. FAR 15.610(a)(4).

2. Statutes and implementing regulations provide little guidance for making this determination. A contracting officer should consider factors such as favorable but noncompliant proposals; unclear proposals; incomplete proposals; unreasonable costs or prices; suspected mistakes; changes or clarifications to specification; and other issues for resolution before award. *See Milcom Sys. Corp.*, B-255448.2, May 3, 1994, 94-1 CPD ¶ 339.

**I. Determining the Competitive Range.**
FAR 15.609.
1. What is a competitive range?
   The group of offerors with which the contracting officer conducts discussions, and from which revised proposals are sought. Proposals outside the competitive range are no longer considered.
2. Which proposals are included in the competitive range?
   All proposals that have a reasonable chance of receiving award. FAR 15.609(a).
3. How is the competitive range determined?
   a. Consider all factors, including price or cost, in making the determination. *National Medical Diagnostics, Inc.*, B-232238, Dec. 2, 1988, 88-2 CPD ¶ 553. However, if a proposal is totally unacceptable technically, an agency may exclude it from the competitive range regardless of its lower cost or the weight accorded to cost in the RFP. *Crown Logistics Servs.*, B-253740, Oct. 19, 1993, 93-2 CPD ¶ 228; *cf. Bay Tankers, Inc.*, B-238162, Apr. 13, 1990, 69 Comp. Gen. 404, 90-1 CPD ¶ 389 (when awarding to low-cost, technically acceptable offeror, agency could not exclude proposal from competitive range without considering price).

   b. Exclude unacceptable offers requiring major revisions to become acceptable; inclusion would be tantamount to allowing a new proposal. *Harris Data Communications v. United States*, 2 Cl. Ct. 229 (1983), *aff'd*, 723 F.2d 69 (Fed. Cir. 1983); *SST Strategic Sciences and Technologies, Inc.*, B-257980, 94-2 CPD ¶ 194 (reasonable to exclude offeror proposing inexperienced key personnel—the most important criteria—from competitive range); *InterAmerica Research Assocs., Inc.*, B-253698.2, Nov. 19, 1993, 93-2 CPD ¶ 288 (exclusion of offeror failing to provide required information, who merely parroted back language from solicitation, was proper).

   c. Exclusion of a technically acceptable proposal, or one susceptible to being made acceptable, is proper if, in comparison with other offers, it stands no reasonable chance of receiving award. *Radio Sys., Inc.*, B-255080, Jan. 10, 1994, 94-1 CPD ¶ 9 (offer was technically acceptable, but 350% higher on price); *Caldwell Consulting Assocs.*, B-252590, July 13, 1993, 93-2 CPD ¶ 18 (offeror ranked 11 of 12 technically, and was only fifth low on price).

   d. If there is doubt about whether to exclude a proposal from the competitive range, leave it in. FAR 15.609(a).
   (1) The GSBCA has awarded bid preparation costs to an offeror who was improperly included in the competitive range. *SMS Data Prods. Group*, GSBCA No. 8589-P, 87-1 BCA ¶ 19,496, *rev'd on other grounds, Federal Data Corp. v. SMS Data Prods. Group*, 819 F.2d 277 (Fed. Cir. 1987). The GSBCA, however, is moving to a more deferential standard of review. *Unisys Corp.*, GSBCA No. 11069-P, 91-2 BCA ¶ 23,879 (GSBCA adopted abuse of discretion standard for reviewing inclusion of offerors in competitive range, and gave substantial weight to regulations directing inclusion of offerors in the range in close cases).

(2) The Comptroller General ordinarily gives great deference to an agency's determination of the competitive range. A protester must make a clear showing that the evaluation was unreasonable, or inconsistent with the stated evaluation factors. *Mainstream Eng'g Corp.*, B-251444, Apr. 8, 1993, 93-1 CPD ¶ 307; *cf. Intertec Aviation*, B-239672, Sept. 19, 69 Comp. Gen. 717, 90-2 CPD ¶ 232 (elimination of proposal unreasonable where alleged technical deficiencies were minor, cost was competitive, and action seriously reduced available competition).

4. When is the competitive range determination made?

    a. After the initial evaluation, and at any time thereafter, an agency may eliminate proposals from the competitive range. FAR 15.609(b). *See SMB, Inc.*, B-252575.2, July 30, 1993, 93-2 CPD ¶ 72 (offeror eliminated from competitive range after submission of revised proposal that did not correct deficiencies noted during discussions).

    b. However, agencies must not make a competitive range determination before they finalize their requirements and cease amending the RFP. *Integrated Sys. Group, Inc. v. Dep't of Agriculture*, GSBCA No. 12552-P, 94-1 BCA ¶ 26,556 (may not preclude offeror from submitting BAFO without giving it opportunity to be responsive to final requirements).

5. Who determines the competitive range? The contracting officer (FAR 15.609) or the Source Selection Authority (AFARS 15.609(b)) determines the competitive range.

6. Common errors.

    a. Reducing competitive range to one proposal. A contracting officer's decision to reduce a competitive range to one offeror will receive "close scrutiny." *Rockwell Int'l Corp. v. United States*, 4 Cl. Ct. 1 (1983); *Aerospace Design, Inc.*, B-247793, July 9,

1992, 92-2 CPD ¶ 11. Even if good reasons exist for reducing a competitive range to one offeror, it may be an abuse of discretion to do so unless it is clear that an excluded offeror has *no* reasonable chance of receiving award. *See Birch & Davis Int'l v. Christopher*, 4 F.3d 970 (Fed. Cir. 1993) (vacating GSBCA decision upholding an agency's reduction of the competitive range to a single offeror). The AFARS prohibits reduction of competitive range to one offeror. AFARS 15.609(b).

    b. Excluding an offeror from the competitive range for omissions easily correctable during discussions. *Essex Electro Eng'rs, Inc.*, B-250862, Feb. 23, 1993, 94-1 CPD ¶ 80 (government excluded offeror for submitting unreasonably low price, even though data demonstrating reasonableness of proposed price could be submitted during discussions).

    c. Using predetermined cutoff scores. *DOT Sys., Inc.*, B-186192, July 1, 1976, 76-2 CPD ¶ 3; *To the Sec'y of Transportation*, B-169645, 50 Comp. Gen. 59 (1970).

    d. Exclusion based on "nonresponsiveness." Material defects in initial offers may be cured in negotiations and do not require exclusion from the competitive range. *Leigh Instruments, Ltd.*, B-233270, Mar. 3, 1989, 89-1 CPD ¶ 232. Concept of "responsiveness" is incompatible with a competitive range. *Consolidated Controls Corp.*, B-185979, Sept. 21, 1976, 76-2 CPD ¶ 261.

**J. Conducting Discussions.**

1. The contracting officer shall conduct written or oral discussions with all responsible offerors who submit proposals within the competitive range. The content and extent of discussions is a matter of the contracting officer's judgment, based on the facts of each acquisition. FAR 15.610(b). Conducting discussions face-to-face with one offeror does not require face-to-face discussions with all offerors, so long as other offerors are not

prejudiced. *Data Sys. Analysts, Inc.*, B-255684, Mar. 22, 1994, 94-1 CPD ¶ 209.

2. Discussions must be meaningful. Meaningful discussions, as a minimum, must notify each offeror in the competitive range of *deficiencies* in its proposal, *and* provide each offeror with an *opportunity to revise* its proposal.

3. A deficiency is a failure to satisfy the government's requirements in any area (e.g., technical, contractual, or cost). FAR 15.601.

4. Cases:

a. Failure to disclose deficiencies. *Price Waterhouse*, B-254492.2, Feb. 16, 1994, 94-1 CPD ¶ 168 (failure to notify that level of effort was too low); *Columbia Research Corp.*, B-247631, June 22, 1992, 92-1 CPD ¶ 536 (agency did not even hint at problems); *Mikalix & Co.*, B-241376.3, June 5, 1991, 70 Comp. Gen. 545, 91-1 CPD ¶ 527 (discussions not meaningful if agency does not advise offeror of weaknesses, excesses, or deficiencies which it must address to be in line for award); *IDA, Inc.*, B-225595, Mar. 16, 1987, 87-1 CPD ¶ 290 (must say if price is unreasonably high or low).

b. Meaningful discussions need not specifically identify each deficiency. It is sufficient if the contracting officer leads the contractor into areas requiring improvement. *CBIS Fed., Inc. v. Dep't of Labor*, GSBCA No. 12302-P, 93-3 BCA ¶ 26,121 (government properly identified weaknesses; no need to give multiple opportunities to revise proposal); *JCI Envtl. Servs.*, B-250752, Apr. 7, 1993, 93-1 CPD ¶ 299 (adequate to advise offeror with unreasonably low prices that its prices were at significant variance with the agency's price analysis).

c. An agency need not actually "bargain" with an offeror. *Northwest Regional Educ. Lab.*, B-222591.3, Jan. 21, 1987, 87-1 CPD ¶ 74.

d. Weaknesses.

(1) An agency need not identify every aspect of a technically acceptable proposal that received less than a maximum score. *SeaSpace Corp.*, B-252476.2, June 14, 1993, 93-1 CPD ¶ 462, *recon. denied*, B-252476.3, Oct. 27, 1993, 93-2 CPD ¶ 251 (all-encompassing discussions not required).

(2) However, an agency must discuss a lack of detail throughout a proposal resulting in a low but acceptable score, to provide the offeror a meaningful chance to improve its proposal. *Eldyne, Inc.*, B-250158, Jan. 14, 1993, 93-1 CPD ¶ 430, *sust'd on recon.*, *Dep't of the Navy—Recon.*, B-250158.4, May 28, 1993, 93-1 CPD ¶ 422; *see also Motorola, Inc.*, B-254489, Dec. 15, 1993, 93-2 CPD ¶ 322; *Andrew M. Slovak*, B-253275.2, Nov. 2, 1993, 93-2 CPD ¶ 263 (discussions are not meaningful if weaknesses significantly affecting score, and precluding reasonable chance of award, are not discussed).

(3) The GAO recently stated its view on this subject in *Management Health-Care Prods. & Servs*, B-251503.2, Dec. 15, 1993, 93-2 CPD ¶ 320:

Agencies are required to discuss weaknesses in an offeror's proposal where the weaknesses have a significant adverse impact on the proposal's technical rating, although discussions need not address every area in which the proposal received less than a perfect score, and the need for meaningful discussions may be constrained to avoid technical leveling, technical transfusion, and an auction.

e. When discussions will not improve a deficiency, an agency may be excused if it fails to point out the deficiency to the offeror. *See Appalachian Council, Inc.*, B-256179, May 20, 1994, 94-1 CPD ¶ 319 (past performance record disclosed by references named in proposal is historical; discussions will not improve it); *Encon Mgmt., Inc.*, B-234679, June 23, 1989, 89-1 CPD

¶ 595 (discussions cannot improve business experience; failure to discuss not error).

f. An agency may be excused from inquiring into omissions or business decisions on matters clearly addressed in the solicitation. *See Wade Perrow Constr.*, B-255332.2, Apr. 19, 1994, 94-1 CPD ¶ 266; *Associated Chem. & Envtl. Servs.*, B-228411.3, Mar. 10, 1988, 67 Comp. Gen. 315, 88-1 CPD ¶ 248.

g. An agency need not tell an offeror that its price is too high, unless the government has reason to believe that the price is unreasonable. *Warren Elec. Constr. Corp.*, B-236173.4, July 16, 1990, 90-2 CPD ¶ 34.

h. An agency must hold discussions about matters the RFP states will be discussed. *Daun-Ray Casuals, Inc.*, B-255217.3, 94-2 CPD ¶ 42 (failure to allow contractor to respond to unfavorable past performance information was improper, despite offeror's receipt of satisfactory rating, because RFP stated contractor would be allowed to address unfavorable reports).

5. Do more than the minimum necessary to satisfy the requirement for meaningful discussions. The purpose of discussions is to ensure a meeting of the minds. FAR 15.610(c) states that the contracting officer must—

a. Control all discussions;

b. Advise the offeror of deficiencies so that the offeror is given an opportunity to satisfy the government's requirements;

c. Provide the offeror a reasonable opportunity to submit revisions to its proposal;

d. Attempt to resolve any uncertainties concerning the technical proposal and other terms and conditions of the proposal; and

e. Resolve suspected mistakes by noting them as specifically as possible without disclosing information about other proposals or their evaluations. *Baytex Marine Communication, Inc.*, B-237183, Feb. 8, 1990, 90-1 CPD ¶ 164 (wide cost disparity required discussion to ensure common understanding of requirements).

6. Prohibited discussions.

a. *See generally* Feldman, *Traversing the Tightrope between Meaningful Discussions and Improper Practices in Negotiated Federal Acquisitions: Technical Transfusion, Technical Leveling, and Auction Techniques*, 17 Pub. Cont. L.J. 211 (Sept. 1987); Rollins, *A Contract Lawyer's Guide to the Requirement for Meaningful Discussions in Negotiated Procurements*, 122 Mil. L. Rev. 221 (Fall 1988).

b. Technical transfusion is government disclosure of one offeror's proposal to another to help the other improve its own proposal. FAR 15.610(d); 15.610(e)(2). There is one reported case of technical transfusion (although not so named) resulting in reversal of award. *Litton Sys., Inc.*, B-234060, May 12, 1989, 68 Comp. Gen. 422, 89-1 CPD ¶ 450. *Cf. Simmonds Precision Prods., Inc.*, B-244559.3, June 23, 1993, 93-1 CPD ¶ 483 (not technical transfusion to ask offeror if it considered alternate approaches to meeting Air Force black box requirement, resulting in that offeror proposing a similar solution to the protester's); *Technical Assessment Sys., Inc.*, B-242436, May 3, 1991, 91-1 CPD ¶ 432 (disclosure of unsolicited advertising material not transfusion).

c. Technical leveling is helping an offeror bring its proposal up to the level of other proposals through successive rounds of discussion. *Planning Research Corp.*, GSBCA No. 10472-P, 90-2 BCA ¶ 22,798 (meaningful discussions must end before technical leveling begins; the contracting officer must discuss deficiencies, not weaknesses).

(1) DOD controls on successive BAFOs (DFARS 215.611(c)(i)-(iii)) should help eliminate this practice.

(2) Revealing information available in commercial literature to competitors during a market survey is not technical leveling, even if protester claims it is proprietary. *Coastal Computer Consul-*

*tants Corp.*, GSBCA No. 12504-P, 94-1 BCA ¶ 26,447.

d. Auctioning is the practice of promoting price bidding between offerors by indicating the price offerors must beat, holding repeated rounds of best and final offers, disclosing other offerors' prices, etc. FAR 15.610(d)(3); *see Integrated Sys. Group v. Dep't of the Navy*, GSBCA No. 12508-P, Nov. 1, 1993, 94-2 BCA ¶ 26,623 (reasonable to request second BAFOs when one offeror offered unsolicited price reduction in conjunction with extension of proposal acceptance period; no disclosure of price information found); *Food Servs., Inc.*, B-241408, Feb. 12, 1991, 91-1 CPD ¶ 150 (repeated discussions about unrealistically low price not an auction, because the government did nothing more than conduct reasonable discussions by identifying deficiencies); *cf. Odetics, Inc.*, GSBCA No. 11506-P, 92-2 BCA ¶ 24,738 (agency failed to discover and disclose deficiencies in proposal until evaluation of BAFOs, but failure to discuss was not prejudicial error; no justification for second round of BAFOs, and illegal auction found); *International Business Mach. Corp.*, GSBCA No. 11324-P, 92-1 BCA ¶ 24,439 (in response to protest, agency reopened discussions, although no error justified the action; held illegal auction).

(1) The GAO holds that there is nothing inherently illegal about an auction. *The Faxon Co.*, B-227835.3, B-227835.5, 67 Comp. Gen. 39, 87-2 CPD ¶ 425 (1987) (there is nothing inherently illegal in conducting an auction in a negotiated procurement; the possibility that a contract may not be competed on an equal basis has a more harmful effect on the integrity of the competitive procurement system than a possible illegal auction).

(2) Agencies and intervenors frequently attempt to use the prohibition against auctions to defend against soliciting another round of BAFOs. Inevitably, however, the GAO finds that preserving the integrity of the competitive process outweighs the risks posed by an auction. *Baytex Marine Communication, Inc.*, B-237183, Feb. 8, 1990, 90-1 CPD ¶ 164.

e. The agency must treat offerors fairly.

(1) Do not mislead an offeror into raising its price unnecessarily, causing it to be too high to receive the award. *See SRS Technologies*, B-254425.2, Sept. 14, 1994, 94-2 CPD ¶ 125 (Navy told offeror its prices were too low when all it needed was better support for offered prices); *Ranor, Inc.*, B-255904, Apr. 14, 1994, 94-1 CPD ¶ 258 (misleading to tell offeror its price is below government estimate, and cause it to raise price, and then award to a lower-priced offeror); *DTH Mgmt. Group*, B-252879.2, Oct. 15, 1993, 93-2 CPD ¶ 227 (agency told offeror its price was too low, based on comparison with government estimate, when agency knew government estimate was faulty).

(2) Provide like information to all offerors. *Securiguard, Inc.*, B-249939, Dec. 21, 1992, 93-1 CPD ¶ 362 (if offeror is advised of weaknesses, agency must advise all); *Grumman Data Sys. Corp. v. Sec'y of the Army*, No. 91-1379, slip op. (D.D.C. June 28, 1991), *recon. denied*, No. 91-1379, slip op. (D.D.C. Aug. 28, 1991) (agency gave out answers, but not questions, misleading other offerors); *Seaspace*, B-241564, Feb. 15, 1991, 70 Comp. Gen. 268, 91-1 CPD ¶ 179 (one offeror in competitive range was told that agency wanted a more powerful computer, which it offered in BAFO; held preferential and prejudicial to others).

**K. Best and Final Offers.**

1. Discussions are concluded by requesting Best and Final Offers (BAFO's). FAR 15.611.

The request must include—

a. Notice that discussions are concluded;

b. Notice that offerors may submit a BAFO;

c. A common cutoff date and time that allows a reasonable opportunity for submission of written BAFOs;[9] and

d. Notice that if a modification is submitted, it must be received by the date and time specified and is subject to the requirements of FAR 52.215-10, Late Submissions, Modifications, and Withdrawals of Proposals, in the RFP. *See SYS v. Nat. Aeronautics & Space Admin.*, GSBCA No. 12154-P, 93-2 BCA ¶ 25,582, *recon. denied*, 93-2 BCA ¶ 25,652; *CardioMetrix*, B-256308, June 6, 1994, 94-1 CPD ¶ 349.

2. Deficiencies introduced in BAFOs do not require an agency to conduct further discussions. *Compliance Corp.*, B-254429, Dec. 15, 1993, 94-1 CPD ¶ 166 (substituted personnel data forms did not indicate that new personnel met minimum requirements); *Saco Defense, Inc.*, B-252066, May 20, 1993, 93-1 CPD ¶ 395 (agency not required to accept and retest a completely redesigned product to verify deficiencies were overcome, when only a minor redesign would have cured problems, and the contractor furnished no test data with its redesign to verify that it met test requirements).

3. Multiple Best and Final Offers.

a. DFARS 215.611(c)(i)-(iii) severely restricts a contracting officer's ability to reopen discussions and then request another round of BAFOs. Requests for subsequent BAFOs shall be approved as follows:

(1) For negotiated acquisitions under formal source selection procedures, by the Source Selection Authority (SSA), and the Service Acquisition Executive (SAE) or the Head of the Contracting Activity (HCA), if so delegated.

(2) For all other negotiated acquisitions, by the HCA. The HCA may delegate this authority to a level no lower than the chief of the contracting office.

b. The contracting officer still must solicit additional BAFOs in appropriate cases. *TRW, Inc.*, B-254045.2, Jan. 10, 1994, 94-1 CPD ¶ 18 (source selection official must resolve significant inconsistencies between technical and cost proposals before making award decision; agency erred in not conducting additional discussions); *Integrated Sys. Group v. Dep't of the Navy*, GSBCA No. 12508-P, Nov. 1, 1993, 94-2 BCA ¶ 26,623 (reasonable to request second BAFOs when one offeror offered unsolicited price reduction in conjunction with extension of proposal acceptance period; no auction found); *Dairy Maid Dairy, Inc.*, B-251758.3, May 24, 1993, 93-1 CPD ¶ 404 (post-BAFO amendment changing contract type from requirements to definite quantity was a material change requiring second BAFOs); *Harris Corp.*, B-237320, Feb. 14, 1990, 90-1 CPD ¶ 276 (contracting officer properly amended RFP to clarify provision and change quantity despite DFARS restriction on multiple BAFOs); *but see Odetics, Inc.*, GSBCA No. 11506-P, 92-2 BCA ¶ 24,738 (agency failed to discover and disclose deficiencies in proposal until evaluation of BAFOs; failure to discuss not prejudicial error, so no justification for second round of BAFOs and illegal auction found).

c. The better practice is to resist asking for your first set of BAFOs until you are confident that:

(1) all questions are asked and answered; and

(2) any last minute changes to the requirements are included in the RFP.

d. Post-BAFO discussions. If the government opens discussions with one offeror after BAFOs, it must open them with all remaining offerors. *Paramax Sys. Corp.*, B-253098.4, Oct. 27, 1993, 93-2 CPD ¶ 282 (offeror's agreement to mandatory fee limitation after BAFOs was discussions); *SmithKline Beecham Pharmaceuticals, N.A.*, B-252226.2, Aug. 4, 1993, 93-2 CPD ¶ 79; *see Government Technology Servs.*,

*Inc.*, GSBCA No. 10389-P, 90-2 BCA ¶ 22,673 (discussions did not occur when agency asked post-BAFO questions to understand an offer, not to determine its acceptability; offer was not modified); *see also Unitor Ships Serv., Inc.*, B-245642, Jan. 27, 1992, 92-1 CPD ¶ 110 (after BAFOs, loser told government that it had misevaluated its proposal; government relooked, agreed, and awarded to loser: held, not improper discussions because BAFO had only one reasonable interpretation); *Booz, Allen & Hamilton, Inc.*, B-236476, Dec. 4, 1989, 89-2 CPD ¶ 513 (need not reopen discussions where key person quits, offeror informs agency and provides replacement resume).

**L. Selection for Award.**

1. Agencies must evaluate BAFOs using the evaluation factors set forth in the solicitation.
   a. Bias in the selection decision is improper. *Latecoere Int'l v. United States*, 19 F.3d 1342 (11th Cir. 1994) (bias against French firm "infected the decision not to award it the contract . . .").
   b. There is no requirement that the same evaluators who did the initial evaluation also evaluate the BAFOs. *Medical Serv. Corp. Int'l*, B-255205.2, April 4, 194, 94-1 CPD ¶ 305.
2. The government normally may not accept an offer that fails to meet a material requirement of the RFP. *Government Micro Resources, Inc.*, GSBCA No. 12493-P, 94-2 BCA ¶ 26,965; *cf. Security Defense Sys., Corp.*, B-237826, Feb. 26, 1990, 90-1 CPD ¶ 321 (agency properly waived 1" deviation from size requirements and awarded to noncompliant proposal; defect was immaterial and protester was not prejudiced); *but see Litton Sys., Inc. v. Department of Transportation*, GSBCA No. 12911-P, 1994 BPD ¶ 213 (solicitation allowed government to waive a mandatory requirement if it determined waiver to be in its interest); *Grumman Data Sys. Corp. v. Dep't of the Air Force*, GSBCA No.

11939-P, 93-2 BCA ¶ 25,776, *aff'd sub nom. Grumman Data Sys. Corp. v. Widnall*, 15 F.3d 1044 (Fed. Cir. 1994) (Air Force awarded contract despite all offers failing to meet minimum requirements; protester did not raise this issue, because it and awardee *both* failed to meet some requirements); *Presearch, Inc.*, B-257889, Nov. 21, 1994, 94-2 CPD ¶ 197 (GAO denied protest that agency improperly relaxed solicitation requirements because record showed no prejudice). If the agency wants to accept an offer that does not comply with material requirements, it **should** issue a written amendment and afford all offerors an opportunity to propose on the new requirement. *4th Dimension Software, Inc.*, B-251936, May 13, 1993, 93-1 CPD ¶ 420.

3. Evaluation is inherently subjective.
   a. The fact that an agency reasonably might have made another selection does not mean that the selection made was unreasonable. *Red R. Serv. Corp.*, B-253671.4, Apr. 22, 1994, 94-1 CPD ¶ 385.
   b. Point scoring techniques do not make it objective. *VSE Corp.*, B-224397, Oct. 3, 1986, 86-2 CPD ¶ 392. Therefore, the RFP should not state that award will be made based on the proposal receiving the most points. *Harrison Sys. Ltd.*, B-212675, May 25, 1984, 84-1 CPD ¶ 572.
4. A cost/technical tradeoff analysis is essential to any source selection decision using a best value basis of award. *See Duke/Jones Hanford, Inc.*, B-249637.10, July 13, 1993, 93-2 CPD ¶ 26. However, more than a mere conclusion is required to support a best value analysis. *B3H Corp. v. Dep't of the Air Force*, GSBCA No. 12813-P, 94-3 BCA ¶ 27,068.
   a. Agencies have broad discretion in making cost/technical tradeoffs, and the extent to which one is sacrificed for the other is tested for rationality and consistency with stated evaluation factors. *Axion Corp.*, B-252812, July 16, 1993, 93-2 CPD ¶ 28. "[A] proposal which is one point better than another but costs millions of dollars

more may be selected if the agency can demonstrate with a reasonable degree of certainty that *the added value of the proposal is worth the higher price.*" *Lockheed Missiles & Space Co. v. Bentsen*, 4 F.3d 955 (Fed. Cir. 1993).

b. Beware of tradeoff techniques that distort the relative importance of the various evaluation criteria. "Dollars per Point" is a scheme in which the technical scores are divided by the cost or price as a method of determining value. This technique has the effect of revising cost/technical factor weights to be equal. *See Billy G. Bassett; Lynch Dev., Inc.*, B-237331, Feb. 20, 1990, 90-1 CPD ¶ 195; *T. H. Taylor, Inc.*, B-227143, Sept. 15, 1987, 87-2 CPD ¶ 252.

c. Comparative consideration of features in competing proposals is permissible, even if those features were not given quantifiable evaluation credit under disclosed evaluation criteria, if the basis for award stated in the RFP provides for an integrated assessment of proposals. *Grumman Data Sys. Corp. v. Dep't of the Air Force*, GSBCA No. 11939-P, 93-2 BCA ¶ 25,776, *aff'd sub nom. Grumman Data Sys. Corp. v. Widnall*, 15 F.3d 1044 (Fed. Cir. 1994) (SSA's head-to-head comparison of proposals may permissibly look at features not directly evaluated).

d. A cost/technical tradeoff analysis may consider relevant matters not disclosed in the RFP as tools to assist in making the tradeoff. *See Advanced Mgmt., Inc.*, B-251273.2, Apr. 2, 1993, 93-1 CPD ¶ 288 (permissible to consider that loss of efficiency in awarding to a new contractor rather than incumbent would reduce effective price difference between them).

e. If the agency requests BAFOs, make the cost/technical tradeoff decision after receipt of BAFOs, not before. *Halter Marine, Inc.*, B-255429, Mar. 1, 1994, 94-1 CPD ¶ 161 (agency failed to consider price reduction in BAFO in its tradeoff analysis).

5. Sound practice requires documentation of the selection decision and its rationale in a written memorandum. A written decision is mandatory for some procurements. *See* AFARS app. AA-201(l); AFR 70-15 (Apr 1988), Attachment 9 (page 83); *see also Colonial Storage Co.*, B-253501.5, Oct. 19, 1993, 93-2 ¶ 234 (if RFP states award will be on a best value basis, failure to document finding that offerors were technically equal in a source selection decision document, and awarding based on low price, was a basis for overturning award, even though agency claimed it made such a finding); *PharChem Labs., Inc.*, B-244385, Oct. 8, 1991, 91-2 CPD ¶ 317 (disclosed evaluation weights were 80% technical, 20% price; source selection authority declared a tie and awarded to slightly lower priced offeror *without* supporting rationale for not accepting a substantially higher-quality offer for a slightly higher price). A well-written source selection memorandum should contain:

a. A summary of the evaluation criteria and their relative importance.

b. A statement of the decision maker's own evaluation of each of the proposals, either adopting recommendations of others or stating a personal evaluation. The statement should identify major advantages and disadvantages (strengths and weaknesses) of each proposal.

c. A description of the reasons for choosing the successful offeror, comparing differences in cost with differences in technical factors.

6. The Source Selection Authority (SSA) need not personally write the decision memorandum. *Latecoere Int'l Ltd.*, B-239113.3, Jan. 15, 1992, 92-1 CPD ¶ 70.

7. The selection decision is subject to review for rationality and consistency with the stated evaluation criteria. *Ogden Plant Maintenance Co.*, B-255156.2, Apr. 7, 1994, 94-1 CPD ¶ 275. The SSA has much discretion.

a. The SSA may consider slightly different scores to be a tie and award to the lower cost offeror. *Tecom, Inc.*, B-257947, Nov. 29, 1994, 94-2 CPD ¶ 212; *Duke/Jones Hanford, Inc.*, B-249637.10, July 13, 1993, 93-2 CPD ¶ 26.

   b. Conversely, the SSA may consider slightly different scores to represent a significant difference justifying the greater price. *Macon Apparel Corp.*, B-253008, Aug. 11, 1993, 93-2 CPD ¶ 93 (identical adjectives earned by two offerors considered to be different, because one was borderline with next lower adjective, and the other was borderline with next higher adjective; 7% price premium reasonable).

   c. In one case, an SSA's decision to award to a substantially lower scored offeror whose cost was only slightly lower was not adequately justified. *TRW, Inc.*, B-234558, June 21, 1989, 68 Comp. Gen. 512, 89-1 CPD ¶ 584. After the SSA's reconsideration, the same outcome was adequately supported. *TRW, Inc.*, B-234558.2, Dec. 18, 1989, 89-2 CPD ¶ 560.

   d. Reliance on the scores of evaluators alone, without looking at strengths and weaknesses of each proposal, may be unreasonable. *See SDA, Inc.*, B-248528.2, Apr. 14, 1993, 93-1 CPD ¶ 320 (failed to detect scoring error).

**M. Debriefings.**[10]
*See* 10 U.S.C. § 2305(b)(5); FAR 15.1001.

1. Notices to unsuccessful offerors.

   a. Notify offerors excluded from the competitive range as soon as practicable, giving the reason. FAR 15.609(c).

   b. In small business set-asides, notify the unsuccessful offerors before award. FAR 15.1001(b)(2).

   c. Notify all losing offerors after award. FAR 15.1001(c).

2. Debriefing unsuccessful offerors who request one is mandatory when the selection decision is based on factors other than price alone. FAR 15.1002.

   a. Debriefings are normally the last opportunity to trigger or avoid a bid protest. *Cf.*

*Information & Telecommunications Strategies J.V. v. Dep't of the Navy*, GSBCA No. 12605-P, Oct. 19, 1993, 94-1 BCA ¶ 26,493 (denying request to suspend delegation of procurement authority pending hearing on merits of protest based on information obtained at a debriefing conducted more than ten days after notice of contract award).

   b. Debriefings generally are limited to the offeror's proposal. Do not make point-by-point comparisons with other proposals. After the enactment of the Federal Acquisition Streamlining Act of 1994, Pub. L. No. 103-355, § 1014, 108 Stat. 2355-56 (1994), debriefings must include as a minimum:

     (1) The agency's evaluation of the offeror's significant weak or deficient factors;

     (2) The overall ratings of the debriefed offeror and of the winning contractor;

     (3) The overall rankings of all offers;

     (4) The rationale for the award decision;

     (5) The make and model number of any commercial item that is an end item offered by the winning contractor; and

     (6) Reasonable responses to questions of the debriefed offeror about the source selection process.

   c. Tailor debriefings to point out how fair source selection procedures are, compliment proposal writers, point out areas for improvement of future proposals, and point out deficiencies which were discussed but not corrected. Avoid arguments with offerors. Leave the room if an argument develops.

## IV. FORMAL SOURCE SELECTION.
FAR 15.612.

**A. Agency Guidance.**
Formal source selections are competitive negotiations with a heavy dose of procedure. *See* AFARS app. AA; NAPS 5215.612; AFFARS app. AA, *Formal Source Selection for Major Acquisitions*; AFFARS app. BB, *Streamlined Source*

*Selection Procedures*; AFARS Manual No. 1, *Source Selection Policy and Procedures*; AMC Pam 715-3, *Source Selection*; AFR 70-15 (Apr. 1988); SECNAVINST 4200.33 (14 July 1986); NASA Handbook 5103.6B (Oct. 1988).

**B. When Used.**

A source selection is considered formal when a specific evaluation group is used to evaluate proposals and select the source for contract award. This approach is generally used in high dollar value acquisitions and may be used in other acquisitions as prescribed in agency regulations. *See* NASA FAR Supp. 1815.613-71(a) (use formal source selection procedures for negotiated procurements exceeding $25 million).

**C. Organization.**

The source selection organization typically includes:

1. Source Selection Evaluation Board (SSEB). This group consists of the evaluators of the offerors' proposals.
2. Source Selection Advisory Council (SSAC). This is a group of senior agency officials who review the report of the SSEB and advise the Source Selection Authority. This group can reassess or rescore proposals after the SSEB completes its work.
3. Source Selection Authority (SSA). An individual at a management level above that of the contracting officer who makes the competitive range determination and the selection decision.

**D. Authority of Source Selection Authorities.**

1. The SSA has broad discretion. *BMY, A Div. of Harsco Corp. v. United States*, 693 F. Supp.

1232 (D.D.C. 1988); *Grey Advertising, Inc.*, B-184825, May 14, 1976, 55 Comp. Gen. 1111, 76-1 CPD ¶ 325.

2. A source selection authority may disagree with the SSEB and SSAC, and re-score the proposals. *Global Assoc.*, B-212820, Apr. 9, 1984, 84-1 CPD ¶ 394. The SSAC may disagree with the SSEB. *Computer Sciences Corp. v. Dep't of the Army*, GSBCA No. 11497-P, 92-1 BCA ¶ 24,703 (each evaluation group is not bound by lower level groups; SSAC can ignore the SSEB's recommendation and exercise its own judgment).
3. If an SSA relies on an SSEB's recommendation that lacks a reasonable basis in arriving at a source selection decision, the SSA's decision also lacks a reasonable basis. *Adelaided Blomfield Mgmt. Co.*, B-253128.2, Sept. 27, 1993, 93-2 CPD ¶ 197.
4. Reversing decisions before award.
   a. Superiors. In *SATO, Inc.*, B-229883, Mar. 29, 1988, 88-1 CPD ¶ 317, the Under Secretary of the Army reviewed and vacated a subordinate SSA's selection. *See Oklahoma Aerotronics, Inc.*, B-237705.2, Mar. 28, 1990, 90-1 CPD ¶ 337 (Assistant Commander, Contracts, may reverse SSA selection).
   b. Successors. In *Lee J. Kriegsfeld*, B-222865, Aug. 27, 1986, 86-2 CPD ¶ 214, the successor to an SSA reversed a predecessor's decision prior to award.

**V. CONCLUSION.**

**A. Advantages.**

**B. Cautions.**

**C. Points to Remember.**

## Endnotes

1. *See Federal Computer Corp. v. Dep't of Justice*, GSBCA No. 12560-P, Sept. 24, 1993, 94-1 BCA ¶ 26,442.

2. Currently only Title 10 requires disclosure of subfactors and their relative weights. When implemented in the FAR, the Federal Acquisition Streamlining Act of 1994 (FASA) will require disclosure of significant subfactors by civilian agencies as well, and an explicit statement by all agencies of whether all non-price or non-cost factors are significantly more important, significantly less important, or approximately equal in importance with cost or price. *See* Pub. L. No. 103-355, §§ 1011(b), 1061(c), 108 Stat. 3243, 3254-55, 3266-67 (1994) (amending 10 U.S.C. § 2305(a) and 41 U.S.C. § 253a(b)).

3. FASA adds similar provisions for civilian agencies, effective upon the issuance of implementing provisions in the FAR.

4. Use of this basis for award often is called "best value" contracting. However, solicitations must clearly state the basis for award that will be used in the source selection decision. A mere reference to "best value" in the solicitation is not sufficient to put offerors on notice that a cost/technical tradeoff will be part of the selection process. *See Systems Resources, Inc. v. Dep't of the Navy*, GSBCA No. 12536-P, 94-1 BCA ¶ 26,388. It is the Army's policy to use the best value basis for award for all formal source selections, and for other procurements whenever appropriate. AFARS 15.602(a)(2)(A).

5. *See* 41 U.S.C. § 253a(b)(2)(B)(i), which continues the 1984 statutory language for civilian agencies until FASA implementation. Under the 1984 version of the statute, an agency could award on initial proposals only if it provided notice in the solicitation. In practice, all solicitations provided this notice. FAR 52.215-16(c).

6. This term does not refer to the revisions made to proposals during the conduct of discussions. FAR 15.412(a).

7. The GAO permits contracting officers to extend closing dates for solicitations, even after the closing date has already passed, to consider late bids, if doing so will enhance competition. *See Varicon Int'l, Inc.*, B-255808, Apr. 6, 1994, 94-1 CPD ¶ 240.

8. FASA will allow civilian agencies to use this authority as well.

9. *See Environmental Control Div., Inc.*, B-255181, Feb. 16, 1994, 94-1 CPD ¶ 115 (BAFO faxed on-time to contracting officer not considered because faxed proposals were not allowed, and hand-carried BAFO that was four minutes late was excluded as well); *FRC Int'l, Inc.*, B-255345, Feb. 18, 1994, 94-1 CPD ¶ 125 (allowing only two and one-half hours for BAFO submission was reasonable where agency reasonably concluded that immediate responses were needed).

10. FASA substantially broadens the debriefing rights of unsuccessful offerors, but these rights are not effective until implementing provisions in the FAR are promulgated.

# SAMPLE EVALUATION FACTORS

## SECTION M. EVALUATION FACTORS FOR AWARD

**M-1. The government will award to the offeror whose proposal is most advantageous to the government considering the evaluation criteria set forth below.**

**M-2. Evaluation Criteria.**
a.  Technical Factors.
(1) Widget Design. The government will evaluate the design of the proposed widget for compliance with the specifications set forth in Section C.
(2) Widget Reliability and Maintainability. The government will evaluate the proposed widget for reliability. Reliability demonstrated through testing is preferred over reliability predicted through analysis. The maintainability of the widget, including ease of repair, use of readily available commercial parts, adequate repair manuals, etc., shall be evaluated.
(3) Key Personnel - The government will evaluate the education, experience, and availability of the offeror's key personnel. Key personnel are those personnel defined in clause H-24, Key Personnel.
b.  Management Factors.
(1) Quality. The offeror's quality control program will be evaluated to determine compliance with MIL-I-45208A and the likelihood that the system will ensure acceptable widgets.
(2) Capability. The proposal will be evaluated on the resources available to perform the contract, including production facilities, financial resources, adequate staffing, etc.
c.  Past Performance.
The offeror will be evaluated on its relevant past performance, including its past performance in supplying similar widgets, and its past performance on other government contracts.
d.  Risk.
The offeror's proposal will be evaluated to assess the risks regarding on time delivery of conforming widgets.
e.  Price.
Only firm-fixed-prices are acceptable. The proposed price will be adjusted for the following price related factors: rental charges for government property and transportation charges.

**M-3. Relative Importance of Evaluation Criteria.**
The technical factors are more important than management factors, past performance, and risk combined. The technical factors are in descending order of importance. The management factors are of equal importance. The management factors, combined, are of equal importance with past performance and risk, individually. Past performance and risk are of equal importance.

Price, adjusted for price-related factors, is of equal importance with the non-cost factors.

**M-4. Selection for Award.**
The government will award to the offeror whose proposal provides the best value to the government. The government may award to an offeror whose proposal is sufficiently more advantageous than lower priced proposals so as to justify payment of the higher price.

# SAMPLE SOURCE SELECTION DECISION
## (AFR 70-15)

*SOURCE SELECTION DECISION*
FOR THE *(Name of System)*

RFP No._____

Pursuant to Air Force Regulation 70-15 as the Source Selection Authority for this acquisition I have determined the *(Name of System) proposed by (Successful Offeror)* provides the best overall value to satisfy Air Force needs. This selection was made based upon the criteria established in Section M of the Request for Proposal (RFP) "Evaluation Factors for Award" and my integrated assessment of the proposals submitted in response to the RFP, the terms and conditions agreed upon during negotiations, and the capability of *(Successful Offeror)* to fulfill the subject requirement.

The *(five)* evaluation criteria against which the potential sources were measured in order of importance, were (1) Operational Utility; (2) Readiness and Support; (3) Life Cycle Cost; (4) Design Approach; and (5) Manufacturing Program and Management.

While all proposals in the competitive range for the _____ system are adequate when measured against the above criteria, the *(Successful Offeror's)* proposal offers significant operational utility and clearly provides the best system in terms of operational effectiveness. _____'s proposal is superior in terms of operational effectiveness, in part because of its excellent instrument arrangement which includes a logically designed and uncluttered instrument panel, in addition to excellent access to all controls. _____'s proposal displayed outstanding consideration for operational supportability by building a full-scale mock-up to refine reliability and maintainability concepts. The system has the strongest characteristics in the area of reliability, maintainability and availability. The design is also the best, meeting or exceeding all RFP requirements. It is exceptional for crew station, escape system and avionics design. The design substantially enhances its reliability and maintainability. _____'s manufacturing approach to the _____ system clearly makes it the leader in this area. Its team of managers and employees, coupled with existing facilities, assure development and fielding of a quality system.

Although the most probable total life cycle cost of _____'s system is not the lowest, it is only _____ percent more than the lowest total life cycle cost and offers the lowest evaluated operating support cost. It is my view that the small difference in total life cycle cost is more than offset by the superior characteristics of _____'s system.

In summary, based on my assessment of all proposals in accordance with the specified evaluation criteria, it is my decision that _____'s proposed system offers the best overall value.

*(Source Selection Authority)*

SOURCE SELECTION AUTHORITY

# NEGOTIATIONS FLOW CHART

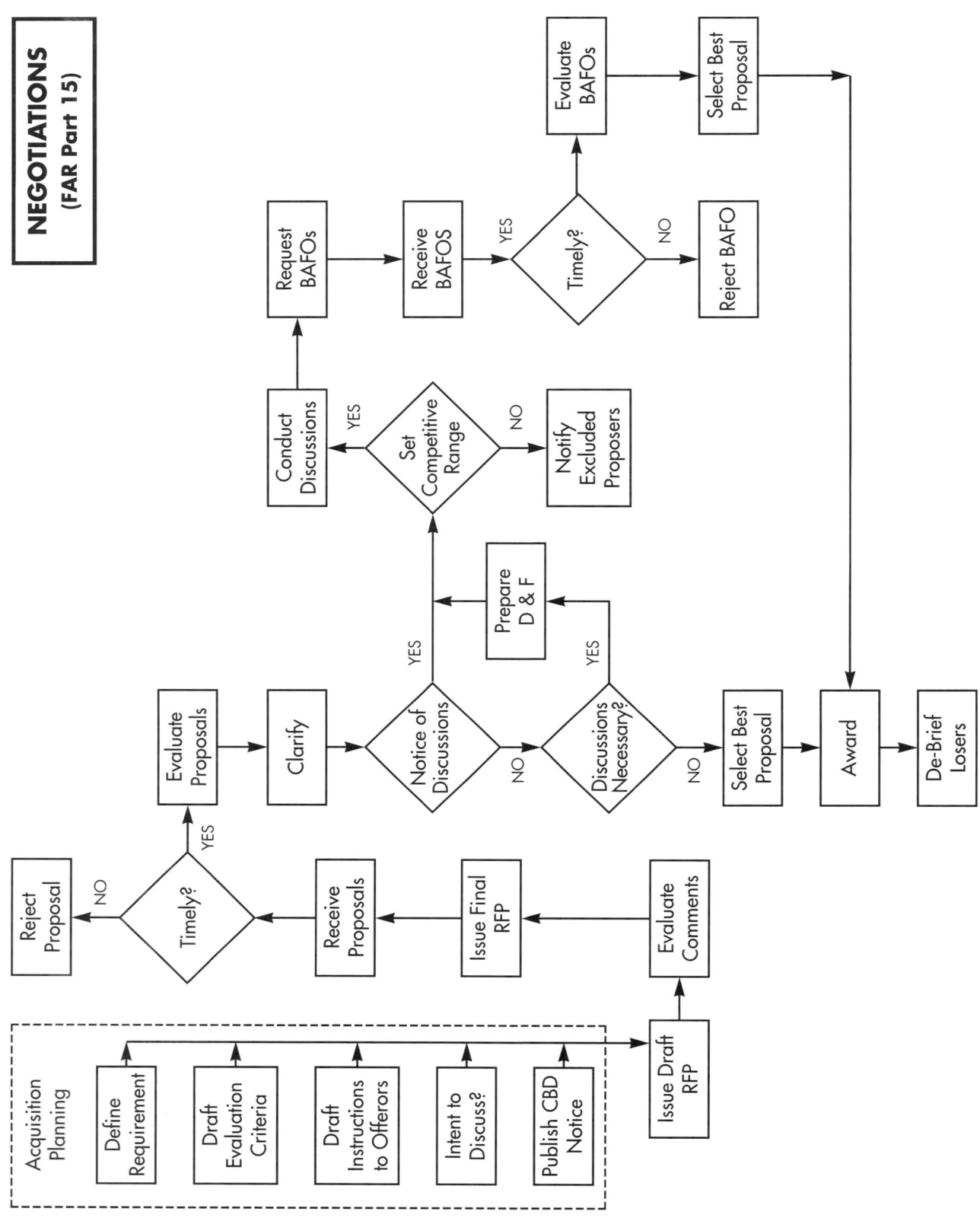

# SPECIAL TYPES OF NEGOTIATED ACQUISITIONS

## I. FOUR-STEP SOURCE SELECTION PROCEDURES.

FAR 15.613; DFARS 215.613.

### A. General.

1. Receive, evaluate, and conduct limited discussions regarding the offerors' technical proposals;
2. Receive, evaluate, establish the competitive range, and conduct discussions of the offerors' cost proposals;
3. Set a common cutoff date for receipt of revised proposals.
4. Negotiation of a definitive contract with the selected offeror.

### B. Why Four-Step Negotiations?

Four-step procedures are designed primarily to: focus attention on technical excellence, maintain the integrity of each offeror's proposal, provide visibility of discriminating features between proposals, reduce the opportunity for buy-ins, preclude the opportunity for the use of auctioning techniques and assure a disciplined and orderly process in the selection of sources.

### C. Issues.

1. Conduct of meaningful discussions prior to selection. There is often an erroneous belief that four-step procedures eliminate the statutory requirement to conduct meaningful discussions. *See To the Administrator of NASA*, B-173677, 51 Comp. Gen. 621 (1972). It is also unwise to use four-step procedures in automatic data processing equipment (ADPE) acquisitions because the GSBCA does not favor them. *CPT Corp;*, GSBCA No. 8134-P-R, 86-1 BCA ¶ 18,727.
2. Scope of post selection discussion. Discussions with the selected offeror shall not involve changes which would affect the basis for selection. DFARS 215.613(i)

## II. ARCHITECT-ENGINEER CONTRACTING. FAR 36.6.

### A. The Brooks Act.

40 U.S.C. §§ 541-544. The Brooks Act sets forth special procedures for the selection of contractors for Architect-Engineering Services (A-E). *See Forest Serv., Dep't of Agriculture, Request for Advanced Decision*, B-233987, July 14, 1989, 68 Comp. Gen. 556, 89-2 CPD ¶ 47 (discussion of what constitutes A-E services).

### B. A-E Procedures Are Considered Competitive.

10 U.S.C. § 2302(2)(A); 41 U.S.C. § 259(b)(1).

### C. Procedures.

1. Solicit proposals. *Asbestos Management, Inc.*, B-237841, Feb. 23, 1990, 90-1 CPD ¶ 325 (if agency loses part of the proposal, it should ask for another copy).
2. Evaluate proposals using the criteria set forth in FAR 36.602-1. Cost is not a factor. Evaluators must score proposals reasonably. *Shah & Assocs.*, B-257405, Sept. 30, 1994, 94-2 CPD ¶ 123.
3. Conduct technical discussions with at least three of the most highly qualified firms.
4. Select and rank the three most highly qualified firms.
5. Negotiate a fair and reasonable price with the most qualified firm. Only if negotiations fail does the contracting officer negotiate with other, less qualified firms. *See Roy F. Weston, Inc.*, B-252541.2, July 19, 1993, 93-2 CPD ¶ 33.

**D. Cases.**

*IDG Architects*, B-235487, Sept. 18, 1989, 89-2 CPD ¶ 236 (no need for an architect on an A-E selection board); *White Shield, Inc.*, B-235522, Sept. 21, 1989, 89-2 CPD ¶ 257 (A-E procedures must be used to buy surveying and mapping services).

## III. BROAD AGENCY ANNOUNCEMENTS. FAR 35.106.

**A. When Used.**

Broad Agency Announcements (BAAs) are used to acquire basic research. In *ABB Lummus Crest Inc.*, B-244440, Sept. 16, 1991, 91-2 CPD ¶ 252, the protester challenged use of a broad agency announcement, alleging the subject matter was not basic research. The GAO ruled the protest untimely because it was not made before receipt of initial proposals. This decision may prove difficult to apply in practice when the broad agency announcement in question has an open period for submission of research proposals, or where the announcement provides for preproposal ("whitepapers").

**B. BAA Procedures Are Considered Competitive.**

10 U.S.C. § 2302(2)(B); 41 U.S.C. § 259(b)(2).

**C. Procedures.**

1. FAR 35.016 and DFARS 235.016 coverage of Broad Agency Announcements is limited. Individual agencies and activities have more detailed procedures. The most detailed procedures appear in DEAR 935.016 (Research Opportunity Announcements). Contracting activities may wish to review Department of Energy procedures for guidance on internal processing of Broad Agency Announcements.

2. Announce the agency's research interest in broadly defined areas.
   a. Describe the contents of a proposal.
   b. Identify the selection criteria and their relative importance.
   c. Specify a period during which proposals will be considered.

3. BAAs do not contain a specific statement of work, and no formal solicitation is issued. *Centre Mfg. Co.*, B-255347.2, Mar. 2, 1994, 94-1 CPD ¶ 162.

4. Evaluate proposals, as received, through a scientific or peer review process. The evaluation must be in accordance with the announced criteria. *See Golden Mfg. Co.*, B-255347, Feb. 24, 1994, 94-1 CPD ¶ 183.

5. Select for award those proposals evaluated as most important for agency programs in accordance with announced criteria.

## IV. SOLE SOURCE AND LIMITED SOURCE NEGOTIATED CONTRACTS.

**A. A Justification and Approval (J&A) is Required.**

Prepare and obtain approval of the Justification and Approval for Other than Full and Open Competition prior to issuing the RFP. AFARS 6.304(90). *But see* FAR 6.303-1(e).

**B. Synopsize in the *Commerce Business Daily* for Awards Over $25,000.**

41 U.S.C. § 416 and 15 U.S.C. § 637.

**C. Limited Competitions.**

A contracting officer must solicit as many offerors as practicable. 10 U.S.C. § 2304(e). The contracting officer must conform to the procedures for full and open competition if appropriate, or any other authorized procedures. FAR 6.301. However, failure to follow competitive procedures precisely is unobjectionable.

*Raytheon Co.*, B-240333, Nov. 9, 1990, 90-2 CPD ¶ 384 (award on initial proposals to other than the low cost offeror permissible because agency justified use of other than competitive procedures).

**D. Sole Source Contracts.**
1. Solicit the identified source.
2. Evaluate the proposal.
3. Negotiate the proposed contract with the sole source.
4. Award the contract.

## V. UNSOLICITED PROPOSALS. FAR 15.5.

**A. Unsolicited Proposals Are Governed by a Number of Statutory Provisions.**
10 U.S.C. § 2304(d); annual DOD Appropriations Act restrictions.

**B. Defense Policy is to Encourage Unsolicited Proposals.**
FAR 15.503.

**C. Advertising Material, Commercial Product Offers, Contributions, or Technical Correspondence as Defined in FAR 15.501 Are Not Unsolicited Proposals.**

**D. Valid Unsolicited Proposals.**
FAR 15.503(c) requires that a valid unsolicited proposal must—
1. Be innovative and unique;
2. Be independently originated and developed by the offeror;
3. Be prepared without government supervision;
4. Include sufficient detail to permit a determination that government support could be worthwhile and the proposed work could benefit the agency's research and development or other mission responsibilities;
5. Not be an advance proposal for a known agency requirement that can be acquired by competitive methods.
6. Unsolicited proposals in response to a publicized general statement of agency needs are considered to be independently originated.
7. Agencies that receive unique and innovative unsolicited proposals not related to their missions may identify for the offeror other agencies whose missions bear a reasonable relationship to the proposal's subject matter.

**E. Procedures.**
1. Conduct an initial review to ensure that the proposal is complete, binding, and marked in accordance with FAR 15.509. FAR 15.506-1.
2. Conduct a comprehensive evaluation of the proposal. FAR 15.506-2. The purpose of the evaluation is to determine whether the agency is interested in the proposal and whether the proposal is eligible for award without further competition as provided by FAR 15.507(b).
3. If the unsolicited proposal is acceptable for award without competition, the agency shall prepare a J&A, then use the proposal as the basis for negotiation of a definitive contract.
4. Otherwise, the proposal shall be returned to the offeror.

## CHAPTER SEVEN

# *Small Purchase Procedures*

## I. INTRODUCTION.

Following this block of instruction, students should:

A. Understand the differences between simplified acquisition procedures and other procurement methods.

B. Understand the various methods used to make simplified acquisitions, and the situations when each method should be used.

C. Understand the differences in competition requirements between simplified acquisition procedures and other procurement methods.

## II. REFERENCES.

A. Federal Acquisition Streamlining Act of 1994, Pub. L. No. 103-355, 108 Stat. 3243 (1994) (hereinafter FASA).

B. FAR Part 13, amended by 60 Fed. Reg. 34741 (effective July 3, 1995).

C. DFARS Part 213.

D. AFARS Part 13.

E. AFFARS Part 5313.

F. NAPS Part 5213.

G. Dep't of Defense Reg. 7000.14-R, *Financial Mgmt. Regulation*, Volume 5, "Disbursing Policies and Procedures" (16 Dec. 1993) [hereinafter DOD Reg. 7000.14-R, vol. 5].

## III. GENERAL.

### A. Purpose.

FAR 13.102. Contracting officers use simplified acquisition procedures and other simplified purchase procedures to:

1. Reduce administrative costs;
2. Increase opportunities for small business concerns and small disadvantaged businesses;
3. Promote efficiency and economy in contracting; and
4. Avoid unnecessary burdens for agencies and contractors.

### B. Definitions.

1. **Simplified acquisition**. Currently, simplified acquisitions are acquisitions of supplies, services, or construction in the amount of $50,000 or less using simplified acquisition procedures. FAR 13.101. Under FASA, this threshold will eventually increase to $100,000. FASA §§ 4001, 4201.

2. **Simplified acquisition procedures**. Those methods prescribed in Part 13 of the FAR, Part 213 of the DFARS, and agency FAR supplements for making simplified acquisitions using imprest funds, purchase orders, credit cards, and blanket purchase agreements. *See* FAR 13.101. Simplified acquisition procedures do not include:

   a. Requirements obtained through the use of delivery orders. FAR 13.101(a). *See Jewett-Cameron Lumber Corp.*, B-229582, Mar. 15, 1988, 88-1 CPD ¶ 265 (no need to reserve plywood requirements contract for small business because requirements contract was not a simplified acquisition procedure).

   b. Contracts with the Small Business Administration (SBA) under section 8(a) of the Small Business Act. 15 U.S.C. § 637(a); FAR 13.101(b). *Cf.* The Judge Advocate

General's School, U.S. Army, *Contract Law Deskbook*, vol. I, ch. 12, *Socioeconomic Policies*, February 1995.

c. Contracts awarded using sealed bidding (see FAR Part 14), negotiation procedures (see FAR Part 15), or small business or labor surplus area set-asides (see FAR Parts 19 and 20), other than small business-simplified acquisition set-asides prescribed in FAR 13.105. FAR 13.101(c).

## C. Policies.

FAR 13.103.

1. Activities shall use simplified acquisition procedures to the "maximum extent practicable" for all purchases of supplies or services not exceeding the simplified acquisition limitation (currently $50,000). 10 U.S.C. § 2304(g)(4); FAR 13.103(a). In support of contingency operations defined by 10 U.S.C. § 101(a)(13), the simplified acquisition threshold increases to $200,000. FASA § 1502 (amending 10 U.S.C. § 2302(7)), DFARS 213.000. § 2302(7); DFARS 213.000.

2. Activities shall not use simplified acquisition procedures to acquire supplies and services initially estimated to exceed the simplified acquisition limitation, or that eventually exceed it. FAR 13.103(b); *All Star Carpet & Bedding, Inc.*, B-242490.3, Apr. 4, 1991, 91-1 CPD ¶ 352.

3. Activities shall not divide requirements that exceed the simplified acquisition threshold into multiple purchases merely to justify using simplified acquisition procedures. FASA § 4201(b); 10 U.S.C. § 2304(g)(3); FAR 13.103(b). *See Mas-Hamilton Group, Inc.*, B-249049, Oct. 20, 1992, 72 Comp. Gen. ___, 92-2 CPD ¶ 259.

## D. Procedures.

1. **Choice of method**. Contracting officers shall use the simplified acquisition method that is most suitable, efficient, and economical. FAR 13.104(a).

2. **Bulk funding**. Agencies shall use bulk funding to the maximum extent practicable to reduce processing time, handling, and documentation. FAR 13.104(c).

3. **Competition**. The government must conduct simplified acquisitions consistent with the concern for fair and equitable competition, even though the competition requirements for large purchases do not apply. *General Metals, Inc.*, B-247560, May 29, 1992, 92-1 CPD ¶ 486 (protest sustained because government issued purchase order to low-priced contractor offering foreign product when solicitation required domestic product).

4. **GSA or DOD specifications**. The FAR specifically exempts simplified acquisitions from the mandatory use of federal specifications, and permits the use of manufacturers' part numbers as item descriptions in simplified acquisitions. FAR 10.006(a); *Mas-Hamilton Group, Inc.*, B-249049, Oct. 20, 1992, 72 Comp. Gen. 6, 92-2 CPD ¶ 259 (manufacturer's part number and national stock number sufficiently described agency's needs); *RMS Indus.*, B-247394, May 19, 1992, 92-1 CPD ¶ 452 (welding torch bodies); *East West Research, Inc.*, B-238551, May 16, 1990, 90-1 CPD ¶ 477 (abrasive wheels).

5. **Inspection and testing**. The government should rely on the contractor to inspect and test to ensure conformity with contract quality requirements, with limited exceptions. FAR 46.202-1(a).

   a. If necessary, the government may inspect and test to ensure compliance with the contract and to evaluate the contractor's internal work processes. FAR 46.202-1(b).

   b. In deciding whether to inspect and test, the contracting officer should consider:

      (1) The nature and intended use of the supplies or services;

      (2) The potential losses if the product is defective;

      (3) The likelihood of uncontested replacement or correction of defective work; and

      (4) The cost of detailed government inspection. FAR 46.202-1; 46.404; and 52.246-1.

6. **Responsibility determinations**. If a contracting officer determines that a responsive small business lacks certain elements of responsibility, the contracting officer normally must withhold contract award and refer the matter to the Small Business Administration (SBA). FAR 13.104(g); FAR Subpart 19.6.

7. **Solicitation of quotes**. The preferred solicitation method is through the Federal Computer Acquisition Network (FACNET). However, if FACNET is not available, buyers should solicit quotes orally. However, buyers must issue written solicitations for construction contracts exceeding $2,000 or when it is uneconomical or impractical to obtain oral quotations. FAR 13.106-1(a)(2).

8. **Notification of unsuccessful offerors**. The contracting officer must notify unsuccessful suppliers upon request. FAR 13.106-1(c)(2).

## IV. SIMPLIFIED ACQUISITION METHODS.

### A. Purchase Orders.

FAR Part 13.5; AFARS Subpart 13.5; AFFARS Subpart 5313.5.

1. Definition. A *purchase order* is a government offer to buy certain supplies, services, or construction, from commercial sources, upon specified terms and conditions. FAR 13.101. A purchase order is different than a delivery order.

2. **Forms**. Within DOD, contracting officers must use the DD Form 1155, Order for Supplies or Services, when using simplified acquisition procedures for unclassified purchases. DFARS 213.505. *See* page 97. Civilian agencies may use Optional Form (OF) 347. *See* page 98.

3. **Standard Form (SF) 44**. Activities normally use SF 44, Purchase Order-Invoice-Voucher, for over-the-counter purchases while away from the purchasing office or at isolated activities. Activities may use the SF 44 as a purchase order, receiving report, invoice, and public voucher. FAR 13.505-3. *See* page 99.

a. Activities may use an SF 44 if:
  (1) The purchase does not exceed $2,500 unless an unusual and compelling urgency exists or the purchase is made overseas in support of a contingency operation. In addition, for DOD, if the purchase is for aviation fuel or oil, the purchase may not exceed $50,000). FAR 13.505-3(b)(1); DFARS 213.505-3(b)(1).
  (2) The supplies or services are available immediately. FAR 13.505-3(b)(2).
  (3) The contractor will make one delivery and the contracting officer will make one payment. FAR 13.505-3(b)(3).
  (4) This method is more economical and efficient than other simplified acquisition methods. FAR 13.505-3(b)(4).

4. **Conditions**. Except as provided under the unpriced purchase order method (FAR 13.502), activities shall issue purchase orders on a fixed-price basis unless authorized by agency procedures. FAR 13.501.

5. **Inspection, acceptance, and delivery**. Orders shall specify free on board (f.o.b.) destination for supplies to be delivered in the United States, except Alaska and Hawaii, unless there are valid reasons why they should not so specify, and generally shall provide for inspection/acceptance at destination. FAR 13.501(d) & (e).

6. **Unpriced purchase orders**. Activities may use unpriced purchase orders only in limited situations. *See* FAR 13.502.

7. **Unsigned electronic purchase orders (EPOs).** Agencies may use unsigned EPOs if the parties agree, the agency does not require formal acceptance, and it is more advantageous to the government. FAR 13.506.

8. **Termination or cancellation of purchase orders**. FAR 13.504. The government may withdraw, amend, or cancel an order at any time before acceptance. *Master Research & Mfg., Inc.*, ASBCA No. 46341, 94-2 BCA ¶ 26,747. The government must notify the vendor in writing. FAR 13.108(c).

a. If the contractor has not accepted a purchase order in writing, the contracting officer may notify the contractor in writing, request the contractor's written acceptance, and:

(1) Cancel the purchase order, if the contractor accepts the cancellation; or

(2) Process the termination action as prescribed in FAR Part 49 if the contractor does not accept the cancellation or claims that it incurred costs as a result of beginning performance. *But see Rex Sys., Inc.*, ASBCA No. 45301, 93-3 BCA ¶ 26,065 (incurring of costs prior to delivery date on purchase order for supplies only created an irrevocable option until delivery date, which the government could later cancel when goods were not timely delivered).

b. Once the vendor accepts a purchase order in writing, the government cannot cancel it; the contracting officer must terminate the contract pursuant to FAR Part 49.

## B. Blanket Purchase Agreements.

FAR Part 13.2; AFARS Subpart 13.2; AFFARS Subpart 5313.2.

1. Definition. A *blanket purchase agreement* (BPA) is a simplified method of filling anticipated repetitive needs for supplies or services by establishing "charge accounts" with qualified sources of supply. FAR 13.201(a). BPAs are not contracts in themselves. *Julian Freeman*, ASBCA No. 46675, 94-3 BCA ¶ 27,280.

2. **Forms**. DOD activities use DD Form 1155 for BPAs. DFARS 213.203-1. FAR 13.203-1(j) requires that BPAs provide:

a. description of agreement;

b. extent of obligation;

c. pricing;

d. purchase limitation (*See* FAR 13.204(b));

e. names of individuals authorized to purchase against the BPA and the dollar limitation per purchase by position or name;

f. delivery ticket/sales slip requirement; and

g. invoice requirement.

3. **Simplified acquisition limitation**. Activities may not use BPAs to avoid the simplified acquisition limitation, such as by fragmenting requirements. FAR 13.204(a).

4. **Subsistence**. Orders for subsistence may exceed the simplified acquisition limit, but such actions must satisfy the competition requirements of FAR Part 6. DFARS 213.204.

5. **Limitations on use**. Use of a BPA does not authorize purchases that are forbidden by law or regulation, justify a sole source purchase, or avoid small business-simplified acquisition set-aside requirements. FAR 13.204(c).

6. **Ordering officials**. A contracting officer may authorize individuals assigned to the purchasing office or requiring activities to place calls under BPAs. AFARS 13.203-1(a). *See also* AFFARS 5313.290.

7. **Recording deliveries**. Formal fiscal recording of individual deliveries and transactions is not required. FAR 13.201(d).

## C. Imprest Funds.

FAR Part 13.4; AFARS Subpart 13.4; AFFARS Subpart 5313.4.

1. Definition. An *imprest fund* is a "cash fund of a fixed amount established by an advance of funds, without charge to an appropriation, from an agency finance or disbursing officer to a duly appointed cashier, for disbursement as needed from time to time in making payment in cash for relatively small amounts." FAR 13.401.

2. **Dollar limits**. Activities may use imprest funds for purchases under $500 or such other limits as have been approved by the agency head. FAR 13.403(a). During contingency operations as defined by 10 U.S.C. § 101 (a)(13), the limit is $2,500 for overseas purchases. DFARS 213.404(a).

3. **Documentary requirements**. An authorized purchase requisition must support each purchase using imprest funds. FAR 13.405(a).

4. **Equitable distribution of orders**. Normally, activities should place orders to suppliers orally and without soliciting competition, if

prices are reasonable. Activities should distribute purchases equitably among qualified suppliers. FAR 13.405(b) & (c).

5. **Establishing funds**. Installation commanders and commanders of activities having contracting authority may establish imprest funds. DFARS 213.403(c).

6. **Separation of duties**. Within DA, imprest fund cashiers may not act as ordering officers and may not make purchases using imprest funds. AFARS 13.403.

7. **Disbursing operations**. DOD Reg. 7000.14-R, vol. 5, sect. 0209 prescribes policy and procedures covering disbursing operations of the DA on the use of imprest funds.

## D. Government Credit Cards.

1. Purpose. The government credit card supplements and simplifies established simplified acquisition procedures, minimizes cost/administrative burdens, and reduces procurement lead time. It does not replace simplified acquisition procedures. AFARS 13.9001.

2. Implementation. The principal assistant responsible for contracting (PARC) is responsible for developing internal operating procedures at the MACOM/major subordinate command level. At the installation level, the Director of Contracting (DOC) has this responsibility. AFARS 13.9002(a).

3. Conditions for Use. In addition to the conditions imposed by the Federal Supply Schedule (FSS) contract, all of the following conditions apply:

   a. One purchase transaction may include multiple items, but may not exceed the amount established by the PARC or DOC.

   b. All over-the-counter purchases must be available immediately. Back ordering is not permitted.

   c. All items purchased during a telephone transaction must be available immediately. Back ordering is not allowed.

   d. Users must inform merchants that the purchase is for official government purposes and is not subject to state or local sales taxes.

   e. Users must receive at least eight hours training before using the card, unless they have received related training previously.

   f. Users must receive procurement ethics training and execute the procurement integrity certification required by FAR 3.104-12, unless the cardholder's authority is limited to $2,500 per purchase and the contracting officer determines that the cardholder will not order more than $20,000 of supplies or services per year. FAR 3.104-4(h)(5).

   g. Cardholders must maintain documentation of all transactions, which reflect items purchased, cost, and item availability.

4. Dollar limits.

   a. Cardholders not assigned to a contracting office shall not exceed the single purchase limitation ($2,500). AFARS 13.9002(i)(1).

   b. Warranted contracting officers shall not authorize transactions over the simplified acquisition limitation ($50,000).

5. Restrictions. AFARS 13.9002(j). Cardholders may not use the credit card to purchase:

   a. meals for reserve training;

   b. non-expendable property, unless approved by the PARC or the DOC, and appropriate property accountability procedures are in place;

   c. other items prohibited under the GSA schedule or under the PARC/DOC internal guidelines; or

   d. purchases from post exchanges greater than $2,500 in CONUS or $50,000 OCONUS.

## V. FAST PAYMENT PROCEDURES.
FAR Part 13.3.

A. The fast payment procedure allows payment before the contracting officer verifies that the government has received and accepted supplies.

B. Payment is based on the contractor's invoice. The invoice represents that: (1) the supplies have been delivered to a post office, common carrier, or point of first receipt by the government; and (2) the contractor agrees to replace, repair, or correct supplies not received at destination, damaged in transit, or not conforming to purchase agreements. FAR 13.301.

C. Generally, individual orders may not exceed $25,000. FAR 13.302(a). Within DOD, there is no dollar limit for purchases of brand name commissary resale subsistence and medical supplies for direct shipment overseas. DFARS 213.302.

## VI. SIMPLIFIED ACQUISITION REQUIREMENTS AND CHARACTERISTICS.

**A. Small Business Set-Aside Requirement.** FAR 13.105.

1. As a general rule, the contracting officer must set aside for small businesses all procurements greater than $2,500 ($2,000 for construction contracts) using simplified acquisition procedures. FASA § 4004; FAR 13.106.

   a. The contracting officer, an offeror, or any other interested party may challenge the small business representation of another offeror. FAR 19.302.

   b. A vendor has 5 days following notification of award to file a timely size status protest. 13 C.F.R. § 121.1603; *American Mobilphone Paging Inc.*, B-238027, Apr. 5, 1990, 69 Comp. Gen. 392, 90-1 CPD ¶ 366.

2. A contracting officer may not consider for award a large business quote which responds to a set-aside request for quotations (RFQ). *See* FAR 52.219-4, Notice of Small Business-Simplified Acquisition Set-Aside.

3. *Exceptions.* The set-aside requirement does not apply when:

   a. There is no reasonable expectation of obtaining quotations from two or more responsible small business concerns that will be competitive in terms of price, qual-

ity, and delivery. FAR 13.105(c)(2). *See American Imaging Servs., Inc.*, B-246124.2, Feb. 13, 1992, 92-1 CPD ¶ 188 (limited small business response to unrestricted solicitation for maintenance services did not justify issuance of unrestricted solicitation for significantly smaller acquisition of similar services);

   b. Purchases occur outside the United States, its territories and possessions, and Puerto Rico. FAR 13.105(b); or

   c. The agency must make purchases from particular sources of supply, such as the Federal Prison Industries, Industries for the Blind and Other Severely Disabled, and mandatory multiple-award Federal Supply Schedule contracts. FAR 13.105(c).

4. Cancelling a small business set-aside. FAR 13.106(a)(3).

   a. If the government does not receive a *reasonable* quote from a responsible small business concern, the contracting officer may cancel the set-aside and complete the purchase on an unrestricted basis. *Stiziel Co.*, B-251560, Apr. 13, 1993, 93-1 CPD ¶ 315.

   b. A protester must establish that its quote is reasonable if the agency has rejected the quote as unreasonable. *Omni Elevator*, B-233450.2, Mar. 7, 1989, 89-1 CPD ¶ 248.

   c. A *prima facie* showing of reasonableness shifts the burden to the government to demonstrate why the quote was unreasonable. GAO will sustain a protest only if the contracting officer's decision had no rational basis or was based on fraud or bad faith. *Interstate Commerce Comm'n — Request for Recon.*, B-237249.2, Apr. 16, 1990, 90-1 CPD ¶ 391 (6% higher than large business courtesy quote was not necessarily unreasonable). *See Omni Elevator, supra* (quote 95% higher than government estimate was unreasonable).

**B. Competition Requirements.** FAR 13.106. *Cambridge Filter Corp.*, B-216519, Feb. 4, 1985, 85-1 CPD ¶ 135 (discussion of differences between small and large purchase requirements).

1. The Competition in Contracting Act of 1984 (CICA) exempts simplified acquisition procedures from the requirement that agencies obtain full and open competition through the use of competitive procedures. 10 U.S.C. § 2304(g)(1); 41 U.S.C. § 253(a)(1)(A) (1988); *J. Sledge Janitorial Serv.*, B-241843, Feb. 27, 1991, 91-1 CPD ¶ 225. For simplified acquisitions, CICA requires only that agencies obtain competition to the "maximum extent practicable." 10 U.S.C. § 2304(g)(4); 41 U.S.C. §§ 253(a)(1)(A), 259(c); *Omni Elevator*, B-233450.2, Mar. 7, 1989, 89-1 CBD ¶ 248.

2. Purchases exceeding $2,500.

   a. Agencies must solicit quotes from a reasonable number of qualified sources to promote competition to the maximum extent practicable and to ensure that the purchase is advantageous to the government, price and other factors considered. FAR 13.106(a)(1); *CardioMetrix*, B-241344, Jan. 31, 1991, 91-1 CPD ¶ 108; *S.C. Servs., Inc.*, B-221012, Mar. 18, 1986, 86-1 CPD ¶ 266.

      (1) Generally, solicitation of three or more vendors is sufficient. FAR 13.106-1(a)(2); *Gateway Cable Co.*, B-223157, Sept. 22, 1986, 65 Comp. Gen. 854, 86-2 CPD ¶ 333.

      (2) Vendors who ask should be permitted to compete. *See Gateway Cable Co., supra; California Properties, Inc.*, B-232323, Dec. 12, 1988, 68 Comp. Gen. 146, 88-2 CPD ¶ 581 (must permit all responsible sources asking to compete to do so). *Cf. Dianne Cooper*, B-229618, Feb. 8, 1988, 88-1 CPD ¶ 123 (permissible to limit competition if done in good faith and a reasonable effort made to secure quotes from a representative number of competitors).

      (3) Normally, the buying activity should solicit the incumbent contractor. *CardioMetrix, supra* (competition obtained despite inadvertent failure to solicit incumbent); *Omni Elevator Co.*, B-246393, Mar. 6, 1992, 71 Comp. Gen. 308, 92-1 CPD ¶ 264 (failure to solicit was inadvertent).

      (4) An agency may not deliberately prevent the incumbent from competing. *J. Sledge Janitorial Serv., supra* (contracting officer's reliance on third party concerning contractor's desire to compete was unreasonable).

      (5) A buyer should request quotes from two sources not included in the previous solicitation, if practical. FAR 13.106-1(a)(4).

   b. The contracting officer should state the basis for determining that a price is reasonable if a price variance between quotes reflects a lack of adequate competition. FAR 13.106(b).

   c. An agency may limit an RFQ to a single source if only one source is reasonably available. FAR 13.106-1(a)(4). If an agency solicits alternate proposals in an anticipated sole-source acquisition, it must evaluate the responses in a timely manner. *Helitune, Inc.*, B-243617.2, Mar. 16, 1992, 92-1 CPD ¶ 285. If an activity solicits only one source, it must document the reason for the lack of competition and how the contracting officer determined that the price was fair and reasonable. FAR 13.106-2(c).

   d. Competition, if any, must be fair and equitable. *Creative Inv. Research, Inc.*, B-255287, Feb. 7, 1994, 94-1 CPD ¶ 84; *Tony's Fine Foods*, B-254959.2, Jan. 31, 1994, 94-1 CPD ¶ 51; *Vocational Resources, Inc.*, B-242396, Apr. 29, 1991, 91-1 CPD ¶ 414 (agency must evaluate quotes in accordance with terms of RFQ); *Ann Riley & Assoc.*, B-241309.2, Feb. 8, 1991, 91-1 CPD ¶ 142; *Armour of Am.*, B-237690, Mar. 19, 1990, 90-1 CPD ¶ 304 (improper to issue a purchase order to a firm whose quote fails to satisfy the RFQ).

3. Purchases of $2,500 ($2,000 for construction) or less ("micropurchases"). FASA § 4301; FAR Subpart 13.6.

a. Competition is not required if the prices offered are reasonable. FAR 13.603(a); *Northern Va. Football Officials Assoc.*, B-231413, Aug. 8, 1988, 88-2 CPD ¶ 120.

b. The contracting officer must verify whether a price is reasonable if:

(1) The buyer suspects or has information indicating that the price may be unreasonable; or

(2) The activity is purchasing an item for which no comparable pricing information is readily available, e.g., an item that is unlike other items that the activity has purchased recently on a competitive basis. FAR 13.603(b).

c. Activities must distribute noncompetitive purchases equitably among qualified sources. FASA § 4301(A); FAR 13.602(b). *See Grimm's Orthopedic Supply & Repair*, B-231578, Sept. 19, 1988, 88-2 CPD ¶ 258 (agency properly distributed orthopedic business based on a rotation list).

d. Agencies may not break down a requirement into several purchases in order to use micropurchase procedures. FAR 13.602(c).

## C. Publication Requirements.

41 U.S.C. § 416; FAR 5.101.

1. Activities must synopsize in the *Commerce Business Daily* (CBD) only those contract actions that are expected to exceed $25,000. FAR 5.101(a)(1). If the agency uses FACNET, then only actions greater than $100,000 need a synopsis. FAR 5.202(a)(13).

2. DOD activities must post in a public place at the contracting office any proposed acquisition expected to exceed $5,000 ($10,000 for non-Defense activities), but which is less than $25,000. The notice must state that all responsible sources may submit a quote that the agency will consider if timely received. The notice must remain for 10 days or until after the quotes are opened, whichever is longer. FAR 5.101(a)(2).

## D. Legal Effect of Quotations.

FAR 13.108.

1. A *quotation* is not an offer. The government may not accept a quotation to form a binding contract. FAR 13.108(a); *Haworth, Inc.*, B-241583.5, Apr. 23, 1991, 91-1 CPD ¶ 398; *Technology Advancement Group*, B-238273, May 1, 1990, 90-1 CPD ¶ 439 (generally, government may solicit and receive new quotations any time before contract formation).

2. An *order* is a government offer to buy supplies or services under specified terms and conditions. A supplier creates a contract when it accepts the government's order. FAR 13.108(a); *Technology Advancement Group*, *supra*; *C&M Mach. Prods., Inc.*, ASBCA No. 39635, 90-2 BCA ¶ 22,787 (bidder's response to purchase order proposing a new price was a counteroffer that the government could accept or reject).

3. A contractor may accept a government order by:

a. notifying the government, preferably in writing;

b. furnishing supplies or services; or

c. proceeding with work to the point of substantial performance. FAR 13.108(b).

## VII. CONCLUSION.

A. Simplified acquisitions are a large part of our business and will play a larger part in the future.

B. Simplified acquisition procedures allows us to accomplish the contracting mission quicker than other procurement methods because simplified acquisitions do not require full and open competition.

# SAMPLE DD FORM 1155

| ORDER FOR SUPPLIES OR SERVICES<br>*(Contractor must submit four copies of invoice.)* | Form approved<br>OMB No. 0704-0187<br>Expires Dec. 31, 1993 | PAGE 1 OF |
|---|---|---|

Public reporting burden for the collection of information is estimated to average 1 hour per response, including the time for reviewing instructions, searching existing data sources, gathering and maintaining the data needed, and completing and reviewing the collection of information. Send comments regarding the burden estimate or any other aspect of this collection of information, including suggestions for reducing this burden, to Department of Defense, Washington Headquarters Services, Directorate for Information Operations and Reports, 1215 Jefferson Davis Highway, Suite 1204, Arlington, VA 22202-4302, and to the Office of Management and Budget, Paperwork Reduction Project (9704-0187), Washington, DC 20503.

## PLEASE DO NOT RETURN YOUR FORM TO EITHER OF THESE ADDRESSES.
## SEND YOUR COMPLETED FORM TO THE PROCUREMENT OFFICIAL IDENTIFIED IN ITEM 6.

| 1. CONTRACT: PURCH. ORDER NO. | 2. DELIVERY ORDER NO. | 3. DATE OF ORDER *(YYMMMDD)* | 4. REQUISITION/PURCH. REQUEST NO. | 5. PRIORITY |
|---|---|---|---|---|

| 6. ISSUED BY          CODE | 7. ADMINISTERED BY *(If other than 6)*          CODE |
|---|---|

8. DELIVERY FOB
☐ DEST
☐ OTHER
*(See Schedule if other)*

| 9. CONTRACTOR          CODE          FACILITY CODE | 10. DELIVER TO FOB POINT BY (DATE) *(YYMMDD)* | 11. MARK IF BUSINESS IS<br>☐ SMALL |
|---|---|---|

Name and address

12. DISCOUNT TERMS

☐ SMALL DISADVANTAGED
☐ WOMEN-OWNED

13. MAIL INVOICES TO

| 14. SHIP TO          CODE | 15. PAYMENT WILL BE MADE BY          CODE | MARK ALL PACKAGES AND PAPERS WITH CONTRACT OR ORDER NUMBER |
|---|---|---|

| 16. TYPE OF ORDER | DELIVERY | This delivery order is issued on another Government agency or in accordance with and subject to terms and conditions of above numbered contract. |
|---|---|---|

Reference your                                   furnish the following on terms specified herein

| | PURCHASE | ACCEPTANCE. THE CONTRACTOR HEREBY ACCEPTS THE OFFER REPRESENTED BY THE NUMBERED PURCHASE ORDER AS IT MAY PREVIOUSLY HAVE BEEN OR IS NOW MODIFIED, SUBJECT TO ALL OF THE TERMS AND CONDITIONS SET FORTH, AND AGREES TO PERFORM THE SAME. |
|---|---|---|

| NAME OF CONTRACTOR | SIGNATURE | TYPED NAME AND TITLE | DATE SIGNED *(YYMMDD)* |
|---|---|---|---|

☐ If this box is marked, supplier must sign Acceptance and return the following number of copies.

17. ACCOUNTING AND APPROPRIATION DATA/LOCAL USE

| 18. ITEM NO. | 19. SCHEDULE OF SUPPLIES/SERVICE | 20. QUANTITY ORDERED/ACCEPTED | 21. UNIT | 22. UNIT PRICE | 23. AMOUNT |
|---|---|---|---|---|---|
| | | | | | |

| * If quantity accepted by the Government is same as quantity ordered, indicate by X. If different, enter actual quantity accepted below quantity ordered and encircle. | 24. UNITED STATES OF AMERICA<br><br>BY:                    CONTRACTING/ORDERING OFFICER | 25. TOTAL |
|---|---|---|
| | | 29. DIFFERENCES |

| 26. QUANTITY IN COLUMN 25 HAS BEEN<br>☐ INSPECTED  ☐ RECEIVED  ☐ ACCEPTED, AND CONFORMS TO THE CONTRACT EXCEPT AS NOTED | 27. SHIP NO.<br><br>☐ PARTIAL<br>  ☐ FINAL | 28. D.O. VOUCHER NO. | 30. INITIALS |
|---|---|---|---|
| DATE   SIGNATURE OF AUTHORIZED GOVERNMENT REPRESENTATIVE | 31. PAYMENT | 32. PAID BY | 33. AMOUNT VERIFIED CORRECT FOR |
| 36. I certify this account is correct and proper for payment. | ☐ COMPLETE<br>☐ PARTIAL<br>☐ FINAL | | 34. CHECK NUMBER |
| DATE   SIGNATURE OF AUTHORIZED GOVERNMENT REPRESENTATIVE | | | 35. BILL OF LADING NO. |

| 37. RECEIVED AT | 38. RECEIVED BY (Print) | 39. DATE RECEIVED | 40. TOTAL CONTAINERS | 41. S.R. ACCOUNT NUMBER | 42. S.R. VOUCHER NO. |
|---|---|---|---|---|---|

NSN 7540-01-152-8070
PREVIOUS EDITION UNUSABLE

30-105-02

STANDARD FORM 30 (Rev. 10-83)
Prescribed by GSA
FAR (48 CFR) 53.243

# SAMPLE OPTIONAL FORM (OF) 347

## ORDER FOR SUPPLIES OR SERVICES

| | PAGE | OF | PAGES |
|---|---|---|---|
| | 1 | | |

IMPORTANT: Mark all packages and papers with contract and/or order numbers.

| 1. DATE OF ORDER | 2. CONTRACT NO. *(If any)* | 3. ORDER NO. | 4. REQUISITION/REFERENCE NO. |
|---|---|---|---|

| 5. ISSUING OFFICE *(Address correspondence to)* | 6. SHIP TO: *(Consignee and address, ZIP Code)* |
|---|---|
| | SHIP VIA: |

**7. TO: CONTRACTOR** *(Name, address and ZIP Code)*

**8. TYPE OF ORDER**

☐ A. PURCHASE—Reference your _____

Please furnish the following on the terms and conditions specified on both sides of this order and on the attached sheets. If any, including delivery as indicated. This purchase is negotiated under authority of:

☐ B. DELIVERY—Except for billing instructions on the reverse this delivery order is subject to instructions contained on this side only of this form and is issued subject to the terms and conditions of the above-numbered contract.

| 9. ACCOUNTING AND APPROPRIATION DATA | 10. REQUISITIONING OFFICE |
|---|---|

**11. BUSINESS CLASSIFICATION** *(Check appropriate box(es))*

☐ SMALL  ☐ OTHER THAN SMALL  ☐ DISADVANTAGED  ☐ WOMEN-OWNED

| 12. F.O.B. POINT | 14. GOVERNMENT B/L NO. | 15. DELIVER TO F.O.B. POINT ON OR BEFORE *(Date)* | 16. DISCOUNT TERMS |
|---|---|---|---|
| 13. PLACE OF INSPECTION AND ACCEPTANCE | | | |

### 17. SCHEDULE *(See reverse for Rejections)*

| ITEM NO. (A) | SUPPLIES OR SERVICES (B) | QUANTITY ORDERED (C) | UNIT (D) | UNIT PRICE (E) | AMOUNT (F) | QUANTITY ACCEPTED (G) |
|---|---|---|---|---|---|---|
| | | | | | | |

| *SEE BILLING INSTRUCTIONS ON REVERSE* | 18. SHIPPING POINT | 19. GROSS SHIPPING WEIGHT | 20. INVOICE NO. | | 17(H). TOT. ◀ *(Cont. pages)* |
|---|---|---|---|---|---|
| | 21. MAIL INVOICE TO: *(Include ZIP Code)* | | | | 17(I). GRAND TOTAL ◀ |

| 22. UNITED STATES OF AMERICA BY *(Signature)* ▶ | 23. NAME *(Typed)* |
|---|---|
| | TITLE: CONTRACTING/ORDERING OFFICER |

NSN 7540-01-152-8083          50347-101          OPTIONAL FORM 347 (10-83)
Prescribed by GSA
FAR (48 CFR) 53.213(e)

# SAMPLE SF 44

## INSTRUCTIONS

*(This form is for official Government use only)*

### 1. Filling in the Form

(a) All copies of the form must be legible. To insure legibility, indelible pencil or ball-point pen should be used. SELLER'S NAME AND ADDRESS MUST BE PRINTED.

(b) Items ordered will be individually listed. General descriptions such as "hardware" are not acceptable. Show discount terms.

(c) Enter project reference or other identifying description in space captioned "PURPOSE." Also, enter proper accounting information, if known.

### 2. Distributing Copies

Copy No. 1—Give to seller for use as the invoice or as an attachment to his commercial invoice.

Copy No. 2—Give to seller for use as a record of the order.

Copy No. 3—

(1) On over-the-counter transactions where delivery has been made, complete receiving report section and forward this copy to the proper administrative office.

(2) On other than completed over-the-counter transactions, forward this copy to location specified for delivery. (Upon delivery, receiving report section is to be completed and this copy then forwarded to the proper administrative office.)

Copy No. 4—Retain in the book, unless otherwise instructed.

### 3. When Paying Cash at Time of Purchase

(a) Enter the amount of cash paid and obtain seller's signature in the space provided in the Seller section of Copy No. 1. If seller prefers to provide a commercial cash receipt, attach it to Copy No. 1 and check the "paid in cash" block at the bottom of the form.

(b) Distribution of copies when payment is by cash is the same as described above, except that Copy No. 1 is retained by Government representative when cash payment is made. Copy No. 1 is used thereafter in accordance with agency instructions pertaining to handling receipts for cash payment.

---

**U.S. GOVERNMENT**

## PURCHASE ORDER—INVOICE—VOUCHER

DATE OF ORDER | ORDER NO.

PRINT NAME AND ADDRESS OF SELLER *(Number, Street, City, and State)*\*

PAYEE

FURNISH SUPPLIES OR SERVICES TO *(Name and address)*\*

| SUPPLIES OR SERVICES | QUANTITY | UNIT PRICE | AMOUNT |
|---|---|---|---|
| | | | |

AGENCY NAME AND BILLING ADDRESS\*

PAYOR

TOTAL

DISCOUNT TERMS
.......... % ..........DAYS

DATE INVOICE RECEIVED

ORDERED BY *(Signature and title)*

PURPOSE AND ACCOUNTING DATA

---

**PURCHASER**—*To sign below for over-the-counter delivery of items*

RECEIVED BY

TITLE | DATE

---

**SELLER**—*Please read instructions on Copy 2*

PAYMENT RECEIVED $..........

PAYMENT REQUESTED $..........

*NO FURTHER INVOICE NEED BE SUBMITTED*

SELLER | DATE

BY .......... *(Signature)*

I certify that this account is correct and proper for payment in the amount of

$..........

DIFFERENCES

ACCOUNT VERIFIED:
CORRECT FOR

.......... *(Authorized certifying officer)* | BY..........

PAID BY ☐ CASH | DATE PAID | VOUCHER NO.

OR .......... *(Check No.)*

\* PLEASE INCLUDE ZIP CODE | 1. SELLER'S INVOICE *(See Instructions on Copy 2)* | STANDARD FORM 44a (Rev. 10-83) PRESCRIBED BY GSA, FAR (48 CFR) 53.213(c)

## CHAPTER EIGHT

# Funding and Fund Limitations

## I. INTRODUCTION.

### A. The Appropriations Process.

1. U.S. Constitution, art. I, § 8, grants to Congress the power to ". . . lay and collect Taxes, Duties, Imports, and Excises, to pay the Debts and provide for the common Defense and general Welfare of the United States. . . ."

2. U.S. Constitution, art. I, § 9, provides that ". . . No Money shall be drawn from the Treasury but in Consequence of an Appropriation made by Law . . ."

3. Congress has limited the ability of executive departments to obligate and expend funds by passage of the "Antideficiency Act." The Act consists of several statutes that authorize administrative and criminal sanctions for the unlawful obligation and expenditure of appropriated funds. *See* 31 U.S.C. §§ 1341, 1342, 1511-19.

4. Congress has directed agency heads to prescribe regulations that restrict obligations and expenditures to the amounts of apportionments and reapportionments, and to fix responsibility for overobligations and overexpenditures. 31 U.S.C. § 1514.

### B. Historical Perspective.

1. Reference: Hopkins and Nutt, *The Anti-Deficiency Act (Revised Statutes 3679) and Funding Federal Contracts: An Analysis*, 80 Mil. L. Rev. 51 (1978).

2. For many years after the adoption of the Constitution, executive departments exerted little fiscal control over the monies appropriated to them. During these years, departments commonly:

   a. Obligated funds in advance of appropriations.

   b. Commingled funds and used funds for purposes other than those for which they were appropriated.

   c. Obligated or expended funds early in the fiscal year and then sought deficiency appropriations to continue operations.

3. Congress passed the so-called Antideficiency Act (ADA), 31 U.S.C. §§ 1301, 1341, 1342, 1350, 1351 and 1511-1519 to curb the abuses of the executive departments in creating coercive deficiencies that required supplemental appropriations.

   a. Initially the statute only prohibited contracts if adequate appropriations were unavailable.

   b. Later, Congress amended the Act to prohibit all obligations unless adequate appropriations were available, to forbid the acceptance of voluntary services, to require apportionment by monthly payments (unless waived), and to impose criminal penalties for violations of the Act.

## II. TERMINOLOGY.

### A. Fiscal Year.

The federal government's Fiscal Year begins on 1 October and ends on 30 September.

### B. Period of Availability.

Most appropriations are available for obligation for a limited period of time, e.g., one fiscal year for operation and maintenance appropriations. If activities do not obligate the funds during the period of availability, the funds expire and are generally unavailable for obligation thereafter.

### C. Obligation.

An obligation is any act that legally binds the government to make payment. Obligations represent the amounts of orders placed, contracts awarded, services received, and similar transactions during an accounting period that will require payment during the same or a future period. AR 37-1, para. 9-1; AFR 177-16; AFR 170-8, para. 2; sec. 22.1; OMB Cir. A-34; DOD Manual 7220.9-M, ch. 24, para. B.3.a.(1).

### D. Budget Authority.

1. Congress finances federal programs and activities by granting budget authority. Budget authority is also called obligational authority.
2. Agencies do not receive cash from appropriated funds to pay for services or supplies. Instead they receive the authority to obligate a specified amount.
3. Budget authority means ". . . authority provided by law to enter into obligations which will result in immediate or future outlay involving government funds . . . ." 2 U.S.C. § 622(2).
4. Budget authority should be distinguished from contract authority, which is a sub-category of budget authority. Contract authority is statutory authority specifically permitting obligations to be incurred in advance of appropriations. *See* 2 U.S.C. § 651(a); 31 U.S.C. § 1301(d).

### E. Authorization Act.

1. An authorization act is a statute, passed annually by Congress, that authorizes programs and the maximum amounts that can be appropriated for programs.
2. An authorization does not provide budget authority.

### F. Appropriation Act.

1. An appropriation act is the most common form of budget authority.
2. An appropriation is "an authorization by an Act of Congress to incur obligations for specified purposes and to make disbursements for them from the U.S. Treasury. It may include authorizations to create obligations in advance of appropriations or other fund authority." AR 37-1, Glossary, sec. II, Terms; AFR 177-16, sec. A.

### G. Apportionment.

1. An apportionment is a distribution of budget authority within the Executive Branch by the Office of Management & Budget (OMB). It limits the amount of obligations allowed during a given period. 31 U.S.C. § 1512; AR 37-1, Glossary, sec. II, Terms; AFR 177-16, sec. A.
2. An appropriation may be apportioned by: months, calendar quarters, operating seasons, or other time periods; activities, functions, projects, or objects; or by a combination of the methods mentioned above. 31 U.S.C. § 1512.

### H. Allocation.

1. An allocation is a distribution of budget authority by the agency to an operating agency for suballocation or allotment to its subordinate activities. AR 37-1, Glossary, sec. II, Terms; AFR 177-16, sec. A.
2. An ADA violation occurs if obligations or expenditures exceed the amount of an allocation. AR 37-1, Glossary, sec. II, Terms.
3. Allocations are formal subdivisions of funds.

### I. Allotment.

1. An allotment is an administrative distribution of budget authority by an operating agency to its subordinate activities. AR 37-1, Glossary, sec. II, Terms; AFR 177-16, sec. A.
2. An ADA violation occurs if obligations or expenditures exceed the amount of an allotment. AR 37-1, Glossary, sec. II, Terms.
3. An allotment is a formal subdivision of funds.

## J. Allowance/Target.

1. An allowance/target is an administrative distribution of budget authority by an operating agency to its subordinate activities. AR 37-1, Glossary, sec. II, Terms; AFR 177-16, para. 24.

2. An allowance is an informal subdivision of funds.

## K. Rate of Obligation.

Appropriations made to the Department of Defense (DOD) or to a military department are available for obligation and expenditure only under scheduled rates of obligation, or changes thereto, that have been approved by the Secretary of Defense. 10 U.S.C. § 2204.

## III. ADMINISTRATIVE CONTROL OF APPROPRIATIONS.

### A. The Administrative Process.

1. General principles.
   a. Executive agencies must establish administrative systems to ensure that obligations and expenditures of appropriated funds do not exceed the amount appropriated, apportioned, or reapportioned. 31 U.S.C. § 1514(a)(1).
   b. The fund control system must enable the agency head to fix responsibility for an obligation that exceeds an appropriation or apportionment. 31 U.S.C. § 1541(a)(2).
   c. Agencies determine the structure of their fund control systems.
   d. Within the DOD, DOD Manual 7220.9-M (being suspended by DOD Financial Management Regulation, DOD 7000.14-R) provides the regulatory framework for the services' fund control systems. AR 37-1 and AFR 177-16, sec. C, provide additional details on the accounting systems of those agencies.

### B. Methods of Administratively Subdividing Funds.

1. **Formal Subdivisions:** After Congress appropriates funds, the Executive Branch subdivides them. Agencies may create absolute limits at each level of the subdivision. These limits are *formal subdivisions* of funds.
   a. These limits may be referred to as apportionments, allocations or allotments.
   b. Exceeding a *formal* subdivision of funds violates the ADA. 31 U.S.C. § 1517(a)(2).

2. *Informal Subdivisions*: Agencies may subdivide funds at lower levels, e.g., within an installation, *without* creating an absolute limitation on obligational authority. These subdivisions are considered funding targets. These limits are *not* formal subdivisions of funds.
   a. These targets also may be referred to as allowances.
   b. Incurring obligations in excess of a target is not necessarily an ADA violation. However, if the governing formal subdivision is thereby exceeded, an ADA violation may occur, and the person responsible for exceeding the target can be held liable for the ADA violation. AR 37-1, Glossary, sec. II, Terms; AFR 177-16, sec. D.
   c. Agencies should establish formal administrative subdivisions of funds at the highest practical level. 31 U.S.C. § 1514(b).
   d. Within DOD, formal subdivisions of funds are established at the highest practical level. Dahoney, *Resource Management*, Feb. 1988, at 19.
   e. Army policy allows formal subdivisions of funds at the Major Command (MACOM) level. AR 37-1, para. 8-10; *see Army Law.*, Apr. 1988, at 62. *Accord* AFR 177-16, para. 25.

## IV. THE ACCOUNTING SYSTEM.

### A. Accounting Classifications.

1. Accounting classifications are codes used to manage appropriations. They are used to implement the administrative fund control system and help to ensure that funds are used correctly.

2. An accounting classification is commonly referred to as a *fund cite*. AR 37-100 and DEP'T OF ARMY, PAMPHLET 37-100-XX, THE ARMY MGMT. STRUCTURE (1 July 1994) (hereinafter

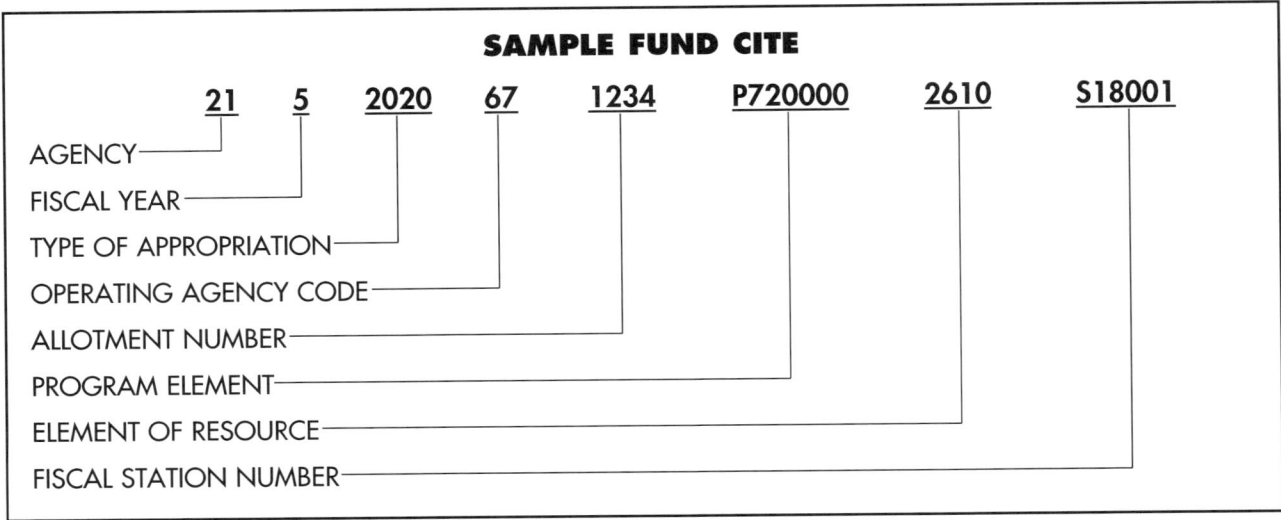

DA 37-100-XX)) provide a detailed break-down of Army accounting classifications. The XX, in DA 37-100-XX, stands for the last two digits of the fiscal year, *e.g.*, AR 37-100-95 is the source for accounting classification data for FY 1995 for the Department of the Army. DA 37-100-XX is published annually. *See* AFI 65-601, vol. 4.

**B. Understanding an Accounting Classification.**

1. Above is a sample fund cite:
2. The first seven numbers in the fund cite are the most important. In the example above the first seven numbers are: 21 5 2020.
   a. The first two digits represent the military department. The "21" in the example shown denotes the Department of the Army.
   b. Other Department codes are:
      (1) 17 - Navy
      (2) 57 - Air Force
      (3) 97 - Department of Defense
   c. The third digit shows the Fiscal Year/Availability of the appropriation. The "5" in the example shown indicates Fiscal Year (FY) 1995 funds (although it could also indicate FY 1985 funds).
      (1) Annual appropriations are frequently used in installation contracting. Several examples of annual appropriations are

set forth below:
      (a) Third digit = 3 = FY 1993 funds;
      (b) Third Digit = 4 = FY 1994 funds;
      (c) Third Digit = 5 = FY 1995 funds;
      (2) Other fiscal year designators which are encountered in installation contracting, less frequently, include:
      (a) Third Digit = X = No Year appropriation, which is available for obligation indefinitely.
      (b) Third Digit = 4/8 = Multi-Year appropriation, in this example, funds appropriated in FY 1994 and available for obligation until FY 1998.
      (c) Third Digit = M = Merged or Merged Surplus Account. *See* para. V.C.5., infra.
   d. The next four digits reveal the type of the appropriation. The following designators are used within DOD fund citations (see page 107).

**V. LIMITATIONS ON THE USE OF APPROPRIATED FUNDS.**

**A. General Limitations on Authority.**

1. The authority of executive agencies to spend appropriated funds is limited. The principal limitations are:
   a. Purpose.

|  | ARMY | NAVY/MC | AIR FORCE | OSD |
|---|---|---|---|---|
| Military Personnel | 2010 | 1453/1105 | 3500 | N/A |
| Reserve Personnel | 2070 | 1405/1108 | 3700 | N/A |
| National Guard Personnel | 2060 | N/A | N/A | N/A |
| O&M | 2020 | 1804/1106 | 3400 | 0100 |
| O&M, Reserve | 2080 | 1806/1107 | 3740 | N/A |
| O&M, National Guard | 2065 | N/A | N/A | N/A |
| O&M, Family Housing | 7025 | 7035(?) | 7045 | |
| Procurement (Aircraft) | 2031 | 1506 | 3010 | N/A |
| Procurement (Missiles) | 2032 | N/A | 3020 | N/A |
| Procurement (Weapons & Tracked Vehicles) | 2033 | 1507 | N/A | N/A |
| Procurement (Ammunition) | 2034 | N/A | N/A | N/A |
| Shipbuilding & Conversion N/A | N/A | 1611 | N/A | |
| Other Procurement | 2035 | 1810/1109 | 3080 | 0300 |
| Research, Development, Test & Evaluation (RDT&E) | 2040 | 1319 | 3060 | 0400 |
| Military Construction | 2050 | 1205 | 3300 | 0500 |
| Family Housing Const. | 7020 | 0703 | 0704 | 0706 |
| Reserve Construction | 2086 | 1235 | 3730 | N/A |
| National Guard Const. | 2085 | N/A | N/A | N/A |
| Stock Fund | 4991 | 4911 | 4921 | N/A |
| Industrial Fund | 4992 | 4912 | 4922 | 4930 |

   b. Time.
   c. Amount.
2. An agency may expend an appropriation only for the purposes for which Congress appropriated it. 31 U.S.C. § 1301(a) ("purpose" statute).
3. A government officer or employee may not make or authorize expenditures or incur obligations exceeding amounts available in an appropriation.
4. A government officer or employee may not make or authorize expenditures or incur obligations in advance of an appropriation.
5. A government officer or employee may not make or authorize expenditures or incur obligations in excess of apportionments or in excess of amounts permitted by regulations.

**B. Limitations Based Upon Purpose.**
1. Major military appropriations accounts characterized by purpose.
   a. Military Personnel: used for pay and benefits of officers and enlisted personnel.
   b. Operations and Maintenance (O&M): used for day-to-day operational costs.
   c. Procurement: used for purchase of high-dollar value, mission-essential, tactical items.
   d. Research, Development, Test, and Evaluation (RDTE): used for basic research; development of new equipment; test of

new, civilian, or foreign equipment; and evaluation of the performance of equipment in use.

e. Military Construction: used for specific construction projects in excess of $1,500,000. Projects less than $1,500,000 are funded with Unspecified Minor Military Construction funds or O&M funds.

2. The purpose rule.
a. 31 U.S.C. § 1301(a), the "purpose statute," provides that appropriations shall be applied only to the objects for which the appropriations were made, except as otherwise provided by law. AR 37-1, para. 7-9; AFR 177-16, para. 40.
b. The DOD has nearly one hundred separate appropriations available to it. These appropriations are used for specific and different purposes.
c. The "purpose statute" does not require that every item of expenditure be specified in an appropriation act. DOD has reasonable discretion to determine how to accomplish the purpose of an appropriation. *Internal Revenue Serv. Fed. Credit Union — Provision of Automatic Teller Mach.*, B-226065, 66 Comp. Gen. 356, 359 (1987). The standard for measuring the propriety of a particular expenditure, not specified in the statute, is whether:
(1) The expenditure is reasonably necessary to carry out an authorized function, or
(2) The expenditure contributes materially to the effective accomplishment of an authorized function.

3. Common Problem: Failure to use procurement appropriations.
a. Operations and Maintenance (O&M) appropriations are generally available to acquire end items which are: (1) locally purchased; and (2) cost less than $50,000.
b. Procurement appropriations are required when acquiring end items which are: (1) centrally managed; or (2) cost more than $50,000.
c. These rules are referred to as the Invest-

ment/Expense threshold. The DOD FINANCIAL MANAGEMENT REGULATION, DOD 7000.14-R, vol. 2A, ch. 1 sets forth the factors that distinguish investments from expenses.
d. Army Audit Agency internal audits have revealed a problem of local activities acquiring computer systems exceeding the investment/expense threshold using O&M funds.

4. Common Problem: Military construction using O&M appropriations. 10 U.S.C. § 2805(c) authorizes use of O&M funds for unspecified minor construction projects. This authorization is limited to $300,000 for each project.

**C. Limitations Based Upon Time.**
1. The Time Rule: An appropriation is available for obligation for a definite period of time, and it must be obligated during this period of availability. If it is not, the authority to obligate expires. 31 U.S.C. § 1552.
2. Moreover, an appropriation is available only for payment of bona fide needs of the time period during which it is available for obligation. 31 U.S.C. § 1502(a).
3. Agencies may not obligate funds until the President signs the Appropriation Act. 31 U.S.C. § 1341 (a)(1)(B). *See Cessna Aircraft Co.*, ASBCA No. 43196, 93-2 BCA ¶ 25,912 (allowing obligation after signature of appropriation act even though agency had not received apportionment from OMB).
4. Types of appropriations characterized by duration.
a. Annual Appropriation: an appropriation account available for obligations only during the fiscal year specified in the appropriation act. AR 37-1, Glossary, sec. II, Terms; AFR 177-16, para. 4(e)(1). Examples include Operations and Maintenance appropriations and Military Personnel account appropriations.
b. Multi-year Appropriation: an appropriation account that is available for incurring obligations for a definite period in excess

of one fiscal year. AR 37-1, Glossary, sec. II, Terms; AFR 177-16, para. 4(e)(2). Examples include Research and Development appropriations (2 years), Procurement appropriations (3 years), and Military Construction appropriations (5 years).

c. No-year Appropriation: an appropriation account that is available for incurring obligations for an indefinite period of time (until exhausted or accomplishment of its stated purpose). AR 37-1, Glossary, sec. II, Terms; AFR 177-16, para. 4(e)(3). Examples include Industrial Funds and Stock Funds.

5. In 1956, Congress established the "M" and merged surplus authority accounts to streamline the method by which an agency may pay obligations after the period of availability for the appropriation. 31 U.S.C. §§ 1551-1557. M accounts ceased to exist on 1 October 1993. Pub. L. No. 101-510, § 1405, 104 Stat. 1675-1679.

a. Funds currently retain their fiscal year identity for five years after the end of the period of availability. During this time, the funds are available to adjust existing obligations or to liquidate prior valid obligations, but not to incur new obligations.

b. The rules governing the use of expired appropriations are complex and detailed. Specific reference to the revised statutory rule is essential to a correct analysis of issues in this area.

6. Practical Applications: There are four important exceptions to the general prohibition against obligating funds after the period of availability.

a. Protests: "[F]unds available to an agency for obligation for a contract at the time a protest is filed in connection with . . . award of such a contract shall remain available for obligation for 90 working days after the date on which the final ruling is made on the protest." 31 U.S.C. § 1558. This statutory provision is incorporated at FAR 33.102(b). 55 Fed. Reg. 55,782 (1990), (Federal Acquisition Circular 90-3).

b. Terminations for default: If a contract or order is terminated for default, and a *bona fide* need still exists for the supplies or services, the original funds remain available for obligation for a reprocurement, even if they otherwise would have expired. The agency must award the reprocurement contract without undue delay, and the contract must be for substantially the same item or service. AR 37-1, para. 12-2(e), *citing Lawrence W. Rosine Co.*, B-185405, 55 Comp. Gen. 1351 (1976).

c. Terminations for convenience, pursuant to court order. If a court or other competent authority determines that the original award of the contract was improper, the agency may use the originally cited funds on the replacement contract. This exception is limited to contracts originally awarded in good faith, for which the agency has a continuing *bona fide* need, which will replaced promptly with a contract of the same size and scope as the original contract. *Matter of Replacement Contracts*, B-232616, 68 Comp. Gen. 158 (1988).

d. The GAO has expanded the principle articulated in *Matter of Replacement Contracts, supra*. An agency may use funds obligated on a contract that is terminated for the convenience of the government, if the government terminates the contract because the government determines the award was improper. The GAO determined that the same rule should apply if the government decides to terminate the contract as the result of an impropriety in the award process or if a court orders the termination. The requirements discussed in para. c, *supra* also apply in this situation. *Navy, Replacement Contract*, B-238548, 91-1 CPD ¶ 117.

7. Limitations Based Upon the *Bona Fide* Need Rule.

a. The statutory basis: "[t]he balance of an appropriation or fund limited for obligation to a definite period is available only for payment of expenses properly incurred during the period of availability, or to complete contracts properly made within that period of availability and obligated consistent with section 1501 of this title. However, the appropriation or fund is not available for expenditure for a period beyond the period otherwise authorized by law." 31 U.S.C. § 1502(a).

b. The government may only obligate appropriated funds for properly incurred expenses. That is, the requirement must be a *bona fide* need of the requiring activity arising during the period of availability of the funds proposed to be used for the acquisition. *See Magnavox - Use of Contract Underrun Funds*, B-207453, Sept. 16, 1983, 83-2 CPD ¶ 401; *To the Secretary of the Army*, B-115736, 33 Comp. Gen. 57 (1953).

c. The *bona fide* need rule applies only to appropriations with limited periods of availability for obligation.

d. The antideficiency act prohibits creating a contract or obligation before an appropriation is made. 31 U.S.C. § 1341(a)(1)(B). The intent of Congress is to avoid situations that require "coercive deficiency" appropriations. *See Project Stormfury - Australia -Indemnification of Damages*, B-198206, 59 Comp. Gen. 369 (1980); AR 37-1, paras. 3-1, 8-1(d)(1); AFR 177-16, sec. D.

e. Each *bona fide* need determination is fact-specific.

f. *Bona fide* need is determined at the time of obligation.

g. The needs of the government and the nature of a product or service determine when a *bona fide* need arises.

h. Factors within the government's control are most important in determining *bona fide* need. *Cf. Theodor Arndt GmbH & Co.*, B-237180, 90-1 CPD ¶ 64 (agency decision to wait until FY90 to award a service contract, with performance commencing on 15 October 1989 is correct, where services are not needed until that date). In analyzing the *bona fide* need for a given item, the following factors are appropriate for consideration:

(1) Evaluate the required delivery date in the contract.

(2) Consider normal rate of consumption.

(3) Determine when the government is making facilities, sites, or tools available.

(4) Determine whether the government controls when the contractor may begin the work. For example, if a barracks will not be available for renovation until 25 December 1994, because the brigade is deploying on the 20th of December and cannot be disrupted between 1 October and 20 December, and the normal lead-time for starting renovation of this type is 15 days, the renovation is the *bona fide* need of FY 1995. Accordingly, the obligation of FY 1994 funds violates the *bona fide* need rule.

(5) Consider normal weather conditions when planning for outdoor construction or renovation projects.

8. *Supply Contracts*: Generally, supplies are the *bona fide* need of the fiscal year in which the agency uses the supplies. *To Chairman, United States Atomic Energy Comm'n*, B-130815, 37 Comp. Gen. 155 (1957); *To Betty F. Leatherman, Dep't of Commerce*, B-156161, 44 Comp. Gen. 695 (1965); *To Adm'r, Small Business Admin.*, B-155876, 44 Comp. Gen. 399 (1965).

a. Lead-Time Exception: It is appropriate to consider the normal production lead-time in determining the *bona fide* need for an acquisition.

b. For example, if the normal lead-time between order and delivery of an item is 45 days, an obligation of FY 1994 funds is appropriate for a delivery on or before 15 November 1994. (Remember: 1 October 1994 is the beginning of FY 1995.) This is a *bona fide* need of FY 1994. If the government permits delivery after 15 November 1994, a question as to whether there is a *bona fide* need for the item in FY 1994 arises.

   c. If the government establishes a delivery date for an item and that delivery date is beyond the normal lead time and in the next fiscal year, it must use funds available for that later fiscal year. In the example above, if the government permits delivery after 15 November 1994, it must use FY 1995 funds. *See Farmers Home Administration*, B-251706, Aug. 17, 1994, 73 Comp. Gen. ____ (agency must correct bona fide need violation by adjusting accounts to charge correct fiscal year funds).

   d. Stock-Level Exception: The government may purchase sufficient supplies to maintain adequate and normal stock levels. For example, an agency may award a contract to maintain a normal stock level of reproduction paper in September 1994, using FY 1994 funds, even if it will not use the paper until early October 1994.

   e. Fiscal year-end stockpiling of supplies in excess of normal usage requirements is prohibited by the *bona fide* need rule.

9. *Service Contracts*: Generally a *bona fide* need for services does not arise until the services are rendered. *Theodor Arndt GmbH & Co.*, B-237180, 90-1 CPD ¶ 64; *EPA Level of Effort Contracts*, B-214597, 65 Comp. Gen. 154 (1985). Thus, severable service contracts generally cannot cross fiscal years. The government must fund such contracts with dollars available for obligation on the date the contractor performs the services.

   a. Exception: If the services produce a single or unified outcome, product, or report, the services are nonseverable. If so, the government must fund the entire effort with dollars available for obligation at the time the contract is executed, and the contract may cross fiscal years. *Incremental Funding of U.S. Fish and Wildlife Serv. Research Work Orders*, B-240264, Feb. 7,

1994 (unpub.); *Proper Appropriation to Charge Expenses Relating to Nonseverable Training Course*, B-238940 70 Comp. Gen. 296 (1991); *Acumenics Research and Technology, Inc. - Contract Extension*, B-224702, Aug. 5, 1987, 87-2 CPD ¶ 128; *Proper Fiscal Year Appropriation to Charge for Contract and Contract Increases*, B-219829, 65 Comp. Gen. 741 (1986).

   b. In DOD, there are four statutory exceptions to the general rule that contracts for severable services are the *bona fide* need of the fiscal year in which the services are performed and must be funded with dollars available when the services are performed. 10 U.S.C. § 2410a. The government may award contracts for the following purposes for a period not to exceed 12 months at any time during the fiscal year:

     (1) Maintenance of tools and facilities;

     (2) The lease of real or personal property, including the maintenance of the property, when contracted for as part of the lease agreement;

     (3) Depot maintenance; and

     (4) Operation and maintenance of equipment.

   c. DFARS 237.106 contains a list of services that are appropriate for cross-year funding using 10 U.S.C. § 2410a.

   d. FASA § 1073 amended title 41 of the United States Code to allow funding of multi-year severable service contracts with funds current when the contract is executed. Applicability of this section to DOD contracts (i.e., title 10) is uncertain. Consult appropriate fiscal decisionmaker within your organization.

10. *Construction*: The government may obligate current funds for construction, to include maintenance and repair contracts involving traditional construction trade skills, near the end of the fiscal year, even if performance may not begin until the next fiscal year. AR 37-1, tbl. 9-2, fn. 5; AFR 170-8, para. 7(c)(1).

This authority is limited to the following situations:

a. The requirement must represent a *bona fide* need of the current or a prior fiscal year;

b. Work must start on or before January 1 of the following calendar year, except in contracts with a foreign government, or contracts entered into pursuant to a binding international agreement. Commencement of work is evidenced by:

    (1) Physical on-site evidence based upon a visual inspection; or

    (2) Documentary evidence of costs incurred or materials ordered.

c. A project that *cannot* reasonably be expected to commence before the onset of winter weather probably is not the *bona fide* need of the prior fiscal year. For example, a contract for paving 37 miles of roads in Alaska probably should not be awarded on 30 September 1994 and funded with FY 1994 dollars.

d. If mission requirements prevent commencement of the work until 1 January, the requirement may not be the *bona fide* need of the prior fiscal year. AR 37-1, para. 9-5. AFR 170-8, para 7.c.(1).

## D. Limitations Based upon the Amount of Funds.

1. "An officer or employee of the United States government . . . may not make or authorize an expenditure or obligation exceeding an amount available in an appropriation . . . ." 31 U.S.C. § 1341(a)1)(A). There must be an available appropriation to support every obligation or expenditure. 31 U.S.C. §§ 1341, 1342, 1511-1519.

2. Executive agencies must establish administrative systems to ensure that obligations and expenditures of appropriated funds do not exceed the amount appropriated, apportioned, or reapportioned. 31 U.S.C. § 1514(a)(1).

3. The rules governing the commitment and obligation of funds are a part of the fund control system used to ensure that appropriation limits are not exceeded. *See, e.g.,* AFR 170-13, para. 7.

## VI. OBLIGATING APPROPRIATED FUNDS.

### A. References.

1. DOD Manual 7220.9-M, ch. 24, para. B(3), ch. 25, para. C; and

2. AR 37-1, ch. 9; AFR 170-8; AFR 177-16; AFR 177-101.

### B. Rules Governing Obligation of Appropriated Funds.

1. Agencies may obligate funds only for the purposes for which they were appropriated. 31 U.S.C. § 1301(a); AR 37-1, para. 9-1; AFR 177-16, para. 40.

2. Agencies may award contracts "subject to the availability of funds" (SAF), if administrative lead time requires a contract to be awarded prior to the receipt of funds to ensure timely delivery of the goods or services. If a SAF clause is used, the government may not accept services or supplies until funds are "available." AR 37-1, para. 9-5; AFR 170-13, para. 9; AFR 177-102, para. 9-18(d).

### C. Rules Governing the Adjustment of Obligations.

1. Agencies must adjust obligation records when changes in circumstance create differences between the original amount obligated and any new liability of the government. AR 37-1, para. 12-5(d); AFR 177-101, ch. 25.

2. In adjusting obligations, the amount of the obligation is usually easy to determine. It is generally more difficult to determine the correct fiscal year's funds to use in the adjustment.

3. The Comptroller General frequently uses a **"relation-back theory"** to analyze which fiscal year's funds are appropriate for use in the adjustment. The "relation-back theory" is based upon the rationale that the price adjustment is not the result of a new liability, but rather "renders fixed and certain the

amount of the government's pre-existing liability to adjust the contract price." *Administrator, Small Business Admin.*, B-155876, 44 Comp. Gen. 399, 401 (1965); *Environmental Protection Agency - Request for Clarification*, B-195732, Sept. 23, 1982, 61 Comp. Gen. 609, 82-2 CPD ¶ 491.

## VII. ENFORCING THE FISCAL LIMITATIONS.

### A. Investigating Violations—General Requirement.

If a statutory violation occurs, the agency must investigate to identify the senior responsible individual. The agency must report the violation to Congress through the ASA(FM) and DOD Comptroller. Violations could result in administrative and/or criminal sanctions on that individual. *See* AR 37-1, paras. 7-6 through 7-8; AFR 177-16, sec. E.

### B. Reporting Requirements.

1. AR 37-1, para. 7-7, requires submission of a flash report within fifteen working days of discovery of the violation. AFR 177-16, para. 49 prescribes a ten day period. The report includes:
   a. Administrative information;
   b. A brief, but comprehensive, statement of facts as known; and
   c. The anticipated date for submission of a formal report.
2. Reports to the President and Congress.
   a. The head of the agency must report to the President and Congress whenever a violation of 31 U.S.C. § 1341(a), § 1342, or § 1517 is discovered. OMB Cir. A-34, para. 32.2; DOD Dir. 7200.1, Encl. 5, para. R; AR 37-1, para. 7-7.
   b. Contents of the report.
      (1) Administrative information;
      (2) Nature of the violation;
      (3) Identification of the responsible individual;
      (4) Cause and circumstances of the violation;

(5) Administrative discipline imposed;
(6) Actions taken to correct the violation; and
(7) A statement of the responsible individual.

### C. Investigations—Procedural Requirements.

1. The commander must appoint a board of officers within thirty days of discovery of the alleged violation. Army investigations are conducted under AR 15-6 (Air Force investigations are conducted in accordance with AFI 90-301. AR 37-1, para. 7-7(a); AFR 177-16, para. 51.
2. Because criminal penalties exist for violations of the Antideficiency Act, responsible individuals must be advised of their rights.
3. The rights include those afforded under Article 31, UCMJ, and the Fifth Amendment. Additionally, if found responsible, an individual has a right to review the report of investigation and submit a statement regarding the alleged violation.

### D. Establishing Responsibility.

1. Responsibility for a violation is fixed at the moment that the improper activity occurs, e.g., overobligation, overexpenditure, etc. AR 37-1, para. 7-7(k); AFR 177-101, para. 53.
2. A responsible party is the person who has authorized or created the overdistribution, obligation, commitment, or expenditure in question. Commanders, budget officers, or finance officers should not be named automatically merely because of their positions. Any investigation should "lead to a specific determination of the *one act* that caused the violation, and the *one individual* who committed the act." DOD Accounting Manual 7220.9-M, ch. 21, para. E.5.b.
3. Generally, the responsible party will be the highest ranking official in the decision making process who had either actual or constructive knowledge of precisely what actions were taken *and* of the impropriety

or questionable nature of such actions. *Cf. To The Honorable Dennis P. McAuliffe*, B-222048, Feb. 10, 1987 (unpub.).

a. Often there will often be officials who had knowledge of either factor. The person in the best position to prevent the error, however, is the highest ranking official with knowledge of both factors.

b. If an accounting error triggers a violation, the person that made the accounting error will be responsible, assuming no other official should have detected the mistake. DOD Accounting Manual 7220.9-M, ch. 21, para. E.4.c.

## CHAPTER NINE

# *Bid Protests*

*"When the defense budget is flush, nobody fights. When the budget is tight, everybody fights for everything."*

Lawyer with prominent D.C. law firm.

*"The Board doesn't view bid protests as a game. We don't grant debating points."*

Stephen M. Daniels
Chairman, GSBCA

## I. INTRODUCTION.

### A. Objectives.

After this class, the student will understand:

1. The application of the Competition in Contracting Act's (CICA's) bid protest process on the federal procurement process.
2. The jurisdictional scope of each of the five fora available for resolving a bid protest.
3. The procedures for resolving a bid protest in each forum.
4. The remedies available from each of the five protest fora.

### B. Background.

The protest system established by the Competition in Contracting Act of 1984 (CICA) and implemented by General Accounting Office (GAO) Bid Protest Regulations is designed to provide for the expeditious resolution of protests with only minimal disruption to the procurement process. *DataVault Corp.*, B-249054.2, Aug. 27, 1992, 92-2 CPD ¶ 133. Similar procedures exist for an even more expeditious treatment of protests brought before the General Services Administration Board of

Contract Appeals (GSBCA). *See* FAR Subpart 33.201; Rules of Procedure of the GSBCA.[1]

### C. Jurisdiction.

1. Multiple fora. An unsuccessful offeror may protest to the agency, the General Accounting Office (GAO), the General Services Board of Contract Appeals (GSBCA), the United States Court of Federal Claims (COFC), or a federal district court.
2. The timing of a protest and the remedy sought frequently governs whether a particular forum can exercise jurisdiction over the action. For example, the Court of Federal Claims has equitable jurisdiction over pre-award protests only.

### D. Remedies.

1. Generally, the fora do not direct the award of a contract and may not award lost profits.
2. Whether the filing of a protest to challenge a contract solicitation or an award creates an automatic stay or suspension of any work on the procurement is of critical importance and varies from forum to forum.

## II. AGENCY PROTESTS.

### A. Authority.

1. Agency protests are protests filed directly with the contracting officer or other cognizant government official within the agency. These protests are governed by FAR 33.103, AFARS 33.103, NAPS 5233.103, AFFARS 5333.102 and 5333.103.
2. Contracting officers must consider and

decide all protests filed with the agency. FAR 33.102(a).

### B. Procedures.

1. FAR 33.103 provides the regulatory authority for agencies to establish bid protest procedures. This FAR provision provides rules for determining the timeliness of a protest and establishes requirements for the contents of a protest.

2. Protesters are *not required to exhaust* agency administrative remedies.

3. Procedures tend to be informal and flexible. For example, the U.S. Army Materiel Command has established a contractually-based agency bid protest procedure.

4. The contracting officer shall *not* make award if an agency protest is filed *before award*. FAR 33.103(a) imposes an *administrative* stay of the contract award. The agency may override the stay. FAR 33.103(a)(2).

5. An agency is *not required* to stay performance of a contract if it receives a protest *after award*. FAR 33.103(b)(2).

6. Contractors generally present protests to the contracting officer; but, they may also submit them to the Competition Advocate, an Agency Ombudsman, or any other *designated* official.

7. Remedies vary with the authority of the individual considering the protest.[2]

8. If unhappy with the agency decision, the protester must file its protest with the appropriate protest forum (e.g. GAO or GSBCA) within 10 working days[3] of receiving the adverse action. 4. C.F.R. § 21.2(a)(1) (1994).

## III. GENERAL ACCOUNTING OFFICE.

### A. Statutory Authority.

The Competition in Contracting Act of 1984, Pub. L. No. 98-369 (1984), 31 U.S.C. §§ 3551-3556, is the current statutory authority for GAO bid protests of federal agency procurements. GAO is authorized to issue implementing regulations, 31 U.S.C. § 3555, and has done so.

### B. Regulatory Authority.

1. The GAO's bid protest rules are set forth at 4 C.F.R. Part 21 (1994). These rules were substantially amended on Jan. 31, 1991. 56 Fed. Reg. 3,759 (1991). As a result of the Federal Acquisition Streamlining Act of 1994 (FASA), the GAO is drafting new provisions revising various procedural rules, to include deadlines and the use of protective orders.[4]

2. FAR provisions governing GAO bid protests are at FAR 33.104. Agency FAR supplements also contain regulatory procedures for managing GAO protests. DFARS 233.1; AFARS 33.104; AFFARS 5333.104; NAPS 5233.104; DLAAR 33.104.

### C. Who May Protest?

1. 31 U.S.C. § 3551(1) and 4 C.F.R. § 21.1(a) (1994) provide that an "interested party" may protest to the GAO.

2. An "Interested Party" is: "An actual or prospective bidder whose direct economic interests would be affected by the award of a contract or failure to award a contract." 31 U.S.C. § 3551(2); 4 C.F.R. § 21.0(a) (1994).

   a. *Before* bid opening, a protester must be a prospective bidder with a direct economic interest. A prospective bidder is one who has expressed an interest in competing. *D.J. Findley, Inc.*, B-221096, Feb. 3, 1986, 86-1 CPD ¶ 121.

   b. *After* bid opening, a protester must be an actual bidder with a direct economic interest.

      (1) An actual bidder must be "next in line" for award. If a protester cannot receive award if it prevails on the merits, then it is not an interested party. *Watkins Sec. Agency, Inc.*, B-248309, Aug. 14, 1992, 92-2 CPD ¶ 108 (highest priced of three technically equal bidders was not in line for award); *Telos Corp.*, B-246177, Jan. 13, 1992, 92-1 CPD ¶ 61 (protester not an interested party where another unsuccessful offeror had a higher technical score and a lower price).

(2) However, a high bidder may show that all lower bidders would be ineligible for award. *Professional Medical Products, Inc.*, B-231743, July 1, 1988, 88-2 CPD ¶ 2.

(3) In a "best value" procurement, the GAO determines whether a protester is an interested party by examining the probable result if the protest is successful. *Northwest EnviroService, Inc.*, B-247380.2, July 22, 1992, 92-2 CPD ¶ 38; *Rome Research Corp.*, B-245797.4, Sept. 22, 1992, 92-2 CPD ¶ 194.

(4) An actual bidder, not in line for award, is an interested party if it would regain the opportunity to compete if the GAO sustains its protest. This occurs if the GAO recommends resolicitation. *Teltara, Inc.*, B-245806, Jan. 30, 1992, 92-1 CPD ¶ 128 (11th low bidder protested the adequacy of the solicitation's provisions concerning a prior collective bargaining agreement; remedy might be resolicitation); *Remtech, Inc.*, B-240402.5, Jan. 4, 1991, 91-1 CPD ¶ 35 (protest by nonresponsive second low bidder challenged IFB as unduly restrictive; interested party because remedy is resolicitation).

c. Non-protesting interested parties, 4 C.F.R. § 21.0(b) (1994), include:

(1) Awardee.

(2) All offerors or bidders who have a substantial prospect of receiving award if protest is denied.

## D. What May Be Protested?[5]

1. Violation of a procurement statute or regulation. 31 U.S.C. § 3552. The GAO will also review allegations of unreasonable agency actions and abuse of discretion. *Building Automation Servs., Inc.*, B-247891, June 5, 1992, 92-1 CPD ¶ 494.

2. 4 C.F.R. § 21.3(m) (1994) provides that GAO will generally *not* consider protests on the following matters:

a. Contract Administration. 4 C.F.R.

§ 21.3(m)(1) (1994). *Bosma Machine and Tool Corp.*, B-257443.2, Oct. 17, 1994, 94-2 CPD ¶ 143 (decision to novate contract to another firm rather than recompete); *Caltech Serv. Corp.*, B-240726.6, Jan. 22, 1992, 92-1 CPD ¶ 94 (modification of contract unless it is a cardinal change); *Neil R. Gross & Co.*, B-237434, Feb. 23, 1990, 90-1 CPD ¶ 212, *aff'd on recon.*, B-237434.2, May 22, 1990, 90-1 CPD ¶ 491; *Casecraft, Inc.*, B-226796.2, June 30, 1987, 87-1 CPD ¶ 647 (decision to terminate a contract for default).

b. Small business size determinations. 4 C.F.R. § 21.3(m)(2) (1994). *Columbia Research Corp.*, B-247073.3, June 4, 1992, 92-1 CPD ¶ 492.

c. Small business Certificate of Competency determinations. 4 C.F.R. § 21.3(m)(3) (1994).

d. Procurements under section 8(a) of the Small Business Act (i.e., small disadvantaged business contracts). 4 C.F.R. § 21.3(m)(4) (1994).

e. Affirmative responsibility determinations. 4 C.F.R. § 21.3(m)(5) (1994); *Imaging Equip. Servs., Inc.*, B-247197, Jan. 13, 1992, 92-1 CPD ¶ 62.

(1) Exception: Where solicitation includes definitive responsibility criteria.

(2) Exception: Where protester alleges fraud or bad faith. *HLJ Management Group, Inc.*, B-225843.6, Mar. 24, 1989, 89-1 CPD ¶ 299.

f. Procurements protested to the GSBCA. 4 C.F.R. § 21.3(m)(6) (1994).

(1) If the protester files both at GAO *and* with the GSBCA, GAO will dismiss the protest. *Resource Consultants, Inc.*, B-218634.2, Nov. 21, 1985, 85-2 CPD ¶ 580.

(2) If the GSBCA dismisses the protest, the GAO will consider the protest if timely filed. *Telos Field Eng'g*, B-233285, Mar. 6, 1989, 89-1 CPD ¶ 238. GAO will dismiss untimely protests. *System*

*Automation Corp.*, B-224166, Oct. 29, 1986, 86-2 CPD ¶ 493.

(3) GAO will consider timely filed protests on an acquisition previously protested to the GSBCA, so long as the issues are different. *Mannsemann Tally Corp.* B-238790.4, Oct. 16, 1990, 90-2 CPD ¶ 293. The GAO will also consider a matter that has been withdrawn from the GSBCA before decision. *Computer Based Sys., Inc.*, B-240963, Jan. 7, 1991, 70 Comp. Gen 173, 91-1 CPD ¶ 14.

g. Procurements by non-federal agencies (e.g., U.S. Postal Service, Federal Deposit Insurance Corporation (FDIC), nonappropriated fund activities). 4 C.F.R. § 21.3(m)(8) (1994).

h. Walsh-Healey (manufacturer or regular dealer) determinations. 4 C.F.R. § 21.3(m)(9) (1994). *Mark Turulski*, B-245592, Jan. 14, 1992, 92-1 CPD ¶ 65.

i. Subcontractor protests. 4 C.F.R. § 21.3(m)(10) (1994). *But see St. Mary's Hosp. of San Francisco, Cal.*, B-243061, June 24, 1991, 91-1 CPD ¶ 597 (subcontractor protest within GAO's jurisdiction because of the degree of governmental control over selection of subcontractor).

j. Solicitations that are the subject of judicial proceedings. 4 C.F.R. § 21.3(m)(11) (1994). The GAO will not hear protests which are the subject of pending federal court litigation unless requested by the court. *Snowblast-Sicard, Inc.*, B-230983.2, Aug. 30, 1989, 89-2 CPD ¶ 190. The GAO also will not hear a protest which has been finally adjudicated, e.g., dismissed with prejudice. *Cecile Indus., Inc.*, B-211475.4, Sept. 23, 1983, 83-2 CPD ¶ 367.

3. What is a Procurement?

a. A procurement of property or services by a federal agency. 31 U.S.C. § 3551. *New York Tel. Co.*, B-236023, Nov. 7, 1989, 89-2 CPD ¶ 435 (solicitation to install pay phones is an acquisition of a service).

b. Sales of government property are excluded. *Fifeco*, B-246925, Dec. 11, 1991, 91-2 CPD ¶ 534 (sale of property by FHA not a procurement of property or services); *Columbia Communications Corp.*, B-236904, Sept. 18, 1989, 89-2 CPD ¶ 242 (GAO declined to review a sale of satellite communications services).

c. The GAO has considered a protest despite the lack of a solicitation or a contract when the agency held "extensive discussions" with a firm and then decided not to issue a solicitation. *Health Servs. Mktg. & Dev. Co.*, B-241830, Mar. 5, 1991, 91-1 CPD ¶ 247. *Accord RJP Ltd.*, B-246678, Mar. 27, 1992, 92-1 CPD ¶ 310.

d. A "Federal Agency" includes executive, legislative, or judicial branch agencies. 31 U.S.C. § 3551(3) (specifically refers to the definition in the Federal Property and Administrative Services Act of 1949 at 40 U.S.C. § 472); 4 C.F.R. § 21.0(c) (1994). However, it *excludes*:

(1) The Senate, House of Representatives, the Architect of the Capitol, and activities under his direction. 40 U.S.C. § 472(b). *Court Reporting Servs., Inc.*, B-25942, Dec. 12, 1994, 10 CGEN ¶ 108,637.

(2) Government corporations identified in 31 U.S.C. § 9101 which are only partially owned by the United States, e.g., FDIC. 31 U.S.C. § 3501; *Cablelink*, B-250066, Aug. 28, 1992, 92-2 CPD ¶ 135. This exclusion does not apply to wholly government-owned corporations, e.g., TVA. *Monarch Water Sys., Inc.*, B-218441, Aug. 8, 1985, 85-2 CPD ¶ 146; *Kennan Auction Co.*, B-248965, June 9, 1992, 92-1 CPD ¶ 503 (Resolution Trust Corporation).

(3) The Postal Service.

e. Generally, procurements by nonappropriated fund instrumentalities (NAFIs) are not "Agency Procurements." *The Brunswick Bowling & Billiards Corp.*, B-224280, Sept. 12, 1986, 86-2 CPD ¶ 295. The GAO *will* consider procurements conducted by federal agencies (i.e. processed by an agency contracting officer) on behalf of a NAFI, even if no appropriated funds are to be obligated. *Americable Int'l, Inc.*, B-251614, Apr. 20, 1993, 93-1 CPD ¶ 336; *Gino Morena Enter.*, B-224235, Feb. 5, 1987, 87-1 CPD ¶ 121; *Artisan Builders*, B-220804, Jan. 24, 1986, 86-1 CPD ¶ 85 (solicitation for construction of cart paths on AAFES-run golf course administered by installation contracting office); AR 215-4, para. 4-40.

### E. When Must a Protest Be Filed?

1. Time limits on protests are set forth in 4 C.F.R. § 21.2 (1994).
   a. Initial protest to GAO:
      (1) GAO must receive protests based on alleged improprieties or errors in a solicitation that are *apparent on the face of the solicitation*, i.e., patent ambiguities or defects, prior to bid opening or the closing date for receipt of initial proposals. 4 C.F.R. § 21.2(a)(1) (1994).
      (2) Protesters challenging a *CBD* notice of intent to make a sole source award must *first* respond to the *CBD* notice in a timely manner. *Norden Sys., Inc.*, B-245684, Jan. 7, 1992, 92-1 CPD ¶ 32 (unless the specification is so restrictive as to preclude a response, the protester must first express interest to the agency).
      (3) When an amendment to a solicitation provides the basis for the protest, then the protest must be filed by the next due date for revised proposals.
      (4) Protests based on any other matter must be submitted within ten *working* days[6] after receiving actual or constructive knowledge of the basis for protest. 4 C.F.R. § 21.2(a)(2) (1994). *See Kaysam Worldwide, Inc.*, B-247743, June 8, 1992, 92-1 CPD ¶ 500; *Ernest A. Cost—Recon.*, B-248969.2, May 4, 1992, 92-1 CPD ¶ 416. *Com-*

*pare Consolidated Indus. Skills Corp.*, B-231669.5, Sept. 19, 1988, 88-2 CPD ¶ 259 (protest alleging specification defect filed before RFP closing date but more than 10 days after denial of agency protest dismissed as untimely) *with* GSBCA rule to the contrary (GSBCA Board Rule 5(b)(3)(iii)).
   b. Initial protest to the agency:
      (1) The agency protest must be filed within the ten working day GAO time limits. 4 C.F.R. § 21.2(a)(2) (1994). *National Envtl. Servs. Co.—Recon.*, B-254377.2, May 20, 1994, 94-1 CPD ¶ 317.
      (2) A subsequent GAO protest must be filed within 10 *working* days[7] of formal notice, actual knowledge, or constructive knowledge of the initial adverse agency decision. 4 C.F.R. § 21.2(a)(3) (1994). Continuing to pursue agency protest after initial adverse decision does not toll the statute of limitations. *Telestar Int'l Corp.—Recon.*, B-247029.2, Jan. 14, 1992, 92-1 CPD ¶ 69.

2. Filing a protest at the GSBCA does *not* toll the requirement that the protest be timely under the GAO's rules. A GAO protest must be filed at the GAO within 10 days of knowledge of the initial adverse agency determination regardless of whether the protester has filed a separate protest at the GSBCA within the 10 day period. *Michigan Data Storage*, B-242219, Dec. 19, 1990, 90-2 CPD ¶ 507.

3. Protesters must use due diligence to obtain the information necessary to pursue the protest. *Products for Industry*, B-257463.2, Oct. 6, 1994, 94-2 CPD ¶ 128 (protest challenging contract award untimely where protester failed to attend bid opening and did not make any post-bid attempt to examine awardee's bid); *Adrian Supply Co.—Recon.*, B-242819.4, Oct. 9, 1991, 91-2 CPD ¶ 321 (use of Freedom of a Information Act (FOIA) request rather than the more expeditious document production rules of the GAO may

result in the dismissal of a protest for lack of due diligence and untimeliness).

4. Exceptions for otherwise untimely protests. 4 C.F.R. § 21.2(c) (1994).

a. *Significant Issue Exception*: The GAO may consider a late protest if it involves an issue significant to the procurement system. *L&L Oil Co.*, B-246560, Mar. 9, 1992, 92-1 CPD ¶ 270.

b. Significant issues generally: 1) have not been previously considered; and 2) are of widespread interest to the procurement community. *DynCorp, Inc.*, B-240980.2, Oct. 17, 1990, 90-2 BCA ¶ 310; *Hunter Envtl. Servs., Inc.*, B-232359, Sept. 15, 1988, 88-2 CPD ¶ 251.

c. The GAO may also consider a protest if there is some good cause, beyond the protester's control, for the lateness. *A.R.E. Mfg. Co.*, B-246161, Feb. 21, 1992, 92-1 CPD ¶ 210; *Surface Combustion, Inc.— Recon.*, B-230112.2, Mar. 3, 1988, 88-1 CPD ¶ 230.

## F. "The CICA Stay"—Automatic Stay.

31 U.S.C. § 3553(c) and (d).

1. *Pre-award Protests*:

a. An agency may *not* award a contract after receiving notice of a protest from the *GAO*. 31 U.S.C. § 3553(c); 4 C.F.R. § 21.4(a) (1994); FAR 33.104(b); AFARS 33.104(b); AFFARS 5333.104(b).

b. The automatic stay is triggered by notice *only* from GAO. *McDonald Welding v. Webb*, 829 F.2d 593 (6th Cir. 1987); *Bendix Field Eng'g Servs., Inc. v. United States*, No. 91-2733, (D.D.C. Nov. 25, 1991), 56 Fed. Contr. Rep. (BNA) 737 (Nov. 25, 1991); *Survival Technology Inc. v. Marsh*, 719 F. Supp. 18 (D.D.C. 1989).

2. *Post-award Protests*: If an agency receives notice of protest **after** contract award but within 10 **calendar** days of the date of contract award,[8] the agency shall, upon receipt of that notice, immediately direct the contractor to cease performance under the contract. 31 U.S.C. § 3553(d); 4 C.F.R. § 21.4(b)

(1994); FAR 33.104(c); AFARS 33.104(c); AFFARS 5333.104(c).

3. *"Proposed Award" Protests*: An agency's decision to cancel solicitation based upon its determination that the costs associated with contract performance would be cheaper if performed in-house (i.e., by federal employees) is subject to the CICA stay. *Inter-Con Security Sys., Inc. v. Widnall*, No. C 94-20442 (D.C. Cal. July 11, 1994).

4. "The CICA Override"—Relief From The CICA Stay. 31 U.S.C. § 3553(c) and (d); 4 C.F.R. § 21.4 (1994); FAR 33.104(b); AFARS 33.104(b); AFFARS 5333.104(b). *See, e.g.*, Appendix 9-C.

a. An agency may authorize the *award* of a contract:

(1) Upon a written finding that urgent and compelling circumstances which significantly affect interests of the United States will not permit waiting for the decision of the Comptroller General; and

(2) The agency is likely to award the contract within 30 days.

b. An agency may authorize *continued performance* under a previously awarded contract upon a written finding that:

(1) Urgent and compelling circumstances which significantly affect the interest of the United States will not permit waiting for the decision of the Comptroller General; or

(2) Continued performance of the contract is in the best interest of the United States.

c. In either case, if the agency is going to override the automatic stay, it must notify the GAO. *Banknote Corp. of America, Inc.*, B-245528, Jan. 13, 1992, 92-1 CPD ¶ 53 (GAO will not review the decision).

5. Override decisions are subject to judicial review. *Dairy Maid Dairy v. United States*, 837 F. Supp. 1370 (E.D. Va. 1993) (Army improperly overrode automatic stay by failing to consider using incumbent contractor to continue services; pre-award and post-

award stays require separate determinations and findings); *DTH Mgmt. Group v. Kelso*, 844 F. Supp. 251 (E.D.N.C. 1993); *Northern Mgmt. Servs., Inc. v. United States*, No. 92-2104, (D.D.C. Sep. 30, 1992) (mem.); *Universal Shipping Co. v. United States*, 652 F. Supp. 668 (D.D.C. 1987).

6. An agency's decision to override a GAO CICA stay based upon its determination that such action is in the best interests of the United States may not be subject to judicial review. *Foundation Health Fed. Servs. v. United States*, No. 93-1717, 39 CCF ¶ 76,681 (D.D.C. 1993).

7. "Blizzard Season": The "end-of-fiscal-year spending spree" (affectionately known among GAO litigators as "Blizzard Season") results in a large volume of protest action during the August-November time frame. To allay worries about the loss of funds pending protest resolution, 31 U.S.C. § 1558 provides that funds will not expire for 90 working days following resolution of the bid protest. FAR 33.102(b).

**G. Scope of GAO Review.**

1. The scope of review is similar to the Administrative Procedures Act. 5 U.S.C. § 706. GAO does not conduct a *de novo* review. Instead, it reviews the agency's actions for violations of procurement statutes or regulations, arbitrary or capricious actions, or abuse of discretion. *Hattal & Assocs.*, B-243357, July 25, 1991, 91-2 CPD ¶ 90.

2. The protester generally has the burden of demonstrating the agency action is clearly unreasonable. *The Saxon Corp.*, B-232694, Jan. 9, 1989, 89-1 CPD ¶ 17.

3. The agency may not, for the first time in a protest, provide its rationale for the decision in a request for reconsideration. *Department of the Army—Recon.*, B-240647, February 26, 1991, 91-1 CPD ¶ 211.

4. Recently, the GAO has demonstrated a greater willingness to probe factual allegations and assumptions made by the agencies. *See, e.g., Secure Servs. Technology, Inc.*, B-

238059, Apr. 25, 1990, 90-1 CPD ¶ 421 (GAO conducted a comparative analysis of competitors' proposals and the alleged deficiencies in them and sustained the protest when it determined that the agency had not evaluated the proposals using the same standards) *Frank E. Basil, Inc.*, B-238354, May 22, 1990, 90-1 CPD ¶ 492 (GAO reviewed source selection plan); *Intertec Aviation*, B-239672, Sept. 19, 1990, 90-2 CPD ¶ 232 (GAO conducted *in camera* comparative review of proposals).

5. If the protester alleges bad faith, the GAO will presume the agency acted in good faith. The protester must present "well-nigh irrefragable proof" of a specific and malicious intent to harm the protester. *Sanstrans, Inc.*, B-245701, Jan. 27, 1992, 92-1 CPD ¶ 112.

6. Timeliness exceptions. When challenging the timeliness of a protest, the burden is on the government. *Packaging Corp. of America*, B-225823, July 20, 1987, 87-2 CPD ¶ 65. If untimely on its face, the protester is required to include "all the information needed to demonstrate . . . timeliness." 4 C.F.R. § 21.2(b) (1994); *Foerster Instruments, Inc.*, B-241685.4, Nov. 18, 1991, 91-2 CPD ¶ 464.

7. When there is a doubt as to whether a protest is timely, the GAO will generally consider the protest. *CAD Language Systems, Inc.*, B-233709, Apr. 3, 1989, 89-1 CPD ¶ 405.

8. If a protester alleges that a requirement is unduly restrictive, the government must make a *prima facie* case that the restriction is necessary to meet agency needs. *Dock Express Contractors, Inc.*, B-223966, Dec. 22, 1986, 86-2 CPD ¶ 695. The burden then shifts to the protester to show that the agency justification is clearly unreasonable. *Morse Boulger, Inc.*, B-224305, Dec. 24, 1986, 86-2 CPD ¶ 715.

9. To prevail, a protester must demonstrate prejudice. *Florida Professional Review Org., Inc.—Advisory Opinion*, B-253908.2, Jan. 10, 1994, 94-1 CPD ¶ 17; *Tektronix, Inc.*, B-

244958, Dec. 5, 1991, 91-2 CPD ¶ 516 (clearly improper relaxation of a specification requirement for a competitor did not result in relief because protester failed to show that its offer would have been any different absent relaxation).

**H. Bid Protest Procedures.**

1. The Protest.
   a. Protests must be *written*, 4 C.F.R. § 21.1(b) (1994), and must include the name, address, and telephone number of the protester, the identity of the contracting activity, the solicitation or contract number, a detailed legal and factual statement of the bases of the protest, copies of relevant documents, a request for relief from the Comptroller General, and a request for a decision by the Comptroller General. 4 C.F.R. § 21.1(c) (1994).
   b. No formal pleadings or briefs are required. 4 C.F.R. § 21.1(e) (1994).
   c. Requests for documents may accompany the protest. 4 C.F.R. § 21.3(e) (1994).
   d. A protest must provide a detailed statement of the legal and factual grounds upon which the protest is based. 4 C.F.R. § 21.1(c)(4) (1994). The GAO may dismiss a protest which is frivolous, or which does not state a valid ground for a protest. 31 U.S.C. § 3554(a)(3); *Federal Computer Int'l Corp.—Recon.*, B-257618.2, July 14, 1994, 94-2 CPD ¶ 24 (mere allegation of improper agency evaluation made "on information and belief" not adequate).
      (1) As a minimum, a protester must make a *prima facie* case asserting improper agency action. *Brackett Aircraft Radio*, B-244831.2, Dec. 27, 1991, 91-2 CPD ¶ 585.
      (2) Generalized allegations of impropriety are not sufficient to sustain the protester's burden under the GAO's Bid Protest Rules. *See* 4 C.F.R. ¶ 21.1 (f) (1994); *Bridgeview Mfg.*, B-246351, Oct. 25, 1991, 91-2 CPD ¶ 378; *Pal-*

*metto Container Corp.*, B-237534, Nov. 5, 1989, 89-2 CPD ¶ 447.
      (3) The protester must show material harm. *Tek Contracting, Inc.*, B-245590, Jan. 17, 1992, 92-1 CPD ¶ 90 (protest that certification requirement was unduly restrictive is denied where protester's product was not certified by any entity); *IDG Architects*, B-235487, Sept. 18, 1989, 89-2 CPD ¶ 236.
   e. The protest must include sufficient information to demonstrate that it is timely. The GAO will not permit protesters to introduce for the first time, in a motion for reconsideration, evidence to demonstrate timeliness. 4 C.F.R. § 21.2(b) (1994). *Management Eng'g Assoc.—Recon.*, B-245284.2, Oct. 1, 1991, 91-2 CPD ¶ 276.

2. The protester must give notice to the contracting activity.
   a. The agency must *receive* the notice within one working day. 4 C.F.R. § 21.1(d) (1994); *Rocky Mountain Ventures*, B-241870.4, Feb. 13, 1991, 91-1 CPD ¶ 169 (failure to give timely notice may result in dismissal of the protest). *But see Management and Technical Support Servs., Inc.—Recon.*, B-232577.2, Mar. 9, 1989, 89-1 CPD ¶ 257 (failure to notify contracting officer in Zaire within one day excused).
   b. If the agency has actual notice of the protest and the basis therefore within one day, the GAO will not dismiss the protest absent prejudice. *Arlington Pub. Schools*, B-228518, Jan. 11, 1988, 88-1 CPD ¶ 16.

3. The GAO provides immediate telephonic notice of protest to the agency. 4 C.F.R. § 21.3(a) (1994).

4. The agency must file an administrative report within 25 *working* days[9] (or any extension granted thereto). 4 C.F.R. § 21.3(c) (1994).
   a. Mandatory contents of an agency report. 4 C.F.R. § 21.3(c) (1994).
      (1) The protest.
      (2) The protester's proposal or bid.
      (3) The successful proposal or bid.

(4) The solicitation.

(5) The abstract of bids or offers.

(6) A statement by the contracting officer.

(7) All evaluation documents.

(8) All *relevant* documents.

b. Also included are:

  (1) Documents requested by the protester. 4 C.F.R. § 21.3(e) (1994).

  (2) A legal memorandum suitable for forwarding to GAO.

5. The agency must forward a copy of the agency report and requested documents to the protester and other interested parties. 4 C.F.R. § 21.3(d) (1994).

a. Late agency reports. *General Elec. Co.*, B-228191, Dec. 14, 1987, 87-2 CPD ¶ 585. GAO will consider a late agency report when the protester is not prejudiced by the delay.

b. New document production rules severely restrict the government's ability to withhold documents in GAO protests.

  (1) Agencies must include all relevant documents in the administrative report. *See Federal Bureau of Investigation— Recon.*, B-245551.2, June 11, 1992, 92-1 CPD ¶ 507 (incomplete report misled GAO about procurement's status).

  (2) Upon request of the agency, the protester, or any interested party, the GAO may issue a protective order. 4 C.F.R. § 21.3(d)(1) (1994).[10]

   (a) The protective order is designed to limit access to trade secrets, confidential business information, and information that would result in an unfair competitive advantage.

   (b) The request for a protective order should be filed as soon as possible, but it must be filed within 20 days of the filing of the protest. 4 C.F.R. § 21.3(d)(1) (1994).

   (c) The GAO shall determine the terms of the protective order prior to the due date for the agency administrative report. 4 C.F.R. § 21.3(d)(2) (1994).

(d) Individuals seeking access to protected information may not be involved in the competitive decision making process of the protester or interested party.

(e) Protesters may retain outside counsel or use in-house counsel, so long as counsel is not in the competitive decision-making process. *Dataproducts New England, Inc.*, B-246149.3, Feb. 26, 1992, 92-1 CPD ¶ 231 (in-house counsel); *Mine Safety Appliance Co.*, B-242379.2, Nov. 27, 1991, 91-2 CPD ¶ 506 (retained counsel).

(f) The GAO grants access to protected information upon application by an individual. The individual must submit a certification of the lack of involvement in the competitive decision making process and a detailed statement in support of the certification. 4 C.F.R. § 21.3(d)((3) (1994). *Atlantic Research Corp.*, B-247650, June 26, 1992, 92-1 CPD ¶ 543.

(g) The GAO may report violations of the protective order to the appropriate bar association of the attorney who violated the order, or may ban the attorney from GAO practice. Additionally, a party whose protected information is improperly disclosed retains all of its remedies at law or equity, including breach of contract. 4 C.F.R. § 21.3(d)(5) (1994).

(h) If the GAO does not issue a protective order, the government has somewhat more latitude in what it must include in the administrative report. If the government chooses to withhold any documents from the report, it must include in the report a list of the documents withheld and the reasons therefor. The agency must furnish all relevant documents and all documents specifically requested by the appellant.

c. If the agency fails to produce all relevant or requested documents, the GAO may impose sanctions. Among the possible sanctions are:

(1) Providing the document to the protester or to other interested parties.

(2) Subpoenaing the documents.

(3) Drawing adverse inferences against the agency. The GAO refused to draw an adverse inference when an agency searched for and was unable to find a document that protester speculated should be in the files. *Textron Marine Sys.*, B-243693, Aug. 19, 1991, 91-2 CPD ¶ 162.

(4) Prohibiting the government from using facts or arguments related to the unreleased documents. 4 C.F.R. § 21.3(i) (1994).

d. Under the "old" rules (i.e., pre-1991) the GAO generally allowed or directed the release of the agency's evaluation of a protester's proposal to the protester. *See G. Marine Diesel; Phillyship*, B-232619, Jan. 27, 1989, 89-1 CPD ¶ 90. With the issuance of its new regulations in April 1991, the GAO allows for the issuance of a protective order. 4 C.F.R § 21.3(d). This arrangement arguably restricts the release of proprietary and source selection sensitive information to parties not admitted under the protective order. *See U.S. Steel Corp. v. United States*, 730 F.2d 1465 (Fed. Cir. 1984); *Telenet Communications Corp.*, GSBCA No. 9925-P, 89-2 BCA ¶ 21,653.

e. Protester may request additional documents within 2 *WORKING* days after receipt of the agency report. 4 C.F.R. § 21.3(f) (1994). *See also C3*, B-233742.9, Mar. 1, 1991, 91-1 CPD ¶ 230 (government may request relevant documents from protester).

6. Protester must comment on the agency report within 10 ***working*** days of receipt.[11] 4 C.F.R. § 21.3(j) (1994). Failure to comment or request decision on the record will result in dismissal. *Piedmont Sys., Inc.*, B-249801, Oct. 28, 1992, 92-2 CPD ¶ 305 (agency's office sign-in log used to establish date when protester's attorney received agency report); *Aeroflex Int'l, Inc.*, B-243603.3, Oct. 7, 1991, 91-1 CPD ¶ 311 (protester held to deadline even though the agency was late in submitting its report); *Kinross Mfg. Co.*, B-232182, Sept. 30, 1988, 88-2 CPD ¶ 309.

7. With the publication of its new regulations in 1991, the GAO abandoned its general practice of holding informal conferences and fact finding conferences in favor of hearing procedures. 4 C.F.R. § 21.5 (1994).

a. The protester, the government, or any interested party may request a hearing. The request shall set forth the reasons why the requester believes a hearing is necessary and why the matter cannot be resolved without oral testimony. 4 C.F.R. § 21.5(a) (1994).

b. The GAO hearing officer has the discretion to determine whether or not to hold a hearing and the scope of the hearing. 4 C.F.R. § 21.5(a) (1994).

(1) As a general rule, the GAO conducts hearings where there is a factual dispute between the parties which cannot be resolved without oral examination or without assessing witness credibility, or where an issue is so complex that developing the protest record through a hearing is more efficient and less burdensome than proceeding with written pleadings only. *Town Dev., Inc.*, B-257585, Oct. 21, 1994, 94-2 CPD ¶ 155.

(2) Absent evidence that a protest record is questionable or incomplete, the GAO will not hold a hearing "merely to permit the protester to orally reiterate its protest allegations or otherwise embark on a fishing expedition for additional grounds of protest" since

such action would undermine GAO's ability to resolve protests expeditiously and without undue disruption of the procurement process. *Town Dev., Inc.*, *supra*.

c. The GAO may hold pre-hearing conferences to resolve procedural matters, including the propriety of issuing a protective order and its scope. 4 C.F.R. § 21.5(b) (1994).

d. Parties are required to be represented by knowledgeable individuals. The GAO retains the discretion to designate individuals to appear on behalf of the parties. 4 C.F.R. § 21.5(d) (1994).

e. If an individual designated by the GAO fails to appear at a hearing, the GAO may draw adverse inferences from that fact. 4 C.F.R. § 21.5(g) (1994).

8. The GAO will issue a decision within 90 ***working*** days.[12] 31 U.S.C. § 3554(a)(1).

9. Express Option. 31 U.S.C. § 3554(a)(2); 4 C.F.R. § 21.8 (1994).

a. Decision in 45 ***calendar*** days.[13]

b. Protester, agency, or other interested party may request the express option in writing within 3 days after protest is filed. The GAO has discretion to decide whether to grant the request. Generally, the GAO reserves use of this expedited procedure for protests involving relatively straightforward facts and issues.

c. The opinion in an express option protest may be in summary form. This requires consent of the parties, and the ultimate decision rests with the GAO. Summary decisions are not precedential. 4 C.F.R. § 21.8(d)(4) (1994).

## I. Remedies.

1. GAO decisions are recommendations. 31 U.S.C. § 3554;[14] *Rice Servs., Ltd. v. United States*, 25 Cl. Ct. 366 (1992); *Wheelabrator Corp. v. Chafee*, 455 F.2d 1306 (D.C. Cir. 1971).

2. Modification of remedy/recommendation. Upon a showing of impracticability by the

agency, the GAO may revise its recommendation. 4 C.F.R. § 21.6(b) (1994); *Department of Health and Human Servs.—Modification of Remedy*, B-254909.2, July 22, 1994, 94-2 CPD ¶ 40 (GAO recommendation that contract be terminated and recompeted not practicable); *Science Applications Int'l Corp.; Dep't of the Navy—Recon.*, B-247036.2, 92-2 CPD ¶ 73.

3. Agencies that choose not to fully implement the GAO's recommendations within 60 days of a decision must report this fact to the GAO. 31 U.S.C. § 3554(e)(1). The GAO, in turn, must report all instances of agency refusal to accept its recommendation to Congress. 31 U.S.C. § 3554(e)(2).

4. By statute, the GAO is authorized to recommend that an agency grant the following remedies:

a. Termination of an existing contract;

b. Refraining from exercising options under an existing contract;

c. Issuance of a new solicitation;

d. Award of the contract consistent with statute and regulation; or

e. All or portions of the remedies listed above, as appropriate. 31 U.S.C. § 3554(b)(1).

5. Additionally, by decision, the GAO has crafted a wide variety of comparable remedies, e.g., reevaluation of the offer to correct an error. *First Fed. Corp.*, B-245891, Feb. 10, 1992, 92-1 CPD ¶ 166.

## J. Protest Costs, Attorneys Fees, and Bid Preparation Costs.

1. Old Rule: A protester must prevail on the merits in order to receive protest costs, attorney's fees, or bid preparation costs. When agency action renders a protest academic, the GAO will dismiss the protest without awarding costs. *H & H Envtl. Servs.—Claim for Costs*, B-235512.2, May 31, 1989, 89-1 CPD ¶ 524; *Pitney-Bowes, Inc.*, B-218241, June 18, 1985, 85-1 CPD ¶ 696.

2. New Rule: The GAO will issue a declaration on the entitlement to costs of pursuing the

protest, to include attorneys' fees, in each case after agencies take corrective action. 4 C.F.R. § 21.6(e) (1994).

   a. In practice, the GAO appears to be following its old rule, i.e., if the agency takes remedial action quickly, it will not award fees. *Oklahoma Indian Corp.*, B-234785.2, June 10, 1991, 91-1 CPD ¶ 558 (no fees where agency reversed prior position and referred matter to SBA for issuance of COC within two weeks of the filing of the protest).

   b. If the agency unreasonably delays taking corrective action, however, the GAO will award fees. *Griner's-A-One Pipeline Servs.*, B-255078.3, July 22, 1994, 94-2 CPD ¶ 41, (corrective action taken two weeks following filing of agency administrative report found untimely). The GAO will consider the complexity of the procurement under protest in determining what is timely agency action. *Lynch Machiner Co., Inc.*, B-256279.2, July 11, 1994, 94-2 CPD ¶ 15 (protester's request for costs denied where agency corrective action taken 3 months following filing of protest complaint).

   c. Agency corrective action must result in some competitive benefit to the protester. *Tri-Ex Tower Corp.*, B-245877, Jan. 22, 1992, 92-1 CPD ¶ 100 (protester not entitled to fees and costs where the agency cancels a competitive solicitation and proposes to replace it with a sole source acquisition; no corrective action taken in response to the protest).

   d. Protester must file its request for declaration of entitlement to costs with the GAO within ten days after learning that the agency is taking corrective action. 4 C.F.R. § 21.6(e) (1994). *Moon Eng'g*, B-247053.6, Aug. 27, 1992, 92-2 CPD ¶ 129.

3. If the GAO determines that the protester is entitled to recover its costs:

   a. The protester must submit a claim for costs within 60 days of the receipt of the GAO decision. Failure to file within 60 days shall result in forfeiture of the right to costs, unless the protester can show good cause for the delay in the filing. 4 C.F.R. § 21.6(f) (1994). *Continental Maritime of San Diego, Ind.—Claim for Cost*, B-249353.5, 93-2 CPD ¶ 323.

   b. Recovery of costs is limited to those costs incurred in pursuing the claim before the GAO. Costs for pursuing the protest before the agency are *not* recoverable. 4 C.F.R. § 21.6(f)(2) (1994); *Diverco, Inc.—Claim for Costs*, B-240639.5, May 21, 1992, 92-1 CPD ¶ 460.

4. Interest on costs is not recoverable. *Techniarts Eng'g—Claim for Costs*, B-234434.2, Aug. 24, 1990, 90-2 CPD ¶ 152.

5. Amount of attorney's fees and protest costs is determined by reasonableness. Equal Access to Justice Act standards do *not* apply.[15] *Bay Tankers, Inc.—Claim for Bid Protest Costs*, B-238162.4, May 31, 1991, 91-1 CPD ¶ 524 (senior partner hourly rate of $300 held to be reasonable); *Pevar Co.—Claim for Costs*, B-242353.3, Sept. 1, 1992, 92-2 CPD ¶ 144 (protester entitled to reimbursement at actual rates of compensation, plus reasonable overhead and fringe benefits, for employees' time).

6. The GAO has refused to establish a maximum limit on the recovery of attorneys fees, ruling that the dollar value of the contract is not directly related to the complexity of the legal issues in the protest. *Armour of Am., Inc.—Claim for Costs*, B-237690.2, Mar. 4, 1992, 92-1 CPD ¶ 257 (agency objects to protester seeking $33,494.20 in fees on a $17,849.28 purchase order; GAO allows $19,798.03).

7. A protester may only recover fees related to those claims on which it prevailed. *Id.* Where the issues are intertwined, however, a protester may recover all of its fees, despite losing some issues. *Omni Analysis—Recon.*, B-233372.2, July 24, 1989, 89-2 CPD ¶ 73.

8. A protester may recover costs on a sustained protest despite the fact that the protester did not raise the issue that the GAO found to be

dispositive. The GAO may award costs even though the protest is sustained on a theory raised by the GAO *sua sponte*. The GAO limits this theory of recovery, however, to those issues that are not so separate and distinct as to constitute a separate protest. *Dep't of Commerce—Recon.*, B-238452.3, Oct. 22, 1990, 90-2 CPD ¶ 322.

9. The protester must document its claim for attorneys fees. *Consolidated Bell, Inc.*, B-220425.4, Mar. 25, 1991, 91-1 CPD ¶ 325 (claim for $376,110 reduced to $490 because no reliable supporting documentation).

10. Bid Preparation Costs. 4 C.F.R. § 21.6(d)(2) (1994).

   a. Anticipatory profits are not recoverable. *DaNeal Constr., Inc.*, B-208469.3, Dec. 14, 1983, 83-2 CPD ¶ 682.

   b. Generally, the GAO will award bid preparation costs only when no other practical relief is available. *Kaysam Worldwide, Inc.*, B-247743, June 8, 1992, 92-1 CPD ¶ 500; *Industrial Storage Equip.- Pacific— Recon.*, B-228123.2, Apr. 1, 1988, 88-1 CPD ¶ 328.

## K. Appeals.

1. Reconsideration of GAO Decisions. The requester must state the factual and legal grounds upon which it seeks reconsideration. Rehashing previous arguments is not fruitful. 4 C.F.R. § 21.12 (1994); *Windward Moving & Storage Co.—Recon.*, B-247558.3, Mar. 31, 1992, 92-1 CPD ¶ 326.

2. Requests for reconsideration must be based upon new facts, unavailable at the time of the initial protest. The GAO does not allow piecemeal development of protest issues. *U.A. Anderson Constr. Co.—Recon.*, B-244711.2, Jan. 23, 1992, 92-1 CPD ¶ 106.

3. A protester may always seek judicial review of an agency action under the Administrative Procedures Act. Courts, however, give great deference to the GAO in light of its considerable procurement expertise. *Shoals American Indus., Inc. v. United States*, 877 F.2d 883 (11th Cir. 1989).

4. This deference is not absolute. A court may still find an agency decision to lack a rational basis, even if the agency complies with the GAO's recommendations in a bid protest. *Commercial Energies, Inc. v. United States*, 20 Cl. Ct. 140 (1990).

## IV. GENERAL SERVICES BOARD OF CONTRACT APPEALS.

### A. Statutory Authority.

1. The Brooks Act provides exclusive authority to the Administrator of the General Services Administration for the acquisition and management of Automatic Data Processing Equipment (ADPE) and Federal Information Processing (FIP) resources[16] for the government. Pub. L. No. 89-306, 79 Stat. 1127 (1965), codified at 40 U.S.C. § 759.

2. The GSBCA received bid protest jurisdiction in the Competition in Contracting Act (CICA) of 1984, Pub. L. No. 98-369, 98 Stat. 1182 (1984), codified at 40 U.S.C. § 759(f).

3. This authority is limited to acquisitions of ADPE. 40 U.S.C. § 759(a)(2)(A) and (B). ADPE is a complex term defined by statute, regulation, and decisional law. The precise scope is not covered in this outline.

4. The GSBCA has the authority to determine which acquisitions fall within its jurisdiction. 40 U.S.C. § 759(f)(1).

### B. Who May Protest?

1. "Interested Parties" may protest to the GSBCA. 40 U.S.C. § 759(f)(1).

   a. The GSBCA and the GAO have identical definitions of interested parties. 40 U.S.C. § 759(f)(9)(B).

      (1) An interested party is an actual or prospective bidder or offeror whose direct economic interest would be affected by the award of the contract or by failure to award the contract. *See ViON Corp.*, GSBCA No. 12736-P, 94-2 BCA ¶ 26,710, *recon. denied*, 94-2 BCA ¶ 26,757 (contractor's protest and

intervention dismissed where it was not an interested party).

(2) Originally, the GSBCA was much less strict than the GAO in finding a protester to have a direct economic interest. *See International Bus. Mach. Corp.*, GSBCA No. 9703-P, 89-1 BCA ¶ 21,367, *recon. denied* 89-1 BCA ¶ 21,372 (interested party status granted despite its negligible chance for award). It has also stated, in dicta, that the definition of "interested party" in Title 40 was broader than that in Title 31. *MCI Telecommunications Corp.*, GSBCA No. 9926-P, 89-2 BCA ¶ 21,650 (a sub- contractor was not an interested party).

(3) The Court of Appeals for the Federal Circuit held that the GAO and GSBCA definitions of "interested party" are identical. *United States v. International Bus. Mach. Corp.*, 892 F.2d 1006 (Fed. Cir. 1989) (third low, nonresponsive bidder not an interested party); *MCI Telecommunications Corp. v. United States*, 878 F.2d 362 (Fed. Cir. 1989), citing with approval, *Waste Mgmt. of No. Am., Inc. v. Weinberger*, 862 F.2d 1393 (9th Cir. 1988) (protester must have actually submitted a bid if protest is filed after date for receipt of bids).

(4) The GSBCA now finds GAO decisions persuasive authority, though not binding. *Laser Digital, Inc.*, GSBCA No. 10810-P, 91-1 BCA ¶ 23,499 (GAO analysis followed regarding treatment of brand name or equal specifications).

b. Subcontractors.

(1) In its early decisions, the GSBCA found subcontractors to be interested parties. It examined each subcontractor individually to see if it was an interested party. *MCI Telecommunications Corp.*, GSBCA No. 9926-P, 89-2 BCA ¶ 21,650.

(2) However, the Court of Appeals for the Federal Circuit has held the GSBCA may not review protests by prospective subcontractors against acquisitions by government prime contractors. *U.S. West Communications Servs., Inc. v. United States*, 940 F.2d 622 (Fed. Cir. 1991).

2. GAO and GSBCA are mutually exclusive fora. 40 U.S.C. § 759(f)(1); 31 U.S.C. § 3552.

a. Forum Shopping. An interested party who has filed at the GAO may not protest before the GSBCA. *Total Procurement Servs., Inc. v. Defense Info. Sys. Agency*, GSBCA No. 12785-P, 94-2 BCA ¶ 26,818 (offeror may not protest a procurement at GSBCA after earlier filing a protest on same procurement at GAO and pursuing to effective conclusion, even if alleging different grounds). Not every communication to GAO is a protest. *Electronic Sys. & Assoc., Inc.*, GSBCA No. 11883-P, 93-1 BCA ¶ 25,278, (the protester's letter to GAO asking for an investigation of the procurement was not a protest).

b. An interested party may file at GAO, then withdraw and pursue the protest before the GSBCA, if its later protest is timely. *See Syscon Corp.*, GSBCA No. 10890-P, 91-1 BCA ¶ 23,523, (protester filed at GAO, by facsimile machine, on Friday, after business hours, getting an automatic stay; on next business day, the protester withdrew and timely filed at GSBCA).

c. GSBCA will hear other protesters raising the same issue. *Design Data Sys.*, GSBCA No. 8934-P, 87-2 BCA ¶ 19,891. GSBCA will hear a protest from another interested party involving implementation of a GAO recommendation on an earlier protest. *Tymnet, McDonnell Douglas Network Sys. Co.*, GSBCA No. 9096-P, 87-3 BCA ¶ 20,202. The GAO will not hear protests involving implementation of a GSBCA decision. *Severn Co.—Request for Recon.*, B-231668.2, Sept. 28, 1988, 88-2 CPD ¶ 293.

3. Intervenors.
   a. "Intervenors of Right" are non-protesting interested parties who timely file a notice of intervention in accordance with Board Rule 5(a)(3)(i), 48 C.F.R. § 6101.5(a)(3)(i) (1994). *Syscon, Corp.*, GSBCA No. 10890-P, 91-1 BCA ¶ 23,496, (intervenor may intervene after 4 day period if protester amends protest or the contracting officer did not provide notice).
   b. "Permissive Intervenors" are interested parties who have filed a protest with the GAO on the same procurement. A permissive intervenor must timely file a motion for intervention under Board Rule 5(a)(3)(iii). 48 C.F.R. § 6101.5(a)(3)(iii) (1994). *Pindar Donnelley Partnership v. Dep't of Commerce*, GSBCA No. 12667-P, 94-2 BCA ¶ 26,672.
   c. "Intervening Agencies" include the GSA when the agency conducts a procurement. FIRMR 201-39.3304-2. An intervening agency must timely file a motion for intervention under 48 C.F.R. § 6101.5(a)(3)(ii) (1994). *Analysis Corp.*, GSBCA No. 10990-P, 91-1 BCA ¶ 23,616, (SBA may intervene to protect interests in interpretation of own regulations).

## C. What May Be Protested?

1. A protester may challenge ADPE acquisitions subject to the Brooks Act. 40 U.S.C. § 759.
2. A protester must allege a violation of statute, regulation, or the Delegation of Procurement Authority (DPA) received from GSA. *Vanguard Technologies Corp.*, GSBCA No. 10217-P-R, 89-3 BCA ¶ 22,116. *See also Sterling Fed. Sys., Inc.*, GSBCA No. 10601-C (10381-P) 1994 WL 323379 (violation of applicable statute and regulation found despite fact that agency had no preaward knowledge of misrepresentations in awardee's proposal).
   a. In *C3, Inc.*, GSBCA No. 10066-P, 89-3 BCA ¶ 22,053, the board held that a Delegation of Procurement Authority (DPA) required the agency to comply with all laws, regulations, and *policies* regarding ADPE acquisitions. Failure to follow a nine-year old DOD policy letter about the AUTODIN system was a fatal flaw in the procurement.
   b. In *Systemhouse Fed. Sys., Inc.*, GSBCA No. 10227-P, 90-1 BCA ¶ 22,435, the board, in *dicta*, stated that a handbook on teleprocessing services was a regulation, even though the handbook specifically stated that it was not a regulation.
3. Even if the agency violates applicable statute or regulation, a protester must also demonstrate it was prejudiced by these actions. *Fortran Corp. v. Dep't of Transportation*, GSBCA No. 12952-P, 1994 BPD ¶ 245 (agency's improper failure to request a second round of BAFOs not prejudicial).
4. "Reverse Protests." A protester may challenge a termination for convenience, if the basis for the termination is the illegality of the underlying award. *Level 6 Sys., Inc.*, GSBCA No. 11410-P, 92-1 BCA ¶ 24,557.
5. A protester may not successfully challenge specifications as not sufficiently restrictive. *Teradata Corp. v. Dep't of the Air Force*, GSBCA No. 11642-P, 92-2 BCA ¶ 24,895. A protester may not successfully challenge an agency's cancellation of a solicitation at the direction of Congress. *Electronic Data Sys. Corp.*, GSBCA No. 11593-P, 92-1 BCA ¶ 24,616.

## D. When Must a Protester File?

1. Time limits are set forth in Board Rule 5(b)(3). 48 C.F.R. § 6101.5(b)(3) (1994).
2. Improprieties in solicitation apparent before bid opening must be protested *before* the bid opening date or date for receipt of initial proposals. Unlike at GAO, this rule applies even if there was an earlier agency protest filed more than 10 days preceding proposal due date. *ViON Corp.*, GSBCA No. 10218-P, 89-3 BCA ¶ 22,190, *recon. denied*, 90-1 BCA ¶ 22,288. GSBCA Board Rule 5(b)(3)(iii).
3. Other alleged errors must be protested within 10 *WORKING* days of actual or construc-

tive knowledge of the basis of protest. This is the same rule as at GAO.[17]

4. If there is an initial protest to the agency, then a protester must file its protest with the board within 10 *WORKING* days of receipt of actual or constructive knowledge of the initial adverse agency action. This is the same rule as at the GAO.

5. Generally, the GSBCA strictly enforces the time limits. *Computer Dynamics, Inc.*, GSBCA No. 10288-P (10209-P), 90-1 BCA ¶ 22,328 (protest untimely because it was filed after hours on the last day by facsimile machine; fact that it was logged in on the last day by a GSBCA clerk working late was immaterial); *Integrated Systems Group, Inc.*, GSBCA No. 11075-P, 91-2 BCA ¶ 23,790 (fax transmission not complete until after closing, therefore was late protest).

**E. Suspension of the Delegation of Procurement Authority.**

1. If a protest is filed before award or within 10 *calendar* days after award,[18] then an interested party may request suspension of the agency's Delegation of Procurement Authority (DPA) and, thus, the acquisition. 40 U.S.C. § 759(f)(2). The GSBCA grants suspensions unless the agency demonstrates cause for relief.

2. The standards for relief from the suspension are similar to those for a GAO protest:
   a. Urgent and compelling circumstances which significantly affect the interests of the United States will not permit waiting for decision; and,
   b. If no award has been made, an award is likely within 30 days. *See Sun Microsystems Fed., Inc. v. Dep't of the Navy*, GSBCA No. 12795-P, 94-2 BCA ¶ 26,881 (Navy request to allow continued evaluation of proposals denied because contract award scheduled several months after protest would be decided).

3. The GSBCA decides whether to lift the stay after a hearing. The agency cannot unilaterally decide to proceed with the acquisition.

4. The GSBCA denies requests for suspension in appropriate cases. Persuasive reasons include:
   a. War. *ViON Corp.*, GSBCA No. 11002-P, 91-1 BCA ¶ 23,615 (gulf war sufficient reason to not suspend computer contract for Strategic Petroleum Reserve); *Electronic Sys. & Assoc., Inc.*, GSBCA No. 11291-P, 91-3 BCA ¶ 24,134 (engineering services in support of the drug war).
   b. Public Health. *Berkshire Computer Prods. v. Dep't of the Army*, GSBCA No. 12228-P, 93-1 BCA ¶ 25,538 (critical hospital computer system which ran out of disk space frequently); *North American Automated Sys. Co.*, GSBCA No. 9098-P, 88-1 BCA ¶ 20,295 (AIDS computer network); *Lockheed Integrated Solutions Co.*, GSBCA No. 11349-P, 91-3 BCA ¶ 24,198 (super computer at the National Cancer Institute urgent and compelling because of the daily loss of life from AIDS and cancer).
   c. Agency shutdown. *Advanced Data Concepts, Inc. v. Dep't of Energy*, GSBCA No. 11707-P, 92-2 BCA ¶ 24,846 (agency successfully opposed suspension of the DPA by showing that no contract meant no continued operation of computer services and substantial impact on agency operations because agency had no in-house capability); *Spectrum Leasing Corp.*, GSBCA No. 9881-P, 89-1 BCA ¶ 21,530 (systems maintenance to support vital function).

5. Compelling circumstances *NOT* found. *I-Net, Inc.*, GSBCA No. 9155-P, 87-3 BCA ¶ 20,096 (increased costs); *Computer Sciences Corp.*, GSBCA No. 9127-P, 87-3 BCA ¶ 20,095 (expiration of funds). The agency must show that no alternatives are available. *Prime Computer, Inc.*, GSBCA No. 9000-P, 87-2 BCA ¶ 19,918.

6. Partial Suspension. The agency may be able to obtain a partial suspension of procurement authority where a total lifting of the suspension would not be appropriate. In those cases, the GSBCA grants partial suspen-

sions to permit the acquisition to progress. *See PRC., Inc. v. Gen'l Servs. Admin.*, GSBCA No. 12713-P, 94-2 BCA ¶ 26,663; *Computer Sciences Corp.*, GSBCA No. 11497-P, 92-1 BCA ¶ 24,524 (board allows agency to perform preparatory tasks required to expeditiously field system critical to national security).

7. Suspensions of Nonexistent DPAs. In *CACI, Inc. v. Stone*, 990 F.2d 1233 (Fed. Cir. 1993), the Court of Appeals for the Federal Circuit reversed the GSBCA's decision in *CACI, Inc.-Fed.*, GSBCA No. 11523-P, 92-1 BCA ¶ 24,590. The GSBCA did not suspend an unauthorized ADPE acquisition because the protest was filed more than 10 days after award, the agency was moving to get a DPA from GSA, and the acquisition was urgent and compelling. The court used a basic authority analysis to hold that the failure to obtain the DPA voided the contract.

## F. Scope of Review.

1. The GSBCA conducts a *de novo* review of agency action. 40 U.S.C. § 759(f)(1). *Grumman Data Sys. Corp.*, GSBCA No. 11939-P, 94-2 BCA ¶ 26,822, *aff'd*, 15 F.3d 1044 (Fed. Cir. 1994) (in reviewing agency evaluations, board's review of information not available to source selection authority is appropriate); *Lanier Bus. Prods., Inc.*, GSBCA No. 7702-P, 85-2 BCA ¶ 8,033. *See also B3H v. Dep't of the Air Force*, GSBCA No. 12813-P, 94-3 BCA ¶ 27,068 (pointed dissent addressing the board's scope of review). Traditionally, the board did not presume that the agency's actions were correct, it gave no deference to agency expertise, nor did it recognize that the agency bears the ultimate burden of erroneous decisions.

2. *De novo* review permits the government to demonstrate that its initial decision was correct, albeit for the wrong reasons. *Storage Technology Corp.*, GSBCA No. 9793-P, 89-2 BCA ¶ 21,498.

3. The GSBCA recognizes that some agency actions are discretionary. These actions are reviewed for an abuse of discretion. *Planning Research Corp.*, GSBCA No. 10697-P, 91-2 BCA ¶ 23,882 (the GSBCA reviews cost realism determinations for abuse of discretion of contracting officer); *Unisys Corp.*, GSBCA No. 11069-P, 91-2 BCA ¶ 23,879 (inclusion of offeror in competitive range not an abuse of discretion, especially in light of agency regulation requiring inclusion in doubtful cases); *Advanced Mgmt., Inc.*, GSBCA No. 11257-P, 91-3 BCA ¶ 24,065 (agency's selection of evaluators reviewed for abuse of discretion, fraud, and actual bias).

4. The GSBCA has described abuse of discretion as conduct which is "clearly erroneous—an abuse of discretion demonstrating a `gross disparity or unfairness'. . . ." *CBIS Fed., Inc. v. Dep't of the Interior*, GSBCA No. 12092-P, 93-2 BCA ¶ 25,590.

5. The protester bears the burden of proof. *Memorex Corp.*, GSBCA No. 7927-P, 85-3 BCA ¶ 18,289. Where the statute or regulation allegedly violated accords the contracting officer discretion, the GSBCA appears to require that the protester demonstrate the agency action was clearly defective. *Honeywell Fed. Sys., Inc.*, GSBCA No. 9807-P, 89-1 BCA ¶ 21,444. *See also Grumman Data Sys. Corp. v. Widnall*, 15 F.3d 1044 (Fed. Cir. 1994) (where solicitation provision susceptible to two interpretations, that interpretation which promotes full and open competition is reasonable). *But see Coastal Computer Consultants Corp.*, GSBCA No. 12869-P, 1994 BPD ¶ 172 (agency failure to justify "new only" requirement for printers held to be overly restrictive).

6. The GSBCA has adopted a harmful error test before granting relief. *Andersen Consulting*, GSBCA No. 10833-P, 91-1 BCA ¶ 23,474 (to set aside an award, the error must have some significance); *Corporate Jets, Inc.*, GSBCA No. 11049-P, 91-2 BCA ¶ 23,998 (agency violated regulation by failing to inform the protester that it was excluded from the competitive range before amending the solic-

itation, but no harm to properly excluded protester); *TRW Inc.*, GSBCA No. 11309-P (evaluator, by an appearance of impropriety, violated regulation; however, he took no action which harmed the protester, so no relief was granted); *The Orkand Corp.*, GSBCA No. 11405-P, 92-1 BCA ¶ 24,624 (failure to disclose deficiency in discussions was not prejudicial because even if protester had perfect score, it would have lost competition).

### G. GSBCA Bid Protest Procedures.

1. Protests must be timely filed in writing and must contain the information set forth in Board Rule 7(b)(2); 48 C.F.R. § 6101.7(b)(2) (1994), including a concise statement of grounds and administrative information concerning the solicitation.

   a. A protester must file its protest with the contracting officer on the same day as it is filed at the GSBCA. Board Rule 3(b)(2); 48 C.F.R. § 6101.3(b)(2) (1994).

   b. The contracting officer must notify other interested parties and agencies, orally or in writing, within one day after receipt of a copy of the protest. Board Rule 5(d); 48 C.F.R. § 6101.5(d) (1994). This triggers the time limits for intervenors.

2. Intervenors must file with the board within four days of receipt of notice. Board Rule 5(b)(4); 48 C.F.R. § 6101.5(b)(4) (1994).

3. Protest File. The government must file a "Rule 4 File" with the board within ten *WORKING* days of date of filing of a protest. Board Rule 4(a); 48 C.F.R. § 6101.4(a) (1994).

   a. Board Rule 4 sets forth the contents of the file.

   b. Submit protectable documents (e.g., proprie-tary sensitive materials) *in camera* to the board.

   c. Serve a copy on all protesters and intervenors.

4. The government's must file its answer within 10 *working* days. Board Rule 7(c)(2); 48 C.F.R. § 6101.7(c)(2) (1994).

5. Conferences.

   a. Prehearing Conference. Board Rule 10; 48 C.F.R. § 6101.10 (1994). The board will hold a prehearing conference to establish a schedule for the proceedings, narrow issues, etc.

   b. Suspension Hearings. Board Rule 19(a)(2); 48 C.F.R. § 6101.19(a)(2) (1994). The GSBCA will hold a hearing on a request for suspension within ten *CALENDAR* days of filing the protest.[19]

6. Discovery. Board Rule 15; 48 C.F.R. § 6101.15 (1994). Board procedures encompass the full range of discovery, i.e., interrogatories, depositions, requests for production of documents, requests for admissions, protective orders, objections, etc.

7. Hearings. Board Rule 19; 48 C.F.R. § 6101.19 (1994).

   a. Hearings on the merits of the protest are conducted within 25 *WORKING* days of the date of filing.

   b. Board hearing procedures. Board Rule 21, 48 C.F.R. § 6101.21 (1994), provides for a full trial with:
      (1) compulsory process;
      (2) sworn testimony;
      (3) cross-examination;
      (4) public hearings;
      (5) Federal Rules of Evidence; and
      (6) verbatim transcripts.

8. The parties shall file post-hearing briefs within five *working* days after receipt by the board of the hearing transcript.

9. The board will render its decision within 45 *working* days.[20] 40 U.S.C. § 759(f)(4)(B).

### H. Remedies.

1. The board may suspend, revise or revoke the Delegation of Procurement Authority (DPA). 40 U.S.C. § 759(f)(5)(B).

   a. This remedy can include suspension of future acquisition authority. *Isyx*, GSBCA No. 9407-P, 88-2 BCA ¶ 20,781, *recon. denied*, 88-2 BCA ¶ 20,815 (agency's DPA withdrawn until agency instituted safeguards in its procurement procedures).

   b. The GSBCA uses the device of modifying

the DPA as a form of injunctive relief. *See National Capitol Sys., Inc.*, GSBCA No. 10823-P, 91-1 BCA ¶ 23,525 (agency directed to disclose evaluation materials to all offerors in the competitive range and request a second round of BAFOs); *Denro, Inc. v. Dep't of Trans.*, GSBCA No. 11736-P-R, 93-1 BCA ¶ 25,315 (board ordered agency to replace evaluators because evaluators believed that protester could not do job). *See also Computer Data Sys., Inc. v. Dep't of Energy*, GSBCA No. 12824-P-R, Aug. 4, 1994, 94-2 BCA ¶ 27,153.

c. The board will consider economic and efficient procurement in fashioning a remedy. 40 U.S.C. § 759(f)(5)(C). *C3, Inc.*, GSBCA No. 10066-P, 89-2 BCA ¶ 22,053; *Storage Technology Corp.*, GSBCA No. 9793-P-R, 89-2 BCA ¶ 21,618 (decision modified to delete requirement to return equipment pending resolicitation); *The Orkand Corp.*, GSBCA No. 11405-P, 92-1 BCA ¶ 24,624, (failure to get pre-award EEO clearance was a *de minimis* violation, thus, no relief).

2. Limits on remedial authority.

a. The GSBCA cannot modify the DPA to adjudicate contract disputes with the awardee. *See Planning Research Corp. v. United States*, 971 F.2d 736 (Fed. Cir. 1992).

b. Directed Awards. In a landmark Federal Circuit decision, *SMS Data Prods. Group, Inc. v. Austin*, 940 F.2d 1514 (Fed. Cir. 1991), the court held that the GSBCA had no authority to direct award of a contract to a successful protester. The board's only authority is to modify the Delegation of Procurement Authority granted by GSA. The decision left unanswered the question of what other actions the board can take under the guise of amending the Delegation of Procurement Authority.

## I. Attorney's Fees, Protest Costs, and Bid Preparation Costs.

1. The board will award attorneys fees and protest costs to "appropriate interested parties" who prevail on a significant issue. *HSQ Technology, Inc.*, GSBCA No. 9985-P, 89-2 BCA ¶ 21,777.

2. The fact that a party did not play the role of "lead protester" does not preclude it from award of protest costs incurred in pursuing the protest count. *Cordant, Inc.*, GSBCA No. 12226-C (12011-P), 94-1 BCA ¶ 26,275; *MBI Business Ctrs.*, GSBCA No. 11030, 93-1 BCA ¶ 25,240 (intervenors on the side of prevailing protester may be awarded protest costs).

3. An intended awardee that intervenes in a protest in support of the government's position is not an "appropriate interested party" for compensation of bid preparation costs. *Litton Sys., Inc.*, GSBCA No. 11915-C-R, 1994 BPD ¶ 81 (costs petition denied on award decision invalidated due to agency's violation of law).

a. EAJA standards *do not* apply.[21] Protest costs are substantial for the protester, the government and intervenors.

b. The board will recognize protest preparation costs even when a protester incur such costs prior to a debriefing. *Science Applications Int'l Corp.*, GSBCA No. 12696-C, 94-2 BCA ¶ 26,943.

c. The board generally regards costs associated with attending a post-award debriefing a routine business expense. Where the protester, however, can demonstrate that it retained outside counsel before debriefing and intended to protest before debriefing, such costs may be allowable. *HSQ Technology, Inc.*, GSBCA No. 12681-P, 94-2 BCA ¶ 26,944 (counsel's presence at debriefing merely a way to gather more facts in support of protest).

d. This does not include fees for subsequent appeal. *Sysorex Info. Sys., Inc.*, GSBCA No. 10781-C (10642-P)-REIN, 93-1 BCA ¶ 25,428.

e. Costs of experts may be recoverable. *Sterling Fed. Sys., Inc. v. NASA*, 16 F.3d 1177 (Fed. Cir. 1994) (vacated a prior GSBCA decision holding expert witness fees not recoverable).

f. The costs of protester's employees, other than in-house counsel, may not be recoverable, except for witness fees. *Id.*

4. The GSBCA may reduce protest costs when a protester prevails on only some of its allegations. *Digital Equip. Corp.*, GSBCA No. 9285-C(9131-P), 89-3 BCA ¶ 22,181. However, in *Planning Research Corp.*, GSBCA No. 10905-C (10694-P), 91-3 BCA ¶ 24,159, the board observed that ". . . a home run that barely clears the fence counts as much as one that hits the upper deck . . ." and awarded full recovery.

5. The board will award bid preparation costs when a prevailing party demonstrates that government misfeasance rendered bid preparation costs unnecessary or wasted. *Xerox, Corp.*, GSBCA No. 12408-C(12322-P), 93-3 BCA ¶ 26,227.

6. The judges are split on whether the GSBCA may order the agency to reimburse the permanent indefinite judgment fund for costs.[22] *See Sysorex Info.*, GSBCA No. 10781-C(10642-P)-REIN, 93-1 BCA ¶ 25,428 n.3.

## J. Appeals.

1. Motion for Reconsideration.
   a. Parties must file a motion for reconsideration of a decision within 7 working days of its receipt. Board Rule 32, 48 C.F.R. § 6101.32 (1994); *Accurate Information Sys. v. Dep't of the Treasury*, GSBCA No. 12978-P-R, 1994 BPD ¶ 236 (telefaxed motion sent on afternoon of seventh day deemed late because motion not printed in its entirety before end of board working day).
   b. The GSBCA will consider newly discovered evidence only where the evidence is likely to produce a new outcome or require amendment of the judgment. *Accurate Information Sys. v. Dep't of the Treasury*, GSBCA No. 12978-P-R, 1994 BPD ¶ 236.

2. The government, protester, or intervenor, may appeal adverse decisions to the U.S. Court of Appeals for the Federal Circuit. The government needs the concurrence of the Attorney General. 40 U.S.C. § 759(f)(6).

## V. UNITED STATES COURT OF FEDERAL CLAIMS.

### A. Statutory Authority.

1. U.S. Court of Federal Claims is granted jurisdiction by the Tucker Act, 28 U.S.C. § 1491, to render judgment upon any claim for damages against the United States founded upon the Constitution, Act of Congress, agency regulation, or express or implied-in-fact contract with the United States not sounding in tort.

2. The Court of Federal Claims was also granted authority by the Federal Courts Improvements Act of 1982, Pub. L. No. 97-164, § 133(a), 96 Stat. 25, 40 (1982), 28 U.S.C. § 1491(a)(3), "to afford complete relief on any contract claim brought before the contract is awarded including declaratory judgments, and such equitable and extraordinary relief as it deems proper" (i.e., injunctive relief).

### B. Who May Protest?

1. Only actual bidders may protest to the Court of Federal Claims. *Motorola, Inc. v. United States*, 988 F.2d 113 (Fed. Cir. 1993); *Hero, Inc. v. United States*, 3 Cl. Ct. 413 (1983); *Indian Wells Valley Metal Trades Council v. United States*, 1 Cl. Ct. 43 (1982).

2. The jurisdiction of the court to review pre-award bid protests flows from an implied-in-fact contract between the government and bidders or offerors to fairly evaluate the bids or offers received in response to a solicitation. *Heyer Prods. Co. v. United States*, 140 F. Supp. 409 (Ct. Cl. 1956).

3. The court permits third party practice. Rules of the United States Court of Federal Claims, Rule 14.

### C. What May Be Protested?

1. The *sole* basis for a bid protest to the court is an alleged breach of the government's implied-in-fact contract with bidders and

offerors to fairly and honestly consider bids or offers received in response to a solicitation.

2. All of the elements of the implied-in-fact contract must be present; none may be inferred. *Howard v. United States*, 21 Cl. Ct. 475 (1990) (a late bid cannot form the basis for the implied-in-fact contract); *Skytech Aero, Inc. v. United States*, 26 Cl. Ct. 251 (1992) (bid extension does not create an implied contract).

3. An allegation of violation of unspecified due process rights in connection with a bid protest is insufficient to support jurisdiction in the court. Due process claims are not money mandating rights under either the Constitution or statute. Accordingly, there is no jurisdiction over them in the Court of Federal Claims. *Howard v. United States*, 21 Cl. Ct. 475 (1990).

## D. When Must a Protest Be Filed?

1. A protester seeking injunctive relief must file its protest prior to award of the contract being protested. *United States v. John C. Grimberg Co.*, 702 F.2d 1362 (Fed. Cir. 1983). If the action is commenced prior to award, the subsequent award of the contract does not deprive the court of jurisdiction. *F. Alderette Gen. Contractors, Inc. v. United States* 715 F.2d 1476 (Fed. Cir. 1983). Transfer of an otherwise timely action from the district court to the Court of Federal Claims is acceptable, even if the transfer occurs after award. *Blackwell v. United States*, 23 Cl. Ct. 746 (1991).

2. An offeror may file a post-award claim for money damages (bid preparation costs) with the Court of Federal Claims within the six year statute of limitations, using a traditional Tucker Act analysis. 28 U.S.C. § 2401(a). *See AT&T Technologies, Inc. v. United States*, 18 Cl. Ct. 315 (1989).

## E. Preliminary Injunctions.

1. Rule 65(a) provides for Temporary Restraining Orders and Preliminary Injunctions. The court applies the traditional four-element test. *We Care, Inc. v. Ultra-Mark, Int'l Corp.*, 930 F.2d 1567 (Fed. Cir. 1991). These elements are:
   a. Likelihood of success on the merits;
   b. Degree of immediate irreparable injury if relief is not granted;
   c. Degree of harm to the party being enjoined if relief is granted; and,
   d. Impact of the injunction on public policy considerations.

2. A protester must post bond in order to obtain a preliminary injunction. Rule 65(c).

## F. Standard of Review.

1. The court uses an arbitrary, capricious, or lack of a rational basis standard of review. *Bean Dredging Corp. v. United States*, 19 Cl. Ct. 561 (1990).

2. The plaintiff must demonstrate either that the agency decision-making process lacks a rational basis or that there is a clear and prejudicial violation of applicable statutes or regulations. *Magellan Corp. v. United States*, 27 Fed. Cl. 446 (1993); *RADVA Corp. v. United States*, 17 Cl. Ct. 812 (1989).

3. To obtain a permanent injunction, the plaintiff must show by a preponderance of the evidence that the challenged action is irrational, unreasonable, or violates an acquisition statute or regulation. *Isratex, Inc. v. United States*, 25 Cl. Ct. 223 (1992). *See also Logicon, Inc.*, 22 Cl. Ct. 776 (1991) (plaintiff need only demonstrate likelihood of success on the merits for temporary restraining order).

4. The court gives decisions by the General Accounting Office great deference. *Honeywell, Inc. v. United States*, 870 F.2d 644 (Fed Cir. 1989). This deference is not absolute. *See Health Sys. Mktg. & Dev. Corp. v. United States*, 26 Cl. Ct. 1322 (1992); *Commercial Energies, Inc. v. United States*, 20 Cl. Ct. 140 (1990).

## G. Procedures.

1. The court conducts a civil proceeding without a jury substantially similar to proceedings

in Federal District Courts. The court has its own rules of procedure.

2. Litigation is generally slower than in the district courts or before the GAO, and distinctly slower than GSBCA actions. Additionally, the plaintiff must be represented by counsel who is admitted to practice before the court. *Finast Metal Prods., Inc. v. United States*, 12 Cl. Ct. 759 (1987).

## H. Remedies.

1. Equitable Relief, i.e., temporary restraining orders, preliminary injunctions, permanent injunctions, and declaratory judgement is available, if a prayer for such relief is filed pre-award. Protesters commencing action in this court usually seek injunctive relief.

2. Bid preparation costs are recoverable.
   a. Anticipatory profits are not recoverable. *Heyer Prods. Co. v. United States*, 135 Ct. Cl. 63, 140 F. Supp. 409 (1956).
   b. Bid preparation costs must be reasonable. *Rockwell Int'l Corp. v. United States*, 8 Cl. Ct. 662 (1985).
   c. The cost of preparing for performance of an anticipated contract is not recoverable. *Celtech, Inc. v. United States*, 24 Cl. Ct. 269 (1991).
   d. The cost of developing a prototype may be recovered. *Coflexip & Servs., Inc. v. United States*, 961 F.2d 951 (Fed. Cir. 1992).

## I. Attorneys' Fees and Protest Costs.

1. The court may award attorneys' fees and protest costs pursuant to the Equal Access to Justice Act. 28 U.S.C. § 2412(d)(1)(A); *Crux Computer Corp. v. United States*, 24 Cl. Ct. 223 (1991); *Bailey v. United States*, 1 Cl. Ct. 69 (1983).

2. The traditional rule is that only those attorneys fees associated with the litigation are recoverable. *Keyava Constr. Co. v. United States*, 15 Cl. Ct. 135 (1988); *Cox v. United States*, 17 Cl. Ct. 29 (1989); *contra Levernier Constr. Co. v. United States*, 21 Cl. Ct. 683 (1990), *rev'd* 947 F.2d 497 (Fed. Cir. 1991)

(costs associated with hiring an expert witness to pursue a claim with the contracting officer, prior to the litigation, not recoverable).

## J. Appeals.

Appeals from decisions of the Court of Federal Claims are taken to the United States Court of Appeals for the Federal Circuit. 28 U.S.C. § 1295(A)(3).

## VI. FEDERAL DISTRICT COURTS.

### A. Statutory Authority.

1. *Scanwell Lab., Inc. v. Shaffer*, 424 F.2d 859 (D.C. Cir. 1970), first recognized the jurisdiction of the Federal District Courts to entertain challenges to agency procurement decisions. It held that these decisions were reviewable under the Administrative Procedures Act, 5 U.S.C. § 702.

2. Currently, a split exists in the Circuits on the impact of the Federal Courts Improvements Act of 1982, Pub. L. 97-164, § 133(a), 96 Stat. 25, 40 (1982). The disagreement is based upon the statutory language that grants the Court of Federal Claims *exclusive* equitable jurisdiction over contract claims before award. *See* 28 U.S.C. § 1491(a)(3).
   a. *Scanwell* suits brought *after award* of the contract are not affected by the language in the Federal Courts Improvement Act. *United States v. John C. Grimberg Co.*, 702 F.2d 1362 (Fed. Cir. 1983).
   b. Disappointed bidder actions or "*Scanwell*" suits may be brought *prior to award* of the contract, depending on the Circuit.
      (1) Concurrent Jurisdiction. The First and Third Circuits recognize concurrent jurisdiction with Court of Federal Claims over preaward claims. *See Coco Bros. v. Pierce*, 741 F.2d 675 (3rd Cir. 1984); *In re Smith & Wesson, Inc.*, 757 F.2d 431 (1st Cir. 1985). At least one district court-level decision within the Sixth Circuit has found concurrent jurisdiction with the Court of Federal

Claims. *North Shore Strapping Co. v. United States*, 788 F. Supp. 344 (N.D. Ohio 1992) (stating that it considers the view of the Sixth Circuit to be that there is concurrent jurisdiction).

(2) Exclusive Jurisdiction. The Ninth, Fourth, and Second Circuits hold that the district courts have no preaward jurisdiction. *J.P. Francis & Assocs. v. United States*, 902 F.2d 740 (9th Cir. 1990); *Rex Sys., Inc. v. Holiday*, 814 F.2d 994 (4th Cir. 1987); *B.K. Instrument, Inc. v. United States*, 715 F.2d 713, 721 n.4 (2nd Cir. 1983). Although their respective courts of appeals have not specifically decided the issue, district courts within the Fifth, Tenth, and Eleventh Circuits have held that the district courts have no preaward jurisdiction. *Neeb-Kearney & Co. v. United States*, 779 F.2d 841 (E.D. La. 1991); *Commercial Energies, Inc. v. Cheney*, 737 F. Supp. 78 (D. Colo. 1990); *Metric Sys. Corp. v. United States*, 673 F. Supp. 439 (N.D. Fla. 1987).

## B. Who May Protest?

A protester must be aggrieved by agency action. Standing to sue is demonstrated by a showing of:

1. Injury-in-Fact. *Scanwell Lab. Inc. v. Shaffer*, 424 F.2d 859 (D.C. Cir. 1970); *AFGE Local v. Callaway*, 398 F. Supp. 176 (N.D. Ala. 1975); or

2. That the protester is within the zone-of-interest of the statute or regulation. *Contractors Eng'rs Int'l, Inc. v. Dep't of Veterans Affairs*, 947 F.2d 1298 (5th Cir. 1991); *Cincinnati Elec. Corp. v. Kleppe*, 509 F.2d 1080 (6th Cir. 1975); *Control Data Corporation v. Baldridge*, 655 F.2d 283 (D.C. Cir. 1981); *Cerberonics, Inc. v. Garrett*, No. 91-0239 (D.D.C. Mar. 20, 1991).

## C. What May Be Protested?

1. Agency actions in violation of the United States Constitution, statute or regulation.

This is a general review of agency action under the Administrative Procedures Act (APA). 5 U.S.C. §§ 701-706.

2. The APA is not, however, a separate waiver of sovereign immunity nor an independent grant of jurisdiction to the District Courts. Plaintiffs must demonstrate an independent basis of jurisdiction. *Eagle-Picher Indus., Inc. v. United States*, 901 F.2d 1530 (10th Cir. 1990). Frequently, plaintiffs allege a violation of the Competition in Contracting Act.

3. A district court will review agency actions that the GAO traditionally declines to review, i.e., small business determinations, responsibility determinations, labor issues, timber sales, etc.

4. The Contract Disputes Act of 1978 (CDA) vests exclusive jurisdiction in the United States Court of Federal Claims and the various Boards of Contract Appeals over contract disputes, i.e., final decisions of contracting officers based upon express contracts with the government. 41 U.S.C. §§ 601-613. Accordingly, the District Courts have no jurisdiction over these CDA matters. *Ingersoll-Rand Co. v. United States*, 780 F.2d 74 (D.C. Cir. 1985); *contra American Airlines, Inc. v. Austin*, 778 F. Supp. 72 (D.D.C. 1991) (district court has jurisdiction over contract claims by GSA against airlines for unused tickets; each ticket is a contract less than $10,000).

5. Terminations for convenience, even if issued shortly after award, are matters of contract administration covered by the Contract Disputes Act (41 U.S.C. §§ 601-613), and are outside the jurisdiction of the district courts. *Mark Dunning Indus., Inc. v. Cheney*, 934 F.2d 266 (11th Cir. 1991); *Ingersoll-Rand Co. v. United States*, 780 F.2d 74 (D.C. Cir. 1985).

## D. When Must the Protest Be Filed?

1. Generally, protests in the District Courts are filed very quickly in order to demonstrate immediate and irreparable harm. Temporary Restraining Order hearings can be held on a

few hours notice. The key to successful defense of these actions is getting credible, factual information to the appropriate United States Attorney's office in a timely manner.

2. Absent a need to show immediate and irreparable harm, actions must be commenced within six years of the date the right of action first accrues. 28 U.S.C. § 2401(a).

### E. Preliminary Injunctions.

1. A plaintiff's primary motive in bringing a disappointed bidder action in a district court is to obtain injunctive relief. The various circuits apply somewhat different standards. Research is required for a complete understanding of the standard applicable in each Circuit. Generally, the traditional four-prong test discussed in Section V.E., above, is applied.

2. If the motion for a TRO or preliminary injunction is defeated, the agency should immediately award the contract. *See Fauconniere Mfg. Corp. v. Secretary of Defense*, 794 F.2d 350 (8th Cir. 1986).

### F. Scope of Review.

1. 5 U.S.C. § 706(2) provides that review of agency action will be limited to determining whether the action was:
   a. Arbitrary, capricious, an abuse of discretion, or otherwise not in accordance with law;
   b. Contrary to constitutional right, power, privilege, or immunity; or
   c. In excess of statutory jurisdiction, authority, or limitations.

2. Judicial construction has established a very high standard of review for agency procurement decisions. Courts should not substitute their own judgment for that of the contracting official, even if the court would have come to a different conclusion given the same set of facts. *See generally Scanwell Lab., Inc. v. Shaffer*, 424 F.2d 859 (D.C. Cir. 1970); *M. Steinthal & Co. v. Seamans*, 455 F.2d 1289 (D.C. Cir. 1971); *Wheelabrator v. Chafee*, 455 F.2d 1301 (D.C. Cir. 1971);

*Princeton Combustion Research Lab. v. McCarthy*, 674 F.2d 1016 (3rd Cir. 1982); *Shoals Am. Indus., Inc. v. United States*, 877 F.2d 883 (11th Cir. 1989).

3. District courts give agency interpretations of statutes and regulations substantial deference. *Shoals Am. Indus., Inc. v. United States*, 877 F.2d 883 (11th Cir. 1989). Even when an agency has erred in its decision-making process, the district courts should not grant injunctive relief absent a strong showing that there is no rational basis for the decision. *See Computer Sciences Corp. v. Garrett*, 36 CCF ¶ 75,841, (D.D.C. Apr. 10, 1990).

4. Many courts find GAO opinions to be instructive in reaching their decisions. *See Professional Bldg. Concepts, Inc. v. City of Central Falls*, 974 F.2d 1 (1st Cir. 1992). A district court may request that the GAO issue an advisory opinion to the court.

5. The review is based on the full administrative record that was before the decision maker at the time the decision was made. *Citizens to Preserve Overton Park v. Volpe*, 401 U.S. 402, 420 (1971).

### G. Procedures.

1. Procedures are those generally followed in federal civil litigation. Litigation is fast-paced. Hearings on requests for temporary restraining orders are frequently heard within 24 hours of filing. Preliminary injunction hearings are often held within several weeks of the commencement of the action.

2. Agencies have had some success in limiting discovery since the court's review is generally limited to the administrative record. This is especially true when a dispositive motion is pending. *See Rosin v. New York Stock Exchange*, 484 F.2d 179 (7th Cir. 1973), *cert. denied*, 415 U.S. 977 (1974); *Brennan v. Local Union No. 639*, 494 F.2d 1092 (D.C. Cir. 1974), *cert. denied*, 429 U.S. 1123 (1976).

### H. Remedies.

1. Equitable and declaratory relief.
2. District courts may not direct the award of a

contract to a particular entity. This decision is vested ultimately in the executive agencies. *Delta Data Sys., Inc. v. Webster*, 744 F.2d 197 (D.C. Cir. 1984).

3. Monetary relief is limited to $10,000. 28 U.S.C. § 1346(a). *Contra American Airlines, Inc. v. Austin*, No. 90-1394 SSH (D.D.C. Nov. 25, 1991), 37 CCF ¶ 76,225 (district court has jurisdiction over contract claims by GSA against airlines for unused tickets; each ticket is a contract less than $10,000).

## I. Attorneys Fees and Cost of Litigation.

District courts may award attorneys' fees and the costs of litigation under the Equal Access to Justice Act. 28 U.S.C. § 2412(d)(1)(a).

## J. Appeals.

1. Where the plaintiff only seeks injunctive relief, appeal from the district court must go to the appropriate regional circuit court of appeals.

2. Where a plaintiff seeks monetary relief under the "Little Tucker Act", however, the Court of Appeals for the Federal Circuit has exclusive jurisdiction over such appeals. 28 U.S.C. § 1346(a)(2); 28 U.S.C. § 1295(a)(2); *Sharp v. Weinberger*, 798 F.2d 1521 (D.C. Cir. 1986) (J. Scalia) (CAFC has exclusive jurisdiction over district court decision where jurisdiction based in whole or in part on "Little Tucker Act").

## Endnotes

1. The Federal Acquisition Streamlining Act of 1994 has made significant changes in the processing of bid protests. This outline will note pertinent changes by citing to the relevant section of the FASA. As of the publication date of this outline, the regulatory changes mandated by FASA exist in draft form only. It behooves the legal advisor to keep abreast of these changes and amend the information contained in this outline accordingly.

2. The FASA allows the agency head to pay a protester its costs for pursuing a meritorious protest. FASA § 1016. *See* 31 U.S.C. § 3554(c)(1) which describes these costs as costs attributable to pursuing a protest, to include "reasonable" attorneys' fees, and bid and preparation costs.

3. Because of FASA, the GAO has issued draft regulations which convert this deadline from 10 working days to 14 calendar days. This change becomes effective once the draft regulations are finalized and implemented.

4. See footnote 3.

5. The FASA will define the term "protest" as a written objection by an interested party to:
   (A) A solicitation or other request by a Federal Agency for offers for a contract for the procurement of property or services.
   (B) The cancellation of such a solicitation or other request.
   (C) An award or proposed award of such a contract.
   (D) A termination or cancellation of an award of such a contract, if the written objection contains an allegation that the termination or cancellation is based in whole or in part on improprieties concerning the award of the contract. FASA § 1401 (amending 31 U.S.C. 3553).

6. Because of the FASA, GAO draft regulations provide 14 calendar days for the filing of a protest.

7. See footnote 6.

8. The FASA provides an alternate deadline that the CICA stay applies when the protest is filed no later than 5 days after the date of the mandatory post-award debriefing. FASA § 1402(b) (amending 31 U.S.C. § 3553). Hence, the CICA stay applies under either deadline, whichever is the later.

9. The FASA changes this deadline to 35 calendar

days. FASA § 1402(a). Additionally, the FASA requires the agency, upon request by an "actual or prospective offeror," to publish a "protest file." FASA § 1015. Under proposed regulations, GAO will allow the agency 20 days to produce this protest file.

10. Proposed changes resulting from the FASA revisions will allow the GAO to issue a protective order without a request from a party.

11. The FASA changes this deadline to 20 calendar days. FASA § 1402.

12. The FASA changes this decisional deadline to 125 calendar days. FASA § 1403(a)(1).

13. The FASA changes this deadline to 65 calendar days. FASA § 1403(a)(2).

14. *See also* FASA § 1403(b) (amending 31. U.S.C. § 3554).

15. The FASA caps attorneys' fees at $150 per hour. These limits, however, do not apply where the protester is a small business. FASA also limits expert witness fees to the "highest rate of compensation for expert witnesses paid by the Federal Government." FASA § 1403(b).

16. The Brooks Act identifies what agencies, contracts, and types of FIP resources fall within its purview. The Federal Information Resource Management Regulation (FIRMR), provides additional guidance regarding the scope of the Brooks Act. The

FIRMR defines FIP resources expansively, to include automatic data processing equipment (ADPE) as that term is used in the Brooks Act. FIRMR 201-4.001.

17. Note that, unlike the GAO, the GSBCA will *not* convert its 10 working day rule to a calendar day rule.

18. Like GAO protests, the FASA adds on a second deadline. A protester's request for suspension may also be timely if it is filed within 5 days of a required post-award debriefing. FASA § 1433.

19. The FASA requires the GSBCA to hold a suspension hearing within 5 days of the protest filing or the required post-award debriefing, whichever is later. FASA § 1433.

20. The FASA converts this deadline to 65 calendar days. FASA § 1433(b).

21. As in GAO protests, the FASA caps attorneys' fees at $150 per hour. These limits, however, do not apply where the protester is a small business. FASA also limits expert witness fees to the "highest rate of compensation for expert witnesses paid by the Federal Government." FASA § 1435.

22. The FASA requires the agency to reimburse any use of the permanent indefinite judgment fund attributable to either board decision or settlement agreement. FASA §§ 1435-36 (amending 40 U.S.C. § 759(f)(5)(C) and (D)).

## CHAPTER TEN

# Government Information Practices

## I. LEARNING OBJECTIVES.

Upon completing this instruction, the student will understand:

A. The scope of the Freedom of Information Act (FOIA) and the scope of the major exemptions that permit the government to withhold records from the public;.

B. The basic procedures in processing a FOIA request; and

C. The circumstances under which plaintiffs may sue the government to obtain records and to recover their costs and attorneys fees.

## II. REFERENCES.

### A. Primary.

1. Freedom of Information Act, 5 U.S.C. § 552, as amended.

2. Department of Defense Directive No. 5400.7, DOD Freedom of Information Act Program (3 Oct. 1990).

3. Department of Defense Regulation No. 5400.7-R, DOD Freedom of Information Act Program (Oct. 1990).

4. Army Regulation No. 25-55, The Department of the Army Freedom of Information Act Program (10 Jan. 1990).

5. Air Force Instruction 37-131, Air Force Freedom of Information Act Program (31 Mar. 1994).

6. Secretary of the Navy Instruction 5720.42E, Department of the Navy Freedom of Information Act Program (5 June 1991), 32 C.F.R. Part 701 (1991), as revised by

56 Fed. Reg. 66574 (Dec. 24, 1991).

7. Marine Corps Order 5720.63, Publication in the Federal Register, Indexing, and Public Inspection of Marine Corps Directives (22 Aug. 1983); Marine Corps Order P5720.56A, Availability to Public of Marine Corps Records (26 Feb. 1985).

### B. Secondary.

1. The Center for National Security Studies, *Litigation Under the Federal Freedom of Information Act and Privacy Act* (18th ed. 1993), 122 Maryland Ave., N.E., Washington, D.C. 20002.

2. *Freedom of Information Act Guide and Privacy Act Overview* (Sept. 1994), U.S. Gov't Printing Office, Washington, D.C. 20402.

3. *Freedom of Information Case List* (Sept. 1994), Sup't of Documents, U.S. Gov't Printing Office, Washington, D.C. 20402.

4. *FOIA UPDATE*, a newsletter issued quarterly by the Justice Department's Office of Information and Privacy (OIP), Room 7238 MAIN, Washington, D.C. 20530.

5. Department of Army Pamphlet No. 27-153 (1989), Chapter 22, "Release of Information."

## III. INTRODUCTION.

### A. History.

### B. Overview of FOIA.

1. Access to agency records.

2. Exemptions/Exclusions.

3. Procedures.

## C. Key concepts.

1. Disclosure is the rule, not the exception.
2. All individuals are entitled to equal access.
3. The government has the burden to justify withholding of information.
4. The requester can get relief if access to government information is improperly denied.

## IV. ACCESS TO AGENCY RECORDS.

### A. Publication.

§ 552(a)(1).

1. How information may be obtained from the agency: DOD Reg. 5400.7-R, AR 25-55, AFI 37-131, SECNAVINST 5720.42E, and MCO 5720.63.
2. Rules of procedure and how to make submittals to the agency: Federal Acquisition Regulation (FAR), DOD FAR Supp. (DFARS), and Army FAR Supp. (AFARS).
3. Substantive rules of general applicability. *See Virgil v. Andrus*, 667 F.2d 931 (10th Cir. 1982); *United States v. Mowat*, 582 F.2d 1194 (9th Cir. 1978). *See also* DAJA-AL 1978/2898.

### B. Index for Public Inspection.

§ 552(a)(2).

1. Final Opinions made in the adjudication of cases.
2. Statements of policy and interpretations of law. *Nat'l Labor Relations Bd. v. Sears*, 421 U.S. 132 (1975).
3. Administrative staff manuals. *Cuneo v. Schlesinger*, 484 F.2d 1086 (D.C. Cir. 1973). *Roberts v. IRS*, 584 F. Supp. 1241 (E.D. Mich. 1984).

### C. Release Upon Request.

§ 552(a)(3).

1. Applies to "agency records."
   a. What is an "agency"? 5 U.S.C. § 552(f).
   b. What is a "record"? AR 25-55, para. 1-402(a); AFI 37-131, Sec. C; SECNAVINST 5720.42E, para. 4b2(1); MCO P5720.56A, para. 2001.
   c. What is *not* a "record"? AR 25-55, para. 1-

402(b); AFI 37-131, para. 3; SECNAVINST 5720.42E, para. 4b(2); MCO P5720.56A, para. 2001.
   (1) Museum material.
   (2) 3-D model.
   (3) Memory or oral communication.
   (4) Personal notes. *Bureau of Nat'l Affairs v. Dep't of Justice*, 742 F.2d 1484 (D.C. Cir. 1984).

2. An agency must possess *and* control the record. AR 25-55, para. 1-402(c); AFR 12-30, para. 2j; SECNAVINST 5720.42E, para. 5f; MCO P5720.56A, para. 2003.
   a. Possession. Agency must have actual possession, not just the right to possess the record. *Kissinger v. Reporters Comm. for Freedom of the Press*, 445 U.S. 136 (1980).
   b. Control.
      (1) Other agency records. *McGehee v. CIA*, 697 F.2d 1095 (D.C. Cir. 1983).
      (2) Records generated from sources outside the Government. Records must be either government-owned or subject to substantial government control or use. *General Electric v. Nuclear Reg. Comm'm*, 750 F.2d 1394 (7th Cir. 1984); *Gov't Sales Consultants, Inc. v. Gen. Servs. Admin.*, No. 77-1294 (D.D.C. Jan. 31, 1979).

3. FOIA does not require agencies to create or retain records. AR 25-55, para. 1-506; AFI 37-131, para. 8; SECNAVINST 5720.42E, para. 5f; MCO P5720.56A, para. 2003.

### D. Other Factors Affecting Access.

1. Rule of segregability. § 552(b).
   a. Portions of documents which should be released must be segregated from those which may be withheld. *Long v. IRS*, 596 F.2d 362 (9th Cir. 1979).
   b. Nonexempt material is not "reasonably segregable" where an inordinate burden would result. *Lead Indus. Assn. v. OSHA*, 610 F.2d 70 (2d Cir. 1979).
2. Status and purpose of requester. As a general rule, the agency cannot consider the status

and purpose of the requester in determining releasability.

3. Release of exempt records. DOD policy is to make records publicly available, unless an exemption applies. Although components may elect to release, a discretionary release is generally not appropriate under exceptions 1, 3, 4, 6, and 7(c). DOD Reg. 5400.7-R para. 1-504; AR 25-55, paras. 1-300 and 3-101; AFI 37-131, para. 1; SECNAVINST 5720.42E, paras. 5a(1) and 7(a); MCO P5720.56A, para. 6000.

## V. NINE EXEMPTIONS PERMIT WITHHOLDING.

### A. Exemption 1: Classified Records.

The FOIA does not apply to records "(A) specifically authorized under criteria established by an Executive order to be kept secret in the interest of national defense or foreign policy and (B) are in fact properly classified pursuant to such Executive order."

1. Executive Order 12,356 (Apr. 6, 1982), implemented by DOD 5200.1-R, AR 380-5, AFR 205-1, and OPNAVINST 5510.1.
2. Proper classification.
   a. Court conducts "de novo" review of both procedural and substantive propriety of classification. *Allen v. CIA*, 636 F.2d 1287 (D.C. Cir. 1980).
   b. Court may conduct "in camera" inspection in its sound discretion, although the court should give substantial weight to agency affidavits. *Ray v. Turner*, 587 F.2d 1187 (D.C. Cir. 1978).
   c. Post-request classification is permitted. E.O. 12356, section 1.6(d); AR 25-55, para. 5-100c; AFI 37-131, para. 10.1.1; SEC-NAVINST 5720.42E, Enclosure (3), para. 1d.
3. Segregability applies even in Exemption 1 cases. *Founding Church of Scientology, Inc. v. Bell*, 603 F.2d 945 (D.C. Cir. 1979).
4. Classified Acquisitions - Glomar Denial. *Phillippi v. CIA*, 546 F.2d 1009 (D.C. Cir. 1976).

### B. Exemption 2: Internal Personnel Rules and Practices.

1. Trivial matters, "Low 2." *See Dep't of the Air Force v. Rose*, 425 U.S. 352 (1976). Agency personnel lists. *Schwaner v. Dep't of the Air Force*, 898 F.2d 793 (D.C. Cir. 1990).
2. Circumvention of agency regulation, "High 2." *Kaganove v. Environ. Protection Agency*, 856 F.2d 884 (7th Cir. 1988), *cert. denied*, 109 S.Ct. 798 (1989); *Crooker v. Bureau of Alcohol, Tobacco, & Firearms*, 670 F.2d 1051 (D.C. Cir. 1981); AR 25-55, para. 3-200, no. 2; AFI 37-131, para. 10.2; SECNAVINST 5720.42E, Enclosure (3), para. 2b; MCO P5720.56A, para. 6002, subpara. 2. *See also* Exemption 7(E), 5 U.S.C. § 552(b)(7)(E).

### C. Exemption 3: Other Federal Withholding Statutes.

— FOIA does not apply to records "specifically exempted from disclosure by statute (other than section 552b of this title), provided that such statute (A) requires that the matters be withheld from the public in such a manner as to leave no discretion on the issue, or (B) establishes particular criteria for withholding or refers to particular types of matter to be withheld." e.g., 41 U.S.C. § 423, Procurement Integrity Act.

### D. Exemption 4: Trade Secrets and Commercial and Financial Information.

1. Trade Secrets. *Public Citizen Health Research Group v. FDA*, 704 F.2d 1280 (D.C. Cir. 1983).

   "[A] secret, commercially valuable plan, formula, process, or device that is used for the making, preparing, compounding, or processing of trade commodities and that can be said to be the end product of either innovation or substantial effort."

2. Commercial or financial information obtained from a person and confidential or privileged.
   a. Commercial or financial information. *See, Washington Post Co. v. Dep't of Health*

*and Human Services*, 690 F.2d 252 (D.C. Cir. 1982).

b. From a person. *See Grumman Aircraft Engineering Corp. v. Renegotiation Board*, 425 F.2d 578 (D.C. Cir. 1970).

c. Confidentiality of information people are "required" to give to the government. The *National Parks* test. *Nat'l Parks & Conservation Ass'n v. Morton*, 498 F.2d 765 (D.C. Cir. 1974). AR 25-55, para. 3-200, no. 4; AFI 37-131, para. 10.4; SECNAVINST 5720.42E, Enclosure (3), para. 4; MCO P5720.56A, para. 6002, subpara. 4.

(1) Would disclosure impair ability of agency to obtain necessary information in the future? *9 to 5 Organization for Women Office Workers v. Board of Governors of Federal Reserve System*, 721 F.2d 1 (1st Cir. 1983); *Orion Research Inc. v. Environ. Protection Agency*, 615 F.2d 551 (1st Cir. 1980).

(2) *Or*, would disclosure cause substantial competitive harm to the supplier? *Hercules, Inc. v. Marsh*, 839 F.2d 1027 (4th Cir. 1988) (holding no competition for Radford Army Ammunition Plant contract); *Gulf & Western Indus. Inc. v. United States*, 615 F.2d 527 (D.C. Cir. 1979); *Ivanhoe Citrus Ass'n v. Handley*, 612 F.Supp. 1560 (D.D.C. 1985) (customer list releasable).

d. Confidentiality: Information given to the Government voluntarily. *Critical Mass Energy Project v. Nuclear Regulatory Comm'm*, 925 F.2d 871 (D.C. Cir. 1992).

(1) Was the information provided voluntarily?

(2) Is it the kind of information that the provider would not customarily make available to the public?

e. Contract bids and proposals are always considered required submissions and therefore only decided under a *National Parks & Conservation Ass'n v. Morton* analysis. *See* DFOISR Memorandum, SUBJECT: FOIA Policy on DOD Application of *Critical Mass Energy Project v. Nuclear*

*Regulatory Commission*, 93-CORR-094, 27 JUL 1993; DFOISR Memorandum, SUBJECT: Interim Guidance on DOD Application of *Critical Mass Energy Project v. Nuclear Regulatory Commission*, 93-CORR-037, 23 MAR 1993.

f. Privileged information. *Washington Post v. Dep't of Health & Human Servs.*, 795 F.2d 205 (D.C. Cir. 1986); *Sharyland Water Supply Corp. v. Block*, 755 F.2d 397 (5th Cir.), *cert. denied*, 471 U.S. 1137 (1985).

3. Determining whether business information is exempt: Notice to the submitter. Executive Order 12600, July 23, 1987; AR 25-55, para. 5-207. Agencies should adopt procedures to develop "an administrative record" to support a decision to release information.

a. Reverse-FOIA suit.

b. Review of agency action under Administrative Procedures Act (APA): review of the administrative record. *Acumenics Research & Technology v. Dep't of Justice*, 843 F.2d 800 (4th Cir. 1988); *General Electric Co. v. Nuclear Regulatory Comm'm*, 750 F.2d 1394 (7th Cir. 1984).

4. Can the agency disclose Exemption 4 information?

*CNA Financial Corp. v. Donovan*, 830 F.2d 1132 (D.C. Cir. 1987), *cert. denied*, 108 S.Ct. 1270 (1988) (18 U.S.C. § 1905 and Exemption 4 held to be congruent).

## E. Exemption 5: Privileged Agency Memoranda & Internal Agency Communications.

— The FOIA does not apply to matters that are "inter-agency or intra-agency memorandums or letters which would not be available by law to a party . . . in litigation with the agency;"

1. Purpose.

2. Scope.

a. Deliberative process privilege.

(1) Purpose. *Wolfe v. Dep't of Health & Human Servs.*, 839 F.2d 768 (D.C. Cir. 1988) (en banc).

(2) "Factual-deliberative" distinction.

(a) Deliberative process privilege does

not generally protect purely factual matters. *Environmental Protection Agency v. Mink*, 410 U.S. 73, 85-91 (1973).

    (b) Facts may be protected if "inextricably intertwined" with deliberative material. *Ryan v. Dep't of Justice*, 617 F.2d 781 (D.C. Cir. 1980); *Jowett, Inc. v. Dep't of Navy*, 729 F. Supp. 871 (D.D.C. 1989).

  (3) "Predecisional - postdecisional" distinction.

    (a) Protects predecisional documents. *NLRB v. Sears*, 421 U.S. 132 (1975).

    (b) Express adoption or incorporation by reference. *NLRB v. Sears*, *supra*; *Swisher v. Dep't of the Air Force*, 660 F.2d 369 (8th Cir. 1981).

  (4) Memoranda prepared by outside consultants fall within the privilege. *Wu v. Nat'l Endowment for Humanities*, 460 F.2d 1030 (5th Cir. 1972), *cert. denied*, 410 U.S. 926 (1973).

  b. Attorney-client privilege. *Mead Data Cent., Inc. v. Dep't of the Air Force*, 566 F.2d 242 (D.C. Cir. 1977).

  c. Attorney work-product privilege. *Fed. Trade Comm'm v. Grolier*, 462 U.S. 19 (1983); *Martin v. Office of Special Counsel*, 819 F.2d 1181 (D.C. Cir. 1987).

  d. Trade secrets or commercial information privilege. *Morrison-Knudsen Co. v. Dep't of the Army*, 595 F. Supp. 352 (D.D.C. 1984), *aff'd* 762 F.2d 138 (D.C. Cir. 1985).

  e. Protection of certain confidential witness statements. *United States v. Weber Aircraft Corp.*, 465 U.S. 792 (1984); *Ahearn v. Department of the Army*, 583 F. Supp. 1123 (D. Mass. 1984).

## F. Exemption 6: Personal Privacy.

1. The balancing test. *Dep't of Justice v. Reporters Committee for Freedom of the Press*, 489 U.S. 749 (1989).

2. Request for wage information on contractor employees. *Painting and Drywall Work Preservation Fund v. Dep't of Housing & Urban Development*, 936 F.2d 1300 (D.C. Cir. 1991)(Union and consumer groups wanted contractor's payroll records to see if wage laws were being enforced.)

3. Release of names and home addresses. *DOD v. Federal Labor Relations Authority*, 114 S.Ct. 1006 (1994).

## G. Exemption 7: Law Enforcement Records.

# VI. ACCESS UPON REQUEST.

## A. What Is A Proper Request?

1. Must request an "agency record." AR 25-55, para. 1-402; AFI 37-131, para. 3; SECNAVINST 5720.42E, para. 4b; MCO P5720.56A, para. 2001.

2. Must reasonably describe the record. AR 25-55, para. 1-507; AFI 37-131, para. 7; SECNAVINST 5720.42E, paras. 5e and 9a(2); MCO P5720.56A, paras. 2003 and 4000. *See Marks v. United States*, 578 F.2d 261 (9th Cir. 1978); *Mason v. Calloway*, 554 F.2d 129 (4th Cir.), *cert. denied*, 434 U.S. 877 (1977).

3. Must comply with agency rules.

  a. Must be in writing. AR 25-55, paras. 1-401 and 1-503; AFI 37-131, paras. 4 and 5; SECNAVINST 5720.42E, para. 9a(1); MCO P5720.56A, paras. 2003 and 4000.

  b. Must express willingness to pay fees. AR 25-55, paras. 1-503 & 6-104; AFI 37-131, para. 5; SECNAVINST 5720.42E, para. 9a(3); MCO P5720.56A, paras. 2003 and 4000.

  c. Must be directed to proper custodian. AR 25-55, para. 1-508; AFI 37-131, para. 5; SECNAVINST 5720.42E, para. 10b; MCO P5720.56A, para. 4003, subpara. 4.

  d. Must expressly or impliedly invoke FOIA or an implementing regulation. AR 25-55, paras. 1-401 and 1-503; AFI 37-131, para. 6; SECNAVINST 5720.42E, para. 9a(1); MCO P5720.56A, paras. 2003 and 4000.

## B. What Must The Agency Do In Response?

1. Statutory time limits. 5 U.S.C. §§ 552(a)(6)(A)(i), (ii).

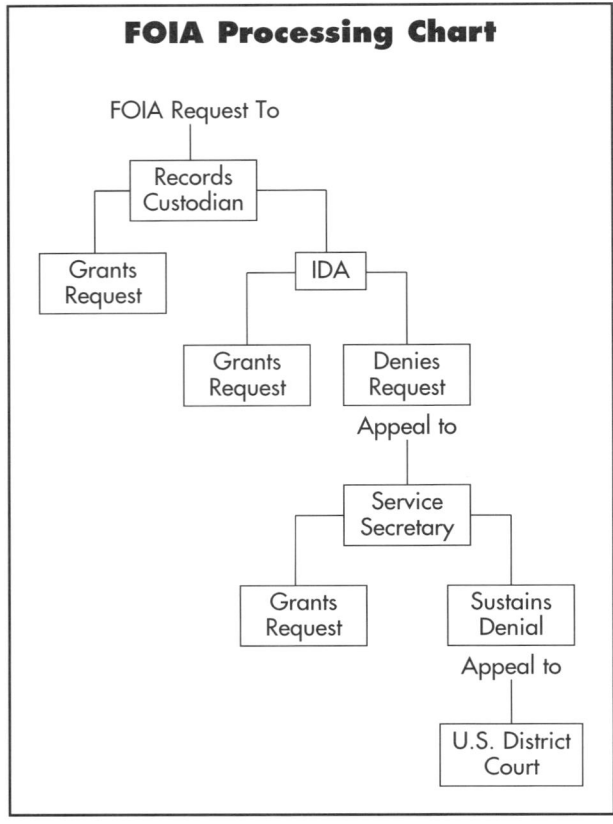

**FOIA Processing Chart**

FOIA Request To

Records Custodian

Grants Request

IDA

Grants Request

Denies Request

Appeal to

Service Secretary

Grants Request

Sustains Denial

Appeal to

U.S. District Court

2. Agency must make "reasonable efforts" to locate records and can be required to demonstrate adequacy of search. *Weisberg v. Dep't of Justice*, 705 F.2d 1344 (D.C. Cir. 1983). *But see Marks v. United States*, 578 F.2d 261 (9th Cir. 1978).

3. Services' release and processing procedures. AR 25-55, ch. V; AFI 37-131, para. 15; SEC-NAVINST 5720.42E, para. 6; MCO P5720.56A, ch. 4.

**C. Fees and Fee Waivers.**

1. Fee charges are based on status and motive of requester, but not on the substance of the information.

   a. First - Most favored category: (1) educational or noncommercial scientific institutions (whose purpose is scholarly or scientific research) or (2) representatives of the news media, are charged only for duplication when records are not sought for commercial use. *National Security Archive v. Dep't of Defense*, 880 F.2d 1381

(D.C. Cir. 1989), *cert. denied*, 494 U.S. 1029 (1990).

   b. Second - Least favored category: requesters of records for commercial use are charged for search, duplication, and *review*.

   c. Third category: All other requesters are charged for search and duplication.

2. Fee waiver also based on status and motive of requester, plus the substance of the information.

   a. Fee waiver standard - if disclosure of the information is in the public interest because it is likely to contribute significantly to public understanding of the operations or activities of the government *and* is not primarily in the commercial interest of the requester.

   b. Automatic waiver applies if costs of routine collection and processing of the fee are likely to equal or exceed the amount of the fee; or for 1st and 3d categories above - first 100 pages of duplication and for 3d category -first two hours of search time will be waived.

3. DOD Exception For Technical Data. 10 U.S.C. § 2328.

**VII. FOIA LITIGATION.**

**A. Administrative Remedies Must Be Exhausted.**
Courts may grant the agency additional time in "exceptional circumstances." 5 U.S.C. § 552(a)(6)(C). *See Open America v. Watergate Special Prosecution Force*, 547 F.2d 605 (D.C. Cir. 1976). *But see Mayock v. Immigration & Naturalization Serv.*, 714 F. Supp. 1558 (N.D. Cal. 1989).

**B. Judicial Review.**
5 U.S.C. § 552(a)(4)(B).

1. Scope of review - *de novo*.

2. *In camera* inspections. *Ingle v. Dep't of Justice*, 698 F.2d 259 (6th Cir. 1983); *Ray v. Turner*, 587 F.2d 1187 (D.C. Cir. 1978).

3. *Vaughn* index. A court may order an agency

to submit a detailed index of the documents sought to be withheld. *Vaughn v. Rosen*, 484 F.2d 820 (D.C. Cir. 1973), *cert. denied*, 415 U.S. 977 (1974).

4. Burden of proof. The burden is on the government to establish that a document is exempt from disclosure. 5 U.S.C. § 552(a)(4)(B).

**C. Attorney Fees and Costs.**
5 U.S.C. § 552(a)(4)(E).

1. Attorney fees are within the discretion of the court when a FOIA plaintiff "substantially prevails." *Education/Instruction Inc. v. Dep't of Housing & Urban Development*, 649 F.2d 4 (1st Cir. 1981).

2. The test to determine whether a plaintiff "substantially prevailed" involves showing that prosecution of action was needed and that the action had causative effect on delivery of the information. *Weisberg v. Dep't of Justice*, 848 F.2d 1265 (D.C. Cir. 1988).

3. Requesters seeking information for commercial gain should be allowed attorney fees only where there is a clear and positive benefit to the public or where the agency withheld information without any reasonable basis in the law. *Aviation Data Serv. v. FAA*, 687 F.2d 1319 (10th Cir. 1982).

4. Generally no attorneys fees for *pro se* litigants. *Carter v. Veterans Admin.*, 780 F.2d 1479 (9th Cir. 1986).

# SAMPLE LETTER TO CONTRACTOR WHEN FOIA REQUEST RECEIVED FOR ITS INFORMATION

The Army has received a request under the Freedom of Information Act (FOIA) for Contract #_____ for the (*on site maintenance of Government owned ADPE Equipment*). Our review of the contract reveals that certain contract data supplied by _____ may fall within exemption 4 to the FOIA.

Under this exemption the Army may refuse to disclose trade secrets and commercial or financial information obtained from a source outside the Government and which is privileged or confidential. Commercial or financial information is considered confidential if its disclosure is likely to cause substantial competitive harm to the source of the information.

In order for us to make a determination regarding the release of the contract under consideration the Army must have a detailed justification of the reasons your firm believes the information requested should not be released under Exemption 4 of the FOIA. We believe that you are in a good position to explain the commercial sensitivity of the information contained in the contract which relates to the (*confidential or privileged information*) from your proposal.

In this regard please provide this office with a specific description concerning how disclosure of (*confidential or privileged information*) or related information in the contract would cause substantial harm to _____'s present or future competitive position. Some factors you may wish to describe are: the general custom or usage in your business regarding this type of information, the number and position of persons who have, or have had, access to the information, the type and degrees of commercial injury that disclosure would cause and the length of time you feel confidential treatment is warranted. Due to the response time limits imposed on the government in these cases we request that you provide your response by _____. If we have not heard from you by that date we will assume that your firm has no objection to disclosure of the contract in its entirety.

We will carefully consider the justification you provide us and will endeavor to protect your proprietary data to the extent permitted under law. Should we disagree with your position regarding some or all of the information requested, and determine it to be releasable, we will provide you with advance notice of our decision so that you may take whatever steps you consider appropriate to protect your interests.

## CHAPTER ELEVEN

# Socioeconomic Policies

## I. INTRODUCTION.

Following this block of instruction, the student will:

A. Understand the procurement policies and procedures which the government uses to support small businesses.

B. Understand the programs established by Congress and DOD to support small disadvantaged businesses.

C. Understand the procedures used to implement the government's preference for domestic products.

## II. POLICY AND PROCEDURE IN SUPPORT OF SMALL BUSINESS.

### A. Policy.

15 U.S.C. §§ 631-650; FAR 19.201.

1. Place a fair proportion of acquisitions with small business concerns.

2. Promote maximum subcontracting opportunity for small businesses.

3. Small business defined. FAR 19.001.
   a. Independently owned and operated;
   b. Not dominant in field; and,
   c. Meets applicable size standards.

4. The Small Business Act applies to all federal agencies, as defined by 5 U.S.C. § 551(1), wherever located. *Discount Mach. & Equip., Inc.*, B-240525, Nov. 23, 1990, 70 Comp. Gen. 108, 90-2 CPD ¶ 420.

### B. Size Determination Procedures.

1. The Small Business Administration (SBA) establishes size standards which are based either on the number of employees or gross receipts. The SBA matches a size standard with a supply, service, or construction classification.

2. The contracting officer adopts an appropriate product or service classification called a Standard Industrial Classification (SIC) code and includes this in the solicitation. FAR 19.102; FAR 52.219-22. *See* page 160.
   a. This classification establishes the applicable size standard for the acquisition. For a supply contract, the size standard for an offeror that does not manufacture a product is 500 employees.
   b. Contractors may appeal the contracting officer's SIC code selection to the SBA. On appeal, the SBA has exclusive authority to determine the proper code for the acquisition. 13 C.F.R. § 121.902.
   c. The contracting officer need not delay bid opening or contract award pending a SIC code appeal. *See Seair Transport Servs., Inc.*, B-249555, Dec. 4, 1992, 92-2 CPD ¶ 390; *Aleman Food Serv., Inc.*, B-216803, Mar. 6, 1985, 85-1 CPD ¶ 277. If the SBA finds the original SIC code improper, the contracting officer must amend the solicitation only if he receives the SBA determination before the date offers are due. *See* FAR 19.303(c)(3).
   d. The GAO and the GSBCA do not review "classification" protests. *Tri-Way Sec. & Escort Serv., Inc.*, B-238115.2, Apr. 10, 1990, 90-1 CPD ¶ 380; *JC Computer Servs., Inc. v. Nuclear Regulatory Comm'n*, GSBCA No. 12731-P, 94-2 BCA ¶ 26,712.

3. Small business certification. FAR 19.301.
   a. Self-certification. To be eligible for award

as a small business, an offeror must certify that it is a small business at the time of the certification. *United Power Corp.*, B-239330, May 22, 1990, 69 Comp. Gen. 477, 90-1 CPD ¶ 494 (offeror must exercise high degree of care when certifying).

b. SBA certification. *Olympus Corp.*, B-225875, Apr. 14, 1987, 87-1 CPD ¶ 407.

c. If an acquisition is set-aside for small business, failure to certify status does not render the bid nonresponsive. *Last Camp Timber*, B-238250, May 10, 1990, 90-1 CPD ¶ 461; *Concorde Battery Corp.*, B-235119, June 30, 1989, 68 Comp. Gen. 524, 89-2 CPD ¶ 17.

d. The contracting officer generally may accept self-certification at face value. 13 C.F.R. § 121.1005(b). However, the government may not award a contract to a bidder that it knows has been declared "other than small" by the SBA at the time of bid opening. *Timothy S. Graves*, B-253813, Oct. 22, 1993, 93-2 CPD ¶ 244, *aff'd on recon.*, B-253813.2, Jan. 18, 1994, 94-1 CPD ¶ 19.

e. Neither the FAR, nor the SBA regulations require a firm to recertify size status before an agency exercises an option where the agency awarded the original contract on a set-aside basis. *See Vantex Serv. Corp.*, B-251102, Mar. 10, 1993, 93-1 CPD ¶ 221.

f. If a contractor misrepresents its status as a small business intentionally, the contract is void or voidable. *C&D Constr., Inc.*, ASBCA No. 38661, 90-3 BCA ¶ 23,256; *J.E.T.S., Inc.*, ASBCA No. 28642, 87-1 BCA ¶ 19,569, *aff'd, J.E.T.S., Inc. v. United States*, 838 F.2d 1196 (Fed. Cir. 1988). *Cf. Danac, Inc.*, ASBCA No. 30227, 92-1 BCA ¶ 24,519 (guilty plea to conspiracy to misrepresent size status is not clear and convincing evidence of a fraudulent act).

4. Size status protests. FAR 19.302.

a. An offeror, a contracting officer, or the SBA may challenge a small business certification. A protest is "timely" if received by the contracting officer within 5 business days after bid opening *or* after the protestor receives notice of the proposed awardee's identity in negotiated actions. A contracting officer's protest is always timely. 13 C.F.R. § 121.1603. *Eagle Design and Mgmt., Inc.*, B-239833, Sept. 28, 1990, 90-2 CPD ¶ 259; *United Power Corp.*, B-239330, May 22, 1990, 69 Comp. Gen. 476, 90-1 CPD ¶ 494.

(1) The contracting officer must forward the protest to the SBA Regional Office and withhold award absent a finding of urgency. FAR 19.302(h)(1). *Aquasis Servs., Inc.*, B-240841.2, June 24, 1991, 91-1 CPD ¶ 592 (urgency determination reasonable); *United Power Corp., supra* (need to award before funding freeze was not sufficient urgency).

(2) The Regional Office must rule within 10 business days or the contracting officer may proceed with award. *Cf. International Ordnance, Inc.*, B-240224, July 17, 1990, 90-2 CPD ¶ 32.

(3) Regional Office decisions are appealable to the Office of Hearings and Appeals. If, however, an activity awards to a firm that the Regional Office initially finds is "small," the activity need not terminate the contract if the SBA reverses the determination. *Verify, Inc.*, B-244401.2, Jan. 24, 1992, 71 Comp. Gen. 158, 92-1 CPD ¶ 107. *See also McCaffery & Whitener, Inc.*, B-250843, Feb. 23, 1993, 93-1 CPD ¶ 168.

b. In negotiated small business set-asides, the agency must inform each unsuccessful offeror prior to award of the name and location of the apparent successful offeror. FAR 15.1001(b)(2); *Phillips Nat'l, Inc.*, B-253875, Nov. 1, 1993, 93-2 CPD ¶ 252 (protester not prejudiced by agency's failure to give pre-award notice where SBA ultimately denies challenge to awardee's size status).

c. Post-award protests generally have no

applicability to the current contract. FAR 19.302(j). *But see* 13 CFR § 121.1603(a)(2) (stating that timely filed protests apply to procurement in question even after award); *Diagnostic Imaging Technical Educ. Ctr., Inc.*, B-257590, Oct. 21, 1994, 74 Comp. Gen. ____, 94-2 CPD ¶ 148 (on small business set-asides, contract award to other than small business should be terminated if possible).

d. The GAO does not review size protests. *McCaffery & Whitener, Inc.*, *supra*; *Correa Enters., Inc.—Recon.*, B-241912.2, July 9, 1991, 91-2 CPD ¶ 35.

e. Courts will not overrule an SBA determination unless it is arbitrary, capricious, an abuse of discretion, or not in accordance with law or regulation. *STELLACOM, Inc, v. United States*, 24 Cl. Ct. 213 (1991).

## C. Responsibility Determinations and Certificates of Competency (COCs).

Federal Acquisition Streamlining Act of 1994, Pub. L. No. 103-355, § 7101, 108 Stat. 3243, 3367 [hereinafter FASA] (repealing § 804, National Defense Authorization Act, 1993, Pub. L. No. 102-484, 106 Stat. 2315, 2447 (1992); FAR Subpart 19.6.

1. The contracting officer must determine an offeror's responsibility. FAR 9.103(b).

2. **OLD RULE for DOD, Coast Guard, and NASA:** if the contracting officer finds a small business nonresponsible, he must notify the firm of its right to request a COC from the SBA. If the firm desires to seek a COC, it must respond to the contracting officer within 14 days. If the contracting officer receives timely notice that the firm intends to seek a COC, the contracting officer must forward the nonresponsibility determination to the SBA. National Defense Authorization Act, 1993, Pub. L. No. 102-484, § 804, 106 Stat. 2315, 2447 (1992); DFARS 219.602-1; 252.219-7009.

3. **NEW RULE for DOD, Coast Guard, NASA, and all other agencies:** if the contracting officer finds a small business nonresponsible,

he must forward the matter to the SBA Regional Office immediately. FASA § 7101; FAR 19.602-1(a)(2).

4. The SBA issues a COC if it finds that the offeror is responsible.

a. The burden is on the offeror to apply for a COC. *Thomas & Sons Bldg. Contr., Inc.*, B-252970.2, June 22, 1993, 93-1 CPD ¶ 482 (COC applicant, not agency, has responsibility to submit rebuttal information concerning its past performance to the SBA).

b. The contracting officer may appeal a decision to issue a COC to the SBA Central Office. FAR 19.602-3.

5. The contracting officer shall award to another offeror if the SBA does not issue a COC within 15 business days of receiving a referral. FAR 19.602-4(c); *Mid-America Eng'g and Mfg.*, B-247146, Apr. 30, 1992, 92-1 CPD ¶ 414. *Cf. Saco Defense, Inc.*, B-240603, Dec. 6, 1990, 90-2 CPD ¶ 462.

6. Once issued, a COC is conclusive as to all elements of responsibility. GAO review of the COC process is limited to determining whether government officials acted in bad faith or failed to consider vital information. *UAV Sys., Inc.*, B-255281, Feb. 17, 1994, 94-1 CPD ¶ 121 (contracting officer's discussions with SBA do not constitute bad faith); *J&J Maint., Inc.*, B-251355.2, May 7, 1993, 93-1 CPD ¶ 373 (protester must make *prima facie* showing that government acted fraudulently, in bad faith, or willfully disregarded vital information). *Accord Accurate Info. Sys., Inc. v. Dep't of the Treasury*, GSBCA No. 12978-P, Sept. 30, 1994, 1994 BPD ¶ 203, *mot. for recon. denied*, 1994 BPD ¶ 236. *But see Pittman Mech. Contractors, Inc. — Recon.*, B-242242.2, May 31, 1991, 70 Comp. Gen. 535, 91-1 CPD ¶ 525 (GAO will review nonresponsibility determination if SBA refuses to issue COC because offeror was not small business).

7. The COC procedure does not apply when an agency eliminates a small business from a procurement due to a material misrepresentation by the small business. *RMTC Sys., Inc.*

*v. Dep't of the Air Force*, GSBCA No. 12346-P-R, 1993 BPD ¶ 169 ("relevant legal issue was neither the offeror's responsibility nor its integrity, but whether the integrity of the bidding process has been compromised.").

8. The COC procedure does not apply when an agency declines to exercise an option because it finds the incumbent nonresponsible. *DOD Contracts, Inc.*, B-250603.2, Mar. 3, 1993, 93-1 CPD ¶ 195 (agency awarded new contract on urgent basis to another contractor).

9. The COC procedure generally does not apply when the contracting officer rejects a technically unacceptable offer. *See Paragon Dynamics, Inc.*, B-251280, Mar. 19, 1993, 93-1 CPD ¶ 248; *Pais Janitorial Serv. & Supplies, Inc.*, B-244157, June 18, 1991, 91-1 CPD ¶ 581. *Cf.* FAR 37.108 (where the government requires highest competence obtainable and proposals are evaluated on technical/management bases, COC process may not apply). *But see Clegg Indus., Inc.*, B-242204.3, Aug. 14, 1991, 70 Comp. Gen. 680, 91-2 CPD ¶ 145 (if agency evaluates responsibility-type factors on "go-no go" basis, it must refer decision to reject small business to SBA); *Envirosol, Inc.*, B-254223, Dec. 2, 1993, 93-2 CPD ¶ 295 (agency's determination that offeror's price is too low concerns the offeror's responsibility — referral to SBA required).

10. The COC procedure applies to service contracts when an agency determines that a small business contractor fails to meet criteria in a prequalification program which relate to the contractor's capability to perform the contract. *Stevens Tech. Serv., Inc.*, B-250515.2, May 17, 1993, 93-1 CPD ¶ 385 (GAO distinguishes contracts for products/supplies— a contracting officer would not be required to refer to SBA a *product's* failure to meet qualification criteria).

## D. Regular Small Business Set-Asides.
FAR Subpart 19.5.

1. The decision to set aside a procurement is within the "discretion" of the agency. FAR 19.501. *Espey Mfg. & Elecs. Corp.*, B-254738.3, Mar. 8, 1994, 94-1 CPD ¶ 180 (contracting officer not required to amend or cancel unrestricted solicitation upon learning of interested small businesses); *State Mgmt. Serv., Inc.*, B-251715, May 3, 1993, 93-1 CPD ¶ 355 (contracting officer made reasonable determination that there was insufficient small business interest, even though more than two small businesses were on bidder's mailing list).

2. The agency must exercise its discretion reasonably and in accordance with statutory and regulatory requirements. *DCT Inc.*, B-252479, July 1, 1993, 93-2 CPD ¶ 1 (agency failed to adequately review potential small business market); *Neal R. Gross & Co.*, B-240924.2, Jan. 17, 1991, 91-1 CPD ¶ 53 (determination not to set aside was abuse of discretion).

3. Types of set-asides.

   a. Total. The entire amount of the acquisition is set aside for exclusive small business participation. FAR 19.502-2. A total set-aside is required when:

      (1) The contracting officer reasonably expects to receive offers from two or more responsible small businesses, and

      (2) Award will be made at a fair market price. *Priscidon Enter., Inc.*, B-238370, Mar. 30, 1990, 90-1 CPD ¶ 345.

   b. Partial. FAR 52.219-6; DFARS 252.219-7001. The contracting officer must set aside a *portion* of an acquisition, except for construction, for exclusive small business participation when:

      (1) A total set-aside is not appropriate;

      (2) The requirement is severable into two or more economic production runs or reasonable lots;

      (3) One or more small business concerns are expected to have the technical competence and capacity to satisfy the requirement at a fair market price; and,

      (4) The acquisition is not subject to small purchase procedures.

——Unless authorized by the head of the contracting activity (HCA), the contracting officer shall not award a partial set-aside if there is a reasonable expectation that only two concerns (one large and one small) will respond with offers.

c. Small business reservation. FASA § 4004 (amending 15 U.S.C. § 644(j)); FAR 13.105.

(1) An activity must set aside for small business concerns any acquisition of supplies or services that has an anticipated value greater than $2,500 but not greater than $100,000.

(2) Exceptions. There is no requirement to set aside if: (i) there is no reasonable expectation of receiving offers from two or more responsible small businesses that will be competitive in terms of market price, quality, and delivery; (ii) purchase will be outside the U.S.; or (iii) the agency is required to make purchases from required sources of supply.

(3) If the contracting officer determines that there are two or more emerging small businesses (ESBs) capable of competing for award, the contracting officer must set aside the acquisition for exclusive ESB competition. FAR 19.1006(c). An ESB is a firm whose size does not exceed 50% of the applicable size standard. FAR 19.1006(c); FAR 19.1002.

4. Contractor Limitations. If the agency sets aside an acquisition, certain subcontracting and domestic end item limitations apply. FAR 52.219-6; FAR 52.219-14; *Kaysam Worldwide, Inc.*, B-247743, June 8, 1992, 92-1 CPD ¶ 500, *Vanderbilt Shirt Co.*, B-237632, Feb. 16, 1990, 69 Comp. Gen. 222, 90-1 CPD ¶ 290.

a. Services. The contractor must spend at least 50% of contract costs on its own employees.

b. Supplies.

(1) A small business manufacturer must perform at least 50% of the cost of manufacturing.

(2) A small business nonmanufacturer (i.e., a dealer) must provide a small business product unless the SBA determines that no small business in the federal market produces the item.

(3) Both manufacturers and nonmanufacturers must provide domestically produced or manufactured items.

c. Construction. The contractor's employees must perform at least 15% of the cost of the contract. If special trade contractors perform construction, the threshold is 25%.

5. Rejecting SBA set-aside recommendations and withdrawal of set-asides. FAR 19.505; DFARS 219.505; DFARS 219.506.

a. The contracting officer may reject an SBA recommendation or withdraw a set-aside before award.

b. The FAR sets forth notice and appeal procedures for resolving disagreements between the agency and the SBA. If the contracting agency and the SBA disagree, the *contracting agency* has the final word on set-aside or withdrawal decisions.

c. Potential offerors also may challenge the contracting officer's decision to issue unrestricted solicitations or withdraw set-asides. *See, e.g., American Imaging Servs.*, B-238969, July 19, 1990, 69 Comp. Gen. 625, 90-2 CPD ¶ 51.

d. If the activity receives no small business offers, the contracting officer may not award to a large business but must withdraw the solicitation and resolicit on an unrestricted basis. *CompuMed*, B-242118, Jan. 8, 1991, 91-1 CPD ¶ 19; *Ideal Serv., Inc.*, B-238927.2, Oct. 26, 1990, 90-2 CPD ¶ 335. *But see* FAR 13.105(d)(3); *Western Filter Corp.*, B-247212, May 11, 1992, 92-1 CPD ¶ 436 (GAO approves award to large business following cancellation of small purchase set-aside).

6. An agency is not required to set aside the reprocurement of a defaulted contract. *Pre-*

*mier Petro-Chemical, Inc.*, B-244324, Aug. 27, 1991, 91-2 CPD ¶ 205.

7. Small Business Competitiveness Demonstration Program (SBCDP). FAR Subpt. 19.10; DFARS Subpt. 219.10.

   a. The SBCDP is designed to test the ability of small businesses to compete successfully in certain industry categories. Generally, set-asides are not required for acquisitions subject to this program.

   b. Designated industry groups (DIGs). As a general rule, for acquisitions involving DIGs, the contracting officer shall not use small business set-asides if the estimated contract value exceeds $25,000. FAR 19.1006(b). This rule does not preclude 8(a) actions or small disadvantaged business (SDB) set-asides. *Sletager, Inc.*, B-241149, Jan. 25, 1991, 91-1 CPD ¶ 74; *Kato Corp.*, B-237965, Apr. 3, 1990, 90-1 CPD ¶ 354 (activity must consider SDB set-aside even though acquisition involves designated industry). The designated industries are:

      (1) Construction;

      (2) Refuse systems and related services;

      (3) Architectural and engineering (A&E) services [A&E services for military projects are exempt from program]; and

      (4) Nonnuclear ship repair.

   c. Emerging small businesses. An emerging small business is a small business whose size is not greater than 50% of the size standard for the acquisition. The contracting officer shall continue to set aside for emerging small businesses, acquisitions in the four designated industry groups with an estimated value equal to or less than the small business reserve amount established by the Office of Federal Procurement Policy [previously $25,000]. FAR 19.1006(b)(2).

   d. Targeted industries. Agency regulations determine what constitutes a targeted industry. The FAR requires that set-asides continue, that acquisitions be tailored to increase small business opportunities in these industries, and that there be increased management attention to such acquisitions. FAR 19.1003(c).

## III. PROGRAMS FOR SMALL DISADVANTAGED BUSINESSES.

### A. Contracting with the SBA under Section 8(a) of the Small Business Act.

15 U.S.C. § 637(a); 13 C.F.R. Part 124; FAR Subpart 19.8; DFARS Subpart 219.8.

1. Section 8(a) authorizes the SBA to enter into contracts with other agencies. The SBA then subcontracts with eligible small disadvantaged businesses.

   a. Either the SBA or the contracting activity may initiate selection of a requirement or a specific contractor for an 8(a) acquisition.

   b. Businesses must meet the criteria set forth in 13 C.F.R. § 124.102 through § 124.109 to be eligible under the 8(a) program.

      (1) The firm must be owned and controlled by socially and economically disadvantaged persons. The regulations require 51% ownership and control by one or more individuals who are <u>both</u> socially *and* economically disadvantaged. *See Software Sys. Assoc. v. Saiki*, No. 92-1776 (D.D.C. June 24, 1993) (woman-owned business not socially disadvantaged).

      (2) The firm must have been in business for two full years in the industry for which it seeks certification.

      (3) The firm must possess the potential for success.

      (4) The firm must have an approved business plan.

   c. Generally, the SBA will not accept an 8(a) reservation if:

      (1) An activity already has issued a solicitation as a small business or SDB set-aside;

      (2) An activity has indicated publicly an intent to issue a solicitation as a small business or SDB set-aside; or

(3) The SBA determines that inclusion of a requirement in the 8(a) program will affect a small business or SDB adversely. 13 C.F.R. § 124.309. *See McNeil Technologies, Inc.*, B-254909, Jan. 25, 1994, 94-1 CPD ¶ 40 (SBA must consider adverse impact even if there are no factors creating a presumption of adverse impact); *State Janitorial Servs.*, B-240646, Dec. 6, 1990, 90-2 CPD ¶ 463 (SBA did not properly consider impact on small business); *American Mutual Protective Bureau*, B-243329.2, June 16, 1994, 94-1 CPD ¶ 371; *cf.* FAR 19.804-2(a)(9); DFARS 219.804-1.

2. Procedures.
   a. If the activity decides that an 8(a) contract is feasible, it offers SBA an opportunity to participate.
   b. If the SBA accepts, the agency or the SBA chooses a contractor, or eligible firms compete for award. In any event, the prime contract is between the SBA and the activity. *See Defense Logistics Agency and Small Bus. Admin. Contract No. DLA100-78-C-5201*, B-225175, Feb. 4, 1987, 87-1 CPD ¶ 115 ("prime contract" existed between the two agencies, but SBA not liable to DLA for reprocurement costs).
   c. Activities must compete acquisitions if:
      (1) The activity expects offers from two eligible responsible 8(a) firms at a fair market price; and
      (2) The value of the contract is expected to exceed $5 million for actions assigned manufacturing SIC codes or $3 million for all other codes. *See* 13 C.F.R. § 124.311(a). The threshold applies to the agency's estimate of the total value of the contract, including all options. *Id.*
   d. The COC procedures do not apply to sole source 8(a) acquisitions. *DAE Corp. v. SBA*, 958 F.2d 436 (1992); *Universal Automation Leasing Corp.*, GSBCA No.

11268-P, 91-3 BCA ¶ 24,255. *See Action Serv. Corp. v. Garrett*, 797 F. Supp. 82 (D.P.R. 1992) (distinguishing *DAE Corp.* as limited to noncompetitive 8(a) acquisitions). The GAO has opined that in a competitive 8(a) acquisition, the agency must refer an action to the SBA if the agency has substantial doubt about a firm's responsibility. This is not under the COC procedures, however. *See Joa Quin Mfg. Corp.*, B-255298, Feb. 23, 1994, 94-1 CPD ¶ 140 (appeal of SBA Regional Office determination to Central Office); *Aviation Sys. & Mfg., Inc.*, B-250625.3, Feb. 18, 1993, 93-1 CPD ¶ 155; *Alamo Contracting Enters.*, B-249265.2, Nov. 20, 1992, 92-2 CPD ¶ 358.

   e. Subcontracting limitations apply to competitive 8(a) acquisitions. *See* FAR 52.219-14; *Data Equip., Inc. v. Dep't of he Air Force*, GSBCA No. 12506-P, 94-1 BCA ¶ 26,446 (Air Force properly withdrew procurement from 8(a) program upon discovering that the required supplies were manufactured only by a large business). *See also Tonya, Inc. v. United States*, 28 Fed. Cl. 727 (1993) (Air Force did not violate Small Business Act by "expecting" that 8(a) contractor would subcontract 49% of the work to a large business); *Jasper Painting Serv., Inc.*, B-251092, Mar. 4, 1993, 93-1 CPD ¶ 204.

   f. Graduation from 8(a) program. Firms graduate from the 8(a) program when they successfully achieve the targets, objectives, and goals set forth in their business plan prior to expiration of the program term. 13 C.F.R. § 124.208. *See Gutierrez-Palmenberg, Inc.*, B-255797.3, 94-2 CPD ¶ 158 (firm remains eligible for award of 8(a) contract if it was a program participant on date specified for receipt of offers).

   g. The GAO will not consider challenges to an award of an 8(a) contract by contractors which are not eligible for the program. *AVW Elec. Sys., Inc.*, B-252399, May

17, 1993, 93-1 CPD ¶ 386. Likewise, the GAO will not consider challenges to an SBA decision that an 8(a) contractor is not competent to perform a contract. *L. Washington & Assocs.*, B-255162, Oct. 19, 1993, 93-2 CPD ¶ 254.

## B. Department of Defense Small Disadvantaged Business Program.
DFARS Subpart 219.5.

1. Background: Congress established an objective for DOD of awarding five percent of its total contract dollars to small disadvantaged business concerns (SDBs). *See* 10 U.S.C. § 2301 note.

2. General. A small disadvantaged business (SDB) is a firm that is at least 51% owned and controlled by one or more individuals who are <u>both</u> socially *and* economically disadvantaged. *See C & S Carpentry Servs.*, B-253615, Oct. 6, 1993, 93-2 CPD ¶ 209 (joint venture did not qualify for SDB set-aside where the SDB would not have control over the management and daily operations of the project). A publicly-owned business also may qualify as a SDB if 51% of its stock is owned by disadvantaged persons, and the management and daily operations are controlled by disadvantaged persons.

   a. The majority of earnings must accrue directly to one or more disadvantaged individuals.

   b. Individuals who certify that they are Black American, Hispanic American, Native American, Asian-Pacific American, or Subcontinent-Asian American are presumed to be socially and economically disadvantaged. 13 C.F.R. § 124.105(b).

   c. The contracting officer shall question the SDB status of any apparent successful offeror whose ownership is based on any categories other than those in b., above. DFARS 219.301(b)(iii).

   d. The SBA will determine a firm's status if status is challenged. DFARS 219.302-70. *Jimenez, Inc.*, B-242663, May 6, 1991, 91-1 CPD ¶ 441.

   e. A firm must be small and disadvantaged at the time of submission of the offer. DFARS 219.301(a)(1). *See also ANDRULIS Research Corp.*, B-253366, Sept. 7, 1993, 93-2 CPD ¶ 156 (previous rule—offeror had to qualify as SDB at time of offer and at the time of award). *Cf.* FAR 19.301(a) (to be eligible for award as a small business, offeror must represent in good faith that it is a small business at the time of certification).

3. Total SDB set-aside. DFARS 219.502-2-70.

   a. The entire amount of an individual acquisition or class of acquisitions is set-aside for exclusive SDB participation. *See Abbott Prods., Inc.*, B-231131, Aug. 8, 1988, 88-2 CPD ¶ 119 (discussion of the SDB set-aside program).

   b. The contracting officer shall initiate a total set-aside if:

   (1) The contracting officer reasonably expects to receive offers from two or more responsible SDBs, *Ryon, Inc.*, B-256752.2, Oct. 27, 1994, 94-2 CPD ¶ 163; *JT Constr. Co.*, B-254257, Dec. 6, 1993, 93-2 CPD ¶ 302;

   (2) The SDBs can meet subcontracting/regular dealer limitations;

   (3) Scientific and/or technological talent consistent with the demands of the acquisition will be offered; and

   (4) The contract price will not exceed the fair market price by more than 10%. *Holmes & Narver Constr. Servs., Inc.* B-252321.2, Aug. 9, 1993, 93-2 CPD ¶ 87 (contracting officer had sufficient information to expect offers from SDBs would not exceed FMP plus 10%); *Godot Enters.*, B-255200, Feb. 16, 1994, 94-1 CPD ¶ 116 (withdrawal of set-aside proper because 10% ceiling exceeded). *Blue Dot Energy Co.*, B-253390, Sep. 27, 1993, 93-2 CPD ¶ 145; *Irvin Tech., Inc.*, GSBCA No. 11581-P, 92-1 BCA ¶ 24,674.

   c. *Exceptions.* Activities *shall not* conduct total SDB set-asides under the following circumstances:

(1) The contracting office has acquired the product or service previously on the basis of a *regular* small business set-aside (unless the SBCDP applies); *W.H. Smith Hardware Co.*, B-250028, Dec. 30, 1992, 92-2 CPD ¶ 454;

(2) The acquisition is for construction, maintenance, or repair under $2 million (unless the SBCDP applies);

(3) The acquisition is for architectural and engineering services or design for military construction projects;

(4) The activity has reserved the acquisition for the 8(a) program; or

(5) The activity conducts the acquisition using simplified acquisition procedures.

4. Evaluation preference for SDBs. DFARS Subpart 219.70.

a. In unrestricted acquisitions, the contracting officer increases non-SDB offers by 10% for evaluation purposes. *Hudson Bay Natural Gas Corp.*, B-237264, Feb. 5, 1990, 69 Comp. Gen. 233, 90-1 CPD ¶ 151. *See Commercial Energies, Inc. v. United States*, 20 Cl. Ct. 140 (1990).

b. The contracting officer, however, shall *not* apply an evaluation preference if:

(1) Simplified acquisition procedures are used;

(2) An acquisition is set aside for total small business or SDB participation, *see Victoria Inn Ltd.; Beige Plane, Ltd.*, B-256724.2, July 21, 1994, 94-2 CPD ¶ 37;

(3) A purchase is for commissary/exchange resale items;

(4) The Small Business Competitiveness Demonstration Program applies; or

(5) An otherwise successful offeror provides either an eligible product under the Trade Agreements Act or a qualifying country end item.

c. The DFARS does not require application of an evaluation preference where award is based on other than price and price-related factors. *Signal Corp.*, B-245376, Sept.

10, 1991, 91-2 CPD ¶ 238. Application of the preference is, however, discretionary. *See* DFARS 219.7001(a); *General Elec. Gov't Servs.*, B-245797.3, Sept. 23, 1992, 92-2 CPD ¶ 196.

d. The preference does not apply to line items funded by civilian agencies. *Commercial Energies, Inc.*, B-243402, July 30, 1991, 91-2 CPD ¶ 102.

e. To be entitled to a preference, an SDB must agree to adhere to certain limitations. *See* DFARS 252.219-7006.

(1) Subcontracting limitations. *Sonicraft, Inc. v. Defense Info. Sys. Agency*, GSBCA No. 11750-P, 93-1 BCA ¶ 25,282.

(2) Nonmanufacturer limitations. *S&W Assocs. Int'l, Inc. v. Dep't of the Navy*, GSBCA No. 12118-P, 1992 BPD ¶ 412; *Baszile Metals Serv. Inc.*, B-237925, Apr. 10, 1990, 90-1 CPD ¶ 378.

f. The contracting officer may not apply this preference if the solicitation does not include the evaluation preference provision. *See American Imaging Servs., Inc.—Recon.*, B-250861.2, Jan. 5, 1993, 93-1 CPD ¶ 13.

5. Partial small business set-aside with preferential consideration for small disadvantaged businesses. DFARS 219.502-3; DFARS 252.219-7001.

a. The contracting officer reserves a portion of an acquisition for small business, and SDBs receive preferential consideration over non-SDBs.

b. The award price of the set-aside portion of the contract may not exceed the fair market price by more than 10%.

6. Set-aside order of precedence (DOD). DFARS 219.504. Defense contracting officers must adhere to the following order of precedence:

a. Total small disadvantaged business (SDB) set-aside;

b. Total set-aside for regular small businesses; and

c. Partial set-aside for small business firms with preferential consideration for SDBs.

## C. Small Disadvantaged Business Program for Civilian Agencies.

1. FASA § 7102 authorizes civilian agencies to enter contracts using SDB set-asides, and to evaluate SDB offers using a 10% evaluation preference.

2. The FAR council has proposed revisions to the FAR to implement this new program. *See* 60 Fed. Reg. 2302, 2306-12 (1995) (amending FAR Subpt. 19.5). Under the proposed rules, the set-aside order of precedence for civilian agencies will be:

   a. Total SDB set-aside.

   b. Total set-aside for small business concerns.

   c. Partial set-aside for small business concerns.

## IV. SUBCONTRACTING OPPORTUNITIES FOR SMALL BUSINESSES.

15 U.S.C. § 637(c); FAR Subpart 19.7; DFARS Subpart 219.7.

### A. Requirements.

1. Any large business that obtains a contract in excess of the simplified acquisition threshold must agree to subcontract with small businesses, small disadvantaged businesses, and women-owned small businesses to the maximum extent practicable.

2. In acquisitions expected to exceed $500,000 ($1 million for construction), large businesses must submit detailed small business subcontracting plans.

3. Contracting officers *may* include incentive clauses in negotiated acquisitions to encourage contractors to exceed their subcontracting goals. FAR 19.705-1; FAR 52.219-10.

### B. The DOD Approach.

1. Generally, an incentive clause is *required* in negotiated acquisitions for which subcontracting plans are required. DFARS 219.708(c)(1)(A); DFARS 252.219-7005.

2. For negotiated procurements of $10 million or more, the contracting officer may use an award fee provision in lieu of the incentive clause. DFARS 219.708(c)(2).

3. For major system, research and development, and other complex acquisitions, the extent to which offerors identify and commit to the use of SDBs shall be a source selection evaluation factor. DFARS 219.705-2(d); 215.605(b).

4. Comprehensive small business subcontracting plans are permitted in limited cases. DFARS 219.702.

### C. Administration of the Subcontracting Program.

1. The contracting officer monitors contractor compliance with the subcontracting plan.

2. If a contractor fails to make a good faith effort to meet its goals, the contractor is in breach of contract, and the contracting officer may assess liquidated damages against it. 15 U.S.C. § 637(c) (4)(F) and § 637(c)(8); FAR 19.702(c); FAR 19.705-7(a).

3. Under DOD comprehensive subcontracting plans, contractors are not subject to liquidated damages. DFARS 219.702.

## V. THE BUY AMERICAN ACT (BAA).

### A. Origin and Purpose.

41 U.S.C. § 10a-10d; Executive Order 10582 (1954), as amended, Executive Order 11051 (1962).

### B. Preference for Domestic Products/Services.

1. As a general rule, under the BAA, agencies may acquire only domestic end items. Unless another law or regulation strictly prohibits the purchase of foreign end items, however, the contracting officer may not reject as non-responsive an offer of such items.

2. The prohibition against the purchase of foreign goods does not apply if: the product is not available in sufficient commercial quantities; domestic preference would be inconsistent with the public interest; the product is for use outside the United States; the cost of the domestic product would be unreason-

able; or the product is for commissary resale. The Trade Agreements Act and the North American Free Trade Agreement may also provide exceptions to the Buy American Act.

**C. Definitions and Applicability.**

FAR 25.101.

1. *Manufactured domestic end products* are those articles, materials, and supplies acquired for public use under the contract that are:

   a. Manufactured in the United States. *General Kinetics, Inc, Cryptek Div.*, 242052.2, May 7, 1991, 70 Comp. Gen. 473, 91-2 CPD ¶ 445 ("manufacture" means completion of the article in the form required for use by the government); *A. Hirsh, Inc.*, B-237466, Feb. 28, 1990, 69 Comp. Gen. 307, 90-1 CPD ¶ 247 (manufacturing occurs when material undergoes a substantial change); *Valentec Wells, Inc.*, ASBCA No. 41659, 91-3 BCA ¶ 24,168; *Ballantine Labs., Inc.*, ASBCA No. 35138, 88-2 BCA ¶ 20,660; and

   b. Comprised of "substantially all" domestic components (over 50% test by cost). [For DOD, the components may be domestic or *qualifying country* components. *See* DFARS 252.225-7001; para. V.C.5, *infra*.]

2. An *unmanufactured* domestic end product must be mined or produced in the United States. Geography determines the origin of an unmanufactured end product.

3. The nationality of the company that manufactures an end item is irrelevant. *Military Optic, Inc.*, B-245010.3, Jan. 16, 1992, 92-1 CPD ¶ 78.

4. *Components* are materials and supplies incorporated directly into the end product. *Orlite Eng'g Co.*, B-229615, Mar. 23, 1988, 88-1 CPD ¶ 300; *Yohar Supply Co.*, B-225480, Feb. 11, 1987, 66 Comp. Gen. 251, 87-1 CPD ¶ 152.

   a. Parts are not components, and their origin is not considered in this evaluation. *Hamilton Watch Co.*, B-179939, June 6, 1974, 74-1 CPD ¶ 306 (watch component is domestic even though all of its parts are foreign).

   b. A component is either entirely foreign or entirely domestic. A component is domestic only if it is manufactured in the United States. *Computer Hut Int'l, Inc.*, B-249421, Nov. 23, 1992, 92-2 CPD ¶ 364.

   c. A foreign-made component may become domestic if it undergoes substantial remanufacturing in the United States. *General Kinetics, Inc, Cryptek Div.*, B-242052.2, May 7, 1991, 70 Comp. Gen. 473, 91-2 CPD ¶ 445.

   d. *Material* that undergoes manufacturing is not a "component" if the material is so transformed that it loses its original identity. *See Orlite Eng'g* and *Yohar Supply Co.*, *supra.*

5. Qualifying country end products/components. *See* DFARS 225.872.

   a. DOD does not apply the restrictions of the BAA when acquiring equipment or supplies which are mined, produced, or manufactured in "qualifying countries." Qualifying countries are countries with which we have reciprocal defense agreements. They are enumerated in DFARS 225.872-1(a).

   b. A manufactured, qualifying country end product must contain over 50 percent (by cost) components mined, produced, or manufactured in the qualifying country or the United States. DFARS 252.225-7001(a)(7).

   c. Qualifying country items thus receive a "double benefit" under the BAA. First, qualifying country components may be incorporated into a product manufactured in the United States to become a *domestic end product* (see para. V.C.1.(b), *supra*). Second, products manufactured by a qualifying country are exempt from the BAA.

**D. Certification Requirement.**

1. A contractor certifies by its offer that each end product is domestic and/or indicates which end products are foreign. FAR 52.225-1; DFARS 252.225-7005.

2. The contracting officer may rely on the offeror's certification that its product is domestic, unless, prior to award, the contracting officer has reason to question the certification. *New York Elevator Co.*, B-250992, Mar. 3, 1993, 93-1 CPD ¶ 196 (construction materials); *Barcode Indus.*, B-240173. Oct. 16, 1990, 90-2 CPD ¶ 299; *American Instr. Corp.*, B-239997, Oct. 12, 1990, 90-2 CPD ¶ 287. *But see Rocky Mountain Trading Co.*, GSBCA No. 10894-P, 91-1 BCA ¶ 23,619 (board will review de novo all timely challenges to BAA evaluations).

### E. Exceptions to the Buy American Act.

As a general rule, the Buy American Act does not apply in the following situations:

1. The required products are not available in sufficient commercial quantities. *Midwest Dynamometer & Eng'g Co.*, B-252168, May 24, 1993, 93-1 CPD ¶ 408; FAR 25.108; DFARS 225.108.

2. An international agreement permits purchase from a certain country. DFARS 225.103; DFARS Subpart 225.8; *Technical Sys. Inc.*, B-225143, Mar. 3, 1987, 66 Comp. Gen. 297, 87-1 CPD ¶ 240.

3. The Trade Agreements Act (TAA) authorizes the purchase. 19 U.S.C. §§ 2501-82; FAR 25.400; *Olympic Container Corp.*, B-250403, Jan. 29, 1993, 93-1 CPD ¶ 89; *Becton Dickinson AcuteCare*, B-238942, July 20, 1990, 90-2 CPD ¶ 55; *IBM Corp.*, GSBCA No. 10532-P, 90-2 BCA ¶ 22,824.

   a. Under the TAA, only domestic products, products from designated foreign countries, qualifying country products, and products which, though comprised of over 50% foreign components, are "substantially transformed" in the United States or a designated country, are eligible for award. *See Compuadd Corp. v. Dep't of the Air Force*, GSBCA No. 12021-P, 93-2 BCA ¶ 25,811 ("manufacturing" standard of the BAA is less stringent than "substantial transformation" required under TAA); *Hung Myung (USA) Ltd.*, B-244686, Nov.

7, 1991, 71 Comp. Gen. 64, 91-2 CPD ¶ 434; *TLT-Babcock, Inc.*, B-244423, Sept. 13, 1991, 91-2 CPD ¶ 242.

   b. The TAA applies if the estimated cost of an acquisition equals or exceeds a threshold (currently $182,000) set by the U.S. Trade Representative.

   c. The TAA does not apply to DOD unless the DFARS lists the product, even if the threshold is met. *See* DFARS 225.403-70.

   d. Because of the component test, the definition of "domestic end product" under the BAA is more restrictive than the definition of "U.S. made end product" under the TAA. Thus, for DOD, if an offeror submits a U.S. made end product, the BAA evaluation factor still may apply. *See* DFARS 225.105(5); DFARS tbl. 25-1; para. V.E.7 *infra*.

4. The North American Free Trade Agreement (NAFTA) Implementation Act authorizes the purchase. Pub. L. No. 103-182, 107 Stat. 2057 (1993); FAR 25.402. Note, however, that NAFTA does not apply to DOD procurements unless the DFARS lists the product. *See* DFARS 225.403-70.

5. The Caribbean Basin Economic Recovery Act authorizes foreign purchases. 19 U.S.C. §§ 2701-05; FAR 25.401.

6. The product is for use outside the United States. FAR 25.102(a)(1). *Note:* Under the Balance of Payments Program, an agency must buy *domestic* even if the end item is to be used overseas. A number of exceptions allow purchase of foreign products under this program. If both domestic and foreign products are offered, and if the low domestic price exceeds the low foreign price by more than 50%, the contracting officer must buy the foreign item. FAR Subpart 25.3; DFARS Subpart 225.3.

7. The cost of the domestic product is unreasonable. FAR 25.102(a)(2); FAR 25.105; DFARS 225.102. Although cost reasonableness normally is a preaward determination, an agency may also make this determination after award. *John C. Grimberg Co. v. United States*, 869 F.2d 1475 (Fed. Cir. 1989).

a. Civilian agencies.

(1) If an offer of a non-domestic product is low and a large business offers the lowest-priced, domestic product, increase the non-domestic product by 6%.

(2) If an offer of a non-domestic product is low and a small business offers the lowest-priced, domestic product, increase the non-domestic product by 12%.

b. DOD agencies increase offers of non-domestic, non-qualifying country products by 50%, regardless of the size of the business that offers the lowest-priced, domestic end product. Under the DFARS, if application of the differential does not result in award on a domestic product, disregard the differential and evaluate offers at face value. DFARS 225.105(2).

c. In a negotiated procurement, agencies may award to a firm offering a technically superior but higher priced non-domestic, non-qualifying country product. *STD Research Corp.*, B-252073.2, May 24, 1993, 93-1 CPD ¶ 406.

## F. Construction Materials.

41 U.S.C. § 10b; FAR Subpart 25.2.

1. This portion of the BAA applies to contracts for the construction, alteration, or repair of any public building or public work in the United States.

2. The Act requires construction contractors to use only domestic materials in the United States.

3. *Exceptions*. This restriction does not apply if:

a. The cost would be unreasonable, as determined by the head of agency;

b. The agency head determines that use of a particular domestic construction material would be impracticable; or,

c. The material is not available in sufficient commercial quantities. FAR 25.108.

4. Application of the restriction. The restriction applies to the material in the form that the contractor brings it to the construction site.

FAR 25.201. *See Mauldin-Dorfmeier Constr., Inc.*, ASBCA No. 43633, 93-2 BCA ¶ 25,790 (board distinguishes "components" from "construction materials"). *S.J. Amoroso Constr. Co. v. United States*, 26 Cl. Ct. 759 (1992), *aff'd*, 12 F.3d 1072 (Fed. Cir. 1993); *Mid-American Elevator Co.*, B-237282, Jan. 29, 1990, 69 Comp. Gen. 211, 90-1 CPD ¶ 125.

5. Post-Award exceptions.

a. Contractors must formally request waiver of the BAA. *C. Sanchez & Son v. United States*, 6 F.3d 1539 (Fed. Cir. 1993) (contractor failed to formally request waiver of BAA; claim for equitable adjustment for supplying domestic wire denied);

b. Failure to grant a request for waiver may be an abuse of discretion. *John C. Grimberg Co. v. United States*, 869 F.2d 1475 (Fed. Cir. 1989) (contracting officer abused discretion by denying post-award request for waiver of BAA, where price of domestic materials exceeded price of foreign materials plus differential).

6. The DOD qualifying country source provisions do not apply to construction materials. DFARS 225.872-2(b).

## G. Remedies for Buy American Act Violations.

1. If the agency head finds a violation of the Buy American Act—Construction Materials, the findings and the name of the contractor are made public. The contractor will be debarred for three years. FAR 25.204.

2. Termination for default is proper if the contractor's product does not contain over 50% (by cost) domestic or qualifying country components. *H&R Machinists Co.*, ASBCA No. 38440, 91-1 BCA ¶ 23,373.

3. A contractor is not entitled to an equitable adjustment for providing domestic end items if required by the BAA. *Valentec Wells, Inc.*, ASBCA No. 41659, 91-3 BCA ¶ 24,168; *LaCoste Builders, Inc.*, ASBCA No. 29884, 88-1 BCA ¶ 20,360; *C. Sanchez & Son v. United States*, *supra*.

| SIC | DESCRIPTION | SIZE |
|---|---|---|

## DIVISION A—AGRICULTURE

### Major Group 01–Agricultural Production-Crops

| 0111- | | |
|---|---|---|
| 0191 | Agricultural Production-Crops | $0.5 |

### Major Group 02–Agricultural Production-Livestock

| 0211 | Beef Cattle Feedlots (Custom) | $1.0 |
|---|---|---|
| 0212- | | |
| 0291 | Agricultural Production-Livestock, except 0211 and 0252 | $0.5 |
| 0252 | Chicken Eggs | $1.0 |

### Major Group 07–Agricultural Services

| All SIC's | | $3.5 |
|---|---|---|

### Major Group 08–Forestry

| All SIC's | | $3.5 |
|---|---|---|

### Major Group 09–Fishing, Hunting, and Trapping

| All SIC's | | $2.0 |
|---|---|---|

## DIVISION B—MINING

### Major Group 10–Metal Mining

| 1011 | Iron Ores | 500 |
|---|---|---|
| 1021 | Copper Ores | 500 |
| 1031 | Lead and Zinc Ores | 500 |
| 1041 | Gold Ores | 500 |
| 1044 | Silver Ores | 500 |
| 1061 | Ferroalloy Ores, Except Vanadium | 500 |
| 1081 | Metal Mining Services | $3.5 |
| 1094 | Uranium-Radium-Vanadium Ores | 500 |
| 1099 | Metal Ores, N.E.C. | 500 |

### Major Group 12–Bituminous Coal and Lignite Mining

| 1221 | Bituminous and Lignite Coal Mining, Surface, and Bituminous Coal Preparation Plants | 500 |
|---|---|---|
| 1222 | Bituminous Coal Mining, Underground | 500 |
| 1231 | Anthracite Mining | 500 |
| 1241 | Coal Mining Services | $3.5 |

### Major Group 13–Oil and Gas Extraction

| 1311 | Crude Petroleum and Natural Gas | 500 |
|---|---|---|
| 1321 | Natural Gas Liquids | 500 |
| 1381 | Drilling Oil and Gas Wells | 500 |
| 1382 | Oil and Gas Field Exploration Services | $3.5 |
| 1389 | Oil and Gas Field Services, N.E.C. | $3.5 |

| SIC | DESCRIPTION | SIZE |
|---|---|---|

### Major Group 14–Mining and Quarrying of Non-Metallic Minerals, Except Fuels

| 1411 | Dimension Stone | 500 |
|---|---|---|
| 1422 | Crushed and Broken Limestone | 500 |
| 1423 | Crushed and Broken Granite | 500 |
| 1429 | Crushed and Broken Stone, N.E.C. | 500 |
| 1442 | Construction Sand and Gravel | 500 |
| 1446 | Industrial Sand | 500 |
| 1455 | Kaolin and Ball Clay | 500 |
| 1459 | Clay and Related Minerals, N.E.C | 500 |
| 1474 | Potash, Soda, and Borate Minerals | 500 |
| 1475 | Phosphate Rock | 500 |
| 1479 | Chemical and Fertilizer Mining, N.E.C. | 500 |
| 1481 | Nonmetallic Minerals (Except Fuels) Services | $3.5 |
| 1499 | Nonmetallic Minerals, N.E.C. | 500 |

## DIVISION C—CONSTRUCTION

### Major Group 15–Building Construction-General Contractors and Operative Builders

| 1521 | General Contractors-Single-Family Houses | $17.0 |
|---|---|---|
| 1522 | General Contractors-Residential Buildings, Other Than Single-Family | $17.0 |
| 1531 | Operative Builders | $17.0 |
| 1541 | General Contractors-Industrial Buildings and Warehouses | $17.0 |
| 1542 | General Contractors-Nonresidential Buildings, Other Than Industrial Buildings and Warehouses | $17.0 |

### Major Group 16–Construction Other Than Building Construction-General Contractors

| 1611 | Highway and Street Construction | $17.0 |
|---|---|---|
| 1622 | Bridge, Tunnel, and Elevated Highway Construction | $17.0 |
| 1623 | Water, Sewer, Pipe Line, Communication and Power Line Construction | $17.0 |
| 1629 | Heavy Construction, Except Dredging, N.E.C. | $17.0 |
| 1629 | Dredging and Surface Cleanup Activities[2] | 13.5 |

### Major Group 17–Construction-Special Trade Contractors

| 1711 | Plumbing, Heating (Except Electric), and Air Conditioning | $7.0 |
|---|---|---|
| 1721 | Painting, Paper Hanging, and Decorating | $7.0 |
| 1731 | Electrical Work | $7.0 |

Notes: Size standards preceded by a dollar sign ($) are in millions of dollars. All others are in number of employees unless specified otherwise. N.E.C.: Not Elsewhere Classified.

## CHAPTER TWELVE

# Contract Changes

## I. INTRODUCTION.

## II. LEARNING OBJECTIVES.

Following this instruction, the student will understand:

A. How to analyze change issues arising in government contracts.

B. How to make formal changes to government contracts.

C. How to recognize constructive changes in government contracts, and to resolve constructive changes issues.

## III. ANALYZING CHANGES ISSUES.

A. Determine whether the contract required "additional" work. If so, then there was no "change" to the contract requirements, and a contract adjustment is unnecessary.

B. If the government changed the contract requirements, determine whether the new work was within or outside the scope of the contract.

1. Within-scope change. The contractor may be entitled to relief pursuant to the Changes clause. FAR 52.243-1 (supplies); FAR 52.243-1, Alternate I (services); FAR 52.243-4 (construction). Under the basic equitable adjustment formula, the contractor is entitled to the difference between the reasonable costs of performing the work as changed and the reasonable costs of performing as originally required. *American Line Builders, Inc. v. United States*, 26 Cl. Ct. 1155 (1992).

2. Outside-the-scope change (cardinal change). This is a new acquisition and

may constitute a breach of contract. *Luria Bros. & Co. v. United States*, 177 Ct. Cl. 676, 369 F.2d 701 (1966).

C. If a change occurred, determine whether the government employee who ordered/caused the change had actual authority to order the change *or* whether the contractor can overcome the employee's lack of actual authority. *J.F. Allen Co. and Wiley W. Jackson Co., a Joint Venture v. United States*, 25 Cl. Ct. 312 (1992).

D. If a change occurred, determine when the change occurred; when the contractor provided, or when the government can be charged with having acquired, notice of the change; and whether the contractor provided timely notice. Determine if untimely notice prejudiced the government.

E. If a change occurred, determine the effect of the change on the costs incurred or saved by the contractor and on the time required for contract performance. *See R.B. Hazard, Inc.*, ASBCA No. 36136, 91-1 BCA ¶ 23,376 (assuming a change occurred, there was no impact).

## IV. CHANGES CLAUSE COVERAGE.

A. **Purposes of the Clause.**

B. **Limitations.**

1. The change must be of a type specified in the Changes clause.

2. The change must be within the general scope of the contract.

C. **Scope Determinations.**

1. In a *protest* action, the test is whether the change so materially altered the contract that

the field of competition for the contract as modified would be significantly different from that obtained for the original contract (scope of competition). *AT&T Communications, Inc. v. Wiltel, Inc.*, 1 F.3d 1201 (Fed. Cir. 1993); *Caltech Serv. Corp.*, B-240726.6, Jan. 22, 1992, 92-1 CPD ¶ 94; *Neil R. Gross & Co.*, B-237434, Feb. 23, 1990, 69 Comp. Gen. 248, 90-1 CPD ¶ 212; *MCI Telecommunications Corp. v. General Servs. Admin.*, GSBCA No. 11963-P, 93-1 BCA ¶ 25,541.

2. In *Neil R. Gross & Co.*, *supra*, the GAO considered the following factors in determining the materiality of a modification:

   a. the extent of any changes in the type of work or the performance period, or the difference in costs between the contract as awarded and as modified;

   b. whether the solicitation for the original contract adequately advised offerors of the potential for the type of changes that actually occurred; and

   c. whether the modification was of a nature that potential offerors reasonably would have anticipated under the Changes clause.

3. In contract *disputes*, the term, "within the general scope," has a broader meaning. Courts and boards focus on whether the contract, as modified, is for essentially the same work that the parties originally bargained for (scope of work). *Edward R. Marden Corp. v. United States*, 194 Ct. Cl. 799, 442 F.2d 364 (1971); *Air-A-Plane Corp. v. United States*, 187 Ct. Cl. 269, 408 F.2d 1030 (1969).

**D. Scope Determination Factors.**

1. Changes in the Function of the Item or the Type of Work.

   a. In determining the materiality of a change, the most important factor to consider is the extent to which a product or service, as changed, differs from the requirements of the original contract. *See E. L. Hamm & Assocs, Inc.* ASBCA No. 43792, 94-2 BCA ¶ 26,724 (change from lease to lease/purchase was out-of-scope); *Aragona Constr.*

*Co. v. United States*, 165 Ct. Cl. 382 (1964).

   b. Substantial changes in the work may be in-scope if the parties entered into a broadly conceived contract. *General Dynamics Corp. v. United States*, 585 F.2d 457 (Ct. Cl. 1978); *AT&T Communciations, Inc. v. Wiltel, Inc.*, 1 F.3d 1201 (Fed. Cir. 1993) (more latitude allowed where the activity requires a state-of-the-art product).

2. Changes in Quantity.

   a. Increases and decreases in the quantity of *major* items or portions of the work are not "within the scope" of a contract. *See, e.g., Liebert Corp.*, B-232234.5, Apr. 29, 1991, 70 Comp. Gen. 449, 91-1 CPD ¶ 413 (order in excess of maximum quantity was a material change). *Cf. Caltech Serv. Corp.*, B-240726.6, Jan. 22, 1992, 92-1 CPD ¶ 94 (increase in cargo tonnage on containeriza- tion requirements contract was within scope). Generally, increases are new procurements, and decreases are partial terminations for convenience. *Cf. Lucas Aul, Inc.*, ASBCA No. 37803, 91-1 BCA ¶ 23,609 (order was deductive change, not partial termination).

   b. Generally, the Changes clause permits increases and decreases in the quantity of *minor* items or portions of the work unless the variation alters the entire bargain. *See Symbolic Displays, Inc.*, B-182247, May 6, 1975, 75-1 CPD ¶ 278 (addition of strobe lights to aircraft manufacturing contract was not an "evident" out-of-scope change). *Cf. Lucas Aul, Inc.*, *supra*.

3. Number and Cost of Changes.

   a. Neither the number nor the cost of changes, alone, dictates whether modifications are beyond the scope of a contract. *Bruce-Andersen Co.*, ASBCA No. 35791, 89-2 BCA ¶ 21,871; *Triax Co. v. United States*, 28 Fed. Cl. 733 (1993).

   b. The cumulative effect of a large number of changes is determinative, however. *Air-A-Plane Corp. v. United States*, 187 Ct. Cl. 269, 408 F.2d 1030 (1969).

4. Changes in Time of Performance.
   a. The supply Changes clause does not authorize unilateral acceleration of performance. FAR 52.243-1; *see* page 175.
   b. Under the services Changes clause, the contracting officer unilaterally may change "when" a contractor is to perform but not the overall performance period. FAR 52.243-1, Alternate I; *see* page 176.
   c. The construction contract Changes clause authorizes unilateral acceleration of performance. FAR 52.243-4(a)(4); *see* page 177.

5. Acceptance of a Change.
   a. If a contractor performs under a change order, it may not argue subsequently that the change constituted a breach of contract. *Silberblatt & Lasker, Inc. v. United States*, 101 Ct. Cl. 54 (1944); *C.E. Lowther & Son*, ASBCA No. 26760, 85-2 BCA ¶ 18,149.
   b. Agreeing to a change does not convert an out-of-scope change into one that is within the scope of the contract for *competition* purposes; it simply means that the parties have agreed to process the change under the Changes clause. The contracting officer may not use modifications to avoid the statutory mandate for competition. *Corbin Superior Composites, Inc.*, B-235019, B-235019.2, July 20, 1989, 89-2 CPD ¶ 67.

**E. The Duty to Continue Performance.**

1. The Changes and Disputes clauses require the contractor to continue performance pending the resolution of a dispute over an in-scope change. *See* FAR 52.233-1, Disputes; FAR 52.243-1(e), Changes-Fixed Price clause.

2. Conversely, under the standard Disputes clause, a contractor has no duty to proceed diligently with performance pending resolution of any dispute concerning a change *outside the scope of the contract* (cardinal change). FAR 52.233-1(h). *Airprep Technology, Inc. v. United States*, 30 Fed. Cl. 488 (1994).

3. Exceptions to the duty to proceed.

   a. The government withholds progress payments improperly. *Sterling Millwrights v. United States*, 26 Cl. Ct. 49 (1992); *DeKonty Corp.*, ASBCA No. 32140, 89-2 BCA ¶ 21,586.
   b. Continued performance is impractical. *United States v. Spearin*, 248 U.S. 132 (1918) (government refused to provide safe working conditions); *Xplo Corp.*, DOT BCA No. 1289, 86-3 BCA ¶ 19,125.
   c. The government fails to provide clear direction to the contractor. *James W. Sprayberry Constr.*, IBCA No. 2130, 87-1 BCA ¶ 19,645 (contractor justified to await clarification of defective specifications).

4. The Alternate Disputes clause requires the contractor to continue to perform even if the government orders a cardinal change, or otherwise breaches the contract. *See* FAR 52.233-1, Alternate I; DFARS 233.214.

**V. FORMAL CONTRACT CHANGES.**

**A. Types of Formal Changes.**

1. Administrative change. A unilateral written change that does not affect the substantive rights of the parties. FAR 43.101.

2. Change order. A unilateral, written order, signed by the contracting officer, directing the contractor to make a change that the Changes clause authorizes the contracting officer to direct, with or without the contractor's consent. FAR 43.101.

3. Bilateral modification (supplemental agreement). A contract modification signed by the contractor and the contracting officer. FAR 43.103(a). Bilateral modifications are used for:
   a. negotiating equitable adjustments that result from the issuance of a change order;
   b. definitizing a letter contract; and
   c. reflecting other agreements of the parties changing the terms of a contract.

**B. Modifying a Contract.**

1. Only contracting officers acting within the scope of their authority may execute con-

163

tract modifications. FAR 43.102; *Daly Constr., Inc.*, ASBCA No. 34322, 92-1 BCA ¶ 24,469; *Commercial Contractors, Inc.*, ASBCA No. 30675, 88-3 BCA ¶ 20,877. *See also* Chapter 2, Authority to Contract.

2. Contracting officers must issue modifications on SF 30, Amendment of Solicitation/Modification of Contract. FAR 43.102; FAR 43.301. *See* page 180. *Texas Instr., Inc. v. United States*, 922 F.2d 810 (Fed. Cir. 1990); *Mil-Spec Contractors, Inc. v. United States*, 835 F.2d 865 (Fed. Cir. 1987); *Daly Constr., Inc.*, ASBCA No. 34322, 92-1 BCA ¶ 24,469. *But see Robinson Contracting Co. v. United States*, 16 Cl. Ct. 676 (1989) (SF 30 not required).

3. The contracting officer must price modifications before executing them if this can be done without adversely affecting the interests of the government. FAR 43.102(b).

4. The contracting officer may order a change at any time prior to final payment. Final payment means payment in the full amount of the contract balance owed, received, and accepted by the contractor after delivery of supplies or the performance of services, with the understanding that no further payments are due. *Design & Prod., Inc. v. United States*, 18 Cl. Ct. 168 (1989); *Gulf & Western Indus., Inc. v. United States*, 6 Cl. Ct. 742 (1984).

## C. Prerequisites for Formal Changes.

1. The government must receive a benefit. *G. Issaias & Co. (Kenya)*, ASBCA No. 30359, 88-1 BCA ¶ 20,441.

2. Proper funds must be available. FAR 43.105; AR 37-1, tbl. 9-9; AFR 172-1, vol. I, para. 8-24.
   a. If a change is within the scope of the contract, obligate funds available at the time of contract award.
   b. A change outside the scope of the contract is a new acquisition. Obligate funds current when the contracting officer executes the modification.

## VI. OVERVIEW OF CONSTRUCTIVE CHANGES.

### A. Elements of a Constructive Change.
*Dan G. Trawick III*, ASBCA No. 36260, 90-3 BCA ¶ 23,222.

1. A change occurred, either as the result of government action or inaction. *Kos Kam, Inc.*, ASBCA No. 34682, 92-1 BCA ¶ 24,546;

2. The contractor did not perform voluntarily. *Jowett, Inc.*, ASBCA No. 47364, 94-3 BCA ¶ 27,110; and

3. The change resulted in an increase (or a decrease) in the cost or the time of performance. *Advanced Mechanical Servs., Inc.*, ASBCA No. 38832, 94-3 BCA ¶ 26,964.

### B. Types of Constructive Changes.
1. contract misinterpretation by the government;
2. defective specifications;
3. interference and failure to cooperate;
4. failure to disclose vital information (superior knowledge); and
5. constructive acceleration.

## VII. CONTRACT INTERPRETATION PRINCIPLES.

### A. Main Issues.
Ralph C. Nash, Jr., *Government Contract Changes*, 11-2 (2d ed. 1989).

1. Did the government's interpretation originate from an employee with authority? *See J.F. Allen Co. and Wiley W. Jackson Co., a Joint Venture v. United States*, 25 Cl. Ct. 312 (1992).

2. Did the contractor perform work that the contract did not require?

3. Did the contractor timely notify the government of the impact of the government's interpretation?

### B. Contract Interpretation Process.
1. A judge must interpret a contract when the parties do not agree on the meaning of its terms. *Fruin-Colon Corp. v. United States*, 912 F.2d 1426 (Fed. Cir. 1990).

2. Framework for analyzing contract interpretation issues.
   a. Seek the intent of the parties by examining:
      (1) the language of the contract; and/or
      (2) the facts and circumstances surrounding contract formation and performance.
   b. If this process fails to reveal the objective intent of the parties, apply the two rules of risk allocation: *contra proferentem* and the duty to seek clarification.
3. The contractor must continue performance even if it does not agree with the contracting officer's interpretation, absent a material breach. *See* FAR 52.233-1, Disputes; *Aero Prods. Co.*, ASBCA No. 44030, 93-2 BCA ¶ 25,868.

**C. Intrinsic Evidence of Intent.**

1. In determining the objective intent of the parties, first examine the terms of the contract. *See, e.g., U.S. Eagle, Inc.*, ASBCA No. 41093, 91-3 BCA ¶ 24,371.
2. Interpret the contract as a whole. *Hol-Gar Mfg. Corp. v. United States*, 169 Ct. Cl. 384, 351 F.2d 972 (1965); *Sheladia Constr. Corp.*, VABCA No. 3313, 91-3 BCA ¶ 24,111 (contractor may not ignore requirement merely because it is not stated in normal section of the specifications). *Okland Constr. Co.*, ASBCA No. 43986, 93-2 BCA ¶ 25,867 (subcontractors did not bid on something required by contract and prime contractor had overall responsibility; specifications were divided up).
   a. Give effect to all provisions and do not render meaningless any term of the contract. *B.D. Click Co. v. United States*, 222 Ct. Cl. 290, 614 F.2d 748 (1980); *Jamsar, Inc. v. United States*, 194 Ct. Cl. 819, 442 F.2d 930 (1971); *Rex Sys., Inc.*, ASBCA No. 45874, 94-1 BCA ¶ 26,370; *Electronic Genie, Inc.*, ASBCA No. 40535, 93-1 BCA ¶ 25,307.
   b. Interpret a contract in harmony with its principal purpose. *Maddox Indus. Contractors, Inc.*, ASBCA No. 36091, 88-3 BCA

¶ 21,037; *Restatement (Second) of Contracts* § 203(a) (1981).

3. How to define terms.
   a. Give ordinary terms their plain and ordinary meaning in defining the rights and obligations of the parties. *Elden v. United States*, 223 Ct. Cl. 239, 617 F.2d 254 (1980).
   b. Give technical terms their technical meanings. Specialized or trade meanings take precedence over "lay" meanings. *See Western States Constr. Co. v. United States*, 26 Cl. Ct. 818 (1992).
      (1) Give scientific and engineering terms their recognized technical meanings unless the context or an applicable usage indicates a contrary intention. *Tri-Cor, Inc. v. United States*, 198 Ct. Cl. 187, 458 F.2d 112 (1972); *Coastal Drydock & Repair Corp.*, ASBCA No. 31894, 87-1 BCA ¶ 19,618.
      (2) Similarly, give terms unique to government contracts their technical meanings. *General Builders Supply Co. v. United States*, 187 Ct. Cl. 477, 409 F.2d 246 (1969) (meaning of "equitable adjustment").
4. Lists of items.
   a. Lists are presumed exclusive unless qualified. *Kimmins Constr. Corp.*, ASBCA No. 43800, 94-2 BCA ¶ 26,608; *Henry J. Korpi*, ASBCA No. 6948, 61-1 BCA ¶ 3030.
   b. Nonexclusive lists are presumed to include only similar, unspecified items. "Words, like men, are known by the company they keep. The meaning of a doubtful word may be ascertained by reference to the meaning of words with which they are associated." *C.W. Roberts Constr. Co.*, ASBCA No. 12348, 68-1 BCA ¶ 6819. *See United States v. Turner Constr. Co.*, 819 F.2d 283 (Fed. Cir. 1987) (unreasonable to include unmentioned item in a list where unmentioned item was most expensive component).
5. Contract clauses.
   a. To resolve inconsistencies, order of precedence clauses establish priorities among

different sections of the contract. *See, e.g.,* FAR 52.214-29, Order of Precedence—Sealed Bidding; FAR 52.215-33, Order of Precedence; FAR 52.236-21, Specifications and Drawings for Construction.

b. In construction contracts, a contractor may rely on the order of precedence clause to resolve a discrepancy between the specifications and drawings even if a discrepancy is patent or known to the contractor prior to bid submission. *Hensel Phelps Constr. Co. v. United States,* 886 F.2d 1296 (Fed. Cir. 1989); *C Constr. Co,* ASBCA No. 38098, 91-2 BCA ¶ 23,923; *Hull-Hazard, Inc.,* ASBCA No. 34645, 90-3 BCA ¶ 23,173.

c. Omissions. In construction contracts, the DFARS states that the contractor shall perform omitted details of work that are necessary to carry out the intent of the drawings and specifications or that are performed customarily. DFARS 252.236-7001; *Single Ply Sys., Inc.,* ASBCA No. 42168, 91-2 BCA ¶ 24,032; *Hull-Hazard, Inc., supra.*

**D. Extrinsic Evidence of Intent.**

1. Do not consider extrinsic evidence if the contract terms are clear. *See C. Sanchez & Son, Inc. v. United States,* 24 Cl. Ct. 14 (1991), *rev'd on other grounds,* 6 F.3d 1539 (Fed. Cir. 1993).

2. Preaward communications.

a. The Explanation to Prospective Offerors clause does not prevent parties from using clarifying statements by "authorized" officials to interpret an ambiguous provision. FAR 52.214-6 (sealed bidding); FAR 52.215-14 (negotiations); *Max Drill, Inc. v. United States,* 192 Ct. Cl. 608, 427 F.2d 1233 (1970); *Turner Constr. Co. v. Gen. Servs. Admin.,* GSBCA No. 11361, 92-3 BCA ¶ 25,115 (contractor could not rely on preaward statement that was inconsistent with terms of solicitation); *Community Heating & Plumbing Co.,* ASBCA No. 37981, 92-2 BCA ¶ 24,870; *Dollar*

*Roofing,* ASBCA No. 36461, 92-1 BCA ¶ 24,695.

b. Statements made at pre-bid conferences may bind the government. *General Atronics Corp.,* ASBCA No. 46784, 94-3 BCA ¶ 27,112. *Cf. Orbas & Assoc.,* ASBCA No. 33359, 87-2 BCA ¶ 19,742 (contractor who did not attend pre-bid conference was not bound by explanation of provision where solicitation should have explained provision).

c. Preaward acceptance of contractor's cost-cutting suggestion was binding on the government. *See Pioneer Enters., Inc.,* ASBCA No. 43739, 93-1 BCA ¶ 25,395.

3. Actions during contract performance. The way in which the parties comport themselves often reveal the intent of the parties. Courts and boards afford these actions great weight when determining the meaning of a provision. *Drytech, Inc.,* ASBCA No. 41152, 92-2 BCA ¶ 24,809; *Tri-States Serv. Co.,* ASBCA No. 37058, 90-3 BCA ¶ 22,953; *Macke Co. v. United States,* 199 Ct. Cl. 552, 467 F.2d 1323 (1972).

4. Prior course of dealing.

a. To determine the meaning of the current contract, consider a prior course of dealing between the parties in earlier contracts. *Superstaff, Inc.,* ASBCA No. 46112, 94-1 BCA ¶ 26,574; *American Transp. Line, Ltd.,* ASBCA No. 44510, 93-3 BCA ¶ 26,156; *L.W. Foster Sportswear Co. v. United States,* 405 F.2d 1285 (Ct. Cl. 1969).

b. The parties must be aware of the prior course of dealing. *Gresham & Co. v. United States,* 470 F.2d 542 (Ct. Cl. 1972); *T. L. Roof & Assocs.,* ASBCA No. 38928; 93-2 BCA ¶ 25,895; *Snowbird Indus.,* ASBCA No. 33027, 89-3 BCA ¶ 22,065.

c. Prior waivers of specifications must be numerous or consistent to vary an unambiguous term. *Doyle Shirt Mfg. Corp.,* 462 F.2d 1150 (Ct. Cl. 1972); *Kvaas Constr. Co.,* ASBCA No. 45965, 94-1 BCA ¶ 26,513 (four waivers not enough); *General Sec.*

*Servs. Corp. v. General Servs. Admin.*, GSBCA No. 11381, 92-2 BCA ¶ 24,897 (no waiver based on waivers in six previous contracts because GSA sought to enforce requirement in current contract).

5. Custom or trade usage/industry standard.

   a. Parties may not use custom and trade usage to contradict unambiguous terms. *WRB Corp. v. United States*, 183 Ct. Cl. 409, 436 (1968); *C. Sanchez & Son, Inc.*, *supra*; *Riley Stoker Corp.*, ASBCA No. 37019, 92-3 BCA ¶ 25,143 (contract terms were ambiguous); *Harold Bailey Painting Co.*, ASBCA No. 27064, 87-1 BCA ¶ 19,601 (used to define "spot painting").

   b. Parties may resort to custom and trade usage to explain or define unambiguous terms. *W.G. Cornell Co. v. United States*, 179 Ct. Cl. 651, 376 F.2d 299 (1967).

   c. Parties also may use an industry standard or trade usage to show that a term is ambiguous. *See Gholson, Byars and Holmes Constr. Co. v. United States*, 173 Ct. Cl. 374, 351 F.2d 987 (1965); *Western States Constr. Co. v. United States*, 26 Cl. Ct. 818 (1992).

   d. The party asserting the industry standard or trade usage bears the burden of proving the existence of the standard or usage. *DWS, Inc., Debtor in Possession*, ASBCA No. 29743, 93-1 BCA ¶ 25,404.

## E. Allocation of Risk for Ambiguous Language.

If contract terms are ambiguous after application of the rules of interpretation, apply risk allocation principles to determine which party is ultimately responsible. An ambiguity exists when the words of a contract are subject to two or more reasonable interpretations. *Community Heating & Plumbing Co. v. Kelso*, 987 F.2d 1575 (Fed. Cir. 1993). The risk allocation principles do not apply to ambiguities in procurement regulations. *Santa Fe Eng'rs, Inc. v. United States*, 801 F.2d 379 (Fed. Cir. 1986).

1. *Contra proferentem. Peter Kiewit Sons' Co. v. United States*, 109 Ct. Cl. 390 (1947).

   a. If one cannot resolve an ambiguity under the contract interpretation rules, construe the ambiguity against the drafter. *Emerald Maint., Inc.*, ASBCA No. 33153, 87-2 BCA ¶ 19,907; *WPC Enter. v. United States*, 163 Ct. Cl. 1, 323 F.2d 874 (1963).

   b. "[*Contra proferentem*] puts the risk of ambiguity, lack of clarity, and absence of proper warning on the drafting party which could have forestalled the controversy; it pushes the drafters toward improving contractual forms; and it saves contractors from hidden traps not of their own making." *Sturm v. United States*, 190 Ct. Cl. 690, 697, 421 F.2d 723 (1970).

   c. Elements of the rule.

     (1) To recover, the contractor's interpretation must be reasonable. *J.C.N. Constr. Co.*, ASBCA No. 42263, 91-3 BCA ¶ 24,095 (contractor interpretation unreasonable);

     (2) The opposing party must be the drafter. This is usually the government, but a contractor also may be the drafter. *See Canadian Commercial Corp. v. United States*, 202 Ct. Cl. 65 (1973); *TRW, Inc.*, ASBCA No. 27299, 87-3 BCA ¶ 19,964; *Prince George Ctr., Inc. v. Gen. Servs. Admin.*, GSBCA No. 12289, 94-2 BCA ¶ 26,889; and

     (3) The non-drafting party must have relied on its interpretation in submitting its bid. *Fruin-Colon Corp. v. United States*, 912 F.2d 1426 (Fed. Cir. 1990); *L. D. Dosca Assocs.*, ASBCA No. 45267, 93-3 BCA ¶ 26,066; *Jamco Constructors, Inc.*, VABCA No. 3271, 94-1 BCA ¶ 26,405.

2. Duty to seek clarification. Do not apply *contra proferentem* if an ambiguity is patent or glaring and the contractor failed to seek clarification. *Interstate Gen. Gov't Contractors, Inc. v. Stone*, 980 F.2d 1433 (Fed. Cir. 1992), *Community Heating & Plumbing Co. v. Kelso*, *supra*; *Gaston & Assocs., Inc. v. United States*, 27 Fed. Cl. 243 (1993) (latent ambiguity); *Technocratica*, ASBCA No.

44134, 94-2 BCA ¶ 26,606; *Allen County Builders Supply*, ASBCA No. 41836, 93-1 BCA ¶ 25,398; *D.E.W., Inc.*, ASBCA No. 36389, 92-3 BCA ¶ 25,029 (patent ambiguity); *Sturm Craft Co.*, ASBCA No. 37832, 91-2 BCA ¶ 23,924; *Jamco Constructors, Inc.*, *supra*; *Stroh Corp. v. Gen. Servs. Admin.*, GSBCA No. 11029, 93-2 BCA ¶ 25,841 (latent ambiguity); *Foothill Eng'g.*, IBCA No. 3119-A, 94-2 BCA ¶ 26,732 ("busy bidder" rule).

## VIII. DEFECTIVE SPECIFICATIONS— OVERVIEW.

### A. Theories of Recovery.

Courts and boards hold the government liable for defects in specifications based upon:

1. The *implied warranty* the government gives for the use of design specifications in a contract.

2. The principles of *impracticability/impossibility* of performance caused by increased costs in attempting to conform to defective performance specifications.

### B. Causation.

This type of constructive change is deemed to have occurred at the time of contract award on the premise that the contracting officer had an immediate duty to issue an order correcting the defective specifications.

## IX. DEFECTIVE SPECIFICATIONS—IMPLIED WARRANTY OF SPECIFICATIONS.

### A. Basis for the Implied Warranty.

1. This "warranty" is based on an implied promise by the government that a contractor can follow the contract drawings and specifications and perform without undue expense. This promise has been called a warranty; however, recovery is based on a breach of the duty to provide drawings and specifications reasonably free from defects. *United States v. Spearin*, 248 U.S. 132 (1918); *Luria Bros. & Co. v. United States*, 177 Ct. Cl. 676, 369 F.2d 701 (1966).

2. Defective specifications constitute constructive changes. *See, e.g., Hol-Gar Mfg. Corp. v. United States*, 175 Ct. Cl. 518, 360 F.2d 634 (1964). In some cases, judges have relied on a breach of contract theory. *See e.g., Big Chief Drilling Co. v. United States*, 26 Cl. Ct. 1276 (1992).

### B. Specification Types.

*Aleutian Constr. v. United States*, 24 Cl. Ct. 372 (1991); *Monitor Plastics Co.*, ASBCA No. 14447, 72-2 BCA ¶ 9626.

1. DESIGN SPECIFICATIONS set forth precise measurements, tolerances, materials, tests, quality control, inspection requirements, and other specific information. *See Q.R. Sys. North, Inc.*, ASBCA No. 39618, 92-2 BCA ¶ 24,793 (specified roofing material inadequate for roof type).

2. PERFORMANCE SPECIFICATIONS set forth the operational characteristics desired for the item. In such specifications, design, measurements, and other specific details are neither stated nor considered important as long as the performance requirement is met. *See Interwest Constr. v. Brown*, 29 F.3d 611 (Fed. Cir. 1994).

3. PURCHASE DESCRIPTIONS are specifications that designate a particular manufacturer's model, part number, or product. The phrase "or equal" may accompany a purchase description.

4. COMPOSITE SPECIFICATIONS are specifications that are comprised of two or more different specification types. *See Transtechnology, Corp., Space Ordnance Sys. Div. v. United States*, 22 Cl. Ct. 349 (1990).

### C. Scope of Government Liability.

1. The scope of government liability depends on the specification type. *Lopez v. A.C. & S., Inc.*, 858 F.2d 712 (Fed. Cir. 1988); *Morrison-Knudsen Co.*, ASBCA No. 32476, 90-3 BCA ¶ 23,208.

2. Design specifications.

   a. The key issue is whether the government required the contractor to use detailed specifications. *Geo-Con, Inc.*, ENG BCA No. 5749, 94-1 BCA ¶ 26,359.

b. The government is responsible for design and related omissions, errors, and deficiencies in the specifications and drawings. *Geo-Con, Inc., supra*; *Neal & Co. v. United States*, 19 Cl. Ct. 463 (1990) (defective design specifications found to cause bowing in wall); *International Foods Retort Co.*, ASBCA No. 34954, 92-2 BCA ¶ 24,994 (bland chicken ala king). *But cf. Hawaiian Bitumuls & Paving v. United States*, 26 Cl. Ct. 1234 (1992) (contractor may vitiate warranty by participating in drafting and developing specifications).

3. Performance specifications.
   a. If the government uses a performance specification, the contractor accepts general responsibility for the design, engineering, and achievement of the performance requirements. *Aleutian Constr. v. United States*, 24 Cl. Ct. 372 (1991).
   b. The contractor has discretion as to the details of the work, but the work is subject to the government's right of final inspection and approval or rejection. *Kos Kam, Inc.*, ASBCA No. 34682, 92-1 BCA ¶ 24,546.

4. Purchase descriptions. *Monitor Plastics Co.*, ASBCA No. 14447, 72-2 BCA ¶ 9626.
   a. If the contractor furnishes or uses in fabrication a specified brand name or an acceptable and approved substitute brand-name product, the responsibility for proper performance generally falls upon the government.
   b. The government's liability is conditioned upon the contractor's correct use of the product.
   c. If the contractor elects to manufacture an equal product, it must ensure that the product is equal to the brand name product.

5. Composite specifications.
   a. If the government uses a composite specification, the parties must examine each portion of the specification to determine which specification type caused the prob-

lem. This determination establishes the scope of the government's liability. *See Penguin Indus. v. United States*, 209 Ct. Cl. 121, 530 F.2d 934 (1976).

b. The contractor must isolate the defective element of the design portion or demonstrate affirmatively that its performance did not cause the problem.

### D. Recovery under the Implied Warranty of Specifications.

*See Transtechnology, Corp., supra.*

1. To recover under the implied warranty of specifications, the contractor must prove that:
   a. it reasonably relied upon the defective specifications and complied fully with them. *Al Johnson Constr. Co. v. United States*, 854 F.2d 467 (Fed. Cir. 1988); *Gulf & Western Precision Eng'g Co. v. United States*, 543 F.2d 125 (Ct. Cl. 1976); *Mega Constr. Co.*, 29 Fed. Cl. 396 (1993); *Santa Fe Eng'rs, Inc.*, ASBCA No. 25549, 82-2 BCA ¶ 15,982.
   b. That the defective specifications caused increased costs. *Chaparral Indus., Inc.*, ASBCA No. 34396, 91-2 BCA ¶ 23,813, *aff'd*, 975 F.2d 870 (Fed. Cir. 1992).

2. The contractor cannot recover if it has actual or constructive knowledge of the defects prior to award. *Centennial Contractors, Inc.*, ASBCA No. 46820, 94-1 BCA ¶ 26,511; *L.W. Foster Sportswear Co. v. United States*, 405 F.2d 1285 (Ct. Cl. 1969) (contractor had actual knowledge from prior contract). Generally, constructive knowledge is limited to patent errors because a contractor has no duty to conduct an independent investigation to determine whether the specifications are adequate. *Jordan & Nobles Constr. Co.*, GSBCA No. 8349, 91-1 BCA ¶ 23,659; *John C. Grimberg Co.*, ASBCA No. 32490, 88-1 BCA ¶ 20,346. *Cf. Spiros Vasilatos Painting*, ASBCA No. 35065, 88-2 BCA ¶ 20,558.

3. A contractor may not recover if it decides unilaterally to perform work knowing that the specifications were defective. *Ordnance Research, Inc. v. United States,*

221 Ct. Cl. 641, 609 F.2d 462 (1979).

4. The government may disclaim this warranty. *See, e.g., Service Eng'g Co.*, ASBCA No. 40272, 92-3 BCA ¶ 25,106; *Bethlehem Steel Corp.*, ASBCA No. 13341, 72-1 BCA ¶ 9186.

## X. DEFECTIVE SPECIFICATIONS— IMPRACTICABILITY/IMPOSSIBILITY OF PERFORMANCE.

Elements. *Oak Adec, Inc. v. United States*, 24 Cl. Ct. 502 (1991); *Gulf and Western Indus., Inc.*, ASBCA No. 21090, 87-2 BCA ¶ 19,881.

### A. An unforeseen or unexpected occurrence.

1. A significant increase in work, usually caused by unforeseen technological problems. Examine the following factors to determine whether a problem was unforeseen or unexpected:
   a. the nature of the contract and specifications, i.e., whether they require performance beyond the state of the art;
   b. the extent of the contractor's effort; and
   c. the ability of other contractors to meet the specification requirements.

2. In some cases, a contractor must show that an extensive research and development effort was necessary to meet the specifications or that no competent contractor can meet the performance requirements. *Hol-Gar Mfg. Corp. v. United States*, 175 Ct. Cl. 518, 360 F.2d 634 (1964); *Numax Elec., Inc.*, ASBCA No. 29080, 90-1 BCA ¶ 22,280.

### B. The contractor did not assume the risk of the unforeseen occurrence by agreement or custom.

*Southern Dredging Co.*, ENG BCA 5843, 92-2 BCA ¶ 24,886; *Fulton Hauling Corp.*, PSBCA No. 2778, 92-2 BCA ¶ 24,886.

1. A contractor may assume the risk of the unforeseen effort by using its own specifications. *See Bethlehem Corp. v. United States*, 199 Ct. Cl. 247, 462 F.2d 1400 (1972); *Austin Co. v. United States*, 161 Ct. Cl. 76, 314 F.2d 518 (1963).

2. By proposing to extend the state of the art, a contractor may assume the risk of impossible performance. *See J.A. Maurer, Inc. v. United States*, 202 Ct. Cl. 813, 485 F.2d 588 (1973).

### C. Performance is *commercially* impracticable or impossible.

1. The contractor must show that the increased cost of performance is so much greater than anticipated that performance is commercially senseless. *See Fulton Hauling Corp., supra; Beeston, Inc.*, ASBCA No. 38969, 91-3 BCA ¶ 24,241. *But see SMC Info. Sys., Inc. v. General Servs. Admin.*, GSBCA No. 9371, 93-1 BCA ¶ 25,485. The increased difficulty cannot be the result of poor workmanship.

2. There is no universal standard for determining "commercial senselessness."
   a. Judges sometimes use a "willing buyer" test to determine whether the increased costs render performance commercially senseless. A contractor must show that there are no buyers willing to pay the increased cost of production plus a reasonable profit. Ralph C. Nash, Jr., *Government Contract Changes*, 13-37 to 13-39 (2d ed. 1989).
   b. Some decisions have stated that it must be "positively unjust" to hold the contractor liable for the increased costs. *Southern Dredging Co., supra; Gulf and Western Indus., supra* (70% increase insufficient); *HLI Lordship Indus.*, VABCA No. 1785, 86-3 BCA ¶ 19,182 (200% increase in gold prices insufficient); *Xplo Corp.*, DOT BCA No. 1289, 86-3 BCA ¶ 19,125 (50% increase in costs was sufficient).

## XI. INTERFERENCE AND FAILURE TO COOPERATE.

### A. Theory of Recovery.

1. Contracting activities have an implied obligation to cooperate with their contractors and not to administer the contract in a manner that hinders, delays, or increases the cost of performance. *R&B Bewachungsgesellschaft*

*mbH*, ASBCA No. 42213, 91-3 BCA ¶ 24,310; *C.M. Lowther, Jr.*, ASBCA No. 38407, 91-3 BCA ¶ 24,296.

2. Generally, a contractor may not recover for "interference" that results from a sovereign act. *See generally Hills Materials Co.*, ASBCA No. 42410, 92-1 BCA ¶ 24,636, *rev'd sub nom.*, *Hills Materials Co. v. Rice*, 982 F.2d 514 (Fed. Cir. 1992); *Orlando Helicopter Airways, Inc.*, ASBCA No. 45778, 94-2 BCA ¶ 26,751 (but government may agree to compensate for a sovereign act); *Henderson, Inc.*, DOT BCA No. 2423, 94-2 BCA ¶ 26,728 (limitation on dredging period created implied warranty); *R&B Bewachungsgesellschaft mbH*, *supra* (criminal investigators took action in government's contractual capacity, not sovereign capacity). *See also Hughes Communications Galaxy, Inc. v. United States*, 998 F.2d 953 (Fed. Cir. 1993) (government may waive sovereign act defense).

**B. Bases for Interference Claims.**

1. Overzealous inspection of the contractor's work. The government must act reasonably. *WRB Corp. v. United States*, 183 Ct. Cl. 409 (1968); *Adams v. United States*, 175 Ct. Cl. 288, 358 F.2d 986 (1966).

2. Incompetence of government personnel. *Harvey C. Jones, Inc.*, IBCA No. 2070, 90-2 BCA ¶ 22,762.

3. Water seepage or flow caused by the government. *See C.M. Lowther, Jr.*, ASBCA No. 38407, 91-3 BCA ¶ 24,296 (water from malfunctioning sump pump was interference); *Caesar Constr., Inc.*, ASBCA No. 41059, 91-1 BCA ¶ 23,639 (melting snow).

4. Disruptive criminal investigations conducted in the government's contractual capacity. *R&B Bewachungsgesellschaft mbH, supra*.

**C. Bases for Failure to Cooperate Claims.**

The government must cooperate with a contractor. *See, e.g., James Lowe, Inc.*, ASBCA No. 42026, 92-2 BCA ¶ 24,835; *Mit-Con, Inc.*, ASBCA No. 42916, 92-1 CPD ¶ 24,539. Bases for claims include:

1. Failure to provide assistance necessary for efficient contractor performance. *Chris Berg, Inc. v. United States*, 197 Ct. Cl. 503, 455 F.2d 1037 (1972) (implied requirement); *Durocher Dock & Dredge, Inc.*, ENG BCA No. 5768, 91-3 BCA ¶ 24,145 (failure to contest sheriff's stop work order was not failure to cooperate); *Hudson Contracting, Inc.*, ASBCA No. 41023, 94-1 BCA ¶ 26,466; *Packard Constr. Corp.*, ASBCA No. 46082, 94-1 BCA ¶ 26,577; *Ingalls Shipbldg. Div., Litton Sys., Inc.*, ASBCA No. 17717, 76-1 BCA ¶ 11,851 (express requirement).

2. Failure to prevent interference by another contractor. Examine closely the good faith effort of the government to administer the other contract to reduce interference. *Stephenson Assocs., Inc.*, GSBCA No. 6573, 86-3 BCA ¶ 19,071.

3. Failure to provide access to the work site. *Summit Contractors, Inc. v. United States*, 23 Cl. Ct. 333 (1991) (absent specific warranty, site unavailability must be due to government's fault); *M.A. Santander Constr., Inc.*, ASBCA No. 35907, 91-3 BCA ¶ 24,050 (interference excused default); *Reliance Enter.*, ASBCA No. 20808, 76-1 BCA ¶ 11,831.

4. Abuse of discretion in the approval process. When the contract makes the precise manner of performance subject to approval by the contracting officer, the duty of cooperation requires that the government approve the contractor's methods unless approval is detrimental to the government's interest. Ralph C. Nash, Jr., *Government Contract Changes* 12-7 (2d ed. 1989). Common bases for claims are:

a. Failure to approve substitute items or components that are equal in quality and performance to the contract requirements. *Page Constr. Co.*, AGBCA No. 92-191-1, 93-3 BCA ¶ 26,060; *Bruce-Anderson Co.*, ASBCA No. 29411, 88-3 BCA ¶ 21,135 (contracting officer gave no explanation for refusal).

b. Unjustified disapproval of shop drawings or failure to approve within a reasonable time. *Vogt Bros. Mfg. Co. v. United States*, 160 Ct. Cl. 687 (1963).

   c. Improper failure to approve the substitution or use of a particular subcontractor. *Hoel-Steffen Constr. Co. v. United States*, 231 Ct. Cl. 128, 684 F.2d 843 (1982); *Liles Constr. Co. v. United States*, 197 Ct. Cl. 164, 455 F.2d 527 (1972); *Richerson Constr., Inc. v. Gen. Servs. Admin.*, GSBCA No. 11161, 93-1 BCA ¶ 25,239. *Cf.* FAR 52.236-5, Material and Workmanship.

## XII. FAILURE TO DISCLOSE VITAL INFORMATION (SUPERIOR KNOWLEDGE).

### A. Theory.

1. Part of the government's duty to cooperate with the contractor and not to hinder or interfere with its performance is a duty to disclose vital information of which the contractor is ignorant. *See Helene Curtis Indus. v. United States*, 312 F.2d 774 (Ct. Cl. 1963); *Miller Elevator Co. v. United States*, 30 Fed. Cl. 662 (1994); *Bradley Const. Inc. v. United States*, 30 Fed. Cl. 507 (1994); *Maitland Bros.*, ENG BCA No. 5782, 94-1 BCA ¶ 26,473.

2. Nondisclosure is a change to the contract because the contracting activity should have disclosed the vital information at contract award.

### B. Elements of the Implied Duty to Disclose Vital Information.

*Hercules, Inc. v. United States*, 24 F.3d 188 (Fed. Cir. 1994).

1. The contractor undertakes to perform without vital knowledge of a fact that affects performance costs or duration. *Sanders Constr. Co.*, IBCA No. 2309, 90-1 BCA ¶ 22,412; *Bradley Const., Inc. v. United States*, 30 Fed. Cl. 507 (1994) (information must have a direct bearing on the cost or duration of contract performance); *Johnson & Son Erector Co.*, ASBCA No. 23689, 86-2 BCA ¶ 18,931. (amount of interference caused by the nondisclosure is a factor in determining whether the

information is vital); *Numax Elec., Inc.*, ASBCA No. 29080, 90-1 BCA ¶ 22,280; *Riverport Indus., Inc.*, ASBCA No. 30888, 87-2 BCA ¶ 19,876 (government must disclose the history of a procurement if the information is necessary to successful performance).

2. The government was aware the contractor had no knowledge of and had no reason to obtain such information. *Hardeman-Monier-Hutcherson v. United States*, 198 Ct. Cl. 472, 458 F.2d 1364 (1972); *Max Jordan Bauunternehmung v. United States*, 10 Cl. Ct. 672 (1986), *aff'd*, 820 F.2d 1208 (Fed. Cir. 1987). *GAF Corp. v. United States*, 932 F.2d 947 (Fed. Cir. 1991) (government need not inquire into the knowledge of an experienced contractor).

3. The contract specification misled the contractor or did not put it on notice to inquire. *Jack L. Olsen, Inc.*, AGBCA No. 87-345-1, 93-2 BCA ¶ 25,767 (information provided in solicitation excused contractor from further inquiry). There is no breach of the duty to disclose vital information if the government shows that the contractor knew or should have known of the information. *H.N. Bailey & Assoc. v. United States*, 449 F.2d 376 (Ct. Cl. 1971) (information was general industry knowledge); *Metal Trades, Inc.*, ASBCA No. 41643, 91-2 BCA ¶ 23,982; *Hydromar Corp. of Del. & Eastern Seaboard v. United States*, 25 Cl. Ct. 555 (1992), *aff'd*, 980 F.2d 744 (Fed. Cir. 1992); (undisclosed information reasonably was available to the contractor); *Maitland Bros. Co.*, ENG BCA No. 5782, 94-1 BCA ¶ 26,473 (information in public domain). *See Kloke Transfer*, ASBCA No. 39602, 91-3 BCA ¶ 24,356 (information not reasonably available); *Panamint, Inc.*, ENG BCA No. 5351, 87-2 BCA ¶ 19,927 (contractor reasonably investigated)

4. The government failed to provide the relevant information. *P.J. Maffei Bldg. Wrecking Corp. v. United States*, 732 F.2d 913 (Fed. Cir. 1984) (contractor failed to prove government had better information than already disclosed); *Bethlehem Corp. v. United States*, 462 F.2d

1400 (Ct. Cl. 1972) (knowledge by one government agency is not attributable to another government agency absent some meaningful connection between the agencies).

## XIII. CONSTRUCTIVE ACCELERATION.

### A. Theory of Recovery.

1. If a contractor encounters an excusable delay, it is entitled to an extension of the contract schedule.

2. Constructive acceleration occurs when the contracting officer refuses to recognize a new contract schedule and demands that the contractor complete performance within the original contract period.

### B. Elements of Constructive Acceleration.
*Trepte Constr. Co.*, ASBCA No. 28555, 90-1 BCA ¶ 22,595.

1. the existence of one or more excusable delays;

2. notice by the contractor to the government of such delay and a request for an extension of time;

3. failure or refusal by the government to grant the extension request;

4. an express or implied order by the government to accelerate; and

5. actual acceleration resulting in increased costs.

### C. Actions That May Lead to Constructive Acceleration.

1. the government threatens to terminate when the contractor encounters an excusable delay, *Intersea Research Corp.*, IBCA No. 1675, 85-2 BCA ¶ 18,058;

2. the government threatens to assess liquidated damages and refuses to grant a time extension, *Norair Eng'g Corp. v. United States*, 666 F.2d 546 (Ct. Cl. 1981); or

3. the government delays approval of a request for a time extension. *Fishbach & Moore Int'l Corp.*, ASBCA No. 18146, 77-1 BCA ¶ 12,300, *aff'd*, 617 F.2d 223 (Ct. Cl. 1980). *But see Franklin Pavlov Constr. Co.*, HUD BCA No. 93-

C-13, 94-3 BCA ¶ 27,078 (mere denial of delay request due to lack of information not tantamount to government order to accelerate).

### D. Measure of Damages.

1. The contractor's acceleration efforts need not be successful; a reasonable attempt to meet a completion date is sufficient. *Fermont Div., Dynamic Corp.*, ASBCA No. 15806, 75-1 BCA ¶ 11,139.

2. The measure of recovery will be the difference between:
   a. the reasonable costs attributable to acceleration or attempting to accelerate; and
   b. the lesser costs the contractor reasonably would have incurred absent its acceleration efforts, plus
   c. a reasonable profit on the above-described difference.

3. Common acceleration costs.
   a. increased labor costs;
   b. increased material cost due to expedited delivery; and
   c. loss of efficiency or productivity. A method to compute this cost is to compare the work accomplished per labor hour or dollar during an acceleration period with the work accomplished per labor hour or dollar during a normal period. *See* Ralph C. Nash, Jr., *Government Contract Changes*, 18-16 and 18-17 (2d ed. 1989).

## XIV. NOTICE REQUIREMENTS.

### A. Notice of an Equitable Adjustment by the Contractor.

1. Formal changes. The standard Changes clauses require the contractor to assert its right to an adjustment within 30 days after receipt of a written change order. Courts and boards, however, do not strictly construe this requirement. A request for an equitable adjustment submitted prior to final payment is timely unless the late notice is prejudicial to the government. *Watson, Rice & Co.*, HUD BCA No. 89-4468-C8, 90-1 BCA ¶ 22,499; *SOSA Y Barbera Constrs., S.A.,* ENG BCA No.

PCC-57, 89-2 BCA ¶ 21,754; *E.W. Jerdon, Inc.*, ASBCA No. 32957, 88-2 BCA ¶ 20,729.

2. Constructive Changes. The standard supply and service contract Changes clauses do not prescribe specific periods within which a contractor must seek an adjustment for a constructive change.

   a. Under the Changes clause for construction contracts, however, a contractor must assert its right to an adjustment within 30 days of notifying the government that it considers a government action to be a change. FAR 52.243-4(b); FAR 52.243-4(e).

   b. In a construction contract, unless the contractor bases its adjustment on defective specifications, it may not recover costs incurred more than 20 days before notifying the government of a constructive change. FAR 52.243-4(d). *But see Martin J. Simko Constr., Inc. v. United States*, 11 Cl. Ct. 257 (1986) (government must show late notice was prejudicial).

   c. Requests for equitable adjustments based on constructive changes submitted *prior to final payment* are timely unless late notice is prejudicial to the government. *Martin J. Simko Constr., supra*; *Technical Food Servs., Inc.*, ASBCA No. 26808, 83-1 BCA ¶ 16,267.

3. Content of notice for *constructive changes*. *McLamb Upholstery, Inc.*, ASBCA No. 42112, 91-3 BCA ¶ 24,081.

   a. A contractor must assert a positive, present intent to seek recovery as a matter of legal right.

   b. Written notice is not required, and there is no formal method for asserting an intent to recover. The notice, however, must be more than an ambiguous letter that evidences a differing opinion. Likewise, merely advising the contracting officer of problems is not sufficient notice.

4. Effect of final payment.

   a. Requests for equitable adjustments raised for the first time after final payment are untimely. *Design & Prod., Inc. v. United States*, 18 Cl. Ct. 168 (1989) (final pay-

ment rule predicated on express contractual provisions); *Electro-Technology Corp.*, ASBCA No. 42495, 93-2 BCA ¶ 25,750.

   b. Final payment does not bar claims for equitable adjustments that were pending or of which the government had constructive knowledge at the time of final payment. *Gulf & Western Indus., Inc. v. United States*, 6 Cl. Ct. 742 (1984); *David Grimaldi Co.*, ASBCA No. 36043, 89-1 ¶ 21,341 (contractor must specifically assert a claim as a matter of right; letter merely presented arguments).

**B. Notice of an Equitable Adjustment by the Government.**

1. The standard Changes clauses do not limit the time within which the government must claim a downward equitable adjustment.

2. Under the Federal Acquisition Streamlining Act of 1994 (FASA), the government must now assert any claims it has against a contractor within six years from the accrual of the claim. FASA § 2351 (amending 41 U.S.C § 605).

3. The government must request an equitable adjustment within a reasonable time unless the contract specifies otherwise. In *Joseph H. Roberts v. United States*, 174 Ct. Cl. 940, 357 F.2d 938 (1966), the court held that to be reasonable, the government must act:

   a. while the facts supporting the claim are readily available; and

   b. before the contractor's position is prejudiced by final settlement with its subcontractors, suppliers, and other creditors.

## XV. CONCLUSION.

A. Changes issues are the heart of contract administration.

B. You must understand when formal changes are proper and the proper procedures for making formal changes.

C. You must understand the various types of constructive changes and the consequences of constructive changes.

# CHANGES CLAUSE (SUPPLIES), FAR 52.243-1

## CHANGES—FIXED-PRICE (AUG 1987)

(a) The Contracting Officer may at any time, by written order, and without notice to the sureties, if any, make changes within the general scope of this contract in any one or more of the following:

    (1) Drawings, designs, or specifications when the supplies to be furnished are to be specially manufactured for the Government in accordance with the drawings, designs, or specifications.

    (2) Method of shipment or packing.

    (3) Place of delivery.

(b) If any such change causes an increase or decrease in the cost of, or the time required for, performance of any part of the work under this contract, whether or not changed by the order, the Contracting Officer shall make an equitable adjustment in the contract price, the delivery schedule, or both, and shall modify the contract.

(c) The Contractor must assert its right to an adjustment under this clause within 30 days from the date of receipt of the written order. However, if the Contracting Officer decides that the facts justify it, the Contracting Officer may receive and act upon a proposal submitted before final payment of the contract.

(d) If the Contractor's proposal includes the cost of property made obsolete or excess by the change, the Contracting Officer shall have the right to prescribe the manner of the disposition of the property.

(e) Failure to agree to any adjustment shall be a dispute under the Disputes clause. However, nothing in this clause shall excuse the Contractor from proceeding with the contract as changed.

# CHANGES CLAUSE (SERVICES), FAR 52.243-1, ALTERNATE 1

### CHANGES—FIXED-PRICE (AUG 1987)

(a) The Contracting Officer may at any time, by written order, and without notice to the sureties, if any, make changes within the general scope of this contract in any one or more of the following:
  (1) Description of services to be performed.
  (2) Time of performance (i.e., hours of the day, days of the week, etc.).
  (3) Place of performance of the services.

(b) If any such change causes an increase or decrease in the cost of, or the time required for, performance of any part of the work under this contract, whether or not changed by the order, the Contracting Officer shall make an equitable adjustment in the contract price, the delivery schedule, or both, and shall modify the contract.

(c) The Contractor must assert its right to an adjustment under this clause within 30 days from the date of receipt of the written order. However, if the Contracting Officer decides that the facts justify it, the Contracting Officer may receive and act upon a proposal submitted before final payment of the contract.

(d) If the Contractor's proposal includes the cost of property made obsolete or excess by the change, the Contracting Officer shall have the right to prescribe the manner of the disposition of the property.

(e) Failure to agree to any adjustment shall be a dispute under the Disputes clause. However, nothing in this clause shall excuse the Contractor from proceeding with the contract as changed.

# CHANGES CLAUSE (CONSTRUCTION), FAR 52.243-4

## CHANGES (AUG 1987)

(a) The Contracting Officer may, at any time, without notice to the sureties, if any, by written order designated or indicated to be a change order, make changes in the work within the general scope of the contract, including changes—

(1) In the specifications (including drawings and designs);

(2) In the method or manner of performance of the work;

(3) In the Government-furnished facilities, equipment, materials, services, or site; or

(4) Directing acceleration in the performance of the work.

(b) Any other written order or oral order (which, as used in this paragraph (b), includes direction, instruction, interpretation or determination) from the Contracting Officer that causes a change shall be treated as a change order under this clause; *provided*, that the Contractor gives the Contracting Officer written notice stating (1) the date, circumstances, and source of the order and (2) that the Contractor regards the order as a change order.

(c) Except as provided in this clause, no order, statement, or conduct of the Contracting Officer shall be treated as a change under this clause or entitle the Contractor to an equitable adjustment.

(d) If any change under this clause causes an increase or decrease in the Contractor's costs of, or the time required for, the performance of any part of the work under this contract, whether or not changed by any such order, the Contracting Officer shall make an equitable adjustment and modify the contract in writing. However, except for an adjustment based on defective specifications, no adjustment for any change under paragraph (b) above shall be made for any costs incurred more than 20 days before the Contractor gives written notice as required. In the case of defective specifications for which the Government is responsible, the equitable adjustment shall include any increased cost reasonably incurred by the Contractor in attempting to comply with such defective specifications.

(e) The Contractor must assert its right to an adjustment under this clause within 30 days after (1) receipt of a written change order under paragraph (a) of this clause or (2) the furnishing of a written notice under paragraph (b) of this clause, by submitting to the Contracting Officer a written statement describing the general nature and amount of the proposal, unless this period is extended by the Government. The statement of proposal for adjustment may be included in the notice under paragraph (b) above.

(f) No proposal by the Contractor for an equitable adjustment shall be allowed if asserted after final payment under this contract.

# STANDARD FORM (SF) 30, AMENDMENT OF SOLICITATION/MODIFICATION OF CONTRACT

## AMENDMENT OF SOLICITATION/MODIFICATION OF CONTRACT

| 1. CONTRACT ID CODE | PAGE OF PAGES |
|---|---|

| 2. AMENDMENT/MODIFICATION NO. | 3. EFFECTIVE DATE | 4. REQUISITION/PURCHASE REQ. NO. | 5. PROJECT NO. (If applicable) |
|---|---|---|---|

| 6. ISSUED BY | CODE | 7. ADMINISTERED BY (If other than Item 6) | CODE |
|---|---|---|---|

8. NAME AND ADDRESS OF CONTRACTOR (No., street, county, state and ZIP code)

(✓)

9A. AMENDMENT OF SOLICITATION NO.

9B. DATED (SEE ITEM 11)

10A. MODIFICATION OF CONTRACT/ORDER NO.

10B. DATED (SEE ITEM 13)

| CODE | FACILITY CODE |
|---|---|

## 11. THIS ITEM ONLY APPLIES TO AMENDMENTS OF SOLICITATIONS

[ ] The above numbered solicitation is amended as set forth in Item 14. The hour and date specified for receipt of Offers [ ] is extended, [ ] is not extended.

Offers must acknowledge receipt of this amendment prior to the hour and date specified in the solicitation or as amended, by one of the following methods:

(a) By completing Items 8 and 15, and returning _____ copies of the amendment; (b) By acknowledging receipt of this amendment on each copy of the offer submitted; or (c) By separate letter or telegram which includes a reference to the solicitation and amendment numbers. FAILURE OF YOUR ACKNOWLEDGMENT TO BE RECEIVED AT THE PLACE DESIGNATED FOR THE RECEIPT OF OFFERS PRIOR TO THE HOUR AND DATE SPECIFIED MAY RESULT IN REJECTION OF YOUR OFFER. If by virtue of this amendment you desire to change an offer already submitted, such change may be made by telegram or letter, provided each telegram or letter makes reference to the solicitation and this amendment, and is received prior to the opening hour and date specified.

12. ACCOUNTING AND APPROPRIATION DATA (If required)

## 13. THIS ITEM APPLIES ONLY TO MODIFICATIONS OF CONTRACTS/ORDERS, IT MODIFIES THE CONTRACT/ORDER NO. AS DESCRIBED IN ITEM 14.

| (✓) | |
|---|---|
| | A. THIS CHANGE ORDER IS ISSUED PURSUANT TO: (Specifiy authority) THE CHANGES SET FORTH IN ITEM 14 ARE MADE IN THE CONTRACT ORDER NO. IN ITEM 10A. |
| | B. THE ABOVE NUMBERED CONTRACT/ORDER IS MODIFIED TO REFLECT THE ADMINISTRATIVE CHANGES (such as changes in paying office, appropriation date, etc.) SET FORTH IN ITEM 14, PURSUANT TO THE AUTHORITY OF FAR 43.103(b). |
| | C. THIS SUPPLEMENTAL AGREEMENT IS ENTERED INTO PURSUANT TO AUTHORITY OF: |
| | D. OTHER (Specify type of modification and authority) |

E. IMPORTANT: Contractor [ ] is not, [ ] is required to sign this document and return _____ copies to the issuing office.

14. DESCRIPTION OF AMENDMENT/MODIFICATION (Organized by UCF section headings, including solicitation/contract subject matter where feasible.)

Except as provided herein, all terms and conditions of the document referenced in Item 9A or 10A, as heretofore changed, remains unchanged and in full force and effect.

| 15A. NAME AND TITLE OF SIGNER (Type or print) | 16A. NAME AND TITLE OF CONTRACTING OFFICER (Type or print) |
|---|---|

| 15B. CONTRACTOR/OFFEROR | 15C. DATE SIGNED | 16B. UNITED STATES OF AMERICA | 16C. DATE SIGNED |
|---|---|---|---|
| (Signature of person authorized to sign) | | BY _____ (Signature of Contracting Officer) | |

NSN 7540-01-152-8070
PREVIOUS EDITION UNUSABLE

30-105-02

STANDARD FORM 30 (Rev. 10-83)
Prescribed by GSA
FAR (48 CFR) 53.243

## CHAPTER THIRTEEN

# *Selected Labor Standards*

## I. INTRODUCTION.

Following this block of instruction, students will understand:

A. The general statutory and regulatory framework of labor standards affecting government contracts.

B. The requirements of the Davis-Bacon, Service Contract, and Walsh-Healey Acts.

C. The remedies for violations of labor standards.

## II. FAIR LABOR STANDARDS ACT OF 1938 (FLSA).

29 U.S.C. §§ 201-219; FAR Subpart 22.10.

### A. Application.

1. The FLSA was the first federal wage-hour law having general applicability; its application is not limited to government contracts.

2. The FLSA covers employees engaged in interstate commerce and the production of goods for interstate commerce.

### B. Purposes.

1. The statute specifies a federal minimum wage.

2. It requires payment of overtime wages.

3. The FLSA restricts the use of child labor.

## III. CONTRACT WORK HOURS AND SAFETY STANDARDS ACT (CWHSSA).

40 U.S.C. §§ 327-333; FAR Subpart 22.3; FAR 22.403-3; DFARS Subpart 222.3.

### A. Application.

1. Types of employees covered—laborers and mechanics.

2. Types of contracts covered.

   a. Contracts exceeding $2,000 for public works of the United States or the District of Columbia.

   b. Other contracts exceeding $2,500 to which the United States or one of its agencies, instrumentalities, and territories, or the District of Columbia, is a party.

3. The CWHSSA usually does not apply to supply contracts. FAR 22.305(c).

### B. Purposes.

1. CWHSSA establishes a forty-hour work week and requires the payment of overtime wages for public works and other covered contracts. *See Maitland Bros. Inc.*, ENG BCA No. 5782, Oct. 13, 1993, 94-1 BCA ¶ 26,473.

2. CWHSSA specifies health and safety requirements.

### C. Government Policy.

It is government policy that contractors perform without using overtime. FAR 22.103-2. The government will not reimburse the contractor for overtime payments unless the contracting officer determines that overtime is in the government's interest. FAR 52.222-2.

## IV. COPELAND (ANTI-KICKBACK) ACT.

18 U.S.C. § 874; 40 U.S.C. § 276c; 29 C.F.R. Part 3; FAR 22.403-2.

### A. Application.

1. The Anti-Kickback Act protects the wages of *any person* engaged in the construction or

repair of a public building or public work (including projects that are *financed at least in part by* federal loans or grants).

2. The Act requires prime contractors and subcontractors to submit a weekly statement of compliance pertaining to the wages paid to each employee during the preceding week. FAR 22.40-32; FAR 52.222.10.

### B. Purpose.

The Act prohibits employers from exacting "kickbacks" from employees as a condition of employment.

### C. Recordkeeping Requirements.

The Act requires contractors and subcontractors to submit weekly payroll reports and statements of compliance. Both the contractors and the agency must keep these records for three years after completion of the contract. FAR 22.406-6.

### V. DAVIS-BACON ACT (DBA).

40 U.S.C. §§ 276a to 276a-7; 29 C.F.R. Part 5; FAR Subpart 22.4; DFARS Subpart 222.4.

### A. Statutory Requirements.

40 U.S.C. § 276a; FAR 22.403-1.

1. Contractors must pay mechanics and laborers a "prevailing wage rate" on federal construction projects performed in the United States that exceed $2,000.

2. The prevailing wage rate is the key to the Davis-Bacon labor standards. The Department of Labor determines the minimum wage which normally is based on the wage paid to the majority of a class of employees in an area. 29 C.F.R. § 1.2 (1994).

   a. A wage rate determination is not subject to review by the General Accounting Office or boards of contract appeals. *American Fed'n of Labor - Congress of Indus. Org., Bldg., and Constr. Trades Dep't*, B-211189, Apr. 12, 1983, 83-1 CPD ¶ 386; *Woodington Corp.*, ASBCA No. 34053, 87-3 BCA ¶ 19,957.

   b. "Wages" under the terms of the DBA

include the basic hourly rates of pay plus fringe benefits.

### B. Application.

FAR 22.402.

1. The DBA applies to federal contracts primarily involving the construction of public buildings.

   a. The DBA only applies to construction activity performed on "the site of the work." Generally, construction activity does not encompass manufacturing, supplying materials, or performing service/maintenance work.

   b. Construction does *not* include transportation of materials to and from the project site. *See Building & Constr. Trades Dep't, AFL-CIO v. Dep't of Labor Wage Appeals Board*, 932 F.2d 985 (D.C. Cir. 1991), *rev'g* 747 F. Supp. 26 (D.D.C. 1990). *Cf.* 29 C.F.R. § 3.2(b) (1994); 29 C.F.R. § 5.2(j) (1994).

   c. The "site of the work" is limited to the geographical confines of the construction jobsite. *Ball, Ball, and Brossamer, Inc. v. Reich*, 24 F.3d 1447 (D.C. Cir 1994), *rev'g Ball, Ball, and Brosamer, Inc. v. Martin, Sec'y of Labor*, 800 F. Supp. 967 (D.D.C. 1992).

   d. "Public building" or "public work" means a construction or repair project which is carried on by the authority, or with the funds, of a federal agency to serve the interests of the general public.

2. Dual coverage. *See* DFARS 222.402-70.

   a. The DBA also may apply to construction work performed under a non-construction contract, e.g., installation support contract. Apply DBA standards if the contract requires a substantial and segregable amount of construction, repair, painting, alteration, or renovation.

   b. The DBA applies to *repairs* but not to *maintenance*. The DFARS provides a bright line test to determine whether work is maintenance (Service Contract Act work) or repair (Davis-Bacon Act work). If a service order requires 32 or more work hours, the work is "repair." Otherwise, consider the work to be "maintenance." For painting, the work is subject to the DBA if the service order requires painting of 200 square feet or more, regardless of workhours.

3. Non-dual coverage. The DBA *does not apply* to construction work to be performed as part of non-construction contracts, if:
   a. The construction work is incidental to other contract requirements; or
   b. The construction work is so merged with nonconstruction work, or so fragmented in terms of the locations or time spans in which it is to be performed, that it cannot be segregated as a separate contractual requirement.

## C. Employees Covered and Exempted.
29 C.F.R. § 5.2(m); FAR 22.401.
1. "Laborers or mechanics" are covered, including:
   a. Manual laborers employed by a contractor or subcontractor *at any tier*.
   b. Working foremen who devote more than 20 percent of their time during a workweek to performing duties as a laborer or mechanic.
2. Office workers, superintendents, technical engineers, scientific workers, and other professionals, executives, and administrative personnel are *exempt*. 29 C.F.R. Part 541.

## D. Types of Wage Determinations.
29 C.F.R. § 1.6 (1994); FAR 22.404-1.
1. *General Wage Determinations*. 29 C.F.R. §§ 1.5(b) and 1.6(a)(2) (1994); FAR 22.404-1(a). A general wage rate determination contains prevailing wage rates for the types of construction specified in the determination, and is used in contracts performed within a specified geographical area. General wage determinations remain valid until modified or cancelled by the Department of Labor.
2. *Project Wage Determinations*. 29 C.F.R. § 1.6(a)(1); FAR 22.404-1(b).

a. The contracting officer uses a project wage determination when no general wage determination applies to the work. The determin-ation is effective for 180 calendar days from the date of its issuance.
b. If the project wage determination expires, the contracting officer must follow special procedures; these vary depending on whether the activity contracted by sealed bidding or negotiation. FAR 22.404-5.

## E. Procedures for Obtaining Wage Determinations.
FAR 22.404-3.
1. General requirements.
   a. If a general wage determination is applicable to the project, the agency may use it without notifying DOL.
   b. If necessary, a contracting officer may request that DOL issue a general wage determination.
   c. A contracting officer may request a project wage determination from DOL by specifying the location of the project and including a detailed description of the types of construction involved and the estimated cost of the project.
   d. Processing time for wage rate determinations is at least 30 days.
   e. DOL (Wage and Hour Division) defines types of construction for use in selecting proper wage rate schedules. FAR 22.404-2(c).
2. If possible, the contracting officer must include the proper wage rate determination in each solicitation covered by the DBA.
   a. Solicitations issued without a wage rate determination must advise that the contracting officer will issue a schedule of minimum wage rates as an amendment to the solicitation. FAR 22.404-4(a). If an offeror fails to acknowledge an amendment that adds or modifies a wage rate, the offer may be nonresponsive. *North Santiam Paving Co.*, B-241062, Jan. 8, 1991, 91-1 CPD ¶ 18. *But see BUI Constr. Co. & Bldg. Supply*, ASBCA No. 28707, 84-

1 BCA ¶ 17,183 (board incorporates missing wage rate as a matter of law).

b. If the activity uses sealed bidding, it may not open bids until a reasonable time after furnishing the wage determination to all bidders.

c. In negotiated acquisitions, the contracting officer may open the proposals and conduct negotiations before obtaining the wage determination but must include the wage determination in the solicitation before calling for best and final offers. FAR 22.404-4(c).

## F. Failure to Incorporate a Wage Determination.

If the contracting officer fails to incorporate a wage determination in a contract upon award, the contracting officer must:

1. Modify the contract to incorporate the required wage rate determination, retroactive to the date of award, and equitably adjust the contract price, if appropriate [FAR 22.404-9(b)(1)]. *See BellSouth Comm. Sys., Inc.*, ASBCA No. 45955, Sept. 27, 1994, 94-3 BCA ¶ 27,231; or

2. Terminate the contract. FAR 22.404-9(b)(2). *Sunspot Garden Ctr. & Country Craft Gift Shop*, B-237065.2, Feb. 26, 1990, 90-1 CPD ¶ 224.

## G. Modifications of Wage Determinations.
FAR 22.404-6.

1. The DOL may modify a general or project wage rate determination at any time. The need to incorporate such wage rate modifications in a solicitation or contract depends upon the type of determination and when the agency receives notice of the proposed modification.

   a. General - Publication of notice in the Federal Register is constructive "receipt."

   b. Project - Actual receipt by the contracting *agency* governs.

2. Sealed bidding procedures. FAR 22.404-6(b).

   a. Before bid opening, a modification is effective if:

(1) The contracting agency receives it, or DOL publishes notice of the modification in the Federal Register 10 or more calendar days before the date of bid opening; or

(2) The agency receives it, or DOL publishes notice less than 10 calendar days before the date of bid opening, unless the contracting officer finds that there is not reasonable time available before bid opening to notify prospective bidders.

   b. If the contracting officer receives an effective modification *before* bid opening, the contracting officer must extend the opening and permit bidders to revise their offers. FAR 22.404-6(b)(3).

   c. If notice of a modification to a general wage determination is published in the Federal Register after bid opening, but before award, the modification will be "effective" if award is not made within 90 days of opening. FAR 22.404-6(b)(6).

   d. If the contracting officer receives an "effective" modification *after* bid opening, but *before* award, the contracting officer may:

      (1) Award the contract and incorporate the new determination to be effective on the date of contract award; or

      (2) Cancel the solicitation.

   e. If the contracting officer receives an effective modification *after award*, the contracting officer shall modify the contract to incorporate the wage modification retroactive to the date of award. FAR 22.404-6(b)(5).

3. If using negotiation procedures:

   a. All modifications received by the contracting agency or published in the Federal Register *before award*, are effective. FAR 22.404-6(c)(1).

   b. If the contracting officer receives an effective wage modification *before award* and it changes a previous determination, the contracting officer must amend the solicitation to include the modification and must allow prospective offerors to revise their proposals if the closing date for receipt of proposals has not yet passed. If the closing date has passed, the contracting officer must notify only offerors who submitted proposals. FAR 22.404-6(c)(2).

c. If the contracting officer receives an effective modification *after award*, he must modify the contract to incorporate the change. FAR 22.404-6(c)(3).

## H. Contract Administration—Compliance Checks and Investigations.

1. The contracting officer must make checks and conduct investigations to ensure compliance with the DBA requirements. FAR 22.406-7; DFARS 222.406-1.

2. Regular compliance checks include:
   a. Employee interviews;
   b. On-site inspections;
   c. Payroll reviews; and
   d. Comparison of information gathered during checks with available data, e.g., inspector reports and construction activity logs.

3. The contracting officer must make special compliance checks when he detects inconsistencies, errors, or omissions during regular checks, or if he receives a complaint.

4. Labor standards investigations. FAR 22.406-8; DFARS 222.406-8.
   a. The contracting agency conducts an investigation when compliance checks indicate that violations are substantial in amount, willful, or uncorrected. The DOL also may perform or request an investigation.
   b. The contracting officer provides notice of preliminary findings, proposed corrective actions, and certain contractor rights. FAR 22.406-8(c).
   c. The contracting officer forwards his report to the agency head who, in certain cases, must forward it to DOL. If the contracting officer suspects criminal activity, the agency head must forward the report to the U.S. Attorney General.

## I. Withholding and Suspending Contract Payments.
FAR 22.406-9.

1. The contracting officer must *withhold* contract payments if the contracting officer believes that a violation of the DBA exists, or upon request by the DOL. *M.E. McGeary Co.*, ASBCA No. 36788, 90-1 BCA ¶ 22,512. *See* 29 C.F.R. § 5.5(a)(2); FAR 22.406-9(a)(1) (allowing cross-withholding).

2. The contracting officer may *suspend* any further payment, advance, or guarantee of funds otherwise due to a contractor if a contractor or subcontractor fails or refuses to comply with the DBA.

## J. Disputes Relating to DBA Enforcement.
FAR 22.406-10; 52.222-14.

1. The DOL settles labor disputes that are not resolved at the local level. Labor disputes are not reviewable under the Disputes clause. *Emerald Maint., Inc. v. United States*, 925 F.2d 1425 (Fed. Cir. 1991); *Page Constr. Co.*, ASBCA No. 39685, 90-3 BCA ¶ 23,012; *M.E. McGeary Co., supra.*

2. Boards of contract appeals and courts review claims relating to labor disputes if the dispute is based on the contractual rights and obligations of the parties. *See, e.g., Central Paving, Inc.*, ASBCA No. 38658, 90-1 BCA ¶ 22,305 (board had jurisdiction to review claim that the original wage rate information in the contract was incorrect). *Compare Page Constr. Co.*, ASBCA No. 39685, 90-3 BCA ¶ 23,012 (no jurisdiction over claim that government breached a statutory obligation); *American Maint. Co.*, ASBCA No. 42011, 92-2 BCA ¶ 24,806 (BCA has jurisdiction over contractor's claim for reimbursement of fringe benefits).

3. Federal district courts have jurisdiction to review DOL's implementation of the DBA, i.e., district courts entertain appeals from DOL decisions. *See, e.g., Building and Constr. Trades Dep't, AFL-CIO v. Sec'y of Labor*, 747 F. Supp. 26 (D.D.C. 1990).

## VI. MCNAMARA-O'HARA SERVICE CONTRACT ACT OF 1965 (SCA).

41 U.S.C. §§ 351-358; 29 C.F.R. Part 4; FAR Subpart 22.10; DFARS Subpart 222.10.

### A. Statutory Requirements.

1. Contractors performing any service contract shall pay their employees not less than the FLSA minimum wage.

2. Service contracts over $2,500 *shall contain* mandatory provisions regarding minimum wages and fringe benefits, safe and sanitary working conditions, notification to employees of the minimum allowable compensation, and equivalent federal employee classifications and wage rates. However, even if omitted from the solicitation, the SCA and applicable wage determinations are binding on contractors. *Kleenco, Inc. d/b/a/ Superior Linen-Laundry*, ASBCA No. 44348, 93-2 BCA 25,619; *Miller's Moving Co.*, ASBCA No. 43114, 92-1 BCA ¶ 24,707.

3. For contracts over $2,500, the minimum wage and fringe benefits are based on either:
   a. Wage and fringe benefit determinations issued by DOL; or
   b. Wages and fringe benefits established by a predecessor contractor's collective bargaining agreement (CBA). 29 C.F.R. §§ 4.5 and 4.152 (1994); FAR 22.1002-2.

### B. Application.

FAR 22.1002; FAR 22.1003. The SCA applies to:
1. Service contracts.
   a. "Service contract" means any federal contract, except as exempted by the SCA, the principal purpose of which is to furnish services in the United States through the use of service employees. 29 C.F.R. § 4.111 (1994); FAR 22.1001.
   b. The SCA does *not* apply if the *principal purpose* of a contract is to provide something other than services of the character contemplated by the SCA. Further, the SCA is not applicable to services performed *incidental* to a non-service contract. *J.L. Assocs.*, B-236698.2, Jan. 17,

1990, 90-1 CPD ¶ 60. *See Westbrook Indus., Inc.*, B-248854, Sept. 28, 1992, 92-2 CPD ¶ 213 (agency reasonably determined that rental of washers and dryers was not subject to SCA).
   c. The SCA applies to service contracts performed in the United States. 29 C.F.R. § 4.112(a) (1994); FAR 22.1003-2. "United States" includes any state, the District of Columbia, Puerto Rico, and certain specified possessions/territories.
2. Performed by service employees.
   a. The SCA applies only to service employees. "Service employee" means any person engaged in the performance of a service contract or subcontract, other than persons employed in bona fide executive, administrative, or professional capacities. 29 C.F.R. § 4.113 (1994); FAR 22.1001. *See* 29 C.F.R. Part 541 (defines executives, professionals, and others).
   b. The term "service employee" includes all nonexempt persons engaged in the performance of a service contract regardless of any contractual relationship alleged to exist between a contractor or subcontractor and such persons. 29 C.F.R. §§ 4.113 and 4.155 (1994); FAR 22.1001.

### C. Statutory Exemptions and Dual Coverage Under the Service Contract Act.

41 U.S.C. § 356; 29 C.F.R. §§ 4.115 to 4.122 (1994); FAR 22.1003-3.
1. Davis-Bacon Act (DBA) coverage.
   a. The SCA does not apply if the principal purpose of a contract is to obtain construction work. In such a situation, the DBA covers all work done under the contract, including any incidental service-type work.
   b. Dual coverage. The DBA requires contracting officers to incorporate DBA provisions and clauses under a service contract if there is a substantial amount of segregable construction work.
2. Walsh-Healey Public Contracts Act (WHA) coverage.

a. The SCA does not apply if the principal purpose of the contract is the manufacture or delivery of supplies, materials, or equipment.

b. Dual coverage. Some work under a service contract may be exempt from the SCA because it entails the manufacture or delivery of supplies, materials, or equipment.

3. Miscellaneous statutory exemptions. *See* FAR 22.1003-3.

## D. Administrative Variances and Exemptions.

1. The DOL may establish reasonable variations, tolerances, and exemptions from SCA provisions. 41 U.S.C. § 353(b).

2. Requirements exempted from SCA coverage by the DOL are found at 29 C.F.R. § 4.123 and FAR 22.1003-4.

## E. Compensation Standards Under the SCA.

1. Regardless of the amount of a contract or subcontract, a contractor or subcontractor on a contract covered by the SCA must pay service employees *at least* the minimum wage specified by the FLSA. 29 C.F.R. §§ 4.159 and 4.160 (1994); FAR 22.1002-4.

2. Service contracts over $2,500. 29 C.F.R. §§ 4.161 through 4.163 (1994); FAR 22.1002-3.

   a. A contractor must pay service employees not less than the wage rate issued by DOL for the contract. DOL's wage determination is based either on a prevailing wage/fringe rate or a collective bargaining agreement (CBA).

   b. If there is no wage determination or effective CBA, the FLSA minimum wage applies.

## F. Obtaining Wage Rate Determinations (WRD).

FAR 22.1007 and 22.1008; DFARS 222.1008; 29 C.F.R. § 4.143 (1994).

1. The contracting officer must obtain wage rate determinations for:

   a. Each new solicitation and contract exceeding $2,500;

   b. A contract modification that increases the contract to over $2,500;

   c. Extends the contract pursuant to an option clause or otherwise; or

   d. Changes the scope of the contract whereby labor requirements are affected *significantly*.

   e. Each multiple year contract in excess of $2,500. The contracting officer must request a wage determination annually if funding is annual, or biennially if funding is not subject to annual appropriations.

2. The contracting officer must request a WRD from DOL by submitting a notice of intent to make a service contract (SF 98). DOL will issue a determination, and the contracting officer must include it in the solicitation and contract. FAR 22.1012-1. *Information Handling Servs., Inc.*, B-240011, Oct. 19, 1990, 90-2 CPD ¶ 306. *Cf. Allen-Norris-Vance Enter., Inc.*, B-243115, July 5, 1991, 91-2 CPD ¶ 23 (contractor that quotes rates below those set forth in the WRD is eligible for award).

   a. The contracting officer shall request a WRD not less than 60 days before initiation or renewal of an acquisition action. If an action is for a nonrecurring or unknown requirement and advance planning was not feasible, only 30 days advance notice is required. FAR 22.1008-7.

   b. There are different rules for determining whether a revised or new WRD will be applicable to a solicitation/contract. Applicability hinges on the method of acquisition, whether there is a CBA, and whether the request for a WRD was timely.

   c. If there is a CBA, the contracting officer must timely notify the incumbent contractor and the collective bargaining agent of planned acquisition dates. FAR 22.1008-3.

## G. "Successor Contractor" Rule.

1. If an activity competes a new contract for substantially the same services, and the contract is to be performed in the same locality, the successor contractor must pay wages and

fringe benefits at least equal to those contained in any *bona fide* CBA *effective* under the previous contract. 29 C.F.R. § 4.163; FAR 22.1008-3(b). *Klate Holt Co. v. Int'l Bhd. of Elec. Workers*, 868 F.2d 671 (4th Cir. 1989); *Professional Servs. Unified, Inc.*, ASBCA No. 45799, 94-1 BCA ¶ 26,580.

2. This rule also applies when the contracting officer exercises an option extending the term of a contract, or changes the scope of the labor requirement, or at any other time that a new WRD is required.

3. Exceptions. The new CBA will not apply to the successor contract if:

   a. The incumbent enters into a CBA for the first time, and the CBA will not be effective until after the incumbent's contract expires;

   b. The agency has timely notified the incumbent contractor and bargaining agent of the applicable acquisition dates, but the agency has not received timely notice of the terms of a new CBA, the new CBA will not apply to the successor contract. FAR 22.1008-3(c); or

   c. DOL determines that the CBA was not negotiated in good faith or that the rates set in the CBA vary substantially from the prevailing rates. *Vigilantes, Inc. v. United States*, 968 F.2d 1412 (1st Cir. 1992).

### H. Price Adjustments for Wage Rate Increases.

1. Generally, the wage rate incorporated at award will not change throughout the life of the contract.

2. If, however, there is an increase in the FLSA minimum wage rate, or a new wage rate incorporated upon exercise of an option increases labor costs, the contractor may be entitled to a price adjustment. FAR 52.222-43; FAR 52.222-44. *See United States v. Serv. Ventures, Inc.*, 899 F.2d 1 (Fed. Cir. 1990); *Williams Servs., Inc.*, ASBCA No. 41121, 91-1 BCA ¶ 23,486; *Gricoski Detective Agency*, GSBCA No. 8901(7823), 90-3 BCA ¶ 23,131 (adjustment not allowed since contract

included priced option years, and contractor did not include vacation pay costs in its option year prices). *Cf. Sterling Servs., Inc.*, ASBCA No. 40475, 91-2 BCA ¶ 23,714 (partial relief on claim arising from corrected wage determination).

3. A contractor is not entitled to a price adjustment for the increased costs of complying with a wage rate determination in existence at the time of contract award. *Holmes & Narver Servs.*, ASBCA No. 40111, 93-3 BCA ¶ 26,246 (SCA Price Adjustment clause does not entitle contractor to an adjustment for complying with an unchanged wage rate determination). *But see Professional Servs. Unified, Inc.*, ASBCA No. 45799, 94-1 BCA ¶ 26,580 (contractor entitled to equitable adjustment on a mutual mistake theory when incorrect wage rate determination incorporated into contract).

## VII. WALSH-HEALEY PUBLIC CONTRACTS ACT OF 1936 (WHA).

41 U.S.C. §§ 35-45; 41 C.F.R. Parts 50-201 to 50-210; FAR Subpart 22.6; DFARS Subpart 222.6.

### A. 1994 Amendments.

Section 7201 of the Federal Acquisition Streamlining Act of 1994, Pub. L. No. 103-355, 108 Stat. 3243 (1994), eliminated the requirement that contractors must be a regular dealer or manufacturer of the items to be furnished under a contract.

### B. What's Left?

1. Wage Rate Determinations. 41 U.S.C. § 35(a).

   a. Under the WHA, DOL determines the prevailing minimum wages based on similar wages in the applicable industry and locale in which the supplies are to be manufactured or furnished under a contract. 41 U.S.C. § 35(b). Presently, however, there is no wage rate determination activity under the Act.

   b. The FLSA minimum wage is the Walsh-Healey Act wage rate.

2. Overtime Provisions. 41 U.S.C. § 35(b).

3. Child and Convict Labor. 41 U.S.C. § 35(c).

4. Health and Safety Requirements. 41 U.S.C. § 35(d).

## VIII. REMEDIES FOR LABOR STANDARDS VIOLATIONS.

### A. Termination for Default.

1. WHA - 41 U.S.C. § 36.

2. DBA - 40 U.S.C. § 276a-1. *See Kelso v. Kirk Bros. Mech. Contractors, Inc.*, 16 F.3d 1173 (Fed. Cir. 1994); *Quality Granite Constr. Co.*, ASBCA No. 43846, 93-3 BCA ¶ 26,073.

3. SCA - 41 U.S.C. § 352(c).

4. CWHSSA - 40 U.S.C. § 333(b) (after DOL makes a determination of noncompliance).

### B. Debarment.

1. WHA - 41 U.S.C. § 37; 41 C.F.R. § 50-203.1 (violation of stipulations or representations of the Act).

2. DBA - 40 U.S.C. § 276a-2(a); 29 C.F.R. § 5.12 (for disregard of its obligations to employees or sub-contractors under the Act).

3. SCA - 41 U.S.C. § 354(a).

4. CWHSSA - 40 U.S.C. § 333; 29 C.F.R. § 5.12 (for aggravated or willful violation).

### C. Withholding Contract Funds.

1. WHA - 41 U.S.C. § 36 (held in account and paid directly to employees on order of DOL).

2. DBA - 40 U.S.C. § 276a-2 (turned over to GAO, which may pay employees directly).

3. SCA - 41 U.S.C. § 352(a); 29 C.F.R. 4.187 (turned over to DOL on order); *Castle Bldg. Maint., Inc.*, GSBCA No. 10003, 90-3 BCA ¶ 23,271; *National Sec. Serv. Co.*, DOT CAB NO. 1033, 80-1 BCA ¶ 14,268. *But see Jeanneate M. Bailey v. Dep't of Labor*, 810 F. Supp. 261 (Alaska D.C., 1993), where the court held that a contracting officer's withholding of underpaid SCA wages arising under another contract was an unconstitutional denial of the contractor's due process.

4. CWHSSA - 40 U.S.C. § 328(b)(2) (held in account and paid directly to employees).

### D. Liquidated Damages ($10.00 a day for each employee improperly paid).

1. WHA - 41 U.S.C. § 36.

2. DBA/SCA (per CWHSSA) - 40 U.S.C. § 328(b)(2); *United States v. Munsey Trust Co.*, 332 U.S. 234 (1947); *To the Secretary of the Air Force*, B-123227, 48 Comp. Gen. 387 (1968).

## CHAPTER FOURTEEN

# *Construction Contracting*

## I. INTRODUCTION.

Following this block of instruction, students should:

A. Understand the unique clauses and procedures used in construction contracting.

B. Understand how to analyze common legal issues that arise in construction contracting.

## II. REFERENCES.

A. FAR Parts 28, 36; DFARS Parts 228, 236; AFARS Part 36; AFFARS Part 5336.

B. Army Regulations.
1. AR 415-10, Military Construction—General (Apr. 1, 1984).
2. AR 415-15, Army Military Construction Program Development and Execution (Aug. 30, 1994).
3. AR 420-10, Management of Installation Directorates of Eng'g and Housing (July 2, 1987).
4. AR 210-50, Housing Mgmt. (Apr. 24, 1990).

C. Air Force Regulations.
1. AFR 85-2, Operations Mgmt. (Oct. 1980).
2. AFR 88-25, Military Family Housing Design and Constr. Mgmt. (Apr. 1990).
3. AFR 90-1, Family Housing Mgmt. (Oct. 1990).

D. Navy Regulation.
OPNAVINST 11010.20E, *Facilities Projects Manual* (July 9, 1985).

## III. CONCEPTS.

A. Construction.
10 U.S.C. § 2801(a); FAR 36.102.

1. "Construction" means any construction, alteration, conversion, renovation, repair, or painting of buildings, structures, or other real property.
2. Work performed on vessels, aircraft, or other personal property is not construction.

B. Fiscal Distinctions.
1. For fiscal purposes only, "construction" does *not* include "repair."
2. Regardless of how an activity funds a construction project, it must award the contract in accordance with FAR Part 36 and its supplements.

## IV. METHODS OF ACQUIRING CONSTRUCTION.

A. Sealed Bidding.
Activities must use sealed bidding procedures to acquire construction if the four conditions of FAR 6.401(a) apply. FAR 36.103(a).

B. Negotiation.
1. Contracting officers must use negotiation procedures if the conditions of FAR 6.401(a) do not apply. *See Michael C. Avino, Inc.*, B-250689, Feb. 17, 1993, 93-1 CPD ¶ 148 (paving contract properly awarded on a best-value basis to other than the lowest-priced offeror); *see also Pardee Constr. Co.*, B-256414, June 13, 1994, 94-1 CPD ¶ 372 (contract for 374 new family housing units awarded using negotiations procedures).
2. Contracting officers may use negotiation pro-

cedures for construction performed outside the United States, its possessions, or Puerto Rico, even if sealed bidding is otherwise required. FAR 36.103(a).

**C. Job Order Contracts (JOC).**
AFARS Subpart 17.91; *Schnorr-Stafford Constr., Inc.*, B-227323, Aug. 12, 1987, 87-2 CPD ¶ 153; *Salmon & Assoc.*, B-227079, Aug. 12, 1987, 87-2 CPD ¶ 152 (JOC/SABER use does not *per se* violate small business set-aside requirements).

1. A JOC is an indefinite quantity, indefinite delivery contract for small to medium-sized repair and construction projects.
2. An activity develops task specifications and a unit price book. Contractors multiply the government unit price by their own coefficients to arrive at bid/proposal prices.
3. The activity orders services specified in a JOC from the contractor at the price set forth in the bid/proposal.
4. Limitations:
   a. Requires approval of Head of Contracting Activity (HCA).
   b. Formerly delivery orders could not exceed $125,000 unless the HCA approved in emergencies; Army Acquisition Letter 93-7 (Aug. 2, 1993) raised the limit for *new* JOC contracts to $300,000 per delivery order.
   c. JOC delivery orders are inappropriate if required work is within the scope of local requirements contracts, within in-house capabilities, or of the type properly set aside for small and disadvantaged businesses (SDBs) or the section 8(a) program.

## V. CONTRACT TYPES.

**A. Firm-Fixed-Price Contracts.**
FAR 36.207. Generally, activities shall award firm-fixed-price contracts for construction. The contracting officer may require pricing on a lump-sum basis, a unit price basis, or a combination of these two methods.
1. With lump-sum pricing, the government pays one sum for the total project or for portions of the project.

2. With unit pricing, a contractor bids a price for a specified quantity of work units. The contracting officer must ensure that the government or the contractor performs quantity surveys to calculate work effort. *See* FAR 52.236-16.
3. Contractors may protest an activity's use of lump sum pricing, and the GAO will review pricing schemes to determine if they are reasonable. *Mid-South Dredging Co.*, B-256219, May 25, 1994, 94-1 CPD ¶ 324 (lump-sum pricing of dredging stations, with adjustments for lift and pipeline lengths, is reasonable); *Tumpane Serv. Corp.*, B-242221, Apr. 12, 1991, 70 Comp. Gen. 407, 91-1 CPD ¶ 369 (lump-sum pricing reasonable); *Four Star Maintenance Corp.*, B-240413, Nov. 2, 1990, 91-1 CPD ¶ 70 (lump-sum pricing unreasonable).

**B. Fixed-Price With Economic Price Adjustment Contracts.**
The government may use this contract type:
1. If the use of this type is customary in the trade;
2. If a significant number of offerors would *not* bid if this contract type was not used; or,
3. If the use of this type would avoid inclusion of unwarranted contingencies in bidders' prices.

**C. Cost-Reimbursement Contracts.**
1. The Assistant Secretary of Defense (Production and Logistics) must approve the award of cost-plus-fixed-fee contracts if:
   a. The activity uses military construction appropriations;
   b. Performance will occur in the United States (Alaska excluded); and
   c. The acquiring activity expects the contract to exceed $25,000.
      *See* Military Construction Appropriations Act, 1995, Pub. L. No. 103-307, § 101, 108 Stat. 1659, 1663 (1994); DFARS 236.271; AFFARS 5336.271.
2. Activities shall not use price incentive, cost-plus-fixed-fee, or other fee contracts with

firm-fixed-price contracts at the same work site without the approval of the HCA. FAR 36.208.

## VI. PRE-BID COMMUNICATIONS WITH OFFERORS.

### A. Pre-Solicitation Notice.
FAR 36.302; SF 1417 (form at FAR 53.301-1417). *See* page 203.
1. The contracting officer must send this notice to prospective offerors when the contract is expected to equal or exceed $100,000.
2. The notice informs offerors of the project magnitude. FAR 36.204.
   a. Along with other information, the notice describes the physical characteristics and states the estimated price range of the project.
   b. The contracting officer shall not disclose the government estimate. FAR 36.203.
3. Distribution of notices. FAR 36.211.
   a. The contracting officer should send notices to contractors on the bidders list and to organizations that have display rooms for such information.
   b. The contracting officer determines the geographical range of distribution.

### B. Commerce Business Daily (CBD).
Publication of both pre-solicitation notice and the solicitation itself is mandatory. FAR 36.302(b)(9).

## VII. SOLICITATION.

### A. Forms.
FAR 36.701; FAR Part 53; DFARS 236.701.
1. The contracting officer uses Standard Form (SF) 1442, Solicitation, Offer, and Award, in lieu of SF 33. If a bidder fails to return this form with its offer, the offer is nonresponsive. *C.J.M. Contractors, Inc.*, B-250493.2, Nov. 24, 1992, 92-2 CPD ¶ 376. *See* page 204.
2. Normally, activities do not use the Uniform Contract Format (UCF) with construction solicitations. FAR 14.201-1.

### B. Statutory Limitations.
FAR 36.205; DFARS 252.236-7006.
1. The solicitation must include any statutory price limit(s). *K.C. Brandon Constr.*, B-245934, Feb. 3, 1992, 92-1 CPD ¶ 139.
2. The government shall reject any offer exceeding a statutory limit, or which is materially unbalanced to avoid such limits. DFARS 252.236-7006; *William G. Tadlock Constr.*, B-252580, June 29, 1993, 93-1 CPD ¶ 502 (reallocation of prices after opening to avoid ceiling, even if total price remains unchanged, is not permissible); *H. Angelo & Co.*, B-249412, Nov. 13, 1992, 92-2 CPD ¶ 344.
3. Some statutory limitations are waivable. *See, e.g.*, 10 U.S.C. § 2853; FAR 36.205; *TECOM, Inc.*, B-240421, Nov. 9, 1990, 90-2 CPD ¶ 386.

### C. Site Familiarization Clauses.
1. The contractor must investigate the job site and conditions affecting the work. FAR 52.236-3.
   a. A contractor must investigate transportation, labor, utility, weather, surface and subsurface conditions, and determine what equipment it needs. *Fred Burgos Constr. Co.*, ASBCA No. 41395, 91-2 BCA ¶ 23,706; *Aulson Roofing, Inc.*, ASBCA No. 37677, 91-2 BCA ¶ 23,720.
   b. However, the contractor need not hire its own geologists or conduct extensive engineering efforts to verify conditions reasonably inferred from site visit or solicitation. *Michael-Mark Ltd.*, IBCA No. 2697, 94-1 BCA ¶ 26,453 ("incompetent rock" encountered during construction of fish passage).
   c. A contractor must perform at the contract price if the contractor could have discovered the condition by a reasonable investigation. *Weeks Dredging & Contracting, Inc. v. United States*, 13 Cl. Ct. 193 (1987); *Avisco, Inc.*, ENG BCA No. 5802, 93-3 BCA ¶ 26,172 (excessive growth and vegetation reasonably discoverable); *Signal Contracting, Inc.*, ASBCA No. 44963,

93-2 BCA ¶ 25,877 (bid deemed to include price of installing conduit because reasonable site investigation would have revealed that conduit was not already installed inside existing communications duct). *Cf. I.M.I., Inc.*, B-233863, Jan. 11, 1989, 89-1 CPD ¶ 30 (failure to inspect does *not* make bid nonresponsive even if solicitation requires inspection).

    d. Generally, a contractor's interpretation of data and government representations that are not included in the solicitation do not bind the government. *Eagle Contracting, Inc.*, AGBCA No. 88-225-1, 92-3 BCA ¶ 25,018.

2. Physical data. FAR 52.236-4.

    a. The contracting officer may provide physical data for the convenience of the contractor.

    b. The government is not responsible for a contractor's erroneous interpretation or conclusion based on data furnished. *But see United Contractors v. United States*, 177 Ct. Cl. 151, 368 F.2d 585 (Ct. Cl. 1966) (liable under differing site condition theory).

3. Changes to site after bid closing date. Generally the government is responsible for increased costs of performance due to changes at a site after the date of bid submission, even if offerors agree to a government request for an extension of the bid acceptance period. *Valley Constr. Co.*, ENG BCA No. 6007, 93-3 BCA ¶ 26,171 (flooding).

**D. Bid Guarantee Requirement.**
FAR 28.101, 52.228-1; SF 24, Bid Bond; *Eagle Asphalt & Oil, Inc.*, B-240340, Nov. 14, 1990, 90-2 CPD ¶ 395. *See* page 205.

1. A bid guarantee ensures that a bidder will not withdraw its bid and will furnish other required bonds.

    a. Generally, noncompliance with the bid guarantee requirement renders a bid nonresponsive. The contracting officer may waive noncompliance only in limited circumstances. FAR 28.101-4(c) (nine excep-

tions); *see Apex Servs., Inc.*, B-255118, Feb. 9, 1994, 94-1 CPD ¶ 95 (contracting officers have discretion to waive or not waive inadequate bid guarantees, depending on the circumstances and needs of the government).

    b. The bid guarantee must be in the form required by the solicitation. *Concord Analysis, Inc.*, B-239730, Dec. 4, 1990, 90-2 CPD ¶ 452; *but see Mid-South Metals, Inc.*, B-257056, Aug. 23, 1994, 94-2 CPD ¶ 78 (bid guaranteed with multiple credit cards was responsive, despite IFB warning that submission of multiple credit cards was unacceptable, because bidder was legally bound by its offer; government was required to waive variance from terms of IFB as a minor irregularity).

    (1) Although the FAR does not require the use of Standard Form 24 (Bid Bond), if the terms of a commercial form deviate from the material terms of the SF 24, then the bond is unacceptable, and the contracting officer must reject the bid as nonresponsive. *Alarm Control Co.*, B-246010, Nov. 18, 1991, 91-2 CPD ¶ 472.

    (2) The FAR permits offerors to use surety bonds, certified or cashier's checks, irrevocable letters of credit, postal money orders, U.S. bonds, or cash. FAR 28.204-2; FAR 52.228-1, Bid Guarantee. *See* Treasury Dep't Cir. 570 for listing of acceptable commercial sureties.

    (3) If a bidder uses an individual surety (versus a corporate surety), the surety must provide a security interest in acceptable assets equal to the penal sum of the bond. FAR 28.203. The adequacy of an individual surety offering apparently adequate and binding security interest is a matter of responsibility, not responsiveness. *Gene Quigley, Jr.*, B-241565, Feb. 19, 1991, 70 Comp. Gen. 273, 91-1 CPD ¶ 182; *but see Harrison Realty Corp.*, B-254461.2, 93-2 CPD ¶ 345 (misrepresentations in

surety affidavit cast doubt on surety's integrity and made bid nonresponsive). A bidder may not be his own individual surety. *Astor V. Bolden*, B-257038, Apr. 26, 1994, 94-1 CPD ¶ 288.

2. The bid bond must equal 20% of the bid (not to exceed $3,000,000). *But see* FAR 28.101-4(c)(2); *S.J. Amoroso Constr. Co.*, B-240687, Nov. 27, 1990, 90-2 CPD ¶ 432 (guarantee sufficient if less than penal sum but greater than difference between low offeror's bid and next higher bid).

3. The contracting officer may not accept a bid accompanied by an apparently unenforceable guarantee. *Conservatek Indus., Inc.*, B-254927, Jan. 26, 1994, 94-1 CPD ¶ 42 (bond with wrong project number rejected); *MKB Constructors, Inc.*, B-255098, Jan. 10, 1994, 94-1 CPD ¶ 10 (discrepancy between bond principal and nominal bidder left doubt about bond's enforceability); *Arlington Constr., Inc.*, B-252535, July 9, 1993, 93-2 CPD ¶ 10 (strict suretyship law requires rejection of bond signed by agent who exceeds stated authority); *Cherokee Enter., Inc.*, B-252948, June 3, 1993, 93-1 CPD ¶ 429 (bond "subject to" another document not accompanying bid is nonresponsive); *Hugo Key & Son, Inc.*, B-245227, Aug. 22, 1991, 91-2 CPD ¶ 189 (stamped signature inadequate); *Techno Eng'g & Constr.*, B-243932, July 23, 1991, 91-2 CPD ¶ 87 (bid rejection proper if power of attorney does not name person signing bond); *Maytal Constr. Corp.*, B-241501, Dec. 10, 1990, 90-2 CPD ¶ 476 (penal sum whited-out and typed over made bond unacceptable); *Bird Constr.*, B-240002, Sept. 19, 1990, 90-2 CPD ¶ 234 (facsimile bond unacceptable; it lacks original signature); *cf. Services Alliance Sys., Inc.*, B-255361, Feb. 22, 1994, 94-1 CPD ¶ 137 (bid responsive when accompanied by bid bond with original signature and photocopied power of attorney which by its own terms was valid in facsimile form).

4. In negotiated acquisitions, the contracting officer must address bid guarantee deficiencies during discussions, unless the contracting officer awards on initial proposals. FAR 28.101-4(b).

**E. Pre-Bid Conferences.**
Contracting officers may hold conferences when necessary to brief bidders and explain complex specifications and requirements. FAR 14.207.

**F. Bid/Proposal Preparation Time.**
FAR 36.303. The contracting officer must afford bidders ample time to conduct site visits, obtain subcontractor bids, examine data, and prepare estimates. *Raymond Int'l of Del., Inc.*, ASBCA No. 13121, 70-1 BCA ¶ 8,341.

## VIII. AWARD.

**A. Responsiveness Issues.**
1. A bid is nonresponsive if it exceeds any statutory dollar limit, or if a bid fails to include a separate bid for a line item subject to a statutory limitation. FAR 36.205(c); *Ward Constr. Co.*, B-240064, July 30, 1990, 90-2 CPD ¶ 87; *cf. Wynn Constr. Co.*, B-220649, Feb. 21, 1986, 86-1 CPD ¶ 184 (bid acceptable when contractor mistakenly bid low on line item not subject to a statutory limitation and overpriced a line item subject to the limitation).

2. If a bid guarantee is unacceptable, the contracting officer must reject the bid. In sealed bidding, offerors may not cure defective bid guarantees after bid opening. FAR 28.101-4(a); *Maytal Constr. Corp.*, B-241501, Dec. 10, 1990, 90-2 CPD ¶ 476.

3. If an offeror provides a shorter bid acceptance period than the solicitation requires, the bid is nonresponsive. *See* page 206, Block 13D.

4. Failure to acknowledge a material solicitation amendment renders a bid nonresponsive. *See, e.g. Dutra Constr. Co.*, B-241202, Jan. 31, 1991, 91-1 CPD ¶ 97 (adding liquidated damages provision).

5. Failure to acknowledge an amendment to a

wage rate determination renders a bid nonresponsive, unless the offeror is otherwise bound by a wage rate equal to or greater than the new rate. *Tri-Tech Int'l, Inc.*, B-246701, Mar. 23, 1992, 92-1 CPD ¶ 304; *Fast Elec. Contractors*, Inc., B-223823, Dec. 2, 1986, 86-2 CPD ¶ 627.

6. Equivocation on a requirement to obtain permits and licenses renders a bid nonresponsive. *Bishop Contractors, Inc.*, B-246526, Dec. 17, 1991, 91-2 CPD ¶ 555.

## B. Responsibility Issues.

1. Prequalification of sources. DFARS 236.272. The contracting officer may establish a list of contractors that are qualified to perform a specific contract.

   a. For DOD, the HCA must determine that a project is so urgent or complex that prequalification is necessary.

   b. If the contracting officer finds a small business unqualified for responsibility reasons, he must refer this finding to the Small Business Administration (SBA) for a preliminary recommendation.

   c. If the SBA determines the small business to be responsible, the contracting officer must allow the firm to bid.

2. The contracting officer may use performance evaluation reports as part of a preaward survey. FAR 36.201(c)(2). Use of these reports is mandatory if the contract will exceed $1 million. DFARS 236.201(c).

3. Evaluation reports grading contractor performance are mandatory for contracts valued at $500,000 or more, and for contracts terminated for default that exceed $10,000. FAR 36.201(a). The North Pacific Division of the Corps of Engineers maintains all reports in a database for a period of six years.

4. Before the contracting officer rejects a small business offeror as nonresponsible, the SBA may review the proposed unfavorable determination. FAR 19.602-1. For DOD, referral is mandatory only if the small business informs the contracting officer that it will seek a Certificate of Competency (COC). National

Defense Authorization Act of 1993, Pub. L. No. 102-484, § 804, 106 Stat. 2315, 2447 (1992).

5. Generally, whether a contractor intends to perform a contractually-required percentage of work with its own labor force is a matter of responsibility, not responsiveness. *Luther Constr. Co.*, B-241719, Jan. 28, 1991, 91-1 CPD ¶ 76. *But see Blount, Inc. v. United States*, 22 Cl. Ct. 221 (1990) (bid *nonresponsive* if offeror indicates in bid that it will subcontract greater percentage of work than solicitation allows); *C. Iber & Sons, Inc.*, B-247920.2, Aug. 12, 1992, 92-2 CPD ¶ 99 (same). The Performance of Work by the Contractor clause (FAR 52.236-1) is not applicable to small business set-asides or 8(a) acquisitions. FAR 36.501(b).

6. The contracting officer shall not award a contract to the firm that designs a project, unless the agency head or delegee approves. FAR 36.209; *Lawlor Corp.*, B-241945.2, Mar. 28, 1991, 70 Comp. Gen. 375, 91-1 CPD ¶ 335.

## C. Price Evaluation.

1. The Buy American Act (BAA) and Balance of Payments Act restrictions apply. FAR Subparts 25.2 and 25.3; DFARS Subparts 225.2 and 225.3.

   a. The BAA requires that only domestic construction materials be used for construction within the United States, unless an exception applies. FAR 25.202(a).

   b. The Balance of Payments Act provides for an evaluation preference for domestic offers in overseas construction equal to fifty percent of the price of the lowest nonqualifying country offer; exceptions may apply. DFARS 225.303(b).

2. The contracting officer must evaluate additive items properly. DFARS 252.236-7007.

   a. The contracting officer shall award to the bidder who submits the low bid for the base project and for additive items which, in order of priority, provide the most features within the amount of available funds.

b. The contracting officer may select the low bidder based only on the funding that is available at bid opening. *Huntington Constr., Inc.*, B-230604, June 30, 1988, 67 Comp. Gen. 499, 88-1 CPD ¶ 619.

## IX. CONTRACT ADMINISTRATION.

### A. Preconstruction Letters.
The contracting officer uses these letters for administrative coordination and to remind the contractor of applicable labor standards. FAR 22.406-1(b); DFARS 222.406-1(b).

### B. Preconstruction Conferences.
Generally these conferences serve the same purposes as preconstruction letters. FAR 36.305.

### C. Performance and Payment Bonds.
FAR Part 28. The Miller Act, 40 U.S.C. §§ 270a-270f, requires performance and payment bonds for any construction contract over $25,000. *Cf. TLC Servs., Inc.*, B-254972.2, Mar. 30, 1994, 94-1 CPD ¶ 235, (requirement also applies if construction line items exceeding $25,000). Failure to provide acceptable bonds justifies default termination. FAR 52.228-1(c); *Pacific Sunset Builders, Inc.*, ASBCA No. 39312, 93-3 BCA ¶ 25,923 (default appropriate unless contracting officer was unreasonable, arbitrary, or capricious in finding bonds unacceptable).
1. *Performance bonds* ensure that a contractor fulfills its obligations after contract award. The penal amount (the maximum amount of the surety's obligation) must equal 100% of the contract price. *See* FAR 28.102-2(a); SF 25; FAR 53.301-25.
2. Payment bonds protect suppliers of services or materials. *See* FAR 28.102-2(a); SF 25-A.
   a. The penal amounts of these bonds are based on contract prices. If a contract price is:
      (1) Not more than $1,000,000, the penal sum must be 50% of the contract price;
      (2) More than $1,000,000 but not more than $5,000,000, the bond must equal 40% of the contract price;

   (3) More than $5,000,000, the bond must equal $2,500,000.
   b. *During contract performance*, agencies generally shall not withhold payments due a contractor because the contractor has not paid its subcontractors or suppliers. FAR 28.106-7. The DFARS, however, requires withholding of payments under certain circumstances, when suppliers complain to a DOD contracting officer that they have not been paid. DFARS 232.970-1. *See also Balboa Ins. Co. v. United States*, 775 F.2d 1158 (Fed. Cir. 1985) (upon notice from surety that payment has not been made, contracting officer must act responsibly with remaining contract funds); *National Surety Corp.*, 31 Fed. Cl. 565 (1994) (improper to release progress payment retainage for which surety was third party beneficiary); *Dan F. Harrison Constr., Inc.*, ASBCA No. 41572, 91-2 BCA ¶ 23,949 (withholding during investigation of subcontractor complaint was reasonable).
   c. If, *after completion of the work*, the surety provides written notice that the contractor failed to pay suppliers or subcontractors, the contracting officer shall withhold final payment. FAR 28.106-7.
      (1) The surety must agree to hold the government harmless for withholding final payment.
      (2) The contracting officer shall release final payment as agreed to by the contractor and surety, or in accordance with a judicial determination.
      (3) Absent agreement between the surety and the contractor, or a judicial determination of entitlement, however, the contracting officer may withhold final payment only if the contract specifically provides a right to do so. *George Bernadot Co.*, ASBCA No. 42943, 94-3 BCA ¶ 27,242.
   d. Failure to pay employees is handled by withholding from payments to the contractor an amount equal to the amount of

the underpayment, or by suspending all further payments until violations cease. *See, e.g.,* FAR 22.406-9 (Davis-Bacon Act violations).

**D. Differing Site Conditions.**
FAR 52.236-2.

1. This clause allows for an equitable adjustment if the contractor provides prompt, written notice of a differing site condition. There are two types of differing site conditions. *Consolidated Constr., Inc.*, GSBCA No. 8871, 88-2 BCA ¶ 20,811.

2. Type I condition. *Praught Constr. Corp.*, ASBCA No. 39670, 93-2 BCA ¶ 25,896. To recover for a Type I condition, the contractor must prove that:

   a. The contract indicated a particular site condition, either positively or implicitly. *See Franklin Pavkov Constr. Co.*, HUD BCA No. 93-C-C13, 94-3 BCA ¶ 27,078 (no recovery where specifications and drawings gave no specific details from which actual site could differ); *Glagola Constr. Co., Inc.*, ASBCA No. 45579, 93-3 BCA ¶ 26,179 (Type I differing site condition recovery allowed due to a combination of bad weather and materially misdescribed soil conditions; solicitation inferred conditions more favorable than they actually were); *Konoike Constr. Co.*, ASBCA No. 36342, 91-1 BCA ¶ 23,440 (implicit representation sufficient); *cf. Jack L. Olsen, Inc.*, AGBCA No. 87-345-1, 93-2 BCA ¶ 25,767 (government liable for nondisclosure of information it had but did not release in solicitation on a superior knowledge theory, i.e., breach of its duty to disclose).

   b. The contractor reasonably interpreted and relied on the indications. *R.D. Brown Contractors, Inc.*, ASBCA No. 43973, 93-1 BCA ¶ 25,368; and

   c. The contractor encountered latent or subsurface conditions which differed materially from those indicated in the contract. *Meredith Constr. Co.*, ASBCA No. 40839, 93-1 BCA ¶ 25,399 (not materially differ-

ent); *Caesar Constr., Inc.*, ASBCA No. 41059, 91-1 BCA ¶ 23,639.

   d. The claimed costs were attributable solely to the differing site condition. *P.J. Dick, Inc.*, GSBCA No. 12036, 94-3 BCA ¶ 27,073.

3. Type II condition. To recover for a Type II condition, the contractor must prove that:

   a. The conditions encountered were unusual physical conditions unknown at the time of award. *Walser v. United States*, 23 Cl. Ct. 591 (1991) (beaver damage not unusual); *Gulf Coast Trailing Co.*, ENG BCA No. 5795, 94-2 BCA ¶ 26,921 (engine blocks and I-beams not unusual); *Soletanche Rodio Nicholson (JV)*, ENG BCA No. 5796, 94-1 BCA ¶ 26,472 (rock subjected to unforeseeable ground stress and difficult to excavate was unusual); and

   b. The conditions differed materially from those ordinarily encountered. *Green Constr. Co.*, ASBCA No. 46157, 94-1 BCA ¶ 26,572 (oversized manhole bottoms); *Virginia Beach Air Conditioning Corp.*, ASBCA No. 42538, 92-1 BCA ¶ 24,432; *Arctic Slope, Alaska Gen./SKW Eskimos, Inc.*, ENG BCA No. 5023, 90-2 BCA ¶ 22,850 (subsurface conditions were not extraordinary).

4. The Differing Site Conditions clause covers only conditions existing at the time of contract award. Acts of nature occurring after award are not differing site conditions. *Arundel Corp. v. United States*, 96 Ct. Cl. 77, 354 F.2d 252 (1942); *Meredith Constr. Co.*, ASBCA No. 40839, 93-1 BCA ¶ 25,399; *PK Contractors, Inc.*, ENG BCA No. 4901, 92-1 BCA ¶ 24,583. *But see Valley Constr. Co.*, ENG BCA No. 6007, 93-3 BCA ¶ 26,171 (flood debris deposited after bid submission but before award).

5. If the contractor could have discovered the condition during a reasonable site investigation, it may not recover. *O.K. Johnson Elec. Co.*, VABCA No. 3464, 94-1 BCA ¶ 26,505 (failure to lift ceiling tiles unreasonable); *Arctic Slope, Alaska Gen., supra; cf. Opera-*

*tional Serv. Corp.*, ASBCA No. 37059, 93-3 BCA ¶ 26,190 (past practice was no proof that planting of additional trees and shrubs would continue in future; contract did not contain differing site conditions clause, but board held for contractor under constructive change theory).

6. A contractor cannot create its own differing site condition. When a hazardous materials cleanup contractor intermingled excavated materials, requiring pH testing to distinguish hazardous from non-hazardous materials, rather than distinguishing by color as stated in the contract, the cost of such testing was not compensable. *Geo-Con, Inc.*, ENG BCA No. 5749, 94-1 BCA ¶ 26,359.

7. The contractor must prove damages. *H.V. Allen Co.*, ASBCA No. 40645, 91-1 BCA ¶ 23,393. *See also Praught Constr. Corp.*, ASBCA No. 39670, 93-2 BCA ¶ 25,896 (injury must be due solely to differing site conditions; recovery substantially denied for damages due *both* to surface water *and* to high ground water differing materially from conditions depicted in solicitation).

8. The contractor must notify the government promptly. *Engineering Technology Consultants, S.A.*, ASBCA No. 43376, 92-3 BCA ¶ 25,100.

   a. Untimely notification may bar differing site conditions claim if late notice prejudices the government. *See Moon Constr. Co. v. Gen. Servs. Admin.*, GSBCA No. 11766, 93-3 BCA ¶ 26,017 (contractor failed to provide proper notice that composition of historic building it was to move was different than indicated on drawings; no prejudice to government, so equitable adjustment allowed); *see Hemphill Contracting Co.*, ENG BCA No. 5698, 94-1 BCA ¶ 26,491 (prejudice found due to lack of notice); *Meisel Rohrbau*, ASBCA No. 35566, 92-1 BCA ¶ 24,434 (prejudice found); *Holloway Constr., Holloway Sand & Gravel Co.*, ENG BCA No. 4805, 89-2 BCA ¶ 21,713 (government did not show prejudice).

   b. If the government's defense to a differing site condition claim is made more difficult but not impossible by late notice, the ASBCA will waive the notice requirement, but place a heavier burden of persuasion on the contractor. *Glagola Constr. Co.*, ASBCA No. 45579, 93-3 BCA ¶ 26,179.

   c. When the government is on notice of differing site conditions, and takes no exceptions to the contractor's notice or its corrective actions, the government must pay contractor's increased costs. *Potomac Marine & Aviation, Inc.*, ASBCA No. 42417, 93-2 BCA ¶ 25,865.

   d. Lack of notice of a differing site condition will not bar a contractor recovery when government breaches duty to cooperate by failing to designate inspector to whom contractor should give notice during scheduled weekend work. *Hudson Contracting, Inc.*, ASBCA No. 41023, 94-1 BCA ¶ 26,466.

9. Final payment bars an unreserved differing site condition claim. FAR 52.236-2(d).

## E. Variation in Estimated Quantity.
FAR 52.212-11.

1. A fixed-price contract may include estimated quantities for unit-priced items of work.

2. If the actual quantity of a unit-priced item varies more than 15% above or below the estimated quantity, the contracting officer shall equitably adjust the contract. The contracting officer shall base an adjustment "upon any increase or decrease in costs due solely to the variation." *Clement-Mtarri Cos.*, ASBCA No. 38170, 92-3 BCA ¶ 25,192, *aff'd sub nom. Shannon v. Clement-Mtarri Cos.*, No. 93-1268, 12 FPD ¶ 114 (Fed. Cir. Nov. 4, 1993).

3. Whether a party may demand repricing of work that falls outside the 15% range, or whether the original contract unit price controls, had been unsettled until recently. *See Foley Co. v. United States*, 26 Cl. Ct. 936 (1992), *aff'd*, 11 F.3d 1092 (Fed. Cir. 1993) (repricing *not* required); *Burnett Constr. Co.*

*v. United States*, 26 Cl. Ct. 296 (1992) (repricing required); *Diversified Technology & Servs. of Va., Inc.*, ASBCA No. 44961, 93-2 BCA ¶ 25,876 (costs incurred under service contract because quantity of work exceeded 15% limitation are fully reimbursable); *Bean Dredging Corp.*, ENG BCA No. 5507, 89-3 BCA ¶ 22,034 (repricing required). Now adjustments are based only on the difference between the unit cost of the original work and the unit cost of work outside the allowable variation range. *Foley Co. v. United States*, 11 F.3d 1092 (Fed. Cir. 1993) (unit price is baseline for equitable adjustment). *But see TECOM, Inc.*, ASBCA No. 44122, 94-1 BCA ¶ 26,483 (adjustment under Variation in Workload clause of supply contract based upon actual costs, not unit prices—decision dated one week before release of *Foley* opinion by Federal Circuit).

4. The contractor may request an extension if the variation in quantity causes an increase in the performance period.

## F. Suspension of Work.

FAR 52.212-12.

1. The contracting officer may suspend, interrupt, or delay work for the convenience of the government. *Valquest Contracting, Inc.*, ASBCA No. 32454, 91-1 BCA ¶ 23,381.

2. A government delay is compensable if:

   a. It is *unreasonable. Southwest Constr. Corp.*, ENG BCA No. 5286, 94-3 BCA ¶ 27,120 (even an extensive time to review contractor's submittals is reasonable if review and approval are important to performance, and require additional data submissions, site visits, meetings, and additional test to resolve technical issues); *C&C Plumbing & Heating*, ASBCA No. 44270, 94-3 BCA ¶ 27,063 (government's piecemeal release of work areas to contractor was unreasonable); *Kimmins Contracting Corp.*, ASBCA No. 46390, 94-2 BCA ¶ 26,869 (reasonable to suspend work until contractor complied with con-

tract requirement for quality control manager at work site).

   b. The contracting officer orders it. *See Mergentime Corp.*, ENG BCA No. 5765, 92-2 BCA ¶ 25,007 (suspension ordered by Secret Service not compensable); *Durocher Dock & Dredge, Inc.*, ENG BCA No. 5768, 91-3 BCA ¶ 24,145 (sheriff's suspension was not an order from the contracting officer). *But see Fruehauf Corp. v. United States*, 218 Ct. Cl. 456, 587 F.2d 486 (1978) (government not at fault, but delay was too long; unreasonable for contractor to bear entire cost); *Henderson, Inc.*, DOT BCA No. 2423, 94-2 BCA ¶ 26,728 (government liable for delay caused when third party prevented contractor from dredging for extended period, because the government warranted in the contract that the site would be available during the period when the delay occurred); *Technocratica*, ASBCA No. 44134, 94-2 BCA ¶ 26,606 (government responsible for delays caused by denial of access to work site for failure to renew clearances for employees, because contract did not require new ones); *Lane Constr. Corp.*, ENG BCA No. 5834, 94-1 BCA ¶ 26,358 (delay ordered by Maryland Highway Department compensable due to its close working relationship with federal agency);

   c. The contractor has not caused the suspension by its own or its subcontractors' negligence or failure to perform. *See Hvac Constr. Co., Inc. v. United States*, 28 Fed. Cl. 690 (1993) (subcontractor's failure to obtain approvals delayed start of work into winter, necessitating a suspension of work during the winter period; no recovery); and,

   d. The cost of performance increases. *Missile Sys., Inc.*, ASBCA No. 46079, 94-3 BCA ¶ 27,091 (supply contract); *Frazier-Fleming Co.*, ASBCA No. 34537, 91-1 BCA ¶ 23,378.

3. The contractor may be entitled to delay costs

even if it finishes work on time, if it proves that it planned to finish the work early, but was delayed by the government. *Oneida Constr., Inc.*, ASBCA No. 44194, 947-3 BCA ¶ 27,237; *Labco Constr., Inc.*, AGBCA No. 90-115-1, 94-2 BCA ¶ 26,910.

4. A contractor may be entitled to a performance period extension even if the delay is reasonable. A contractor also may raise government delay as a defense to a default termination or an assessment of liquidated damages. *See Farr Bros., Inc.*, ASBCA No. 42658, 92-2 BCA ¶ 24,991.

5. A contractor may not recover costs incurred more than 20 days before the contractor notifies the government of the delay. This rule applies only in "constructive" suspension cases, and is subject to a prejudice test.

6. If both the contractor and the government contribute to a delay, and the causes of delay are intertwined such that the periods and costs of delay cannot be apportioned clearly, neither party can recover for the delay. *Wilner v. United States*, 994 F.2d 783, 786 (Fed. Cir. 1993); *cf. G. Bliudzius Contractors*, ASBCA No. 42366, 93-3 BCA ¶ 26,074 (critical path analysis or similar method of demonstrating causation required for recovery).

7. A constructive suspension of work may arise if:
   a. The government fails to issue a notice to proceed within a reasonable time after contract award. *M.E. Brown*, ASBCA No. 40403, 91-1 BCA ¶ 23,293.
   b. The government fails to provide timely directions following a reasonable request for guidance. *Tayag Bros. Enters., Inc.*, ASBCA No. 42097, 94-2 BCA ¶ 26,962.

8. Profit is not recoverable, and final payment bars unreserved suspension claims.

9. Distinguish delay costs associated with differing site conditions or change orders from those resulting from government delay in deciding how to correct a condition or proceed with a change. *See CCM Corp. v. United States*, 20 Cl. Ct. 649 (1990); *Berrios Constr. Co.*, VABCA No. 3152, 92-2 BCA ¶ 24,828; *James Reeves Contractor, Inc.*, ASBCA No. 33744, 88-1 BCA ¶ 20,426.

10. The clause limits suspensions to 45 days, but an informal extension of work suspensions beyond 45 days is treated no differently than the initial 45-day suspension. *Debcon, Inc.*, ASBCA No. 45050, 93-3 BCA ¶ 25,906.

## G. Permits and Responsibilities.
FAR 52.236-7.

1. A contractor must obtain applicable permits and licenses, and comply with laws and regulations, at no additional cost to the government. *GEM Eng'g Co.*, DOT BCA No. 2574, 94-3 BCA ¶ 27,202 (contractor must pay for insurance above coverage required by contract to meet local requirement at its own expense); *C'n R Indus. of Jacksonville, Inc.*, ASBCA No. 42209, 91-2 BCA ¶ 23,970 (contractor must pay environmental fines); *Holk Dev., Inc.*, ASBCA No. 40137, 90-2 BCA ¶ 22,852 (asbestos removal license); *but see Hills Materials v. Rice*, 982 F.2d 514 (Fed. Cir. 1992) (Accident Prevention clause shifted liability to government for cost of complying with amended OSHA regulation, despite Permits and Responsibilities clause); *Hemphill Contracting Co.*, ENG BCA No. 5698, 94-1 BCA ¶ 26,491 (specifically requiring a debris disposal technique during negotiations, when that techniques does not meet state law, entitles contractor to compensation for change despite Permits and Responsibilities clause). *Cf. Gartrell Constr., Inc. v. Aubry*, 940 F.2d 437 (9th Cir. 1991) (state may not require contractor on federal project to obtain contractor's license).

2. Normally, licensing is a question of responsibility, not responsiveness. *See Restec Contractors, Inc.*, B-245862, Feb. 6, 1992, 92-1 CPD ¶ 154; *Computer Support Sys., Inc.*, B-239034, Aug. 2, 1990, 69 Comp. Gen. 645, 90-2 CPD ¶ 94; *but see Bishop Contractors, Inc.*, B-246526, Dec. 17, 1991, 91-2 CPD ¶ 555 (bid was nonresponsive because it indi-

cated that offer excluded all costs for permits and fees).

3. A contractor assumes the risk of loss or damage to its equipment. It also is responsible for injuries to third persons. *Potashnick Constr., Inc.*, ENG BCA No. 5551, 92-2 BCA ¶ 24,985; *Aulson Roofing, Inc.*, ASBCA No. 37677, 91-1 BCA ¶ 23,720. The contractor may bear similar responsibilities under a Government Furnished Property clause (e.g., FAR 52.245-4) as well. *See Technical Servs.— K.H. Nehlsen GmbH*, ASBCA No. 43869, 94-1 BCA ¶ 26,377 (contractor assumed risk of sabotage).

4. A contractor is responsible for work in progress until the government accepts it. *Labco Constr., Inc.*, ASBCA No. 44945, 93-3 BCA ¶ 26,027 (responsibility also continues during periods of contract extension, when the contractor agreed to the modifications extending the contract); *Tyler Constr. Co.*, ASBCA No. 39365, 91-1 BCA ¶ 23,646 (occupancy by the government is not necessarily acceptance); *D.J. Barclay & Co.*, ASBCA No. 28908, 88-2 BCA ¶ 20,741; *but see Fraser Eng'g Co.*, VABCA No. 3265, 91-3 BCA ¶ 24,223 (contractor not responsible for damage caused by the government); *Joseph Beck & Assocs.*, ASBCA No. 31126, 88-1 BCA ¶ 20,428 (contractor not responsible for fire damage to other parts of building).

## H. Specifications and Drawings.
FAR 52.236-21; DFARS 252.236-7001.

1. The omission or misdescription of details of work necessary to carry out intent of contract drawings and specifications, or which customarily are performed, does not relieve contractors from performing the omitted or misdescribed details of work. Contractors must perform as if the drawings and specifications describe the details fully and correctly. DFARS 252.236-7001; *Wood & Co. v. Dep't of Treasury*, GSBCA No. 12452-TD, 94-1 BCA ¶ 26,365 (shingle removal); *Single Ply Sys., Inc.*, ASBCA No. 42168, 91-2 BCA ¶ 24,032 (siding).

2. The contractor must review all drawings before beginning work, and is responsible for any errors that a reasonable review might detect. *But see Wick Constr. Co.*, ASBCA No. 35378, 89-1 BCA ¶ 21,239 (unreasonable to require reinsulation of pipe to meet safety requirements at no cost, after contractor properly removed asbestos from 420 feet of pipe, because requirement was relatively minor and not apparent from drawings or specifications).

3. If specifications contain provisions that conflict with contract drawings, the specifications govern. The parties may rely on this order of precedence regardless of whether an ambiguity is patent. FAR 52.236-21; *Hensel Phelps Constr. Co.*, 886 F.2d 1296 (Fed. Cir. 1989) (contractor may rely on order of precedence even if discrepancy known before bid or is patent); *see, e.g., Shemya Constructors*, ASBCA No. 45251, 94-1 BCA ¶ 26,346 (contractor must install tank gage as required by specification, even though not shown on drawings); *Rohr, Inc.*, ASBCA No. 44193, 93-2 BCA ¶ 25,871 (metallic conduit required when called for in specifications despite drawings indicating PVC conduit was to be used); *but see J.S. Alberici Constr. Co v. Gen. Servs. Admin*, GSBCA No. 12386, 94-2 BCA ¶ 26,776 (drawings took precedence over specifications when contract also stated that explicit requirements took precedence over industry standards, and drawings contained explicit sprinkler locations while specifications only reference industry standards).

4. Contractors must prove damages to recover for a constructive change if the government directs work in accordance with the drawings rather than the specifications. Likewise, the government may not recover for a change in a more stringent specification to match a less stringent drawing if the contractor based its bid on the drawing. *McGhee Constr., Inc.*, ASBCA No. 45175, 93-3 BCA ¶ 26,154 (inequitable for government to receive price reduction in addition to already lower bid).

## I. Labor Issues.

1. Payrolls. FAR 22.406-6; 52.222-8.
   a. The contractor must submit payroll records for examination.
   b. The government may withhold progress payments if the contractor fails to furnish records within seven calendar days after the regular payment date for the pay period covered.

2. Compliance checks. FAR 22.406-7.
   a. The government may conduct employee interviews to verify that a contractor has correctly classified and paid its employees.
   b. The government may perform on-site inspections to ensure that general working conditions comply with statutory and regulatory requirements.
   c. The contracting officer must investigate further if compliance checks indicate a willful or substantial violation by a contractor or subcontractor. FAR 22.406-8.
   d. Applicable labor standards include:
      (1) Davis-Bacon Act. 40 U.S.C. §§ 276a to 276a-7; FAR 22.403-1; FAR 52.222-6.
      (2) Contract Work Hours and Safety Standards Act, 40 U.S.C. §§ 327-333; FAR 22.403-3 and 52.222-4.
      (3) Copeland "Anti-Kickback" Act, 18 U.S.C. § 874 and 40 U.S.C. § 276c (requirement for weekly payroll submissions); FAR 22.403-2 and 52.222-10.

## J. Payments Under Fixed-Price Construction Contracts.

FAR 32.103; FAR 32.905(c); FAR 52.232-5.

1. The government pays the contractor periodically in an amount related to the percentage of work completed. These payments are subject to the Prompt Payment Act. *Toombs & Co.*, ASBCA No. 35085, 91-1 BCA ¶ 23,403; *Zinger Constr. Co.*, ASBCA No. 31858, 87-3 BCA ¶ 20,043.

2. If the contracting officer determines that the contractor made adequate progress during a pay period, the contracting officer pays the full percentage due. If progress is unsatisfactory, the contracting officer may retain up to 10%.

3. Failure to make progress payments for completed work constitutes a breach of contract unless withholding/suspension is pursuant to the contract. *Nexus Constr. Co.*, ASBCA No. 31070, 91-3 BCA ¶ 24,303. *See United States v. DeKonty Corp.*, 922 F.2d 826 (Fed. Cir. 1991) (no breach where contracting officer delayed progress payment until he had checked contract status).

## K. Liquidated Damages (LDs).

FAR 12.202; FAR 36.206; FAR 52.212-5; DFARS 212.204.

1. The government may assess LDs if:
   a. The parties intended to provide for LDs;
   b. Anticipated damages attributable to untimely performance were uncertain or difficult to quantify at the time of award; and
   c. The LDs bear a reasonable relationship to anticipated government losses resulting from delayed completion. Unreasonable damages are unenforceable. *D.E.W., Inc.*, ASBCA No. 38392, 92-2 BCA ¶ 24,840; *JEM Dev. Corp.*, ASBCA No. 42645, 91-3 BCA ¶ 24,428 (unreasonable); *Brooks Lumber Co.*, ASBCA No. 40743, 91-2 BCA ¶ 23,984 (use of Navy manual to calculate damages was reasonable); *Dave's Excavation*, ASBCA No. 35956, 88-3 BCA ¶ 20,911 (rate at twice agency guidelines was unenforceable penalty); *see P&D Contractors, Inc. v. United States*, 25 Cl. Ct. 237 (1992) (contractor must challenge reasonableness of damages at time of contract execution).

2. If the damage forecast was reasonable, the government may assess LDs even though no actual damages occurred. *Cegers v. United States*, 7 Cl. Ct. 615 (1985); *American Constr. Co.*, ENG BCA No. 5728, 91-2 BCA ¶ 24,009. Use of rate from agency manual that is part of its procurement regulations is presumed reasonable. *Fred A. Arnold, Inc. v. United States*, 18 Cl. Ct. 1 (1989), *aff'd in*

*part*, 979 F.2d 217 (Fed. Cir. 1992); *JEM Dev. Corp.*, ASBCA No. 45912, 94-1 BCA ¶ 26,407.

3. The government may not assess damages if a project is substantially complete. *Hill Constr. Corp.*, ASBCA No. 43615, 93-3 BCA ¶ 25,973 (work substantially complete despite air conditioning that was only partially operational); *Wilton Corp.*, ASBCA No. 39876, 93-2 BCA ¶ 25,897 (work not substantially complete when remaining work priced at 11% of contract total). Nor may the government collect LDs if it is partly responsible for the completion delay. *H.G. Reynolds Co., Inc.*, ASBCA No. 42351, 93-2 BCA ¶ 25,797 (excessive and conflicting government punchlists, including some items not required by the contract, contributed to the delay; contractor also responsible, however, so it could also not recover on its delay claims).

4. Contractor may be excused from liquidated damages if it shows that delays were excusable or beyond its control, and without the fault or negligence of it or its subcontractors. *Potomac Marine & Aviation, Inc.*, ASBCA No. 42417, 93-2 BCA ¶ 25,865.

5. Contracting officers must ensure that project completion dates are reasonable to avoid contractors "padding" their bids to protect against LDs.

6. Another contract clause that sets an alternate rate of compensation for standby time may be enforceable, even if it is quite high, if it serves a different purpose in the contract than a liquidated damages clause. *Stapp Towing Co.*, ASBCA No. 41584, Oct. 25, 1993,

94-1 BCA ¶ 26,465 ($450 per hour for "demurrage" time).

**L. Use/Possession Prior to Completion.**
FAR 52.236-11.

1. The government may take possession of a construction project prior to its completion (beneficial occupancy).

2. Possession does not necessarily constitute acceptance. *Tyler Constr. Co.*, ASBCA No. 39365, 91-1 BCA ¶ 23,646. The contractor must complete a project as required by the contract, including all "punch list" items. *Toombs & Co.*, ASBCA No. 34590, 91-1 BCA 23,403.

3. The contractor is not responsible for any loss or damage that the government causes. *Fraser Eng'g Co.*, VABCA No. 3265, 91-3 BCA ¶ 24,223.

4. The contractor may be due an equitable adjustment if possession by the government causes a delay.

## X. CONCLUSION.

A. General contracting principles still apply, but unique clauses and procedures make construction contracting different.

B. Contractors have additional remedies and additional responsibilities in construction contracting.

C. Special rules allocate risks, and ensure the government's interests are protected when it does business with the construction industry.

# STANDARD FORM (SF) 1417

| **PRE-SOLICITATION NOTICE** *(Construction Contract)* | 1. PROJECT NO. | 2. DATE OF NOTICE | 3. DATE SOLICITATION DOCUMENTS AVAILABLE *(Approx)* | FORM APPROVED OMB NUMBER 9000-0037 |
|---|---|---|---|---|

Public reporting burden for this collection of information is estimated to average 10 minutes per response, including the time for reviewing instructions, searching existing data sources, gathering and maintaining the data needed, and completing and reviewing the collection of information. Send comments regarding this burden estimate or any other aspect of this collection of information, including suggestions for reducing this burden, to the FAR Secretariat (VRS), Office of Federal Acquisition Policy, GSA, Washington, DC 20405; and to the Office of Management and Budget, Paperwork Reduction Project (9000-0037), Washington, DC 20503.

NOTE: The project number in Items 1 and 16 may be the same as the invitation or Proposal Number.

| 4. OFFERS TO BE RECEIVED BY (at place specified for receipt of offers) ▶ | A. TIME A.M. P.M. | B. DATE *(Month, day, year)* | 5. TIME FOR COMPLETION *(Calendar days)* |
|---|---|---|---|

| 6A. ISSUING OFFICE *(Name, address, and ZIP code)* | 7. PROJECT TITLE AND LOCATION |
|---|---|

RETURN NOTICE TO THIS ADDRESS

| 6B. ROOM NO. | 6C. TELEPHONE NO. *(Include area code)* | |
|---|---|---|

INSTRUCTIONS: a. Solicitation Documents will be issued upon receipt of your affirmative response to this Pre-Solicitation Notice by the DUE DATE set forth in Item 15. b. If a charge is required under Item 8A, your affirmative response must include a check or money order in the applicable amount, made payable to Agency (shown in Item 9). Refund (when specified in Item 8B) will be made upon your return of the bid documents in good condition, without marks, notes, or mutilations, within 20 calendar days after the final date for receipt of offers. c. The Issuing Office, at its discretion, may make bid documents available to plan rooms of the Associated General Contractors, Chambers of Commerce, Dodge Reports, and other similar contractors' commercial service facilities. d. Bid guarantee is required with any bid in excess of $25,000. Bid guarantee shall be on the amount of 20 percent of the amount of the bid, or $3,000,000, whichever is less. For bid guarantee purposes, the amount of the bid is the aggregate of the Lump Sum Base Bid, all Alternates (if any), and the product(s) of each unit price (if any) multiplied by the applicable number of units shown on the Bid Form. e. NOTICE TO SMALL BUSINESS FIRMS: A program for the purpose of assisting qualified small business concerns in obtaining certain bid payment, or performance bonds that are otherwise not obtainable is available through the Small Business Administration (SBA). For information concerning SBA's surety bond guarantee assistance, contact your SBA District Office.

| 8A. CHARGE FOR SOLICITATION DOCUMENTS | 8B. IS THIS CHARGE REFUNDABLE? ☐ YES ☐ NO | 9. MAKE CHACK PAYABLE TO: | |
|---|---|---|---|

| 10. ESTIMATED COST RANGE OF PROJECT | | 11. OFFERS COVERING THE PROJECT RESTRICTED TO SMALL BUSINESS? | 12. SUBCONTRACTING PLAN REQUIRED? |
|---|---|---|---|
| A. FROM $ | B. TO $ | ☐ YES ☐ NO | ☐ YES ☐ NO |

13. DESCRIPTION OF WORK *(Physical characteristics)*

*(If additional space is needed use reverse)*

IMPORTANT: FAILURE TO COMPLETE AND RETURN THIS PART OF THE NOTICE TO THE ISSUING OFFICE, AT THE ADDRESS IN ITEM 6A, ON OR BEFORE THE DUE DATE SHOWN IN ITEM 15, MAY RESULT IN YOUR NAME BEING REMOVED FROM OUR MAILING LIST.

| 14. ACTION REQUESTED *(Check applicable box)* | | 15. DUE DATE |
|---|---|---|
| A. I AM INTERESTED IN BIDDING ON THIS PROJECT AS A: ☐ PRIME CONTRACTOR   ☐ PRINCIPAL SUBCONTRACTOR | B. I AM NOT INTERESTED IN BIDDING ON THIS PROJECT. RETAIN MY NAME ON YOUR MAILING LIST. | |
| NO. OF SET(S) YOU REQUIRE OF SOLICITATION DOCUMENTS | C. REMOVE MY NAME FROM YOUR MAILING LIST. | 16. PROJECT NO. |

17. NAME, ADDRESS *(City, State, ZIP Code)* AND TELEPHONE NUMBER OF FIRM

| 18. NAME AND TITLE OF FIRM REPRESENTATIVE | 19. SIGNATURE OF REPRESENTATIVE | 20. DATE SIGNED |
|---|---|---|

NSN 7540-01-148-3931
Previous edition usable

EXPIRATION DATE 1-31-93

1417-104

STANDARD FORM 1417 (REV. 1-90)
Prescribed by GSA-FAR (48 CFR) 53.236-XX

# STANDARD FORM (SF) 1442

| **SOLICITATION, OFFER AND AWARD** *(Construction, Alteration, or Repair)* | 1. SOLICITATION NO. | 2. TYPE OF SOLICITATION ☐ SEALED BID (IFB) ☐ NEGOTIATED (RFP) | 3. DATE ISSUED | PAGE OF PAGES |
|---|---|---|---|---|

IMPORTANT—The "offer" section on the reverse must be fully completed by offeror.

| 4. CONTRACT NO. | 5. REQUISITION/PURCHASE REQUEST NO. | 6. PROJECT NO. |
|---|---|---|

| 7. ISSUED BY          CODE | 8. ADDRESS OFFER TO |
|---|---|

| 9. FOR INFORMATION CALL: ▶ | A. NAME | B. TELEPHONE NO. *(Include area code) (NO COLLECT CALLS)* |
|---|---|---|

## SOLICITATION

NOTE: In sealed bid solicitations "offer" and "offeror" mean "bid" and "bidder."

10. THE GOVERNMENT REQUIRES PERFORMANCE OF THE WORK DESCRIBED IN THESE DOCUMENTS *(Title, identifying no., date):*

11. The Contractor shall begin performance within _____ calendar days and complete it within _____ calendar days after receiving

☐ award, ☐ notice to proceed. This performance period is ☐ mandatory, ☐ negotiable. (See _____.)

| 12A. THE CONTRACTOR MUST FURNISH ANY REQUIRED PERFORMANCE AND PAYMENT BONDS? *(If "YES," indicate within how many calendar days after award in Item 12B.)* ☐ YES   ☐ NO | 12B. CALENDAR DAYS |
|---|---|

13. ADDITIONAL SOLICITATION REQUIREMENTS:

A. Sealed offers in original and _____ copies to perform the work required are due at the place specified in Item 8 by _____ (hour) local

time _____ (date). If this is a sealed bid solicitation, offers must be publicly opened at that time. Sealed envelopes containing

offers shall be marked to show the offeror's name and address, the solicitation number, and the date and time offers are due.

B. An offer guarantee ☐ is, ☐ is not required.

C. All offers are subject to the (1) work requirements, and (2) other provisions and clauses incorporated in the solicitation in full text or by reference.

D. Offers providing less than _____ calendar days for Government acceptance after the date offers are due will not be considered and will be rejected.

# STANDARD FORM (SF) 24

| **BID BOND**<br>*(See instructions on reverse)* | DATE BOND EXECUTED<br>*(Must not be later than bid opening date)* | FORM APPROVED OMB NO.<br><br>9000-0045 |
|---|---|---|

Public reporting burden for this collection of information is estimated to average 25 minutes per response, including the time for reviewing instructions, searching existing data sources, gathering and maintaining the data needed, and completing and reviewing the collection of information. Send comments regarding this burden estimate or any other aspect of this collection of information, including suggestions for reducing this burden, to the FAR Secretariat (VRS), Office of Federal Acquisition Policy, GSA, Washington, DC 20405; and to the Office of Management and Budget, Paperwork Reduction Project (9000-0045), Washington, DC 20503.

| PRINCIPAL *(Legal name and business address)* | TYPE OF ORGANIZATION ("X" one) |
|---|---|
| | ☐ INDIVIDUAL   ☐ PARTNERSHIP<br>☐ JOINT VENTURE   ☐ CORPORATION |
| | STATE OF INCORPORATION |

SURETY(IES) *(Name and business address)*

| PERCENT OF BID PRICE | PENAL SUM OF BOND | | | | BID IDENTIFICATION | |
|---|---|---|---|---|---|---|
| | AMOUNT NOT TO EXCEED | | | | BID DATE | INVITATION NO. |
| | MILLION(S) | THOUSAND(S) | HUNDRED(S) | CENTS | | |
| | | | | | FOR *(Construction, Supplies or Services)* | |

**OBLIGATION:**

We, the Principal and Surety(ies) are firmly bound to the United States of America (hereinafter called the Government) in the above penal sum. For payment of the penal sum, we bind ourselves, our heirs, executors, administrators, and successors, jointly and severally. However, where the Sureties are corporations acting as co-sureties, we, the Sureties, bind ourselves in such sum "jointly and severally" as well as "severally" only for the purpose of allowing a joint action or actions against any or all of us. For all other purposes, each Surety binds itself, jointly and severally with the Principal, for the payment of the sum shown opposite the name of the Surety. If no limit of liability is indicated, the limit of liability is the full amount of the penal sum.

**CONDITIONS:**

The Principal has submitted the bid identified above.

**THEREFORE:**

The above obligation is void if the Principal—(a) upon acceptance by the Government of the bid identified above, within the period specified therein for acceptance (sixty (60) days if no period is specified), executes the further contractual documents and gives the bond(s) required by the terms of the bid as accepted within the time specified (ten (10) days if no period is specified) after receipt of the forms by the principal; or (b) in the event of failure to execute such further contractual documents and give such bonds, pays the Government for any cost of procuring the work which exceeds the amount of the bid.

Each Surety executing this instrument agrees that its obligation is not impaired by any extension(s) of the time for acceptance of the bid that the Principal may grant to the Government. Notice to the surety(ies) of extension(s) are waived. However, waiver of the notice applies only to extensions aggregating not more than sixty (60) calendar days in addition to the period originally allowed for acceptance of the bid.

**WITNESS:**

The Principal and Surety(ies) executed this bid bond and affixed their seats on the above date.

| | PRINCIPAL | | | |
|---|---|---|---|---|
| SIGNATURE(S) | 1.<br>(Seal) | 2.<br>(Seal) | 3.<br>(Seal) | Corporate Seal |
| NAME(S) & TITLE(S) *(Typed)* | 1. | 2. | 3. | |

| | INDIVIDUAL SURETY(IES) | | |
|---|---|---|---|
| SIGNATURE(S) | 1.<br>(Seal) | 2.<br>(Seal) | |
| NAME(S) & TITLE(S) | 1. | 2. | |

| | CORPORATE SURETY(IES) | | | |
|---|---|---|---|---|
| **SURETY A** | NAME & ADDRESS | | STATE OF INC. | LIABILITY LIMIT<br>$ |
| | SIGNATURE(S) | 1. | 2. | Corporate Seal |
| | NAME(S) & TITLE(S) *(Typed)* | 1. | 2. | |

NSN 7540-01-152-8059<br>Previous edition not usable   EXPIRATION DATE 12-31-92   24-106   STANDARD FORM 24 (REV. 1-90)<br>Prescribed by GSA-FAR (48 CFR) 53.228(a)

## CHAPTER FIFTEEN

# *Pricing of Contract Adjustments*

## I. INTRODUCTION.

Following this block of instruction, the student should be able to:

A. Distinguish the different types of adjustments and damages.

B. Know how to measure an adjustment.

C. Know how to prove the amount of an adjustment.

## II. OVERVIEW.

### A. Entitlement to an Adjustment and/or Damages.

1. In an equitable adjustment, the contractor receives its allowable costs plus a reasonable profit on those costs. Equitable adjustments are based on contract clauses granting that remedy, including:
   a. FAR 52.243-1 thru -7, Changes;
   b. FAR 52.245-2, -4, -5, and -7, Government Furnished Property;
   c. FAR 52.248-1 thru -3, Value Engineering;
   d. FAR 52.212-11, Variation in Estimated Quantity;
   e. FAR 52.212-13, Stop Work Order;
   f. FAR 52.236-2, Differing Site Conditions.

2. Adjustments are similar to equitable adjustments, except that adjustments exclude profit. Adjustments arise under the following clauses:
   a. FAR 52.212-12, Suspension of Work;
   b. FAR 52.212-15, Government Delay of Work.

3. Adjustments under some labor standards clauses include only the increased costs of direct labor. FAR 52.222-44, Fair Labor Standards Act and Service Contract Act-Price Adjustment; *KIME Plus, Inc.*, ASBCA No. 38840, 91-3 BCA ¶ 24,045 (the labor clauses of the contract allowed an adjustment for cost increases due to increase in minimum wages; increase includes wages and fringes only, not overhead or profit).

4. Damages are recoverable for breach of contract, i.e. the failure of a party to fulfill the obligations assumed when the contract was formed. Damages are measured under common law principles, rather than remedy granting clauses in the contract. The cost principles, however, may apply. *See AT&T Technologies, Inc.*, 18 Cl. Ct. 315 (1989).

### B. Pricing Formula.

1. The basic equitable adjustment formula is the difference between what it would have reasonably cost to perform the work as originally required, and what it reasonably cost to perform the work as changed, plus a reasonable profit. *Pacific Architects and Eng'rs, Inc. v. United States*, 203 Ct. Cl. 499, 491 F.2d 734 (1974) (contractor could not use an equitable adjustment to convert a loss contract into a profitable one); *Bruce Andersen Co.*, ASBCA No. 29412, 89-2 BCA ¶ 21,872 (deductive change).

2. Agencies price additional work based on the reasonable costs actually incurred in performing the new work. *Delco Elecs. Corp. v. United States*, 17 Cl. Ct. 302 (1989), *aff'd*, 909 F.2d 1495 (Fed. Cir. 1990). The contrac-

tor should segregate and accumulate these costs.

3. Agencies price deleted work based on the difference between the estimated costs of the original work and the actual costs of performing the work after the change. *Knights' Piping, Inc.*, ASBCA No. 46985, 94-3 BCA ¶ 27,026; *Anderson/Donald, Inc.*, ASBCA No. 31213, 86-3 BCA ¶ 19,036 (measure of deductive change is costs saved). *But see Condor Reliability Servs, Inc.*, ASBCA No. 40538, 90-3 BCA ¶ 23,254 (deletion of a loss item).

4. Where the contractor shares the fault, it shares the added costs. *See Dickman Builders, Inc.*, ASBCA No. 32612, 91-2 BCA ¶ 23,989 (added costs of installing hot water branch piping to heating coils were shared because contractor failed to enquire about the patent ambiguity and government failed to clarify after another bidder asked questions).

### C. Recoverable Costs.

1. Cost determinations as part of a contract adjustment must comply with the cost principles in FAR Part 31 and DFARS Part 231 applicable on the date of contract award. FAR 31.102; DFARS 252.243-7001, Pricing of Adjustments (no civilian agency equivalent). To recover a particular cost, the incurred cost, either direct or indirect, must be reasonable, allocable to the contract, measured in accordance with accounting standards, and not specifically disallowed. FAR 31.201-2(a).

2. Reasonableness. A cost is reasonable if, in its nature and amount, it does not exceed that which a prudent person would incur in the conduct of a competitive business. FAR 31.201-3.
   a. Cost held unreasonable in amount. *DeMauro Constr. Co.*, ASBCA No. 12514, 73-1 BCA ¶ 9,830; *Air Repair, GmbH*, ASBCA No. 10288, 67-1 BCA ¶ 6115.
   b. Nature of cost held unreasonable. *Lockheed-Georgia Co., Div. of Lockheed Corp.*, ASBCA No. 27660, 90-3 BCA ¶ 22,957 (air

travel to the Greenbriar resort for executive physicals unreasonable because competent physicians were available in Atlanta).

3. Allocability. A cost is allocable if incurred specifically for the contract; or the cost benefits both the contract and other work, and is distributed to them in reasonable proportion to the benefits received; or is necessary for the overall operation of the business. FAR 31.201-4.

4. Measured in accordance with accounting standards. Contractors can determine costs by using any generally accepted cost accounting method that is equitably and consistently applied. FAR 31.201-1. The contractor's method must comply with the Cost Accounting Standards (CAS), FAR Part 30, if applicable.

5. Not specifically disallowed. FAR 31.205 sets forth the cost principles applicable to government contracts. The government does not pay certain costs, even if they are actually incurred, reasonable, allocable, and properly accounted for. Similarly, the parties may specify in the contract that certain costs will not be allowable under a specific contract.

### D. Certification Requirements.

1. In DOD, requests for equitable adjustments exceeding $100,000, at the time of submission, must be certified by a person with knowledge of the basis for the request, the accuracy and completeness of the supporting data, and the request itself. 10 U.S.C. § 2410e; DFARS 233.7000.
   a. The certifying official must be an individual who is "authorized to bind the contractor." 10 U.S.C. § 2410e(a)(2); DFARS 233.7000 (a)(2).
   b. The above certificate is different from the certification required under the Contract Disputes Act, 41 U.S.C. §§ 601-13, for claims exceeding $100,000. DFARS 233.7000(c).

2. Similarly, after negotiating an agreement on a modification settling a request for equitable

adjustment on a negotiated contract, the contractor must furnish a certificate of current cost and pricing data if the modification exceeds $500,000 under the Truth in Negotiations Act. 10 U.S.C. § 2306a.

## III. MEASUREMENT OF THE ADJUSTMENT.

### A. Total Costs.
The total cost of an adjustment is the sum of allowable direct and indirect costs, incurred or to be incurred, less any allowable credits, plus cost of money. FAR 31.201-1. If it is an *equitable* adjustment, one must also calculate the profit on the allowable costs.

### B. Direct Costs.
1. A direct cost is any cost which is identified specifically with a particular final cost objective. Direct costs are not limited to items which are incorporated in the end product as material or labor. Costs identified specifically with a claim are direct costs of that claim. FAR 31.202.
2. Direct costs generally include direct labor, direct material, subcontracts, and other direct costs.

### C. Indirect Costs.
1. Indirect costs are any costs not directly identified with a single final cost objective, but identified with two or more final cost objectives, or with at least one intermediate cost objective. FAR 31.203.
   a. Overhead. Allocable to a cost objective based on benefit conferred. Typical overhead costs include: the costs of personnel administration, depreciation of plant and equipment, utilities, and management.
   b. General and administrative (G&A). Not allocable based on benefit, but necessary for overall operation of the business. FAR 31.201-4.
2. Calculating indirect cost rates. The indirect cost pool divided by the allocation base equals the indirect cost rate. For example, if

a contractor has indirect costs totalling $100,000 an accounting period, and direct costs totalling $1,000,000 in the same accounting period, the indirect cost rate is 10%.
3. Some agencies limit the recoverable overhead through contract clauses. *Reliance Ins. Co. v. United States*, 931 F.2d 863 (Fed. Cir. 1991) (court upheld clause which limited recoverable overhead for change orders).

### D. Profit and Loss.
An equitable adjustment includes a reasonable and customary allowance for profit. *United States v. Callahan Walker Constr. Co.*, 317 U.S. 56 (1942). Adjustments under the Suspension of Work clause do not include profit. FAR 52.212-12. Profit is calculated as:
1. The rate earned on the unchanged work;
2. A lower rate based on the reduced risk of equitable adjustments; or
3. The rate calculated using weighted guidelines. *See Doyle Constr. Co.*, ASBCA No. 44883, 94-2 BCA ¶ 26,832 (board is not bound by the weights applied by the agency).

## IV. PROVING THE AMOUNT OF THE ADJUSTMENT.

### A. Burden of Proof.
1. The burden is on the party claiming the benefit of the adjustment. *Globe Constr. Co.*, ASBCA No. 21069, 78-2 BCA ¶ 13,337.
2. What must the party prove?
   a. Entitlement—the government did something that changed the contractor's costs, for which the government is legally liable. *T.L. James & Co.*, ENG BCA No. 5328, 89-1 BCA ¶ 21,643 (no liability for increased costs caused by a sovereign act).
   b. Causation—there must be a causal nexus between the basis for liability and the claimed increase (or decrease) in cost. *Boyajian v. United States*, 191 Ct. Cl. 233 (1970).
3. Presumptions.
   a. Actual costs are no longer presumed rea-

sonable. 10 U.S.C. § 2324(j) (no presumption that indirect costs are reasonable); FAR 31.201-3 (no presumption that *any* cost is reasonable).

b. Above reverses *Bruce Constr. v. United States*, 163 Ct. Cl. 97, 324 F.2d 516 (1963) (actual costs incurred presumed reasonable). The burden of proof of the reasonableness of incurred costs is on the contractor (a preponderance standard).

c. No reported decision addresses the conflict between *Bruce Construction* and FAR 31.201-3.

## B. Actual Costs Preferred.

1. A contractor must prove its costs using the best evidence available under the circumstances. The preferred method is actual cost data. *Cen-Vi-Ro of Texas, Inc. v. United States*, 210 Ct. Cl. 684, 538 F.2d 348 (1976).

2. The contracting officer may include the Change Order Accounting clause, FAR 52.243-6, in a contract. This clause permits the contracting officer to order accumulation of actual costs. A contractor must indicate in its proposal which proposed costs are actual and which are estimates.

3. Failure to accumulate actual cost data may result in either a substantial reduction or total disallowance of the claimed costs. *Delco Elecs. Corp. v. United States*, 17 Cl. Ct. 302 (1989), *aff'd*, 909 F.2d 1495 (Fed. Cir. 1990) (recovery reduced for unexcused failure to segregate); *Togaroli Corp.*, ASBCA No. 32995, 89-2 BCA ¶ 21,864 (costs not segregated despite the auditor's repeated recommendation to do so; no recovery beyond final decision); *Assurance Co.*, ASBCA No. 30116, 86-1 BCA ¶ 18,737 (lack of cost data prevented reasonable approximation of damages for jury verdict, therefore, the appellant recovered less than the amount allowed in the final decision); *Barrow Utilities & Elec. Coop. Inc. v. United States*, 20 Cl. Ct. 113 (1990) (claim barred by laches demonstrated where fire destroyed records of costs incurred during period contractor failed to submit claim).

## C. Use of Estimates.

1. Good faith estimates are preferred when actual costs are not available. *Lorentz Brunn Co.*, GSBCA No. 8505, 88-2 BCA ¶ 20,719 (estimates of labor hours and rates admissible). Estimates are generally required when negotiating the cost of a change in advance of performing the work. Estimates are an acceptable method of proving costs where they are supported by detailed substantiating data or are reasonably based on verifiable cost experience. *J.M.T. Mach. Co.*, ASBCA No. 23928, 85-1 BCA ¶ 17,820 (1984), *aff'd on other grounds*, 826 F.2d 1042 (Fed. Cir. 1987).

2. If the contractor uses detailed estimates based on analyses of qualified personnel, the government will not be able to successfully allege that the contractor used the disfavored total cost method of adjustment pricing. *Illinois Constructors Corp.*, ENG BCA No. 5827, 94-1 BCA ¶ 26,470.

3. Estimates based on *Mean's Guide* must be disregarded where actual costs are known. *Anderson/Donald, Inc.*, ASBCA No. 31213, 86-3 BCA ¶ 19,036.

## D. Total Cost Method.

1. The total cost method is not preferred because it assumes the entire overrun is solely the government's fault. The total cost method calculates the difference between the bid price on the original contract and the actual total cost of performing the contract as changed. *David J. Tierney, Jr., Inc.*, GSBCA No. 7107, 88-2 BCA ¶ 20,806; *Concrete Placing Inc. v. United States*, 25 Cl. Ct. 369 (1992). *Cf. Servidone Constr. Corp. v. United States*, 19 Cl. Ct. 346 (1990), *aff'd*, 931 F.2d 860 (Fed. Cir. 1991) (total cost appropriate when pricing a differing site condition claim for material that was more difficult than expected to remove).

2. To use the total cost method, the contractor must establish four factors:

a. The nature of the particular cost is impossible or highly impracticable to determine with a reasonable degree of certainty;

b. The contractor's bid was realistic;

c. The contractor's actual incurred costs were reasonable; and

d. The contractor was not responsible for any of the added costs.

3. Modified total cost method. The court or board of contract appeals allows the contractor to adjust the total cost method to account for other factors, usually because the bid was not realistic or because there were other causes for the extra costs. *Olsen v. Espy*, 26 F.3d 141 (Fed. Cir. 1994); *Hardrives, Inc.*, IBCA No. 2319, 94-1 BCA ¶ 26,267; *Servidone Constr. Corp.*, ENG BCA No. 4736, 88-1 BCA ¶ 20,390; *Teledyne McCormick-Selph v. United States*, 218 Ct. Cl. 513 (1978).

## E. Jury Verdicts.

1. Jury verdicts are not a method of proof, but a means of resolving disputed facts. *Paragon Energy Corp.*, ENG BCA No. 5302, 88-3 BCA ¶ 20,959; *Joseph Pickard's Sons v. United States*, 209 Ct. Cl. 643 (1976); *Delco Elecs. Corp. v. United States*, 17 Cl. Ct. 302 (1989), *aff'd*, 909 F.2d 1495 (Fed. Cir. 1990).

2. Courts and boards may adopt a jury verdict approach when:

a. There is clear proof of injury;

b. No more reliable method exists, *see Dawco Constr. Co. v. United States*, 930 F.2d 872 (Fed. Cir. 1991) (actual costs are preferred; where contractor offers no evidence of justifiable inability to provide actual costs, then it is not entitled to a jury verdict); *Service Eng'g Co.*, ASBCA No. 40274, 93-2 BCA ¶ 25,885; and

c. The evidence is sufficient for a fair approximation of the damages.

## V. SPECIAL ITEMS.

### A. Unabsorbed Overhead.

1. Two types of costs associated with certain types of claims are unabsorbed or extended overhead. Extended overhead results when work is added to the contract and the performance period is extended. Unabsorbed overhead results when work is suspended. For example, assume there is a one day delay on a ship building contract. During the one day delay, the drydock continues to depreciate, to incur property taxes, to require insurance, etc. However, during the one day delay, no additional work is done to absorb these overhead costs. Nor can the half built ship be removed from the drydock so that work can start on another contract, thereby absorbing the costs.

2. In construction contracts, the *Eichleay* formula is the principal means of calculating unabsorbed overhead. *Wickham Contracting Co. v. Fischer*, 12 F.3d 1574 (Fed. Cir. 1994).

a. Under this method, calculate the daily overhead rate during the contract period, then multiply the daily rate by the number of days of delay.

b. Standby and the inability to take on additional work are prerequisites to recovery under *Eichleay*. *Interstate Gen. Gov't Contractors, Inc.*, 12 F.3d 1053 (Fed. Cir. 1993). The contractor is not required to show, however, that its workers were standing by idly. *Id.*

3. In manufacturing contracts, reviewing authorities use the *Allegheny* method, which deletes the variable overhead costs from the pool of unabsorbed overhead. *See Do-Well Mach. Shop, Inc.*, ASBCA No. 35867, 92-2 BCA ¶ 24,843 (*Eichleay* generally only apples to construction contracts). *But see So-Pak-Co.*, ASBCA No. 38906, 93-3 BCA ¶ 26,215 (*Eichleay* applied to a manufacturing contract).

4. Recovery of unabsorbed overhead is not automatic. The contractor must offer credible proof of increased costs resulting from the government delay. *Beaty Elec. Co.*, EBCA 403-3-88, 91-2 BCA ¶ 23,687. When added work causes a delay, the additional overhead is absorbed by the additional costs and *Eich-*

*leay* does not apply. *Community Heating & Plumbing Co. v. Kelso*, 987 F.2d 1575 (Fed. Cir. 1993) (*Eichleay* recovery denied because overhead was "extended" as opposed to "unabsorbed"); *accord C.B.C. Enters., Inc. v. United States*, 978 F.2d 669 (Fed. Cir. 1992).

## B. Loss of Efficiency.

The disruption caused by changes may cause labor inefficiency and/or loss of learning. Contractors may recover for these damages, if proven. Thomas E. Shea, *Proving Productivity Losses in Government Contracts*, 18 Pub. Cont. L. J. 414 (March 1989).

## C. Other Delay Damages.

The contractor may recover the increased costs of performing work during later periods when weather or other factors makes the work more difficult. *Charles G. Williams Constr., Inc.*, ASBCA No. 42592, 92-1 BCA ¶ 24,635 (contractor recovered costs of performing during worse weather).

## D. Breach Damages.

1. Consequential Damages. The general rule is that consequential damages are not recoverable unless they are foreseeable and caused directly by the government's breach. *Prudential Ins. Co. of America v. United States*, 801 F.2d 1295 (Fed. Cir. 1986); *Hadley v. Baxendale*, 9 Exch. 341, 156 Eng. Rep. 145 (1854); *Land Movers Inc. and O.S. Johnson - Dirt Contractor (JV)*, ENG BCA No. 5656, 91-1 BCA ¶ 23,317 (no recovery of lost profits based on loss of bonding capacity; also no recovery related to bankruptcy, emotional distress, loss of business, etc.).

2. Compensatory Damages. A contractor whose contract was breached by the government is entitled to be placed in as good of a position as it would have been by full performance. *PHP Healthcare Corp.*, ASBCA No. 39207, 91-1 BCA ¶ 23,647 (the measure of damages for failure to order the minimum quantity is not the contract price; the contractor must

prove actual damages). Compensatory damages include a reliance component (costs incurred as a consequence of the breach), and an expectancy component (lost profits). *Keith L. Williams*, ASBCA No. 46068, 94-3 BCA ¶ 27,196.

## E. Attorneys' Fees.

Costs related to prosecuting and defending claims and appeals against the federal government are generally unallowable. FAR 31.205-47; *Singer Co., Librascope Div. v. United States*, 215 Ct. Cl. 281, 568 F.2d 695 (1977). This is consistent with the general rule that attorneys' fees are not allowed in suits against the United States in the absence of an express statutory provision allowing recovery. *Piggly Wiggly Corp. v. United States*, 112 Ct. Cl. 391, 81 F. Supp 819 (1949).

1. The Equal Access to Justice Act, 5 U.S.C. § 504, authorizes courts and boards to award attorneys' fees to qualifying prevailing parties unless the government can show that its position was "substantially justified." *See, e.g., Midwest Holding Corp.*, ASBCA No. 45222, 94-3 BCA ¶ 27,138.

2. Consultant and professional costs are unallowable even if incurred to prepare a demand for payment that does not meet the CDA definition of a "claim." *Bill Strong Enters.*, ASBCA No. 42946, 93-3 BCA ¶ 25,961.

3. Legal fees unrelated to presenting or defending claims against the government are generally allowable. *Bos'n Towing and Salvage Co.*, ASBCA No. 41357, 92-2 BCA ¶ 24,864 (costs of professional services, including legal fees, are generally allowable, except where specifically disallowed).

## F. Interest.

1. Interest generally is based upon the rate established by the Secretary of the Treasury as provided by the CDA, 41 U.S.C. § 611. Interest prior to the submission of a claim is generally unallowable. FAR 31.205-20. However, under the Prompt Payment Act (31

U.S.C. §§ 3901-3907) the contractor could be entitled to interest if the contractor submits a proper voucher and the government fails to make payment within 30 days.

2. Interest begins to run upon the contracting officer's receipt of a properly certified claim *Dawco Constr., Inc. v. United States*, 930 F.2d 872 (Fed. Cir. 1991), or upon submission of a defectively certified claim that is subsequently certified. Federal Courts Administration Act of 1992, Title IX, Pub. L. No. 102-572, 106 Stat. 4506, 4518. Interest runs regardless whether the claimed costs have actually been incurred at the date of submission of a claim. *Servidone Constr. Co. v. United States*, 931 F.2d 860 (Fed. Cir. 1991).

3. When the contracting officer pays a claim, the payment is applied first to accrued interest. Then the payment is applied to the principle amount due. Any unpaid principle continues to accrue interest. *Paragon Energy Corp.*, ENG BCA No. 5302, 91-3 BCA ¶ 24,349.

## VI. CONCLUSION.

A. Distinguish equitable adjustments and adjustments. Know which is applicable in a given situation.

B. Elements of Adjustments. Direct costs plus indirect costs, minus allowable credits, plus the cost of money. Should profit be included?

C. How to prove the amount of the adjustment.
   1. Actual cost method;
   2. Estimates;
   3. Total Cost Method;
   4. Jury Verdicts;
   5. The *Eichleay* Formula.

## CHAPTER SIXTEEN

# Inspection, Acceptance, and Warranty

## I. INTRODUCTION.

Following this block of instruction, students should:

A. Understand the fundamental concepts of inspection and testing.

B. Understand the government's remedies under the Inspection clauses when a contractor tenders nonconforming goods or services.

C. Understand how the government accepts goods and services, and the three exceptions to the finality of acceptance.

D. Understand how warranties operate in government contracts, and how the government asserts warranty claims.

## II. FUNDAMENTAL CONCEPTS OF INSPECTION AND TESTING.

### A. General.

1. The Inspection clauses, which are remedy granting clauses, vest the government with significant rights and remedies.

2. In any dispute, the parties must identify the correct theory of recovery and applicable contractual provisions. The theory of recovery normally flows from a contractual provision. *See Morton-Thiokol, Inc.*, ASBCA No. 32629, 90-3 BCA ¶ 23,207 (government denial of cost reimbursement rejected — board noted government's failure to cite Inspection clause). Additionally, a party may recover in the event of breach of a contract by the other party.

### B. Origin of the Government's Right to Inspect.

FAR Part 46.

1. The government has the right to inspect to ensure that it receives conforming goods and services. Additionally, the particular Inspection clauses, if any, contained in a contract, determine the government's right to inspect a contractor's performance. *See* page 225.

2. Contract inspections fall into three general categories, depending on the extent of quality assurance needed by the government for the acquisition involved. These include:

   a. Government reliance on inspection by the contractor. FAR 46.202-1;

   b. Standard inspection requirements. FAR 46.202-2; and

   c. Higher-level contract quality requirements. FAR 46.202-3.

3. The FAR contains several different Inspection clauses. In determining which clause to use, consider:

   a. The *contract type* (e.g., fixed-price, cost-reimbursement, time-and-materials and labor-hour); and,

   b. The *nature of the item procured* (e.g., supply, service, construction, transportation, or research and development).

### C. Operation of the Inspection Clauses.

1. Definitions. FAR 46.101

   a. "Inspection" means examining and testing supplies or services to determine whether they conform to contract requirements.

b. "Testing" is that element of inspection that determines the properties or elements of products, including the functional operation of supplies or their components, by the application of established scientific principles and procedures.

2. Depending upon the specific clauses in the contract, the government has the right to inspect and test supplies, services, materials furnished, work required by the contract, facilities, and equipment at all places and times, and, in any event, before acceptance. *See, e.g.*, FAR 52.246-2 (supplies—fixed-price), -4 (services—fixed-price), -5 (services—cost-reimbursement), -6 (time-and-materials and labor-hour), -8 (R&D—cost-reimbursement), -9 (R&D), -10 (facilities), and -12 (construction).

3. The government may require a contractor to maintain an inspection system that is adequate to ensure delivery of supplies and services that conform to the requirements of the contract. *David B. Lilly Co.*, ASBCA No. 34678, 92-2 BCA ¶ 24,973 (government ordered contractor to submit new inspection plan to eliminate systemic shortcomings in the inspection process).

4. Inspection and testing reasonably must relate to determining whether performance is in compliance with contractual requirements.

   a. Contractually specified inspections or tests are presumed reasonable unless they conflict with other contract requirements. *General Time Corp.*, ASBCA No. 22306, 80-1 BCA ¶ 14,393.

   b. If the contract specifies a test, the government may not require a higher level of performance than measured by the method specified. *United Technologies Corp., Sikorsky Aircraft Div. v. United States*, 27 Fed. Cl. 393 (1992). However, the government may use tests other than those specified in the contract provided the tests do not impose a more stringent standard of performance. *Donald C. Hubbs, Inc.*, DOT BCA No. 2012, 90-1 BCA ¶ 22,379 (use of rolling straightedge

permitted after initial inspection determined that road was substantially nonconforming). *See also Puroflow Corp.*, ASBCA No. 36058, 93-3 BCA ¶ 26,191 (board upholds government's rejection of First Article Test Report for contractor's failure to perform an unspecified test).

   c. Absent contractually specified tests, the government may use any tests that do not impose different or more stringent standards than those required by the contract. *Nash Metalware Co. v. Gen. Servs. Admin.*, GSBCA No. 11951, 94-2 BCA ¶ 26,780 (government reasonably measured capacity of ladles); *Davey Compressor Co.*, ASBCA No. 38671, 94-1 BCA ¶ 26,433; *Al Johnson Constr. Co.*, ENG BCA No. 4170, 87-2 BCA ¶ 19,952.

   d. If the contract specifies no particular tests, consider the following factors in selecting a test or inspection technique:

      (1) Consider the intended use of the product or service. *A-Nam Cong Ty*, ASBCA No. 14200, 70-1 BCA ¶ 8,106 (unreasonable to test coastal water barges on the high seas while fully loaded).

      (2) Measure compliance with contractual requirements, and inform the contractor of the standards it must meet. *Service Eng'g Co.*, ASBCA No. 40275, 94-1 BCA ¶ 26,382 (board refused to impose a military standard on contract for ship repair, where contract simply required workmanship in accordance with "best commercial marine practice"); *Tester Corp.*, ASBCA No. 21312, 78-2 BCA ¶ 13,373, *mot. for recon. denied*, 79-1 BCA ¶ 13,725.

      (3) Use standard industry tests, if available. *DiCecco, Inc.*, ASBCA No. 11944, 69-2 BCA ¶ 7,821 (use of USDA mushroom standards upheld). *But see Chelan Packing Co.*, ASBCA No. 14419, 72-1 BCA ¶ 9,290 (government inspector failed to apply industry standard properly).

5. The government must inspect and test cor-

rectly. *Baifield Indus., Div. of A-T-O, Inc.*, ASBCA No. 13418, 77-1 BCA ¶ 12,308 (cartridge cases/rounds fired at excessive pressure).

6. Generally, the government is not required to perform inspections. *Cannon Structures, Inc.*, AGBCA No. 90-207-1, 93-3 BCA ¶ 26,059.

   a. The government's failure to discover defects during inspection does not relieve the contractor of the requirement to tender conforming supplies. FAR 52.246-2(c); *Boes Iron Works, Inc.*, ASBCA No. 46159, 94-3 BCA ¶ 27,230.

   b. However, the government may not deny unreasonably a contractor's request to perform preliminary or additional testing. *Alonso & Carus Iron Works, Inc.*, ASBCA No. 38312, 90-3 BCA ¶ 23,148 (no liability for defective fuel tank because government refused to allow a preliminary water test not prohibited by the contract); *Praoil, S.R.L.*, ASBCA No. 41499, 94-2 BCA ¶ 26,840 (government unreasonably refused contractor request, per industry practice, to perform retest of fuel; termination for default overturned).

7. The government constructively changes a contract when it requires a contractor to perform tests not specified in the contract, entitling the contractor to an equitable adjustment of the contract price. *CBI NA-CON, Inc.*, ASBCA No. 42268, 93-3 BCA ¶ 26,187.

## III. GOVERNMENT REMEDIES UNDER THE INSPECTION CLAUSE.

### A. Introduction.

1. The Inspection clauses give the government significant remedies.

2. The government's remedies under the Inspection clauses operate in two phases. Initially, the government may demand correction of deficiencies. If this proves to be unsuccessful, the government may obtain corrective action from other sources.

3. Under the Inspection clauses, the government's remedies depend upon when the contractor delivers nonconforming performance.

### B. Defective Performance before the Required Delivery Date.

1. If the contractor delivers defective products or performance before the required delivery date, the government may:

   a. Reject the tendered product or performance, *Andrews, Large & Whidden, Inc. and Farmville Mfg. Corp.*, ASBCA No. 30060, 88-2 BCA ¶ 20,542 (government demand for replacement of non-conforming windows sustained); *Centric/Jones Constr.*, IBCA No. 3139, 94-1 BCA ¶ 26,404 (government failed to prove that rejected work was noncompliant with specifications; contractor entitled to equitable adjustment for performing additional tests to secure government acceptance);

   b. Require the contractor to correct the nonconforming product or service, giving the contractor a reasonable opportunity to do so, *see Premiere Bldg. Servs., Inc.*, B-255858, Apr. 12, 1994, 94-1 CPD ¶ 252 (government may charge reinspection costs to contractor); or

   c. Accept the nonconforming product or performance at a reduced price. *Federal Boiler Co.*, ASBCA No. 40314, 94-1 BCA ¶ 26,381 (change in cost of performance to the contractor, not the damages to the government, is the basis for adjustment); *Blount Bros. Corp.*, ASBCA No. 29862, 88-2 BCA ¶ 20,644 (government entitled to a credit totalling the amount saved by contractor for using nonconforming concrete). *But cf. Valley Asphalt Corp.*, ASBCA No. 17595, 74-2 BCA ¶ 10,680 (although runway built to wrong elevation, only nominal price reduction allowed because no loss in value to the government).

2. The government may not terminate the contract for default based on the tender of non-

conforming products or performance before the required delivery date.

## C. Defective Performance on the Required Delivery Date.

1. If the contractor delivers nonconforming products or performance on the required delivery date, the government may:
   a. Reject or require correction of the nonconforming product or performance;
   b. Reduce the contract price and accept the nonconforming product; or
   c. Terminate for default if performance is not in substantial compliance with the contract requirements. *See* FAR 52.249-6 to 52.249-12.

2. If the contractor has complied substantially with the requirements of the contract, the government must give the contractor notice and the opportunity to correct minor defects before terminating the contract for default. *Radiation Tech., Inc. v. United States*, 366 F.2d 1003 (Ct. Cl. 1966).

## D. Defective Performance after the Required Delivery Date.

1. Generally, the government may terminate the contract for default.

2. If the contractor has complied substantially with the requirements of the contract, albeit after the required delivery date, the government should give the contractor notice of the defects and an opportunity to correct them. *See Franklin E. Penny Co. v. United States*, 524 F.2d 668 (Ct. Cl. 1975) (late nonconforming goods may substantially comply with contract requirements); Section IV, para. B.6, *infra*.

3. The government may accept nonconforming performance at a reduced price.

## E. Remedies if the Contractor Fails to Correct Defective Performance.

1. If the contractor fails to correct defective performance after receiving notice and a reasonable opportunity to correct the work, the government may:
   a. Contract with a commercial source to correct or replace the defective performance (often, obtaining funding is difficult and may make this remedy impracticable), *George Bernadot Co.*, ASBCA No. 42943, 94-3 BCA ¶ 27,242;
   b. Correct or replace the defective performance itself;
   c. Accept the nonconforming performance at a reduced price; or
   d. Terminate the contract for default. When the government terminates a contract for default, it acquires rights and remedies under the termination clause, including the right to reprocure supplies or services similar to those terminated. *See* FAR 52.249-8(b).

## F. Special Rules for Service Contracts.

1. The Inspection clause for fixed-price *service* contracts, FAR 52.246-4, is different than FAR 52.246-2, which pertains to fixed-price *supply* contracts.

2. The government's remedies depend on whether it is possible for the contractor to perform the services correctly.
   a. Normally, the government should permit the contractor to re-perform the services and correct the deficiencies, if possible.
   b. Otherwise, the government may:
      (1) Require the contractor to take adequate steps to ensure future compliance with the requirements of the contract; and
      (2) Reduce the contract price to reflect the reduced value of services received. *Teltara, Inc.*, ASBCA No. 42256, 94-1 BCA ¶ 26,485 (government properly used random sampling inspections to calculate contract price reductions); *Orlando Williams*, ASBCA No. 26099, 84-1 BCA ¶ 16,983 (although T4D of janitorial contract was sustained, the government acted unreasonably by withholding maximum payments when some work had been performed satisfactorily).

c. Authorities disagree about whether the same failure in contract performance can support both a reduction in contract price and a termination for default. *Compare W.M. Grace, Inc.*, ASBCA No. 23076, 80-1 BCA ¶ 14,256 (monthly deductions due to poor performance waived right to terminate for default during those months) and *Wainwright Transfer Co.*, ASBCA No. 23311, 80-1 BCA ¶ 14,313 (deduction for HHG shipments precluded termination) *with Cervetto Bldg. Maint. Co. v. United States*, 2 Cl. Ct. 299 (1983) (reduction in contract price and termination are cumulative remedies).

## IV. STRICT COMPLIANCE VS. SUBSTANTIAL COMPLIANCE.

### A. Strict Compliance.

1. As a general rule, the government is entitled to strict compliance with its specifications. *Blake Constr. Co. v. United States*, 28 Fed. Cl. 672 (1993); *Meisel Rohrbau, GmbH*, ASBCA No. 35622, 93-3 BCA ¶ 26,222, *aff'd on recon.*, 94-1 BCA ¶ 26,530 (government properly insisted that contractor use brand name steel pipe rather than an "equal" brand). *See also Cascade Pac. Int'l v. United States*, 773 F.2d 287 (Fed. Cir. 1985); *Ace Precision Indus.*, ASBCA No. 40307, 93-2 BCA ¶ 25,629 (government rejection of line block final assemblies that failed to meet contract specifications was proper). *But see Zeller Zentralheizungsbau GmbH*, ASBCA No. 43109, 94-2 BCA ¶ 26,657 (government improperly rejected contractor's use of "equal" equipment where contract failed to list salient characteristics of brand name equipment).

2. Contractors must comply with specifications even if they vary from standard commercial practice. *R.B. Wright Constr. Co. v. United States*, 919 F.2d 1569 (Fed. Cir. 1990) (contract required three coats over painted surface although commercial practice was to apply only two); *Graham Constr., Inc.*, ASBCA No. 37641, 91-2 BCA ¶ 23,721 (specification

requiring redundant performance sustained).

3. Slight defects are still defects. *Mech-Con Corp.*, GSBCA No. 8415, 88-3 BCA ¶ 20,889 (installation of 2" pipe insulation did not satisfy 1-1/2" requirement).

### B. Substantial Compliance.

1. "Substantial compliance" is a judicially created concept to avoid the harsh result of termination for default based upon a minor breach, and to avoid economic waste. The concept originated in construction contracts and has been extended to other types of contracts. *See Radiation Tech., Inc. v. United States*, 366 F.2d 1003 (Ct. Cl. 1966).

2. Substantial compliance gives the contractor the right to attempt to cure defective performance. The elements of substantial compliance are:
   a. Timely delivery;
   b. Contractor's good faith belief that it has complied with the contract's requirements;
   c. Minor defects;
   d. Defects that can be corrected within a reasonable time; and
   e. Time is *not* of the essence, i.e., the government does not require strict compliance with the delivery schedule.

3. Generally, the doctrine of substantial compliance does not require the government to accept defective performance by the contractor. *Cosmos Eng'rs, Inc.*, ASBCA No. 19780, 77-2 BCA ¶ 12,713.
   a. The doctrine of economic waste, however, may require the government to accept noncompliant construction if the work, as completed, is suitable for its intended purpose and the cost of correction would far exceed the gain that would be realized. *Granite Constr. Co. v. United States*, 962 F.2d 998 (Fed. Cir. 1992), *cert. denied*, 113 S. Ct. 965 (1993).
   b. The economic waste doctrine applies only when the contractor has substantially complied with the contract. *Triple M Contractors*, ASBCA No. 42945, 94-3 BCA ¶ 27,003 (no economic waste where initial place-

ment of reinforcing materials in drainage gutters reduced useful life from 25 to 20 years); *Shirley Constr. Corp.*, ASBCA No. 41908, 93-3 BCA ¶ 26,245 (concrete slab not in substantial compliance even though it could support the design load; without substantial compliance, doctrine of economic waste inapplicable).

4. Except in those rare situations involving economic waste, the doctrine of substantial compliance affects only when the government may terminate for default. It does not preclude termination for default if the contractor fails to correct defective performance. The government —

   a. Must give the contractor a reasonable amount of time to correct its work, including, if necessary, an extension beyond the original required delivery date.

   b. May terminate for default if the contractor fails to correct defects within a reasonable period of time.

5. The contractor must have believed that the defective goods conformed to the requirements of the contract when it delivered the goods. *Norwood Precision Prods.*, ASBCA No. 38095, 90-3 BCA ¶ 23,200 (no substantial compliance because contractor knew that engine rings, when delivered, were placed improperly).

6. *Radiation Technology*, *supra*, established the concept of substantial compliance for the timely delivery of nonconforming goods. *Franklin E. Penny Co. v. United States*, 524 F.2d 668 (Ct. Cl. 1975), arguably expanded the concept to include late delivery of nonconforming goods. The courts and boards have not widely followed *Penny*; however, they have not overruled it.

## V. PROBLEM AREAS IN TESTING AND INSPECTION.

### A. Claims Resulting from Unreasonable Inspections.

1. Government inspections may give rise to equitable adjustment claims if they delay the contractor's performance or cause additional work. The government—

   a. Must perform reasonable inspections. FAR 52.246-2. *Donald C. Hubbs, Inc.*, DOT BCA No. 2012, 90-1 BCA ¶ 22,379 (more sophisticated test than specified, rolling straightedge, was reasonable).

   b. Must avoid overzealous inspections. The government may not inspect to a level beyond that authorized by the contract. Overzealous inspection may impact adversely upon the government's ability to reject the contractor's performance, to assess liquidated damages, or to otherwise assert its rights under the contract. *See Gary Aircraft Corp.*, ASBCA No. 21731, 91-3 BCA ¶ 24,122 ("overnight change" in inspection standards was unreasonable).

   c. Must exercise reasonable care when performing tests and inspections prior to acceptance of the products or services, and may not rely solely on destructive testing after acceptance to discover a deficiency it could have discovered before acceptance. *Ahern Painting Contractors, Inc.*, GSBCA No. 7912, 90-1 BCA ¶ 22,291.

   d. Must resolve ambiguities involving inspection requirements in a timely manner. *P & M Indus.*, ASBCA No. 38759, 93-1 BCA ¶ 25,471.

2. Improper inspections may excuse a contractor's delay, thereby delaying or preventing termination for default. *Puma Chem. Co.*, GSBCA No. 5254, 81-1 BCA ¶ 14,844 (contractor justified in refusing to proceed when government test procedures subjected contractor to unreasonable risk of rejection).

3. Improper inspections may justify claims for increased costs of performance under the Delay of Work or Changes clauses in the contract. *See, e.g., Hull-Hazard, Inc.*, ASBCA No. 34645, 90-3 BCA ¶ 23,173 (contract specified joint inspection, however, government conducted multiple inspections and bombarded contractor with "punch lists"); *H.G. Reynolds Co.*, ASBCA No. 42351, 93-2 BCA ¶ 25,797; *Harris Sys. Int'l, Inc.*, ASBCA No.

33280, 88-2 BCA ¶ 20,641 (10% "spot mop-ping" specified, government demanded 100% for "uniform appearance"). *But see Space Dynamics Corp.*, ASBCA No. 19118, 78-1 BCA ¶ 12,885 (defects in aircraft carrier cata-pult assemblies justified increased govern-ment inspection).

4. It is a constructive change to test a standard commercial item to a higher level of perfor-mance than is required in commercial prac-tice. *Max Blau & Sons, Inc.*, GSBCA No. 9827, 91-1 BCA ¶ 23,626 (insistence on exten-sive deburring and additional paint on a com-mercial cabinet was a constructive change).

5. Improper inspection, if extreme, may give rise to a claim of government breach of con-tract. *Adams v. United States*, 358 F.2d 986 (Ct. Cl. 1966) (government breached con-tract when inspector disregarded inspection plan, doubled inspection points, complicated construction, delayed work, increased stan-dards, and demanded a higher quality tent pin than specified); *Electro-Chem Etch Metal Markings, Inc.*, GSBCA No. 11785, 93-3 BCA ¶ 26,148. *But see Southland Constr. Co.*, VABCA No. 2217, 89-1 BCA ¶ 21,548 (gov-ernment engineer's "harsh and vulgar" lan-guage, when appellant contributed to the tense atmosphere, did not justify refusal to continue work).

6. Government breach of its duty to cooperate with the contractor may shift the cost of damages caused by testing to the govern-ment. *See Alonso & Carus Iron Works, Inc.*, ASBCA No. 38312, 90-3 BCA ¶ 23,148 (gov-ernment refusal to permit reasonable, prelim-inary test proposed by contractor shifted the risk of loss to the government).

## B. Waiver, Prior Course of Dealing, and Other Acts of Government Employees Affecting Testing and Inspection.

1. By his actions, an authorized government official may waive contractual requirements. *See generally Longmire Coal Corp.*, ASBCA No. 31569, 86-3 BCA ¶ 19,110. The elements of waiver are:

    a. Authorized government official;
    b. Knowledge by government official of true facts;
    c. Ignorance by contractor of true facts; and
    d. Detrimental reliance by the contractor.

2. Normally, previous government acceptance of similar nonconforming performance is insufficient to demonstrate waiver of specifi-cations.

    a. Government acceptance of nonconform-ing performance by other contractors nor-mally does not waive contractual requirements. *Moore Elec. Co.*, ASBCA No. 33828, 87-3 BCA ¶ 20,039 (government's allowing deviation to another contractor on prior contract for light pole installation did not constitute waiver, even where both contractors used the same subcon-tractor).

    b. Government acceptance of nonconform-ing performance by the same contractor normally does not waive contractual requirements. *Basic Marine, Inc.*, ENG BCA No. 5299, 87-1 BCA ¶ 19,426.

    c. Government acceptance of similar non-conforming performance by the same con-tractor over a prolonged period of time may waive the requirements of that partic-ular specification. *Gresham & Co. v. Unit-ed States*, 470 F.2d 542 (Ct. Cl. 1972) (acceptance of dishwashers without deter-gent dispensers eventually waived require-ment to equip with dispensers); *Astro Dynamics, Inc.*, ASBCA No. 28381, 88-3 BCA ¶ 20,832 (acceptance of 7 shipments of rocket tubes with improper dimensions precluded termination for default for same reason on shipment #8); *but see Kvass Constr. Co.*, ASBCA No. 45965, 94-1 BCA ¶ 26,513 (Navy's acceptance on four prior construction contracts of "expansion com-pensation devices" for a heat distribution system did not waive contract require-ment for "expansion loops").

3. Generally, an inspector's failure to require correction of defects is insufficient to waive the right to demand correction. *Hoboken*

*Shipyards, Inc.*, DOT BCA No. 1920, 90-2 BCA ¶ 22,752 (government not bound by an inspector's unauthorized agreement to accept improper type of paint if a second coat was applied).

## VI. ACCEPTANCE.

### A. Definition.

*Acceptance* is the act of an authorized representative of the government that asserts ownership of identified supplies tendered or approves specific services performed in partial or complete fulfillment of contractual requirements. FAR 46.101.

### B. General Principles of Acceptance.

1. Acceptance is conclusive except for latent defects, fraud, gross mistakes amounting to fraud, or as otherwise provided for in the contract, e.g., warranties. FAR 52.246-2(k).
2. Acceptance entitles the contractor to payment and is the event that marks the passage of title from the contractor to the government.
3. Acceptance may be express or implied. The following may indicate acceptance.
   a. DD Form 250 is the most common document used to memorialize acceptance.
   b. Final payment operates as an act of acceptance. *Norwood Precision Prods.*, ASBCA No. 24083, 80-1 BCA ¶ 14,405. *See also Farruggio Constr. Co.*, DOT CAB No. 75-2-75-2E, 77-2 BCA ¶ 12,760 (progress payments on wharf sheeting contract did not shift ownership and risk of loss to the government).
   c. Unconditional acceptance of initial, partial deliveries of a segregable, multi-year contract may waive the right to demand that the final product perform satisfactorily. *See Infotec Dev., Inc.*, ASBCA No. 31809, 91-2 BCA ¶ 23,909 (multi-year contract for minuteman missile software).
   d. Government use of the product or service, or unreasonable delay in accepting the tendered performance, may constitute

constructive acceptance. *See, e.g., Cudahy Packing Co. v. United States*, 109 Ct. Cl. 833, 75 F. Supp. 239 (1948); *Mann Chem. Labs, Inc. v. United States*, 182 F. Supp. 40 (D. Mass. 1960).
   e. Government changes to a product which render the product nonfunctional may preclude rejection. *The Interlake Cos., v. Gen. Servs. Admin.*, GSBCA No. 11876, 93-2 BCA ¶ 25,813 (government changes to material handling system rendered computer's preprogrammed logic useless).
   f. Payment, even if no more monies are due under a contract, does not necessarily constitute final acceptance. *Spectrum Leasing Corp.*, GSBCA No. 7347, 90-3 BCA ¶ 22,984 (in a partial termination for default of computer software contract, there was no acceptance because contract provided that final testing and acceptance would occur after the last payment).
4. As a general rule, contractors bear the risk of loss or damage to the contract work prior to acceptance. *See* FAR 52.246-16, Responsibility for Supplies (supply); FAR 52.236-7, Permits and Responsibilities (construction). *See also Meisel Rohrbau GmbH*, ASBCA No. 40012, 92-1 BCA ¶ 24,716 (damage caused by children); *DeRalco Corp.*, ASBCA No. 41306, 91-1 BCA ¶ 23,576 (structure destroyed by 180 MPH hurricane winds although construction was 97% complete and only required to withstand 100 MPH winds).
   a. If the contract specifies f.o.b. destination, the contractor bears the risk of loss during shipment even if the government accepted the supplies prior to shipment. FAR 52.246-16; *KAL M.E.I. Mfg. & Trade Ltd.*, ASBCA No. 44367, 94-1 BCA ¶ 26,582 (contractor liable for full purchase price of cover assemblies lost in transit, even though cover assemblies had only scrap value);
   b. In construction contracts, the government may use and possess the building prior to completion. *See* FAR 52.236-11, Use and

Possession Prior to Completion. The contractor is relieved of responsibility for loss of or damage to work resulting from the government's possession or use. *See Fraser Eng'g Co.*, VABCA No. 3265, 91-3 BCA ¶ 24,223 (government responsible for damaged cooling tower when damage occurred while tower was in its sole possession and control).

## C. Exceptions to the Finality of Acceptance.

1. Latent defects may enable the government to avoid the finality of acceptance. To be latent, a defect must have been—
   a. Unknown to the government. *See Gavco Corp.*, ASBCA No. 29763, 88-3 BCA ¶ 21,095;
   b. In existence at the time of acceptance. *See Santa Barbara Research Ctr.*, ASBCA No. 27831, 88-3 BCA ¶ 21,098; *mot. for recon. denied*, 89-3 BCA ¶ 22,020 (failure to prove crystalline growths were in laser diodes at the time of acceptance and not reasonably discoverable); and
   c. Not discoverable by a reasonable inspection. *Tricon-Triangle Contractors*, ENG BCA No. 5553, 92-1 BCA ¶ 24,667 (government failure to inspect waterline waived contractor's liability); *Wickham Contracting Co.*, ASBCA No. 32392, 88-2 BCA ¶ 20,559 (failed spliced telephone and power cables were latent defects and not discoverable); *Dale Ingram, Inc.*, ASBCA No. 12152, 74-1 BCA ¶ 10,436 (mahogany plywood was not a latent defect because a visual examination would have disclosed).

2. Contractor fraud allows the government to avoid the finality of acceptance. To establish fraud, the government must prove that—
   a. The contractor intended to deceive the government;
   b. The contractor misrepresented a material fact; and
   c. The government relied on the misrepresentation to its detriment. *D&H Constr. Co.*, ASBCA NO. 37482, 89-3 BCA ¶ 22,070 (sub-

contractor's substitution of counterfeit underwriter's labels on nonconforming freezers was fraud); *United States v. Aerodex, Inc.*, 469 F.2d 1003 (5th Cir. 1972)

3. A gross mistake amounting to fraud may avoid the finality of acceptance. The elements of a gross mistake amounting to fraud are—
   a. A major error, without intent to deceive, causing the government to accept nonconforming performance;
   b. The contractor's misrepresentation of a fact; and
   c. Detrimental government reliance on the misrepresentation. *Z.A.N. Co.*, ASBCA No. 25488, 86-1 BCA ¶ 18,612 (gross mistake amounting to fraud established where the government relied on Z.A.N. to verify watch caliber and Z.A.N. accepted watches from subcontractor without proof that the caliber was correct).

4. Warranties. Warranties operate to revoke acceptance if the nonconformity is covered by the warranty. *See* discussion in Section VII, *infra*.

5. Once the government revokes acceptance, its normal rights under the Inspection, Disputes, and Default clauses of the contract are revived. FAR 52.246-2(l) (Inspection-Supply clause expressly revives rights). *Jo-Bar Mfg. Corp.*, ASBCA No. 17774, 73-2 BCA ¶ 10,311 (the contractor's failure to heat treat aircraft bolts entitled government to recover purchase price paid); *cf.* FAR 52.246-12 (Inspection-Construction clause is silent on reviving rights).

## VII. WARRANTY.

### A. General Principles.

1. Warranties may be express or implied.
2. Normally, warranties are defined by the time and scope of coverage.
3. The use of warranties is not mandatory. FAR 46.703. In determining whether a warranty is appropriate for a specific acquisition, consider:
   a. Nature and use of the supplies or services;
   b. Cost;

c. Administration and enforcement;

d. Trade practice; and

e. Reduced quality assurance requirements, if any.

4. Special regulations govern weapons systems warranties. *See* DFARS Subpart 246.770.

**B. Asserting Warranty Claims.**

1. When asserting a warranty claim, the government must prove:

   a. That there was a defect when the contractor completed performance, *Vistacon Inc. v. Gen. Servs. Admin.*, GSBCA No. 12580, 94-2 BCA ¶ 26,887;

   b. That the warranted defect was the most probable cause of the failure, *A.S. McGaughan Co.*, PSBCA No. 2750, 90-3 BCA ¶ 23,229; *R.B. Hazard, Inc.*, ASBCA No. 41061, 91-2 BCA ¶ 23,709 (government denied recovery under warranty theory because it failed to prove that pump failure was not the result of government misuse and that defective material or workmanship was the most probable cause of the damage);

   c. That the defect was within the scope of the warranty;

   d. That the defect arose during the warranty period;

   e. That the contractor received notice of the defect and its breach of the warranty; and

   f. The cost to repair the defect, if not corrected by the contractor. *Hoboken Shipyards, Inc.*, DOT BCA No. 1920, 90-2 BCA ¶ 22,752. *See Globe Corp.*, ASBCA No. 45131, 93-3 BCA ¶ 25,968 (board reduced government's claim against the contractor because the government inconsistently allocated the cost of repairing the defects).

2. The government may invalidate a warranty through improper maintenance, operation, or alteration.

3. A difficult problem in administering warranties on government contracts is identifying and reporting defects covered by the warranty.

4. The Changes clause does not vest the government with the unilateral power to change a warranty provision. *BMY - A Div. of Harsco Corp.*, ASBCA No. 36926, 91-1 BCA ¶ 23,565 (Changes clause permits government to change *specifications*, however, the warranty clause is not a specification).

**C. Remedies for Breach of Warranty.**

1. The FAR provides the basic outline for governmental remedies. *See* FAR 52.246-17 and 52.246-18. If the contractor breaches a warranty clause, the government may—

   a. Order the contractor to repair or replace the defective product;

   b. Retain the defective product at a reduced price;

   c. Correct the defect in-house or by contract if the contractor refuses to honor the warranty; or

   d. Permit an equitable adjustment in the contract price. The adjustment cannot reduce the price below the scrap value of the product.

**D. Mitigation of Damages.**

1. The government must attempt to mitigate its damages.

2. The government may recover consequential damages. *Norfolk Shipbldg. and Drydock Corp.*, ASBCA No. 21560, 80-2 BCA ¶ 14,613 (government entitled to cost of repairs caused by ruptured fuel tank).

**VIII. CONCLUSION.**

The government has numerous rights and remedies arising under the Inspection clauses of the contract. Unfortunately, it sometimes forfeits these rights by failing to understand them and to enforce them correctly. Judge advocates and government attorneys can contribute to the success of the government procurement process by working with government inspectors, contracting officer representatives, and contracting officers to insure that each of these individuals understands the government's rights and obligations with regards to the inspection, acceptance, and warranty of government contracts.

# SUPPLY INSPECTION CLAUSE

**52.246-2 Inspection of Supplies—Fixed-Price.**

As prescribed in 46.302, insert the following clause:

INSPECTION OF SUPPLIES—FIXED-PRICE

(JUL 1985)

(a) Definition. "Supplies," as used in this clause, includes but is not limited to raw materials, components, intermediate assemblies, end products, and lots of supplies.

(b) The Contractor shall provide and maintain an inspection system acceptable to the Government covering supplies under this contract and shall tender to the Government for acceptance only supplies that have been inspected in accordance with the inspection system and have been found by the Contractor to be in conformity with contract requirements. As part of the system, the Contractor shall prepare records evidencing all inspections made under the system and the outcome. These records shall be kept complete and made available to the Government during contract performance and for as long afterwards as the contract requires. The Government may perform reviews and evaluations as reasonably necessary to ascertain compliance with this paragraph. These reviews and evaluations shall be conducted in a manner that will not unduly delay the contract work. The right of review, whether exercised or not, does not relieve the Contractor of the obligations under the contract.

(c) The Government has the right to inspect and test all supplies called for by the contract, to the extent practicable, at all places and times, including the period of manufacture, and in any event before acceptance. The Government shall perform inspections and tests in a manner that will not unduly delay the work. The Government assumes no contractual obligation to perform any inspection and test for the benefit of the Contractor unless specifically set forth elsewhere in this contract.

(d) If the Government performs inspection or test on the premises of the Contractor or a subcontractor, the Contractor shall furnish, and shall require subcontractors to furnish, without additional charge, all reasonable facilities and assistance for the safe and convenient performance of these duties. Except as otherwise provided in the contract, the Government shall bear the expense of Government inspections or tests made at other than the Contractor's or subcontractor's premises: *provided,* that in case of rejection, the Government shall not be liable for any reduction in the value of inspection or test samples.

(e) (1) When supplies are not ready at the time specified by the Contractor for inspection or test, the Contracting Officer may charge to the Contractor the additional cost of inspection or test.

(2) The Contracting Officer may also charge the Contractor for any additional cost of inspection or test when prior rejection makes reinspection or retest necessary.

(f) The Government has the right either to reject or to require correction of nonconforming supplies. Supplies are nonconforming when they are defective in material or workmanship or are otherwise not in conformity with contract requirements. The Government may reject nonconforming supplies with or without disposition instructions.

(g) The Contractor shall remove supplies rejected or required to be corrected. However, the Contracting Officer may require or permit correction in place, promptly after notice, by and at the expense of the Contractor. The Contractor shall not tender for acceptance corrected or rejected supplies without disclosing the former rejection or requirement for correction, and, when required, shall disclose the corrective action taken.

(h) If the Contractor fails to promptly remove, replace, or correct rejected supplies that are required to be removed or to be replaced or corrected, the Government may either (1) by contract or otherwise, remove, replace, or correct the supplies and charge the cost to the Contractor or (2) terminate the contract for default. Unless the Contractor corrects or replaces the supplies within the delivery schedule, the Contracting Officer may require their delivery and make an equitable price reduction. Failure to agree to a price reduction shall be a dispute.

(i) (1) If this contract provides for the performance of Government quality assurance at source, and if requested by the Government, the Contractor shall furnish advance notification of the time (i) when Contractor inspection or tests will be performed in accordance with the terms and conditions of the contract and (ii) when the supplies will be ready for Government inspection.

(2) The Government's request shall specify the period and method of the advance notification and the Government representative to whom it shall be furnished. Requests shall not require more than 2 workdays of advance notification if the Government representative is in residence in the Contractor's plant, nor more than 7 workdays in other instances.

(j) The Government shall accept or reject supplies as promptly as practicable after delivery, unless otherwise provided in the contract. Government failure to inspect and accept or reject the supplies shall not relieve the Contractor from responsibility, nor impose liability on the Government, for nonconforming supplies.

(k) Inspections and tests by the Government do not relieve the Contractor of responsibility for defects or other failures to meet contract requirements discovered before acceptance. Acceptance shall be conclusive, except for latent defects, fraud, gross mistakes amounting to fraud, or as otherwise provided in the contract.

(l) If acceptance is not conclusive for any of the reasons in paragraph (k) hereof, the Government, in addition to any other rights and remedies provided by law, or under other provisions of this contract, shall have the right to require the Contractor (1) at no increase in contract price, to correct or replace the defective or nonconforming supplies at the original point of delivery or at the Contractor's plant at the Contracting Officer's election, and in accordance with a reasonable delivery schedule as may be agreed upon between the Contractor and the Contracting Officer; *provided,* that the Contracting Officer may require a reduction in contract price if the Contractor fails to meet such delivery schedule, or (2) within a reasonable time after receipt by the Contractor of notice of defects or nonconformance, to repay such portion of the contract as is equitable under the circumstances if the Contracting Officer elects not to require correction or replacement. When supplies are returned to the Contractor, the Contractor shall bear the transportation cost from the original point of delivery to the Contractor's plant and return to the original point when that point is not the Contractor's plant. If the Contractor fails to perform or act as required in (1) or (2) above and does not cure such failure within a period of 10 days (or such longer period as the Contracting Officer may authorize in writing) after receipt of notice from the Contracting Officer specifying such failure, the Government shall have the right by contract or otherwise to replace or correct such supplies and charge to the Contractor the cost occasioned the Government thereby.

## CHAPTER SEVENTEEN

# *Financing of Government Contracts*

## I. INTRODUCTION.

### A. Contractor and Government Interests.

1. Finance and accounting considerations.
2. Avoidance of interest penalties.
3. Debt collection by government.
4. Effect on contract performance.

### B. Invoice Payments v. Finance Payments.

1. Invoice payments are payments made upon delivery of goods or performance of services and *acceptance* thereof by the government. Invoice payments include:
   a. Final payments of the contract price, costs, or fee in accordance with the contract or as settled by the government and the contractor.
   b. Payments for partial deliveries or partial performance under fixed-price contracts.
2. Contract financing payments are payments made to a contractor *before* acceptance of goods or services by the government. Such payments are a means of financing the contractor's performance. Finance payments include:
   a. Advance payments.
   b. Progress payments. *Note*: Progress payments under fixed-price construction and fixed-price architect-engineer contracts are treated as invoice payments under the Prompt Payment Act.
   c. Interim payments on cost-type contracts.

## II. CONTRACT FINANCING METHODS.

41 U.S.C. § 255; 10 U.S.C. § 2307; FAR Subpart 32.1. Whenever practicable, agencies must make financing payments based on performance, as opposed to incurred costs. FEDERAL ACQUISITION STREAMLINING ACT OF 1994, Pub. L. No. 103-355, § 2001, 108 Stat. 3243 (to be codified at 10 U.S.C. § 2307(b)).

### A. Partial Payments.

1. Partial payments are payments made under fixed-price contracts for supplies or services that are accepted by the government but are only part of the contract requirements. *See* page 233.
2. Unless otherwise specified in the contract, the government must make payment under fixed-price contracts when it *accepts* partial deliveries if:
   a. The amount due on the deliveries warrants it; or
   b. The contractor requests payment and the amount due on partial deliveries is at least $1,000 or 50% of the total contract price. FAR 52.232-1.

### B. Advance Payments.

FAR Subpart 32.4; FAR 52.232-12, Advance Payments.

1. Advance payments are advances of money by the government to a prime contractor before, in anticipation of, and for the purpose of complete performance under one or more contracts.
2. This is the least preferred method of contract financing.
3. Requirements:
   a. The contractor must give adequate security.

b. Advance payments cannot exceed the unpaid contract price.

c. The agency head or designee must determine that advance payment is in the public interest or facilitates the national defense.

4. Advance payments can be authorized *in addition to* progress or partial payments on the same contract.

5. The government charges interest on the daily unliquidated balance of advance payments, except under specified types of contracts that the agency head or designee may exempt from interest charges.

### C. Progress Payments.

1. Progress payments can be made on the basis of costs incurred by the contractor as work progresses under the contract. FAR Subpart 32.5; FAR 52.232-16, Progress Payments.

   a. Customary v. Unusual progress payments. FAR 32.501-1 and FAR 32.501-2. DFARS 232.5 provides customary and uniform progress payment rates.

   b. The FY94 Appropriations Act directed DOD to lower customary progress payment rates from 85% to 75%. Interim DFARS Rule 232.501 makes this change permanent for solicitations issued after November 11, 1993.

   c. Contractor may be liable for treble damages under the False Claims Act, 31 U.S.C. § 3729, for submitting a payment request in advance of cost incurrence. *Young-Montenay, Inc. v. United States*, 15 F.3d 1040 (Fed. Cir. 1994).

2. Progress payments can also be based on a percentage or stage of contract completion, if authorized by agency procedures. This type of progress payment is subject to three general restrictions:

   a. The agency must ensure that payments are commensurate with the work accomplished. *Greenhut Constr. Co.*, ASBCA No. 41777, 93-1 BCA ¶ 25,374.

   b. The work accomplished must meet the quality standards established under the contract; and

   c. Such payments cannot exceed 80 percent of the eligible costs of work accomplished if the contractual terms, specifications, and price are indefinite, i.e., under undefinitized contract actions.

3. Consideration for progress payments. FAR 32.501-4.

   a. If the contract contains progress payment terms when awarded, no specific consideration is required for inclusion of those terms or for subsequent changes in progress payment or liquidation rates provided for in the contract.

   b. New monetary or nonmonetary contract consideration is required, however, if the parties amend the contract by adding progress payment provisions.

4. Subcontract progress payment arrangements. FAR 32.504. The contracting officer must encourage the prime contractor to provide progress payments to subcontractors at "customary" rates. If the prime pays the subcontractor at a higher rate without government approval, the prime may not include the excess amount in its progress payment request. FAR 32.504(c).

### D. Progress Payments on Construction Contracts.

FAR 32.103; *see* page 234.

1. When a construction contract provides for progress payments and the contractor fails to achieve satisfactory performance for a period for which a progress payment is to be paid, the government may retain a percentage of the progress payment. The retainage shall not exceed 10 percent of the progress payment.

2. The government is not required to make progress payments for the value of construction materials stored at the construction site prior to installation. *Webb Elec. Co. of Florida*, ASBCA No. 40557, 93-2 BCA ¶ 25,715.

### E. Loan Guarantees.

Loan guarantees are made by Federal Reserve banks on behalf of one or more specific guaranteeing agencies to enable the contractor to obtain financing from private sources under contracts for the acquisition of supplies or services for the national defense. 50 U.S.C. app. § 2091, Defense Production Act of 1950, sec. 301; FAR Subpart 32.3.

### F. Interim Payments under Cost-Type Contracts.

*See infra* para. III.A.3.(e), pertaining to the Prompt Payment Act.

### III. CONTRACT PAYMENT PROCEDURES AND THE PROMPT PAYMENT ACT.

31 U.S.C. §§ 3901-06, *as amended by* the Prompt Payment Act Amendments of 1988, Pub. L. 100-496, 102 Stat. 2455; OMB Cir. A-125; FAR Subpart 32.9.[1]

### A. Applicability of the Prompt Payment Act (PPA).

1. Background.
2. Contracts covered.
   a. The PPA applies to *all government contracts* (including simplified acquisitions as defined in FAR Subpart 13.1), *except* for contracts where payment terms and late payment penalties have been established by other governmental authority, e.g., tariffs.
   b. There are *no* geographical limitations to applicability of the PPA's procedural requirements. FAR 32.901. *Held & Franke Bauaktiengesellschaft mbH*, ASBCA No. 42463, 92-1 BCA 24,712 (1992).
3. Applicability to types of payments. The PPA applies to invoice payments—i.e., payments made for supplies or services accepted by the government. For purposes of applying the PPA, invoice payments include (FAR 32.902):
   a. Final cost or fee payments where the government and the contractor have settled the amounts owed.
   b. Payments for partial deliveries accepted by the government under fixed-price contracts. FAR 32.902.
   c. Progress payments under fixed-price archi-

tect-engineer contracts. *Reddick & Sons of Gouverneur, Inc. v. United States*, 31 Fed. Cl. 558 (1994).
   d. Progress payments under fixed-price construction contracts.
   e. Payments under cost-reimbursement contracts where the government has already received the services. *Technology for Communications Int'l*, ASBCA No. 36265, 93-3 BCA ¶26,139; *Northrop Worldwide Aircraft Servs., Inc. v. Dep't of Treasury*, GSBCA No. 11162-TD, 92-2 BCA ¶ 24,765.
4. The PPA *does not apply* to contract financing payments—those made prior to acceptance of supplies or services. FAR 32.907-2. For purposes of applying the PPA, contract financing payments include (FAR 32.902):
   a. Advance payments;
   b. Progress payments based on cost;
   c. Progress payments based on percentage or stage of completion (except for those made under the fixed-price construction and fixed-price architect-engineer payments clauses noted above); and
   d. Interim payments in cost-type contracts where the government has not received performance.

### B. Invoice Payment Procedures.

1. *Proper invoice required*. The contractor must submit a proper invoice. FAR 32.902; FAR 32.905(e). *Ralcon Inc.*, ASBCA No. 43176, 94-2 BCA ¶ 26,935.
   a. To be proper, an invoice must include:
      (1) Name and address of contractor.
      (2) Invoice date.
      (3) Contract number or other authorization.
      (4) Description, quantity, unit of measure, and cost of supplies delivered or services performed.
      (5) Shipping and payment terms.
      (6) Name and address of contractor official to whom payment is to be sent.
      (7) Name, telephone number, and mailing address of person to notify if the invoice is defective.

(8) Any other information or documentation required by the contract, such as evidence of shipment.

b. Notice of defective invoice. The government must notify the contractor of any defective invoice within 7 days (less for certain perishable commodities) after receipt of the invoice at the designated payment office. The notice should include a statement identifying the defect in the invoice. FAR 32.905(e). *Technocratica*, ASBCA No. 44347, 94-1 BCA ¶ 26,584.

c. Supporting documentation is required. FAR 32.905(f).

(1) A receiving report or some other government document authorizing payment must support all invoice payments. A receiving report is evidence that the government accepted the supplies delivered or services performed by the contractor.

(2) The contractor must forward supporting documentation by the 5th working day after government acceptance or approval, unless the parties have made other arrangements. This period of time does not extend the payment due dates.

2. *Payment due date*. The payment due date for invoice payments is the later of (FAR 32.905):

a. The 30th day after the designated billing office receives a proper invoice; or

b. The 30th day after government acceptance of supplies delivered or services performed by the contractor.

(1) On a final invoice where the payment amount is subject to contract settlement actions, acceptance occurs on the effective date of the settlement.

(2) For the sole purpose of computing an interest penalty, government acceptance occurs constructively on the 7th day after the contractor has delivered the supplies or performed the services, unless there is a disagreement over quantity, quality, or contractor compliance with a contract requirement.

(3) The contracting officer may specify a longer period for constructive acceptance.

c. Special payment periods. The payment due date on contracts for perishable agricultural commodities is shorter. FAR 32.905(d).

d. It is DOD *policy* to assist small disadvantaged businesses by paying them as quickly as possible after receipt of a proper invoice. This policy does not alter the payment due date for purposes of the Prompt Payment Act. DFARS 232.903.

3. *Interest penalty for late payment*. The government incurs an interest penalty for late invoice payment, including late payment of progress payments under fixed-price architect-engineering contracts and fixed-price construction contracts. FAR 32.907-1.

a. Accrual. The interest penalty accrues when the government pays the contractor after the contract payment due date. There is *no grace period* for payment by the government (formerly there was a 15 day grace period).

b. Automatic payment. The interest penalty accrues automatically and must be paid by the government without request by the contractor.

c. Late payment *penalty on penalty*.

(1) The interest penalty is increased if the agency fails to make a required interest penalty payment within 10 days after the date the invoice amount is paid *and* the contractor then makes a written demand for the penalty within 40 days after the payment.

(2) This additional penalty applies to contracts *awarded* on or after 1 October 1989.

d. Non-excusability. The interest penalty is not excused by temporary unavailability of funds. FAR 32.903.

4. Distinguish Contract Disputes Act interest from Prompt Payment Act interest.

a. Under the Contract Disputes Act (CDA), the government pays interest on amounts found to be due to a contractor on claims submitted to the contracting officer. Such CDA interest accrues from the date the contracting officer receives a proper claim until payment of the amount due on the claim. 41 U.S.C. § 611. *See Paragon Energy Corp.*, ENG BCA No. 5302, 91-3 BCA ¶ 24,349 (payment of CDA claim presumed to include interest).

b. The interest payable under the PPA is an interest penalty that is payable when the agency fails to pay a business concern by the payment due date for property or services that have been delivered or completed.

(1) This interest penalty may also apply to a failure to pay interest due to a contractor by the due date of that interest.

(2) Payment of PPA interest is not dependent on a contractor submitting a claim for the interest penalty; however, the business concern must submit a proper invoice or voucher for payment. 31 U.S.C. § 3902.

c. PPA and CDA interest is based on the rate established by the Secretary of the Treasury and published in the Federal Register. 31 U.S.C. § 3902 and 41 U.S.C. § 611. Under the CDA, the government pays simple interest and adjusts the rate every six months to accord with the current Treasury rate. In contrast, PPA interest is compounded and is not adjusted during the one year accrual period.

## C. Fixed-Price Construction Contracts.

FAR 52.232-5, Payments Under Fixed-Price Construction Contracts (APR 1989); FAR 52.232-27, Prompt Payment for Construction Contracts.

1. The government must pay interest on approved construction contract progress payments that remain unpaid for more than 14 days after a proper payment request is received by the designated billing office.

a. The contracting officer may specify a longer period if necessary to adequately inspect work in process.

b. The contractor must certify such progress payment requests.

2. Similarly, the contractor must pay interest on unearned progress payments, e.g., when the contractor's performance for which progress payments are made does not conform to contract terms.

3. The government must pay interest on any retained amount that is approved for release if the government does not pay the retained amount to the contractor by the 30th day (unless specified otherwise in contract) after release.

## D. Fixed-Price Architect-Engineer Contracts.

FAR 52.232-10, Payments Under Fixed-Price Architect-Engineer Contracts; FAR 52.232-26, Prompt Payment for Fixed-Price Architect-Engineer Contracts. The government must pay interest penalties on approved contract progress payments that remain unpaid for more than 30 days after government approval of contractor estimates of work or services accomplished.

## E. Prompt Payment Discounts.

FAR 32.903.

1. The government may take prompt payment discounts offered by a contractor only when it makes payment within the specified discount period. *Jay Dee Militarywear, Inc.*, ASBCA No. 46539, 94-2 BCA ¶ 26,720.[2]

2. The PPA imposes an interest penalty on improperly taken discounts, and the agency must pay the penalty without request by the contractor.

## Endnotes

1. Several clarifications to FAR Subpart 32.9, Prompt Payment have been proposed as FAR case 91-91, 59 Fed. Reg. 23,776 (1994).

2. For a discussion on the propriety of taking a prompt payment discount for progress payments made in the normal course of contract administration, *see Prompt Payment Discounts Based on Progress Payments*, ARMY LAW., July 1994, at 54.

# FAR CLAUSE 52.232-1
# PAYMENTS (APR 1984)
# AND
# FAR CLAUSE 52.232-2
# PAYMENTS UNDER FIXED-PRICE
# RESEARCH AND DEVELOPMENT CONTRACTS (APR 1984)

**52.232-1 Payments.**

As prescribed in 32.111(a)(1), insert the following clause, appropriately modified with respect to payment due date in accordance with agency regulations, in solicitations and contracts when a fixed-price supply contract, a fixed-price service contract, or a contract for nonregulated communication services is contemplated:

PAYMENTS (APR 1984)

The Government shall pay the Contractor, upon the submission of proper invoices or vouchers, the prices stipulated in this contract for supplies delivered and accepted or services rendered and accepted, less any deductions provided in this contract. Unless otherwise specified in this contract, payment shall be made on partial deliveries accepted by the Government if—

(a) The amount due on the deliveries warrants it; or

(b) The Contractor requests it and the amount due on the deliveries is at least $1,000 or 50 percent of the total contract price.

(End of clause)

(R 7-103.7 1958 JAN)

(R 1-7.102-7)

**52.232-2 Payments under Fixed-Price Research and Development Contracts.**

As prescribed in 32.111(a)(2), insert the following clause, as appropriately modified with respect to payment due dates in accordance with agency regulations, in solicitations and contracts when a fixed-price research and development contract is contemplated:

PAYMENTS UNDER FIXED-PRICE RESEARCH AND DEVELOPMENT CONTRACTS (APR 1984)

The Government shall pay the Contractor, upon submission of proper invoices or vouchers, the prices stipulated in this contract for work delivered or rendered and accepted, less any deductions provided in this contract. Unless otherwise specified, payment shall be made upon acceptance of any portion of the work delivered or rendered for which a price is separately stated in the contract.

(End of clause)

(R 7-302.2 1959 JUN)

(R 1-7.302-2)

# FAR CLAUSE 52.232-5
## PAYMENTS UNDER FIXED-PRICE
## CONSTRUCTION CONTRACTS (APR 1989)

**52.232-5 Payments under Fixed-Price Construction Contracts.**

As prescribed in 32.111(a)(5), insert the following clause:

PAYMENTS UNDER FIXED-PRICE CONSTRUCTION CONTRACTS (APR 1989)

(a) The Government shall pay the Contractor the contract price as provided in this contract.

(b) The Government shall make progress payments monthly as the work proceeds, or at more frequent intervals as determined by the Contracting Officer, on estimates of work accomplished which meets the standards of quality established under the contract, as approved by the Contracting Officer. The Contractor shall furnish a breakdown of the total contract price showing the amount included therein for each principal category of the work, which shall substantiate the payment amount requested in order to provide a basis for determining progress payments, in such detail as requested by the Contracting Officer. In the preparation of estimates the Contracting Officer may authorize material delivered on the site and preparatory work done to be taken into consideration. Material delivered to the Contractor at locations other than the site may also be taken into consideration if—

(1) Consideration is specifically authorized by this contract; and

(2) The Contractor furnishes satisfactory evidence that it has acquired title to such material and that the material will be used to perform this contract.

(c) Along with each request for progress payments, the Contractor shall furnish the following certification, or payment shall not be made:

I hereby certify, to the best of my knowledge and belief, that—

(1) The amounts requested are only for performance in accordance with the specifications, terms, and conditions of the contract;

(2) Payments to subcontractors and suppliers have been made from previous payments received under the contract, and timely payments will be made from the proceeds of the payment covered by this certification, in accordance with subcontract agreements and the requirements of chapter 39 of Title 31, United States Code; and

(3) This request for progress payments does not include any amounts which the prime contractor intends to withhold or retain from a subcontractor or supplier in accordance with the terms and conditions of the subcontract.

_____
(Name)

_____
(Title)

_____
(Date)

(d) If the Contractor, after making a certified request for progress payments, discovers that a portion or all of such request constitutes a payment for performance by the Contractor that fails to conform to the specifications, terms, and conditions of this contract (hereinafter referred to as the "unearned amount"), the Contractor shall—

(1) Notify the Contracting Officer of such performance deficiency; and

(2) Be obligated to pay the Government an amount (computed by the Contracting Officer in the manner provided in 31 U.S.C 3903(c)(1)) equal to interest on the unearned amount from the date of receipt of the unearned amount until—

(i) The date the Contractor notifies the Contracting Officer that the performance deficiency has been corrected; or

(ii) The date the Contractor reduces the amount of any subsequent certified request for progress payments by an amount equal to the unearned amount.

(e) If the Contracting Officer finds that satisfactory progress was achieved during any period for which a progress payment is to be made, the Contracting Officer shall authorize payment to be made in full. However, if satisfactory progress has not been made, the Contracting Officer may retain a maximum of 10 percent of the amount of the payment until satisfactory progress is achieved. When the work is substantially complete, the Contracting Officer may retain from previously withheld funds and future progress payments that amount the Contracting Officer considers adequate for protection of the Government and shall release to the Contractor all the remaining withheld funds. Also, on completion and acceptance of each separate building, public work, or other division of the contract, for which the price is stated separately in the contract, payment shall be made for the completed work without retention of a percentage.

(f) All material and work covered by progress payments made shall, at the time of payment, become the sole property of the Government, but this shall not be construed as —

(1) Relieving the Contractor from the sole responsibility for all material and work upon which payments have been made or the restoration of any damaged work; or

(2) Waiving the right of the Government to require the fulfillment of all of the terms of the contract.

(g) In making these progress payments, the Government shall, upon request, reimburse the Contractor for the amount of premiums paid for performance and payment bonds (including coinsurance and reinsurance agreements, when applicable) after the Contractor has furnished evidence of full payment to the surety. The retainage provisions in paragraph (e) of this clause shall not apply to that portion of progress payments attributable to bond premiums.

(h) The Government shall pay the amount due the Contractor under this contract after—

(1) Completion and acceptance of all work;

(2) Presentation of a properly executed voucher; and

(3) Presentation of release of all claims against the Government arising by virtue of this contract, other than claims, in stated amounts, that the Contractor has specifically excepted from the operation of the release. A release may also be required of the assignee if the Contractor's claim to amounts payable under this contract has been assigned under the Assignment of Claims Act of 1940 (31 U.S.C. 3727 and 41 U.S.C. 15).

(i) Notwithstanding any provision of this contract, progress payments shall not exceed 80 percent on work accomplished on undefinitized contract actions. A "contract action" is any action resulting in a contract, as defined in FAR Subpart 2.1, including contract modifications for additional supplies or services, but not including contract modifications that are within the scope and under the terms of the contract, such as contract modifications issued pursuant to the Changes clause, or funding and other administrative changes.

(End of clause)

# FAR CLAUSE 52.232-7
## PAYMENTS UNDER TIME-AND-MATERIAL
## AND LABOR-HOUR CONTRACTS (APR 1984)

**52.232-7 Payments under Time-and-Materials and Labor-Hour Contracts.**

As prescribed in 32.111(b), insert the following clause:

PAYMENTS UNDER TIME-AND-MATERIALS AND LABOR-HOUR CONTRACTS (APR 1984)

The Government shall pay the Contractor as follows upon the submission of invoices or vouchers approved by the Contracting Officer:

(a) *Hourly rate.* (1) The amounts shall be computed by multiplying the appropriate hourly rates prescribed in the Schedule by the number of direct labor hours performed. The rates shall include wages, indirect costs, general and administrative expense, and profit. Fractional parts of an hour shall be payable on a prorated basis. Vouchers may be submitted once each month (or at more frequent intervals, if approved by the Contracting Officer), to the Contracting Officer or designee. The Contractor shall substantiate vouchers by evidence of actual payment and by individual daily job timecards, or other substantiation approved by the Contracting Officer. Promptly after receipt of each substantiated voucher, the Government shall, except as otherwise provided in this contract, and subject to the terms of (e) below, pay the voucher as approved by the Contracting Officer.

(2) Unless otherwise prescribed in the Schedule, the Contracting Officer shall withhold 5 percent of the amounts due under this paragraph (a), but the total amount withheld shall not exceed $50,000. The amounts withheld shall be retained until the execution and delivery of a release by the Contractor as provided in paragraph (f) below.

(3) Unless the Schedule prescribes otherwise, the hourly rates in the Schedule shall not be varied by virtue of the Contractor having performed work on an overtime basis. If no overtime rates are provided in the Schedule and overtime work is approved in advance by the Contracting Officer, overtime rates shall be negotiated. Failure to agree upon these overtime rates shall be treated as a dispute under the Disputes clause of this contract. If the Schedule provides rates for overtime, the premium portion of those rates will be reimbursable only to the extent the overtime is approved by the Contracting Officer.

(b) *Materials and subcontracts.* (1) Allowable costs of direct materials shall be determined by the Contracting Officer in accordance with Subpart 31.2 of the Federal Acquisition Regulation (FAR) in effect on the date of this contract. Reasonable and allocable material handling costs may be included in the charge for material to the extent they are clearly excluded from the hourly rate. Material handling costs are comprised of indirect costs, including, when appropriate, general and administrative expense allocated to direct materials in accordance with the Contractor's usual accounting practices consistent with Subpart 31.2 of the FAR. The Contractor shall be reimbursed for items and services purchased directly for the contract only when cash, checks, or other forms of actual payment have been made for such purchased items or services. Direct materials, as used in this clause, are those materials which enter directly into the end product, or which are used or consumed directly in connection with the furnishing of the end product.

(2) The cost of subcontracts that are authorized under the subcontracts clause of this contract shall be reimbursable costs under this clause; *provided,* that the costs are consistent with subparagraph (3) below. Reimbursable costs in connection with subcontracts shall be limited to the amounts paid to the subcontractor in the same manner as for items and services purchased directly for the contract under subparagraph (1) above; however, this requirement shall not apply to a Contractor that is a small business concern. Reimbursable costs shall not include any costs arising from the letting, administration or supervision of performance of the subcontract, if the costs are included in the hourly rates payable under (a)(1) above.

(3) To the extent able, the Contractor shall—

(i) Obtain materials at the most advantageous prices available with due regard to securing prompt delivery of satisfactory materials; and

(ii) Take all cash and trade discounts, rebates, allowances, credits, salvage, commissions, and other benefits. When unable to take advantage of the benefits, the Contractor shall promptly notify the Contracting Officer and give the reasons. Credit shall be given to the Government for cash and trade discounts, rebates, allowances, credits, salvage, the value of any appreciable scrap, commissions, and other amounts that have accrued to the benefit of the Contractor, or would have accrued except for the fault or neglect of the Contractor. The benefits lost without fault or neglect on the part of the Contractor, or lost through fault of the Government, shall not be deducted from gross costs.

(c) *Total cost.* It is estimated that the total cost to the Government for the performance of this contract shall not exceed the ceiling price set forth in the Schedule and the Contractor agrees to use its best efforts to perform the work specified in the Schedule and all obligations under this contract within such ceiling price. If at any time the Contractor has reason to believe that the hourly rate payments and material costs that will accrue in performing this contract in the next succeeding 30 days, if added to all other payments and costs previously accrued, will exceed 85 percent of the ceiling price in the Schedule, the Contractor shall notify the Contracting Officer giving a revised estimate of the total price to the Government for performing this contract with supporting reasons and documentation. If at any time during performing this contract, the Contractor has reason to believe that the total price to the Government for performing this contract will be substantially greater or less than the then stated ceiling price, the Contractor shall so notify the Contracting Officer, giving a revised estimate of the total price for performing this contract, with supporting reasons and documentation. If at any time during performing this contract, the Government has reason to believe that the work to be required in performing this contract will be substantially greater or less than the stated ceiling price, the Contracting Officer will so advise the Contractor, giving the then revised estimate of the total amount of effort to be required under the contract.

(d) *Ceiling price.* The Government shall not be obligated to pay the Contractor any amount in excess of the ceiling price in the Schedule, and the Contractor shall not be obligated to continue performance if to do so would exceed the ceiling price set forth in the Schedule, unless and until the Contracting Officer shall have notified the Contractor in writing that the ceiling price has been increased and shall have specified in the notice a revised ceiling that shall constitute the ceiling price for performance under this contract. When and to the extent that the ceiling price set forth in the Schedule has been increased, any hours expended and material costs incurred by the Contractor in excess of the ceiling price before the increase shall be allowable to the same extent as if the hours expended and material costs had been incurred after the increase in the ceiling price.

(e) *Audit.* At any time before final payment under this contract the Contracting Officer may request audit of the invoices or vouchers and substantiating material. Each payment previously made shall be subject to reduction to the extent of amounts, on preceding invoices or vouchers, that are found by the Contracting Officer not to have been properly payable and shall also be subject to reduction for overpayments or to increase for underpayments. Upon receipt and approval of the voucher or invoice designated by the Contractor as the "completion voucher" or "completion invoice" and substantiating material, and upon compliance by the Contractor with all terms of this contract (including, without limitation, terms relating to patents and the terms of (f) and (g) below), the Government shall promptly pay any balance due the Contractor. The completion invoice or voucher, and substantiating material, shall be submitted by the Contractor as promptly as practicable following completion of the work under this contract, but in no event later than 1 year (or such longer period as the Contracting Officer may approve in writing) from the date of completion.

(f) *Assignment.* The Contractor, and each assignee under an assignment entered into under this contract and in effect at the time of final payment under this contract, shall execute and deliver, at the time of and as a condition precedent to final payment under this contract, a release discharging the Government, its officers, agents, and employees of and from all liabilities, obligations, and claims arising out of or under this contract, subject only to the following exceptions:

(1) Specified claims in stated amounts, or in estimated amounts if the amounts are not susceptible of exact statement by the Contractor.

(2) Claims, together with reasonable incidental expenses, based upon the liabilities of the Contractor to third parties arising out of performing this contract, that are not known to the Contractor on the date of the execution of the release, and of which the Contractor gives notice in writing to the Contracting Officer not more than 6 years after the date of the release or the date of any notice to the Contractor that the Government is prepared to make final payment, whichever is earlier.

(3) Claims for reimbursement of costs (other than expenses of the Contractor by reason of its indemnification of the Government against patent liability), including reasonable incidental expenses, incurred by the Contractor under the terms of this contract relating to patents.

(g) *Refunds.* The Contractor agrees that any refunds, rebates, or credits (including any related interest) accruing to or received by the Contractor or any assignee, that arise under the materials portion of this contract and for which the Contractor has received reimbursement, shall be paid by the Contractor to the Government. The Contractor and each assignee, under an assignment entered into under this contract and in effect at the time of final payment under this contract, shall execute and deliver, at the time of and as a condition precedent to final payment under this contract, as assignment to the Government of such refunds, rebates, or credits (including any interest) in form and substance satisfactory to the Contracting Officer.

(End of clause)

# FAR CLAUSE 52.232-8
# DISCOUNTS FOR PROMPT PAYMENT (APR 1989)

**52.232-8 Discounts for Prompt Payment.**

As prescribed in 32.111(c)(1), insert the following clause:

DISCOUNTS FOR PROMPT PAYMENT (APR 1989)

(a) Discounts for prompt payment will not be considered in the evaluation of offers. However, any offered discount will form a part of the award, and will be taken if payment is made within the discount period indicated in the offer by the offeror. As an alternative to offering a prompt payment discount in conjunction with the offer, offerors awarded contracts may include prompt payment discounts on individual invoices.

(b) In connection with any discount offered for prompt payment, time shall be computed from the date of the invoice. For the purpose of computing the discount earned, payment shall be considered to have been made on the date which appears on the payment check or the date on which an electronic funds transfer was made.

(End of clause)

## CHAPTER EIGHTEEN

# *Contracting for Information Resources*

## I. INTRODUCTION.

Upon completing this instruction, the student will understand:

A. The definition of automatic data processing equipment (ADPE) under the Brooks Act.

B. The procedural differences between ADPE procurements and other procurements.

## II. REFERENCES.

A. Brooks Automatic Data Processing Act, Pub. L. No. 89-306, 79 Stat. 1127 (1965), 40 U.S.C. § 759 (hereinafter Brooks Act). This act assigns responsibility for acquisition of all ADPE to the General Services Administration.

B. Federal Information Resource Management Regulation (FIRMR), 41 C.F.R. Chapter 201, 55 Fed. Reg. 53386 (1990) (revised rule effective Apr. 29, 1991). These are the GSA regulations which implement the Brooks Act. FIRMR Part 39 also is published as FAR Appendix A.

C. Defense Federal Acquisition Regulation Supplement Part 239 supplements the FIRMR.

D. OMB Cir. A-130, *Management of Federal Information Resources*, June 25, 1993. This circular sets forth management policies on information resources and authorizes the implementing regulations listed below.

E. DOD Dir. 7740.1, *DOD Information Resources Mgmt. Program*, June 20, 1983.

F. AR 25-1, *The Army Information Resources Mgmt. Program*, Nov. 18, 1988; AFR 700 series; SECNAVINST 5231 series.

G. Richard C. Bean, *Practical Considerations in*

*ADP Acquisitions*, A.F.L. Rev. 265 (1988); Jerome S. Gabig and Richard C. Bean, *A Primer on Federal Information Systems Acquisitions*, 17 Pub. Cont. L. J. 31-76 & 553-594 (1988).

H. *ADP Protest Report*, General Services Administration. Free by writing ADP Protest Report, GSA-IRMS-KMAD, Room 5116, 18th and F Streets, N.W., Washington, DC 20405.

I. Trade Journals: *Federal Computer Week* and *Government Computer News*.

## III. LEGISLATIVE BACKGROUND.

A. Brooks Act.

B. Warner Amendment, Pub. L. No. 97-86, § 908(a)(1), 95 Stat. 1117-1118 (1981), 10 U.S.C. § 2315 (exempted certain DOD acquisitions).

C. Competition in Contracting Act, Pub. L. No. 98-369, § 2713, 98 Stat. 1182-1184 (1984), 40 U.S.C. § 759(f). In 1984 Congress gave the General Services Board of Contract Appeals (GSBCA) temporary bid protest jurisdiction for ADPE acquisitions.

D. *Electronic Data Sys. Fed. Corp. v. Gen. Servs. Admin. Board of Contract Appeals*, 792 F.2d 1569 (Fed. Cir. 1986), curtailed the GSBCA's efforts to expand its jurisdiction.

E. Paperwork Reduction Reauthorization Act of 1986, Pub. L. No. 99-500, Title VIII, §§ 822-824, 100 Stat. 1783-342 to 1783-344 (1986). Congressman Brooks' reaction to the EDS case was quick and definitive.

F. Federal Computer Security Act, Pub. L. No.

100-235, § 4, 101 Stat. 1728 (1988), 40 U.S.C. § 759(d) (made minor amendments to the Brooks Act authorizing the promulgation of standards on computer security).

G. Federal Acquisition Streamlining Act of 1994, Pub. L. No. 103-355, §§ 1433-1438, 108 Stat. 3243, 3291-3294 (made changes to GSBCA jurisdiction and expanded processing time for protests).

## IV. ACQUISITIONS SUBJECT TO THE BROOKS ACT.

### A. Statutory Definition of Automatic Data Processing Equipment (ADPE).

40 U.S.C. § 759(a); *see* FIRMR 201-1.002-1; FIRMR 201-39.101-3.

(1) Automatic Data Processing Equipment means any equipment or interconnected system or subsystems of equipment that is used in the automatic acquisition, storage, manipulation, management, movement, control, display, switching, interchange, transmission, or reception of data or information -

(i) By a Federal agency, or

(ii) Under a contract with a federal agency which

(A) Requires the use of such equipment, or

(B) Requires the performance of a service or the furnishing of a product which is performed or produced making significant use of such equipment.

(2) The term automatic data processing equipment includes -

(i) Computers;

(ii) Ancillary equipment;

(iii) Software, firmware, and similar procedures;

(iv) Services, including support services; and

(v) Related resources as defined by regulations issued by the Administrator of General Services.

### B. What Are ADPE/FIP Resource Contracts Under the Brooks Act?

1. FIRMR Bulletin A-1. The Administrator of GSA has published guidance to assist in distinguishing between covered and noncovered contracts. FIRMR Bulletin A-1, Jan. 31, 1991, provides a decision diagram (*see* page 252) which sets forth a methodology for analyzing whether the Brooks Act and the FIRMR applies to a particular acquisition. The GSBCA and U.S. Court of Appeals for the Federal Circuit recognize FIRMR Bulletin A-1 as the definitive statement on covered acquisitions. *Best Power Technology Sales Corp. v. Austin*, 984 F.2d 1172 (Fed. Cir. 1993); *Pindar Donnelly Partnership v. Dep't of Commerce*, GSBCA No. 12667-P, 94-2 BCA ¶ 26,673; *Liebert Corp.*, GSBCA No. 11300-P, 91-3 BCA ¶ 24,330 (citing with approval FIRMR Bulletin A-1).

2. Does the solicitation require the delivery of ADPE or FIP resources?

a. Look to the solicitation requirements, not the proposals received. *Best Power Technology Sales Corp. v. Austin, supra; Citicorp v. Gen. Servs. Admin.*, GSBCA No. 12631-P, 94-1 BCA ¶ 26,492.

b. Look to the primary deliverables, not all deliverables. *CSC Credit Servs., Inc. v. Dep't of Veterans Affairs*, GSBCA No. 11414-P, 92-2 BCA ¶ 24,778 (the GSBCA examined the "primary deliverable" under the contract and concluded the solicitation did not seek ADPE). Must the contractor deliver hardware or software? Must the contractor's employees have strong computer skills to perform the services? *See Michigan Data Storage*, GSBCA No. 10954-P, 91-1 BCA ¶ 23,471 (warehousing of computer tapes); *Merrimac Mgmt. Inst., Inc.*, GSBCA No. 11139-P, 91-2 BCA ¶ 23,962 (training managers in use of reports generated by shipyard management information system); *Mandex, Inc.*, GSBCA No. 9786-P, 89-3 BCA ¶ 21,914 (TEMPEST testing of ADPE); *Sector Technology*, GSBCA No. 10566-P, 90-2 BCA ¶ 22,908 (security guard services which required operation of a computer system).

c. FIP resources include:
(1) Computer hardware.
(2) Telecommunications equipment. *See The Elec. Genie, Inc.*, GSBCA No. 10571-P, 90-3 BCA ¶ 23,045 (ordinary telephones).
(3) Telecommunications services. *See EDS Fed. Corp.*, GSBCA 8416-P, 86-2 BCA ¶ 18,898 (data communications).
(4) Ancillary equipment. *Best Power Sales Corp. v. Austin*, *supra* (uninterruptable power supplies not ancillary equipment); *S&W Assoc. Int'l Inc. v. Dep't of the Navy*, GSBCA No. 12118-P, 1992 GSBCA LEXIS 601 (Dec. 18, 1992) (a cesium clock was ancillary equipment, not a mere clock with an embedded microprocessor).
(5) Software and firmware.
(6) Support services, including maintaining and operating computer systems.
(7) Systems.
d. Embedded FIP resources are excluded. FIRMR 201-1.002-2(e) and FIRMR 201-39.101-3(b)(5) exclude ADPE which is embedded in a product whose principal function is other than automatic acquisition, storage, manipulation, management, movement, control, display, switching, interchange, transmission, or reception of data or information, and which:
(1) cannot be used for other purposes without substantial modification; *OR*
(2) costs less than the lesser of $500K or 20% of the product's value. In *Liebert Corp.*, GSBCA No. 11300-P, 91-3 BCA ¶ 24,330, the board held an uninterruptable power supply was not ADPE because the protester had not shown that the embedded microprocessor exceeded the above thresholds.
e. Recent FIRMR amendments exclude the following FIP resource contracts:
(1) contracts for FIP resources to replace or upgrade "embedded FIP resources." FIRMR 201-1.002-2(g).
(2) contracts

(a) where the value of the FIP resources is $500,000 or less and the FIP resources are a minimal part of the contract, or
(b) are of little consequence to the major purpose of the contract. FIRMR 201-1.002(d).
3. Incidental and insignificant use of ADPE/FIP resources.
a. Where the solicitation does not specify the delivery of FIP resources, you must still examine whether the contract makes a significant use of FIP resources.
b. If the solicitation explicitly requires the contractor to use FIP resources, then the use is not incidental or insignificant. *See National Biosystems, Inc.*, GSBCA No. 10332-P, 90-1 BCA ¶ 22,459 (statement of work required creation of database); *Corporate Jets, Inc.*, GSBCA No. 11049-P, 91-2 BCA ¶ 23,765 (statement of work required the contractor to maintain computer database).
c. If the contractor can reasonably perform the contract without using FIP resources then any use is incidental.
d. If the use of FIP resources is reasonably necessary, though not specifically required, and the expected value of the FIP resources expended is less than:
(1) $500,000, or
(2) 20% of the contract cost, then the use is insignificant. FIRMR § 201-1.002-1(b)(3) and FIRMR § 201-39.101-3(a)(2)(iii). *See also National Loan Servicenter v. Dep't of Housing & Urban Dev.*, GSBCA No. 12193-P, 93-2 BCA ¶ 25,853.
4. The contracting officer should consider including FIRMR 201.39.5202-1, FIRMR Applicability (OCT 90 FIRMR), in the solicitation when a contract makes a non-significant use of ADPE. FIRMR 201-39.101-3(c).
5. Agencies should consider severing the ADPE effort in a contract from the non-ADPE effort where feasible. FIRMR 201-20.305(b)(3).

## C. Covered Agencies.

Federal agencies are defined as any executive agency or any establishment in the legislative or judicial branch of government (except the Senate, the House of Representatives, and the Architect of the Capitol). 40 U.S.C. § 472(b).

1. Nonappropriated Funds. The Brooks Act does not apply to DOD nonappropriated fund instrumentalities (NAFIs). *Consulting Assocs. Inc. v. Dep't of the Air Force*, GSBCA No. 13194-P, 95-1 BCA ¶ 27,602. It may apply to civilian agency NAFIs. *See Rocky Mt. Trading Co.*, GSBCA No. 8958-P, 87-2 BCA ¶ 19,840 (Office of the Comptroller of the Currency covered, even though not funded with appropriated funds).

2. Private Corporations. It does not apply to private corporations. *U.S. Sprint Communications Co., Ltd. Partnership*, GSBCA No. 11490-P, 92-1 BCA ¶ 24,622, (no jurisdiction over acquisitions by individual federal reserve banks; they are not a federal agency because they are privately owned by member banks).

3. Post Office. The U.S. Postal Service is exempted by statute. *United States v. Elec. Data Sys. Fed. Corp.*, 857 F.2d 1444 (Fed. Cir. 1988).

4. Recipients of federal grants. Grantees are not subject to the Brooks Act. *Systems Eng'g & Software, Inc.*, GSBCA No. 9593-P, 88-3 BCA ¶ 21,075.

## D. Exclusions From the Definition of ADPE.

40 U.S.C. § 759(A)(3); FIRMR 201-1.002-2; FIRMR 201-39.101-3(b).

1. Actions pursuant to separate statutory authority. *See United States v. Citizens & S. Nat'l Bank*, 889 F.2d 1067 (Fed. Cir. 1989) (procurement under the National Bank Act, 12 U.S.C. § 90, is not an ADPE contract despite the requirement for extensive use of ADPE). *Electronic Data Sys. Corp.*, GSBCA No. 11593-P, 92-1 BCA ¶ 24,616 (GSBCA held it had no jurisdiction over cancellation of a procurement taken at specific congressional direction).

2. Radar, Sonar, Radio, and Television. *Wilcox Elec., Inc.*, GSBCA No. 9640-P, 89-1 BCA ¶ 21,217 (instrument landing system was a radio); *Bulloch Int'l, Inc.*, GSBCA No. 10977-P, 91-2 BCA ¶ 23,737, (T-1 satellite communications circuit not a radio).

3. Central Intelligence Agency acquisitions are exempt.

4. Warner Amendment Exclusions. 10 U.S.C. § 2315; 40 U.S.C. § 759(a)(3)(C); DFARS 239.001-70.

   a. Contracting activities must obtain approval for use of the Warner Amendment. DFARS 239.001(c). AFARS 39.001-70 sets forth Army approval procedures. Failure to obtain determination does not prevent assertion of exclusion. *Cyberchron Corp.*, 867 F.2d 1407 (Fed. Cir. 1989).

   b. Intelligence. ADPE for intelligence purposes is excluded. *Tetra Indus., Inc.*, GSBCA No. 9243-P, 88-1 BCA ¶ 20,301 (Army threat and intelligence production system); *TBC Corp.*, GSBCA No. 9471-P, 88-2 BCA ¶ 20,817 (procurement need not be classified); *Data Gen. Serv., Inc.*, GSBCA No. 9727-P, 89-1 BCA ¶ 20,817 (Defense Mapping Agency); *Cryptek, Inc.*, GSBCA No. 10680-P, 90-3 BCA ¶ 23,277 (fax machines for the war on drugs were held to involve intelligence activities); *Wiltel, Inc. v. Defense Info. Sys. Agency*, GSBCA No. 12310-P, 93-3 BCA ¶ 25,982 (incidental use of phone circuits primarily used for intelligence purposes for non-classified purposes does not destroy exemption). Mere occasional use of a phone system for intelligence purposes, however, does not exclude the entire system. *Contel Fed. Sys., Inc.*, GSBCA No. 11060-P, 91-2 BCA ¶ 23,764 (Fort Belvoir telecommunications upgrade was not Warner Amendment exempt because it did not *primarily* involve intelligence, citing DOD guidance).

   c. Cryptologic. ADPE for encryption efforts is excluded. *Wiltel, Inc. v. Defense Info. Sys. Agency*, *supra*; *Cyberchron Corp.*, GSBCA No. 9445-P, 88-2 BCA ¶ 20,783, *aff'd*, 867 F.2d 1407 (Fed. Cir. 1989) (ruggedized disk drives for a combat cryptologic support console).

d. Command and control of military forces. ADPE for fighting generals is excluded. *Automated Data Mgmt., Inc.*, GSBCA No. 9486-P, 88-3 BCA ¶ 20,848 (Theater Automated Command and Control System-Korea); *Contel Fed. Sys., Inc.*, GSBCA No. 11060-P, 91-2 BCA ¶ 23,764 (ordinary phone system did not involve command and control any more than any other DOD phone system); *Lockheed/MDB v. Dep't of the Navy*, GSBCA No. 12097-P, 93-2 BCA ¶ 25,589 (commercial disk drives for an antisubmarine operations center involved command and control).

e. Integral part of a weapon or weapons system. The microchips for "smart weapons" are excluded. This exception normally applies to "embedded" ADPE and software. *Julie Research Lab., Inc.*, GSBCA No. 8070-P, 85-3 BCA ¶ 18,295. Flight training systems are not embedded ADPE. *Communications Technology Applications*, GSBCA No. 9978-P, 89-3 BCA ¶ 21,941.

f. Critical to the direct fulfillment of a military mission.

(1) Administrative, financial, and logistics systems are not within this exception. *Systems Mgmt. Am. Corp.*, GSBCA No. 9773-P, 89-1 BCA ¶ 21,357 (shipboard ADP system to support maintenance, supply, financial accounting, administration, pay and personnel).

(2) Test is whether the agency can demonstrate a real and convincing nexus between the contract and the fulfillment of a military mission. *Electronic Sys. Assoc., Inc.*, GSBCA No. 9966-P, 89-2 BCA ¶ 21,759 (microprocessor R&D for "Star Wars"); *Pacificorp Capitol, Inc. v. United States*, 852 F.2d 549 (Fed. Cir. 1988) (ADPE for software maintenance on embedded weapons systems software).

(3) In *Information Sys. & Networks Corp.*, GSBCA No. 10775-P, 91-1 BCA ¶ 23,354, *aff'd* 946 F.2d 876 (Fed. Cir. 1991), the GSBCA found that an intrusion detection system was critical to the direct fulfillment of a military mission. The mission was safeguarding lives and property. The fact that the alarm systems were congressionally mandated, for use on bases overseas, and responded to specific terrorist threats, appeared to influence heavily the board's decision.

## V. AUTHORITY TO ACQUIRE ADPE.

FIRMR 201-20.305.

### A. The Administrator of GSA Has Sole Authority to Acquire ADPE.

40 U.S.C. § 759(b)(1). GSA may, and usually does, delegate its authority to other agencies. 40 U.S.C. § 759(b)(2). If an agency enters into a contract for ADPE without a proper delegation of procurement authority (DPA) from GSA, the contract is void. *CACI, Inc. v. Stone*, 990 F.2d 1233 (Fed. Cir. 1993).

### B. Blanket Delegations.

FIRMR 201-20.305-1 (effective Oct. 24, 1994).

1. The FIRMR delegates certain ADPE authority to all agencies. GSA need not give additional approval when agencies act within this blanket delegation.

2. The FIRMR places federal agencies into three categories for delegation purposes based on the size of their information technology budgets. These categories are:

a. Large—DOD (including all military departments and defense agencies); Energy; Health and Human Services; Transportation; Treasury; and NASA.

b. Medium—Agriculture; Commerce; EPA; GSA; Justice; Interior; State; and Veterans Affairs.

c. Small—All other federal agencies.

3. Based on their category, agencies may competitively acquire Federal Information Pro-

cessing (FIP) equipment, software, services, and support services where the dollar value of the FIP resources acquired under the contract does not exceed the following levels:

a. Large agencies—$20 million.

b. Medium agencies—$10 million.

c. Small agencies—$5 million.

4. Agencies may acquire Federal Information Processing equipment, software, services, and support services, from a sole source or use a specific make and model specification, where the dollar value of the FIP resources acquired under the contract does not exceed:

a. Large agencies—$2 million.

b. Medium agencies—$1 million

c. Small agencies—$500,000.

5. Agencies may acquire related supplies regardless of amount.

6. PROBLEM: A large agency wishes to competitively acquire $15 million in IBM compatible computers, $3 million in MS-DOS 6.22 operating systems, and five option years of maintenance at $600,000 per year.

7. Agencies may not fragment requirements to avoid the ceilings. FIRMR 201-20.305(b)(2); *Digital Serv. Group, Inc.*, GSBCA No. 8735-P, 87-1 BCA ¶ 19,555.

8. Modified Blanket DPAs. FIRMR 201-20.305-2. Some agencies have higher blanket DPAs. *See* Acquisition Letter 94-11, dated Dec. 19, 1994 (Army delegation now $30 million for competitive procurements). Some have lower blanket DPAs. *See Data Switch Corp.*, GSBCA No. 10034-P-R, 89-3 BCA ¶ 22,137, *stayed* 89-3 BCA ¶ 22,138 (GSBCA suspended the Blanket DPA for a Navy contracting office as an enforcement mechanism); *ISYX*, GSBCA No. 9407-P-R, 88-2 BCA ¶ 20,781, *recon. denied*, 88-2 BCA ¶ 20,815 (revocation of blanket DPA for abuse of GSA schedule contracts).

### C. Obtaining Specific DPA's.

FIRMR Bulletin C-5; AFARS 39.002; AFR 700-3, AFR 700-4; SECNAVINST 5231.1.

1. If any part of the acquisition exceeds a blanket delegation or a previous specific delega-

tion, a new or revised specific DPA is required for the whole acquisition. FIRMR 201-20.305-3.

2. The vehicle for requesting authority is an Agency Procurement Request. *See* FIRMR Bulletin C-5; AFARS 39.002.

3. GSA will accept APRs only from designated points of contact. For DOD, these are:

a. Army - Information Systems Selection and Acquisition Agency, Alexandria, VA.

b. Air Force - USAF/SCM, Washington, D.C.

c. Navy - Information Technology Acquisition Center, Washington, D.C.

4. Specific delegations are granted by a letter from GSA.

5. The agency conducts the acquisition after the DPA is received.

6. If the acquisition "materially" deviates from the terms and conditions of the DPA, the agency must obtain an amendment. Material deviations include:

a. Exceeding dollar threshold on the DPA. *Integral Biomedical Eng'g, Inc.*, IBCA No. 2069, 88-2 BCA ¶ 20,570.

b. Slip of award date. *Computer Sys. & Resources, Inc.*, GSBCA No. 9176-P, 88-1 BCA ¶ 20,331.

c. Early receipt of proposals. *U.S. West Info. Sys., Inc.*, GSBCA No. 9103-P, 1987 GSBCA LEXIS 584, (Sept. 25, 1987), as amended (Feb. 8, 1988).

d. Violation of internal agency policies is a material deviation from the DPA. *C3, Inc.*, GSBCA No. 10063-P, 89-3 BCA ¶ 22,053.

## VI. CONTRACT FORMATION ISSUES.

### A. Funding Acquisition of ADPE.

*See* page 250.

1. Purchase and capital leases.[1]

a. Over $50,000 - Procurement.

b. Under $50,000 - Operations and Maintenance.

2. Operating leases - Operations and Maintenance.

3. Training - Operations and Maintenance.

4. Software.

a. Off the shelf with a single payment - add to hardware costs.

b. Software development - Operations and Maintenance or Research, Development, Testing, and Evaluation (RDTE) funds.

c. Commercial software with initial fee plus annual fee - annual fee is Operations and Maintenance, while initial fee is funded as Procurement, if over $50,000.

## B. Acquisition Alternatives to New Contracts.

1. Reuse of existing equipment. FIRMR 201-20.203-1(a)(4); FIRMR 201-24.202. Allows for reuse of excess equipment with an original acquisition cost of over $1 million.

2. Sharing resources. FIRMR 201-20.203-1(a)(5).

3. GSA Multiple Award Schedule Contracts. FIRMR 201-39.501-3; FIRMR 201-39.803.

   a. GSA schedules normally have a Maximum Order Limitation (MOL) of $500,000.

   b. Most favored customer clause - normally can be beaten in a competition.

   c. The agency must have Justification and Approval for sole source acquisitions from a schedule. *Telos Field Eng'g*, GSBCA No. 9802-P, 89-1 BCA ¶ 21,533.

   d. The agency may not materially deviate from schedule contract terms. *American Mgmt. Software Sys., Inc.*, B-216998, July 1, 1985, 85-2 CPD ¶ 3.

4. DOD requirements contracts.

   a. An example of a DOD requirements contract was the Desktop IV microcomputer contract administered by the Air Force.

   b. Mandatory for some agencies and equipment.

   c. Low prices through competitive large purchases.

   d. Fiscal conveniences. Delivery orders may cite appropriate funds.

## C. Defining ADPE Requirements.
FIRMR 201-20.1.

1. FIRMR 201-20.1 requires agencies to analyze ADPE requirements and a range of alternatives prior to acquiring ADPE.

2. The GSA may not substitute its judgment for that of the agency regarding its ADPE requirements. 40 U.S.C. § 759(e).

   a. This limitation extends to the GSBCA. *Data Gen. Prod. Corp. v. United States*, 915 F.2d 1544 (Fed. Cir. 1990).

   b. The GSBCA, however, has not followed *Data General*. In *RMTC Sys., Inc. v. Nuclear Regulatory Comm'n*, GSBCA No. 11734-P, 92-3 BCA ¶ 25,113, the board distinguished *Data General* as a post award protest, not a challenge to unduly restrictive specifications. In *Amdahl v. Dep't of Health and Human Servs.*, GSBCA No. 11998-P, 93-2 BCA ¶ 26,612, the GSBCA distinguished nonreviewable "agency needs" from unduly restrictive specifications.

3. Specific make or model specifications. Must be justified as other than full and open competition despite multiple sources. 40 U.S.C. § 759(i); FIRMR 201-39.601. Restriction to a specific make and model software is permissible where well substantiated. *North Am. Automated Sys. Co.*, GSBCA No. 8638-P, 87-1 BCA ¶ 19,402.

4. Restrictive ADPE specifications.

   a. "There are limitations on competition inherent in all procurements. A decision to purchase an electronic calculator excludes . . . the abacus. There is only one issue: are the agency's needs such that it acted properly - reasonably, legitimately, permissibly - in narrowing competition. . . ." *Memorex Corp.*, GSBCA No. 7929-P, 85-3 BCA ¶ 18,289.

   b. Compatibility limited requirements. Agencies must justify use of compatibility-limited requirements, e.g., plug compatible. FIRMR 201-20.103-4; *Federal Sys. Group, Inc.*, GSBCA No. 10551-P, 90-3 BCA ¶ 22,960 (government not required to formally justify compatibility-limited requirement and perform software conversion study where requirements analysis justified limitation); *Digital Equip. Corp.*,

GSBCA No. 9131-P, 88-1 BCA ¶ 20,254 (use of a privately developed standard upheld where FIPS had not yet been issued).

c.  All or none requirements.

(1) Bundling different types of equipment. In *PacifiCorp Capital, Inc.*, GSBCA No. 9733-P, 89-1 BCA ¶ 21,378, the GSBCA rejected a Navy requirement that offerors propose on all line items in a hardware acquisition, which was to be a ten-year requirements contract. The requirement was unduly restrictive of competition because it limited competition for some items on which several vendors could have competed if the procurement had not been an "all or none" competition.

(2) Bundling maintenance of different items. Requiring a single vendor for hardware, software, and maintenance of a specific make and model improperly restricts competition. *Telos Field Eng'g*, GSBCA No. 9802-P, 89-1 BCA ¶ 21,533; *DSI, Inc.*, GSBCA No. 8568-P, 87-1 BCA ¶ 19,407.

(3) The GAO gives much more deference to agencies' needs determinations. *Institutional Communications Co.*, B-233058.5, Mar. 18, 1991, 91-1 CPD ¶ 292 (decision to acquire Pentagon's phone system as total package rather than in bits and pieces was reasonable even though it limited competition to large firms).

d.  Used equipment. The used equipment vendors have aggressively challenged solicitation requirements which exclude used equipment. In *InSyst Corp.*, GSBCA No. 9946-P, 89-3 BCA ¶ 21,911, the GSBCA ordered the General Services Administration to consider offers of used equipment for their multiple award schedule program. Other vendors have successfully settled protests against the inclusion of "new only" requirements. *See Federal Sys. Group, Inc.*, GSBCA No. 10114-P, 1989 BPD ¶ 178 (Order of Dismissal, June 22, 1989); *Integrated Sys. Group, Inc.*, GSBCA No. 12127-P, 93-2 BCA ¶ 25,726 (new only restriction is unduly restrictive; record bare of any evidence that used equipment not as good as new equipment).

5.  Commercial product requirements/waivers.

a.  Agencies frequently require some degree of commercial availability to minimize the risk of immature technology. Extra care should be taken in drafting such requirements and waiver provisions to afford maximum flexibility and minimum protest exposure. In *C & P Tel. Co.*, GSBCA No. 10331-P, 90-2 BCA ¶ 22,883, the GSBCA directed termination of a contract awarded to AT&T because the offered ADPE was not commercially available as defined in the RFP. In *AT&T Paradyne Corp.*, GSBCA No. 10598-P, 90-3 BCA ¶ 23,062, the GSBCA permitted the agency to waive a commercial-off-the-shelf requirement and to award to AT&T's competitor. The difference in the two cases was that in the latter acquisition, the government reserved the right to approve noncommercial products. Any solicitation which requires commercial availability should have a similar waiver provision to avoid a similar protest.

b.  The commercial availability clause should also specify the date on which the agency will evaluate the product's commercial availability and what stage in the marketing process the product should have reached (e.g., announcement, order taking, delivery to customers, etc.). *See Syscon Corp. v. Dep't of the Army*, GSBCA No. 12803-P, 94-3 BCA ¶ 27,007 (agency provision defining "commercially available" as available at time of delivery upheld).

6.  Federal Information Processing Standards (FIPS). FIRMR 201-20.303; FIRMR 201-39.1002.

a.  All federal agencies shall use FIPS when applicable, unless waived. 40 U.S.C. § 487(b). Agency heads may waive FIPS. FIRMR § 201-20.303(d).

b. Use of FIPS eliminates many problems discussed above.

## D. Evaluation of ADPE Proposals.

1. Capability and Performance Validation. FIRMR § 201-20.304; FIRMR Bulletin C-4.

   a. FIRMR Bulletin C-4 describes several methods that agencies may use to insure that FIP resources purchased actually meet agency needs. The most common method used is commonly known as "benchmarking."

   b. Benchmarks are capability and performance validation tests. Live Test Demonstrations (LTDs) are performed on complete systems. Functional Test Demonstrations (FTDs) are performed on partial systems. Agencies may perform benchmarks before or after award of the contract. Agencies may make benchmarks either pass/fail or use test data in the technical evaluation.

   c. Benchmark problems.

      (1) The GAO disfavors pass/fail evaluation criteria in negotiated procurements. *CompuChem Lab., Inc.*, B-242889, June 17, 1991, 91-1 CPD ¶ 572.

      (2) Tightly control benchmarks so all offerors are fairly treated and test results provide valid comparisons.

         (a) Personnel conducting preaward benchmarks must have knowledge of solicitation provisions and waiver criteria. *Computer Sys. & Resources, Inc.*, GSBCA No. 9176-P, 88-1 BCA ¶ 20,331.

         (b) Waivers of benchmarks are acceptable if other offerors are not prejudiced. *Computer Sciences Corp.*, GSBCA No. 9127-P, 88-1 BCA ¶ 20,338.

         (c) Offerors may not substitute equipment during benchmarks unless solicitation permits. *Morton Mgmt., Inc.*, GSBCA No. 8419-P, 86-3 BCA ¶ 19,019.

      (3) Scope of benchmark testing. *Denro, Inc. v. Dep't of Trans.*, GSBCA No.

11736-P, 93-1 BCA ¶ 25,315 (protesters thought benchmark tests would be simple demonstrations; instead, government thoroughly tested features and stressed the proposed systems to failure point).

      (4) Benchmark testing after Best and Final Offers is generally limited to validation of the acceptability of systems. *Data Sys. Mktg. Corp.*, B-228888, Dec. 18, 1987, 87-2 CPD ¶ 609.

2. Evaluation of cost and price.

   a. ADPE acquisitions are generally evaluated based upon the total life-cycle cost of the acquisition. FIRMR § 201-39.1501-1 lists specific cost evaluation factors agencies must include in their RFPs. These factors include:

      (1) all basic and option prices.

      (2) in-house costs of installing, operating, and disposing of the ADPE, if quantifiable and different based on different offers.

      (3) conversion costs.

      (4) present value analysis using OMB Cir. A-94, if the timing of payments is expected to differ. (The contracting officer must disclose the methodology and rates in the solicitation). FIRMR 201-39.1502.

   b. Agencies no longer must solicit for acquisition methods (purchase, lease, lease with option to purchase, and lease to ownership plan).

   c. Take extra care in disclosing the cost evaluation criteria. *Systemhouse Fed. Sys., Inc.*, GSBCA No. 9313-P, 88-2 BCA ¶ 20,603.

3. The solicitation should identify all evaluation criteria. 10 U.S.C. § 2305(b)(2)(A)(i); *Richard S. Carson & Assoc., Inc.*, GSBCA No. 9313-P, 88-2 BCA ¶ 20,778; *Honeywell Fed. Sys., Inc.*, GSBCA No. 9807-P, 89-1 BCA ¶ 21,444.

4. Evaluation criteria must address all elements of the acquisition. *Julie Research Lab., Inc.*, GSBCA No. 8919-P, 87-2 BCA ¶ 19,919.

## VII. CONTRACT PERFORMANCE PROBLEMS.

### A. General.

The problems which arise in the administration and performance of ADPE contracts are, as a general matter, no different than those in non-ADPE contracts. ADPE contracts include the same remedy granting clauses as other contracts. Nevertheless, certain problems occur more often then others.

### B. Validating System Performance.

ADPE specifications often identify performance thresholds which the equipment and software must meet. Normally, these performance thresholds are expressed in terms of work performed per unit of time. Benchmarking is an attempt to identify nonconforming systems prior to award. After award, testing to determine compliance with performance specifications creates many problems. For example, testing may include government-furnished equipment, software, or data creating questions regarding the cause of test failures. Tests may not specify the beginning and end of measurable time periods. Performance thresholds such as "user friendly" are difficult to measure for compliance. Lastly, test personnel may be unfamiliar with the performance standards specified.

### C. System Reliability.

One system performance parameter which is difficult to test at the time of hardware acceptance is system reliability. System reliability is a function of equipment design, hardware and software conflicts, preventive maintenance, and on-call remedial maintenance. The government frequently specifies that the ADPE system must operate a specified percentage of the time, e.g., 95%. When the system fails to do so, the government may have rights surviving acceptance ranging from damages and maintenance credits to revocation of acceptance and default termination. Three problems arise from reliability specifications: how to count the nonoperational time, what caused the problem, and keeping adequate records. The first is a terminology problem; what is up time, what is down time, and when does each start and stop. The causation problem is especially difficult when the system is operated by government personnel, uses government furnished software and hardware, and interacts with other vendor's equipment. It is not unusual to find that separate vendors are quick to blame someone else. The record keeping problem is difficult to enforce on government personnel, especially when service calls start the period of chargeable down time.

### D. Future Requirements Clauses.

The information resources industry has been marked by rapid technological change and improvements. Equally unique is the inability of government to measure its needs accurately when automating a previous manual system; first no one wants to change, then everyone wants their own computer yesterday. Government agencies acknowledge these trends by including future requirements clauses in their contracts. The purpose of such clauses is to define the general scope of the contract broadly so future modifications adding effort need not be competed. *See AT&T Communications, Inc. v. Wiltel, Inc.*, 1 F.3d 1201 (Fed. Cir. 1993).

### E. Rights in Computer Software.

1. The intellectual property rights in computer software are defined by DFARS 252.227-7013, Rights in Technical Data and Computer Software. However, standard commercial license agreements usually conflict with this provision, as well as other standard clauses. For this reason, and because there is a widespread ignorance of intellectual property law in both industry and government, intellectual property issues are a recurring problem. *See also* AFARS 27.7009-2; AFARS 52.227-9003.

2. Time bombs. One technique used by software vendors to ensure continued license payments is to write software which will automatically self destruct and, occasionally destroy data, when routine "maintenance" is

not performed. Thus, when a dispute arises over payment, the vendor simply allows the time bomb to go off.

3. Bugs, upgrades, etc. A recurring problem with software is what rights the buyer has to future upgrades and/or defect corrections, and at what cost. No computer program of any size is perfect. As problems are identified, they are corrected. Some vendors deliver the corrections for free, and some vendors charge for correcting defective software. Corrections may be combined with other changes providing added capability and delivered at an increased price.

### Endnote

1. The FY 1995 DOD Appropriations Act authorized DOD to increase the threshold for purchasing investment items with O&M funds to $50,000 from $25,000. Department of Defense Apppropriations Act, 1995, Pub. L. 103-335, § 8076, 108 Stat. 2599, 2635 (1994). DOD has exercised this new authority. *See* Message, DFAS-IN-AP, subject: Change (03) to DA Pamphlet 37-100-95 (Oct. 26, 1994).

# FIRMR APPLICABILITY
## Determining FIRMR Applicability to a Contract Action

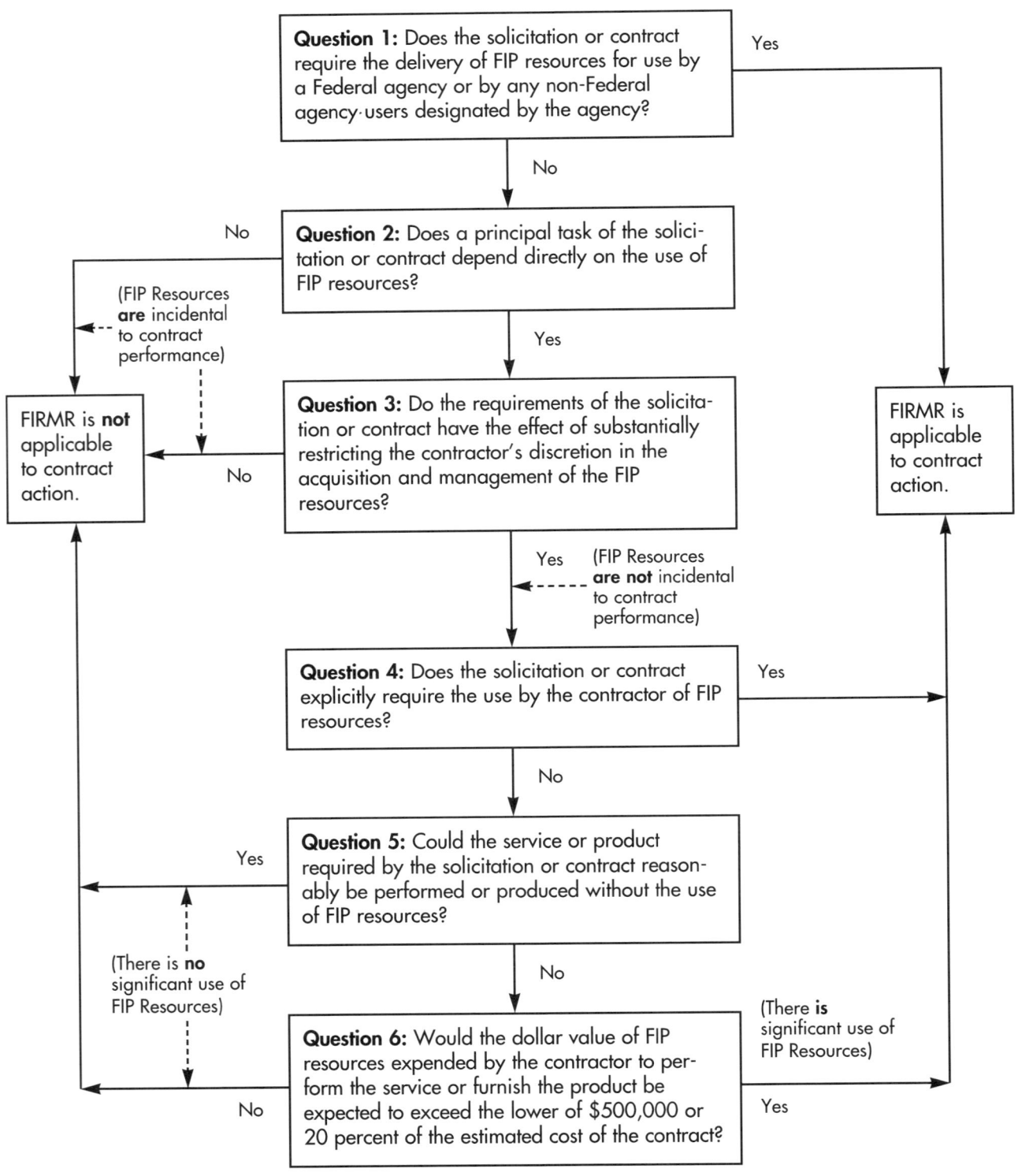

**Question 1:** Does the solicitation or contract require the delivery of FIP resources for use by a Federal agency or by any non-Federal agency·users designated by the agency?

Yes

No

**Question 2:** Does a principal task of the solicitation or contract depend directly on the use of FIP resources?

No

(FIP Resources **are** incidental to contract performance)

Yes

**Question 3:** Do the requirements of the solicitation or contract have the effect of substantially restricting the contractor's discretion in the acquisition and management of the FIP resources?

No

FIRMR is **not** applicable to contract action.

FIRMR is applicable to contract action.

Yes (FIP Resources **are not** incidental to contract performance)

**Question 4:** Does the solicitation or contract explicitly require the use by the contractor of FIP resources?

Yes

No

**Question 5:** Could the service or product required by the solicitation or contract reasonably be performed or produced without the use of FIP resources?

Yes

No

(There is **no** significant use of FIP Resources)

(There **is** significant use of FIP Resources)

**Question 6:** Would the dollar value of FIP resources expended by the contractor to perform the service or furnish the product be expected to exceed the lower of $500,000 or 20 percent of the estimated cost of the contract?

No

Yes

Note: Exceptions for intelligence and related activities and radar, sonar, radio, television and embedded equipment do not appear on this chart.

# ARMY ADPE FUNDING GUIDANCE

9. Automatic Data Processing Costs
   a. For all Army facilities/activities, the following rules apply:
      (1) Development and acquisition of ADP hardware/software (see Appendix A for expense/investment criteria).
         (a) General Purpose (see Appendix A).
         (b) Special purpose (see AR 70-15, Chapter 4).
      (2) Acquisition of Software (see Appendix A).

## D. Special Guidance Concerning Information Mission Area (IMA) Software and Hardware

1. General
   a. Congressional direction and DoD and Army guidance state that the acquisition, modification, and support costs for purchase of IMA software and hardware must be funded with Operation and Maintenance, Army (OMA) funds if the cost is less than the expense/investment threshold (currently $50,000) and with Other Procurement, Army (OPA) funds if the cost is equal to or greater than the threshold. The only exception to this rule is that the acquisition of all ADPE at Research, Development, Test and Evaluation (RDTE)-funded facilities may be financed with RDTE funds, regardless of cost.
   b. The "system" concept must be considered in evaluating the procurement of IMA end items. A system exists if a number of components are designed primarily to function within the context of a whole and will be interconnected to satisfy an approved Army requirement. Fragmented or piecemeal acquisition of the documented requirement will not be used as a basis to circumvent the "system" concept. A matrix showing the criteria for determining IMA expense and investment costs is shown at Figure 2.
   c. Installation—Normal installation costs will be included as part of the total IMA system cost.
   d. Training—IMA training will normally be funded separately with Operation and Maintenance funds (e.g., Operation and Maintenance, Army, Operation and Maintenance, Army National Guard and Operation and Maintenance, Army Reserve) or Research Development test and Evaluation Army funds (if a RDTE funded installation) and not included within the cost of the total system. However, when the cost of training is included as part of the original contract and is inseparable (not separately priced) it then becomes part of the total system cost and is funded with the same color of money as the system.
   e. Maintenance—Annual fees for maintenance will normally be funded separately with Operation and Maintenance or Research Development, Test and Evaluation, Army funds (if a RDTE funded installation) and not included within the cost of the total system. However, when the cost of maintenance/warranty service is inseparable (not separately priced) it then becomes part of the total IMA system cost and is funded with the same color of money as the IMA system.

2. Communications/ADPE Procurement
   a. New Equipment/System Procurement—The aggregate cost of an end item/system procured to address a valid requirement (including peripherals, installation and system unique software) will be used to determine whether it should be treated as an expense or investment cost. Determination of what comprises an end item/system will be based on the primary function of the hardware and software to be acquired as stated in the approved requirements document.

      For example, the appropriate color of money for the purchase of 5 stand-alone computers is determined by deciding whether the primary function of the computers is to operate as independent workstations (i.e., five systems) or as a part of a larger system. If the computers are designed to primarily operate independently, they should be considered as separate end items and applied against the expense/investment criteria individually. If they function as a component of a larger system (i.e., interconnected and primarily designed to operate as one), then they should be considered a system and the total cost applied against the expense/investment criteria.

b. Additional or Replacement Equipment/System Procurement—When requirements necessitate adding/replacing or modifying equipment/software which is a component of, or supports the functioning of an existing system, only the additional equipment/software procurement costs (including installation) will be used to determine whether the purchase is an expense or an investment.

3. Communications/ADP Software Acquisition

a. Off-the-Shelf Software

(1) Acquisition of a standard off-the-shelf software where no modification is required will be subject to the expense/investment criteria as follows:

(a) When the purchase is part of an initial hardware/software acquisition. The cost of the off-the-shelf software will be included as part of the total system cost and determination of the appropriate color of money will be based on application of the total system cost against the dollar threshold.

(b) When the purchase is adding to or upgrading an existing system. The total cost of the add-on/upgrade will be applied against the dollar threshold.

(2) Acquisition of off-the-shelf software where modification is required will be funded as follows:

(a) Acquisition of the off-the-shelf software will be funded as in paragraph (1) above.

(b) Modification of the off-the-shelf software is not considered to be a part of the total system cost, is not subject to the dollar threshold and will be financed with Operation and Maintenance or Research, Development, Test and Evaluation, Army funds (if a RDTE funded installation).

(3) Development of application software is not considered to be a part of the total system cost, is not subject to the dollar threshold and will be financed with Operation and Maintenance or Research, Development, Test and Evaluation, Army funds (if a RDTE funded installation).

b. Modification of existing software—The modification (e.g., enhancement, conversion, etc.) of an existing software end item is not considered to be a part of the total system costs, is not subject to the dollar thresholds and will be financed with Operation and Maintenance or Research, Development, Test and Evaluation, Army funds (if a RDTE funded installation).

*Example 1.* The Army enters into a contractual arrangement to purchase 5 off-the-shelf software packages to upgrade an existing system at a cost of $20,000 each. The software packages will require modification at a total cost of $30,000. The total cost of the 5 software packages ($100,000) would be applied against the dollar threshold and finance with procurement funds. The modification effort ($30,000) would be financed with Operation and Maintenance or Research, Development, Test and Evaluation, Army funds (if a RDTE funded installation).

*Rationale.* The 5 off-the-shelf software packages constitute an upgrade to an existing system. The rule (paragraph 3a(1)(b)) provides, "When the purchase is adding to or upgrading an existing system. The total cost of the add-on/upgrade will be applied against the dollar threshold." The modification effort is financed in accordance with paragraph 3a(2)(b) using Operation and Maintenance or Research, Development, Test and Evaluation, Army funds (if a RDTE funded installation).

*Example 2.* The Army enters into a contractual arrangement to purchase 5 off-the-shelf application software packages to upgrade 5 stand-alone PCs at a cost of $20,000 each. The software packages will require modification at a total cost of $30,000. The 5 software packages would be applied individually against the dollar threshold and financed with Operation and Maintenance or Research, Development, Test and Evaluation, Army funds (if a RDTE funded installation). The modification effort ($30,000) would also be financed with Operation and Maintenance or Research, Development, Test and Evaluation, Army funds (if a RDTE funded installation).

*Rationale.* The cost of each off-the-shelf application software package ($20,000) is applied individually against the dollar threshold because they are being purchased to upgrade 5 individual systems/end items (i.e., 5 stand-alone PCs). The rule (paragraph 3a(1)(b)) which provides, "When the purchase is adding to or upgrading an existing system. The total cost of the add-on/upgrade will be applied against the dollar threshold," would be applied under this scenario against each of the 5 systems individually. Therefore, the total cost to upgrade each system is $20,000 which is below the current threshold and the use of Operation and Maintenance or Research, Development, Test and Evaluation, Army funds (if a RDTE funded installation) would be appropriate. The modification effort is financed in accordance with paragraph 3a(2)(b) with Operation and Maintenance or Research, Development, Test and Evaluation, Army funds (if a RDTE funded installation).

*Example 3.* The Army enters into a contractual arrangement with a contractor to develop an application software for $30,000. The development effort is not subject to the dollar threshold and will be financed with Operation and Maintenance or Research, Development, Test and Evaluation, Army funds (if a RDTE funded installation).

*Rationale.* In this case, the Army is contracting to develop an application software package. Determination of the appropriate color of money will be in accordance with paragraph 3a(3) which states, "Development of application software is not considered to be a part of the total system cost, is not subject to the dollar threshold and will be financed with Operation and Maintenance or Research, Development, Test and Evaluation, Army funds (if a RDTE funded installation)." Therefore, the use of Operation and Maintenance or Research, Development, Test and Evaluation, Army funds (if a RDTE funded installation) would be appropriate.

c. "Off-the-Shelf" Software Licensing
   (1) When the purchase of an "off-the-shelf" software package includes a one-time up-front payment for the use of the software over the life of the system, the color of money will be determined by applying the rules in paragraph b.1. above.
   (2) When the purchase of an "off-the-shelf" software package includes an annual licensing fee the following will apply:
      • The appropriate color of money for acquisition of the software package will be determined by applying the rules in paragraph a above.
      • The annual licensing fees are not subject to the expense/investment dollar threshold and will be financed by the Operation and Maintenance or Research, Development, Test and Evaluation, Army appropriation.
      • Annual fees. Annual for the use of the license itself with additional annual fees for maintenance or modifications provided by the vendor would be financed within the O&M or RDTE appropriations.
   (3) Local Area Network (LAN) and Wide Area Network (WAN). Local Area Networks and Wide Area Network are considered to be systems. As such, the total cost of all component parts must be applied against the dollar threshold to determine the appropriate color of money when the LAN or WAN is purchased as an add-on or upgrade to an existing system. If the WAN or LAN is part of the initial hardware/software acquisition, the cost will be included as part of the total system cost.
   (4) Centrally managed systems. Acquisitions for any system which is centrally managed is considered an investment regardless of the amount. Systems managed by an Army-Acquisition-Executive-Chartered Program Executive Officer or Program Manager are considered centrally managed systems.

(5) Turnkey Acquisition. Acquisitions wherein a single or prime contractor provides a complete system to include hardware, software, installation, etc., may be entirely financed with procurement funds. A turnkey system is typically large and at the point of contracting the appropriate color of money cannot be readily determined due to the nature of the system. Therefore, it is appropriate to budget and execute the entire acquisition within the procurement appropriations.

d. Military Interdepartmental Purchase Requests (MIPR) and Reimbursable Orders (RO). Using a MIPR or RO to acquire IMA hardware and/or software from another Army activity or Federal agency is proper and legal, provided the appropriate color of money is cited. Neither the MIPR nor the RO can be used to circumvent the expense/investment criteria or to change the color of money. It is illegal for one activity to MIPR Operation and Maintenance funds to another Federal Agency to purchase IMA equipment and software which should be financed with procurement funds.

## F. Definitions Used in Determining Expense and Investment Costs

1. Requirement. This is the basic determining factor for all expense/investment criteria decisions. A requirement consists of the set of capabilities which are necessary to perform the mission. This set of capabilities directs the decision as to what is or is not part of a system, or what is an independent upgrade. Neither the capability nor the requirement will be fragmented to circumvent application of the expense/investment criteria.

   a. System. There are two considerations for the definition of a system. The first consists of an automation capability which is centrally managed and must be considered by a Major automated Information Systems Review Committee (MAISRC). The second is generic and could be any combination of components/items which work together to perform a function or to satisfy an approved requirement as defined above.

   b. Centralized Item Management and Asset Control. The management in the central supply system or a DoD-wide/Service-wide acquisition and control system in which the manager has the authority for management and procurement of items of equipment. This includes such functions as requirements determination, distribution management, procurement direction, configuration control and disposal direction. Asset control includes the authority to monitor equipment availability and take such actions as necessary to restock to approved stockage levels.

   c. Modification. The alteration, conversion, or modernization of an end item of investment equipment which changes or improves the original purpose or operational capacity in relation to effectiveness, efficiency, reliability or safety of that item.

   d. Maintenance. The routine, recurring effort conducted to maintain an end item of investment equipment at its intended capability or designed performance level.

   e. Construction. The erection, installation, or assembly of a new facility; the addition, expansion, extension, alteration, conversion, or replacement of an existing facility; or the relocation of a facility from one installation to another.

   f. Real Property Maintenance. The various functions for the maintenance and repair of facilities and the accomplishment of minor construction financed by an operations appropriation.

   g. Facility Maintenance. The recurrent, day-to-day, periodic or scheduled work required to preserve real property in such condition that it may be used for its designated purposes.

   h. Facility Repair. The restoration of real property to such condition that it may be used for its designated purpose.

   i. System. The combination of a number of components that are functioning with the context of a whole to satisfy a documented requirement.

# EXPENSE/INVESTMENT DECISION MATRIX

## Investment Cost Decision Diagram

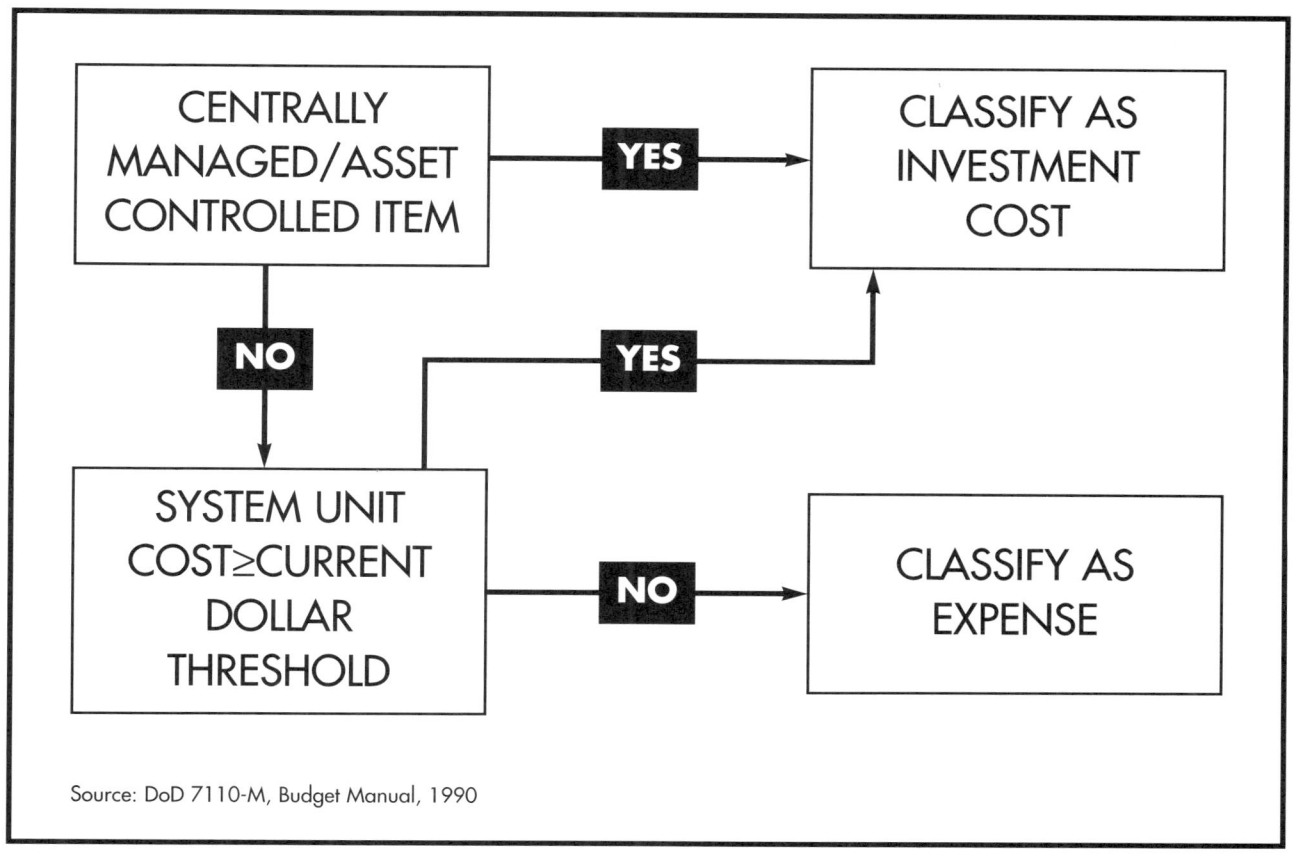

Source: DoD 7110-M, Budget Manual, 1990

# INFORMATION MISSION AREA
# EXPENSE/INVENTORY DECISION MATRIX

| | Include as Part of System? | Centrally Managed System? | Less Than Dollar Threshold? | Greater than Dollar Threshold? | Funding |
|---|---|---|---|---|---|
| **New Equipment** | | | | | |
| System Purchase | YES | YES | N/A | N/A | Procurement |
| • peripherals | YES | NO | NO | YES | Procurement |
| • software and installation | YES | NO | YES | N/A | OPM/RDTE 1* |
| **Add-on or Replacement** | | | | | |
| Equipment/System | YES | YES | N/A | N/A | Procurement |
| Total cost of | | | | | |
| • Add-on | YES | NO | NO | YES | Procurement |
| • Replacement | YES | NO | YES | N/A | O&M/RDTE 1* |
| **Related Costs:** | | | | | |
| Installation | | | | | |
| • Contracted | YES | N/A | N/A | N/A | 2* |
| • In house (Military or Civilian) | NO | N/A | N/A | N/A | N/A |
| Training | | | | | |
| • Separately priced | NO | N/A | N/A | N/A | O&M/RDTE 1* |
| • Inseparable | YES | N/A | N/A | N/A | Procurement |
| Maintenance | | | | | |
| • Separately priced | NO | N/A | N/A | N/A | O&M/RDTE 1* |
| • Inseparable | NO | N/A | N/A | N/A | Construction |
| Real Property Preparation | | | | | |
| • Non structural changes | YES | N/A | N/A | N/A | 2* |
| • Structural changes | NO | N/A | N/A | N/A | Construction |
| **Off-the-Shelf Software** | | | | | |
| Acquisition | | | | | |
| • Part of initial (new system) hardware and software acquisition | YES | N/A | N/A | N/A | 2* |
| • Add or upgrade existing system | YES | N/A | N/A | N/A | 2* |
| • Modification required to above software purchases | NO | N/A | N/A | N/A | O&M/RDTE 1* |
| Modification of Existing Off-the-Shelf Software | NO | N/A | N/A | N/A | O&M/RDTE 1* |
| Development of Application Software | NO | N/A | N/A | N/A | O&M/RDTE 1* |
| **Software Licensing Fees** | | | | | |
| • One time up-front/part of initial new system purchase | YES | N/A | N/A | N/A | 2* |
| • Add or upgrade existing system | YES | N/A | N/A | N/A | 2* |
| • Annual licensing fee | NO | N/A | N/A | N/A | O&M/RDTE 1* |
| • Annual Fees (License use and annual fees for maintenance/modification provided by the vendor) | NO | N/A | N/A | N/A | O&M/RDTE 1* |
| **Local Area Network (LAN) and Wide Area Network (WAN)** | | | | | |
| • Part of initial hardware/software acquisition | YES | N/A | N/A | N/A | 2* |
| • Add or upgrade existing system acquisition | YES | N/A | N/A | N/A | 2* |
| • Add or upgrade existing system | YES | N/A | N/A | N/A | 2* |
| **Turnkey Acquisition** | N/A | N/A | NO | YES | Procurement |

FOOTNOTES

1* RDTE funding is appropriate for RDTE funded installations regardless of cost.

2* Included as part of the total system cost. Color of money determination in accordance with rules governing New Equipment/System Purchases or Add-on or Replacement Equipment/System Purchases.

Source: ASA(FM) memoranda, May 25, 1990 and December 13, 1991

# AIR FORCE ADPE FUNDING GUIDANCE

**Figure 4.1. Exceptions to the 20-Percent Limit on Obligations in August and September.**

| Don't Apply the Limit | | |
|---|---|---|
| **A. If You're In** | **B. And the Obligation Concerns** | **C. Because** |
| Any command | programs assigned to Military Personnel Appropriations | The Deputy Asst Secretary (Budget) administers this appropriation centrally with compensating controls to stay under the limit |
| Any command | reprogrammings and supplemental budget authority approved or appropriated and received during the last 2 months of the fiscal year | Statutes don't require |
| AFRES or AETC | supporting active duty Reserve Personnel projects for training of components, summer camp training of ROTC, or active duty for training (summer field training) of participants in the Health Professions Scholarship Program | DoD Appropriations Act excludes |

## Section B—Information Processing Equipment (IPE) and Resources

**4.3. Budgeting and Funding for General Purpose IPE.** Whether you're in an Active or Reserve component, follow this section to select the correct appropriation for funding to develop, buy, lease, and maintain Information Processing (IP) Resources. Acquisition of IPE may involve procurement actions ranging from base-wide, organization, or functional community local area network (LAN) systems down to ancillary equipment (e.g., personal computers, printers, etc.) and software which operates totally independent of a LAN. When commands can't agree to funding responsibilities, refer the matter to SAF/FMBM.

4.3.1. **LAN Acquisition.** LANs consist of any equipment that is integral to the operation of a LAN system to include file servers, cable, personal computers (PCs) and other support components (e.g., line drivers, multiplexers, etc.). A LAN is further subdivided into its lowest system form: base-wide, organizational (e.g., wing, squadron, division, branch, etc.), or functional community (e.g., logistics, maintenance, civil engineering, etc.).

- Include the total cost of each independent LAN system when applying the expense and investment criteria to a procurement action. Include any additional LAN installation costs (e.g., quality assurance, system engineering. equipment installation, testing, etc.) in the aggregate cost of all equipment items being acquired to make the LAN system operate. You must apply the expense and investment threshold to the aggregate cost of the entire system.
- LAN system modifications or upgrades of equipment essential to LAN operations obligated within any 12-month period should be considered part of the same requirement and the total cost will be subject to the expense and investment criteria. Cost each upgrade or modification separately from the original purchase. The same applies to parts purchased to replace components which are functioning but "are no longer logistically supportable." Ensure that LAN system modifications or upgrades are not an attempt to fragment the requirement to circumvent the expense and investment threshold.

4.3.2. **Ancillary IPE Acquisition.** Ancillary IPE consists of personal computers (PC), printers, etc., whose primary purpose is to operate independently from the LAN, as well as repair parts, components, network spares, and PC upgrades (i.e., 286,386, etc.). In these cases apply the expense and investment threshold to each individual equipment purchased on a "cost per component" basis. Repair parts or components should be functionally equivalent to the unit being replaced and purchased to replace a failed component. Use O&M funds for these type of requirements if each component purchased is less than $25,000 (current threshold). The overriding rule is that stand-alone operational integrity of an ancillary IPE must be maintained in deciding to procure, upgrade, or modify IPE using O&M funding.

**4.3.3. PC Application Software Loaded on Network File Server.** MAJCOMs and installations must implement management controls to ensure that sufficient applications software is procured to permit implementation of stand-alone operation of each PC, should the network fail for an extended period of time. The major task is to ensure that only the authorized number of copies of application software are procured, installed and used throughout the network, whether in a networked mode (launched from the file server) or from the individual PC hard drives. Where the application software is to be loaded or stored, doesn't determine the type of expense and investment funding to be used for a PC, only whether the PC can operate independently or is integral to a LAN's system operation. Purchase sufficient application software at the same time network PCs are procured using O&M funds to ensure stand-alone PC operational integrity is maintained. *EXCEPTION:* Those requirements where the procurement of a PC is intended to upgrade older, less capable computer equipment (i.e., 286, 386, etc.) and the application software can be reused on a one-for-one basis on the upgraded PC.

**4.4. O&M Funded Facilities and Activities.** Finance the acquisition and operation of IP resources supporting O&M funded facilities and activities as follows:

**4.4.1. Leasing or Maintaining IPE.** Use O&M funds.

**4.4.2. Acquiring IPE.** Apply the $25,000 expense and investment threshold criteria to the total cost of the IPE system to determine which appropriation to use. (If the threshold is raised to an expected $50,000 level in FY 95, a message will confirm the change.) (*NOTE:* an IPE system is a group of components that are interconnected, designed mainly to operate together, and procured at the same time.)
 • Use O&M if the total system cost is under $25,000.
 • Use Other Procurement if the total system costs $25,000 or more.
 • Use Other Procurement funds for centrally managed equipment items. (The $25,000 threshold doesn't apply; see figure 4.3.)

4.4.2.1. Exclude contract costs associated with the preparation of real property (e.g., building modification, cable trenching, etc.; see figure 4.1).

4.4.2.2 Don't fragment the validated requirement XXXX or upgrade to a communications or automation processing system or acquire IP in a piecemeal XXXXX order to circumvent the expense end of investment criteria guidance.

4.4.2.3. Apply the determination of expense or investment cost on the basis of each system in the requirements document (e.g., Communications Systems Requirements Document, Base Communications-Computer Systems Comprehensive Blueprint, etc.), if the document includes more than one system. Purchasing several items at same time does not necessarily mean the items are part of one system. For example, if you are buying four small computers for administrative offices in an organization, which may be interconnected (e.g., for sending electronic mail), consider these as four separate systems *if their primary purpose is to operate independently.* Regarding LANS, a basic rule to follow is that separate requirements documents should be prepared for items integral to an independent LAN's operation and items not integral to a LAN's operation.

### 4.4.3. **Acquiring Software:**

4.4.3.1. Use O&M funds (without regard to investment threshold and without including software in the total system cost) for:
- Software obtained via a software development contract (i.e., where the acquiring activity pays a contractor for the software development services).
- Proprietary software (i.e., software obtained with limited data rights or licensed to the Air Force). (This applies to FY 1994 and prior years only. For FY 1995 and beyond, see paragraph 4.4.3.2.)
- Software maintenance and modification, and for other IP contractual services.
- Software that is not obtained from a development or services contract and for which the Air Force obtains unlimited data rights (i.e., the Air Force will actually own the software and be free to use, duplicate, distribute, and dispose of the software without restriction from its publisher or developer).

4.4.3.2. Use O&M or investment funds based on the expense/investment threshold (and include in the total system cost, if applicable) for application software with limited data rights or licensed to the Air Force (applies in FY 1995 and beyond).

4.4.3.3. Air Force organizations may accept investment funds from organizations outside of the Air Force for the purpose of buying software with limited data rights or that is licensed.

### 4.4.4. **Communications Cable Funding:**

4.4.4.1. For maintenance and repair of existing cable (e.g., metallic, fiber optic, premise wiring, etc.) regardless of whether or not the cable is located inside a building or between buildings, Commands will always use O&M funds for these requirements.

4.4.4.2. For an entire information transport system (e.g., cable plant) purchase and installation the expense and investment criteria will be applied. Other Procurement funds will be used for information transport systems (ITS) (that are $25,000 or more. O&M funds may be used if the system cost is less than $25,000.

4.4.4.3. For ITS expansion (e.g., jobs requiring new fiber optic cable to accommodate base population growth, new building construction, or a cable expansion to accommodate LAN users in other buildings (in order to provide solely E-mail or file transfer type connectivity between LANs that operate independently of each other), Commands will follow rules of minor construction projects. If the specific requirement is less than $300,000, then Commands will use O&M funds. If an expansion is above $300,000, Commands will document the requirement in the Base Communications-Computer Systems Comprehensive Blueprint (BCB) where it can be centrally funded (e.g., Air Force C4I Superhighway-2000) using Other Procurement funds. LAN expansion efforts within a particular building will continue to be governed by the LAN acquisition guidance in paragraph 4.3.1. above. In short, an independent LAN that is spread between buildings will include cable connectivity costs within the aggregate costs of the overall LAN since the cable is an integral part of the LAN system operation.

4.4.4.4. The large majority of organic engineering and installation teams cost should covered under paragraph 4.4.4.3 above. Commands are basically "contracting" with the Communications Systems Center (CSC) for these type of cable jobs and are providing a cost reimbursement for the expenses accrued by the CSC to complete the particular job. Paragraph 4.4.4.3. will also apply to commercial contractors working the same type of cable jobs.

4.4.5. **Using Productivity Programs.** If you are purchasing IPE under provisions of productivity enhancing capital investment (PECI) programs, group the IPE to comprise an integrated system (or systems) capable of amortizing all investment costs within the criteria established in AFI 38-301. Apply the expense/investment rule criteria to determine correct funding.

**4.5. RDT&E-funded Facilities and Activities.** Use RDT&E for all of the costs identified in 4.6, above, for funding by the O&M and Other Procurement appropriations.

4.5.1. **Defense Business Operations Fund (DBOF) Facilities and Activities.** Use DBOF funds to finance all costs identified in 4.6, above, for funding by the O&M and Other Procurement appropriations. DFAS-DE Regulation 170-10, Chapter 2 has special guidance for funding of management systems development costs for DBOF activities.

**4.6. Site Preparation.** Figure 4.1 contains guidance for determining the type of funds to use for IPE site preparation. Additional guidance is in paragraph 8.16.7.1.

4.6.1. Figure 4.1 covers two situations: alteration of an existing facility to accommodate new IPE or to better accommodate IPE currently housed in the facility (columns 2 and 3); and addition to an existing facility or construction of a new facility to accommodate IPE (columns 4 and 5).

4.6.2. Types of funds are denoted by **CON** for construction, **EQP** for investment equipment, and **EXP** for expense.

**4.7. Embedded Computers.** Apply the following rules to determine how to fund embedded Information Processing Equipment (IPE) and software developed or acquired under the systems management procedures (acquisition series of instructions).

4.7.1. Use RDT&E to:
- Fund all initial IPE and software development efforts up to the point where an operational configuration baseline has been tested, evaluated, and accepted or qualified.
- Finance the design, development, test and evaluation of embedded IPE and software. This includes all costs related to feasibility studies, system design, preparation, integration (including interface with other systems or subsystems), and associated documentation.
- Design and develop training devices, such as simulators, that employ new or off-the-shelf computers and system components, but have software and interface components unique to the training system. Use RDT&E for the initial system and all of its support cost through acceptance by the Air Force. Typically, these training devices have small quantity requirements and the initial system is eventually used for operational training.

4.7.2. Don't use RDT&E funds beyond the initial system unless the training organization needs more than one full system to demonstrate the training device performance before accepting it.

**Table 4.1 Funding for Information Processing Equipment (IPE) Site Preparation**

| Categories | Alteration of Existing Facility | | Addition or new construction | |
|---|---|---|---|---|
| | Materials | Installing | Materials | Installing |
| 1. Raised flooring (see chapter 8, paragraph 8.19.4 for exception). | EXP | EXP | CON | CON |
| 2. Air conditioning for: <br> a. Equipment space directly related to IPE operations and not in associated space. <br> b. Equipment space directly related to IPE operations and concurrently in associated space. | (note 2) <br><br><br> CON | EXP <br><br><br> CON | CON (note 1) <br><br><br> CON (note 1) | CON (note 1) <br><br><br> CON (note 1) |
| 3. Utility work: <br> a. Secondary utility work necessary to connect IPE to the building services. <br> b. Primary utility work and secondary utility work not described in 3a. | (note 2) <br><br> CON | EXP <br><br> CON | CON <br><br> CON | CON <br><br> CON |
| 4. Removal and installation of interior partitions, etc.: <br> a. To permit installation of IPE. <br> b. For other than the installation of IPE. | EXP <br> CON | EXP <br> CON | CON <br> CON | CON <br> CON |
| 5. Uninterrupted power supply (UPS). | EQP | EXP (note 3) | EQP | (note 3) |
| 6. Real property installed generator. | CON | CON | CON | CON |
| 7. Fire protection system: <br> a. Built into the facility such as a sprinkler system. <br> b. HALON 1301 total flooding system. | REP <br> (note 4) | REP <br> (note 4) | REP <br> CON | REP <br> CON |

NOTES:

1. You may use either Military Construction (3300) or O&M Minor Construction (3400) funds, depending on the total cost, when you procure or install air conditioning systems as RPIE in conjunction with new construction or construction of an addition to a new facility (see Section E, chapter 8).

2. Purchase individual equipment items costing $25,000 and over with investment equipment funds; all other items are expense.

3. Use investment equipment funds if you purchase the UPS on an installed basis; otherwise, installation is an expense. The associated site preparation is always construction for addition or new construction.

4. If you purchase the HALON 1301 total flooding system on an installed basis, use investment equipment funds; otherwise, purchase individual equipment items costing $25,000 and over with investment equipment funds; all other costs are expense.

4.7.3. To buy fully developed and tested IPE and software, use the same appropriation that funds the acquisition of the weapon or support system of which it is a part. Fund fully developed and tested IPE and software associated with an equipment modification with the same appropriation that funds the production mod kits (see also paragraph chapter 8, section G for guidance on modification funding).

4.7.4. Use O&.M-type funds to finance the maintenance of embedded IPE and software, except for investment items necessary for maintenance. Use procurement appropriations to finance investment items which are funded by the procurement appropriations. Paragraph 4.7. applies for embedded IPE and software used in research and development programs or owned by RDT&E funded activities.

4.7.5. Fund changes to existing operational software as follows:

4.7.5.1. Use O&M-type appropriations or funds for changes designed to correct latent errors or deficiencies in software programs that otherwise meet criteria for operational suitability and usefulness.

4.7.5.2. Use O&M-type appropriations or funds for changes designed to improve reliability, maintainability, safety, or that otherwise qualify as normal life-cycle support.

4.7.5.3. Use RDT&E funds for changes designed to increase the capability of the system to perform its mission, to add new capability, or to remove an existing capability. However, use the O&M-type appropriation that funds the maintenance for software changes (or blocks of such changes) that are relatively minor in scope and cost, and that can be accomplished during regular software maintenance.

4.7.6. See chapter 8, section G for instruction on funding software changes related to equipment modification engineering tasks. Use O&M, RDT&E or DBOF funds for other software changes associated with end item modification programs as discussed elsewhere in paragraphs 4.9 and 8.24.

**4.8. Funding Other Equipment with Computers.** This category includes equipment items such as materiel handling equipment that contain or depend upon computer devices but are not C4 systems.
- Use procurement accounts to finance the initial acquisition cost.
- Finance software changes as an expense.
- Finance such charges from the DBOF for DBOF-funded facilities and activities.

**8.16. Base Procured Equipment:**

8.16.1. Use appropriation 57*3080 (BPAC 84XXXX) to fund annual requirements for base-level procurement of authorized investment equipment items if these items cost $25,000 or more and aren't available through Air Force central procurement. (At time of printing, the expense/investment threshold was expected to be raised to $50,000 and SAF/FMB will notify the field of any new threshold amount.) Use the same appropriation for authorized related costs. If you're a host installation, include tenant requirements in your annual programs (see paragraph 7.7 for guidance and exception).

8.16.2. Although appropriation 57*3080 funds are available by law for obligation for 3 years, the Air Force finances the program requirements of the year for which the funds are appropriated. Therefore, MAJCOMs and installations must:
- Treat BPAC 84501X (base procured equipment) as an annual program.
- Fully commit this program by the end of the first fiscal year (FY).
- Obligate it no later than 3 months after the end of the first FY.
- Defer equipment requirements identified too late to be on contract within the 15 months to a later FY for funding. If you have questions, ask SAF/FMBIO or HQ USAF/LGSP.

**8.17. Finance the Following Items with 57*3080, BPAC 84XXXX Funds:** (Unless equipment is being replaced as part of an O&M-type fund repair project)(See paragraph 8.2 for changes to the 3080 BP 8400 program due to stock funding of Depot Level Reparables.)
- Investment equipment items with a source of supply from General Services Administration, Defense

Logistics Agency, other services, or local purchase (including replacement Real Property Installed Equipment (RPIE)).

- Non-stock-listed investment equipment items that are locally procured (including replacement RPIE).
- Installation costs of investment items dictated by technical considerations or warranty conditions, or if installation charges are included in the cost of equipment offered for public sale as quoted in manufacturers' or vendors' price lists. Installation includes unpacking, assembling components, placement, and connecting necessary utilities in a space previously prepared for operating the equipment.
- Relocatable buildings purchased as items of war reserve stock (see chapter 9 of this volume).
- Portable buildings if their cost is $25,000 or more. (See chapter 9 of this volume.)
- Fast pay back capital (FASCAP) investment items approved by AF/MOQ-DMR per AFI 38-301.

**8.18. Don't Finance the Following Items with 57\*3080, BPAC 84XXXX Funds:** (See paragraph 8.1.4 for changes to 3080 BP 8400 program due to stock funding of Depot Level Reparables.)

- Equipment costing less than $25,000.
- Spares, components, assemblies, repair parts, and other materiel (expense or investment) that do not qualify as end items of equipment.
- Centrally managed equipment items or substitutes for such items, such as aircraft, vehicles, etc.
- Initial or replacement RPIE to be installed as part of a construction project (either in-house or by contract), except as shown in figure 4.1.
- Replacement equipment (RPIE) as part of an O&M funded repair project.
- Initial or replacement electric power generators classified as RPIE.
- Installation, erection, local fabrication, construction, checkout or other service (done by organic work-force or contract) connected to acquiring or purchasing equipment, except as provided in paragraph 8.13.
- Preparing a site to install of leased, transferred, issued, or newly procured equipment.

8.22.4. If specifically approved by HQ USAF, AFMC or Air Force Intelligence Command (AFIC) may procure equipment financed from the 57\*3080 appropriation and required for a fixed operation on a **system** or a **packaged** basis.

- Under the **system** approach, the equipment procurement contract includes one or more pieces of equipment, components, installation material, and engineering and installation charges. Use the 57\*3080 appropriation.
- Under the **packaged** approach, use the 57\*3080 appropriation to finance the system and the necessary directly related construction under one contract (see paragraph 8.19 and 8.21).

8.22.5. Procure computer-raised flooring for new production flight simulators as part of the simulator complex using the "package procurement" approach. Include the costs to acquire and install this flooring in the procurement specification packages for all new production flight simulators using Aircraft Procurement, Air Force (57\*3010) funds. This is an exception to chapter 4 (figure 4.1.).

## CHAPTER NINETEEN

# *Ethics in Government Contracting*

## I. INTRODUCTION.

Upon completing this instruction, the student will understand:

A. The coverage of the Procurement Integrity Act.

B. The restrictions on procurement officials seeking employment upon leaving government service.

## II. THE PROCUREMENT INTEGRITY ACT.

Section 27, Office of Federal Procurement Policy Act (OFPPA) Amendments of 1988, 41 U.S.C. § 423; FAR 3.104; DFARS 203.104.

### A. Coverage.

1. Applies to all federal agency contracts and modifications awarded on or after December 1, 1990.
2. Applies "during the conduct of the procurement."
3. Applies to procurement officials.
4. Applies to competing contractors. Any entity that is reasonably likely to become a competitor or recipient of a contract or subcontract.
5. Applies to officers, employees, representatives, agents, or consultants of competing contractors.
6. Applies to the incumbent contractor in the case of a modification.

### B. Prohibited Conduct.

1. **Procurement Official**. FAR 3.104-3(b). "During the conduct of any federal agency procurement," no PROCUREMENT OFFICIAL of such agency shall *knowingly*:
   a. SOLICIT, ACCEPT, or DISCUSS future employment or business opportunity with any officer, employee, representative, agent, or consultant of a competing contractor;
   b. SOLICIT or RECEIVE any money, gratuity or any thing of value from any officer, employee, representative, agent, or consultant of a competing contractor; or
   c. DISCLOSE any proprietary or source selection information except as authorized by the contracting officer or agency head.

2. **Competing Contractors**. FAR 3.104-3(a). "During the conduct of any federal agency procurement," no COMPETING CONTRACTOR, or those acting for it, shall *knowingly*:
   a. ENGAGE in certain employment or business opportunity discussions with a procurement official;
   b. OFFER gratuities to a procurement official; or
   c. SOLICIT or RECEIVE certain proprietary and source selection information from agency personnel.

3. "During the conduct of any federal agency procurement," *no PERSON* who is given authorized or *unauthorized access* to proprietary or source selection information shall *knowingly* disclose such information to any person other than one authorized by the agency head or the contracting officer to receive such information. FAR 3.104-3(c).

4. Penalties apply only to persons who "knowingly" engage in prohibited conduct.

## C. Definitions.

1. Procurement official.
   a. Any civilian or military official or employee of an agency who has participated "personally and substantially" in any of certain specific activities for a particular procurement. FAR 3.104-4(h)(l).
   b. The activities include:
      (1) Drafting a specification or statement of work.
      (2) Review and approval of a specification or statement of work.
      (3) Preparation or development of a procurement or purchase request.
      (4) Preparation or issuance of a solicitation.
      (5) Evaluation of bids or proposals.
      (6) Source selection.
      (7) Contract negotiations.
      (8) Review *and* approval of a contract award or modification.
   c. To participate "personally and substantially" means active and significant involvement of the individual in activities directly related to the procurement. FAR 3.104-4(g).
2. Competing contractor.
   a. Any entity that is, or is reasonably likely to become, a competitor for or recipient of a contract or subcontract under such procurement. FAR 3.104-4(b)(1).
      (1) Includes any other person acting on behalf of such an entity.
      (2) Includes the incumbent contractor in case of a contract modification.
   b. An entity shall not be considered a competing contractor whenever it is clear that the entity will not, or will no longer, participate in a particular procurement. FAR 3.104-4(b)(3).
3. "During the conduct of any federal agency procurement of property or services" means:
   a. The period beginning on the earliest date upon which an identifiable specific action

is taken for a particular procurement. FAR 3.104-4(c)(1).
   b. "Identifiable specific action" includes:
      (1) Drafting a specification or statement of work.
      (2) Review and approval of a specification.
      (3) Requirements computation at an inventory control point.
      (4) Development of a procurement or purchase request.
      (5) Preparation or issuance of a solicitation.
      (6) Evaluation of bids or proposals.
      (7) Source selection.
      (8) Conduct of negotiations.
      (9) Review *and* approval of a contract or modification.
   c. In no event shall the conduct of the procurement be deemed to have begun prior to a decision by an authorized official to satisfy a specific agency need or requirement by procurement. FAR 3.104(c)(1).
4. Gratuity or other thing of value. FAR 3.104-4(f)(1).
   a. Includes entertainment, gift, or other item:
      (1) Services, conference fees, lodging, meals, transportation, and vendor promotional training.
      (2) Discounts not available to the general public.
      (3) Loans extended by anyone other than a bank or financial institution.
   b. Does not include:
      (1) Anything paid for by someone other than a competing contractor, or a representative, agent, or consultant of a competing contractor.
      (2) Anything paid for by the government under a government contract or accepted by the government under specific statutory authority.
      (3) Plaques or certificates with no intrinsic value.
      (4) Vendor training when the vendor's products are furnished under contract to the government *and* the training facilitates the use of the product.

(5) Anything other than money having a market value of $10.00 or less.

 c. *But see* 5 C.F.R. § 2635.201 (1994) (Office of Government Ethics regulation allows gifts up to $20.00 in value). Despite the general rule contained in that regulation, the more restrictive FAR provision controls for procurement officials. 5 C.F.R. § 2635.202(c)(4)(iii) (1994).

## D. Ethics Advisory Opinion.

FAR 3.104-8(e).

1. Employees may request an ethics advisory opinion as to whether specific conduct would violate the Act, or for the purpose of determining the individual's status as a procurement official.

2. An employee who engages in conduct in good faith reliance upon the advisory opinion may not be found to have knowingly violated the restrictions at issue.

## E. Recusal of Procurement Officials.

FAR 3.104-6.

1. Procurement officials, including procurement officials who are not government officers or employees, may propose to disqualify themselves from participation in a procurement.

2. Proposal must be submitted and approved prior to entering into any discussions of employment or business opportunity with a competing contractor.

3. Procurement officials who have personally and substantially participated in the evaluation of bids or proposals, selection of sources, or conduct of negotiations may not be recused.

4. Competing contractors may discuss employment or business opportunities with a procurement official *only after* the procurement official has been recused.

## F. Competing Contractor and Contracting Officer Certifications.

FAR 3.104-9.

1. *Certifications Requirements*. Apply to contracts or modifications in excess of $100,000.

2. *Competing Contractor Certifications*. FAR 3.104-9(b). Submitted by an officer or employee of the competing contractor responsible for the offer, bid, or modification. Each competing contractor must certify that:

 a. to his or her *best knowledge and belief*, such officer or employee has no information concerning a violation or possible violation of Subsection 27(a), (b), (d) or (f) of the Procurement Integrity Act (see FAR 3.104-3) as implemented in the FAR pertaining to the specific procurement;

 b. he or she has disclosed information to the contracting officer and certifies all such information has been disclosed; and

 c. he or she has received supporting certifications from each officer, employee, agent, representative, and consultant who on or after December 1, 1990 has participated personally and substantially in the preparation or submission of such bid, offer, or modification. *Hein-Werner Corp.*, B-245766, Jan. 30, 1992, 71 Comp. Gen. 193; 92-1 CPD ¶ 126 (contracting officer's identity irrelevant).

3. *Supporting Certifications to the Competing Contractor*. FAR 3.104-9(b)(iii). Submitted by each officer, employee, agent, representative, and consultant of the competing contractor who has participated personally and substantially in the preparation or submission of the offer, bid, or modification. Each of these individuals must certify that he or she:

 a. is familiar with and will comply with the requirements of Section 27(a) of the OFPPA (see FAR 3.104-3) as implemented in the FAR pertaining to the specific procurement; *and*

 b. will report immediately to the officer or employee of the competing contractor responsible for the offer, bid, or modification any information concerning a violation or possible violation of Section 27(a), (b), (d) or (f) of the Procurement Integrity Act (see FAR 3.104-3) as implemented in the FAR pertaining to the specific procurement.

4. *Submission of Competing Contractor Certification*. FAR 3.104-9.
   a. For sealed bids, by each bidder with bid submission.
   b. For two-step sealed bidding procedures, with submission of the step two bid.
   c. For other than sealed bids, by the successful offeror, within the time the contracting officer specifies.
   d. For letter contracts, one certification prior to contract award and one prior to definitization.
5. *Contracting Officer Certification*. FAR 3.104-9(c).
   a. Submitted by the contracting officer responsible for the procurement. The contracting officer must:
      (1) certify to the agency head that the contracting officer, to the *best of his or her knowledge and belief*, has no information concerning a violation or possible violation of Section 27(a), (b), (d) or (f) of the Procurement Integrity Act (see FAR 3.104-3) as implemented in the FAR pertaining to the specific procurement; *or*
      (2) disclose such information to the agency head and certifies all such information has been disclosed.
   b. The contracting officer shall execute the certification required immediately prior to contract award or execution of a modification.
6. *Additional Certifications*. The agency head may, at any time during the conduct of a procurement, require any procurement official or competing contractor to execute additional certifications. FAR 3.104-9(d)(1).
7. *Certification Requirement Waived*. Certification requirements do not apply to:
   a. Contracts with a foreign government or international organization awarded non-competitively.
   b. Exceptional cases for which the agency head waives the requirements. FAR 3-104-9(f).

**G. Penalties.**
41 U.S.C. § 423(g)-(j).
1. *Contractual Remedies*.
   a. Competing contractor is subject to remedies stated in FAR 52.203-10, a clause required in all contracts over $100,000.
   b. Remedies include loss of profits and termination for default.
   c. Contracting officers may impose any other appropriate remedy. FAR 3.104-11.
2. *Administrative Remedies*.
   a. Government employees are subject to removal or other appropriate adverse action in accordance with Chapter 75 of Title 5 (for civilians) or other laws and regulations.
   b. Competing contractor and its employees are subject to immediate suspension and possible initiation of debarment proceedings.
   c. Competing contractor may also have its contract voided or rescinded, or it may be disqualified for award.
3. *Civil Penalties*.
   a. Government and contractor employees may be fined up to $100,000.
   b. Competing contractors may be fined up to $1,000,000.
4. *Criminal Penalties*.
   a. Applies only to the knowing and willful solicitation or receipt of, or, in the case of a government employee, the unauthorized disclosure of source selection or proprietary information to a competing contractor.
   b. Possible imprisonment of up to five years and/or a fine. *See* 18 U.S.C. § 3571 for range of possible fines.

## III. POST-EMPLOYMENT RESTRICTIONS.

### A. General.
1. Civilian and military federal employees engaged in government contracting are subject to a number of statutory and regulatory provisions concerning their post-employment activities as well as their attempts to

acquire post-government employment. These restrictions are summarized on page 275, Summary of Post Employment Restrictions. The restrictions are also discussed in 5 C.F.R. Part 2635 (1994), Subpart F and in DOD 5500.7-R, Joint Ethics Regulation (JER), chs. 8 and 9 (Aug. 30, 1993).

2. In general, these provisions are designed to protect the integrity of the procurement process.

3. The post-employment provisions impose restrictions on such activities as selling to the government, representation of others before the government, and employment of personnel previously involved in the procurement process by defense contractors.

## B. Restrictions on Government Employees Seeking Employment.

1. *Conflicts of Interest.* FAR 3.104-6; 5 C.F.R. § 2635.604(a) (1994). During the course of a federal agency procurement, a procurement official may not knowingly solicit, accept, or discuss future employment or business opportunity with any officer, employee, representative, agent, or consultant of a competing contractor.

2. *Financial Conflicts of Interest.* 18 U.S.C. § 208; 5 C.F.R. § 2635.402(a) (1994). Prohibits persons from participating in their official capacity in any matter in which that person, a family member, a business associate, certain organizations, or a contractor or person with whom the government employee is negotiating for employment has a financial interest.

   a. The term "negotiating" is interpreted broadly. *United States v. Schaltenbrand,* 930 F.2d 1554 (11th Cir. 1991).

   b. Government personnel may not "personally and substantially" participate as a representative of the government in any particular matter in which, to his knowledge, he, his spouse, minor child, partner, or entity with which he is connected or is seeking employment, has a financial inter-

est. 18 U.S.C. § 208; 5 C.F.R. § 2635.402 (1994).

   c. Violation of the statute can result in imprisonment up to one year, and if willful, five years. In addition, a fine of $50,000 to $250,000 is possible. *See* 18 U.S.C. § 3571.

3. *Duty to Report Employment Contacts.* 10 U.S.C. § 2397a.

   a. All officers in the grade of O-4 and above and all civilian employees in the grade of GS-11 and above must report to their immediate supervisors and designated agency ethics officials any contact regarding future employment by the awardee of a contract in which the government employee performed a "procurement function."

      (1) "Procurement function" includes:

         (a) the negotiation, award, administration, or approval of the contract;

         (b) the selection of the contractor;

         (c) the approval of changes in the contract;

         (d) quality assurance, operation and developmental testing, the approval of payment, or auditing under the contract; or

         (e) the management of the procurement program.

      (2) The reporting must take place if either the employee or the contractor initiates the contact EXCEPT if the contractor initiates the contact and the employee immediately rejects the offer. However, if the contractor persists with repeated contacts, the employee must report all the contacts.

   b. Failure to report may result in a 10-year employment ban (from date of leaving federal service) with the contractor involved and a fine of up to $10,000.

## C. Restrictions on Government Employees After Departure from Government Service.

1. *Providing Assistance to Competing Contractors.* 41 U.S.C. § 423(f); FAR 3.104-3(d).

a. No individual, who was a procurement official with respect to a particular procurement, may knowingly help a "competing contractor" by participating in negotiations for the contract, for a modification of the contract, or for an extension of the contract.

b. No individual, who was a procurement official with respect to a particular procurement, may knowingly help a "competing contractor" to perform a procurement in which the individual participated as a procurement official.

c. The restriction lasts for two years from the date of the procurement official's last personal and substantial participation in the procurement concerned.

2. *Selling To and Prosecuting Claims Against the U.S.* 18 U.S.C. § 281. Prohibits retired military officers for two years after retirement from:

a. Representing others for compensation in the sale of anything to the branch of the service from which the officer retired, or

b. Prosecuting or assisting in the prosecution of a claim against the military department from which the officer retired, or

c. Prosecuting or assisting in the prosecution of a claim involving any subject matter with which the officer was directly connected while in an active-duty status.

d. Violation of the sales representation prohibition can result in two years imprisonment and a fine up to $250,000. Violation of the claims prosecution provisions can result in one year imprisonment and a fine up to $100,000.

e. Section 6001 of the Federal Acquisition Streamlining Act of 1994, Pub. L. No. 103-355, 108 Stat. 3243 (1994) [hereinafter FASA], suspended the application of this statute through Dec. 31, 1996. The suspension took effect on Oct. 13, 1994.

f. Section 6001 of the FASA also repealed 37 U.S.C. § 801. This statute had prohibited retired regular officers from collecting retirement pay while engaging in the selling of tangible property to any DOD agency or activity.

3. *Prohibited Post-Employment.* 10 U.S.C. § 2397b. Prohibits certain former DOD procurement officials from working for specific contractors for two years after separation from DOD.

a. Applies only to officers and civilian employees in grades *above* O-3 or GS-12 who spent a majority of their working days in their last two years of DOD service either:

(1) Performing procurement functions relating to a DOD contract at a plant or site owned or operated by a DOD contractor, or

(2) Performing procurement functions relating to a major defense system and in the performance of such function the individual participated personally and substantially in decision-making responsibilities through personal contact with the contractor.

b. The statute also applies to officers and civilian employees above the grade of O-6 and GS-15 who served as a primary representative of the U.S. in negotiations with a defense contractor of a contract or claim in an amount in excess of $10 million.

4. Scenario:

a. It is Friday afternoon and you are looking forward to a relaxing weekend with your two-year-old twins, when suddenly, LTC Sanders, the Deputy Inspector General, walks into your office and closes the door. She tells you that, while investigating a sexual harassment complaint in the 2nd Brigade Headquarters, she interviewed MAJ Malfunction, the 2nd Brigade Automation Officer. MAJ Malfunction denied any sexual harassment, and then stated that he really didn't care anyway because he was getting out of the Army. Upon further questioning, LTC Sanders discovered that MAJ Malfunction has accepted a job with Lapple Computers, which will begin when he gets out of the military on 1

October 1995, and will pay him twice what he is making as a Major. LTC Sanders also learned that MAJ Malfunction was on the source selection committee for a recent acquisition of computer hardware for the 2nd Brigade, and that he conducted most of the negotiations personally. Lapple Computers won the contract, which was worth over $500,000. MAJ Malfunction has 11 years in service. LTC Sanders asks you if anything should be done about this situation. What is your response?

b. Assume that MAJ Malfunction had not been hired by Lapple Computers and, in fact, was planning on staying in the Army forever (or at least until his second nonselection to LTC). LTC Sanders has learned, however, that MAJ Malfunction's spouse has a financial interest (a big chunk of preferred stock) in Electric Digits, Inc., a proposed subcontractor of Lapple Computers for the computer hardware contract. LTC Sanders also tells you that Lapple Computers, as part of its offer, proposed to hire local teenage "computer nerds" (of which MAJ Malfunction has two). LTC Sanders asks whether this information raises any issues. What would your advice be?

5. *Representational Restrictions*. 18 U.S.C. § 207.

a. Applies to *all* former officers and civilian employees.

b. Imposes a lifetime prohibition on the former employee against communicating or appearing with the intent to influence concerning a particular matter, on behalf of anyone other than the government, when:
(1) the government is a party or has a direct and substantial interest,
(2) the former officer or employee participated personally and substantially in the matter while in his official capacity, and
(3) at the time of the participation, specif-

ic parties other than the government were involved.

c. Prohibits for two years after leaving federal service communicating or appearing with the intent to influence concerning a particular matter, on behalf of anyone other than the government, when:
(1) the government is a party or has a direct and substantial interest,
(2) the former officer or employee knew or should have known that the matter was pending under his official responsibility during the one-year period prior to leaving federal service, and
(3) at the time of the participation, specific parties other than the government were involved.

d. Prohibits "senior employees" (officers above the grade of O-6 and civilian employees above the grade of GS-15) from communicating or appearing with the intent to influence concerning a particular matter, on behalf of anyone other than the government, for one year after leaving federal service when:
(1) the matter involves the department or agency the officer or employee served during his last year of federal service as a senior employee, and
(2) the person represented by the former officer or employee seeks official action by the department or agency concerning the matter.

## D. Dealings with Contractors.

1. *General Rule*: Government business shall be conducted in a manner that is above reproach, with complete impartiality, and with preferential treatment for none. FAR 3.101-1.

2. Some pre-contract contacts with industry are permissible, and in fact are encouraged where the information exchange is beneficial (e.g., necessary to learn of industry's capabilities or to keep them informed of our future needs). FAR Part 5. Some examples are:

a. Research and development. Industrial, educational, research, and non-profit organizations will be informed of current and future military RDTE requirements. However, the information release will be supervised by a contracting officer. AR 70-35, para. 1-5.

b. Unsolicited proposals. Companies are encouraged to make contacts with agencies before submitting proprietary data or spending extensive effort or money on these efforts. FAR 15.504.

c. Market surveys. FAR 7.101.

**E. Release of Acquisition Information.**

1. Integrity of the acquisition process requires a high level of business security.

2. Contracting officers may make available the maximum amount of information to the public *except* information (FAR 5.401(b)):

   a. On plans that would provide undue discriminatory advantage to private or personal interests.

   b. Received in confidence from offerors. 18 U.S.C. § 1905; FAR 15.508; FAR 15.509.

   c. Otherwise requiring protection under the Freedom of Information Act.

   d. Pertaining to internal agency communications (e.g., technical reviews).

3. Information regarding unclassified long-range acquisition estimates is releasable as far in advance as practicable. FAR 5.404.

4. General limitations on release of acquisition information. FAR 14.203-2; FAR 15.402.

   a. Agencies should furnish identical information to all prospective contractors.

   b. Agencies should release information as nearly simultaneously as possible, and only through designated officials (i.e., the contracting officer).

   c. Agencies should not give out advance information concerning future solicitations to anyone.

5. Interim DOD Directive, Release of Acquisition-Related Information. 32 C.F.R. Part 286h (1994).

a. General Policy. DOD policy is to make the maximum amount of acquisition-related information available to the general public, except information for which release is restricted.

b. Information for which release is restricted:

   (1) Information for which release is subject to statutory restrictions.

   (2) Classified information.

   (3) Contractor bid or proposal information.

   (4) Source selection information.

   (5) Planning, programming, and budgetary information.

6. Scenario.

It is 0615 and you have just finished mandatory PT (a nice little 4-mile run.) Before you get a chance to shower, your installation commander, BG Dynamics, calls you over and tells you what a terrific run you had, and that it's a great day to be a soldier. Then he says, "Come on over to my office, judge. I need to ask your opinion about something." When you get there, he tells you that he has a meeting at 0800 with his former Chief of Staff, who is recently retired and is working for a small but growing consulting firm. Mr. (formerly Colonel) Klink simply wants to introduce BG Dynamics to the other members of his firm, who will brief BG Dynamics on the capabilities of the company. The briefing will not occur until after Mr. Klink has finished the introductions and has departed, nor will the briefings be related to any particular ongoing procurement. What do you tell BG Dynamics?

## IV. CONCLUSION.

A. The ethical rules governing procurement officials are more strict than the general rules governing federal employees.

B. You must be familiar with the various ethical rules stated in the Procurement Integrity Act and in other statutes governing employment by former federal employees.

# SUMMARY OF POST-EMPLOYMENT RESTRICTIONS

## 1. Applicable to all officers and civilian employees.
**IF you were a Government officer or employee (including a special Government employee), THEN you may not—**

| | | | |
|---|---|---|---|
| ever— | make, on behalf of anyone else, with the intent to influence, any communication to or appearance before— | any Government officer or employee regarding— | any particular matter involving specific parties in which you ever participated personally and substantially for the Government (18 USC 204(a)(1); JER, para. 9-300. |
| within 2 years after termination of your Government service— | make, on behalf of anyone else, with the intent to influence, any communication to or appearance before— | any Government officer or employee regarding— | any particular matter involving specific parties that you know (or reasonably should know) was pending under your official responsibility in the last year of Government employment (18 USC 207(a)(2); JER, para. 9-300). |

## 2. Applicable only to officers and civilian employees who participated in treaty or trade negotiations.
**IF you participated personally and substantially in any treaty or trade negotiations and had access to covered information, THEN you may not—**

| | | | |
|---|---|---|---|
| within 1 year after termination of your Government service— | represent, aid, or advise— | anyone else concerning— | an ongoing trade or treaty negotiation in which during your last year of Government service you participated personally and substantially (18 USC 207(b); JER, para. 9-300). |

## 3. Applicable only to "senior employees."
**IF you held an Executive Level position, a military grade 0-7 or above, or an SES position at ES-5 or above, THEN you may not—**

| | | | |
|---|---|---|---|
| within 1 year after termination of service in a "senior employee" position— | make, on behalf of anyone else, with the intent to influence, any communication to or appearance before— | any officer or employee of a department or agency in which you served during your last year as a "senior employee" regarding— | any matter on which you seek official action (18 USC 207(c); JER, para. 9-300). |
| within 1 year after termination of service in a "senior employee" position— | aid or advise a foreign entity, or represent a foreign entity before the Government, with the intent to influence— | any Government entity, officer, or employee regarding— | any official decision (18 USC 207(f); JER, para. 9-300). |

## 4. Applicable only to officers and civilian employees who participated in the conduct of a procurement.
**IF you participated personally and substantially in the conduct of a particular procurement, or personally reviewed and approved the award, modification, or extension of any contract for that procurement, THEN you may not—**

| | | | |
|---|---|---|---|
| within 2 years after the date of your last participation in that procurement— | participate on behalf of any competing contractor (i.e., any entity likely to be a competitor for or recipient of a Government-contract or sub-contract)— | in any manner whatsoever in— | any negotiations leading to the award, modification, or extension of any contract for that procurement (41 USC 423(e)(1); JER, para. 9-601). |
| within 2 years after the date of your last participation in that procurement— | participate on behalf of any competing contractor— | personally and substantially in— | the performance of that contract (41 USC 423(e)(2); JER, para. 9-601). |

## 5. Applicable to certain other procurement officials.

### a. Officers and Civilian Employees in Grades Above 0-3 or GS-12.

IF during the 2 years prior to separation you performed a procurement function on a majority of your working days, either:

(1) At a site owned or operated by a particular DOD contractor, or

(2) Relating to a major defense system supplied by a particular DOD contractor with regard to which you participated personally and substantially in decision-making responsibilities through contact with that contractor, THEN you may not—

| | | | |
|---|---|---|---|
| for 2 years after separation from DOD— | accept compensation from that particular contractor— | for any service whatsoever— | regardless of whether it involves any DOD matter (10 USC 2397b; JER, para. 9-600(a)). |

### b. Officers in Grades Above 0-6 and SES employees:

IF, at any time during the 2 years prior to separation, you ever acted as one of the primary representatives of the United States in the negotiation of any DOD contract over $10 million, or in the settlement of a contract claim for over $10 million, THEN you may not—

| | | | |
|---|---|---|---|
| for 2 years after separation from DOD— | accept compensation from that particular contractor— | for any service whatsoever— | regardless of whether it involves any DOD matter (10 USC 2397b; JER, para. 9-600(a)(3)). |

## 6. Applicable only to retired military officials.

### IF you are a retired military officer, THEN you may not—

| | | | |
|---|---|---|---|
| within 2 years after retirement— | prosecute or assist in prosecuting any claim against the U.S. Government before— | any Government entity, officer, or employee regarding— | any matter with which you were directly connected while on active duty (18 USC 281(b)(2); JER, para. 9-701). |
| within 2 years after retirement— | prosecute or assist in prosecuting any claim against the U.S. Government before— | any Government entity, officer, or employee regarding— | any matter with which you were directly connected while on active duty (18 USC 281(b)(1); JER, para. 9-701). |
| within 2 years after retirement— | represent another, for compensation, in connection with selling to, | the department in which you hold a retired status— | anything, either goods or services (18 USC 281(a)(1); JER, para. 9-700(a)(1)). |
| within 3 years after retirement as a Regular military officer— | engage in selling, or contracting or negotiating in connection with a sale, to— | any Department of Defense agency, including the military departments and all DOD non-appropriated fund activities— | any tangible property (but not personal or professional services) (37 USC 801(b); JER, para. 9-700(a)(2)). |

## CHAPTER TWENTY

# *Claims and Remedies*

## I. INTRODUCTION.

As a result of this instruction, the student will understand:

A. The claims submission and disputes resolution process provided by the Contract Disputes Act (CDA).

B. The jurisdiction of the Armed Services Board of Contract Appeals (ASBCA) and the U.S. Court of Federal Claims (COFC) to decide appeals of contracting officer final decisions.

C. The role of the contracts attorney in addressing contractor claims, defending against contractor appeals, and prosecuting government claims.

## II. OVERVIEW.

### A. Historical Development.

1. **Pre-Civil War**. Before 1855, government contractors had no forum in which to sue the United States. In 1855, the Congress created the Court of Claims as an Article I (legislative) court to consider claims against the United States and to recommend private bills to Congress. Act of February 24, 1855, 10 Stat. 612. Ordinarily, however, service secretaries resolved contractor-submitted claims. As early as 1861, the Secretary of War appointed a board of three officers to consider and decide specific contract claims. *See Adams v. United States*, 74 U.S. 463 (1868). Upon receipt of an adverse agency board decision, a contractor's only recourse was to request a private bill from Congress.

2. **Civil War reforms**. In 1863, Congress expanded significantly the power of the Court of Claims by authorizing it to enter judgments against the United States. Act of March 3, 1863, 12 Stat. 765. In 1887, Congress passed the Tucker Act, which expanded and clarified the Court of Claims' jurisdiction. Act of March 3, 1887, 24 Stat. 505, codified at 28 U.S.C. § 1491. In that Act, Congress granted the Court authority to consider claims based on express or implied-in-fact contracts, but not implied-in-law contracts. For the first time, a government contractor could sue the United States as a matter of right.

3. **Final decision**. The agencies responded to the increased oversight by the Court of Claims. They added contract clauses appointing specific agency officials, generally the contracting officer or the service secretary, as the final decision maker for questions of fact. The Supreme Court upheld the finality of these officials' decisions in *Kihlberg v. United States*, 97 U.S. 398 (1878). The tension between the agencies' desire to decide contract disputes without outside interference, and the contractors' desire to resolve disputes in the Court of Claims, continued until 1978. This tension resulted in considerable litigation and a substantial body of case law.

4. **Boards of contract appeals**. During World War I, the War and Navy Departments established full-time boards of contract appeals to hear claims involving wartime contracts. The War Department board was abolished in 1922, but the Navy board continued in name, if not fact, until replaced during World War II. Between the wars, an interagency group developed a standard disputes clause.

This clause made contracting officer decisions final as to all questions of fact. World War II again showed that boards of contract appeals were needed to resolve the massive number of wartime contract disputes. *See Penker Constr. Co. v. United States*, 96 Ct. Cl. 1 (1942). Thus, the War Department created a board of contract appeals, and the Navy revived its board. In 1949, the Department of Defense (DOD) merged the two boards to form the current Armed Services Board of Contract Appeals (ASBCA).

5. **Supreme Court weighs in**. The Supreme Court, in a series of cases culminating in *Wunderlich v. United States*, 342 U.S. 98 (1951), upheld the finality, absent fraud, of agency factual and legal decisions issued under the disputes clauses. It further held that the Court of Claims could not review board decisions de novo. Congress reacted by passing the Wunderlich Act, 41 U.S.C. §§ 321-322, which reaffirmed that the Court of Claims could review factual and legal decisions by agency boards of contract appeals. At about the same time, Congress changed the Court of Claims from an Article I (legislative) to an Article III (judicial) court. Pub. L. No. 83-158, 67 Stat. 226 (1953). Later, the Supreme Court clarified the relationship between the Court of Claims and the agency boards of contract appeals by limiting the jurisdiction of boards of contract appeals to cases "arising under" remedy granting clauses in the contract. *See Utah Mining and Constr. Co. v. United States*, 384 U.S. 394 (1966).

6. **Congress reacts**. In 1978, Congress enacted the Contract Disputes Act (CDA), which revised extensively the claims and disputes process. *See* Contract Disputes Act of 1978, 41 U.S.C. §§ 601-613. This Act replaced the previous system with a comprehensive statutory description of jurisdiction and procedures. In 1982, Congress overhauled the Court of Claims and created the Claims Court, a new Article I court, from the old Trial Division of the Court of Claims, and merged the Court of Claims and the Court of Customs and Patent Appeals to create the Court of Appeals for the Federal Circuit. Federal Courts Improvement Act of 1982, Pub. L. No. 97-164, 96 Stat. 25. The Act substantially revised the jurisdiction of the new courts.

7. **Recent changes**.
a. The Federal Acquisition Streamlining Act of 1994 (FASA) made significant changes to the CDA disputes resolution process. Pub. L. No. 103-355, 108 Stat. 3243 (1994). As of this outline's publication date, most FASA changes remain in draft form only. This outline will refer the student to proposed regulatory changes throughout the outline. It behooves the student to be aware of these upcoming revisions and amend the information contained in this outline accordingly. (Footnote citations to FASA sections refer to the Public Law section designations.)
b. In 1992, Congress passed the Federal Courts Administration Act, which changed the name of the Claims Court to the United States Court of Federal Claims and expanded the jurisdiction of the court to include the adjudication of nonmonetary claims. Federal Courts Administration Act of 1992, Title IX, Pub. L. No. 102-572, 106 Stat. 4506.

**B. The Disputes Process.**
1. The CDA establishes procedures and requirements for asserting and resolving claims subject to the Act.
2. The disputes process flowchart. (*See* page 277.)
3. Distinguishing bid protests from disputes.
   a. In bid protests, disappointed bidders or offerors seek relief from improper actions leading to contract award. *See* FAR Subpart 33.1, *Protests*.
   b. In contract disputes, contractors seek relief from government actions and events that occur following contract award. *See* FAR Subpart 33.2, *Disputes and Appeals*.
   c. Except for the General Services Board of Contract Appeals, the boards of contract

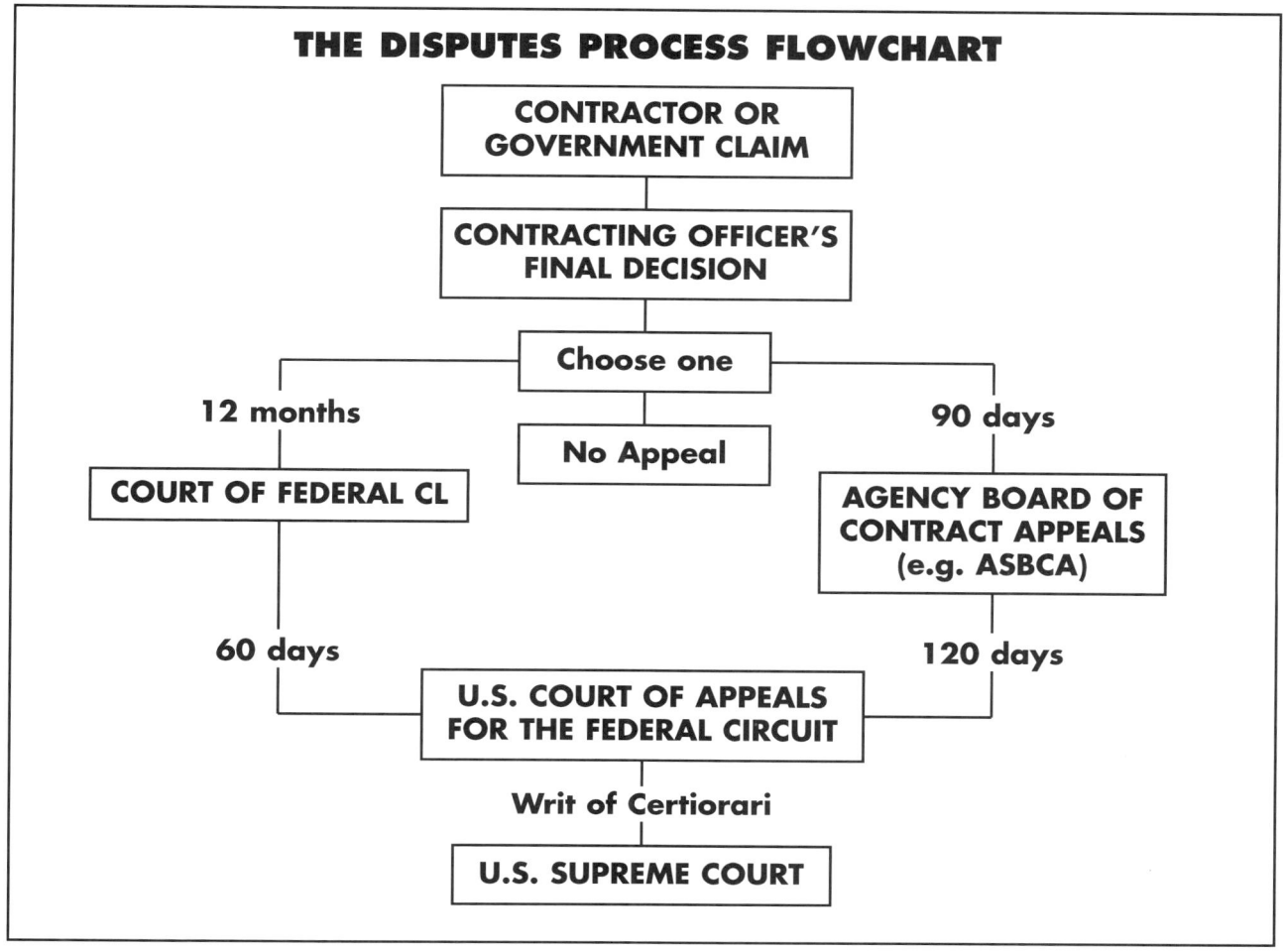

**THE DISPUTES PROCESS FLOWCHART**

CONTRACTOR OR GOVERNMENT CLAIM

CONTRACTING OFFICER'S FINAL DECISION

Choose one

12 months

No Appeal

90 days

COURT OF FEDERAL CL

AGENCY BOARD OF CONTRACT APPEALS (e.g. ASBCA)

60 days

120 days

U.S. COURT OF APPEALS FOR THE FEDERAL CIRCUIT

Writ of Certiorari

U.S. SUPREME COURT

appeals lack jurisdiction over bid protest actions. *See, e.g., Commercial Sound and Safety, Inc.*, VABCA No. 3750, 93-1 BCA ¶ 25,498.

## III. APPLICABILITY OF THE DISPUTES CLAUSE.

### A. Appropriated Fund Contracts.

1. Disputes Clause. The standard Disputes clause, FAR 52.233-1, applies to all express or implied contracts covered by the FAR, except, at the discretion of the agency head, a contract with a foreign government or an international organization. FAR 33.203. *See G.E. Boggs & Assocs.*, ASBCA No. 34841, 91-1 BCA ¶ 23,515 (contractual agreement conferred "Disputes clause jurisdiction").

2. The Disputes clause implements the CDA, as amended, and obligates a contractor to continue to perform a government contract pending resolution of disputes *"arising under"* a remedy granting clause in the contract. *See* page 291.

3. Mission critical contracts may include FAR 52.233-1, Alternate I, Disputes; DFARS 233.214. *See* page 291. This clause obligates a contractor to continue performance pending resolution of disputes *"arising under or relating to"* a contract, including those involving government breach.

### B. Nonappropriated Fund Contracts.

1. The CDA is generally inapplicable to contracts funded solely with nonappropriated funds (NAF), except Army Air Force Exchange Service (AAFES) contracts. *See* FAR 33.203. The government, however, may

include a disputes clause in a NAF contract, thereby giving a contractor recourse to the disputes process.

2. The right to dispute an adverse final decision arising under a NAF contract is a contractual right, not a statutory one. *See* Disputes clause, DA Form 4074-R, I-25 (SEP 1984) (NAF contracts); *but see Recreational Enters.*, ASBCA No. 32176, 87-1 BCA ¶ 19,675 (disputes clause incorporated into NAF contract by operation of law).

## IV. CONTRACTOR CLAIMS.

### A. Settlement.

1. It is government policy to resolve claims by mutual agreement, if possible. FAR 33.204; FAR 33.210. *See also Pathman Constr. Co., Inc. v. United States*, 817 F.2d 1573 (Fed. Cir. 1987) (a "major purpose" of the CDA is to "induce resolution of contract disputes with the government by negotiation rather than litigation").

2. Only the contracting officer or his authorized representatives may settle contract claims. *J.H. Strain & Sons, Inc.*, ASBCA No. 34432, 88-3 BCA ¶ 20,909. The Department of Justice has plenary authority to settle cases pending before the U.S. Court of Federal Claims. *Executive Business Media v. Dep't of Defense*, 3 F.3d 759 (4th Cir. 1993).

### B. Definition of a Claim.

1. The CDA does not define "claim."

2. The FAR defines a "claim" as a written demand or written assertion by one of the contracting parties seeking, as a matter of right, the payment of money, adjustment or interpretation of contract terms, or other relief arising under or related to a contract. A claim arising under a contract, unlike a claim relating to a contract, is a claim that can be resolved under a contract clause providing for the relief sought by the claimant. FAR 33.201; FAR 52.233-1.

3. The submission of a voucher, invoice, or other routine request for payment is *not* a claim when submitted. The submission may become a CDA claim if the contractor complies with the submission and certification requirements of the Disputes clause, if the parties dispute the submission either as to liability or amount, or if the contracting officer fails to act on the request in a reasonable time. FAR 33.201; FAR 52.233-1. *S-TRON*, ASBCA No. 45890, 94-3 BCA ¶ 26,957, *citing Transamerica Ins. Corp. v. United States*, 973 F.2d 1572, 1579 (Fed. Cir. 1992) (stating that a "common sense analysis" should be used when reviewing a purported claim).

4. Letters to the government merely notifying the government of performance difficulties and delays, or summarizing the parties' positions without demanding payment of money, an adjustment or interpretation of contract terms, or other relief, are not claims. *B.L.I. Constr. Co.*, ASBCA No. 40855, 91-2 BCA ¶ 24,037; *Oman-Fischbach Int'l, J.V.*, ASBCA No. 41474, 91-2 BCA ¶ 24,018. *But see Essex Electro Eng'rs, Inc.*, ASBCA No. 40553, 91-2 BCA ¶ 23712, *aff'd on recon.*, 91-2 BCA ¶ 23900 (letter, including documentation and certification, identifying contents as a claim, was a claim despite language asking contracting officer to schedule date for negotiations).

### C. Elements of a Claim.

1. **Submitted in writing**. Contractors shall submit, in writing and to the contracting officer for decision, all claims relating to a contract. 41 U.S.C. § 605(a); *Blake Constr. Co.*, ASBCA No. 34480, 88-2 BCA ¶ 20,552; *Honig Industrial Diamond Wheel, Inc.*, ASBCA No. 46711, 94-2 BCA ¶ 26,955 (government motion to strike monetary claims granted in an appeal involving a termination for default in which contractor asserted affirmative monetary claims that it had not previously submitted to contracting officer).

2. **Supporting data**. A claim must contain sufficient detail to enable the contracting officer to render an informed decision about it. *Contract Cleaning Maint., Inc. v. United*

*States*, 811 F.2d 586, 592 (Fed. Cir. 1987); *Scientific Mgmt. Assocs.*, ASBCA No. 42971, 92-2 BCA ¶ 24,912 (chart, alone, failed to support claims); *Bay Area Crane-Hoist Co.*, ASBCA No. 35700, 90-1 BCA ¶ 22,356; *Holk Dev., Inc.*, ASBCA No. 40579, 90-3 BCA ¶ 23,086 (failure to explain cause and effect of alleged damages). Contracting officers should deny an insufficient claim or request additional information.

3. **Sum certain**. Where the essence of a dispute is the increased cost of performance, the contractor must demand a sum certain as a matter of right. *Essex Electro Eng'rs, Inc. v. United States*, 22 Cl. Ct. 757, *aff'd* 960 F.2d 1576, (Fed. Cir. 1992), *cert. denied*, 113 S. Ct. 408 (1992) (submission of cost proposals for change orders and inspection reports did not seek a sum certain as a matter of right); *East West Research, Inc.*, ASBCA No. 35401, 88-3 BCA ¶ 29,931 (request for future savings under VECP was a "sum certain"); *Atlantic Indus., Inc.*, ASBCA No. 34832, 88-1 BCA ¶ 20,244; *Jepco Petroleum*, ASBCA No. 40480, 91-2 BCA ¶ 24,038 (claim was quantified properly since the contracting officer could determine the amount of the claim by simple arithmetic). *See also Winding Specialist Co.*, ASBCA No. 37765, 89-2 BCA ¶ 21,737 (contractor may not seek contract interpretation while holding a monetary claim in abeyance).

4. **Certification, generally**. Contractors must certify all contractor claims exceeding $50,000.[1] 41 U.S.C. § 605(c)(1); FAR 33.207.

   a. Until recently, proper certification was a jurisdictional prerequisite before the courts and boards. *W.M. Schlosser Co. v. United States*, 705 F.2d 1336 (Fed. Cir. 1983); *B&M Roofing & Painting Co.*, ASBCA No. 37839, 91-2 BCA ¶ 23,975.

   b. As of 29 October 1992, certification is no longer a jurisdictional prerequisite. Federal Courts Administration Act of 1992, Title IX, Pub. L. No. 102-572, 106 Stat. 4506, 4518. *SAE/American - Mid-Atlantic, Inc.*, GSBCA No. 12294, 94-2 BCA ¶ 26,890 (contractor's "certificate of current cost or pricing data" held to meet CDA certification requirements). *But see Eurostyle, Inc.*, ASBCA No. 45934, 94-1 BCA ¶ 26,458 (applying a "common sense" analysis, the board finds the *complete* absence of a certification rendered the claim invalid and precluded board from exercising jurisdiction); *see also Hamza v. United States*, 31 Fed. Cl. 315 (1994). For claims exceeding $100,000 within DOD, *see also* DFARS 252.233-7000.

   c. The contractor must execute its CDA certification *after* the date the matter is considered to have become "in dispute." Certification which predates the actual "dispute" is not acceptable. *R.W. Elec. Corp.*, ASBCA No. 46592, 1994 WL 682319.

   d. When required to certify a claim, contractors must certify that:
      (1) **THE CLAIM IS MADE IN GOOD FAITH; AND**
      (2) **SUPPORTING DATA ARE ACCURATE AND COMPLETE TO THE BEST OF THE CONTRACTOR'S KNOWLEDGE AND BELIEF; AND**
      (3) **THE AMOUNT REQUESTED ACCURATELY REFLECTS THE CONTRACT ADJUSTMENT FOR WHICH THE CONTRACTOR BELIEVES THE GOVERNMENT IS LIABLE; AND**
      (4) **THE PERSON SUBMITTING THE CLAIM IS DULY AUTHORIZED TO CERTIFY THE CLAIM ON BEHALF OF THE CONTRACTOR.** 41 U.S.C. § 605(c)(1); FAR 33.207.

   e. As noted above, a defective claim certification is not a jurisdictional bar. Instead, the court or board shall require the contractor to correct any defect prior to entry of a final judgment or decision. 41 U.S.C. § 605(c)(6); FAR 33.207(f).

   f. Absent extraordinary circumstances, the board will not question the accuracy of the statements in a contractor's certification. *D.E.W., Inc.*, ASBCA No. 37332, 94-3

BCA ¶ 27,004. A prime contractor is expected only to believe there are good grounds for the claim, not that it is certain as to the government's liability or amount recoverable. *Oconto Elec., Inc.*, ASBCA No. 45856, 94-3 BCA ¶ 26,958 (contractor lacked personal knowledge of the amount claimed but did not disagree with the claim.) *See also Arnold M. Diamond, Inc. v. Dalton*, 25 F.3d 1006 (Fed. Cir. 1994) (contractor submission of claim pursuant to court order held to meet "good faith" criteria).

   g. A contractor may not separate one claim exceeding $50,000[2] into multiple claims to avoid the certification requirement. *Warchol Constr. Co. v. United States*, 2 Cl. Ct. 384 (1983).

     (1) Separate claims less than $50,000 require no certification even if the total of all of them exceeds $50,000.[3] *B. D. Click Co.*, ASBCA No. 25609, 81-2 BCA ¶ 15,394; *Phillips Constr. Co.*, ASBCA No. 27055, 83-2 BCA ¶ 16,618.

     (2) Claims that are based on a "common or related set of operative facts" constitute one claim. *Placeway Constr. Corp. v. United States*, 920 F.2d 903, 907 (Fed. Cir. 1990).

     (3) A contractor need not certify a claim that grows to exceed $50,000[4] after submission to the contracting officer. *John R. Glenn v. United States*, 858 F.2d 1577 (Fed. Cir. 1988); *TECOM v. United States*, 732 F.2d 935 (Fed. Cir. 1984); *T.E. Deloss Equip. Rentals*, ASBCA No. 35374, 88-1 BCA ¶ 20,497; *AAI Corp. v. United States*, 22 Cl. Ct. 541 (1991) (court refused to dismiss element of claim that had been $0 when submitted to the contracting officer but had increased to $500,000 by the time the suit came before the court).

5. **Proper certifying official**. In an effort to clarify who must sign the certificate, the Federal Courts Administration Act provides that certifications "may be executed by any person duly authorized to bind the contractor with respect to the claim." Federal Courts Administration Act, *supra*, § 907; FAR 33.207(e).

**D. Submission to the Contracting Officer.**
41 U.S.C. § 605(a).

1. Who may submit a claim?

   a. Generally, only contractors may submit claims. *United States v. Johnson Controls*, 713 F.2d 1541 (Fed. Cir. 1983) (dismissing subcontractor claim). *Cf. Choe-Kelly*, ASBCA No. 43481, 92-2 BCA ¶ 24,910 (board had jurisdiction to consider subcontractor's unsponsored claim alleging implied-in-fact contract).

   b. Sureties. Absent privity of contract, sureties may not file claims. *William A. Ransom and Robert D. Nesen v. United States*, 900 F.2d 242 (Fed. Cir. 1990).

   c. Dissolved/suspended corporations. *Allied Prod. Mgmt., Inc., and Richard E. Rowan, J.V.*, DOT CAB No. 2466, 92-1 BCA ¶ 24,585 (contractor could appeal despite suspended corporate status). *Cf. Micro Tool Eng'g, Inc.*, ASBCA No. 31136, 86-1 BCA ¶ 18,680 (dissolved corporation could not sue under New York law).

2. A contractor must submit its claims to the contracting officer. FAR 52.233-1(d)(1). However, a contractor may submit a claim through other government officials to the contracting officer. *Dawco Constr., Inc. v. United States*, 930 F.2d 872 (Fed. Cir. 1991) (claim submitted through resident officer in charge of construction); *Roy McGinnis & Co.*, ASBCA No. 40004, 91-1 BCA ¶ 23,395. However, claims trigger CDA interest and decision time limits *only upon receipt by the contracting officer*. 41 U.S.C. § 611 (interest); 41 U.S.C. § 605(c)(1) (decision time limits).

**E. Interest.**
Interest on CDA claims is calculated every six months based on a rate established by the Secretary of the Treasury pursuant to Public Law 92-41 (85 Stat. 97) for the Renegotiation Board (31 U.S.C. § 3902). 41 U.S.C. § 611; FAR 33.208.

The Commerce Clearing House (CCH) Government Contracts Reporter (Vol. 4) lists these interest rates from 1971 to the present. *Cf. Ruhnau-Evans-Ruhnau v. United States*, 3 Cl. Ct. 217 (1983) (contractor who acceded to government demand for payment and then successfully appealed government's right to payment not entitled to interest because appeal was on a government claim).

## V. GOVERNMENT CLAIMS.

### A. General.

1. The government may assert claims against a contractor. A claim by the government against the contractor shall be subject to a written final decision by the contracting officer. 41 U.S.C. § 605(a); FAR 52.233-1(d)(1); *P.J. Dick Contracting, Inc. v. Gen. Servs. Admin.*, GSBCA No. 11646, 92-2 BCA ¶ 24,847 (failure to issue final decision regarding government claim involving cost of utilities). Generally, the government may not assert at hearing counterclaims that were not the subject of a final decision.

2. Once the contracting officer's decision becomes final (i.e., the appeal period has passed) on a government claim, the contractor cannot judicially challenge the merits of that decision. *Seaboard Lumber Co. v. United States*, 903 F.2d 1560, 1562 (Fed. Cir. 1990), *cert. denied*, 111 S. Ct. 1308 (1991); 41 U.S.C. § 605(a).

3. A contracting officer's decision to terminate a contract for default is a government claim, immediately appealable by the contractor. *Independent Mfg. & Serv. Cos. of Am., Inc.*, ASBCA No. 47636, 94-3 BCA ¶ 27,233 (contract modification terminating contract for default constitutes government claim). *See also Malone v. United States*, 849 F.2d 1441, 1443 (Fed. Cir. 1988).

4. Not all government claims are appealable final decisions. *Boeing Co.*, 25 Cl. Ct. 441 (1992) (post-termination letter demanding return of unliquidated progress payments was not appealable).

### B. Opportunity to Comment.
Before issuing a final decision on a government claim, a contracting officer must give the contractor notice and an opportunity to comment. FAR 33.211; *Instruments & Controls Serv. Co.*, ASBCA No. 38332, 89-3 BCA ¶ 22,237; *Keystone Coat & Apron Mfg. Corp. v. United States*, 150 Ct. Cl. 277 (1960).

### C. Certification.
Neither party is required to certify a government claim. *Placeway Constr. Corp. v. United States*, 920 F.2d 903, 906 (Fed. Cir. 1990). *See* 41 U.S.C. § 605(a), (c)(1). However, a contractor must certify its request for interest on money deducted by the government. *General Motors Corp.*, ASBCA No. 35634, 92-3 BCA ¶ 25,149.

### D. Interest.
Interest on a government claim begins to run when the contractor receives the government's initial written demand for payment. FAR 52.232-17.

## VI. FINAL DECISIONS.

### A. Consideration by a Contracting Officer.
All claims, whether government or contractor, must be the subject of a final decision by the contracting officer. 41 U.S.C. § 605(a); FAR 33.206. *But see McDonnell Douglas Corp.*, ASBCA No. 44637, 93-2 BCA ¶ 25,700 (contractor's appeal from government claim for non-compliance with cost accounting standards dismissed because decision issued by the procuring contracting officer instead of by the cognizant administrative contracting officer, as required by the FAR and DFARS).

### B. Issuing a Final Decision.
1. Opportunity to comment. Government claims relating to a contract shall be the subject of a decision by the contracting officer, who must give the contractor an opportunity to comment before issuing a final decision. FAR 52.233-1(d); *Martin J. Simko Constr.,*

*Inc. v. United States*, 852 F.2d 540 (Fed. Cir. 1988); *Wilner Constr. Co. v. United States*, 23 Cl. Ct. 241, 263 (1991) (government counterclaim for liquidated damages disallowed). *Cf. BMY-Combat Sys. Div. of Harsco Corp. v. United States*, 26 Cl. Ct. 846 (1992) (fraud counterclaim required no final decision).

2. Time limits. Upon request, contracting officers must issue a final decision on a contractor's claim within specified statutory time limits. 41 U.S.C. § 605(c)(1); FAR 33.211. Upon receipt of a written request from a contractor that a decision be issued within that period, the contracting officer must issue a final decision as follows:[5]

   a. Claims of $50,000 or less—within 60 days.

   b. Certified claims exceeding $50,000—within 60 days, the contracting officer must:

      (1) Issue a final decision; or

      (2) Notify the contractor of a firm date when the decision will be issued. 41 U.S.C. § 605(c)(2)(B); *Boeing Co. v. United States*, 26 Cl. Ct. 257 (1992); *Westclox Military Prod.*, ASBCA No. 25592, 81-2 BCA ¶ 15,270.

   c. The contracting officer has no obligation to issue a final decision on any claim exceeding $50,000[6] which contains a defective certification. If the claim certification is defective, the CO must notify the contractor, in writing, within 60 days after receipt of the claim of the reasons why any attempted certification was found to be defective. 41 U.S.C. § 605(c)(6); FAR 33.211(e).

3. If the contracting officer delays unduly in issuing a final decision, the contractor may ask the board to direct the contracting officer to issue a final decision. 41 U.S.C. § 606(c)(4); *American Indus.*, ASBCA No. 26930-15, 82-1 BCA ¶ 15,753 (model order directing the contracting officer to issue a final decision).

4. The board may not direct the contracting officer to issue a more detailed final decision than issued already. *A.D. Roe Co.*, ASBCA No. 26078, 81-2 BCA ¶ 15,231.

5. A contractor may treat the contracting officer's failure to issue a final decision within the specified time period as an appealable final decision (a "deemed denial"). 41 U.S.C. § 605(c)(5).

**C. Format.**

1. A contracting officer must issue a *written* final decision. *Tyger Constr. Co.*, ASBCA No. 36100, 88-3 BCA ¶ 21,149. FAR 33.211 provides that a final decision should include:

   a. A description of the claim or dispute;

   b. A reference to the pertinent or disputed contract terms;

   c. A statement of the disputed and undisputed facts;

   d. A statement of the contracting officer's decision and rationale; and,

   e. A demand for repayment of any indebtedness (to start interest running).

2. Every final decision must inform the contractor of its appeal rights. 41 U.S.C. § 605(a); Federal Courts Administration Act of 1992, *supra* § 907(b); FAR 33.211(a)(4)(v). The FAR specifies that the rights advisement should state:[7]

   This is a final decision of the Contracting Officer. You may appeal this decision to the [Armed Services Board of Contract Appeals, Skyline Six, 5109 Leesburg Pike, 7th Floor, Falls Church, Virginia 22041-3208]. If you decide to appeal, you must, within 90 days from the date you receive this decision, mail or otherwise furnish written notice to the [Armed Services] Board of Contract Appeals and provide a copy to the Contracting Officer from whose decision the appeal is taken. The notice shall indicate that an appeal is intended, reference this decision, and identify the contract by number. With regard to appeals to the agency board of contract appeals, you may, solely at your election, proceed under the board's small claim procedure for claims of $10,000 or less or its accelerated procedure for claims of $50,000 or less. Instead of appealing to the [Armed Services] Board of Contract Appeals, you may bring an action directly in the United States Court of Federal Claims (except as provided in the Contract Disputes Act of 1978, 41 U.S.C. § 603, regarding Maritime Contracts) within 12 months of the date you receive this decision.

3. The government must give the final decision to the contractor.
   a. Use certified mail, return receipt requested. FAR 33.211(b).
   b. Hand delivery and telefax are acceptable. Keep evidence of the date the contractor received the decision with the final decision, and confirm receipt.

## D. Independent Act of a Contracting Officer.

1. The FAR requires contracting officers to request and consider the advice of specialists, as appropriate, but to exercise independent judgment. FAR 1.602-2(c). A contracting officer's final decision must be the contracting officer's personal, independent act. *Climatic Rainwear Co. v. United States*, 88 F. Supp. 415 (Ct. Cl. 1950).

2. Although required to act independently, contracting officers may seek assistance from engineers, attorneys, auditors, and other advisors. *Max Jordan Bauunternehmung*, ASBCA No. 23055, 82-1 BCA ¶ 15,685. Indeed, the FAR requires contracting officers to seek assistance from others, including legal advisors. FAR 33.211(a)(2). *See General Kinetics, Inc., Cryptek Secure Communications Div.*, B-243078.2, Jan. 22, 1992, 92-1 CPD ¶ 95 (contracting officer commended by GAO for considering legal advice concerning Buy American Act).

## E. Finality.

1. A final decision, unless timely appealed, is binding on the contractor and all courts, boards of contract appeals, and federal agencies. 41 U.S.C. § 605(b). Once the appeal period has run, the government may enforce

the decision and is entitled to summary judgment based on it. *United States v. Roarda, Inc.*, 671 F. Supp. 1084 (D. Md. 1987); *United States v. Dabbs*, 608 F. Supp. 507 (S.D. Miss. 1985).

2. Reconsideration—a trap for the unwary.
   a. A contracting officer may reconsider or withdraw a final decision before expiration of the appeal period. *General Dynamics Corp.*, ASBCA No. 39866, 91-2 BCA ¶ 24,017; *Daniels & Shanklin Constr. Co.*, ASBCA No. 37102, 89-3 BCA ¶ 22,060; *but see McDonnell Douglas Astronautics Co.*, ASBCA No. 36770, 89-3 BCA ¶ 22,253.
   b. A contracting officer may vacate his or her final decision and extend the appeal period by agreeing to meet with the contractor to discuss the matters in dispute. *Royal Int'l Builders Co.*, ASBCA No. 42637, 92-1 BCA ¶ 24,684.
   c. To restart the appeal period after reconsidering a final decision, the contracting officer must issue a new, written, final decision. *Information Sys. & Networks Corp. v. United States*, 17 Cl. Ct. 527 (1989); *Birken Mfg. Co.*, ASBCA No. 36587, 89-2 BCA ¶ 21,581.

3. Fulford Doctrine. A contractor may dispute the underlying, unappealed, default termination as part of a timely appeal from a government demand for excess reprocurement costs. *Fulford Mfg. Co.*, ASBCA No. 2143, 6 CCF ¶ 61,815 (May 20, 1955); *Kellner Equip., Inc.*, ASBCA No. 26006, 82-2 BCA ¶ 16,077 (applying *Fulford* to CDA appeals).

## VII. APPEALS TO THE ARMED SERVICES BOARD OF CONTRACT APPEALS.

### A. The Right of Appeal.

A contractor may appeal a contracting officer's final decision to an agency board of contract appeals. 41 U.S.C. § 606. The agency board reviews the dispute, including the contracting officer's final decision, *de novo*, and is not bound by the contracting officer's findings of fact or law. *Space Age Eng'g, Inc.*, ASBCA No. 26028, 82-1 BCA ¶ 15,766.

## B. The Armed Services Board of Contract Appeals (ASBCA).

1. The ASBCA consists of 31-32 administrative judges who dispose of approximately 1600 appeals per year (over 60% of all contract disputes under the CDA).

2. BCA judges are administrative judges who specialize in contract disputes and who come from the government and private sectors. Each judge has at least five years of experience working in the field of government contract law.

3. The Rules of the Armed Services Board of Contract Appeals appear in Appendix A of the DFARS.

## C. Perfecting an ASBCA Appeal.

1. A contractor has 90 days following receipt of a final decision to file an appeal, and a board of contract appeals may not waive a late filing. *Cosmic Constr. Co. v. United States*, 697 F.2d 1389 (Fed. Cir. 1982), *aff'g* ASBCA No. 26537, 82-1 BCA ¶ 15,541. In computing the appeal period, exclude the day the contractor receives the final decision and count the day the contractor mails notice of appeal. ASBCA Rule 33(b).

   a. The government must prove that the contractor actually or constructively received the final decision, and the date of receipt. *Alco Mach. Co.*, ASBCA No. 38183, 89-3 BCA ¶ 21,955; *Joseph Morton Co.*, GSBCA No. 4707, 77-1 BCA ¶ 12,320 (actual notice); *Sancolmar Indus.*, ASBCA No. 16879, 73-1 BCA ¶ 9,812 (constructive notice).

   b. Issuing defective appellate rights instructions extends the appeal period. indefinitely. *Caesar Constr. Co.*, ASBCA No. 46023, 94-2 BCA ¶ 26,956 (appeal filed three years after initial "claim" found timely due to failure of final decision to set out contractor's appeal rights).

   c. The Federal Circuit has determined that

the Tucker Act six-year limitation does not apply to CDA appeals.[8] *Pathman Constr. Co. v. United States*, 817 F.2d 1573 (Fed. Cir. 1987).

   d. Methods of filing notice of appeal with the ASBCA.

   (1) Placing the appeal in the U.S. Postal System is a filing. ASBCA Rule 1(a); *Micrographic Technology, Inc.*, ASBCA No. 25577, 81-2 BCA ¶ 15,357 (normal mailing procedures proved appeal had been filed).

   (2) Only the U.S. mail counts; Federal Express is not "mailing." *North Coast Remfg., Inc.*, ASBCA No. 38599, 89-3 BCA ¶ 22,232. *See also Kenneth Dolan*, AGBCA No. 94-152-1, 94-2 BCA ¶ 26,734 (contractor's use of incorrect zip code made its (unreceived) board appeal untimely).

   (3) Notifying the contracting officer of an appeal is a filing if it reflects dissatisfaction with the final decision and states an intent to appeal to a board of contract appeals. *Kos Kam, Inc.*, ASBCA No. 34633, 88-1 BCA ¶ 20,311. *See also Birken Mfg. Co.*, ASBCA No. 37064, 89-1 BCA ¶ 21,248; *Brunner Bau GmbH*, ASBCA No. 35678, 89-1 BCA ¶ 21,315 (mailing a notice of appeal to government counsel is a filing).

   (4) An adequate notice of appeal must express dissatisfaction with the contracting officer's decision and must manifest an intention to appeal the decision to the board. *Larry D. Paine*, ASBCA No. 41273, 93-2 BCA ¶ 25,702. *See also Stewart-Thomas Indus., Inc.*, ASBCA No. 38773, 90-1 BCA ¶ 22,481 (intent to appeal to the board must be unequivocal).

   (5) Whenever the 90th day is a Saturday, Sunday, or federal holiday, the appeal period ends at the close of the next business day. ASBCA Rule 33(b).

2. An election to appeal to the agency board of contract appeals is irrevocable. The contrac-

tor may not withdraw its appeal and later appeal the same decision to the Court of Federal Claims. *Bonneville Assoc. v. United States*, 1994 WL 703381 (Fed. Cir. Dec. 19, 1994); *National Neighbors, Inc. v. United States*, 839 F.2d 1539 (Fed. Cir. 1988).

## D. Procedure.

1. Regular appeals.
   a. The ASBCA Recorder dockets the Notice of Appeal. The Recorder assigns the appeal a docket number and forwards it to the Chief Trial Attorney for the agency. The Chief Trial Attorney notifies the contracting officer.
   b. Complaint. Absent board-granted extensions, the appellant must file a complaint within 30 days after the appeal is docketed. ASBCA Rule 6(a). If sufficiently detailed, the notice of appeal may constitute the complaint.
   c. Answer. The government must answer the complaint within 30 days after receipt. ASBCA Rule 6(b). In an appeal from a government claim, the board may direct the government to file the complaint.
   d. Appeal file (Rule 4 File). The contracting officer prepares a file containing the final decision, the contract and specifications, correspondence, and other documents relevant to the dispute. ASBCA Rule 4(a). The government furnishes the Rule 4 file to the board and the contractor within 30 days after receipt of the notice of appeal. Later, the appellant may supplement the Rule 4 file with additional relevant matters.
   e. Discovery. The parties may begin discovery after the complaint has been filed. ASBCA Rule 14, 15. Discovery may include depositions, interrogatories, requests for production of documents, and requests for admission.
   f. Prehearing conferences. Occasionally, the ASBCA holds a prehearing, telephonic conference after it receives the answer.
   g. Motions. Parties must file jurisdictional motions promptly. ASBCA Rule 5.
   h. Record submissions. The parties may submit the case for decision on the record. ASBCA Rule 11. When submitting a case on the record, the parties may supplement the record with affidavits, depositions, admissions, and stipulations. *See Solar Foam Insulation*, ASBCA No. 46921, 94-2 BCA ¶ 26,901.
   i. Hearings. The board may hold a hearing. ASBCA Rules 17-25. At the hearing, the board hears sworn testimony and receives exhibits into evidence, generally in accordance with the Federal Rules of Evidence. The parties and the board may subpoena witnesses and documents. Witnesses testify under oath, subject to cross examination. A court reporter prepares a verbatim transcript of the proceedings.
   j. Briefs. The parties may elect to file post-hearing briefs after receipt of the transcript or after the record is closed. ASBCA Rule 23.
   k. Decision. The board issues a written decision. ASBCA Rule 28. Normally, the presiding judge drafts the decision. The presiding judge, with the concurrence of a vice chairman, or by a majority among these two and the chairman, decides the appeal.
   l. Appeals. Either party may appeal to the Court of Appeals for the Federal Circuit within 120 days. The government needs the consent of the U.S. Attorney General to appeal. 41 U.S.C. § 607(g)(1).
2. Accelerated appeal procedures.[9] 41 U.S.C. § 607(f); ASBCA Rule 12.3. In an accelerated appeal:
   a. The amount in dispute may not exceed $50,000, including government counterclaims;
   b. The presiding judge hears the appeal and drafts the decision, which he and one other judge then issue. In case of disagreement, the presiding judge, with the concurrence of a vice chairman, or by a majority among these two and the chairman, decides the appeal;

c. The board encourages parties to limit briefs and discovery;

d. The board must render its decision within 180 days from the date of appellant's election, unless appellant withdraws its election; and

e. Either party may appeal to the Federal Circuit within 120 days. The government needs the consent of the U.S. Attorney General to appeal. 41 U.S.C. § 607(g)(1).

3. Small claims (expedited) procedures.[10] 41 U.S.C. § 608; ASBCA Rule 12.2. In an expedited appeal:

a. The amount in dispute may not exceed $10,000, including government counterclaims;

b. The presiding judge, alone, decides the appeal, and may issue an oral decision from the bench, followed by a memorandum formalizing the decision;

c. The parties use streamlined procedures (accelerated filings, limited discovery) and receive few time extensions;

d. The board must decide the appeal within 120 days from the date of appellant's election, unless appellant withdraws its election; and

e. Neither party may appeal the decision and the decision has no precedential value.

## E. Remedies.

1. Boards of contract appeals may grant any relief that would be available to a litigant asserting a contract claim in the Court of Federal Claims. 41 U.S.C. § 607(d). Boards need not find a remedy granting clause to grant relief. *S&W Tire Serv., Inc.*, GSBCA No. 6376, 82-2 BCA ¶ 16,048 (boards may award anticipatory profits). Remedies may include reformation, rescission, and voiding the contract, as well as money damages and an equitable adjustment.

2. Boards of contract appeals do not grant specific performance or injunctive relief. *General Elec. Automated Sys. Div.*, ASBCA No. 36214, 89-1 BCA ¶ 21,195.

3. Boards may award attorney's fees pursuant to the Equal Access to Justice Act (EAJA) for disputes processed under the CDA. 5 U.S.C. § 504; *Cape Tool & Die, Inc.*, ASBCA No. 46433, 1994 WL 393329 (although $75 per hour used as guideline for attorney's fees rates in some cases, rates in excess of that amount found reasonable for Washington D.C. area attorneys with government contracting expertise—$225/hr. for partner; $80-$110/hr. for associate).

4. Declaratory judgments. Most boards of contract appeals hold that they may issue declaratory judgments. FAR 33.201; *Malone v. United States*, 849 F.2d 1441 (Fed. Cir. 1988).

5. Payment of judgments. 41 U.S.C. § 612.

a. Agencies initially pay judgments from the judgment fund established by 31 U.S.C. § 1304.

b. Agencies repay the judgment fund from current appropriations. 41 U.S.C. § 612(c).

c. Department of Defense normally pays settlements from original contract funds.

## F. Appealing an Adverse Decision.

1. Either party may file a motion for reconsideration within 30 days after receipt of an adverse decision. ASBCA Rule 29. Motions filed after 30 days are untimely. *Arctic Corner, Inc.*, ASBCA No. 33347, 92-2 BCA ¶ 24,874.

2. Absent unusual circumstances, appellant cannot use a motion for reconsideration to correct errors in its initial presentation to the board. *Metric Constructors, Inc.*, ASBCA No. 46279, 94-2 BCA ¶ 26,827.

3. Board decisions are final unless appealed to the Federal Circuit within 120 days after receipt. 41 U.S.C. § 607(g)(1). The agency must obtain prior approval of the Attorney General to appeal an adverse decision. 41 U.S.C. § 607(g)(l)(B).

4. The Federal Circuit must receive appeals within 120 days. Federal Circuit Rule 15(a)(2); *Placeway Constr. Corp. v. United States*, 713 F.2d 726 (Fed. Cir. 1983).

5. The CDA adopts the language of the Wunder-

lich Act, 41 U.S.C. §§ 321-322, regarding the scope of review. 41 U.S.C. § 609(b).

   a. Board decisions concerning *questions of law* are neither final nor conclusive.

   b. Board decisions concerning *questions of fact* are final and conclusive unless fraudulent, arbitrary, capricious, or so grossly erroneous as to imply bad faith, or if the decision is not supported by substantial evidence.

6. Contractors and the government appeal relatively few ASBCA decisions.

## VIII. APPEALS TO THE UNITED STATES COURT OF FEDERAL CLAIMS.

### A. Background.

1. The United States Claims Court was an Article I court created by the Federal Courts Improvement Act of 1982, Pub. L. No. 97-164, 96 Stat. 25. In 1992, Congress changed the name of the U.S. Claims Court to the U.S. Court of Federal Claims (COFC). *See* Federal Courts Administration Act of 1992, Title IX, Pub. L. No. 102-572, 106 Stat. 4516, (amending 28 U.S.C. § 1491(a)(1)). The court hears contract and noncontract claims.

2. The Court of Federal Claims has Tucker Act jurisdiction over *all* monetary claims against the United States founded upon the Constitution, any statute or agency regulation, or upon an express or implied contract for amounts in excess of $10,000. 28 U.S.C. §§ 1491(a)(1) and 1346(a)(2); *United States v. Hohri*, 482 U.S. 64, 66 n.1. (1987); *Gould, Inc.*, 29 Fed. Cl. 758 (1993).

3. Additionally, the CDA specifically vests the COFC with authority to consider appeals from contracting officers' final decisions concerning disputes under express contracts with the United States. 41 U.S.C. § 609.

4. The Federal Courts Administration Act of 1992 expanded the jurisdiction of the Court of Federal Claims to include both monetary and nonmonetary claims arising under the CDA. Hence, the Court of Federal Claims now has jurisdiction over disputes "concerning termination of a contract, rights in tangible or intangible property, compliance with cost accounting standards, and other non-monetary disputes" which are the subject of a contracting officer's final decision. 28 U.S.C. § 1491(A)(2).

5. The COFC receives approximately 300 CDA appeals annually.

### B. Perfecting an Appeal.

1. A contractor may bring an action directly on a claim in the Court of Federal Claims. 41 U.S.C. § 609(a)(1). In such an action, the court will proceed *de novo* in accordance with the rules of the court. 41 U.S.C. § 609(a)(3). For example, a contracting officer's findings of fact and conclusions of law which are adverse to a contractor or the government receive no presumption of validity. Hence, a contracting officer's final decision is treated as only one piece of documentary evidence to be weighed with all other evidence in the record. *Wilner v. United States*, 24 F.3d 1397 (Fed. Cir. 1994) (en banc) (over-ruling previous case law that a contracting officer's final decision constitutes a "strong presumption or an evidentiary admission" of the extent of government liability).

2. An appellant must file its complaint with the Clerk of the Court within twelve months from the date of the receipt by the contractor of the contracting officer's final decision to perfect an appeal. 41 U.S.C. § 609(a)(1) and (3); *White Buffalo Constr., Inc. v. United States*, 28 Fed. Cl. 145 (1992) (filing one day after expiration of twelve month period was untimely).

3. Exceptions. Rule of the United States Court of Federal Claims (RCFC) 3(b)(2)(C) permits the court to deem a late complaint to be timely if:

   a. The appellant sent the complaint by properly addressed registered or certified mail, with return receipt requested;

   b. The appellant deposited the complaint in the mail sufficiently in advance to provide for receipt by the clerk by the due date in the ordinary course of the mail; and

c. The appellant exercised no control over the mailing from after deposit in the mail until delivery. *See B.D. Click Co. v. United States*, 1 Cl. Ct. 239 (1982) (contractor failed to demonstrate the applicability of exceptions to timeliness rules).

4. The Court follows the "Fulford Doctrine" as developed by the ASBCA. *D. Moody & Co. v. United States*, 5 Cl. Ct. 70 (1984); *but see Z.A.N. Co. v. United States*, 6 Cl. Ct. 298 (1984).

### C. Procedure.

1. The Clerk of the Court forwards the complaint to the U. S. Attorney General. RCFC 4(a).

2. The government has 60 days to answer the complaint. RCFC 12(a). Attorneys assigned to the Commercial Branch, Civil Division, Department of Justice, Washington, D.C., generally represent the government. These attorneys coordinate with the agency for information and assistance. The government's answer must respond to the allegations in the complaint, raise affirmative defenses and counterclaims, if any, and make appropriate motions.

3. The U.S. Court of Federal Claims permits third-party practice. RCFC 14.

4. Discovery and pretrial procedures are regulated extensively by court rules, and the court may impose monetary sanctions for noncompliance with discovery orders. *M.A. Mortenson Co. v. United States*, 996 F.2d 1177 (Fed. Cir. 1993). *But see, Southwest Marine, Inc.*, ASBCA No. 39472, 94-1 BCA ¶ 26,487 (board rules do not permit imposition of monetary sanctions against the government).

5. Decisions may result from either Motion for Summary Judgment (RCFC 56), or by trial. Procedures generally mirror those of trials without juries before federal district courts. The judges make written findings of fact and state conclusions of law.

### D. Remedies Available.

1. Money damages are the principal remedy available and relief sought by appellants.

2. The court has no authority to issue injunctive relief or specific performance, except reformation in aid of monetary judgment or rescission instead of money damages. *John C. Grimberg Co. v. United States*, 702 F.2d 1362 (Fed. Cir. 1983); *Paragon Energy Corp. v. United States*, 645 F.2d 966 (Ct. Cl. 1981); *Rash v. United States*, 360 F.2d 940 (1966).

3. The COFC may award EAJA attorneys' fees. 28 U.S.C. § 2412.

4. Declaratory judgment. Since the COFC has jurisdiction over cases involving "a dispute concerning termination of a contract, rights in tangible or intangible property, compliance with cost accounting standards, and other nonmonetary disputes," the court effectively may provide declaratory relief for these nonmonetary CDA claims. 28 U.S.C. § 1491(a)(2); *Sharman Co., Inc. v. United States*, 2 F.3d 1564 (Fed. Cir. 1993).

5. The court has a voluntary alternative disputes resolution program. Federal Claims Court General Order No. 13.

### E. Appealing an Adverse Decision.

Parties may appeal adverse decisions to the Federal Circuit within 60 days following receipt of a decision. 28 U.S.C. § 2522; RCFC 72; FRAP 4(a).

## IX. APPEALS TO THE UNITED STATES COURT OF APPEALS FOR THE FEDERAL CIRCUIT (CAFC).

### A. National Jurisdiction.

The Federal Circuit has national jurisdiction. *Dewey Elec. Corp. v. United States*, 803 F.2d 650 (Fed. Cir. 1986); *Teller Envtl. Sys., Inc. v. United States*, 802 F.2d 1385 (Fed. Cir. 1986). It has exclusive jurisdiction of an appeal from a final decision of the U.S. Court of Federal Claims and of an agency board of contract appeals pursuant to section 8(g)(1) of the CDA. 28 U.S.C. § 1295(a)(3) and (10).

## B. Frivolous Appeals.

The court will assess damages against parties filing frivolous appeals. *Dungaree Realty, Inc. v. United States*, 30 F.3d 122 (Fed. Cir. 1994); *Wright v. United States*, 728 F.2d 1459 (Fed. Cir. 1984).

## C. Supreme Court Review.

The U.S. Supreme Court reviews decisions of the Federal Circuit by writ of certiorari. Rule 17.2, U.S. Supreme Court.

## X. CONTRACT ATTORNEY RESPONSIBILITIES IN THE DISPUTES PROCESS.

### A. Actions upon Receipt of a Claim.

1. Review the claim—check facts and theories.
2. Verify that the contractor has certified properly all claims exceeding $50,000.[11]
3. Advise the contracting officer to consider business judgment factors, as well as legal issues.

### B. Contracting Officer's Final Decision.

1. Prior to reviewing the final decision, determine whether the claim should be certified. If the claim exceeds $50,000,[12] ensure the claim is properly certified by a person authorized to bind the contractor.
2. Ensure that a pre-existing dispute over payment is the subject of the final decision as opposed to a contractor's invoice or preliminary request for an adjustment.
3. Review the final decision.
4. Check the validity of the reasoning.
5. Ensure that the decision letter properly sets forth the contractor's appellate rights.

### C. Appeal File.

1. If possible, coordinate with the trial counsel assigned to the appeal as to what documents to include/omit from the Rule 4 file.
2. Oversee preparation of the Rule 4 file.

3. Put privileged documents in a separate litigation file for transmission to the trial attorney.

### D. Discovery.

1. Assist the trial attorney in formulating a discovery plan.
2. Identify knowledgeable persons, to include both government and contractor personnel. Conduct preliminary interviews of government witnesses.
3. Draft interrogatories, discovery requests, and requests for admissions; and prepare responses to the appellant's corresponding submissions to the government.
4. Assist the trial counsel in the conduct of depositions, to include the identification of key contractor personnel and pertinent documents related to the dispute. Coordinate with trial counsel regarding the feasibility of field counsel conducting depositions.

### E. Hearings.

1. Coordinate with the trial attorney and consider entering an appearance to participate in the case-in-chief.
2. To the extent practicable, assist in witness and evidence preparation.
3. Assist in the preparation and/or review of post-hearing briefs.

### F. Client Expectations.

Assist the trial attorney in providing the contracting officer and relevant persons regular status updates regarding the appeal.

### G. Settlement.

Work with the contracting officer and the trial attorney regarding the costs and benefits of litigating the claim. Whatever the circumstances, the contract attorney should strive for a position that reflects sound business judgment and protects the interests of the government.

## Endnotes

1. The FASA increases the CDA certification requirement threshold to $100,000. FASA § 2351(b) (amending 40 U.S.C. § 605).

2. See footnote 1.

3. See footnote 1.

4. See footnote 1.

5. The FASA increases this CDA decisional threshold to $100,000. FASA § 2351(b) (amending 40 U.S.C. § 605).

6. See footnote 5.

7. The FASA has raised the CDA the accelerated procedures threshold to $100,000 and small claims jurisdiction to $50,000. FASA § 2351(c)&(d) (amending 40 U.S.C. §§ 607(f) and 608(a)).

8. The FASA will impose a six-year statue of limitation for the filing of CDA claims. This six-year period begins with the "accrual of the claim." This provision does not apply to claims involving fraud. FASA § 2351(a) (amending 40 U.S.C. § 605).

9. The FASA has increased the accelerated appeals threshold to $100,000. FASA § 2351(c) (amending 41 U.S.C. § 607(f)).

10. The FASA has increased the small claims threshold to $50,000. FASA § 2351(d) (amending 41 U.S.C. § 608(a)).

11. See footnote 1.

12. See footnote 1.

# DISPUTES CLAUSES

## PART 52—SOLICITATION PROVISIONS AND CONTRACT CLAUSES 52.233-1

**52.233-1 Disputes.**

As prescribed in 33.215, insert the following clause:

DISPUTES (MAR 1994)

(a) This contract is subject to the Contract Disputes Act of 1978, as amended (41 U.S.C. 601-613).

(b) Except as provided in the Act, all disputes arising under or relating to this contract shall be resolved under this clause.

(c) "Claim," as used in this clause, means a written demand or written assertion by one of the contracting parties seeking, as a matter of right, the payment of money in a sum certain, the adjustment or interpretation of contract terms, or other relief arising under or relating to this contract. A claim arising under a contract, unlike a claim relating to that contract, is a claim that can be resolved under a contract clause that provides for the relief sought by the claimant. However, a written demand or written assertion by the Contractor seeking the payment of money exceeding $50,000 is not a claim under the Act until certified as required by subparagraph (d)(2) below. A voucher, invoice, or other routine request for payment that is not in dispute when submitted is not a claim under the Act. The submission may be converted to a claim under the Act by complying with the submission and certification requirements of this clause, if it is disputed either as to liability or amount or is not acted upon in a reasonable time.

(d) (1) A claim by the Contractor shall be made in writing and submitted to the Contracting Officer for a written decision. A claim by the Government against the Contractor shall be subject to a written decision by the Contracting Officer.

(2) (i) Contractors shall provide the certification specified in subparagraph (d)(2)(iii) of this clause when submitting any claim—

(A) Exceeding $50,000; or

(B) Regardless of the amount claimed, when using—

(1) Arbitration conducted pursuant to 5 U.S.C. 575-580; or

(2) Any other alternative means of dispute resolution (ADR) technique that the agency elects to handle in accordance with the Administrative Dispute Resolution Act (ADRA).

(ii) The certification requirement does not apply to issues in controversy that have not been submitted as all or part of a claim.

(iii) The certification shall state as follows: "I certify that the claim is made in good faith; that the supporting data are accurate and complete to the best of my knowledge and belief; that the amount requested accurately reflects the contract adjustment for which the Contractor believes the Government is liable; and that I am duly authorized to certify the claim on behalf of the Contractor."

(3) The certification may be executed by any person duly authorized to bind the Contractor with respect to the claim.

(e) For Contractor claims of $50,000 or less, the Contracting Officer must, if requested in writing by the Contractor, render a decision within 60 days of the request. For Contractor-certified claims over $50,000, the Contracting Officer must, within 60 days, decide the claim or notify the Contractor of the date by which the decision will be made.

(f) The Contracting Officer's decision shall be final unless the Contractor appeals or files a suit as provided in the Act.

(g) At the time a claim by the Contractor is submitted to the Contracting Officer or a claim by the Government is presented to the Contractor, the parties, by mutual consent, may agree to use ADR. When using arbitration conducted pursuant to 5 U.S.C. 575-580, or when using any other ADR technique that the agency elects to handle in accordance with the ADRA, any claim, regardless of amount, shall be accompanied by the certification described in subparagraph (d)(2)(iii) of this clause, and executed in accordance with subparagraph (d)(3) of this clause.

(h) The Government shall pay interest on the amount found due and unpaid from (1) the date that the Contracting Officer receives the claim (certified, if required); or (2) the date that payment otherwise would be due, if that date is later, until the date of payment. With regard to claims having defective certifications, as defined in FAR 33.201, interest shall be paid from the date that the Contracting Officer initially receives the claim. Simple interest on claims shall be paid at the rate, fixed by the Secretary of the Treasury as provided in the Act, which is applicable to the period during which the Contracting Officer receives the claim and then at the rate applicable for each 6-month period as fixed by the Treasury Secretary during the pendency of the claim.

(i) The Contractor shall proceed diligently with performance of this contract, pending final resolution of any request for relief, claim, appeal, or action arising under the contract, and comply with any decision of the Contracting Officer.

(End of clause)

*Alternate I* (DEC 1991). If it is determined under agency procedures, that continued performance is necessary pending resolution of any claim arising under or relating to the contract, substitute the following paragraph (i) for the paragraph (i) of the basic clause:

(i) The Contractor shall proceed diligently with performance of this contract, pending final resolution of any request for relief, claim, appeal, or action arising under or relating to the contract, and comply with any decision of the Contracting Officer.
(AV 7-103.12(h) 1980 JUN)

## 52.233-2 Service of Protest.

As prescribed in 33.106, insert the following provision:

SERVICE OF PROTEST (NOV 1988)

(a) Protests, as defined in section 33.101 of the Federal Acquisition Regulation, that are filed directly with an agency, and copies of any protests that are filed with the General Accounting Office (GAO) or the General Services Administration Board of Contract Appeals (GSBCA), shall be served on the Contracting Officer (addressed as follows) by obtaining written and dated acknowledgment of receipt from _____ *[Contracting Officer designate the official or location where a protest may be served on the Contracting Officer.]*

(b) The copy of any protest shall be received in the office designated above on the same day a protest is filed with the GSBCA or within one day of filing a protest with the GAO.

(End of provision)

## 52.233-3 Protest after Award.

As prescribed in 33.106(b), insert the following clause:

PROTEST AFTER AWARD (AUG 1989)

(a) Upon receipt of a notice of protest (as defined in 33.101 of the FAR) the Contracting Officer may, by written order to the Contractor, direct the Contractor to stop performance of the work called for by this contract. The order shall be specifically identified as a stop-work order issued under this clause. Upon receipt of the order, the Contractor shall immediately comply with its terms and take all reasonable steps to minimize the incurrence of costs allocable to the work covered by the order during the period of work stoppage. Upon receipt of the final decision in the protest, the Contracting Officer shall either—

(1) Cancel the stop-work order; or

(2) Terminate the work covered by the order as provided in the Default, or the Termination for Convenience of the Government, clause of this contract.

(b) If a stop-work order issued under this clause is canceled either before or after a final decision in the protest, the Contractor shall resume work. The Contracting Officer shall make an equitable adjustment in the delivery schedule or contract price, or both, and the contract shall be modified, in writing, accordingly, if—

(1) The stop-work order results in an increase in the time required for, or in the Contractor's cost properly allocable to, the performance of any part of this contract; and

(2) The Contractor asserts its right to an adjustment within 30 days after the end of the period of work stoppage; *provided,* that if the Contracting Officer decides the facts justify the action, the Contracting Officer may receive and act upon a proposal at any time before final payment under this contract.

(c) If a stop-work order is not canceled and the work covered by the order is terminated for the convenience of the Government, the Contracting Officer shall allow reasonable costs resulting from the stop-work order in arriving at the termination settlement.

(d) If a stop-work order is not canceled and the work covered by the order is terminated for default, the Contracting Officer shall allow, by equitable adjustment or otherwise, reasonable costs resulting from the stop-work order.

(e) The Government's rights to terminate this contract at any time are not affected by action taken under this clause.

(End of clause)

*Alternate I* (JUN 1985). As prescribed in 33.106(b), substitute in paragraph (a)(2) the words "the Termination clause of this contract" for the words "the Default, or the Termination for Convenience of the Government clause of this contract." In paragraph (b) substitute the words "an equitable adjustment in the delivery schedule, the estimated cost, the fee, or a combination thereof, and in any other terms of the contract that may be affected" for the words "an equitable adjustment in the delivery schedule or contract price, or both."

## 52.234—52.235 Reserved.

## 52.236-1 Performance of Work by the Contractor.

As prescribed in 36.501(b), insert the following clause in solicitations and contracts when a fixed-price construction contract is contemplated and the contract amount is expected to exceed $1,000,000. The Contracting Officer may insert the clause in solicitations and contracts when a fixed-price construction contract is contemplated and the contract amount is expected to be $1,000,000 or less. Complete the clause by inserting the appropriate percentage consistent with the complexity and magnitude of the work and customary or necessary specialty subcontracting (see 36.501(a)).

PERFORMANCE OF WORK BY THE CONTRACTOR
(APR 1984)

The Contractor shall perform on the site, and with its own organization, work equivalent to at least _____ [*insert the appropriate number in words followed by numerals in parentheses*] percent of the total amount of work to be performed under the contract. This percentage may be reduced by a supplemental agreement to this contract if, during performing the work, the Contractor requests a reduction and the Contracting Officer determines that the reduction would be to the advantage of the Government.

(End of clause)
(R 7-603.15 1965 JAN)
(R 1-18.104)

## CHAPTER TWENTY-ONE

# Nonappropriated Fund Contracting

## I. INTRODUCTION.

Upon completing this instruction, the student will understand:

A. The persons involved in nonappropriated fund (NAF) contracting,

B. The basic procedures and procurement methods used in NAF contracting, and

C. The rules governing special types of NAF contracting, including the Commercial Sponsorship Program.

## II. REFERENCES.

A. 10 U.S.C. § 3013(b)(9).

B. DOD Instr. No. 4105.67, Nonappropriated Fund (NAF) Procurement Policy (2 Oct. 1981) [hereinafter, DOD Instr. 4105.67].

C. Army Fed. Acquisition Reg. Supp. (AFARS) 1.9001, Acquisitions Using Nonappropriated Funds (30 Nov. 1994).

D. Army Regulations. The principal Army NAF regulations are compiled in a single volume, entitled "Morale, Welfare, and Recreation Update," dated 10 October 1990. Additionally, ARs 420-10, 415-15, and 415-35, govern construction contracting.

## III. DEFINITIONS AND STATUTORY CONTROLS.

### A. Nonappropriated Fund Instrumentality (NAFI).

DOD Instr. No. 4105.67, encl. 2, para. I; AR 215-1, Consolidated Glossary, sec. II, Terms. A NAFI is an integral DOD organizational entity that performs a government function. It acts in its own name to provide or assist DOD components in providing morale, welfare, and recreational programs for military personnel and authorized civilians . . . . As a fiscal entity, it maintains custody of, and control over, its nonappropriated funds . . . . It is not incorporated under the law of any state or the District of Columbia, and it enjoys the legal status of an instrumentality of the United States.

### B. Nonappropriated Funds (NAFs).

AR 215-1, Consolidated Glossary, sec. II, Terms. Cash and other assets received by NAFIs from sources other than monies appropriated by the Congress of the United States. NAFs are government funds used for the collective benefit of those who generate them: military personnel, their dependents, and authorized civilians. These funds are separate and apart from funds that are recorded in the books of the Treasurer of the United States.

### C. Statutory Controls on Funds.

Congress has directed DOD to issue regulations governing the management and use of NAFs, and has made DOD civilians and military personnel subject to penalties for their misuse. 10 U.S.C. § 2783. *See* Appendix 22-A. Congress has imposed other controls, as well, on the use of nonappropriated funds. For example:

1. NAFIs in the United States may purchase beer and wine only in the state where the NAFI is located. 10 U.S.C. § 2488. *See* AR 215-2, para. 4-13b; AR 215-4, para. 5-57.

2. NAFIs located on military installations outside the United States must distribute and price wines produced in the United States equitably when compared with wines produced by the host nation. 10 U.S.C. § 2489. *Cf.* AR 215-2, para. 4-13a (MACOMs determine policy governing the source of alcoholic beverages).

## IV. AUTHORITY TO CONTRACT.

### A. General.

Generally, only warranted contracting officers have the authority to enter into, administer, and terminate NAF contracts. The authority of a contracting officer is limited by his warrant.

1. Emergency purchase procedure exception. When unforeseeable events occur that are likely to cause a loss of NAFI property or assets if immediate action is not taken, specific unwarranted individuals may incur obligations on behalf of a NAFI. AR 215-4, para. 2-16.

2. The chief of the NAF contracting office may appoint individuals to make purchases totalling $2,500 or less after normal duty hours. These buyers must obtain funding before making a purchase. AR 215-4, paras. 2-16a(2)(b) and 3-5c.

### B. Contracting Officers.

Three types of contracting officers support Army NAFIs. AR 215-4, paras. 1-6 through 1-9; AR 215-4, paras. 3-11 and 3-12; AFARS 1.9001. These include:

1. Installation NAF contracting officer.
   a. An installation commander or his designee may appoint, in writing, a NAF contracting officer, who must meet mandatory training requirements and act within the limitations set forth in the officer's warrant.
   b. There are regulatory dollar limitations on a NAF contracting officer's authority to contract. AR 215-4, para. 1-6h and app. B.
      (1) For supplies, services, entertainment, or construction, the NAF contracting officer may obligate up to $25,000.

      (2) For resale merchandise, the NAF contracting officer may obligate up to $50,000. *See* AR 215-4, para. 5-48.
      (3) The NAF contracting officer's authority to issue delivery orders against competitively awarded contracts is unlimited, except as set forth in the basic contract or as limited by the installation commander. *See* AR 215-4, para. 4-17.
   c. The installation NAF contracting officer may use small purchase procedures similar to those in FAR Part 13. AR 215-4, ch. 4.

2. Appropriated fund (APF) contracting officer.
   a. An APF contracting officer may manage NAF acquisitions for supplies and services if the contract value is expected to exceed the warrant of the NAF contracting officer. AR 215-4, paras. 1-8d and 3-11.
   b. An APF contracting officer or a NAF contracting officer assigned to the United States Army Community and Family Support Center (USACFSC) must solicit, award, and administer all NAFI construction contracts and all architect-engineer contracts expected to exceed $25,000. AR 215-4, paras. 5-14 and 5-15.
   c. An APF contracting officer must adhere to NAF policies and procedures when procuring supplies or services on behalf of an Army NAFI. AR 215-4, para. 3-11; AFARS 1.9001(a)(2).

3. NAF contracting officer, USACFSC.
   a. Contracting officers assigned to the USACFSC contracting office may solicit, award, and administer supply and service contracts that exceed the limitations of an installation NAF contracting officer. AR 215-4, para. 3-12.
   b. Installations purchasing ADPE and information management services and items above the warrant level of the installation NAF contracting officer shall forward purchase requests through the MACOM to the USACFSC Contracting Division for action. AR 215-4, para. 1-13.1.a.

## V. NONAPPROPRIATED FUND ACQUISITIONS: APPROVAL AND COORDINATION.

AR 215-4, para. 1-12 and app. B.

### A. Army NAF Purchase Request (DA Form 4065-R).

The requesting activity begins the NAF acquisition process by submitting to the contracting officer a DA Form 4065-R, which shows that funds are available and that the activity has obtained required approvals.

### B. Approval Authorities.

1. The Assistant Director of Community and Family Activities (ADCFA) is the approval authority for:
   a. Purchases of supplies, services, or entertainment costing $25,000 or less.
   b. Purchases of resale merchandise, without limitation as to cost.
2. The installation commander or the commander's designee must approve purchase requests that exceed $25,000.

### C. Additional Requirements for Construction Projects.

AR 215-1, ch. 6.
1. NAFIs must coordinate with the servicing Director of Engineering and Housing (DEH) concerning all operation, maintenance, repair, and construction of real property facilities used to support morale, welfare, and recreation (MWR) activities. AR 215-1, para. 6-2a.
2. Construction of real property facilities must conform to Army Corps of Engineers (USACE) Architectural and Engineering Instructions. AR 215-1, para. 6-2b. If available, USACE standard designs will be used for all MWR facility requirements. AR 215-1, para. 6-2n.
3. Funding approval limitations for MWR construction projects are set forth in AR 215-1, para. 6-2d through h; para. 6-3; and in the corresponding Army regulations governing construction. For projects financed wholly by NAFs, see ARs 215-1 and 415-19.
4. There are limitations on combining APFs and NAFs or private funds, or both, in a single construction project. Before combining funds, the contracting officer must obtain prior written approval, as follows:
   a. For construction projects costing $200,000 or less ($500,000 or less if only NAFs are used) - MACOM commander.
   b. For construction projects costing between $200,000 and $1,000,000 - Assistant Chief of Staff for Installation Management (DAIM-FD).
   c. For construction projects costing more than $1,000,000 - Secretary of the Army.
5. Installations may not use facilities that have been designed and constructed or converted by major renovation for MWR activities for other purposes without specific DA approval. This restriction applies whether funded from APFs or NAFs. AR 215-1, para. 6-2o.

## VI. COMPETITION AND SOURCES OF SUPPLIES AND SERVICES.

### A. Competition.

The competition requirements of the Armed Services Procurement Act (ASPA) do not apply to NAFIs unless appropriated funds are obligated. 10 U.S.C. § 2303; *Gino Morena Enter.*, B-224235, Feb. 5, 1987, 66 Comp. Gen. 231, 87-1 CPD ¶ 121.
1. Although the Competition in Contracting Act (CICA) is inapplicable to NAFI acquisitions involving only NAFs, AR 215-4 requires competition for some procurement actions.
   a. For purchases of $2,500 or less, NAFIs need not seek competition provided the price obtained is fair and reasonable and purchases are distributed equitably among qualified suppliers.
   b. For purchases costing more than $2,500, NAFIs must compete the acquisitions, except those for commercial entertainment, unless a sole source acquisition is justified. AR 215-4, para. 1-11b.
   c. Competition exists if the activity solicits at

least three responsible offerors; the offerors submit offers independently; and the activity receives at least two responsive offers.

   d. NAFIs may, but need not, synopsize acquisitions in the *Commerce Business Daily* (CBD). AR 215-4, para. 4-6.

2. Sole source acquisitions. AR 215-4, para. 3-10, indicates when a sole source acquisition is appropriate. A contracting officer must approve all sole source acquisitions except those due to an unusual and compelling urgency, which the installation commander or designee must approve.

**B. Approved Sources.**

1. Government sources of supply for NAFI requirements include the General Services Administration (GSA), Defense Supply Depots, and commissaries. AR 215-4, para. 4-1.

2. Other NAF sources include, but are not limited to, the Army and Air Force Exchange Service (AAFES), Navy Resale System Office, and Marine Corps Exchange System. AR 215-4, para. 4-1.

3. FAR Subparts 8.6 and 8.7, which require activities to purchase certain supplies from the Federal Prison Industries, Inc., and from the blind and severely handicapped, apply to NAF acquisitions. AR 215-4, para. 4-2.

4. NAFIs may solicit commercial vendors. Activities may use solicitation mailing lists developed by the NAF contracting office or obtained from the APF contracting office. AR 215-4, para. 4-4.

**C. Prohibited Sources.**

1. NAFIs may not contract with government or NAFI employees unless they cannot meet their needs otherwise or unless there is some other compelling reason for so doing. AR 215-4, para. 4-3. The installation commander or designee must approve any exception.

2. Generally, NAFIs may not solicit or consent to subcontracts with firms or individuals that have been suspended or disbarred, or proposed for debarment. AR 215-4, para. 4-5.

3. Generally, APF activities may not contract with NAFIs. *See Departments of the Army and Air Force, Army and Air Force Exchange Serv.*, B-235742, Apr. 24, 1990, 90-1 CPD ¶ 410. However, 10 U.S.C. § 2424 allows a limited exception for in-stock purchases from overseas exchanges.

## VII. ACQUISITION METHODS.

**A. DOD Policy.**

DOD Instr. 4105.67, para. D.1, provides that NAFs shall conduct procurements:

1. Primarily through competitive negotiation;

2. By trained procurement personnel;

3. In a fair, equitable, and impartial manner; and

4. To the advantage of the applicable NAFI.

**B. Small Purchases.**

AR 215-4, ch. 4, sec. II.

1. When making small purchases, the NAF contracting officer may solicit price quotations orally, but AR 215-4 requires written solicitations for construction contracts exceeding $2,000, and service contracts exceeding $2,500. AR 215-4, paras. 4-9 and 4-10.

2. The contracting officer may issue purchase orders for purchases of $10,000 or less, for the future delivery of supplies, or for the future performance of nonpersonal services. AR 215-4, para. 4-14. The purchase order obligates the NAFI to pay the amount stated on the order if the contractor performs. AR 215-4, para. 4-15.

3. Blanket Purchase Agreements (BPAs) provide a simplified method of making small purchases. By establishing a BPA with a vendor, the NAFI eliminates the need for repetitive purchase orders. AR 215-4, paras. 4-12 and 4-13.

4. Contracting officers may issue delivery orders against an *existing contract* for the future delivery of supplies or nonpersonal services. The NAFI must pay the amount on the order if the contractor performs. AR 215-4, para. 4-17.

## C. Negotiated Acquisitions.

AR 215-4, ch. 4, sec. III.

1. Negotiation is the preferred method of contracting for supplies and services that NAFIs cannot procure using small purchase procedures.
2. Negotiation procedures.
   a. Request for proposals (RFP). AR 215-4, paras. 4-22 through 4-30.
   b. Late proposals and late modifications. AR 215-4, para. 4-31.
   c. Evaluation of offers. AR 215-4, paras. 4-33 through 4-37.
   d. Contract award. AR 215-4, paras. 4-38 and 4-39.
   e. Mistakes. AR 215-4, para. 4-41.
   f. Protests. AR 215-4, para. 4-40. *See infra,* sec. IX.

## D. Sealed Bidding.

AR 215-4, ch. 4, sec. IV.

1. Sealed bidding is not preferred for NAFI contracting. It may be used only if:
   a. Price is the only evaluation factor;
   b. Current and accurate purchase descriptions or specifications have been developed;
   c. Time permits the solicitation, submission, and evaluation of bids;
   d. Discussions with bidders are unnecessary; and
   e. There is a reasonable expectation of receiving more than one sealed bid. *See* AR 215-4, para. 4-43.
2. Sealed bidding procedures. AR 215-4, paras. 4-44 through 4-47.
   a. Invitations for bids (IFB). AR 215-4, para. 4-44.
   b. Late bids, late bid modifications, and late bid withdrawals. AR 215-4, para. 4-45.7.
   c. Amendment and cancellation of bids. AR 215-4, paras. 4-45.5 and 4-45.6.
   d. Mistakes. AR 215-4, paras. 4-46.1 and 4-46.2.
   e. Contract award. AR 215-4, para. 4-47.
   f. Protests. AR 215-4, para. 4-48. *See infra,* sec. IX.

## VIII. CONTRACT TYPES.

AR 215-4, ch. 5.

### A. Fixed-Price or Cost-Reimbursement?

AR 215-4, ch. 5, sec. I.

1. If possible, NAFI contracts will be *fixed-price.* AR 215-4, para. 5-1b.
2. A NAF contracting officer may use other than a fixed-price contract only if its use is justified in writing, if it is reviewed for legal sufficiency (regardless of dollar value), and if it is approved by the MACOM and HQ, USACFSC. AR 215-4, para. 5-1b.

### B. Service Contracts.

AR 215-4, ch. 5, sec. II.

1. The contracting officer must ensure that the proposed contract is for *nonpersonal* services.
2. NAFIs use a service contract format if an acquisition involves a lease, and not the purchase, of equipment. AR 215-4, para. 5-4b; *WestByrd, Inc.,* B-237515, Feb. 7, 1990, 69 Comp. Gen. 194, 90-1 CPD ¶ 159 (Walsh-Healey inapplicable to lease of personal property).
3. Labor standards requirements. The Service Contract Act (SCA) applies to all service contracts expected to exceed $2,500. AR 215-4, para. 5-9.
4. Socioeconomic policies. The Small Business Act does not apply to NAF service contracts. AR 215-4, para. 1-16.

### C. Construction and Architect-Engineer (A-E) Contracts.

AR 215-4, ch. 5, sec. III.

1. The process for awarding NAF construction projects and A-E service contracts is similar to that for the same type of APF contracts.
2. Performance and payment bonds are required for construction projects that exceed $25,000. AR 215-4, para. 5-14l.
3. Labor standards. The Davis-Bacon and Copeland Acts apply to construction contracts that exceed $2,000. AR 215-4, paras. 1-19 and 1-20. The Contract Work Hours and

Safety Standards Act also applies. *See* DA Form 4075-R, dated August 1990.

4. Socioeconomic policies.
   a. The Small Business Act does not apply.
   b. The Buy American Act applies. AR 215-4, para. 1-17.

## D. Supply and Equipment Contracts.

AR 215-4, ch. 5, sec. VIII.

1. If an acquisition involves both supplies and services, the contracting officer may require contractors to submit separate line item offers or quotes for each. AR 215-4, para. 5-59b.
2. NAFIs may order from federal supply schedules. AR 215-4, para. 5-72a.
3. Socioeconomic policies.
   a. The Small Business Act does not apply.
   b. The Buy American and Trade Agreement Acts, and the Balance of Payments Program apply to NAFI supply acquisitions. AR 215-4, paras. 1-17, 1-21, and 1-22.

## E. Concession Contracts.

AR 215-4, ch. 5, sec. IV.

1. A concession contract is essentially a license or permit for an activity/business to sell goods and services to authorized patrons.
2. Before a concession contract is awarded, the installation commander must determine that the need cannot be met through a NAF direct-hire. AR 215-4, para. 5-19.
3. The NAFI receives a flat fee or percentage of gross sales from the concessionaire. AR 215-4, para. 5-17.
4. If a service is involved, the contract must contain a SCA wage rate determination. AR 215-4, para. 5-22.

## F. Entertainment Contracts.

AR 215-4, ch. 5, sec. V.

1. Generally, AR 215-4 does not require competition for these contracts, but does prohibit exclusive use of one entertainer or agent. AR 215-4, para. 5-31.
2. The SCA may apply if the entertainment requires the use of stage hands or other technicians.

3. The contract must contain a cancellation and liquidated damages clause. AR 215-4, para. 5-32.

## G. Contracts with Amusement Companies and Traveling Shows.

AR 215-4, ch. 5, sec. VI.

1. The installation commander or designee must approve these activities.
2. Competition is required unless a nationally known company is involved.
3. Responsibility determinations are particularly important in these acquisitions. Contractors must provide references.

## H. Resale—Consumables and Subsistence Contracts.

AR 215-4, ch. 5, sec. VII. The ADCFA has unlimited dollar approval authority for resale items.

1. Alcoholic beverages are considered subsistence items. Only a contracting officer may purchase them.
2. Purchases of wine and malt beverages must be from in-state sources. There are special rules for the State of Washington. All alcoholic beverage purchases (including hard liquor) in Alaska and Hawaii must be from in-state sources.

## I. Commercial Sponsorship.

1. Definition. "Commercial sponsorship is the act of providing assistance, funding, goods, equipment (including fixed assets), or services to an MWR program or event by . . . [a sponsor] . . . for a specific (limited) period of time in return for public recognition or advertising promotions." Memorandum, Deputy Assistant Secretary of Defense (Personnel Support, Families & Education), Office of the Assistant Secretary of Defense, subject: Morale, Welfare, and Recreation (MWR) Commercial Sponsorship (May 19, 1992). *See* Appendix 22-B.
2. Procedures. The DOD components using commercial sponsorship procedures must ensure that:
   a. Obligations and entitlements of the spon-

sor and the MWR program are set forth in a written agreement that is not longer than one year.

b. The component disclaims any endorsement of any commercial supplier, product, or service in any public recognition or advertising media.

c. The commercial sponsor certifies in writing that it shall not charge its costs of the sponsorship to any part of the federal government.

d. Officials responsible for procurement or contracting are not directly or indirectly involved with the solicitation of commercial vendors, except for those officials whose function is to administer NAF contracts.

3. Commercial sponsorship agreements. See Appendix 22-C.

## IX. LITIGATION INVOLVING NONAPPROPRIATED FUND CONTRACTS.

### A. Protests.

AR 215-4, para. 4-40.

1. GAO jurisdiction.

a. NAFI procurement. The GAO has no jurisdiction over NAF procurements by a NAFI. 31 U.S.C. §§ 3551-3553; GAO Bid Protest Rules, 4 C.F.R. § 21.3(m)(8); *DSV, GmbH*, B-253724, Jun. 16, 1993, 93-1 CPD ¶ 468. Protests are resolved in accordance with AR 215-4, para. 4-40.

b. Procurement conducted by an APF contracting officer. The GAO has jurisdiction over procurements conducted "by or for a federal agency," regardless of the source of funds involved. *Barbarosa Reiseservice GmbH*, B-225641, May 20, 1987, 87-1 CPD ¶ 529. *See also* AR 215-4, para. 4-40a(2).

c. The GAO will consider a protest involving a NAFI when the protester alleges that the agency is using the NAFI to avoid competition requirements. *Premier Vending*, B-256560, July 5, 1994, 94-2 CPD ¶ 8.

2. GSBCA jurisdiction (only automatic data processing equipment acquisitions are subject to the Brooks Automatic Data Processing (ADP) Act). The GSBCA has decided that it has no jurisdiction over protests of procurements conducted by DOD NAFIs, because NAFIs are not federal agencies subject to the Brooks ADP Act. Consulting Assocs. Inc. v. Dep't of the Air Force, GSBCA No. 13194-P, 95-1 BCA ¶ 27,602.

### B. Disputes.

AR 215-4, ch. 7, sec. II.

1. The requirement for a final decision.

a. If the contracting officer fails to resolve a dispute arising under or relating to the contract with the contractor, he issues a final decision in accordance with the Disputes clause, if any, contained in the NAF contract. AR 215-4, paras. 7-11 and 7-12.

b. The contracting officer's final decision lacks finality if it advises the contractor incorrectly of its appeal rights under the contract. *Wolverine Supply, Inc.*, ASBCA No. 39250, 90-2 BCA ¶ 22,706.

2. No judicial forum has jurisdiction over NAFI contract disputes, except those disputes arising under contracts involving the exchange services, as indicated below.

a. As instrumentalities of the United States, NAFIs are immune from suit. Congress has not waived immunity for NAFIs in general under the Tucker Act [28 U.S.C. § 1346(a)(2)], the Contract Disputes Act [41 U.S.C. § 602(a)], or the Administrative Procedures Act. *Borden v. United States*, 116 F. Supp. 873 (E.D.N.Y. 1953); *Swiff-Train Co. v. United States*, 443 F.2d 1140 (5th Cir. 1971); *Commercial Offset Printers, Inc.*, ASBCA No. 25302, 81-1 BCA ¶ 14,900.

b. Exception. Express or implied contracts entered into by DOD, Coast Guard, and NASA exchange services, although NAFIs, are contracts of the United States for purposes of determining jurisdiction under the Tucker Act and under the Contract Disputes Act of 1978.

c. The Federal Circuit has held that the Court of Federal Claims (formerly "Claims Court") would have jurisdiction over a contract dispute between the Navy Resale and Services Support Office (NAVRESSO), although it is a NAFI, and that the Tucker Act does not waive explicitly sovereign immunity for that NAFI. *McDonald's Corp. v. United States*, 926 F.2d 1126 (Fed. Cir. 1991).

3. The ASBCA has jurisdiction over NAF contract disputes if:

a. The contract incorporates a disputes clause that grants such jurisdiction. *COVCO Hawaii Corp.*, ASBCA No. 26901, 83-2 BCA ¶ 16,554; or

b. The contract contains no disputes clause, but DOD regulations require incorporation of a jurisdiction-granting clause in the NAF contract. *Recreational Enter.*, ASBCA No. 32176, 87-1 BCA ¶ 19,675.

# TITLE 10, SECTION 2783

## Nonappropriated Fund Instrumentalities:
## Financial Management and Use of Nonappropriated Funds

(a) REGULATION OF MANAGEMENT AND USE OF NONAPPROPRIATED FUNDS.—The Secretary of Defense shall prescribe regulations governing —

(1) the purposes for which nonappropriated funds of a nonappropriated fund instrumentality of the United States within the Department of Defense may be expended; and

(2) the financial management of such funds to prevent waste, loss, or unauthorized use.

(b) PENALTIES FOR VIOLATIONS. —

(1) A civilian employee of the Department of Defense who is paid from nonappropriated funds and who commits a substantial violation of the regulations prescribed under subsection (a) shall be subject to the same penalties as are provided by law for misuse of appropriations by a civilian employee of the Department of Defense paid from appropriated funds. The Secretary of Defense shall prescribe regulations to carry out this paragraph.

(2) The Secretary shall provide in regulations that a violation of the regulations prescribed under subsection (a) by a person subject to chapter 47 of title 10, United States Code (the Uniform Code of Military Justice), is punishable as a violation of section 892 of such title (article 92) of the Uniform Code of Military Justice).

(c) NOTIFICATION OF VIOLATIONS. —

(1) A civilian employee of the Department of Defense (whether paid from nonappropriated funds or from appropriated funds), and a member of the Armed Forces , whose duties include the obligation of nonappropriated funds, shall notify the Secretary of Defense of information which the person reasonably believes evidences —

(A) a violation by another person of any law, rule, or regulation regarding the management of such funds; or

(B) other mismanagement or gross waste of such funds.

(2) The Secretary of Defense shall designate civilian employees to receive a notification described in paragraph (1) and ensure the prompt investigation of the validity of information provided in the notification.

(3) The Secretary shall prescribe regulations to protect the confidentiality of a person making a notification under paragraph (1).

# DOD COMMERCIAL SPONSORSHIP POLICY AND REPORTING PROCEDURES

**DEPARTMENT OF THE ARMY**
U.S. ARMY COMMUNITY AND FAMILY SUPPORT CENTER
ALEXANDRIA, VA 22331-05

S: 15 June 1992

CFSC-AE-MA

MEMORANDUM FOR SEE DISTRIBUTION

SUBJECT: DoD Commercial Sponsorship Policy and Reporting Procedures

1. Policy memorandum from the Deputy Assistant Secretary of Defense (Personnel Support, Families & Education) provides further guidance on MWR commercial sponsorship (Enclosure 1). Army implementation of the revised policy is being developed.

2. The policy memorandum requires certain commercial sponsorship information for CY 91. Request this information be submitted in the format provided at Enclosure 2 to the following address by 19 June 1992:

> Commander
> U.S. Army Community and Family Support Center
> ATTN: CFSC-AE-MA
> 2461 Eisenhower Avenue, Room 1434
> Alexandria, VA 22331-0507
> (FAX 703-325-4686/DSN 221-4686)

3. The commercial sponsorship program has been a tremendous success. It has been used to offset the cost of existing events, to support new events, and to enhance the quality of life for soldiers and family members. The new guidance will open the door to greater success in the commercial sponsorship arena.

4. The POC for this action is Robin Donohoe, DSN 221-2473/Commercial 703-325-2473.

FOR THE COMMANDER:

2 Encls

AGGIE BYERS
Acting Director
Plans and Policy

DISTRIBUTION:
COMMANDER IN CHIEF
U. S. ARMY EUROPE AND SEVENTH ARMY
FORCES COMMAND

CFSC-AE-MA
SUBJECT: DoD Commercial Sponsorship Policy and Reporting Procedures

DISTRIBUTION: (cont)
COMMANDER
U.S. ARMY TRAINING AND DOCTRINE COMMAND
U.S. ARMY MATERIEL COMMAND
U.S. INFORMATION SYSTEMS COMMAND
U.S. ARMY HEALTH SERVICES COMMAND
U.S. ARMY TRAFFIC MANAGEMENT COMMAND
U.S. ARMY MILITARY DISTRICT OF WASHINGTON
U.S. ARMY SOUTH
EIGHTH U.S. ARMY
U.S. ARMY PACIFIC
U.S. MILITARY ENTRANCE PROCESSING COMMAND

SUPERINTENDENT, U.S. MILITARY ACADEMY
DIRECTOR, DEFENSE LOGISTICS AGENCY

**THE OFFICE OF THE ASSISTANT SECRETARY OF DEFENSE**
WASHINGTON, D.C. 20301-4000

FORCE MANAGEMENT
AND PERSONNEL

MAY 19, 1992

MEMORANDUM FOR DEPUTY ASSISTANT SECRETARY OF THE ARMY
(MILITARY PERSONNEL MANAGEMENT AND EQUAL OPPORTUNITY POLICY)

SUBJECT: Morale, Welfare, and Recreation (MWR) Commercial Sponsorship

Our draft DoDD 1015.1 is being withheld from publication pending the results of our review of morale, welfare, and recreation. The results of this review may have a major impact on how we conduct MWR operations and, therefore, publishing DoDD 1015.1 at this time would be premature. However, policy memoranda will be issued for certain critical areas.

The purpose of this memorandum is to provide updated policy and to request information to assist the Services and CSD in the oversight of the commercial sponsorship of MWR events. The attached guidelines (Attachment 1) replace all previous policy issued by this office concerning commercial sponsorship.

Commercial sponsorship for MWR events has met with outstanding success. It has not only contributed to the enhanced quality of events but also in generating new revenues to support MWR programs. This success can be largely attributed to the MWR professionals in the Service headquarters and at local installations who have actively promoted sponsorship opportunities while closely adhering to the commercial sponsorship policy during its initial and developmental phases.

The attached information at Attachment 2 should be completed for the calendar year and submitted to the Deputy Assistant Secretary of Defense (PSF&E), Attention: Director, Personnel Support Policy and Services.

Calendar Year 1991 information should be submitted by July 1.

Millicent W. Woods
Deputy Assistant Secretary of Defense
(Personnel Support, Families & Education)

Attachments:
As Stated

# COMMERCIAL SPONSORSHIP POLICY

## A. GENERAL.

1. Commercial sponsorship is the act of providing assistance, funding, goods, equipment (including *fixed assets*), or services to an *MWR program(s)* or *event(s)* by an individual, agency, association, company or corporation or other entity (sponsor) for a *specific (limited)* period of time in return for public recognition or *advertising promotions.* Commercial sponsorship is either unsolicited or solicited and is authorized only for support of DoD MWR programs. It does not include volunteer work or activities or outright donations where no volunteer or donor recognition or acknowledgment is expected or required. This program does not include nor refer to those products and services that are considered gifts or donations nor those items considered to be premiums, coupons or limited samples. Any funds, products, services or items resulting from the commercial sponsorship programs will be used only within the MWR program.

2. Commercial sponsorship is authorized only if the DoD component has established standard procedures to ensure the following:

a. *Education and training* procedures are developed and administered to those individuals authorized to work with the commercial sponsorship program.

b. Obligations and entitlements of the sponsor and the MWR program are incorporated into a written agreement that shall be for a 1-year period or less. The period covered by the original agreement and any annual renewals will not exceed a total of 5 years. All agreements will receive a legal review.

c. Assistance provided is commensurate with the level of sponsorship offered.

d. Special concessions or favored treatment are not provided to sponsors, with the exception of public recognition and *advertising entitlements* addressed in the agreement. In addition, individuals or entities not providing sponsorship are not treated with disfavor or suffer any form of reprisal.

e. Appropriate disclaimers are required in any public recognition or advertising media since DoD does not endorse nor favor any commercial supplier, product, or service.

f. The contents of all public recognition and advertising media to be used by or for the sponsor, that refers to any part or program of DoD, are reviewed by the DoD components for consistency with DoD and component policies, and are otherwise appropriate under the agreement.

g. Agreements concerning television and radio broadcast rights to MWR events, and pre-event publicity related thereto, are entered into after coordination with OASD (PA) for DoD inter-service events, or the public affairs office of the military component concerned where only one Military Department is involved.

h. Tobacco and alcoholic beverage (including beer) sponsorship is not solicited. If offered, sponsorship may be accepted only if unsolicited and not directed predominately or exclusively at the military, provided a responsible *use campaign and/or surgeon general's warning* is part of the sponsorship.

i. The commercial sponsor certifies in writing that its costs of the sponsorship *shall not be charged to* any part of the *Federal Government.*

j. The DoD Component shall maintain a record of all MWR sponsored events to include the sponsor's name and organization, the type and amount of the sponsor's assistance, funding, goods, or services provided and the disposition and use of that assistance, funding, goods, or services provided within the MWR programs.

3. Commercial sponsorship is *authorized* for MWR events at *open houses* only *when* specifically *approved* by the *Service* Secretary or his designated representative. Military open house programs are primarily public affairs activities. They are not intended as MWR events. This does not preclude MWR involvement in these events as long as generating MWR revenue does not become the primary objective. OSD approved Service procedures and guidelines for MWR commercial sponsorship must be followed at open houses.

## B. SOLICITED.

1. This sponsorship is specifically solicited on behalf of the MWR event from a potential sponsor willing to provide support for the mutual benefit of the sponsor and the MWR program.

# COMMERCIAL SPONSORSHIP INFORMATION
## CALENDAR YEAR JANUARY 1 - DECEMBER 31, 199X
### ($ in 000)

| VALUE OF CS | SOLICITED | UNSOLICITED (ALCOHOL) | UNSOLICITED (TOBACCO) | UNSOLICITED (OTHER) | SUBTOTAL |
|---|---|---|---|---|---|
| CASH | | | | | |
| MERCHANDISE/ IN-KIND SERVICES | | | | | |
| TOTAL | | | | | |

2. Commercial sponsorship may be solicited only after submission of a proposed solicited commercial sponsorship implementation plan prescribing written procedures and guidelines in compliance with this memorandum to DASD (PSF&E). When approved by DASD (PSF&E), each component will use the implementation plan to develop and demonstrate competence in conducting the commercial sponsorship program. The component will provide an *annual update* on its program *to DASD (PSF&E),* Attention: Director, Personnel Support Policy and Services. The update will include the value of commercial sponsorship funding by solicited and unsolicited with a breakout for unsolicited alcohol and tobacco sponsorship.

3. Each component's procedures and guidelines will include requirements that solicited commercial sponsorship be based on principles similar to those that guide NAF contracting, e.g., competition, evaluation of offers, etc. Additionally:

a. Each installation authorized to accept solicited commercial sponsorship products and services, will *designate* the *individual(s)* by name who will work with this type of sponsorship.

b. Sponsors will be solicited competitively from an adequate number of known U.S. sources and generally limited to firms and organizations involved with consumer products. Where feasible, announcements of solicitations will be placed in appropriate publications to reach the maximum number of potential sponsors. NAF contracting officials should act in an advisory capacity.

c. Officials responsible for procurement or contracting may not be directly or indirectly involved with the solicitation of commercial sponsors. This does not limit the involvement of those officials whose function is to administer NAF contracts.

4. In overseas areas, solicitation of non-U.S. firms is authorized with the commander's approval provided solicitation is not in violation of SOFA or treaty agreements or in direct competition with the armed service exchanges.

## C. UNSOLICITED.

Unsolicited commercial sponsorship shall be treated the same as solicited commercial sponsorship except that it has been *wholly and entirely initiated by the prospective sponsor without prior knowledge of the needs* of the MWR program or installation. After an appropriate inquiry from a prospective sponsor, the installation point-of-contact for sponsorship may inform sponsor of the needs. The unsolicited sponsor should then furnish a letter or memorandum of intent to the installation. *Unsolicited sponsorship* is otherwise *subject* to the *policies* outlined above in *paragraph A.*

## THE OFFICE OF THE ASSISTANT SECRETARY OF DEFENSE
### WASHINGTON, D.C. 20301-4000

OCT 26, 1992

MEMORANDUM FOR DEPUTY ASSISTANT SECRETARY OF THE ARMY
(PERSONNEL SUPPORT)

SUBJECT: Morale, Welfare, and Recreation (MWR) Commercial Sponsorship

My memorandum of May 19, 1992, provided updated policy and guidelines on MWR Commercial Sponsorship. The purpose of this memorandum is to modify those guidelines to help clarify an issue that has been brought to my attention. The issue concerns coordination between MWR and Armed Forces Exchanges on commercial sponsorship opportunities. While it is important that we not be over restrictive, we must ensure that MWR does not violate existing understandings or agreements with armed forces exchanges when pursuing commercial sponsorship opportunities.

It is, therefore, requested that you promulgate the following modifications to my memorandum of May 19, 1992:

Add paragraph 2.k. to read "Commercial sponsorship opportunities will be coordinated with the local Armed Forces Exchange to insure they do not violate existing understandings or agreements." Delete the words in paragraph B.4. after the word "agreements" and end the sentence with a period.

The above modifications are intended to enhance MWR programs, while insuring the income generating capability of our exchanges to provide funds for MWR. In 1991 the Services reported an increase in DoD MWR commercial sponsorship of approximately 55% from the previous year. My congratulations and encouragement for your continued success in pursuing new commercial sponsorship opportunities.

Millicent W. Woods
Deputy Assistant Secretary of Defense
(Personnel Support, Families & Education)

# COMMERCIAL SPONSORSHIP AGREEMENT

**DEPARTMENT OF THE ARMY**
**U.S. ARMY COMMUNITY AND FAMILY SUPPORT CENTER**
**ALEXANDRIA, VA 22331-05**

August 12, 1992

Marketing Division

Mr. Jim Finelli
M&M Mars
High Street
Hackettstown, New Jersey 07840

Dear Mr. Finelli:

It is our pleasure to welcome the M&M Mars as a sponsor of the 1992 BOSS Concert Tour. Your support is appreciated by all involved with the concert series.

If the terms outlined in the enclosed agreement meet with your approval, please sign where indicated and return one copy of the agreement to Ms. Robin Donohoe, Marketing Division, U.S. Army Community and Family Support Center, 2461 Eisenhower Avenue, Room 1434, Alexandria, Virginia 22331-0507. Please feel free to contact Ms. Donohoe ar (703) 325-6120 with any questions.

We look forward to working with you on the 1992 BOSS Concert Tour.

Sincerely,

Douglas J. Middleton
Colonel, U.S. Army
Chief of Staff

Enclosure

# COMMERCIAL SPONSORSHIP AGREEMENT

## BOSS CONCERT SERIES

This sponsorship agreement is made and entered into by and between the U.S. Army Community and Family Support Center (CFSC), 2461 Eisenhower Avenue, Alexandria, VA 22331-0507 and M&M Mars, High Street, Hackettstown, NJ 07840.

In consideration of the mutual promises set forth herein below, the parties, intending to be legally bound hereby agree as follows:

1. *Event.* The 1992 BOSS Concert Series has been developed to provide quality entertainment that appeals to the BOSS target audience of 18-24 year old soldiers, living in the barracks, and single. The head-line performer is Alyson Williams, the opening act will be EX-GIRLFRIEND. Artists and schedule are sub-ject to change. The proposed schedule for the 1992 tour is as follows:

> August 22, 1992 - Ft. Jackson, SC
> August 23, 1992 - Ft. Bragg, NC
> August 29, 1992 - Ft. Stewart, GA
> September 12, 1992 - Ft. Knox, KY
> September 13, 1992 - Ft. Campbell, KY

Admission to all performances will be approximately $5.00 per ticket. Concerts will be open to the public at the installations' discretion.

2. *CFSC Responsibilities.*

   a. M&M Mars name and logo will appear on all BOSS Concert Series promotional collateral that is produced by the Army. This includes posters, flyers, banners, marquees, signs, programs and other printed materials.

   b. M&M Mars will be recognized as a sponsor in all publicity produced by the Army, in whichever media that is used to publicize the BOSS Concert Series.

   c. Press clippings will be provided to M&M Mars.

   d. CFSC will coordinate retail tie-in of M&M Mars products with AAFES at installations hosting BOSS concerts.

   e. M&M Mars will be recognized as a Sponsor in AAFES displays held in conjunction with the tour, where feasible and approved by AAFES officials.

   f. Two 3'x6' M&M Mars banners will be displayed at each BOSS concert.

   g. Fifteen VIP passes will be provided to M&M Mars. These passes will allow possessor entry to backstage VIP area, reserved seating and reserved parking.

   h. M&M Mars will be recognized as a sponsor of the BOSS Concert Series via the public address sys-tem at each concert performance.

   i. Exclusivity: CFSC reserves the right to engage co-sponsors. CFSC represents and warrants that it will not authorize any corporation competitive to M&M Mars to be an additional sponsor or supplier or to be associated with the BOSS Concert Series.

   j. An after-action report detailing attendance figures at all performances will be submitted to M&M Mars no later than October, 31, 1992.

3. *M&M Mars Responsibilities.*

   a. M&M Mars will sponsor the BOSS Concert Series for $25,000 product support.

   b. M&M Mars will provide camera-ready logo and graphic guidelines for correct staging of the logo. Use of logo shall be limited solely to the sponsorship of the event and any advertising or promotional activities relating thereto. CFSC will not use the sponsor's trademarks in a way which would cause any person reasonably to infer, or would otherwise convey the impression that CFSC is in any way affiliated with or acting on behalf of M&M Mars or which may be detrimental to the sponsor's interest.

    c. All printed materials will display CFSC approved disclaimer.

    d. All promotional material produced by M&M Mars to promote the BOSS Concert Series such as posters, flyers, banners, premiums, and advertisements will be submitted to CFSC for review and approval.

4. *Term and Termination.* The term of this Agreement shall commence on the date signed and shall continue until 31 October 1992. Any party may immediately terminate this agreement upon a material breach of any term or condition set forth herein. Notice in writing shall be provided the party in breach.

5. *Sponsorship Costs.* No costs incurred by M&M Mars in association with the sponsorship of the BOSS Concert Series shall be charged to any part of the Federal Government.

6. *Independent Contractor.* Sponsor, Co-sponsor(s) and CFSC shall be and act as independent contractors, and under no circumstances shall this agreement be construed as one of agency, partnership or joint venture of employment between CFSC, Sponsor and Co-Sponsor (s). None of the personnel under contract to, employed by or volunteering for CFSC shall be deemed in any way to have any contractual relationship with Sponsor(s) whatsoever. The Department of the Army shall be solely responsible for the conduct of its employees, personnel, and agents in connection with their performance hereunder.

7. *Force Majeure.* No party shall be responsible for events that are unforeseeable and beyond its reasonable control, such as acts of God, weather delays, government restrictions, or unforeseen commercial delays.

8. *Assignment.* This agreement is not assignable in whole or part by any party hereto in the absence of the prior written consent of the parties.

9. *Entire Agreement.* This Agreement contains the entire understanding between the parties hereto relating to the subject matter contained herein and supersedes any and all prior agreements, arrangements, communications or representations, whether oral or written. This Agreement may not be amended, altered, modified or changed except by an addendum signed by all parties hereto.

    IN WITNESS WHEREOF, the parties hereto have caused this Agreement to be executed.

Community and Family Support Center

By: _____

Title: _____

Date: _____

M&M Mars

By: _____

Title: _____

Date: _____

## CHAPTER TWENTY-TWO

# *Minor Construction Funding*

## I. INTRODUCTION.

### A. Objectives.
Following this block of instruction, students will:
1. Understand the statutes and regulations governing the fiscal aspects of military construction.
2. Understand how to apply minor construction funding rules to routine problems.

### B. Practitioners Must Stay Current.
New developments occur frequently in this area of the law due to changes promulgated through annual authorization and appropriations acts.

## II. REFERENCES.

A. 10 U.S.C. §§ 2801-65 (Military Construction Codification Act); 41 U.S.C. § 12; 10 U.S.C. § 401.
B. DOD Dir. 4270.36, DOD Emergency, Contingency, and Other Unprogramed Constr. (May 16, 1991).
C. AR 37-1, Army Accounting and Fund Control (Apr. 30, 1991).
D. AR 210-50, Housing Mgmt. (Apr. 24, 1990).
E. AR 415-15, Military Constr., Army (MCA) Program Development (Aug. 30, 1994).
F. AR 420-10, Management of Installation Directorates of Eng'g and Housing (July 2, 1987).
G. AFR 86-1, vol. I, Programming Civil Eng'r Resources— Appropriated Fund Resources (May 1984), ch. 5.

H. AFR 88-25, Military Family Housing Design and Constr. Mgmt. (Apr. 1990).
I. AFR 172-1, vol. I, USAF Budget and Procedures (Oct. 15, 1990), ch. 9.
J. SECNAVINST 11013.13E, Unspecified Minor Constr., Emergency Constr., and Restoration or Replacement of Facilities Damaged or Destroyed (Oct. 14, 1983).
K. OPNAVINST 11010.20E, Facilities Projects Manual (July 9, 1985).
L. Munns, *An Analysis of the Military Constr. Codification Act*, The Army Lawyer, Nov. 1987.

## III. MILITARY CONSTRUCTION APPROPRIATIONS.

### A. Congressional Oversight of the Military Construction Program.
Congressional oversight is extensive and pervasive. Military services may accomplish *only* minor construction projects (i.e., $1.5 million or less in cost) without prior approval of Congress.

### B. The Military Construction Codification Act.
1. The Act's *purpose* was to revise and codify in a new chapter (Chapter 169) of Title 10, U.S.C., the recurring and permanent provisions of law related to military construction and family housing.
2. In the *"Specified" Military Construction Program*, Congress provides annual approval and funding for the DOD military construc-

tion program. Congress funds *specific construction projects* in the annual Military Construction Appropriation (MCA) Act with a lump sum appropriation. The conference report provides a by-project break down for this lump sum amount. The specified military construction program normally consists of construction projects projected to exceed $1.5 million.

3. In the *"Unspecified" Minor Construction Program*, Congress provides annual funding and approval to each military department for minor construction projects not specified in the conference report accompanying the MCA Act. Congress appropriates such Minor Military Construction (MMC) funds to each military department. The Army's share of the MMC funds is titled "Minor Military Construction, Army" (MMCA) in the appropriation acts. Pursuant to the "unspecified" minor construction authority of 10 U.S.C. § 2805(a), service secretaries may use MMC funds for minor projects not specifically approved by Congress. This authority is limited to $1.5 million for *each project*.

4. The service secretary must notify Congress before certain minor military construction projects are commenced. *See, e.g.*, 10 U.S.C. § 2805(b)(2) (minor construction exceeding $500,000).

## C. The Operation and Maintenance (O&M) Appropriation.

1. Most installations fund their routine operations with O&M funds. The military services use O&M funds for military construction activities performed in furtherance of specific operational requirements of the services *only* pursuant to specific authorization from Congress.

   a. As a general rule, no public contract relating to erection, repair, or improvements to public buildings shall bind the government for funds in excess of the amount specifically appropriated for that purpose. 41 U.S.C. § 12.

   b. The General Accounting Office (GAO)

interprets this code provision to require that Congress specifically authorize in an appropriations act all military construction projects, and that general appropriations are not ordinarily available for such projects.

2. The authorization of 10 U.S.C. § 2805(c) to use O&M funds of up to $300,000 for unspecified MMC projects is a statutory exception to this requirement. This authorization is limited to $300,000 for *each project*.

3. In FY 1992, Congress established and funded the Real Property Maintenance (RPM), Defense account to finance only the backlog of DOD maintenance and repair projects. Department of Defense Appropriations Act, 1992, Pub. L. No. 102-172, 105 Stat. 1152 (1991). The DOD Appropriations Act for 1993 provided that RPM funds were available to finance the backlog of maintenance and repair projects, minor construction projects, and major repair of real property. Pub. L. No. 102-396, 106 Stat. 1885 (1992). However, the Department of Defense Appropriations Act, 1994, Pub. L. No. 103-139, 107 Stat. 1418 (1993), contained no RPM funding, and restored the former practice of funding all maintenance, repair, and minor construction below $300,000 with O&M funds. FY 1993 RPM funds remained available for obligation only until the end of FY 1994.

## D. Prohibition on Use of O&M Funds for Minor Construction During JCS Exercises Outside the United States.

1. DOD must fund from the services' unspecified minor construction accounts all exercise-related construction projects coordinated or directed by the Joint Chiefs of Staff (JCS) outside the United States. Furthermore, Congress has limited the authority for exercise-related construction to no more than $5 million per military department per fiscal year. 10 U.S.C. § 2805(a)(2).

2. This statute resulted from an opinion issued

by the GAO regarding construction and related activities undertaken during joint/combined exercises in Honduras in 1983—the Ahuas Tara (Big Pine) II exercise. *To The Honorable Bill Alexander, U.S. House of Representatives*, B-213137, 63 Comp. Gen. 422 (1984).

3. The statute does not affect funding of minor and temporary structures such as tent platforms, field latrines, shelters, and range targets that forces remove once the exercise is completed. These may continue to be funded with the O&M accounts.

4. Potential expansion of permissible uses of O&M funds during contingency operations.

   a. Units may use O&M funds for the acquisition of materials and/or cost of erection of structures which:

      (1) Are of a temporary operational nature and operational forces intend to use for only a *temporary period* as required to facilitate operations; and

      (2) Will not be used to sustain permanent or contingency operations, or to facilitate future exercises at the conclusion of the relief efforts.

   b. Example: Road work during Operation Restore Hope.

   c. Military construction criteria apply in all other situations, including construction for which the United States will have follow-on or contingency uses after terminating the operations necessitating the construction.

## E. Notification Requirement for Military Exercise Construction Spending in Excess of $100,000.

Congress requires the Secretary of Defense to give prior notice of the plans and scope of *any* proposed military exercise involving United States personnel if the estimated amount for construction, either temporary or permanent, will exceed $100,000. Military Construction Appropriations Act, 1995, Pub. L. 103-307, § 113, 108 Stat. 1659, 1664 (1994).

## F. Statutory Authorization to Restore or Replace a Facility That Is Damaged or Destroyed.

1. 10 U.S.C. § 2854 provides that a service secretary may repair, restore, or replace a facility that is damaged or destroyed. O&M funds will be used if the cost of replacement is less than $300,000. If MMCA funds are used, they are from the "urgent-minor" subaccount. *See* DOD Dir. 4270.36; AR 415-15, app. D; AFR 172-1, vol. I, ch. 9.

2. If the cost of such repair, restoration, or replacement exceeds the maximum amount for a minor military construction project, the secretary must notify Congress of the amount and the source of the funds to be used at least twenty-one days prior to commencement of the project.

3. The secretary may carry out such projects only after the end of the 21-day period, or after congressional approval, if received prior to the expiration of the 21-day period.

## G. Emergency Construction Authorities.

1. 10 U.S.C. § 2808 provides that, upon Presidential Declaration of National Emergency, the Secretary of Defense may undertake construction projects, not otherwise authorized by law, that are necessary to support the armed forces. *See* AR 415-15, app. D, para. D-2.

   a. Funds for such projects come from unobligated military construction *and* family housing appropriations.

   b. On November 14, 1990, President Bush invoked emergency construction authority under 10 U.S.C. § 2808 to support Operation Desert Shield. *See* Executive Order 12734 of Nov. 14, 1990, 55 Fed. Reg. 48,099.

2. Two other emergency construction authorities require prior notice and waiting periods:

   a. Emergency Construction, 10 U.S.C. § 2803. *See* AR 415-15, para. 1-6.b.(2).

      (1) Requires prior notification to Congressional appropriations committees;

      (2) Must justify projects as vital to the national defense;

(3) Must wait 21 days after notification before beginning projects; and

(4) Must use unobligated military construction funds, and must not exceed $30 million in any fiscal year.

b. Contingency Construction, 10 U.S.C. § 2804. *See* AR 415-15, para. 1-6.b.(6).

(1) Requires prior notification to Congressional appropriations committees;

(2) Must justify the project;

(3) Must wait 21 days after notification before beginning the project; and

(4) Must use funds appropriated for this purpose.

3. During Operation Desert Shield, emergency authorities were not timely exercised. Future operational plans should include provisions for the timely exercise of these authorities, so construction and improvement of logistics facilities can commence immediately, and so these efforts will be funded by the proper appropriations.

**H. Statutory Restriction on Base Closure and Realignment Construction.**

Unspecified minor construction projects required in connection with base closures and realignments shall comply with 10 U.S.C. § 2687.

1. Evaluate fiscal, local economic, environmental, and operational consequences of the project.

2. Congressional notification and waiting period required.

## IV. A METHODOLOGY FOR REVIEW OF MINOR MILITARY CONSTRUCTION ACQUISITIONS.

A. Define the Scope of the Project—work needed to produce a complete and useable facility or improvement to an existing facility.

B. Define the Work—determine its nature in terms of statutory and regulatory definitions of military construction and minor military construction:

1. Maintenance?

2. Repair?

3. Construction?

4. Combination of above?

C. Determine the Funded Cost of the Project.

D. Select the Proper Appropriation.

1. Statutes (e.g., 10 U.S.C. § 2805(c)).

2. Regulations (e.g., AR 415-15).

3. Messages, Funding Authorization Documents, etc.

E. Verify Who Is the Proper Approval Authority for the Project. Ensure that the command obtains approval to undertake the project before commencing work. *See infra* paras. VIII. B. & C.

## V. SCOPING CONSTRUCTION PROJECTS.

Project Splitting Is Prohibited!

1. An agency may not treat "clearly interrelated" construction activities as separate projects. *The Honorable Bill Alexander, House of Representatives*, B-213137, Jan. 30, 1986 (unpub.).

2. A "project" includes all work necessary to produce a complete and usable facility or a complete and usable improvement to an existing facility. *See The Honorable Michael B. Donley*, B-234326.15, Dec. 24, 1991 (unpub.) (Air Force improperly split project involving a group of twelve related buildings into multiple projects).

## VI. IDENTIFYING CONSTRUCTION WORK.

**A. Statutory Definition of "Military Construction."**

10 U.S.C. § 2801(a) & (b).

1. It includes any construction, development, conversion, or extension of any kind carried out with respect to a military installation.[1]

2. It includes all work necessary to produce a complete and usable facility or a complete and usable improvement to an existing facility.

**B. Statutory Definition of "Minor Military Construction."**

10 U.S.C. §§ 2801, 2805.

1. Congress distinguishes "minor military construction project" from "military construction project" by adding additional terms to the definition of a military construction project.

2. It includes the two factors defining military construction (VI.A.1 & 2, above).

3. Additionally, minor military construction is for a "single undertaking" at an installation, and it must have an approved cost less than or equal to $1,500,000.

**C. Services' Definition of "Construction."**
AR 415-15, Glossary, sec. II; AFR 172-1, vol. I, para. 9-2.

1. The acquisition, erection, installation, or assembly of a *new facility*.

2. Construction includes some types of work on an *existing facility*.

   a. A change to a real property facility, such as *expansion* or *extension* of, the facility that adds to its overall external dimensions.

   b. *Alteration* of the interior or exterior arrangements of a facility to improve its current purpose. This includes installation of equipment made a part of the existing facility. Additions, expansions, and extensions of facilities are not alterations.

   c. *Conversion* of the interior or exterior arrangements of a facility so that the facility can be used for a new purpose. This includes installation of equipment made a part of the existing facility.

   d. *Replacement* of a real property facility, which is a complete rebuild of a facility that has been destroyed or damaged beyond economical repair.

3. Construction includes *relocation* of a facility from one location to another.

   a. Construction encompasses efforts to move a structure from one site to another. A facility may be disassembled and later reassembled, or moved intact. Work includes connection of new utility lines, but excludes relocation of roads, pavements, or airstrips.

   b. Relocation of two or more facilities into a single facility is a single project.

   c. Section 107 of the 1995 Military Construction Appropriation Act prohibits the use of funds appropriated under that Act for minor construction to transfer or relocate any activity from one base or installation to another, without prior notification to Senate and House Committees on Appropriations. Military Construction Appropriations Act, 1995, Pub. L. No. 103-307, § 107, 108 Stat. 1659, 1663 (1994).

4. Construction also includes:

   a. *Installed equipment* in a facility.

   b. *Site preparation*, excavation, filling, landscaping, or other land improvements.

**D. *An Illustrative Case:* The Letterkenny Army Depot Case.**
GAO/NSIAD-87-112BR (May 1987). The Letterkenny Automated Storage and Retrieval System was installed in a building specifically constructed to contain it; therefore, the facility should have been classified as military construction, not as an industrial equipment acquisition. The Army improperly used Army industrial funds rather than construction funds. By improperly charging construction costs to industrial funds, the Army violated the purpose restriction of 31 U.S.C. § 1301(a). Also, because the expenditures were properly chargeable to military construction funds, but Congress had not funded this work, the project violated the Antideficiency Act.

**E. Maintenance and Repair.**
Maintenance and repair *are not* construction. AR 420-10; AFR 172-1, vol. I, ch. 9.

1. *Maintenance* is recurrent work to prevent deterioration. It is work required to preserve or maintain a facility in such condition that it may be used for its designated purpose.

2. *Repair* is restoration for use for a designated purpose by overhaul, reprocessing, or replacing parts or materials that have deteriorated from the elements or wear and tear in use,

and which have not been corrected through maintenance.

3. Construction work accomplished simultaneously with maintenance or repair—where does maintenance or repair end and construction begin? *See* AR 420-10, para. 3-1.

4. Caveat: The *replacement* of a real property facility that has been destroyed or damaged *is* construction. 10 U.S.C. § 2854.

## VII. UNFUNDED v. FUNDED COSTS: PROJECT LIMITS APPLY ONLY TO FUNDED COSTS.

*See* AR 420-10, Glossary, sec. II; AFR 172-1, vol. I, ch. 9.

### A. Unfunded Costs.

1. Unfunded costs are costs charged against appropriations other than those directly paying for the construction project. They include:
   a. Costs funded by Military Personnel, Army (MPA) Appropriations, e.g., salaries of military personnel.
   b. Planning and design costs (architect-engineer efforts, environmental studies, etc.).
   c. Depreciation of government equipment used in the project; *but* equipment maintenance and operation costs *are* funded costs.
   d. Materials, supplies, and equipment received for the project as excess distributions from another service or federal agency on a non-reimbursable basis; *but* transportation costs are funded.
   e. Nonappropriated funds; *but* secretarial approval is required. *See* AR 415-19.

2. Report unfunded costs to higher headquarters, even though they do not apply toward the military construction appropriation limitations.

### B. Funded Costs. All other costs <u>are</u> funded. For example:

1. Materials and supplies applicable to the project.
2. Labor (except that of military personnel).

3. Costs for temporary duty (TDY) of military personnel.
4. Maintenance and operation costs of government equipment used in the project.
5. Value of real property relocated within an installation.
   a. The purchase cost of new land is funded.
   b. Transportation and relocation costs of moving buildings are funded.

## VIII. PROJECT LIMITATIONS AND APPROVAL LEVELS.

### A. Key Limitations.

1. Do not subdivide projects to reduce the cost per project to meet construction funding limitations.
2. Planned incremental construction or phasing of construction is prohibited.
3. Minor construction authority may not be used to begin or complete projects financed under other authorizations. AR 420-10, para. 3-1.
4. Commercial Activities Program (CAP) issue: FAR 36.101(c) permits inclusion of minor construction tasks in a services contract. *See A.J. Fowler Corp.*, B-227955, Nov. 13, 1987, 87-2 CPD ¶ 482.

### B. Approval of Construction Projects.

AR 415-15, app. B, para. B-1.

1. MACOM Commanders may approve projects up to $300,000. Delegation is allowed; this authority usually is delegated to installation commanders.
2. The Assistant Chief of Staff for Installation Management (DAIM-FD) is the approval authority for projects over $300,000 and up to $500,000.
3. The Secretary of the Army (DASA(IH)) approves construction projects over $500,000 and up to $1,500,000.
4. Congressional notification is required on projects over $500,000; work on the project cannot begin for 21 days to permit Congress time to disapprove. *See* AR 415-15, app. B, para. B-2.f.

## C. Approval of Maintenance & Repair Projects.

1. Approval of Army repair and maintenance projects. AR 420-10, para. 3-2.
   a. MACOM commanders *normally* approve projects costing $2 million or less.
   b. Projects exceeding MACOM approval level must be approved by the Secretary of the Army.
2. For all services, secretarial approval is required for all repair projects exceeding $5 million in cost. 10 U.S.C. § 2811(b).

## IX. COST VARIATIONS.

AR 415-15, para. 5-12; 10 U.S.C. § 2853.

### A. Variation from the Approved Cost.

Variation from the approved cost of the MIL-CON/MMC project, after the project is approved, is permitted only if:

1. An increase is required solely to meet unusual variations in cost.
2. The cost variation could not have been reasonably anticipated.
3. The cost variation is not requested to increase the scope of the project.
4. The cost variation meets percentage of increase/total cost limitations.

### B. Congressional Notification of Cost Variations.

Congress must be notified of cost variations when the total project value exceeds $1.5 million.

### C. Application of Cost Variation Rules:

1. If the amount approved for a project is less than the minor construction project ceiling, the approved amount may be increased to the amount of such ceiling if the secretary concerned determines (1) that such an increase is required for the sole purpose of meeting unusual variations in cost, and (2) that such variations in cost could not have been reasonably anticipated at the time the project was originally approved.

2. If, based upon offers received, the adjusted estimate of the cost of a project is more than 200% of the minor construction ceiling *or* is more than 125 percent of the original approved amount for the project, the project may not be placed under contract until the secretary concerned notifies Congress and receives approval.

## X. CONGRESSIONAL CONCERN OVER USE OF O&M FUNDS.

A. In 1989, the House Armed Services Committee criticized the DOD's use of O&M funding for renovation and repair projects as follows (H.R. Rep. No. 21, 101st Cong., 1st Sess. 188-189 (1989)):

> Limits on the use of [O&M] funding for maintenance and repair are inadequate and effectively allow both circumvention of military construction oversight and inappropriate use of O&M funds. . . . [I]n many cases the construction funding review does not occur because these projects are categorized as repair and maintenance even though, in many cases, their cost is far greater than major construction. . . .

B. The committee cited three of the numerous examples it had uncovered "of installation commanders substituting O&M funds for construction funds because of expediency or concern that these projects would not survive the budget competition with other major construction projects."

1. The Air Force built a new officers club using $10 million in O&M funds.
2. An Army installation used over $26 million in O&M funds to gut a building and then completely upgrade the interior.
3. The Navy used over $13 million in O&M funds to completely restore the exterior of a building.

## XI. CONCLUSION.

A. Use a structured methodology to analyze construction funding issues.

B. Document rationale for funding decisions.

C. Different rules may apply during overseas exercises and contingency operations.

### Endnote

1. "The term 'military installation' means a base, camp, post, station, yard, center, or other activity under the jurisdiction of the Secretary of a military department or, in the case of an activity in a foreign country, *under the operational control* of the Secretary of a military department or the Secretary of Defense." 10 U.S.C. § 2801(c)(2) (emphasis added).

## CHAPTER TWENTY-THREE

# *Contract Terminations for Convenience*

## I. INTRODUCTION.

Following this block of instruction, the student should:

A. Understand the right of the government to terminate a contract for convenience, and limitations on that right.

B. Understand when and how the contracting officer should terminate a contract for convenience.

C. Understand the factors which the contracting officer must consider when settling termination for convenience claims.

## II. THE RIGHT TO TERMINATE FOR CONVENIENCE.

A. **Historical Development of Termination for the Convenience of the Government.**

1. Inherent Authority.

   a. The government has inherent authority to suspend contracts. *United States v. Corliss Steam Engine Co.*, 91 U.S. 321 (1875).

   b. A contractor can recover breach of contract damages, which include anticipatory (lost) profits, as a result of a termination or suspension based on inherent authority. *United States v. Speed*, 75 U.S. 77 (1868).

2. Contractual Authority.

   a. Settlement of war-related contracts led to the federal procurement policy that the parties to a federal contract must bilaterally agree that the government can terminate the contract at will.

   b. Convenience termination clauses preclude the contractor from recovering anticipatory or lost profits when the government terminates for its convenience—an action that would constitute a breach of contract absent the termination for convenience clause.

B. **Termination for Convenience Clauses.**
FAR 52.249-1 through 52.249-6; FAR Subpart 49.

1. These clauses:

   a. Give the government a broad contractual right to terminate the contract *without cause*.

   b. *Limit the contractor's recovery* to costs incurred, profit on work done, and the costs of preparing the termination settlement proposal. The contractor cannot recover anticipated (lost) profits, which would be recoverable under common law breach of contract principles. *Rhen v. United States*, 17 Cl. Ct. 140 (1989); *American Geometrics Constr. Co.*, ASBCA No. 37734, 92-1 BCA ¶ 24,545.

2. Termination is for the convenience *of the government*. When a contractor is performing at a loss, termination may be beneficial to the contractor, but the government has no duty to the contractor to exercise the government's right to terminate for the contractor's benefit. *Rotair Indus.*, ASBCA No. 27571, 84-2 BCA ¶ 17,417.

3. There are three basic types of convenience termination clauses. *See* FAR 49.502.

   a. "Short form" clauses governing fixed-price contracts not to exceed $100,000: settlement per FAR Part 49. *See* pages 329 and 330.

b. Fixed-price contract "long form" clauses (contracts exceeding $100,000) specify contractor obligations and termination settlement provisions. *See Arrow, Inc.*, ASBCA No. 41330, 94-1 BCA ¶ 26,353 (board denied claim for useful value of special machinery and equipment because service contract properly contained short form termination clause). *See* page 331.

c. Cost-reimbursement contract clauses, which cover both convenience and default terminations, specify detailed termination settlement provisions.

4. The "*Christian* Doctrine." If a termination for convenience clause is omitted from the contract, it will be read into the contract by operation of law. *G.L. Christian & Assoc. v. United States*, 312 F.2d 418 (Ct. Cl. 1963), *reh. denied*, 320 F.2d 345 (Ct. Cl. 1963), *cert. denied*, 375 U.S. 954 (1964). *See also S.J. Amoroso Constr. Co. v. United States*, 12 F.3d 1072 (Fed. Cir. 1993) (*Christian* doctrine applies when agency includes wrong clause in contract); *Chamberlain Mfg. Corp.*, ASBCA No. 18103, 74-1 BCA ¶ 10,368. *But see Montana Refining Co.*, ASBCA No. 44250, 94-2 BCA ¶ 26,656 (*Christian* doctrine inapplicable when government uses authorized deviation to termination for convenience clause); *Michael Grinberg*, DOT BCA No. 1543, 87-1 BCA ¶ 19,573 (*Christian* doctrine applicable only when clause is mandatory).

## C. Termination by Conversion.

The termination for default clauses provide that an erroneous default termination converts to a termination for convenience. FAR 52.249-8(g); FAR 52.249-10(c); *Darwin Constr. Co. v. United States*, 811 F.2d 593 (Fed. Cir. 1987); *Rhen v. United States*, 17 Cl. Ct. 140 (1989); *Spectrum Leasing Corp.*, GSBCA No. 7425, 92-1 BCA ¶ 24,394. *But see Apex Int'l Mgmt. Servs., Inc.*, ASBCA No. 38087, 94-2 BCA ¶ 26,842, *aff'd on recon.*, 94-2 BCA ¶ 26,852 (board refuses to convert default termination to a termination for convenience where government officials acted in bad faith; contractor entitled to breach damages).

## D. Constructive Termination for Convenience.

1. Courts and boards have developed a doctrine under which a governmental breach of contract may be construed as a termination for the convenience of the government when changed circumstances justify the reallocation of risk to the contractor. *Maxima Corp. v. United States*, 847 F.2d 1549 (Fed. Cir. 1988); *Peter A. Foreman*, ASBCA No. 33284, 88-3 BCA ¶ 21,055.

2. The constructive termination for convenience doctrine is based on the concept that a contracting party who is sued for breach may ordinarily defend on the ground that there existed at the time a legal excuse for nonperformance, although that party was then ignorant of the fact. *College Point Boat Corp. v. United States*, 267 U.S. 12 (1925). Therefore, if the government, for reasons that turn out to be questionable or invalid, issues a directive to end performance of a contract, that directive will be considered a termination for convenience instead of a breach. *G.C. Casebolt Co. v. United States*, 421 F.2d 710 (Ct. Cl. 1970); *Building Maint. Specialist, Inc.*, ENG BCA No. 5654, 90-3 BCA ¶ 23,032.

3. The government cannot, however, use the constructive termination for convenience theory to retroactively terminate a fully performed contract in an effort to limit its liability for failing to order the contract's minimum amount of services. *PHP Healthcare Corp.*, ASBCA No. 39207, 91-1 BCA ¶ 23,647. Further, the government may not require bidders to agree in advance that the government's failure to order the contract's minimum quantity would be treated as a termination for convenience. *Southwest Lab. of Okla., Inc.*, B-251778, May 5, 1993, 93-1 CPD ¶ 368.

## E. Deductive Change versus Partial Termination for Convenience.

1. The contracting officer must determine whether deleted work is a deductive change or a termination for convenience. Generally, the courts and boards will not overturn the contracting officer's determination that the deleted work is a deductive change if the parties consistently treated the deletion as such. *Dollar Roofing*, ASBCA No. 36461, 92-1 BCA ¶ 24,695; *Kinetic Eng'g & Constr.*, ASBCA No. 30726, 89-1 BCA ¶ 21,397. *But see Griffin Servs., Inc.*, GSBCA No. 11022, 92-3 BCA ¶ 25,181 (board characterized deleted work as a partial termination for convenience, but ordered recovery based on the changes clause).

2. If the contractor disputes the contracting officer's treatment of the deletion, courts and boards will examine the relative significance (dollar value, scope of the change) of the deleted work. If major portions of the work are deleted and no additional work is substituted in its place, the termination for convenience clause must be used. *Nager Elec. Co. v. United States*, 442 F.2d 936 (Ct. Cl. 1971). The deletion of relatively minor and segregable items of work are usually treated as a deductive change. *Lionsgate Corp.*, ENG BCA No. 5425 90-2 BCA ¶ 22,730.

## III. THE DECISION TO TERMINATE FOR CONVENIENCE.

### A. Regulatory Guidance.

1. The FAR clauses give the government the right to terminate a contract in whole or in part if the contracting officer determines that termination is *in the government's interest*. *See John Massman Contracting Co. v. United States*, 23 Cl. Ct. 24 (1991) (no duty to terminate when it would be in the contractor's best interest).

2. The FAR provides no guidance on factors that the contracting officer should consider when determining whether termination is "in the government's interest." FAR 49.101(b)

and the convenience termination clauses merely provide that contracting officers shall terminate contracts *only* when it is in the government's interest to do so.

3. The FAR does provide guidance concerning circumstances in which contracting officers normally cannot or should not use a convenience termination. For example, a negotiated no-cost settlement is appropriate instead of a termination for convenience or default when:
   a. The contractor will accept it;
   b. Government property was not furnished; and,
   c. There are no outstanding payments due to the contractor, debts due by the contractor to the government, or other contractor obligations. FAR 49.101(b).

4. The government normally should not terminate a contract, but should allow it to run to completion, when the price of the undelivered balance of the contract is less than $5,000. FAR 49.101(c).

5. The government should not normally terminate a contract for convenience if the contractor is in unexcused default and the government has a legal right to terminate for default, even if the government's requirements no longer exist. AFARS 49.101(91); AFFARS 49.101-90(c)(2); DLAR 49.101. However, the contracting officer shall obtain a no cost settlement when appropriate, even if the contractor is in unexcused default. *See* FAR 49.101.

6. In many cases, the contracting officer must obtain authorization before exercising his or her authority to terminate a contract for convenience. AFARS 49.101(90); AFFARS 49.101-90. However, there is no requirement to give the contractor a hearing before the termination decision. *Melvin R. Kessler*, PSBCA No. 2820, 92-2 BCA ¶ 24,857.

### B. Discretionary Decision.

The courts and boards recognize the government's broad right to terminate a contract for convenience. *Salsbury Indus. v. United States*,

17 Cl. Ct. 47 (1989), *aff'd* 905 F.2d 1518 (Fed. Cir. 1990). The bad faith or abuse of discretion standard that applies generally to discretionary decisions by government officials also applies to a contracting officer's decision to terminate a contract for the convenience of the government.

1. Bad faith. Both courts and boards of contract appeals (BCAs) require that contracting officers exercise their authority to terminate a contract for convenience in good faith. A contractor must prove that contracting officials had a specific intent to injure the contractor to establish a bad faith termination. *TLT Constr. Corp.*, ASBCA No. 40501, 93-3 BCA ¶ 25,978 (inept government actions do not constitute bad faith); *Kalvar Corp. v. United States*, 543 F.2d 1298 (Ct. Cl. 1976); *Special Waste, Inc.*, ASBCA No. 36775, 90-2 BCA ¶ 22,935; *Systems Architects, Inc.*, ASBCA No. 28861, 90-2 BCA ¶ 22,860.

2. Abuse of discretion. A contracting officer's decision to terminate for convenience cannot be arbitrary or capricious. *Pacificorp Capital, Inc. v. United States*, 25 Cl. Ct. 707 (1992); *Air-Flo Cleaning Sys.*, ASBCA 39608, 90-3 BCA ¶ 23,071.

3. The Court of Claims enunciated four factors to apply in determining whether a contracting officer's discretionary decision is arbitrary or capricious. *Keco Indus. v. United States*, 492 F.2d 1200 (Ct. Cl. 1974) (award decision); *United States Fidelity & Guaranty Co. v. United States*, 676 F.2d 622 (Ct. Cl. 1982) (decision to pay progress payments). These factors are:
   a. Evidence of subjective bad faith on the part of the government official;
   b. Lack of a reasonable basis for the decision;
   c. The amount of discretion given to the government official; i.e., the greater the discretion granted, the more difficult it is to prove that the decision was arbitrary and capricious; and,
   d. A proven violation of an applicable statute or regulation [this factor alone may be enough to show that the conduct was arbitrary and capricious].

4. The *Torncello v. United States* "change in circumstances" test:
   a. A 1982 Court of Claims case and a line of cases following it appeared to hold that a contracting officer cannot exercise his or her authority to terminate a contract for convenience unless there has been a change in the circumstances of the bargain or in the expectations of the parties. *Torncello v. United States*, 681 F.2d 756 (Ct. Cl. 1982) (government awarded a requirements contract knowing it would divert a portion of the work to another contractor). *See also Embrey v. United States*, 17 Cl. Ct. 617 (1989); *Municipal Leasing v. United States*, 7 Cl. Ct. 43 (1984); *Maxima Corp. v. United States*, 847 F.2d 1549 (Fed. Cir. 1988) (Federal Circuit appeared to endorse *Torncello*).
   b. A 1990 Federal Circuit case, however, limits application of *Torncello* to circumstances in which the government contracts with a party *knowing full well* that it will not honor the contract. The Court opined that *Torncello* only means that the government cannot obtain the benefits of its termination for convenience rights when to do so would permit the government to avoid its contractual obligations with impunity. *Salsbury Indus. v. United States*, 905 F.2d 1518 (Fed. Cir. 1990). *Accord Pacificorp Capital, Inc. v. United States*, 25 Cl. Ct. 707 (1992); *SMS Data Prods. Group, Inc. v. United States*, 19 Cl. Ct. 612 (1990).
   c. The Armed Services Board of Contract Appeals has discussed but never really applied the "change in circumstances" test of *Torncello*. Rather, the Board considers it to be an abuse of discretion for the government to terminate for convenience under circumstances such as arose in *Torncello* because it is not in the government's best interests to avoid contractual responsibilities as would have resulted from a convenience termination under the facts of that case. *Operational Serv. Corp.*,

ASBCA No. 37059, 93-3 BCA ¶ 26,190 (government exercised option year of contract while knowing that it would award a commercial activities contract or perform the work in house); *C.F.S. Air Cargo, Inc.*, ASBCA No. 36113, 91-1 BCA ¶ 23583; *Special Waste, Inc.*, ASBCA No. 36775, 90-2 BCA ¶ 22,935; *Vec-Tor, Inc.*, ASBCA No. 25807, 85-1 BCA ¶ 17,755.

5. The effects of an improper termination for convenience may be substantial. By terminating in bad faith or arbitrarily and capriciously, the government breaches the contract, permitting the contractor to recover common law breach of contract damages, including anticipatory (lost) profits.

## C. Revocation of a Termination for Convenience.

1. Reinstatement of the contract. FAR 49.102(d).
   a. A terminated portion of a contract may be reinstated in whole or in part if the contracting officer determines in writing that there is a requirement for the terminated items and that the reinstatement is advantageous to the government. *To the Administrator, Gen. Servs. Admin.*, 34 Comp. Gen. 343 (1955).
   b. The contracting officer may not reinstate a contract unilaterally; the written consent of the contractor is required.

2. A termination for default cannot be substituted for a termination for convenience. *Roged, Inc.*, ASBCA No. 20702, 76-2 BCA ¶ 12,018; *Cecile Indus.*, ASBCA No. 24600, 81-1 BCA ¶ 15,122. *But see Amwest Surety Ins. Co.*, ENG BCA No. 6036, 94-2 BCA ¶ 26,648 (conditional termination for convenience).

## IV. CONVENIENCE TERMINATION SETTLEMENTS.

### A. Procedures.

FAR Part 49.

1. After termination for convenience, the parties must:

   a. Stop the work.
   b. Dispose of termination inventory.
   c. Adjust the contract price.

2. Convenience termination settlements are based on incurred costs, plus a reasonable profit on the incurred costs, plus the costs of preparing the settlement proposal. If the contractor has incurred no costs, it may not recover. The contractor has the burden of reasonably establishing the amount of incurred costs. *American Geometrics Constr. Co.*, ASBCA No. 37734, 92-1 BCA ¶ 24,545; *Techno Eng'g & Constr., Ltd.*, ASBCA No. 36869, 90-1 BCA ¶ 22,566.

3. Timing of the termination settlement claim.
   a. The contractor must submit its termination claim within one year of the termination for convenience. FAR 49.206; *Do-Well Mach. Shop, Inc. v. United States*, 870 F.2d 637 (Fed. Cir. 1989); *see also Harris Corp.*, ASBCA No. 37940, 89-3 BCA ¶ 22,145 (contractor's submission of an otherwise timely and complete termination settlement proposal was not rendered a legal nullity for not being certified within the required one year period).
   b. Timely submittal is defined as mailing the proposal within one year after receipt of the termination notice. *Jo-Bar Mfg. Corp.*, ASBCA No. 39572, 93-2 BCA ¶ 25,756.
   c. In a contract for commercial items under DFARS 211.70, the contractor must submit its proposal within 90 days following receipt of the termination notice, unless extended. DFARS 252.211-7000.
   d. If a contractor fails to submit its termination settlement claim within the required time period, or any extension granted by the contracting officer, the contracting officer may then unilaterally determine the amount due the contractor. The contractor may not appeal this decision under the contract's Disputes clause. FAR 52.249-2; DFARS 252.211-7000; *Cedar Constr.*, ASBCA No. 42178, 92-2 BCA ¶ 24,896 (contracting officer's refusal to extend the period for submission of the claim is *not* an appeal-

able decision; submittal of the termination for convenience claim is still required).

4. Methods of settlement. FAR 49.103.
   a. Bilateral negotiations between the contractor and the government.
   b. Unilateral determination of the government. This method is appropriate only when the contractor fails to submit a proposal or a settlement cannot be reached by agreement.

## B. Special Considerations.

FAR Part 49.

1. As a general rule, a termination for convenience converts the terminated portion of a fixed-price contract to a cost-reimbursement type of contract, so costs on the settlement proposal are determined under FAR Part 31—Cost Principles and Procedures. *Bos'n Towing & Salvage Co.*, ASBCA No. 41357, 92-2 BCA ¶ 24,864.

2. Nevertheless, the cost principles must be applied subject to the fairness principle set forth at FAR 49.201(a), which states:

   A settlement should compensate the contractor fairly for the work done and the preparations made for the terminated portions of the contract, including a reasonable allowance for profit. Fair compensation is a matter of judgment and cannot be measured exactly. In a given case, various methods may be equally appropriate for arriving at fair compensation. The use of business judgment, as distinguished from strict accounting principles, is the heart of a settlement.

   *See Codex Corp. v. United States*, 226 Ct. Cl. 693 (1981) (board decision disallowing precontract costs based on strict application of cost principles was remanded for further consideration by the board based on the court's determination that cost principles must be applied "subject to" the fairness concept in DAR 8-301 (now FAR 49.201)). *See also J.W. Cook & Sons*, ASBCA No. 39691, 92-3 BCA ¶ 25,053 (board definition of "fairness").

3. Merger. Claims against the government are generally merged with the termination for convenience settlement proposal; therefore, it is not necessary to distinguish equitable adjustment costs from normal performance costs unless the contract is in a loss status. *Worsham Constr. Co.*, ASBCA No. 25907, 85-2 BCA ¶ 18,016.

4. Cost of Defective Work. Generally, a contractor can recover costs of defective work when a contract is terminated for the convenience of the government. *Morton-Thiokol, Inc.*, ASBCA No. 32629, 90-3 BCA ¶ 23,207; *but see Lisbon Contractors, Inc. v. United States*, 828 F.2d 759 (Fed. Cir. 1987); *Air Cool, Inc.*, ASBCA No. 32838, 88-1 BCA ¶ 20,399.

## C. Limitations on Termination for Convenience Settlements.

1. **Overall contract price for fixed-price contracts**. The total settlement may not exceed the contract price (less payments made or to be made under the contract) plus the amount of the settlement expenses. FAR 49.207; FAR 52.249-2(e); *Tom Shaw, Inc.*, ENG BCA No. 5540, 93-2 BCA ¶ 25,742. *See also Alta Constr. Co.*, PSBCA No. 1463, 92-2 BCA ¶ 24,824. *Compare Okaw Indus.*, ASBCA No. 17863, 77-2 BCA ¶ 12,793 (the contract price of items terminated on an indefinite quantity contract is the price of the ordered quantity, not of the estimated quantity, where the government has ordered the minimum quantity) *with Aviation Specialists, Inc.*, DOT BCA No. 1967, 91-1 BCA ¶ 23,534 (the only reasonable measure of the maximum recovery under a requirements contract is the government estimate.)

2. Add the price of valid pending claims for government delay, defective specifications, etc., to the original contract price to establish the "ceiling" of convenience termination recovery. *See, e.g., Wolfe Constr. Co.*, ENG BCA No. 5309, 88-3 BCA ¶ 21,122.

3. A contractor is not entitled to anticipatory profits. *Dairy Sales Corp. v. United States*, 593 F.2d 1002 (Ct. Cl. 1979).

4. A contractor is not entitled to consequential damages. *William Green Constr. Co. v. United States*, 477 F.2d 930 (Ct. Cl.) *cert. denied*, 417 U.S. 909 (1973).

5. Usable items. The cost of common items that the contractor can use on other work is not allowable.

   a. FAR 31.205-42(a) provides that "[t]he costs of items reasonably usable on the contractor's other work shall not be allowable unless the contractor submits evidence that the items could not be retained at cost without sustaining a loss."

   b. Courts and boards have applied this provision to more than just materiel costs. *Dairy Sales Corp. v. United States*, 593 F.2d 1002 (Ct. Cl. 1979) (cost of butter wrapping machine not allowed in a partial termination of a butter packing contract); *Hugo Auchter GmbH*, ASBCA No. 39642, 91-1 BCA ¶ 23,645 (general purpose off-the-shelf computer equipment); *Globe Air, Inc.*, AGBCA No. 76-119, 78-1 BCA ¶ 13,079 (helicopter provided under helicopter rental contract); *American Packers, Inc.*, ASBCA No. 14275, 71-1 BCA ¶ 8846 (pickup trucks under contract for packing and hauling household goods).

6. Mutual fault. In some situations, if both the government and the contractor are responsible for the causes resulting in termination of a contract, contractors have been denied full recovery of termination costs.

   a. In *Dynalectron Corp. v. United States*, 518 F.2d 594 (Ct. Cl. 1975), the court allowed the contractor only one-half of the allowable termination for convenience costs because the contractor was at fault in continuing to incur costs while trying to meet impossible government specifica-

tions without notifying the government of its efforts. *See also Martin J. Simko Constr., Inc. v. United States*, 11 Cl. Ct. 257 (1986).

   b. In *Insul-Glass, Inc.*, GSBCA No. 8223, 89-1 BCA ¶ 21,361, the board denied termination for convenience recovery because of the contractor's deficient administration of the contract. The board noted that under the default clause, if the default is determined to be improper, "the rights and obligations of the parties shall be the same as if a notice of termination for convenience of the government had been issued. We may exercise our equitable powers, however, to fashion, in circumstances where both parties share in the blame for the predicament which engenders an appeal, a remedy which apportions costs fairly." *See also A.J.C.A. Constr. v. Gen. Servs. Admin.*, GSBCA No. 11541 (May 17, 1994), 94-2 BCA ¶ 26,949 (default termination converted to no-cost termination for convenience).

**D. Loss Contracts.**

1. A contracting officer may not allow profit in settling a termination claim if it appears that the contractor would have incurred a loss had the entire contract been completed. FAR 49.203.

2. If the contractor would have suffered a loss on the contract in the absence of the termination for convenience, the contractor may recover only the same percentage of costs incurred as would have been recovered had the contract gone to completion. The rate of loss is applied to costs incurred to determine the cost recovery. FAR 40.203. The termination for convenience recovery equation for a contract in a loss status is:

$$\frac{\text{Contract price}}{\text{Expected cost-full performance}} \times \text{cost incurred} = \text{contractor recovery}$$

3. The government has the burden of proving that the contractor would have incurred a loss at contract completion. *R&B Bewachungs, GmbH*, ASBCA No. 42214, 92-3 BCA ¶ 25,105; *Specon, Inc.*, ASBCA No. 29137, 86-3 BCA ¶ 19,163.

### E. Subcontract Settlements Upon Termination for Convenience.

Subcontractors generally are entitled to the same recovery from the prime contractor as the prime is against the government. FAR 49.108. Such subcontractor recovery amounts are allowable as part of the prime's termination for convenience settlement with the government. FAR 31.205-42(h); *Bos'n Towing & Salvage Co.*, ASBCA No. 41357, 92-2 BCA ¶ 24,864.

### F. Fiscal Considerations.

1. An agency must analyze *each* contract that it plans to terminate for convenience to determine whether termination for convenience or completion of the contract is less costly or otherwise in the best interests of the government.

2. An agency must determine whether the convenience termination settlement would be governed by:
   a. Standard FAR convenience termination clause provisions, or
   b. Contract-specific terms, such as termination ceilings, multi-year contract termination costs, or other specific contractual terms.

3. An agency must determine the disposition of funds obligated for the contract to be terminated.
   a. The general rule is that a prior year's funding obligation is extinguished upon termination of a contract, and funds will not remain available to fund a replacement contract in a subsequent year where a contracting officer terminates a contract for the convenience of the government.
   b. The GAO adopted an important exception to this rule in *Funding of Replacement Contracts*, B-232616, 68 Comp. Gen. 158 (1988), and *Navy, Replacement Contract*, B-238548, 70 Comp. Gen. 230 (1991). Funds originally obligated in one fiscal year for a contract that is later terminated for convenience *in response to* a court order or to a determination by the General Accounting Office or other competent authority that the award was improper, *or as a result of* the contracting officer's determination that the award was clearly erroneous, remain available in a subsequent fiscal year to fund a replacement contract, subject to the following conditions:
      (1) The original award was made in good faith;
      (2) The agency has a continuing *bona fide* need for the goods or services involved;
      (3) The replacement contract is of the same size and scope as the original contract;
      (4) The replacement contract is executed without undue delay after the original contract is terminated for convenience; and
      (5) If the termination for convenience is issued by the contracting officer, the contracting officer's determination that the award was improper is supported by findings of fact and law.

# SHORT FORM TERMINATION FOR CONVENIENCE CLAUSE FOR FIXED-PRICE CONTRACTS

**52.249-1 Termination for Convenience of the Government (Fixed-Price) (Short Form).**

As prescribed in 49.502(a)(1), insert the following clause in solicitations and contracts when a fixed-price contract is contemplated and the contract amount is expected to be $100,000 or less, except (a) if use of the clause at 52.249-4, Termination for Convenience of the Government (Services) (Short Form) is appropriate, (b) in contracts for research and development work with an educational or nonprofit institution on a no-profit basis, (c) in contracts for architect-engineer services, or (d) if one of the clauses prescribed or cited at 49.505(a), (b), or (e), is appropriate:

TERMINATION FOR CONVENIENCE OF THE GOVERNMENT
(FIXED-PRICE) (SHORT FORM) (APR 1984)

The Contracting Officer, by written notice, may terminate this contract, in whole or in part, when it is in the Government's interest. If this contract is terminated, the rights, duties, and obligations of the parties, including compensation to the Contractor, shall be in accordance with Part 49 of the Federal Acquisition Regulation in effect on the date of this contract.

(End of clause)
(R 1-8.705-1)
(R 1-8.705-2)
(R 7-103.21(a) 1968 FEB)
(R 7-602.29(b) 1965 JAN)

*Alternate I* (APR 1984). If the contract is for dismantling, demolition, or removal of improvements, designate the basic clause as paragraph (a) and add the following paragraph (b):

(b) Upon receipt of the termination notice, if title to property is vested in the Contractor under this contract, it shall revest in the Government regardless of any other clause of the contract, except for property that the Contractor (a) disposed of by bona fide sale or (b) removed from the site.

(R 7-2101.8(b) 1976 OCT)

# SHORT FORM TERMINATION FOR CONVENIENCE CLAUSE FOR SERVICES CONTRACTS

**52.249-4 Termination for Convenience of the Government (Services) (Short Form).**

As prescribed in 49.502(c), insert the following clause in solicitations and contracts for services, regardless of value, when a fixed-price contract is contemplated and the Contracting Officer determines that because of the kind of services required, the successful offeror will not incur substantial charges in preparation for and in carrying out the contract, and would, if terminated for the convenience of the Government, limit termination settlement charges to services rendered before the date of termination:

TERMINATION FOR CONVENIENCE OF THE GOVERNMENT
(SERVICES) (SHORT FORM) (APR 1984)

The Contracting Officer, by written notice, may terminate this contract, in whole or in part, when it is in the Government's interest. If this contract is terminated, the Government shall be liable only for payment under the payment provisions of this contract for services rendered before the effective date of termination.

(End of clause)
(R 7-1902.16 1968 FEB)
(R 1-8.705-1)

# FAR CLAUSE 52.249-2
# LONG FORM TERMINATION FOR CONVENIENCE
# CLAUSE FOR FIXED-PRICE CONTRACTS

**52.249-2 Termination for Convenience of the Government (Fixed-Price)**

As prescribed in 49.502(b)(1)(i), insert the following clause in solicitations and contracts when a fixed-price contract is contemplated, and the contract amount is expected to be over $100,000, except in contracts for (a) dismantling and demolition, (b) research and development work with an educational or non-profit institution on a no-profit basis, or (c) architect-engineer services. It shall not be used if the clause at 52.249-4, Termination for Convenience of the Government (Services) (Short Form), is appropriate (see 49.502(c)), or one of the clauses prescribed or cited at 49.505(a), (b), or (e), is appropriate.

TERMINATION FOR CONVENIENCE OF THE GOVERNMENT
(FIXED-PRICE) (APR 1984)

(a)  The Government may terminate performance of work under this contract in whole or, from time to time, in part if the Contracting Officer determines that a termination is in the Government's interest. The Contracting Officer shall terminate by delivering to the Contractor a Notice of Termination specifying the extent of termination and the effective date.

(b)  After receipt of a Notice of Termination, and except as directed by the Contracting Officer, the Contractor shall immediately proceed with the following obligations, regardless of any delay in determining or adjusting any amounts due under this clause:

(1)  Stop work as specified in the notice.

(2)  Place no further subcontracts or orders (referred to as subcontracts in this clause) for materials, services, or facilities, except as necessary to complete the continued portion of the contract.

(3)  Terminate all subcontracts to the extent they relate to the work terminated.

(4)  Assign to the Government, as directed by the Contracting Officer, all right, title, and interest of the Contractor under the subcontracts terminated, in which case the Government shall have the right to settle or to pay any termination settlement proposal arising out of those terminations.

(5)  With approval or ratification to the extent required by the Contracting Officer, settle all outstanding liabilities and termination settlement proposals arising from the termination of subcontracts; the approval or ratification will be final for purposes of this clause.

(6)  As directed by the Contracting Officer, transfer title and deliver to the Government (i) the fabricated or unfabricated parts, work in process, completed work, supplies, and other material produced or acquired for the work terminated, and (ii) the completed or partially completed plans, drawings, information, and other property that, if the contract had been completed, would be required to be furnished to the Government.

(7)  Complete performance of the work not terminated.

(8)  Take any action that may be necessary, or that the Contracting Officer may direct, for the protection and preservation of the property related to this contract that is in the possession of the Contractor and in which the Government has or may acquire an interest.

(9)  Use its best efforts to sell, as directed or authorized by the Contracting Officer, any property of the types referred to in subparagraph (6) above; *provided,* however, that the Contractor (i) is not required to extend credit to any purchaser and (ii) may acquire the property under the conditions prescribed by, and at prices approved by, the Contracting Officer. The proceeds of any transfer or disposition will be applied to reduce any payments to be made by the Government under this contract, credited to the price or cost of the work, or paid in any other manner directed by the Contracting Officer.

(c)  After expiration of the plant clearance period as defined in Subpart 45.6 of the Federal Acquisition Regulation, the Contractor may submit to the Contracting Officer a list, certified as to quantity and quality, of termination inventory not previously disposed of, excluding items authorized for disposition by the Contracting Officer. The Contractor may request the Government to remove those items or enter into an agreement for their storage. Within 15 days, the Government will accept title to those items and remove them or enter into a storage agreement. The Contracting Officer may verify the list upon removal of the items, or if stored, within 45 days from submission of the list, and shall correct the list, as necessary, before final settlement.

(d) After termination, the Contractor shall submit a final termination settlement proposal to the Contracting Officer in the form and with the certification prescribed by the Contracting Officer. The Contractor shall submit the proposal promptly, but no later than 1 year from the effective date of termination, unless extended in writing by the Contracting Officer upon written request of the Contractor within this 1-year period. However, if the Contracting Officer determines that the facts justify it, a termination settlement proposal may be received and acted on after 1 year or any extension. If the Contractor fails to submit the proposal within the time allowed, the Contracting Officer may determine, on the basis of information available, the amount, if any, due the Contractor because of the termination and shall pay the amount determined.

(e) Subject to paragraph (d) above, the Contractor and the Contracting Officer may agree upon the whole or any part of the amount to be paid because of the termination. The amount may include a reasonable allowance for profit on work done. However, the agreed amount, whether under this paragraph (e) or paragraph (f) below, exclusive of costs shown in subparagraph (f)(3) below, may not exceed the total contract price as reduced by (1) the amount of payments previously made and (2) the contract price of work not terminated. The contract shall be amended, and the Contractor paid the agreed amount. Paragraph (f) below shall not limit, restrict, or affect the amount that may be agreed upon to be paid under this paragraph.

(f) If the Contractor and the Contracting Officer fail to agree on the whole amount to be paid because of the termination of work, the Contracting Officer shall pay the Contractor the amounts determined by the Contracting Officer as follows, but without duplication of any amounts agreed on under paragraph (e) above:

(1) The contract price for completed supplies or services accepted by the Government (or sold or acquired under subparagraph (b)(9) above) not previously paid for adjusted for any saving of freight and other charges.

(2) The total of—

(i) The costs incurred in the performance of the work terminated, including initial costs and preparatory expense allocable thereto, but excluding any costs attributable to supplies or services paid or to be paid under subparagraph (f)(1) above;

(ii) The cost of settling and paying termination settlement proposals under terminated subcontractors that are properly chargeable to the terminated portion of the contract if not included in subdivision (i) above; and

(iii) A sum, as profit on subdivision (i) above, determined by the Contracting Officer under 49.202 of the Federal Acquisition Regulation, in effect on the date of this contract, to be fair and reasonable; however, if it appears that the Contractor would have sustained a loss on the entire contract had it been completed, the Contracting Officer shall allow no profit under this subdivision (iii) and shall reduce the settlement to reflect the indicated rate of loss.

(3) The reasonable costs of settlement of the work terminated, including—

(i) Accounting, legal, clerical, and other expenses reasonably necessary for the preparation of termination settlement proposals and supporting data;

(ii) The termination and settlement of subcontracts (excluding the amounts of such settlements); and

(iii) Storage, transportation, and other costs incurred, reasonably necessary for the preservation, protection, or disposition of the termination inventory.

(g) Except for normal spoilage, and except to the extent that the Government expressly assumed the risk of loss, the Contracting Officer shall exclude from the amounts payable to the Contractor under paragraph (f) above, the fair value, as determined by the Contracting Officer, of property that is destroyed, lost, stolen, or damaged so as to become undeliverable to the Government or to a buyer.

(h) The cost principles and procedures of Part 31 of the Federal Acquisition Regulation, in effect on the date of this contract, shall govern all costs claimed, agreed to, or determined under this clause.

(i) The Contractor shall have the right of appeal, under the Disputes clause, from any determination made by the Contracting Officer under paragraph (d), (f),or (k), except that if the Contractor failed to submit the termination settlement proposal within the time provided in paragraph (d) or (k), and failed to request a time extension, there is no right of appeal. If the Contracting Officer has made a determination of the amount due under paragraph (d), (f), or (k), the Government shall pay the Contractor (1) the amount determined by the Contracting Officer if there is no right of appeal or if no timely appeal has been taken, or (2) the amount finally determined on an appeal.

(j) In arriving at the amount due the Contractor under this clause, there shall be deducted—

(1) All unliquidated advance or other payments to the Contractor under the terminated portion of this contract.

(2) Any claim which the Government has against the Contractor under this contract; and

(3) The agreed price for, or the proceeds of sale of, materials, supplies, or other things acquired by the Contractor or sold under the provisions of this clause and not recovered by or credited to the Government.

(k) If the termination is partial, the Contractor may file a proposal with the Contracting Officer for an equitable adjustment of the price(s) of the continued portion of the contract. The Contracting Officer shall make any equitable adjustment agreed upon. Any proposal by the Contractor for an equitable adjustment under this clause shall be requested within 90 days from the effective date of termination unless extended in writing by the Contracting Officer.

(l) (1) The Government may, under the terms and conditions it prescribes, make partial payments and payments against costs incurred by the Contractor for the terminated portion of the contract, if the Contracting Officer believes the total of these payments will not exceed the amount to which the Contractor will be entitled.

(2) If the total payments exceed the amount finally determined to be due, the Contractor shall repay the excess to the Government upon demand, together with interest computed at the rate established by the Secretary of the Treasury under 50 U.S.C. App. 1215(b)(2). Interest shall be computed for the period from the date the excess payment is received by the Contractor to the date the excess is repaid. Interest shall not be charged on any excess payment due to a reduction in the Contractor's termination settlement proposal because of retention or other disposition of termination inventory until 10 days after the date of the retention or disposition, or a later date determined by the Contracting Officer because of the circumstances.

(m) Unless otherwise provided in this contract or by statute, the Contractor shall maintain all records and documents relating to the terminated portion of this contract for 3 years after final settlement. This includes all books and other evidence bearing on the Contractor's costs and expenses under this contract. The Contractor shall make these records and documents available to the Government, at the Contractor's office, at all reasonable times, without any direct charge. If approved by the Contracting Officer, photographs, microphotographs, or other authentic reproductions may be maintained instead of original records and documents.

(End of clause)
(R 1-8.701)
(R 7-103.21(b) 1974 OCT)

*Alternate I* (APR 1984). If the contract is for construction, substitute the following paragraph (f) for paragraph (f) of the basic clause:

(f) If the Contractor and Contracting Officer fail to agree on the whole amount to be paid the Contractor because of the termination of work, the Contracting Officer shall pay the Contractor the amounts determined as follows, but without duplication of any amounts agreed upon under paragraph (e) above:

(1) For contract work performed before the effective date of termination, the total (without duplication of any items) of—

(i)  The cost of this work;

(ii) The cost of settling and paying termination settlement proposals under terminated subcontracts that are properly chargeable to the terminated portion of the contract if not included in subdivision (i) above; and

(iii) A sum, as profit on (i) above, determined by the Contracting Officer under 49.202 of the Federal Acquisition Regulation, in effect on the date of this contract, to be fair and reasonable; however, if it appears that the Contractor would have sustained a loss on the entire contract had it been completed, the Contracting Officer shall allow no profit under this subdivision (iii) and shall reduce the settlement to reflect the indicated rate of loss.

(2) The reasonable costs of settlement of the work terminated, including—

(i)  Accounting, legal, clerical, and other expenses reasonably necessary for the preparation of termination settlement proposals and supporting data;

(ii) The termination and settlement of subcontracts (excluding the amounts of such settlements); and

(iii) Storage, transportation, and other costs incurred, reasonably necessary for the preservation, protection, or disposition of the termination inventory.

(R 1-8.703)

(R 7-602.29(a) 1974 APR)

*Alternate II* (APR 1984). If the contract is with an agency of the U.S. Government or with State, local, or foreign governments or their agencies, and if the Contracting Officer determines that the requirement to pay interest on excess partial payments is inappropriate, delete subparagraph (l)(2) of the basic clause. (R 8-701(c))

*Alternate III* (APR 1984). If the contract is for construction and with an agency of the U.S. Government or with State, local, or foreign governments or their agencies, substitute the following paragraph (f) for paragraph (f) of the basic clause. Subparagraph (l)(2) may be deleted from the basic clause if the Contracting Officer determines that the requirement to pay interest on excess partial payments is inappropriate.

(f)  If the Contractor and Contracting Officer fail to agree on the whole amount to be paid the Contractor because of the termination of work, the Contracting Officer shall pay the Contractor the amounts determined as follows, but without duplication of any amounts agreed upon under paragraph (e) above:

(1) For contract work performed before the effective date of termination, the total (without duplication of any items) of—

(i)  The cost of this work;

(ii) The cost of settling and paying termination settlement proposals under terminated subcontracts that are properly chargeable to the terminated portion of the contract if not included in subdivision (i) above; and

(iii) A sum, as profit on (i) above, determined by the Contracting Officer under 49.202 of the Federal Acquisition Regulation, in effect on the date of this contract, to be fair and reasonable; however, if it appears that the Contractor would have sustained a loss on the entire contract had it been completed, the Contracting Officer shall allow no profit under this subdivision (iii) and shall reduce the settlement to reflect the indicated rate of loss.

(2) The reasonable costs of settlement of the work terminated, including—

(i)  Accounting, legal, clerical, and other expenses reasonably necessary for the preparation of termination settlement proposals and supporting data;

(ii) The termination and settlement of subcontracts (excluding the amounts of such settlements); and

(iii) Storage, transportation, and other costs incurred, reasonably necessary for the preservation, protection, or disposition of the termination inventory.

(R 1-8.703)

(R 7-602.29(a) 1974 APR)

(R 8-701(c))

## CHAPTER TWENTY-FOUR

# *Contract Terminations for Default*

## I. INTRODUCTION.

### A. Goals of Instruction.

Following this block of instruction, the student will:

1. Understand the right of the government to terminate a contract for default.

2. Understand the bases for which the government may terminate a contract for default.

3. Understand common contractor defenses to a default termination.

### B. Definition of Default.

A contractor's unexcused present or prospective failure to perform in accordance with the contract's terms, specifications, or delivery schedule constitutes contractual default under government contracts.

### C. Review of Default Terminations by the Courts and Boards.

1. "[A] termination for default is a drastic sanction that should be imposed upon a contractor only for good cause and in the presence of solid evidence." *Lisbon Contractors, Inc. v. United States*, 828 F.2d 759 (Fed. Cir. 1987); *Mega Constr. Co. v. United States*, 25 Cl. Ct. 735 (1992); *Sun Cal, Inc. v. United States*, 21 Cl. Ct. 31 (1990).

2. Burden of Proof. It is the government's burden to prove, by a preponderance of the evidence, that the termination for default was proper. *Lisbon Contractors, Inc. v. United States*, 828 F.2d 759 (Fed. Cir. 1987); *Sterling Millwrights, Inc. v. United States*, 26 Cl. Ct. 49 (1992).

Once the government has met its burden of demonstrating the appropriateness of the default, the burden shifts to the contractor to prove that the default was excusable. *International Elec. Corp. v. United States*, 646 F.2d 496 (Ct. Cl. 1981); *Composite Int'l, Inc.*, ASBCA No. 43359, 93-2 BCA ¶ 25,747.

## II. THE RIGHT TO TERMINATE FOR DEFAULT.

### A. Contractual—Termination for Default Clauses.

The FAR contains a complete set of Default clauses for use in government contracts (*see* pages 347-355). FAR Parts 49 and 52. These clauses vary according to contract type and identify the conditions that permit the government to terminate the contract for default.

### B. Common-Law Doctrine.

1. The standard FAR Default clauses provide as follows:

   "The rights and remedies of the government in this clause are in addition to any other rights and remedies provided by law or under this contract." *See* FAR 52.249-8 and FAR 52.249-10.

2. Courts commonly cite the above-quoted provision as a basis to support the government's termination of a contract for default based on common-law doctrines such as anticipatory repudiation. *Cascade Pac. Int'l v. United States*, 773 F.2d 287 (Fed. Cir. 1985).

## III. GROUNDS FOR TERMINATION.

### A. Failure to Deliver or Perform on Time.

1. The contract default clauses provide this ground for termination. It is commonly referred to as an "(a)(1)(i)" termination. FAR 52.249-8(a)(1)(i); FAR 52.249-1(a); FAR 52.249-6(a).

2. Generally, time is of the essence in all government contracts containing fixed dates for delivery or performance. *See Kit Pack Co.*, ASBCA No. 33135, 89-3 BCA ¶ 22,151. Upon non-delivery of a contract requirement, the government has an immediate right to terminate the contract. *West Coast Research Corp.*, ASBCA No. 37354, 89-2 BCA ¶ 21,684.

3. Additionally, the government is entitled to strict compliance with its specifications. *Mega Constr. Co. v. United States*, 25 Cl. Ct. 735 (1992); *Kurz-Kasch, Inc.*, ASBCA No. 32486, 88-3 BCA ¶ 21,053.

4. Courts and boards recognize the common-law principle of substantial compliance to protect the contractor where performance departs in minor respects from that required by the contract. *F&D Constr. Co.*, ASBCA No. 41441, 91-2 BCA ¶ 23,983. If the following five (5) factors exist, the government may not terminate the contract for default immediately, but must give the contractor additional time to complete performance, *Radiation Technology, Inc. v. United States*, 366 F.2d 1003 (Ct. Cl. 1966):

   a. The contractor delivers on time;
   b. The contractor believes in good faith that it delivered goods that conform to the contract;
   c. The defects are minor in nature;
   d. The defects are capable of being corrected within a reasonable period of time; and,
   e. Time is not of the essence; i.e., the government has no special need for the contractor to comply strictly with the delivery schedule. *See Kurz-Kasch, Inc.*, ASBCA No. 32486, 88-3 BCA ¶ 21,053.

5. Late delivery of conforming goods. Two opposing lines of cases deal with the question of whether a slightly late delivery or performance justifies termination for default.

   a. In *Franklin E. Penny Co. v. United States*, 207 Ct. Cl. 842 (1975), the Court of Claims stated that, "save in situations where 'time is of the essence,' the timeliness of a contractor's performance is as much a factor to be considered in evaluating the substantiality of that performance as are all other factors which might bear upon the adequacy of completeness of that performance".

   b. In both earlier and later cases, however, the Court of Claims and the boards of contract appeals have expressed the strict view that time *is* of the essence in all government contracts containing fixed dates for delivery or performance, unless the government has waived the delivery date. Thus, a failure to meet the delivery or performance date generally is cause for default termination. *DeVito v. United States*, 413 F.2d 1147 (Ct. Cl. 1969); *Simmons Precision Prods., Inc. v. United States*, 546 F.2d 886 (Ct. Cl. 1976); *Kit Pack Co.*, ASBCA No. 33135, 89-3 BCA ¶ 22,151; *National Farm Equip. Co.*, GSBCA No. 4921, 78-1 BCA ¶ 13,195; *Cosmos Eng'rs, Inc.*, ASBCA No. 19780, 77-2 BCA ¶ 12,713.

### B. Failure to Make Progress so as to Endanger Performance.

1. The Default clauses for fixed-price supply and service contracts, fixed-price construction contracts and cost-reimbursement contracts all provide for termination when the contractor fails to make progress or prosecute the work in a manner so as to ensure completion within the time specified in the contract. This is commonly referred to as an "(a)(1)(ii)" termination. FAR 52.249-8(a)(1)(ii); FAR 52.249-1(a); FAR 52.249-6(a).

2. The government is not required to show that it was impossible for the contractor to complete performance. *California Dredging Co.*, ENG BCA No. 5532, 92-1 BCA ¶ 24,475;

*Ener-Tech Automated Control Sys., Inc.*, ASBCA No. 31527, 89-3 BCA ¶ 22,091.

3. The contracting officer must have a reasonable belief that the contractor cannot perform the entire contract effort within the time remaining for contract performance. *Technocratica*, ASBCA No. 44134, 94-2 BCA ¶ 26,606 (termination for "poor progress" improper); *Pipe Tech, Inc.*, ENG BCA No. 5959, 94-2 BCA ¶ 26,649, *mot. for recon. denied*, 94-2 BCA ¶ 26,825 (termination improper where 92% of contract performance time remained and reprocurement contractor fully performed within the time allowed in defaulted contract); *Delta Marine, Inc.*, ASBCA No. 39649, 93-3 BCA ¶ 26,164; *Lisbon Contractors, Inc. v. United States*, 828 F.2d 759 (Fed. Cir. 1987); *Skip Kirchdorfer, Inc.*, ASBCA No. 32367, 91-1 BCA ¶ 23,380.

## C. Failure to Perform Any Other Provision of the Contract.

1. The default clause in fixed-price supply and service contracts specifically provides this ground for termination. It is commonly referred to as an (a)(1)(iii) termination. FAR 52.249-8(a)(1)(iii).

2. This basis for default may also exist in other types of contracts (e.g., construction contracts) based on:

    a. Violations of other contract clauses. *Engineering Technology Consultants, S.A.*, ASBCA No. 43454, 94-1 BCA ¶ 26,586 (construction contractor's failure to maintain required liability insurance); *H&R Machinists Co.*, ASBCA No. 38440, 91-1 BCA ¶ 23,373 (violation of the Buy American clause of the contract).

    b. Violations of other regulatory requirements. *"K" Servs.*, ASBCA No. 41791, 92-1 BCA ¶ 24,568 (false certification as to debarment status); *National Med. Staffing, Inc.*, DOT BCA No. 2568, 94-1 BCA ¶ 26,542 (to support termination for false certification as to prior default termination, government must demonstrate that contracting officer was unaware of prior default termination at time of award).

    c. Violations of statute. *Kirk Bros. Mech. Contractors, Inc. v. Kelso*, 16 F.3d 1173 (Fed. Cir. 1994) (violation of the Davis-Bacon Act). The Act specifically provides for termination as a right of the government. 40 U.S.C. § 276(a).

    d. An implied or common-law right to terminate or cancel a contract provided by the courts or boards to effectuate the public policy embodied in a statute or regulation. *Cosmos Eng'rs, Inc.*, ASBCA No. 23529, 84-2 BCA ¶ 17268 (contractor convicted of fraud under the False Statements Act, 18 U.S.C. § 1001; board upheld default termination in summary judgment motion). *But see Fleischzentrale Sudwest, GmbH*, ASBCA No. 37273, 92-1 BCA ¶ 24,612 (default termination improper because criminal conduct not by contractor employee).

3. Courts and boards will not sustain a default termination unless that "other provision" of the contract is a "material" or "significant" requirement. *Stone Forest Indus. v. United States*, 973 F.2d 1548 (Fed. Cir. 1992); *Precision Prods.*, ASBCA No. 25280, 82-2 BCA ¶ 15981.

## D. Anticipatory Repudiation.

1. Each party to a contract has the common-law right to terminate a contract upon *actual or anticipatory repudiation* of the contract by the other party. *Ortec Sys., Inc.*, ASBCA No. 43467, 92-2 BCA ¶ 24,859 (abandonment is actual repudiation).

    a. Anticipatory repudiation must be express. *Swiss Prods., Inc.*, ASBCA No. 40031, 93-3 BCA ¶ 26,163 (refusal to perform until government provided advance payments); *Western States Mgmt. Servs., Inc.*, ASBCA No. 40212, 92-1 BCA ¶ 24,714; *Scott Aviation*, ASBCA No. 40776, 91-3 BCA ¶ 24,123.

    b. The repudiation must be unequivocal and manifest either a clear intention not to perform or an inability to perform the contract. *Ateron Corp.*, ASBCA No. 46352, 94-3 BCA ¶ 27,229 (contractor's statement that continued contract performance is impossible constitutes repudiation); *Engineering & Professional Servs., Inc.*, ASBCA No. 39164, 94-2 BCA ¶ 26,762 (contractor's statement that "government financing must be provided to assure contract completion" not a repudiation of contract); *Beeston, Inc.*, ASBCA No. 38969, 91-3 BCA ¶ 24,241; *Premier Microwave Corp.*, ASBCA No. 36546, 88-3 BCA ¶ 20,984.

2. This common-law basis for default also applies to all government contracts, since contract clauses do not address and thereby supersede this principle. *See* DFARS 252.211-7000 (adds anticipatory repudiation as a specific contractual basis for default termination).

### E. Demand For Assurance.

1. Failure by one party to give adequate assurances that it would complete a contract is a valid basis for a default termination under common-law. Uniform Commercial Code § 2-609; *Restatement (Second) of Contracts* § 251. This doctrine is also applicable to government contracts. DFARS 252.211-7000; *Engineering & Professional Servs., Inc.*, ASBCA No. 39164, 94-2 BCA ¶ 26,762; *Hannon Elec. Co. v. United States*, 13 FPD ¶ 34 (Fed. Cl. 1994); *National Union Fire Ins. Co.*, ASBCA No. 34744, 90-1 BCA ¶ 22,266; *but see Ranco Constr., Inc. v. Gen. Servs. Admin.*, GSBCA No. 11923, 94-2 BCA ¶ 26,678 (board questions whether demand for assurance under UCC 2-609 applies to construction contracts).

2. The government's "cure notice" may be the equivalent of a demand for assurance. *Fairfield Scientific Corp.*, ASBCA No. 21151, 78-1 BCA ¶ 13082.

### F. Proper Ground(s) for Termination Must Exist at Time of Termination.

Generally, the contracting officer makes a termination decision. Upon appeal, the government is not bound by the contracting officer's reasons for the termination stated in the termination notice. If a proper ground for the default termination existed at the time of the termination, regardless of whether the contracting officer relied on or was even aware of that basis, the termination is proper. *See Kirk Bros. Mech. Contractors, Inc. v. Kelso*, 16 F.3d 1173 (Fed. Cir. 1994); *Quality Granite Constr. Co.*, ASBCA No. 43846, 93-3 BCA ¶ 26,073 (government not required to give notice to contractor when unaware of basis for termination); *Pots Unlimited, Ltd. v. United States*, 220 Ct. Cl. 405 (1979); *Cox & Palmer Constr. Corp.*, ASBCA No. 38739, 92-1 BCA ¶ 24,756.

## IV. NOTICE REQUIREMENTS.

### A. Cure Notice.

1. For fixed-price contracts, the government must notify the contractor, in writing, of its failure to make progress ((a)(1)(ii)) or its failure to perform any other provision of the contract ((a)(1)(iii)) *and* give the contractor 10 days in which to cure such failure before it may terminate the contract. FAR 52.249-8; FAR 52.249-9. *See Delta Indus.*, DOT BCA No. 2602, 94-1 BCA ¶ 26,318 (cure notice not required where contractor timely delivers supplies not in substantial compliance with the specifications); *cf. "K" Servs.*, ASBCA No. 41791, 92-1 BCA ¶ 24,568 (cure notice not required where failure to provide certification could not be cured).

a. A proper cure notice must inform the contractor *in writing*:
   (1) That the government intends to terminate the contract for default;
   (2) Of the reasons for the termination; and
   (3) That the contractor has a right to cure the specified deficiencies within the cure period (10 days). FAR 49.607(a) (format).

b. The government must give the contractor a minimum of ten days to cure the deficiency. *Red Sea Trading Assoc.*, ASBCA No. 36360, 91-1 BCA ¶ 23,567 (the ten day period need not be specifically stated in the notice if a minimum of ten days was actually afforded the contractor). *But see Contract Automotive Repair & Mgt.*, ASBCA No. 45316, 94-1 BCA ¶ 26,516 (although government terminated contract without providing contractor ten days to cure, board denies contractor's motion for summary judgment because contractor did not demonstrate that it could have cured deficiencies prior to expiration of cure period).

c. To support a default decision, the cure notice must clearly identify the nature and extent of the performance failure. *Insul-Glas, Inc.*, GSBCA No. 8223, 89-1 BCA ¶ 21,361; *Insul-Glas, Inc.*, GSBCA No. 9910-C (8223), 89-3 BCA ¶ 22,223.

2. Agencies may terminate cost-reimbursement contracts for default if the contractor fails to perform the contract *and* fails to cure the defect in performance within ten (10) days of receiving a proper cure notice from the contracting officer. FAR 52.249-6(a)(2).

3. Commercial Products. For contracts awarded under the provisions of DFARS Part 211, a cure notice is required before a default termination may be issued for *any* reason. DFARS 252.211-7000.

4. Except as stated above for commercial items, the government is not required to issue a cure notice when the basis for termination is anticipatory repudiation. DFARS 252.211-7000; *Beeston, Inc.*, ASBCA No. 38969, 91-3 BCA ¶ 24,241; *Scott Aviation*, ASBCA No. 40776, 91-3 BCA ¶ 24,123. **NOTE:** A response to a cure notice is often the best medium in which to obtain an unequivocal statement by the contractor concerning its intent to perform.

### B. Show Cause.

If a termination for default appears appropriate, the government should, if practicable, notify the contractor in writing of the possibility of the termination. FAR 49.402-3(e)(1). This notice is referred to as a "show cause" notice. FAR 49.607.

1. The show cause notice should:
   a. Call the contractor's attention to the contractual liabilities if the contract is terminated for default.
   b. Request the contractor to show cause why the contract should not be terminated for default.
   c. State that the failure of the contractor to present an explanation may be taken as an admission that no valid explanation exists.

2. The default clauses do not require the use of a show cause notice. *See* FAR 52.249-8 (Supply and Service); FAR 52.249-9 (Research and Development); FAR 52.249-10 (Construction); *International Foods Retort Co.*, ASBCA No. 34954, 92-2 BCA ¶ 24,994; *Kit Pack Co.*, ASBCA No. 33135, 89-3 BCA ¶ 22,151. However, the courts and boards may *require* a "show cause" notice if its use was practicable. *Udis v. United States*, 7 Cl. Ct. 379 (1985); *Enginetics Corp.*, ASBCA No. 40834, 92-2 BCA ¶ 24,965.

## V. CONTRACTOR DEFENSES TO A TERMINATION FOR DEFAULT.

### A. Excusable Delay.

1. A contractor's failure to deliver or to perform is excusable if the failure is *beyond the control and without the fault or negligence* of the contractor. FAR 52.249-8(c); FAR 52.249-14(a); *Sterling Millwrights, Inc. v. United States*, 26 Cl. Ct. 49 (1992); *Pyramid Packing, Inc.*, AGBCA No. 86-128-1, 92-2 BCA ¶ 24,831. For construction contracts, the cause must be unforeseeable *and* the contractor must notify the contracting officer within 10 days of the cause(s) of the delay. FAR 52.249-10(b)(1).

2. The contractor has the burden of proving that its failure to perform was excusable. *JR & Assoc.*, ASBCA No. 41377, 92-1 BCA ¶ 24,654; *Orlando Williams*, ASBCA No. 26099, 84-1 BCA ¶ 16,983. There are three elements:
   a. The occurrence of an event was unforeseeable, beyond its control, and without

its fault or negligence. *Local Contractors, Inc.*, ASBCA No. 37108, 92-1 BCA ¶ 24,491; *Charles H. Siever*, ASBCA No. 24814, 83-1 BCA ¶ 16,242.

b. Timely performance was actually prevented by the claimed excuse. *Sonora Mfg.*, ASBCA No. 31587, 91-1 BCA ¶ 23,444; *Beekman Indus.*, ASBCA No. 30280, 87-3 BCA ¶ 20,118.

c. The specific period of delay caused by the event. *Conquest Constr., Inc.*, PSBCA No. 2350, 90-1 BCA ¶ 22,605.

3. The Default clauses specifically identify some causes of excusable delay. These include:

a. Acts of God or of the public enemy. *See Nogler Tree Farm*, AGBCA No. 81-104-1, 81-2 BCA ¶ 15,315 (eruption of Mount St. Helens volcano); *Centennial Leasing v. Gen. Servs. Admin.*, GSBCA No. 12037, 94-1 BCA ¶ 26,398 (death of chief operating officer not an act of God).

b. Acts of the government in either its sovereign or contractual capacity.

(1) Sovereign capacity refers to public acts of the government not directed to the contractor. *Pyramid Packing, Inc.*, AGBCA No. 90-154-1, 92-2 BCA ¶ 24,831 (government- inspected raisins failed to meet required standards); *Woo Lim Constr. Co.*, ASBCA No. 13887, 70-2 BCA ¶ 8451 (imposition of security restrictions in a hostile area).

(2) Acts of the government in its contractual capacity are most common and include delays caused by defective specifications, unreasonable government inspections and late delivery of government furnished property. *See John Glenn*, ASBCA No. 31260, 91-3 BCA ¶ 24,054.

c. Fires. *Hawk Mfg. Co.*, GSBCA No. 4025, 74-2 BCA ¶ 10,764.

d. Floods. *Wayne Constr.*, ENG BCA No. 4942, 91-1 BCA ¶ 23,535.

e. Epidemics and quarantine restrictions. *Ace Elecs. Assoc.*, ASBCA No. 11496, 67-2 BCA ¶ 6456.

f. Strikes, freight embargoes, and similar work stoppages. *Woodington Corp.*, ASBCA No. 37885, 91-1 BCA ¶ 23,579.

g. Unusually severe weather. *TCH Indus.*, AGBCA No. 88-224-1, 91-3 BCA ¶ 24,364 (eight inches of snow in northern Idaho in November is neither unusual nor unforeseeable); *Joseph T. Yamin*, ASBCA No. 35373, 90-2 BCA ¶ 22,657.

h. Acts of another contractor in performance of a contract for the government (construction contracts). FAR 52.249-10(b)(1). *Modern Home Mfg. Corp.*, ASBCA No. 6523, 66-1 BCA ¶ 5367.

i. Defaults or delays *by subcontractors or suppliers*. The general rule is that if a failure to perform is caused by the default of a subcontractor or supplier at any tier, the default is excusable if:

(1) The cause of the default was beyond the control and without the fault or negligence of *either* the contractor or the subcontractor; *and,*

(2) The subcontracted supplies, services, or construction were not obtainable from other sources in time for the contractor to meet the required delivery schedule. FAR 52.249-8(d); FAR 52.249-10(b)(1); FAR 52.249-6(b); FAR 52.249-14(a). *Progressive Tool Corp.*, ASBCA No. 42809, 94-1 BCA ¶ 26,413; *C&M Mach. Prods.*, ASBCA No. 43348, 93-2 BCA ¶ 25,748; *Fleetwood Portable Bldg. Co.*, ASBCA No. 31711, 90-2 BCA ¶ 22,843.

4. Additional excuses commonly asserted by contractors include:

a. Material breach of contract by the government. *Todd-Grace, Inc.*, ASBCA No. 34469, 92-1 BCA ¶ 24,742 (breach of implied duty not to interfere with contractor); *Bogue Elec. Mfg. Co.*, ASBCA No. 25184, 86-2 BCA ¶ 18,925 (defective GFE).

b. Lack of financial capability. Generally, this is *not* an excuse. *Southeastern Airways Corp. v. United States*, 673 F.2d 368 (Ct. Cl. 1982); *Local Contractors, Inc.*, ASBCA

No. 37108, 92-1 BCA ¶ 24,491; *Kit Pack Co.*, ASBCA No. 33,135, 89-3 BCA ¶ 22,151. *But*, if the financial difficulties are caused by wrongful acts of the government, the delay may be excused. *See Durable Metal Prods.*, ASBCA No. 41446, 94-3 BCA ¶ 26,963; *Nexus Constr. Co.*, ASBCA No. 31070, 91-3 BCA ¶ 24,303; *Murdock Mach. & Eng'g Co. of Utah*, ASBCA No. 20409, 88-1 BCA ¶ 20,354; *DWS, Inc.*, ASBCA No. 33245, 87-3 BCA ¶ 19,960.

  c. Bankruptcy. Although filing a petition of bankruptcy is not an excuse, it does preclude termination. *Communications Technology Applications, Inc.*, ASBCA No. 41573, 92-3 BCA ¶ 25,211 (government's right to terminate stayed when bankruptcy filed, not when government notified); *Harris Prods., Inc.*, ASBCA No. 30426, 87-2 BCA ¶ 19,807 (a contract is property of the estate under 11 U.S.C. § 541 and is protected by the automatic stay provisions at 11 U.S.C. § 362(a)(3) of the Bankruptcy Code). *See In Re West Electronics, Inc.*, 852 F.2d 79 (3d Cir. 1988) (legal basis for lifting stay).

  d. Commercial impracticability. *Soletanche Rodio Nicholson (JV)*, ENG BCA No. 5796, 94-1 BCA ¶ 26,472 (performance might take 17 years and cost $400 million, rather than 2 years and $16 million); *C&M Mach. Prods.*, ASBCA No. 43348, 93-2 BCA ¶ 25,748 (no commercial impracticability where costs increased 105%); *Beeston, Inc.*, ASBCA No. 38969, 91-3 BCA ¶ 24,241; *Naughton Energy, Inc.*, ASBCA No. 33044, 88-2 BCA ¶ 20,800; *National Oil & Supply Co.*, ASBCA No. 28148, 87-3 BCA ¶ 20,058 (excellent discussion).

5. If a delay is found to be excusable, the contractor is entitled to additional time and/or money. *Batteast Constr. Co.*, ASBCA No. 35818, 92-1 BCA ¶ 24,697. <u>NOTE</u> - Constructive acceleration of the delivery date often occurs when the contracting officer, under threat of termination, directs compliance

with the contract delivery or performance date without extending the delivery or performance date by the time period attributable to an excusable delay.

**B. Waiver.**

1. The government must terminate a contract within a reasonable period of time after the contractor fails to deliver or perform, otherwise the concept of "waiver of the delivery schedule" will preclude termination by the government. *Devito v. United States*, 413 F.2d 1147 (Ct. Cl. 1969); *S.T. Research Corp.*, ASBCA No. 39600, 92-2 BCA ¶ 24,838; *Motorola Computer Sys., Inc.*, ASBCA No. 26794, 87-3 BCA ¶ 20,032.

2. The government may "forbear" for a reasonable period after the default occurs before taking some action. Reasonableness depends on the specific facts of each case. *See Eraklis Eraklidis*, ASBCA No. 40110, 91-3 BCA ¶ 24,188; *Kit Pack Co.*, ASBCA No. 33135, 89-3 BCA ¶ 22,151; *Orion Elec. Corp.*, ASBCA No. 18918, 80-1 BCA ¶ 14,219.

  a. Periods longer than thirty days engender close scrutiny. *Progressive Tool Corp.*, ASBCA No. 42809, 94-1 BCA ¶ 26,413 (although forbearance for 42 days after show cause notice was "somewhat long," T4D sustained because government did not encourage contractor to continue working and contractor did not perform substantial work during that period).

  b. Government actions during "forbearance period" may waive delivery date. *Applied Cos.*, ASBCA No. 43210, 94-2 BCA ¶ 26,837 (government waived delivery date for First Article Test Report by seeking information, making progress payments, directing the contractor to rerun tests, and incorporating engineering change proposals into the contract after the delivery date).

3. The contractor must show detrimental reliance on the government's inaction before the government will be deemed to have waived the delivery schedule. *Ordnance*

*Parts & Eng'g Co.*, ASBCA No. 44327, 93-2 BCA ¶ 25,690 (no detrimental reliance where contractor repudiated contract); *J.J. Seifert Mach. Co.*, ASBCA No. 41398, 91-2 BCA ¶ 23,705; *Hi-Shear Technology Corp.*, ASBCA No. 36041, 90-2 BCA ¶ 22,643; *Korean Maint. Co.*, ASBCA No. 31796, 88-3 BCA ¶ 21,155.

4. A delivery schedule that the government waived can be re-established either bilaterally or unilaterally. *Sermor, Inc.*, ASBCA No. 30576, 94-1 BCA ¶ 26,302 (contract modification not required, but new delivery date must be reasonable and specific).

   a. A new delivery date the parties establish bilaterally is presumed to be reasonable. *Trans World Optics, Inc.*, ASBCA No. 35976, 89-3 BCA ¶ 21,895; *ASC Sys. Corp.*, DOT CAB No. 73-37, 78-1 BCA ¶ 13,119. *See also Sermor, Inc., supra* (by agreeing to new delivery schedule, contractor waives excusable delay).

   b. A new delivery date the government unilaterally establishes must in fact be reasonable in light of the contractor's abilities in order to be enforceable. *Oklahoma Aerotronics, Inc.*, ASBCA No. 25605, 87-2 BCA ¶ 19,917. The schedule proposed by the contractor is presumed reasonable. *Tampa Brass & Aluminum Corp.*, ASBCA No. 41314, 92-2 BCA ¶ 24,865 ("[h]owever ill-considered [the schedule] may have been"). *But see S.T. Research Corp.*, ASBCA No. 39600, 92-2 BCA ¶ 24,838 (schedule proposed by contractor under 24-hour requirement *not* reasonable.)

   c. A cure notice, by itself, does not reestablish a waived delivery schedule. *Lanzen Fabricating*, ASBCA No. 40328, 93-3 BCA ¶ 26,079.

5. If a contract requires multiple deliveries, each successive increment represents a severable obligation to deliver on the contract delivery date. Thus, the government may accept late delivery of one or more installments without waiving the delivery date for future installments. *Allstate Leisure Prods.,*

*Inc.*, ASBCA No. 40532, 94-3 BCA ¶ 26,992; *Container Sys. Corp.*, ASBCA No. 40611, 94-1 BCA ¶ 26,354.

6. The waiver doctrine generally does not apply to construction contracts. *Nexus Constr. Co.*, ASBCA No. 31070, 91-3 BCA ¶ 24,303. *But see Luther Benjamin Constr. Co.*, ASBCA No. 40401, June 29, 1992 (unpub.). *See also Ultrasystems Defense & Space, Inc.*, ASBCA No. 41460, 93-2 BCA ¶ 25,752 (board refused to consider summary judgment "on a waiver issue in the somewhat novel context of a default termination for failure to make progress").

## VI. THE DECISION TO TERMINATE FOR DEFAULT.

FAR Subpart 49.1.

### A. Abuse of Discretion or Bad Faith Standard.

1. Termination for default is a discretionary act of the government.

   a. The standard FAR clauses generally grant the "government" the authority to terminate. FAR 52.249-5 thru 52.249-10. The contracting officer exercises this authority, and may receive extensive staff assistance from other government employees, including supervisory approval. *See PLB Grain Storage Corp.*, AGBCA No. 89-152-1, 92-1 BCA ¶ 24,731.

   b. The default clauses do not compel termination; rather, they permit termination for default if such action is appropriate in the business judgment of the responsible government officials. *Schlesinger v. United States*, 182 Ct. Cl. 571, 390 F.2d 702 (1968) (the Navy default-terminated a contract because of pressure from a Congressional committee, not based upon its own assessment of the government's and contractor's interests. The default termination was overturned and converted to a convenience termination).

   c. Contractors may challenge the default termination decision on the basis that the terminating official abused his or her discretion or acted in bad faith. *See Darwin Constr. Co. v. United States*, 811 F.2d 593 (Fed. Cir. 1987), which overruled a long-standing rule announced in *Nuclear Research Assoc.*, ASBCA No. 13563, 70-1 BCA ¶ 8,237, that a contracting officer's motivation in terminating for default—that is, the contracting officer's reasons for exercising his or her discretion to terminate—was irrelevant. *See also Nuclear Research Corp. v. United States*, 814 F.2d 647 (Fed. Cir. 1987); *National Med. Staffing, Inc.*, ASBCA No. 40391, 92-2 BCA ¶ 24,837; *Professional Window & Housecleaning, Inc.*, GSBCA No. 8268, 90-3 BCA ¶ 22,982.

2. Presumption and burden of proof.

   a. Government officials are presumed to have acted conscientiously in making a default termination decision. *Mindeco Corp.*, ASBCA No. 45207, 94-1 BCA ¶ 26,410; *Local Contractors, Inc.*, ASBCA No. 37108, 92-1 BCA ¶ 24,491. A contractor that asserts abuse of discretion or that the termination decision was arbitrary or capricious can overcome this presumption by a preponderance of the evidence. *Walsky Constr. Co.*, ASBCA No. 41541, 94-1 BCA ¶ 26,264, *aff'd on recon.*, 94-2 BCA ¶ 26,698 (lieutenant colonel's directive to the contracting officer "tainted the termination"); *Quality Env't Sys., Inc.*, ASBCA No. 22178, 87-3 BCA ¶ 20,060.

   b. Proof of "bad faith" by contracting officials, however, must meet a much higher standard. The courts and boards require "well nigh irrefragable proof" to overcome the presumption that public officials act in good faith in the exercise of their powers and responsibilities. *Apex Int'l Mgt. Servs., Inc.*, ASBCA No. 38087, 94-2 BCA ¶ 26,842, *aff'd on recon.*, 94-2 BCA ¶ 26,852 (Navy officials acted in bad faith; board overturns default termination and awards contractor breach damages); *Mindeco Corp.*, ASBCA No. 45207, 94-1 BCA ¶ 26,410; *Kalvar Corp. v. United States*,

211 Ct. Cl. 192 (1976); *T.A. Indus.*, VABCA No. 2941, 90-3 BCA ¶ 22,967; *Arnold V. Hedberg*, ASBCA No. 31747, 90-1 ¶ 22,577.

   c. Courts and boards review the contracting officer's actions according to the circumstances as they existed at the time of the default. *Local Contractors, Inc.*, ASBCA No. 37108, 92-1 BCA ¶ 24,491.

3. Regulatory guidance. The FAR provides detailed procedures which the contracting officer must follow to terminate a contract. FAR 49.402-3.

   a. The contracting officer's decision must reflect consideration of the relevant factors listed at FAR 49.402-3(f) (e.g., the contractor's excuses for failure to perform, availability of the supplies from other sources, urgency of the need for the supplies, the time required to obtain the supplies from other sources, etc.). *S.T. Research Corp.*, ASBCA No. 39600, 92-2 BCA ¶ 24,838.

   b. Failure to consider all information available prior to issuing a termination notice could be an abuse of discretion. *Jamco Constructors, Inc.*, VABCA No. 3271, 94-1 BCA ¶ 26,405, *aff'd on recon.*, 94-2 BCA ¶ 26,792 (contracting officer abused discretion by failing to reconcile contradictory information and "blindly" accepting technical representative's estimates for completion of the contract by another contractor); *National Med. Staffing, Inc.*, ASBCA No. 40391, 92-2 BCA ¶ 24,837; *but see Container Sys. Corp.*, ASBCA No. 40611, 94-1 BCA ¶ 26,354 (contracting officer's failure to consider one or more of the factors listed in FAR 49.402 "is not an automatic admission ticket to a termination for convenience"); *Lafayette Coal Co.*, ASBCA No. 32174, 89-3 BCA ¶ 21,963.

   c. Contracting officers must consider alternatives to termination. FAR 49.402-4.

   d. The contracting officer must explain the decision in a supporting memorandum. FAR 49.402-5.

## B. The Default Termination Notice.

1. Contents of the termination notice. FAR 49.102; FAR 42.601; FAR 49.402-3(g). The written notice must clearly state (FAR 49.102):

    a. That the contract or the applicable portion thereof is being terminated for default.

    b. The effective date of the termination.

    c. Any special instructions (including reduction in work force notice of FAR 49.601-2).

    d. The factual basis for the termination. *Kisco Co. v. United States*, 221 Ct. Cl. 806, 610 F.2d 742 (1979).

2. A default termination is a final decision that can be appealed. *Malone v. United States*, 849 F.2d 1441 (Fed. Cir. 1988) (boards of contract appeals have jurisdiction to hear appeals from default terminations). Under the Federal Courts Administration Act of 1992, Title IX, Pub. L. No. 102-572, the Court of Federal Claims may hear a dispute concerning the termination of a contract.

    a. The termination notification *must* give notice to the contractor of rights to appeal the default termination. If such notice is not given, the termination may be effective, but the contractor's appeal period will not begin to run. *Fleetwood Portable Bldg. Co.*, ASBCA No. 31711, 90-2 BCA ¶ 22,843.

    b. A default termination notice is effective when delivered to the contractor. *Fred Schwartz*, ASBCA No. 20724, 76-1 BCA ¶ 11,916, *recon. denied*, 76-2 BCA ¶ 11,976.

## VII. RIGHTS AND LIABILITIES ARISING FROM TERMINATIONS FOR DEFAULT.

### A. Contractor Liability.

Upon termination of a contract, the contractor is liable to the government for any excess costs incurred in acquiring supplies or services similar to those terminated for default (see FAR 49.402-6) and for any other damages, whether or not repurchase is effected (see FAR 49.402-7). FAR 49.402-2(e).

1. Excess Reprocurement Costs.

    a. Under fixed-price supply and service contracts, the government can acquire supplies or services similar to those terminated and the contractor will be liable for any excess costs of those supplies or services. FAR 52.249-8(b); *Ed Grimes*, GSBCA No. 7652 (7345)-REIN, 89-1 BCA ¶ 21,528; FAR 49.402-6. The government must show that its assessment was proper by establishing the following:

        (1) The reprocured supplies or services are the same as or similar to those involved in the termination. *International Foods Retort Co.*, ASBCA No. 34954, 92-2 BCA ¶ 24,994.

        (2) The government actually incurred excess costs. *Sequal, Inc.*, ASBCA No. 30838, 88-1 BCA ¶ 20,382; and

        (3) The government acted reasonably to minimize the excess costs resulting from the default. *Daubert Chem. Co.*, ASBCA No. 46752, 94-2 BCA ¶ 26,741 (government acted reasonably where it reprocured quickly, obtained seven bids, and awarded to lowest bidder); *Cascade Pac. Int'l v. United States*, 773 F.2d 287 (Fed. Cir. 1985); *Luther Benjamin Constr. Co.*, ASBCA No. 40401, June 29, 1992 (unpub.).

    b. Mitigation of damages: The government has an affirmative duty to mitigate damages on repurchase. *Al Bosgraaf & Son's*, ASBCA No. 45526, 94-2 BCA ¶ 26,913; *Ronald L. Collier*, ASBCA No. 26972, 89-1 BCA ¶ 21,328; *Kessler Chem., Inc.*, ASBCA No. 25293, 81-1 BCA ¶ 14,949.

        (1) Generally, the government is not required to solicit an offer from the defaulted contractor on a repurchase contract. *Morton Mfg., Inc.*, ASBCA No. 30716, 89-1 BCA ¶ 21,326. However, the government must solicit the defaulted contractor if it is the most suitable and readily available source for the reprocurement. *Tom W. Kaufman Co.*, GSBCA No. 4623, 78-2 BCA ¶ 13,288.

The government does not have to allow surety to complete a construction project. *Milner Constr. Co.*, DOT BCA No. 2043, 91-3 BCA ¶ 24,195.

(2) If the repurchase is for a quantity of goods in excess of the quantity that was terminated for default, the contracting officer must treat the entire quantity as a new acquisition. FAR 49.402-6(b).

(3) If a repurchase is for a quantity not in excess of the quantity that was terminated, the government must obtain the maximum practicable amount of competition. FAR 49.402-6(b). *See Al Bosgraaf & Son's*, ASBCA No. 45526, 94-2 BCA ¶ 26,913 (reprocurement by modification of another contract inadequate to mitigate costs); *International Technology Corp.*, B-250377.5, Aug. 18, 1993, 93-2 CPD ¶ 102 (government may award a reprocurement contract to the next-low offeror on the original solicitation when there is a short time span between the original competition and default).

c. When the repurchase is defective — when the government does not mitigate damages — the defaulting contractor may be relieved of liability for excess costs. *Ross & McDonald Contracting, GmbH*, ASBCA No. 38154, 94-1 BCA ¶ 26,316 (government failed to mitigate damages when exercising option on reprocurement contract); *Astra Prods. Co. of Tampa*, ASBCA No. 24474, 82-1 BCA ¶ 15,497.

2. Other Damages.

a. Liquidated Damages. Liquidated damages serve as a contractually agreed upon substitute for actual damages caused by late delivery or late completion of work. The government may recover both liquidated damages and an assessment of excess costs (either for reprocurement or for completion of the work) from a contractor upon terminating a contract for default. FAR 49.402-7.

(1) The common law rule that liquidated damages will not be enforced if they constitute a penalty applies to government acquisitions. *Southwest Eng'g Co. v. United States*, 341 F.2d 998 (8th Cir.), *cert. denied*, 382 U.S. 819 (1965).

(2) A liquidated damages clause will be enforced as reasonable where, at the inception of the contract, the damages are based on a reasonable forecast of possible damages in the event of failure of performance. *American Constr. Co.*, ENG BCA No. 5728, 91-2 BCA ¶ 24,009.

(3) If a contract does not have a liquidated damages clause or if the liquidated damages provision of a contract is unenforceable because it is punitive, the government may recover actual damages to the extent that they are proved. FAR 52.249-10.

b. The government may also recover common law damages, which may be in lieu of or in addition to excess costs assessed under the default termination clause. FAR 52.249-8(h); *ERG Consultants, Inc.*, VABCA No. 3223, 92-2 BCA ¶ 24,905 (damages must be forseeable); *Hideca Trading, Inc.*, ASBCA No. 24161, 87-3 BCA ¶ 20,040; *Cascade Pac. Int'l v. United States*, 773 F.2d 287 (Fed. Cir. 1985). The government has the burden of proving that the damages are foreseeable, direct, material, or the proximate result of the contractor's breach of contract. *Gibson Forestry*, AGBCA No. 87-325-1, 91-2 BCA ¶ 23,874.

c. Advance and progress payments: The government is entitled to repayment by the contractor of advance and progress payments, if any, attributable to the undelivered work. FAR 49.402-2(a). *Smith & Smith Aircraft Co.*, ASBCA No. 39316, 90-1 BCA ¶ 22,475.

**B. The Government's Liabilities.**

1. Upon termination of a fixed-price *supply* contract for default, the government is liable only

for the contract price for completed supplies delivered and accepted. FAR 52.249-8(f).

2. Upon termination of a fixed-price service contract or of a fixed-price construction contract, the government is liable only for the reasonable value of work done before termination, whether or not the services or construction have been contractually accepted by the government. *Sphinx Int'l, Inc.*, ASBCA No. 38784, 90-3 BCA ¶ 22,952.

3. The government may also require the contractor to transfer title and deliver to the government its manufacturing materials, for which the government will pay the reasonable value. FAR 52.249-8(e); FAR 52.249-10(a).

4. Upon termination of a cost-reimbursement type of contract for default, the government is generally liable for all of the reasonable, allowable, and allocable costs incurred by the contractor, whether or not accepted by the government, plus a percentage of the contract fee. The fee is somewhat limited, however, as the amount of the contract fee payable to the contractor is based on the work accepted by the government, rather than on the amount of work done by the contractor. FAR 52.249-6.

## VIII. MISCELLANEOUS.

### A. Portion of the Contract That May Be Terminated for Default.

1. Total or partial termination. A default termination may be total or partial. FAR 52.249-8(a)(1), (b); *General Floorcraft, Inc.*, GSBCA No. 10493, 91-2 BCA ¶ 24,023; *Associated Cleaning, Inc.*, GSBCA No. 8360, 91-1 BCA ¶ 23,360.

2. Incremental delivery schedule. Where a contractor defaults on one delivery under a contract that specifies an incremental delivery schedule, the entire contract may be terminated. *Sonora Mfg., Inc.*, ASBCA No. 31587, 91-1 BCA ¶ 23,444; *Novelty Prods. Co.*, ASBCA No. 21077, 78-1 BCA ¶ 12,989.

3. Severable contract requirements. Where a contract includes severable undertakings,

default on one effort may not justify termination of the entire contract. *T.C. & Sarah C. Bell*, ENG BCA No. 5872, 92-3 BCA ¶ 25,076; *ITRA Coop. Ass'n*, GSBCA No. 7974, 90-1 BCA ¶ 22,410; *Murphy v. United States*, 164 Ct. Cl. 332 (1964).

### B. Availability of Funds.

Funds that have been obligated but have not been disbursed at the time of termination for default *and* funds recovered as excess costs on a defaulted contract remain available for a replacement contract awarded in a subsequent fiscal year; that is, the recovered funds may be expended for the purposes for which the original funds were authorized and appropriated, but without the time of availability limitation applicable to the original funds. *Funding of Replacement Contracts*, B-198074, July 15, 1981, 81-2 CPD ¶ 33; *Bureau of Prisons—Disposition of Funds Paid in Settlement of Breach of Contract Action*, B-210160, Sep. 28, 1983, 84-1 CPD ¶ 91.

### C. Conversion to Termination for Convenience.

All FAR default clauses provide that if, after termination of the contract or of the contractor's right to proceed, it is determined that the contractor was not in default, or that a default or delay was excusable, the rights and obligations of the parties shall be the same as if the termination had been issued for the convenience of the government. FAR 52.249-8(g); FAR 52.249-10(c); FAR 52.249-6(b). *But see Apex Int'l Mgmt. Servs., Inc.*, ASBCA No. 38087, 94-2 BCA ¶ 26,842, *aff'd on recon.*, 94-2 BCA ¶ 26,852 (board refuses to convert improper default termination to a termination for convenience where government officials acted in bad faith; contractor entitled to breach damages); *Delfour, Inc.*, VABCA No. 3803, 94-1 BCA ¶ 26,385 (default clause does not preclude contractor from asserting a monetary claim for improper default termination; board rejects government argument that claim was a "premature settlement proposal").

# TERMINATION FOR DEFAULT CLAUSE FOR FIXED-PRICE SUPPLY AND SERVICE CONTRACTS

**52.249-8 Default (Fixed-Price Supply and Service).**

As prescribed in 49.504(a)(1), insert the following clause in solicitations and contracts when a fixed-price contract is contemplated and the contract amount is expected to exceed the small purchase limitation. The clause may also be used when the contract amount is not expected to exceed the small purchase limitation, if appropriate (e.g., if the acquisition involves items with a history of unsatisfactory quality).

DEFAULT (FIXED-PRICE SUPPLY AND SERVICE) (APR 1984)

(a) (1) The Government may, subject to paragraphs (c) and (d) below, by written notice of default to the Contractor, terminate this contract in whole or in part if the Contractor fails to—

(i) Deliver the supplies or to perform the services within the time specified in this contract or any extension;

(ii) Make progress, so as to endanger performance of this contract (but see subparagraph (a)(2) below); or

(iii) Perform any of the other provisions of this contract (but see subparagraph (a)(2) below).

(2) The Government's right to terminate this contract under subdivisions (1) (ii) and (1)(iii) above, may be exercised if the Contractor does not cure such failure within 10 days (or more if authorized in writing by the Contracting Officer) after receipt of the notice from the Contracting Officer specifying the failure.

(b) If the Government terminates this contract in whole or in part, it may acquire, under the terms and in the manner the Contracting Officer considers appropriate, supplies or services similar to those terminated, and the Contractor will be liable to the Government for any excess costs for those supplies or services. However, the Contractor shall continue the work not terminated.

(c) Except for defaults of subcontractors at any tier, the Contractor shall not be liable for any excess costs if the failure to perform the contract arises from causes beyond the control and without the fault or negligence of the Contractor. Examples of such causes include (1) acts of God or of the public enemy, (2) acts of the Government in either its sovereign or contractual capacity, (3) fires, (4) floods, (5) epidemics, (6) quarantine restrictions, (7) strikes, (8) freight embargoes, and (9) unusually severe weather. In each instance the failure to perform must be beyond the control and without the fault or negligence of the Contractor.

(d) If the failure to perform is caused by the default of a subcontractor at any tier, and if the cause of the default is beyond the control of both the Contractor and subcontractor, and without the fault or negligence of either, the Contractor shall not be liable for any excess costs for failure to perform, unless the subcontracted supplies or services were obtainable from other sources in sufficient time for the Contractor to meet the required delivery schedule.

(e) If this contract is terminated for default, the Government may require the Contractor to transfer title and deliver to the Government, as directed by the Contracting Officer, any (1) completed supplies, and (2) partially completed supplies and materials, parts, tools, dies, jigs, fixtures, plans, drawings, information, and contract rights (collectively referred to as "manufacturing materials" in this clause) that the Contractor has specifically produced or acquired for the terminated portion of this contract. Upon direction of the Contracting Officer, the Contractor shall also protect and preserve property in its possession in which the Government has an interest.

(f) The Government shall pay contract price for completed supplies delivered and accepted. The Contractor and Contracting Officer shall agree on the amount of payment for manufacturing materials delivered and accepted and for the protection and preservation of the property. Failure to agree will be a dispute under the Disputes clause. The Government may withhold from these amounts any sum the Contracting Officer determines to be necessary to protect the Government against loss because of outstanding liens or claims of former lien holders.

(g) If, after termination, it is determined that the Contractor was not in default, or that the default was excusable, the rights and obligations of the parties shall be the same as if the termination had been issued for the convenience of the Government.

(h) The rights and remedies of the Government in this clause are in addition to any other rights and remedies provided by law or under this contract.

(End of Clause)

(R 1-8.707)

(R 7-103.11 1959 AUG)

*Alternate I* (APR 1984). If the contract is for transportation or transportation-related services, delete paragraph (f) of the basic clause, redesignate the remaining paragraphs accordingly, and substitute the following paragraphs (a) and (e) for paragraphs (a) and (e) of the basic clause:

(a) (1) The Government may, subject to paragraphs (c) and (d) below, by written notice of default to the Contractor, terminate this contract in whole or in part if the Contractor fails to—

(i) Pick up the commodities or to perform the services, including delivery services, within the time specified in this contract or any extension.

(ii) Make progress, so as to endanger performance of this contract (but see subparagraph (a)(2) below); or

(iii) Perform any of the other provisions of this contract (but see subparagraph (a)(2) below).

(2) The Government's right to terminate this contract under subdivisions (1)(ii) and (1)(iii) above, may be exercised if the Contractor does not cure such failure within 10 days (or more if authorized in writing by the Contracting Officer) after receipt of the notice from the Contracting Officer specifying the failure.

(e) If this contract is terminated while the Contractor has possession of Government goods, the Contractor shall, upon direction of the Contracting Officer, protect and preserve the goods until surrendered to the Government or its agent. The Contractor and Contracting Officer shall agree on payment for the preservation and protection of goods. Failure to agree on an amount will be a dispute under the Disputes clause.

(R 1-7.703-8)

# TERMINATION FOR DEFAULT CLAUSE
# FOR FIXED-PRICE CONSTRUCTION CONTRACTS

**52.249-10 Default (Fixed-Price Construction).**

As prescribed in 49.504(c)(1), insert the following clause in solicitations and contracts for construction when a fixed-price contract is contemplated and the contract amount is expected to exceed the small purchase limitation. The clause may also be used when the contract amount is not expected to exceed the small purchase limitation, if appropriate (e.g., if completion dates are essential).

DEFAULT (FIXED-PRICE CONSTRUCTION)
(APR 1984)

(a) If the Contractor refuses or fails to prosecute the work or any separable part, with the diligence that will insure its completion within the time specified in this contract including any extension, or fails to complete the work within this time, the Government may, by written notice to the Contractor, terminate the right to proceed with the work (or the separable part of the work) that has been delayed. In this event, the Government may take over the work and complete it by contract or otherwise, and may take possession of and use any materials, appliances, and plant on the work site necessary for completing the work. The Contractor and its sureties shall be liable for any damage to the Government resulting from the Contractor's refusal or failure to complete the work within the specified time, whether or not the Contractor's right to proceed with the work is terminated. This liability includes any increased costs incurred by the Government in completing the work.

(b) The Contractor's right to proceed shall not be terminated nor the Contractor charged with damages under this clause, if—

(1) The delay in completing the work arises from unforeseeable causes beyond the control and without the fault or negligence of the Contractor. Examples of such causes include (i) acts of God or of the public enemy, (ii) acts of the Government in either its sovereign or contractual capacity, (iii) acts of another Contractor in the performance of a contract with the Government, (iv) fires, (v) floods, (vi) epidemics, (vii) quarantine restrictions, (viii) strikes, (ix) freight embargoes, (x) unusually severe weather, or (xi) delays of subcontractors or suppliers at any tier arising from unforeseeable causes beyond the control and without the fault or negligence of both the Contractor and the subcontractors or suppliers; and

(2) The Contractor, within 10 days from the beginning of any delay (unless extended by the Contracting Officer), notifies the Contracting Officer in writing of the causes of delay. The Contracting Officer shall ascertain the facts and the extent of delay. If, in the judgment of the Contracting Officer, the findings of fact warrant such action, the time for completing the work shall be extended. The findings of the Contracting Officer shall be final and conclusive on the parties, but subject to appeal under the Disputes clause.

(c) If, after termination of the Contractor's right to proceed, it is determined that the Contractor was not in default, or that the delay was excusable, the rights and obligations of the parties will be the same as if the termination had been issued for the convenience of the Government.

(d) The rights and remedies of the Government in this clause are in addition to any other rights and remedies provided by law or under this contract.

(End of clause)
(R 1-8.709-1)
(R 7-602.5 1969 AUG)

*Alternate I* (APR 1984). If the contract is for dismantling, demolition, or removal of improvements, substitute the following paragraph (a) for paragraph (a) of the basic clause:

(a) (1) If the Contractor refuses or fails to prosecute the work, or any separable part, with the diligence that will insure its completion within the time specified in this contract, including any extension, or fails to complete the work within this time, the Government may, by written notice to the Contractor, terminate the right to proceed with the work or the part of the work that has been delayed. In this event, the Government may take over the work and complete it by contract or otherwise, and may take possession of and use any materials, appliances, and plant on the work site necessary for completing the work.

(2) If title to property is vested in the Contractor under this contract, it shall revest in the Government regardless of any other clause of this contract, except for property that the Contractor has disposed of by bona fide sale or removed from the site.

(3) The Contractor and its sureties shall be liable for any damage to the Government resulting from the Contractor's refusal or failure to complete the work within the specified time, whether or not the Contractor's right to proceed with the work is terminated. This liability includes any increased costs incurred by the Government in completing the work.

(R 7-2101.7 1976 OCT)

*Alternate II* (APR 1984). If the contract is to be awarded during a period of national emergency, subparagraph (b)(1) below may be substituted for subparagraph (b) (1) of the basic clause:

(1) The delay in completing the work arises from causes other than normal weather beyond the control and without the fault or negligence of the Contractor. Examples of such causes include (i) acts of God or of the public enemy, (ii) acts of the Government in either its sovereign or contractual capacity, (iii) acts of another Contractor in the performance of a contract with the Government, (iv) fires, (v) floods, (vi) epidemics, (vii) quarantine restrictions, (viii) strikes, (ix) freight embargoes, (x) unusually severe weather, or (xi) delays of subcontractors or suppliers at any tier arising from causes other than normal weather beyond the control and without the fault or negligence of both the Contractor and the subcontractors or suppliers; and

(R 7-602.5 1969 AUG)

(R 1-16.404(e))

*Alternate III* (APR 1984). If the contract is for dismantling, demolition, or removal of improvements and is to be awarded during a period of national emergency, substitute the following paragraph (a) for paragraph (a) of the basic clause. The following subparagraph (b)(1) may be substituted for subparagraph (b)(1) of the basic clause:

(a) (1) If the Contractor refuses or fails to prosecute the work, or any separable part, with the diligence that will insure its completion within the time specified in this contract, including any extension, or fails to complete the work within this time, the Government may, by written notice to the Contractor, terminate the right to proceed with the work or the part of the work that has been delayed. In this event, the Government may take over the work and complete if by contract or otherwise, and may take possession of and use any materials, appliances, and plant on the work site necessary for completing the work.

(2) If title to property vested in the Contractor under this contract, it shall revest in the Government regardless of any other clause of this contract, except for property that the Contractor has disposed of by bona fide sale or removed from the site.

(3) The Contractor and its sureties shall be liable for any damage to the Government resulting from the Contractor's refusal or failure to complete the work within the specified time, whether or not the Contractor's right to proceed with the work is terminated. This liability includes any increased costs incurred by the Government in completing the work.

(b) The Contractor's right to proceed shall not be terminated nor the Contractor charged with damages under this clause, if—

(1) The delay in completing the work arises from causes other than normal weather beyond the control and without the fault or negligence of the Contractor. Examples of such causes include (i) acts of God or of the public enemy, (ii) acts of the Government in either its sovereign or contractual capacity, (iii) acts of another Contractor in the performance of a contract with the Government, (iv) fires, (v) floods, (vi) epidemics, (vii) quarantine restrictions, (viii) strikes, (ix) freight embargoes, (x) unusually severe weather, or (xi) delays of subcontractors or suppliers at any tier arising from causes other than normal weather beyond the control and without the fault or negligence of both the Contractor and the subcontractors or suppliers; and

(R 7-2101.7 1976 OCT)

# TERMINATION CLAUSE (DEFAULT & CONVENIENCE) FOR COST-REIMBURSEMENT CONTRACTS

**52.249-6 Termination (Cost-Reimbursement).**

As prescribed in 49.503 (a)(1), insert the following clause:

TERMINATION (COST-REIMBURSEMENT)

(MAY 1986)

(a) The Government may terminate performance of work under this contract in whole or, from time to time, in part, if—

(1) The Contracting Officer determines that a termination is in the Government's interest; or

(2) The Contractor defaults in performing this contract and fails to cure the default within 10 days (unless extended by the Contracting Officer) after receiving a notice specifying the default. "Default" includes failure to make progress in the work so as to endanger performance.

(b) The Contracting Officer shall terminate by delivering to the Contractor a Notice of Termination specifying whether termination is for default of the Contractor or for convenience of the Government, the extent of termination, and the effective date. If, after termination for default, it is determined that the Contractor was not in default or that the Contractor's failure to perform or to make progress in performance is due to causes beyond the control and without the fault or negligence of the Contractor as set forth in the Excusable Delays clause, the rights and obligations of the parties will be the same as if the termination was for the convenience of the Government.

(c) After receipt of a Notice of Termination, and except as directed by the Contracting Officer, the Contractor shall immediately proceed with the following obligations, regardless of any delay in determining or adjusting any amounts due under this clause:

(1) Stop work as specified in the notice.

(2) Place no further subcontracts or orders (referred to as subcontracts in this clause), except as necessary to complete the continued portion of the contract.

(3) Terminate all subcontracts to the extent they relate to the work terminated.

(4) Assign to the Government, as directed by the Contracting Officer, all right, title, and interest of the Contractor under the subcontracts terminated, in which case the Government shall have the right to settle or to pay any termination settlement proposal arising out of those terminations.

(5) With approval or ratification to the extent required by the Contracting Officer, settle all outstanding liabilities and termination settlement proposals arising from the termination of subcontracts, the cost of which would be reimbursable in whole or in part, under this contract; approval or ratification will be final for purposes of this clause.

(6) Transfer title (if not already transferred) and, as directed by the Contracting Officer, deliver to the Government (i) the fabricated or unfabricated parts, work in process, completed work, supplies, and other material produced or acquired for the work terminated, (ii) the completed or partially completed plans, drawings, information, and other property that, if the contract had been completed, would be required to be furnished to the Government, and (iii) the jigs, dies, fixtures, and other special tools and tooling acquired or manufactured for this contract, the cost of which the Contractor has been or will be reimbursed under this contract.

(7) Complete performance of the work not terminated.

(8) Take any action that may be necessary, or that the Contracting Officer may direct, for the protection and preservation of the property related to this contract that is in the possession of the Contractor and in which the Government has or may acquire an interest.

(9) Use its best efforts to sell, as directed or authorized by the Contracting Officer, any property of the types referred to in subparagraph (6) above; *provided, however,* that the Contractor (i) is not required to extend credit to any purchaser and (ii) may acquire the property under the conditions prescribed by, and at prices approved by, the Contracting Officer. The proceeds of any transfer or disposition will be applied to reduce any payments to be made by the Government under this contract,

credited to the price or cost of the work, or paid in any other manner directed by the Contracting Officer.

(d) After expiration of the plant clearance period as defined in Subpart 45.6 of the Federal Acquisition Regulation, the Contractor may submit to the Contracting Officer a list, certified as to quantity and quality, of termination inventory not previously disposed of, excluding items authorized for disposition by the Contracting Officer. The Contractor may request the Government to remove those items or enter into an agreement for their storage. Within 15 days, the Government will accept the items and remove them or enter into a storage agreement. The Contracting Officer may verify the list upon removal of the items, or if stored, within 45 days from submission of the list, and shall correct the list, as necessary, before final settlement.

(e) After termination, the Contractor shall submit a final termination settlement proposal to the Contracting Officer in the form and with the certification prescribed by the Contracting Officer. The Contractor shall submit the proposal promptly, but no later than 1 year from the effective date of termination, unless extended in writing by the Contracting Officer upon written request of the Contractor within this 1-year period. However, if the Contracting Officer determines that the facts justify it, a termination settlement proposal may be received and acted on after 1 year or any extension. If the Contractor fails to submit the proposal within the time allowed, the Contracting Officer may determine, on the basis of information available, the amount, if any, due the Contractor because of the termination and shall pay the amount determined.

(f) Subject to paragraph (e) above, the Contractor and the Contracting Officer may agree on the whole or any part of the amount to be paid (including an allowance for fee) because of the termination. The contract shall be amended, and the Contractor paid the agreed amount.

(g) If the Contractor and the Contracting Officer fail to agree in whole or in part on the amount of costs and/or fee to be paid because of the termination of work, the Contracting Officer shall determine, on the basis of information available, the amount, if any, due the Contractor, and shall pay that amount, which shall include the following:

(1) All costs reimbursable under this contract, not previously paid, for the performance of this contract before the effective date of the termination, and those costs that may continue for a reasonable time with the approval of or as directed by the Contracting Officer; however, the Contractor shall discontinue those costs as rapidly as practicable.

(2) The cost of settling and paying termination settlement proposals under terminated subcontracts that are properly chargeable to the terminated portion of the contract if not included in subparagraph (1) above.

(3) The reasonable costs of settlement of the work terminated, including—

(i) Accounting, legal, clerical, and other expenses reasonably necessary for the preparation of termination settlement proposals and supporting data;

(ii) The termination and settlement of subcontracts (excluding the amounts of such settlements); and

(iii) Storage, transportation, and other costs incurred, reasonably necessary for the preservation, protection, or disposition of the termination inventory. If the termination is for default, no amounts for the preparation of the Contractor's termination settlement proposal may be included.

(4) A portion of the fee payable under the contract, determined as follows:

(i) If the contract is terminated for the convenience of the Government, the settlement shall include a percentage of the fee equal to the percentage of completion of work contemplated under the contract, but excluding subcontract effort included in subcontractors' termination proposals, less previous payments for fee.

(ii) If the contract is terminated for default, the total fee payable shall be such proportionate part of the fee as the total number of articles (or amount of services) delivered to and accepted by the Government is to the total number of articles (or amount of services) of a like kind required by the contract.

(5) If the settlement includes only fee, it will be determined under subparagraph (g)(4) above.

(h) The cost principles and procedures in Part 31 of the Federal Acquisition Regulation, in effect on the date of this contract, shall govern all costs claimed, agreed to, or determined under this clause.

(i) The Contractor shall have the right of appeal, under the Disputes clause, from any determination made by the Contracting Officer under paragraph (e) or (g) above or paragraph (k) below, except that if the Contractor failed to submit the termination settlement proposal within the time provided in paragraph (e) and failed to request a time extension, there is no right of appeal. If the Contracting Officer has made a determination of the amount due under paragraph (e), (g) or (k), the Government shall pay the Contractor (1) the amount determined by the Contracting Officer if there is no right of appeal or if no timely appeal has been taken, or (2) the amount finally determined on an appeal.

(j) In arriving at the amount due the Contractor under this clause, there shall be deducted—

(1) All unliquidated advance or other payments to the Contractor, under the terminated portion of this contract;

(2) Any claim which the Government has against the Contractor under this contract; and

(3) The agreed price for, or the proceeds of sale of materials, supplies, or other things acquired by the Contractor or sold under this clause and not recovered by or credited to the Government.

(k) The Contractor and Contracting Officer must agree to any equitable adjustment in fee for the continued portion of the contract when there is a partial termination. The Contracting Officer shall amend the contract to reflect the agreement.

(l) (1) The Government may, under the terms and conditions it prescribes, make partial payments and payments against costs incurred by the Contractor for the terminated portion of the contract, if the Contracting Officer believes the total of these payments will not exceed the amount to which the Contractor will be entitled.

(2) If the total payments exceed the amount finally determined to be due, the Contractor shall repay the excess to the Government upon demand, together with interest computed at the rate established by the Secretary of the Treasury under 50 U.S.C. App. 1215(b)(2). Interest shall be computed for the period from the date the excess payment is received by the Contractor to the date the excess is repaid. Interest shall not be charged on any excess payment due to a reduction in the Contractor's termination settlement proposal because of retention or other disposition of termination inventory until 10 days after the date of the retention or disposition, or a later date determined by the Contracting Officer because of the circumstances.

(m) The provisions of this clause relating to fee are inapplicable if this contract does not include a fee.

(End of clause)

*Alternate I* (APR 1984). If the contract is for construction, substitute the following subparagraph (g)(4) for subparagraph (g)(4) of the basic clause:

(4) A portion of the fee payable under the contract determined as follows:

(i) If the contract is terminated for the convenience of the Government, the settlement shall include a percentage of the fee equal to the percentage of completion of work contemplated under the contract, but excluding subcontract effort included in subcontractors' termination settlement proposals, less previous payments for fee.

(ii) If the contract is terminated for default, the total fee payable shall be such proportionate part of the fee as the actual work in place is to the total work in place required by the contract.

(R 7-605.26 1974 APR)

(R 1-8.700-2(a)(3))

*Alternate II* (APR 1984). If the contract is with an agency of the U.S. Government or with State, local, or foreign governments or their agencies, and if the Contracting Officer determines that the requirement to pay interest on excess partial payments is inappropriate, delete subparagraph (1)(2) from the basic clause.

(R 8-702(d))

*Alternate III* (APR 1984). If the contract is for construction with an agency of the U.S. Government or with State, local, or foreign governments or their agencies, the following subparagraph (g)(4) shall be substituted for subparagraph (g)(4) of the basic clause. Subparagraph (l)(2) may be deleted from the basic clause if the Contracting Officer determines that the requirement to pay interest on excess partial payments is inappropriate.

(4) A portion of the fee payable under the contract determined as follows:

(i) If the contract is terminated for the convenience of the Government, the settlement shall include a percentage of the fee equal to the percentage of completion of work contemplated under the contract, but excluding subcontract effort included in subcontractors' termination settlement proposals, less previous payments for fee.

(ii) If the contract is terminated for default, the total fee payable shall be such proportionate part of the fee as the actual work in place is to the total work in place required by the contract.

(R 7-605.26 1974 APR)

(R 1-8.700-2(a)(3))

(R 8-702(d))

*Alternate IV* (APR 1984). If the contract is a time-and-material or labor-hour contract, substitute the following paragraphs (g) and (k) for paragraphs (g) and (k) of the basic clause:

(g) If the Contractor and the Contracting Officer fail to agree in whole or in part on the amount to be paid because of the termination of work, the Contracting Officer shall determine, on the basis of information available, the amount, if any, due the Contractor and shall pay the amount determined as follows:

(1) If the termination is for the convenience of the Government, include—

(i) An amount for direct labor hours (as defined in the Schedule of the contract) determined by multiplying the number of direct labor hours expended before the effective date of termination by the hourly rate(s) in the Schedule, less any hourly rate payments already made to the Contractor;

(ii) An amount (computed under the provisions for payment of materials) for material expenses incurred before the effective date of termination, not previously paid to the Contractor;

(iii) An amount for labor and material expenses computed as if the expenses were incurred before the effective date of termination, if they are reasonably incurred after the effective date, with the approval of or as directed by the Contracting Officer; however, the Contractor shall discontinue these expenses as rapidly as practicable;

(iv) If not included in (i), (ii), or (iii) above, the cost of settling and paying termination settlement proposals under terminated subcontracts that are properly chargeable to the terminated portion of the contract; and

(v) The reasonable costs of settlement of the work terminated, including—

(A) Accounting, legal, clerical, and other expenses reasonably necessary for the preparation of termination settlement proposals and supporting data;

(B) The termination and settlement of subcontracts (excluding the amounts of such settlements); and

(C) Storage, transportation, and other costs incurred, reasonably necessary for the protection or disposition of the termination inventory.

(2) If the termination is for default of the Contractor, include the amounts computed under (1) above but omit—

(i) Any amount for preparation of the Contractor's termination settlement proposal; and

(ii) The portion of the hourly rate allocable to profit for any direct labor hours expended in furnishing materials and services not delivered to and accepted by the Government.

(k) If the termination is partial, the Contractor may file with the Contracting Officer a proposal for an equitable adjustment of price(s) for the continued portion of the contract. The Contracting Officer shall make any equitable adjustment agreed upon. Any proposal by the Contractor for an equitable adjustment under this clause shall be requested within 90 days from the effective date of termination, unless extended in writing by the Contracting Officer.

(R 7-901.4 1974 OCT)

*Alternate V* (APR 1984). If the contract is a time-and-material or labor-hour contract with an agency of the U.S. Government or with State, local or foreign governments or their agencies, substitute the following paragraphs (g) and (k) for paragraphs (g) and (k) of the basic clause. Subparagraph (l)(2) may be deleted from the basic clause if the contracting officer determines that the requirement to pay interest on excess partial payments is inappropriate.

(g)  If the Contractor and the Contracting Officer fail to agree in whole or in part on the amount to be paid because of the termination of work, the Contracting Officer shall determine, on the basis of information available, the amount, if any, due the Contractor and shall pay the amount determined as follows:

(1)  If the termination is for the convenience of the Government, include—

(i)  An amount for direct labor hours (as defined in the Schedule of the contract) determined by multiplying the number of direct labor hours expended before the effective date of termination by the hourly rate(s) in the Schedule, less any hourly rate payments already made to the Contractor;

(ii)  An amount (computed under the provisions for payment of materials) for material expenses incurred before the effective date of termination, not previously paid to the Contractor;

(iii) An amount for labor and material expenses computed as if the expenses were incurred before the effective date of termination if they are reasonably incurred after the effective date, with the approval of or as directed by the Contracting Officer; however the Contractor shall discontinue these expenses as rapidly as practicable;

(iv) If not included in (i), (ii), or (iii) above, the cost of settling and paying termination settlement proposals under terminated subcontracts that are properly chargeable to the terminated portion of the contact; and

(v)  The reasonable costs of settlement of the work terminated, including—

(A)  Accounting, legal, clerical, and other expenses reasonably necessary for the preparation of termination settlement proposals and supporting data;

(B)  The termination and settlement of subcontracts (excluding the amounts of such settlements); and

(C)  Storage, transportation, and other costs incurred, reasonably necessary for the protection or disposition of the termination inventory.

(2)  If the termination is for default of the Contractor, include the amounts computed under (1) above but omit—

(i)  Any amount for preparation of the Contractor's termination settlement proposal; and

(ii)  The portion of the hourly rate allocable to profit for any direct labor hours expended in furnishing materials and services not delivered to and accepted by the Government.

(k)  If the termination is partial, the Contractor may file with the Contracting Officer a proposal for an equitable adjustment of the price(s) for the continued portion of the contract. The Contracting Officer shall make any equitable adjustment of the price(s) for the continued portion of the contract. The Contracting Officer shall make any equitable adjustment agreed upon. Any proposal by the Contractor for an equitable adjustment under this clause shall be requested within 90 days from the effective date of termination, unless extended in writing by the Contracting Officer.

(R 7-901.4 1974 OCT)

## CHAPTER TWENTY-FIVE

# Environmental Contracting Issues*

## I. OBJECTIVES.

Following this block of instruction, the student will:

A. Understand the government's obligation to eliminate environmentally hazardous substances from goods and services it procures;

B. Understand the government's obligation to require the use of recycled materials to the maximum extent practicable;

C. Know the contracting processes that implement the government's environmental obligations; and

D. Know the cost and funding limitations involved in environmentally responsible contracting.

## II. INTRODUCTION.

In the post-Cold War era, DOD's approach to environmental problems must rest on two basic premises. First, our national security must include protection of the environment, and environmental concerns must be fully integrated into our defense policies. Second, to protect our nation we must also have a strong economy; protecting the environment and growing the economy must go hand in hand.

> —Secretary of Defense Les Aspin,
> *Report on the Bottom-Up Review*,
> October 1993

---

* This outline is based in part on a thesis written by Lt. Col. James L. Conrad, Elmendorf AFB, AK in partial satisfaction of the Master of Laws requirements of George Washington University. The Army Judge Advocate General's School is grateful for Lt. Col. Conrad's contribution.

## A. Impact of Environmental Laws on the Federal Procurement Process.

Congress and the President, recognizing the influential effect of the billions of dollars spent through the federal procurement process, view this process as a vehicle for environmental change. These efforts fall into two distinct categories:

1. Environmentally Safe Contracting. There are several statutes and executive orders that require the purchase of certain environmentally sound goods and services to create and sustain markets for them; and

2. Restrictions on Purchases. These are also requirements that restrict purchases of environmentally harmful goods and services to limit or phase out their use by federal agencies.

## B. Overview of the Issues.

1. Compliance vs. Clean-Up. Environmental issues in federal procurement generally arise in two contexts: First, agencies must ensure that their procurement practices and contractors comply with current environmental requirements (environmentally safe contracting and purchase restrictions, discussed above, are included in this context); second, issues arise regarding proportionate responsibility and funding when agencies or their contractors become obligated to clean-up contaminated sites.

2. Scope of the Problem. In July 1993, the General Accounting Office (GAO) reported that as of February 1993, federal agencies report-

ed owning or operating over 1,900 contaminated facilities, including military installations. What are the likely effects of this situation?

a. Agencies will have to remediate contaminated facilities, usually by contracting for clean-up services; and

b. Agencies will attempt to contract in an environmentally responsible manner to minimize the potential for future environmental problems.

## III. PHASE OUT OF OZONE DEPLETING SUBSTANCES (ODS) PROCURED UNDER FEDERAL CONTRACTS.

### A. Background.

The United States is a party to the Montreal Protocol, which is an international treaty requiring the phase out of ODS use and production.

### B. Products Containing ODS.

Halons are primarily used as firefighting agents and for vector control in some missile systems. Chlorofluorocarbons are primarily used as refrigerants and cleaning solvents.

### C. Statutory Prohibition.

Section 326(a) of the FY 1993 Authorization Act, Pub. L. No. 102-484, 106 Stat. 2315 (hereinafter Pub. L. 102-484) provides:

No [DOD] contract awarded after June 1, 1993, may include a specification or standard that requires the use of a class I [ODS] or that can be met only through the use of such a substance unless the inclusion of the specification or standard in the contract is approved by the senior acquisition official (SAO) for the procurement covered by the contract. *See also* Exec. Order No. 12843, 58 Fed. Reg. 21,881 (1993); DFARS 210.002-71(a); AFFARS 5310.002-71(90)(a).

### D. Nature of Requirement.

Section 326 of Pub. L. 102-484 only prohibits federal contracting activities from *requiring* the use of ODS.

1. Contractors may choose to use ODS on their own initiative.

2. Contractor screening.

   a. In addition to the screening conducted by the government, the contracting office should encourage contractors to share with the government any special knowledge they have regarding ODS required at any level of contract performance. Memorandum, Secretary of the Army for Research, Development, and Acquisition (SARDA), subject: *Ozone-Depleting Substances* (2 July 1993) [hereafter July SARDA Memo].

   b. Agencies should ensure that their solicitations and contracts do not obligate contractors to identify ODS use in production, performance, or in the end item. Memorandum, Director of Defense Procurement subject: *Ozone-Depleting Substances*, 20 October 1993. *But see* AFFARS 5352.210-9000.

3. DOD has issued a list of military specifications and standards that require the use of ODS. *See* DOD Policy Memorandum, subject: *Ozone Depleting Chemicals* (20 May 1993).

   a. No contract awarded after 1 June 1993 may include a listed specification or standard unless the appropriate authority has granted a waiver. To obtain the latest version of this list, contact the DOD Standardization Program Division (Mr. John Tasher) at (703) 756-0815 (FAX: (703) 756-7622). AFI 32-7080, para. 3.1.3.

   b. Agencies must screen all new contract actions and solicitations for specifications and standards identified by DOD as calling for the use of ODS.

      (1) This initial review does not have to be performed by the Approved Technical Representative (ATR). July SARDA Memo.

      (2) If the reviewer determines that the specifications and standards are not on the DOD list, the reviewer should submit a statement to the contracting office stating his/her conclusion. July SARDA Memo.

(3) The reviewer should submit this statement to the contracting office with the requirements document and the contract file should contain both documents. July SARDA Memo.

c. The ATR must review all solicitations and existing contracts to determine if they include specifications or standards that require use of class I ODS. Memorandum, Secretary of the Army for Research, Development, and Acquisition (SARDA), subject: *Implementation of the Requirements of the National Defense Authorization Act for FY93* (9 June 1993) [hereafter June SARDA Memo].

4. If the solicitation *prohibits* using ODS in the manufacturing process or as components in the end item, but the contractor chooses to use them, the contracting officer must find these offers non-responsive.

### E. DOD Policy.

DOD published an interim rule addressing the elimination of ODS in DOD contracts which amends the DFARS. *See* DFARS 207.105, Contents of Written Acquisition Plans, 58 Fed. Reg. 32,061 (to be codified at 48 C.F.R. Part 207). The rule essentially tracks the language of Section 326 of Pub. L. 102-484. The Director of Defense Procurement, has determined that "urgent and compelling reasons exist to promulgate this rule before affording the public an opportunity to comment in order to meet the statutory implementation date of June 1, 1993." 58 Fed. Reg. 32,061 (1993).

### F. Contracts Awarded Before 1 June 1993.

The following rules apply only if the contract as awarded exceeds $10,000,000 and is modified or extended so that contract performance period will expire more than one year after the effective date of the modification or extension.

1. If a contract awarded before 1 June 1993 is modified or extended after 1 June 1993, forward the contract file to the agency's SAO so he/she may determine whether the contract requires use of a class I ODS and whether

the contract can be performed with an economically feasible substitute. Pub. L. 102-484, § 326(a)(2)(A).

2. If the SAO determines that an economically feasible ODS substitute is available, the cognizant contracting officer must enter into negotiations to modify the contract to require use of the substitute. Pub. L. 102-484, § 326(a)(2) (B); DFARS 210.002-71(b)(2).

3. The agency may adjust the price of the contract modified if use of an ODS substitute affects the costs of performance. Pub. L. 102-484, § 326(b).

### G. Executive Order No. 12843.

On 21 April 1993, the President issued an executive order titled, "Procurement Requirements and Policies for Federal Agencies for Ozone-Depleting Substances," Exec. Order No. 12843, Fed. Reg. 21,881 (1993). This order addresses many of the same concerns as Section 326 of Pub. L. 102-484 and the implementing DFARS provisions discussed above. The order states that:

1. It is federal policy that federal agencies give a preference to the procurement of alternative chemicals, products, and manufacturing processes that reduce overall risks to human health and the environment by lessening the depletion of ozone in the upper atmosphere. Exec. Order No. 12843, sec. 3. For example, the Secretary of the Air Force has directed SAF/AQ and AF/LG to implement procedures making non-use of ODS a salient characteristic of any item or process. ODS Policy Ltr. Further the non-use of ODS should normally be a technical requirement in all federal acquisitions.

2. Federal agencies, where economically practicable, must minimize the procurement of products containing or manufactured with class I ODS and maximize the use of safe alternatives. Exec. Order No. 12843, sec. 3(a). *See, e.g.*, AFI 32-7080, para. 2.4.3.

3. Agencies must amend existing contracts, "to the extent permitted by law," and, where

practicable, make them consistent with the phaseout schedules for class I substances. Exec. Order No. 12843, sec. 3(b).

4. While revisions to the FAR are pending, agencies must implement the order to the extent that implementation is not dependent on regulatory revision. Exec. Order No. 12843, sec. 7.

5. The order does not create any right or benefit, substantive or procedural, enforceable by a non-federal party against the United States, its officers or employees, or any other person. Exec. Order No. 12843, sec. 9.

### H. Waivers.

1. Section 326(a) of Pub. L. 102-484, states that contracts must not include a specification or standard that requires the use of a class I ODS or that can be met only through the use of such a substance unless the SAO approves the inclusion of the specification or standard in the contract. *See also* Exec. Order No. 12843, 58 Fed. Reg. 21,881 (1993); DFARS 210.002-71(a); AFFARS 5310.002-71(90)(a); AFI 32-7080, para. 3.1.3.

2. After the phase out dates specified in the Montreal Protocol, only the President may grant a waiver. 42 U.S.C. § 7671c(f). The phase out date for halon was 1 Jan 94 and the phase out date for chloroflourocarbon is 1 Jan 96.

3. Exceptions.

   a. A waiver is not required for off-the-shelf items, even if they include class I ODS in their production. These items were not "developed from military specifications," although DOD activities may use them for military purposes. Thus, a contracting activity does not violate section 326(a) of Pub. L. 102-484 by contracting for off-the-shelf items produced with or including ODS because the government did not require the use of the ODS. AF Waiver Ltr; Memorandum, ASA, subject: Elimination of Ozone-Depleting Chemicals (20 May 1993) [hereafter Army ODS Policy Ltr.].

   b. Waivers are not required for government

acquisition or use of ODS-containing products already in DOD inventories. AF Waiver Ltr. However, waivers are required to obtain ODS from the Defense Logistic Agency ODC bank for mission critical applications.

### I. Contract Review Checklist.

Because several layers of rules pertaining to ODS impact the federal procurement process, attorneys reviewing contracts should consider the following items:

1. Review by the Requiring Activity. If the requiring activity has determined that the specifications and standards are not on the DOD list of specifications and standards requiring use of ODS, the file should contain a statement from the reviewer. July SARDA Memo.

2. ATR Review. The file should contain a statement from the ATR. This statement may take essentially two forms:

   a. If the ATR determines that the contract does not require the use an ODS, but that such use is an option, the ATR statement should be accompanied by a statement by the SAO recommending that the contracting officer amend the specification or standard to require the contractor to give preference to non-ODC alternatives; or

   b. If the ATR determines that the contract does require the use an ODS, the file should contain a certification from the ATR that either a known substitute exists or that there are no known substitutes.

3. SAO Determination. If the contract requires the use of an ODS, the file must contain a document from the SAO approving either the use of an ODS substitute or the use of the required ODS.

4. MAJCOM/MACOM Review. If a contracting office uses locally drafted ODS clauses, it should obtain approval from the appropriate MAJCOM/MACOM before incorporating such clauses into a contract.

5. Red Herrings. When reviewing statements of work and specifications, be especially alert

to requirements for refrigerants, solvents, and halons. *See generally* Roberts, Captain Walter C., *ODS-An Odious Burden*, The [Air Force] Reporter, September 1993, at 7.

## IV. PROCUREMENT OF ITEMS COMPOSED OF RECOVERED MATERIALS.

### A. Statutory Requirements.

Federal agencies must procure items composed of the highest percentage of recovered materials practicable, . . . consistent with maintaining a satisfactory level of competition. 42 U.S.C. § 6962(c)(1); FAR 23.403.

### B. Definitions.

1. Recovered Materials. Waste material and by-products which have been recovered from solid waste, but not materials generated from and commonly reused within an original manufacturing process. OMB Ltr. 92-4, para. 4.b. *See also* FAR 23.402.

2. Cost-Effective Procurement Preference. A program that favors, *where price and other factors are equal*, the procurement of products and services that are more environmentally sound or energy-efficient than other competing products and services. OFPP Ltr. 92-4, para. 4.f.

### C. Agency Responsibilities.

Agencies must consider energy conservation and efficiency data along with estimated cost and other evaluation factors, in the development of purchase requests and solicitations. OFPP Ltr. 92-4, para. 6(a). In discharging this responsibility, agencies must:

1. Use product descriptions and specifications that reflect cost-effective use of recycled products, recovered materials, remanufactured products and energy-efficient goods and services. Exec. Order No. 12873, sec. 501; OFPP Ltr. 92-4, para. 7.a.(4); FAR 23.401(b).

2. Require that offerors certify the percentage of recovered material used when the agency awards contracts wholly or in part on the basis of utilization of recovered materials. 42 U.S.C. § 6962(c)(3)(A); OFPP Ltr. 92-4, para. 7.a.(6).

3. Use life cycle cost analysis whenever feasible and appropriate, to assist in making source selection decisions. OFPP Ltr. 92-4, para. 7.a.(3). AFI 32-7080, para. 1.3.1.3.

4. When drafting or reviewing specifications, ensure that the specifications:
    a. do not exclude the use of recovered materials;
    b. do not unnecessarily require the item to be manufactured from virgin materials; and
    c. require the use of recovered materials and environmentally sound components to the maximum extent practicable without jeopardizing the intended end use of the item. OFPP Ltr. 92-4, para. 7a.(7).

### D. Implementation.

1. OFPP Policy Letter No. 92-4 states that it is the policy of the federal government that executive agencies implement cost-effective procurement preference programs favoring the purchase of environmentally sound, energy-efficient products and services. OFPP Policy Ltr. No. 92-4, para. 6.

2. The OFPP Policy Letter states that "it is expected that agencies will take all appropriate actions . . . to implement those aspects of the policy that are not dependent upon regulatory change." OFPP Policy Ltr. No. 92-4, para. 10.

3. Developing a Preference Program. 42 U.S.C. § 6962(i)(3); OFPP Ltr. 92-4, para. c.(1)(e). In developing a preference program, agencies must consider the following options:
    a. Provide open competition between products made of virgin materials and products containing recovered materials and provide a preference to the latter; or
    b. For guideline items, establish minimum content standards which identify the minimum content of recovered materials that an item must contain for award.

4. Sealed Bidding. Since agencies cannot con-

sider factors unrelated to price in awarding sealed bid contracts, preferences for environmentally sound goods and services are relevant during the acquisition planning process or when the agency receives two equally priced bids.

### E. Affirmative Procurement Programs.

42 U.S.C. § 6962; Exec. Order No. 12873, 58 Fed. Reg. 54,914 (1993) (hereafter Exec. Order No. 12873); OFPP Ltr. 92-4, para. 7.c. Within one year after publication of guidelines issued pursuant to 42 U.S.C. § 6962(e), each procuring agency must develop an "affirmative procurement program" which will assure that items composed of recovered materials will be purchased to the *maximum extent practicable*. 42 U.S.C. § 6962(i). The use of the guideline-specified material must not "jeopardize the intended end use of the item." 42 U.S.C. § 6962 (d)(2). AFI 32-7080, para. 3.5.

1. EPA has established guidelines for the following materials:
   a. Cement and concrete containing fly ash. 40 C.F.R. § 249;
   b. Paper products. 50 Fed. Reg. 14,076 (1985);
   c. Re-refined lubricating oil. 40 C.F.R. § 252;
   d. Retread tires. 40 C.F.R. § 253; and
   e. Building insulation containing recovered materials. 40 C.F.R. § 248.
2. Applicability. The statutory requirement to purchase EPA guideline items only applies to procurements over $10,000 or where the purchased quantity of such items, or of functionally equivalent items, procured in the prior fiscal year exceeds $10,000. The broader requirement for recovered material purchases have no price threshold.
3. Exec. Order No. 12873 directed federal agencies to implement the EPA procurement guidelines for re-refined lubricating oil and retread tires. It specifically requires that product managers revise specifications to maximize procurement of these items. Exec. Order No. 12873, sec. 506(a).
4. EPA Proposes Additional Items. Exec. Order

No. 12873 directs the EPA to develop a process for designating items that contain recovered materials so that agencies can give a preference to these items in their procurements. On 20 April 1994, EPA published a list of 21 items it proposed to add to the category of "guideline items." 59 Fed. Reg. 18,852 (1994).

### F. Exceptions.

42 U.S.C. § 6962(c)(1); AFI 32-7080, para. 3.5.3. Under The Resource Conservation and Recovery Act (RCRA), 42 U.S.C. §§ 6901-6901i, a procurement is not subject to these requirements if the procuring contracting officer determines that the items meeting the statutory requirements:

1. are not reasonably available within a reasonable period of time;
2. fail to meet the performance standards set forth in the specifications or fail to meet the reasonable performance standards of the procuring agencies;
3. are only available at an unreasonable price; or
4. are not available from a sufficient number of sources to maintain a satisfactory level of competition. 42 U.S.C. § 6002(c).

### V. HAZARDOUS MATERIAL POLLUTION PREVENTION.

DOD Directive 4210.15, Hazardous Material Pollution Prevention (27 July 1989).

### A. DOD Policy.

When procuring hazardous substances, DOD agencies must select, use, and manage hazardous material over its life-cycle so that DOD incurs the lowest cost required to protect human health and the environment. Emphasis must be on less use of hazardous materials in processes and products, as distinguished from end-of-pipe management of hazardous waste. DOD Dir. 4210.15 para. (D).

### B. Implementing Provisions.

Heads of DOD components must revise specifications and standards requiring the use of a hazardous material when a less hazardous alternative is available. DOD Dir. 4210.15 para. F(4)(b)-(d); AFI 32-7080, para. 2.1. Available alternatives include:

1. substituting less hazardous or nonhazardous material;
2. redesigning a component so that hazardous material is not needed in its manufacture, use, or maintenance;
3. modifying processes or procedures, including the use of waste as raw material in other manufacturing. DOD 4210.15, encl. 1, para. 7.

### C. Economic Analysis.
Heads of DOD components must evaluate hazardous materials decisions by economic analysis techniques that consider cost factors and intangible factors.

1. Cost factors refer to the direct and indirect costs attributable to hazardous material that are encountered in operations such as acquisition, manufacture, supply, use, storage, inventory control, treatment, recycling, emission control, training, work place safety, labeling, hazard assessments, engineering controls, personal protective equipment, medical monitoring, regulatory overhead, spill contingency, disposal, remedial action, and liability.
2. Intangible factors include influences bearing on the use or effects of hazardous material, which may not be reduced to monetary terms. For example, the quality of defense and the quality of environment both have intangible characteristics that are not mutually exclusive but which could be overriding factors in a hazardous material issue. Other intangible factors include public emotion and potential litigation.

### VI. ENERGY EFFICIENT COMPUTER EQUIPMENT.

Exec. Order No. 12845, Requiring Agencies to Purchase Energy Efficient Computer Equipment, 58 Fed. Reg. 21,887 (1993); FIRMR Interim Rule 1, Energy Efficient Computer

Equipment, 41 C.F.R. pts. 201-17 and 201-20) (1994).

### A. General Requirements.

1. Agencies must ensure that all acquisitions of microcomputers (including personal computers, monitors and printers) meet "EPA Energy Star" requirements for energy efficiency. Agency heads may grant case-by-case exemptions based on the commercial availability of qualifying equipment, significant cost differences between qualifying and nonqualifying equipment, the agency's performance requirements, and the agency's mission. Exec. Order No. 12845, sec. 1.
2. Under EPA's Energy Star program, computers, printers, and monitors must include an automatic low-power standby feature.

### B. Implementation.
Specifications must require that microcomputers be equipped with the energy efficient low-power standby feature as defined by the EPA Energy Star computers program. To the extent permitted by law, agencies must include this specification in all existing and future contracts, "if both the Government and the contractor agree, and if any additional costs would be offset by the potential energy savings." Exec. Order No. 12845, sec. 1(b).

### C. Judicial Review.
Section 12845 or Exec. Order No. 12845 states that "[t]his order does not create any right or benefit, substantive or procedural, enforceable by an non-Federal party against the United States, its officers or employees, or any other person."

### D. General Services Administration (GSA) Interim Rule.
The GSA issued FIRMR Interim Rule 1, effective 7 January 1994, to implement Exec. Order No. 12845. The interim rule, which is codified at 41 C.F.R. pts. 201-17 and 201-20, closely tracks the language of the Executive Order. The rule also requires agencies to consider the guidance con-

tained in FIRMR Bulletin C-35, issued on 19 November 1993.

## VII. THE NOISE CONTROL ACT OF 1972.

### A. The Noise Control Act of 1972.
42 U.S.C. §§ 4901-18. This Act creates a preference for "low-noise emission" products.

### B. Definition.
A low-noise emission product is: "[A]ny product which emits noise in amounts significantly below the levels specified in noise emission standards under regulations applicable under section 4905 of this title at the time of procurement to that type of product." 42 U.S.C. § 4914(a)(3).

### C. Requirements.
The EPA must determine that a product is a "suitable substitute" for a currently procured item and the GSA must determine that the cost of the product is no more than 125% of the retail cost of the product for which it is a substitute. Once these determinations are made, federal agencies must procure these items in preference to their non-certified substitutes. 42 U.S.C. § 4914.

### D. Implementation.
1. The EPA has promulgated regulations for the low-noise products preference at 40 C.F.R. § 203. EPA's regulations exempt from its requirements aircraft and certain aircraft components, military weapons designed for combat use, certain National Aeronautics and Space Administration (NASA) rockets, and government experimental machinery and equipment. 40 C.F.R. § 203.1(a)(4)

2. Before a product may be certified as a low-noise emission product, the product must be one for which the EPA has promulgated low-noise standards under section 6 of the act. 40 C.F.R. § 203.4 (a)(1). To date, EPA has only promulgated standards pertaining to motorcycles (40 C.F.R. § 205.152), portable air compressors (40 C.F.R. § 204.52), and

medium and heavy duty trucks (40 C.F.R. § 205.52).

3. DOD agencies have formally incorporated the Noise Control Act's low-noise emission products procurement preference into their environmental noise abatement programs. *See, e.g.,* AFR 19-10 and AR 200-1. Under AR 200-1, the Army must:

   a. Procure commercial equipment and products, or those adapted for military use, that are in compliance with established federal noise standards and give priority to use of low-noise-emission products within reasonable cost and mission limitations; and

   b. Incorporate noise control provisions in the design and procurement of vehicles, aircraft, weapons systems and military equipment for use in combat operations to the extent that essential operational capabilities are not significantly impaired. AR 200-1.

## VIII. ENERGY POLICY AND CONSERVATION ACT OF 1975 (EPCA)
42 U.S.C. §§ 6201-6422.

### A. Statutory Requirements.
The EPCA provides that the President shall: [E]stablish or coordinate Federal agency actions to develop mandatory standards with respect to energy conservation and energy efficiency to govern procurement policies and decisions of the Federal Government and all Federal agencies, and shall take such steps as are necessary to cause such standards to be implemented. 42 U.S.C. § 6361(a)(1).

1. The statute prescribes energy conservation standards for various consumer-type products. Federal agencies purchasing such products must ensure that their specifications incorporate these standards. 42 U.S.C. § 6295.

2. Any person may commence a civil action against any federal agency where there is an alleged failure of such agency to perform any

act or duty under the EPCA that is not discretionary. United States District Courts have jurisdiction over such actions, without regard to the amount in controversy. 42 U.S.C. § 6305(a).

### B. Implementation.

The EPCA is implemented by Exec. Order No. 11912, sec. 3 (41 Fed. Reg. 15,825 (1976)); and Exec. Order No. 12759, sec. 5 (56 Fed. Reg. 16,257 (1991)). Section 5 of Exec. Order No. 12759 requires that each agency select for procurement those energy consuming goods or products which are the most life cycle cost-effective, pursuant to the requirements of the Federal Acquisition Regulation. *See also* OFPP Letter 94-2 (57 Fed. Reg. 53,365 (1992)).

### C. FAR Requirements.

FAR 23.203 sets forth the policy that energy conservation and efficiency criteria be applied to acquisitions "whenever the results would be meaningful, practical, and consistent with agency programs and needs." Agencies must consider energy conservation and efficiency criteria "along with price and other relevant factors" when preparing specifications and making awards. When acquiring "covered products," agencies must consider energy use and efficiency labels and energy efficiency standards.

## IX. ENVIRONMENTALLY RESPONSIBLE CONTRACTING AND COMPETITION.

### A. General Requirements.

1. Full and Open Competition. With limited exceptions, contracting officers shall promote full and open competition through the use of competitive procedures in soliciting offers and awarding government contracts. 10 U.S.C. § 2304(a)(1); 41 U.S.C. § 253(a)(1); FAR Subpart 6.1.
2. Defined. "Full and open competition" means that all responsible sources are permitted to compete. FAR 6.003. Full and open competition may not actually *achieve* competition.

### B. Environmental Issues.

The easiest way to comply with the various environmental purchasing preference requirements is to use specifications that restrict competition to only those who can supply items meeting the mandated requirements. Balanced against this strategy is the legal rule that specifications cannot unduly restrict competition.

### C. General Rule.

To implement a collateral policy (such as environmental protection) that restricts the number of offerors eligible for award, the GAO once held that an agency needed a clear grant of authority from Congress. *To the Sec'y of Defense*, B-148930, 42 Comp. Gen. 1 (1962) (requiring labor rates not mandated by statute was improper). Subsequently, the GAO held that a specification is not unduly restrictive if it furthers a strong express or implied public policy. *American Can Co.*, B-187658, Mar. 17, 1977, 77-1 CPD ¶ 196 (reclaimed fiber content requirement).

1. Executive Order 12873 requires agencies to procure recycled and environmentally sound products. In conjunction with the environmental statutes it furthers and GAO decisions that are generally supportive of restrictive specifications that further environmental goals, the order expresses a *strong federal policy* that justifies use of environmental specifications that may narrow the competition for federal requirements.
2. Specifications that are more environmentally restrictive than required by current law are not necessarily unduly restrictive. *See Trilectron Indus.*, B-248475, Aug. 27, 1992, 92-2 CPD ¶ 130 (agency requirement for use of an air conditioner refrigerant with an ozone depletion potential of zero is reasonable, even though it prevents protestor from competing).
3. If the government decides to restrict competition based on its consideration of the environment, GAO normally will not disturb the government's decision even when a protest-

er alleges that the required product or service is actually harmful to the environment. *Integrated Forest Mgmt.*, B-204106, Jan. 4, 1982, 82-1 CPD ¶ 6. *But see Bardex Corp.*, B-252208, June 14, 1993, 93-1 CPD ¶ 461 (GAO grants protest because agency could not show that protester's product was unable to satisfy the agency's environmental concerns).

4. Protesters have been generally unsuccessful in contending that the government should have imposed more restrictive requirements. *See, e.g., Trimble Navigation Ltd.*, B-247913, July 19, 1992, 92-2 CPD ¶ 17; *Container Prods. Corp.*, B-232953, Feb. 6, 1989, 89-1 CPD ¶ 117. GAO has applied this rule even though the protestor had a clear statutory and regulatory basis for its argument to restrict competition in furtherance of environmental policies. *Sunbelt I*, B-214414.2, Jan. 29, 1985, 85-1 CPD ¶ 113.

### D. Executive Order No. 12873.

This Executive Order, which requires agencies to procure recycled and environmentally sound products, states that the order is not intended to create "any right or benefit, substantive or procedural, enforceable at law by a party against the United States, its agencies, its officers, or any other person. Exec. Order No. 12873, sec. 902.

### E. Use of Performance Specifications.

OFPP Policy Letter 91-2, requires maximum use of performance specifications for service contracts. 56 Fed. Reg. 15,112 (1991). DOD published its proposed FAR changes to implement OFPP Letter 91-2 on 30 July 1992, at 57 Fed. Reg. 33,702 (1992). Use of performance specifications more readily allows bidders to propose environmentally-sound processes and products without fear of being held nonresponsive. *See also* FEDERAL ACQUISITION STREAMLINING ACT OF 1994, Pub. L. No. 103-355, § 8104, 108 Stat. 3243, 3390 (amending 10 U.S.C. § 2377), PREFERENCE FOR ACQUISITION OF COMMERCIAL ITEMS.

## X. ACQUISITION PLANNING.

### A. Exec. Order 12873, 58 Fed. Reg. 54,911 (1993)

Applies to all executive agency procurements. It states:

> *Sec. 401.* Acquisition Planning. In developing plans, drawings, work statements, specifications, or other product descriptions, agencies shall consider the following factors: elimination of virgin material requirements; use of recovered materials; reuse of product; life cycle cost; recyclability; use of environmentally preferable products; waste prevention (including toxicity reduction or elimination); and ultimate disposal, as appropriate. These factors should be considered in acquisition planning for all procurements and in the evaluation and award of contracts, as appropriate. Program and acquisition managers should take an active role in these activities.

### B. Formal Acquisition Plans.

Heads of federal agencies must conduct advance procurement planning. 10 U.S.C. § 2305(a)(1)(A). In the DOD, formal, written acquisition plans are required for R&D contracts with an estimated acquisition cost of $5 million or more and supply or service contracts with an estimated cost of $30 million or more for all program years or $15 million or more for any one fiscal year. DFARS 207.103(c)(i). The FY 1995 DOD Authorization Act requires DOD to implement guidance directing consideration of environmental costs as part of the life-cycle cost analysis in major weapons systems procurements. Pub. L. No. 103-337, § 812, 108 Stat. 2663, 2815-6 (1994).

1. The plan must discuss:
   a. Environmental issues associated with the acquisition;
   b. Whether 40 C.F.R. § 1502 requires an environmental assessment or an environmental impact statement;
   c. The proposed resolution of environmental issues; and

    d. Any environment-related provisions to be included in the solicitations and contracts. FAR 7.105(b)(15).

2. Under DFARS interim rule 207.105(b)(15), the formal acquisition plan must also discuss actions taken to eliminate use of ODS or actions taken to obtain authorization for their use. 58 Fed. Reg. 32,061 (1993).

## C. Market Research.

Market research involves collecting and analyzing information about the ability of the market to meet the agency's needs. FAR 10.001.

1. The contracting officer should obtain information on the availability of environmentally sound, non-hazardous products that meet the agency's minimum needs.

2. Price-preference issues often arise during this phase of planning, as an agency determines whether supplies made with recovered materials or in compliance with other environmental guidelines "are only available at an unreasonable cost." *See* 42 U.S.C. § 6962(c)(1)(C).

3. Agencies may reasonably define their minimum needs around environmentally-sound products and pay more for doing so. *Victor Graphics*, B-238290, Apr. 20, 1990, 69 Comp. Gen. 410, 90-1 CPD ¶ 407 (GPO paid 11.5% more for paper with required recovered material content than price offered by protester that did not meet requirement).

## D. Market Surveys.

Once market research discloses the existence of environmentally-sound products, agencies determine the existence of sources for those products by means of a market survey. Market surveys may be informal, such as telephonic surveys of federal or civilian experts, to a more formal Commerce Business Daily (CBD) or scientific journal "sources sought" announcements. FAR 7.101. The contracting officer also may issue solicitations as a means of gathering information. FAR 15.405-1.

## E. Pre-Award Surveys.

A pre-award survey evaluates "a prospective contractor's capability to perform a proposed contract." FAR 9.101. The FAR requires pre-award surveys when there is insufficient information available for the contracting officer to make a determination of contractor responsibility. FAR 9.106-1. Contracting officers request pre-award surveys using Standard Form (SF) 1403, Preaward Survey of Prospective Contractor (General).

## F. EPA List of Violators.

The EPA must list facilities or individuals convicted of certain criminal violations of clean air and clean water standards. The EPA Administrator has discretionary authority to list facilities or individuals for civil violations.

1. Once listed, the offending facility, or, at the Administrator's discretion, the entire corporation (if convicted of a violation of the Clean Air Act), may not be awarded or used to perform a government contract. *See* 42 U.S.C. § 7606; 33 U.S.C. § 1368.

2. FAR Subpart 23.1 implements these provisions. FAR 23.103(b) provides: "Except as provided in 23.104, executive agencies shall not enter into, renew, or extend contracts with firms proposing to use facilities listed by EPA (40 C.F.R. Part 15) as violating facilities under the Clean Air Act [42 U.S.C. §§ 7401-7642] or Clean Water Act [33 U.S.C. §§ 1251-1376]."

    a. This ban does not apply to contracts of $100,000 or under, unless the facility is on the list because of a conviction under either act.

    b. The agency head may exempt any contract or subcontract from the ban for one year if it is in the paramount interest of the United States to do so. FAR 23.104(c). The agency head must notify the EPA that it has granted an exemption and must explain that the paramount interest of the United States required the exception. FAR 23.104(c)(2).

## XI. COST ISSUES IN ENVIRONMENTAL CONTRACTING.

### A. Overview.
Department of Defense (DOD) contractors annually spend millions of dollars to comply with federal and state environmental cleanup laws, and these costs are likely to increase. GAO/NSIAD-92-253FS, DOD Environmental Cleanup (26 June 1992). Contractors will often attempt to charge these costs to their government contracts. This section focuses on the allowability of contractors' environmental costs.

### B. Distinguish Indirect From Direct Costs.
1. Indirect Costs.
   a. Costs not directly identified with any particular contract but instead included in the contractor's overhead or general and administrative (G & A) pools will often be charged to government contracts as indirect costs. FAR 31.203. Clean-up costs will generally be treated as indirect costs.
   b. To be allocable to a government contract, indirect environmental cleanup costs must either benefit that contract and other contracts or must be "necessary to the overall operation of the [contractor's] business." FAR 31.201-4.
   c. Remediation of environmental problems created under prior contracts generally will not confer any benefit on current contracts and would, therefore, only be allocable if necessary to "the overall operation" of the contractor's business. FAR 31.201-4(c).
   d. Costs incurred in one accounting period are not allocable to contracts in a different accounting period. Thus, contractors cannot allocate their environmental cleanup costs to government contracts in the current accounting period if those costs were incurred in a prior accounting period. Cost Accounting Standard (CAS) 410.40(b)(1).
2. Direct Costs. Costs allocable to only one government contract are direct costs of that con-

tract. *See, e.g.*, FAR 52.223-3(b)(3), which obligates contractors to "use best efforts to comply with clean air standards and clean water standards at the facility in which the contract is being performed." If the costs of complying with this provision benefit only one government cost-reimbursement contract, they should be directly charged only to that contract.

### C. Allowability of a Contractor's Environmental Clean-up Costs.
Contractors may incur clean-up costs in response to an environmental agency's determination that the contractor's operations have violated federal or state environmental laws or as the result of an independent management decision to investigate and correct environmental problems to forestall an agency finding of non-compliance.
1. Generally, environmental expenses qualify as normal business expenses which the contractor may allocate as indirect costs, unless the expenses are in the nature of fines or penalties. 10 U.S.C. § 2324(e)(D); FAR 31.205-15.
2. On 14 October 1992, the Defense Contract Audit Agency (DCAA) issued guidance that states "environmental costs are normal costs of doing business and are generally allowable if reasonable and allocable." DCAA Letter, "Audit Guidance on the Allowability of Environmental Costs," (14 October 1992). However, environmental costs that are in the nature of fines or penalties are unallowable. 10 U.S.C. § 2324(e)(D); FAR 31.205-15. *But see* Section 322 of the FY 1993 Authorization Act, Pub. L. 102-484, stating that fines and penalties may be paid from the Defense Environmental Restoration Account (DERA) if, "the act or omission for which the fine or penalty is imposed arises out of activities funded by the account."
   a. The DCAA guidance provides for the disallowance of "unreasonable" costs and explains that environmental costs are unreasonable if the contractor could have

avoided the contamination that is generating the costs.

b. To be allowable under the DCAA guidance, the contamination must have occurred despite the contractor's due care to avoid the contamination, and despite the contractor's compliance with applicable law.

c. Since it is unreasonable for a contractor to allow contamination to continue once it becomes aware of the problem, increased costs due to contractor delay in taking action after discovery of the contamination are not allowable.

3. On April 13, 1994, the DCAA and the Defense Contract Management Command (DCMC) jointly addressed questions arising from guidance issued by DCAA on October 14, 1992. *See* page 372. The DCAA/DCMC Guidance states, *inter alia*, that:

a. an environmental violation (which would render associated costs unallowable), may be established without a formal citation by a government agency.

b. contractors should expense costs to remediate property which was not contaminated when acquired by the contractor, but costs to remediate property that was contaminated when acquired by the contractor should be capitalized as an improvement, rather than expensed in a single accounting period.

c. if a contractor incurs costs as a PRP and cannot collect from another PRP because that PRP no longer exists, such costs are not "bad debts," and therefore not unallowable under FAR 32.205-3.

## D. Specifically Allowable Costs.

Independent research and development (IR&D) and bid and proposal (B&P) costs are allowable to the extent they are incurred for "projects that are of potential interest to DOD." DFARS 231.205-18(c)(1)(i)(C)(2). This includes IR&D/B&P costs incurred to develop efficient technologies for environmental data gathering, environmental clean-up and restoration, pollution reduction in manufacturing, environmental conservation, and environmentally safe management of facilities. DFARS 231.205-18(c)(1)(i)(C)(2)(v).

# DCAA/DCMC GUIDANCE

## Text of Memorandum from Robert P. Scott, Executive Director, Contract Management, and Michael J. Thibault, Assistant Director, Policy and Plans

AQCP (Environmental)/PAD 730.47/94-9
MEMORANDUM FOR ENVIRONMENTAL PILOT PROJECT TEAMS
SUBJECT: Guidance Addressing Questions Raised Related to the 14 October 1992
Guidance Paper on Environmental Costs

Defense Contract Management Command (DCMC) and Defense Contract Audit Agency (DCAA) have jointly developed the enclosed guidance which addresses questions raised by the environmental pilot teams related to the 14 October 1992 Guidance Paper on Environmental Costs.

We would like to thank the teams for their comments and questions. All comments will be considered when we make our recommendations to the Direct of Defense Procurement at the completion of the pilot project.

The DCMC team members should direct any questions regarding this memorandum to Mr. Ken Siler, Environmental Program Team Leader, at (703) 274-7710. The DCAA team members should direct any questions regarding this memorandum to Ms. Susan Katterheinrich, Program Manager, Accounting Policy Division, at (703) 274-6343.

*(Text of Guidance Paper)*

### Guidance Addressing Questions Raised Related to the 14 October 1992 Guidance Paper on Environmental Costs

Capitalization Questions

*Question 1*: Should soil and groundwater remediation costs associated with the contractor's own property be expensed in the period incurred or capitalized and amortized over future periods? (Assume the costs have been determined to be allowable in accordance with the FAR 31.201-2 criteria.)

*Guidance*

*1. Costs to Acquire Property/Equipment Designed to Reduce, Eliminate, or Contain the Environmental Contamination*

Costs to acquire property/equipment designed to reduce, eliminate, or contain the environmental contamination should be accounted for in accordance with CAS 404. If the costs meet the capitalization threshold, then they should be capitalized and depreciated over future periods.

If the costs of the property/equipment do not meet the capitalization threshold and the costs are being incurred to clean up the contractor's own property which was not contaminated when acquired, then see section 2 for the accounting treatment.

If the property/equipment were acquired to clean up the contractor's own property which was already contaminated when acquired, then see section 3 for the accounting treatment.

*2. Costs to Clean Up Property Which Was Not Contaminated When Acquired*

If the soil and groundwater were not contaminated when acquired by the contractor, the costs incurred to remediate the soil and groundwater should be expensed in accordance with CAS 404 and generally accepted accounting principles (GAAP) as discussed in Emerging Issues Task Force (EITF) Issue No. 90-8, unless

   a. The costs are being incurred to prepare the property for sale. See Property Held for Sale. Question 1 for guidance clarification related to property held for sale.

   b. The costs are being incurred to acquire property/equipment, and these costs meet the CAS 404 capitalization threshold. See section 1 for accounting treatment.

CAS 404.40(d) states "costs incurred for repairs and maintenance to a tangible capital asset which either restore the asset to, or maintain it at, its normal or expected service life or production capacity shall be treated as costs of the current period." If the property were not contaminated when acquired, then cleaning up the soil or groundwater only restores the property to its former uncontaminated state. While the CAS does not specifically provide guidance addressing environmental cleanup costs, the cleanup is analogous to a repair as described in CAS 404.40(d). It is not a betterment of the property. Therefore, the costs should be expensed.

Furthermore, paragraph (a)(3) of FAR 31.201-2 (Determining allowability) states that one factor to consider when determining whether a cost is allowable is Standards promulgated by the CAS Board, if applicable; otherwise, generally accepted accounting principles and practices appropriate to the particular circumstances. As noted above, the CAS does not specifically address environmental cleanup costs. However, generally accepted accounting principles (GAAP) as discussed in EITF Issue No. 90-8 state that, in general, environmental contamination treatment costs should be expensed in the period the costs are incurred. EITF Issue No. 90-8 further states that the costs may be capitalized if recoverable but only if any one of the following criteria is met:

a. The costs extend the life, increase the capacity, or improve the safety or efficiency of property owned by the company. For purposes of this criterion, the condition of that property after the costs are incurred must be improved as compared with the condition of that property when originally constructed or acquired, if later.

b. The costs mitigate or prevent environmental contamination that has yet to occur and that otherwise may result from future operations or activities. In addition, the costs improve the property compared with its condition when constructed or acquired, if later.

c. The costs are incurred in preparing for sale the property current held for sale.

Costs incurred to remediate the soil and groundwater do not meet EITF 90-8 capitalization criteria a. or b. If the property is held for sale and the costs are realizable from the sale, then the costs of preparing the property for sale should be capitalized. However, see Property Held for Sale, Question 1 for clarifying guidance.

### 3. Costs to Clean Up Property Which Was Already Contaminated When Acquired
#### a. Accounting Treatment

If the property was already contaminated when acquired by the contractor, then the soil and groundwater remediation costs should be capitalized as an improvement to the land in accordance with CAS 404 and GAAP to the extent that the total book value does not exceed the fair market value of the property. The costs would not be amortized over future periods since land is not a depreciable asset.

CAS 404.40(d) states betterments and improvements are to be capitalized. This accounting treatment is consistent with criterion a. of EITF Issue No. 90-8 (see section 2). Under this criterion, the costs may be capitalized because the soil and groundwater remediation improves the property's safety over its original condition when acquired.

EITF Issue No. 90-8 states costs may be capitalized when the expenditure represents an improvement. However, the 14 October 1992 guidance states capitalization is required because such treatment is appropriate for Government cost accounting purposes (CAS 404.40(d) and FAR 31.201-2(a)(3)). It would be unreasonable for the Government to accept as current period costs, expenditures which improve the contractor's assets.

#### b. Examples of Costs To be Capitalized

Examples of costs which should be capitalized as an improvement to the land, if the property was contaminated when acquired, include the following: cost of the feasibility study which identified the possible alternatives and objectives for remediation, the remediation project management fees, the costs of the actual remediation activities (labor, materials, permits, etc.), and the cost of equipment purchased specifically for the remediation project.

#### c. Examples of Costs—Condition of the Property When Acquired Doesn't Impact Accounting Treatment

The condition of the property when acquired only impacts the accounting treatment of costs which were incurred as part of the remediation project. Legal costs incurred to seek recovery from the insurance companies or other potentially responsible parties are examples of costs which are not part of the remediation project. In addition, costs incurred prior to the decision to clean up the property should not be considered as part of the remediation project. If the contractor's effort to assess the contamination problem is in response to a regulatory agency's notification, then the contractor should begin capitalizing costs at the point when the regulatory agency decides that a cleanup action is necessary.

### d. Determinination of When the Contamination Occured or How Much of the Contamination is Attributable to the Prior Owners

The determination of when the contamination occured or how much of the contamination is attributable to the prior owners must be made on a case-by-case basis, considering all the available data in any specific circumstance. In some cases it may be clear that all of the contamination is attributable to the prior owner. For example, if the contamination was caused by a substance or process which was unique to the operation of a prior owner, then we can conclude that the property was contaminated when acquired by the contractor.

However, in some cases it may be difficult to precisely determine when the contamination occurred or how much of the contamination is attributable to the prior owner. If a review of the available data and the site usage discloses that contamination occurred both before and after acquisition, then the cleanup costs should be apportioned to the responsible parties using a reasonable allocation method (e.g., time occupied). See section titled Calculation of the Contractor's Share of the Allowable Cleanup Costs for further guidance on apportioning the costs. The portion of the cleanup costs which is attributable to the prior owners' contamination should be capitalized as part of the cost of the land, if the costs are determined to be otherwise allowable.

*Question 2:* Rather than cleansing the contaminated soil, the contractor installs a structure in the ground which contains the contamination on the polluted property. Should the cost of the containment structure be capitalized?

*Guidance*
The cost of the containment structure should be capitalized and depreciated over the structure's useful life. CAS 404.40(a) requires that acquisition costs of tangible capital assets be capitalized if the assets will be used over future periods.

### Property Held for Sale

*Question 1:* Should costs incurred to clean up a property held for sale be expensed or capitalized under the following circumstances?

a. The contractor is cleaning up the property under a regulatory agency's order. The cleanup costs will be realizable from the sale. The cleanup effort will not improve the property beyond its condition at acquisition.

b. There is no regulatory agency's order to clean up the property. However, the property is unsafe and in its present condition cannot be used for the contractor's normal operations.

*Guidance*
In both of these situaions, the cleanup costs should be expensed. Costs incurred to either comply with a regulatory agency's order or to make the property safe for the contractor's normal operations should not be classified as costs of preparing the property for sale. These cleanup costs are necessary whether or not the contractor decides to sell the property.

However, if the costs of either complying with the regulatory agency's order or improving the safety result in an improvement to the property compared to its condition when acquired, then the costs should be capitalized. In addition, costs to acquire property/equipment designed to reduce, eliminate, or contain the environmental contamination should be capitalized if the costs meet the CAS 404 capitalization threshold. See Capitalization Questions for further guidance.

Costs incurred directly relates to the sale (e.g., a site survey required in preparation for the sale) should be offset against the sales proceeds.

*Question 2:* When is a property considered held for sale? For example, is the property considered to be held for sale in the following situation?

The contractor purchased the plant in 1950, but has never used it. The property was contaminated when acquired. The property is available for sale; however, the contractor is not actively pursuing its sale.

*Guidance*

The determination of whether a property is held for sale must be made on a case-by-case basis. If a property is idle, the costs associated with continuing ownership should be evaluated considering the requirements of FAR 31.205-17 (Idle facilities and idle capacity costs). In the above example, whether or not the property is considered held for sale is irrelevant because the costs should be questioned for all of the following reasons:

- The facility has been idle since its acquisition (over 40 years ago); thus, the costs associated with its ownership are unallowable under FAR 31.205-17.
- The property was already contaminated when acquired; thus, the cleanup costs represent a betterment and should be capitalized.

In addition, if the company that caused the contamination either continues in business or a successor company (other than the contractor) has assumed the former company's liabilities, then the costs are unallowable based on FAR 31.205-3 and 31.204(c). See Potentially Responsible Party (PRP) Questions for clarifying guidance on this issue.

*Question 3:* When are costs realizable from the sale? How do we segregate what portion of the difference between book value and sales price is due to inflation and changing market values and what portion is the result of "cleaning up" the property? Is the entire sales price "realizable" if the property is worthless prior to the clean up because it can't be sold until cleaned up?

*Guidance*

The guidance refers to costs being realizable from a sale to address the EITF Issue No. 90-8 criterion that capitalization costs be recoverable. Costs are realizable from the sale when the sales price exceeds the book value. The amount realizable from the sale is the difference between the sales price and the book value without regard to various factors such as inflation or changing market values. The entire sales price is realizable if the book value of the property is zero.

See Property Held for Sale, Question 1 for clarification of when cleanup costs are incurred to prepare a site for sale.

Potentially Responsible Party (PRP) Questions

*Question 1:* Under CERCLA, the contractor is responsible for the cleanup costs attributable to contamination caused by other PRPs. Are these other PRPs' costs allowable under the following set of circumstances:

a. *Other PRP Is No Longer in Business with No Successor Company*

Another PRP caused all or part of the contamination (e.g., contamination from the other PRP's operation leaked onto the contractor's property). The PRP is no longer in business and no successor company has assumed its liabilities.

b. *Other PRP Continues in Business or a Successor Company Has Assumed the other PRP's Liabilities*

Same circumstances as item a., except the other PRP either continues in business or a successor company (other than the contractor) has assumed the other PRP's liabilities.

*Guidance*

The following from the 14 October 1992 DCAA Guidance Paper applies to the circumstances described under the above item b.

If a contractor cannot collect contribution or subrogation claims from other PRPs, the uncollected amounts are, in their essential nature, bad debts. Bad debts and associated collection costs, including legal fees, are unallowable costs (FAR 32.205-3 and 31.204(c)).

However, the Director of Defense Procurement (DDP) has concluded that this guidance does not apply to the circumstances described under the above item a. (See 8 February 1994 DDP Memorandum for DCMC Acting Executive Director, Subject: Allowability of Environmental Cleanup Costs Attributable to Other PRPs) In accordance with DDP's decision, when a contractor is legally required to pay another PRP's share of the cleanup costs and that PRP is out of business (with no successor company having assumed its liabilities), then the costs should not be characterized as bad debt type expenses (FAR 31.205-3 and 31.204(c)) since there is no one against whom the contractor can take recovery action.

*Question 2:* Aren't the costs incurred by the contractor as described in the example under PRP Question 1, item b. (uncollectible other PRP's expenses when PRP continues in business or a successor company has assumed the other PRP's liabilities) allocable to Government contracts under FAR 31.201-4? FAR 31.201-4(c) states a cost is allocable to a Government contract if it is necessary to the overall operation of the business, although a direct relationship to any particular cost objective cannot be shown. The costs incurred by the contractor to clean up the other PRP's contamination are necessary because the contractor is liable under the law and because penalties for failure to take remedial action could be so significant as to lead the the failure of the business.

*Guidance*

The costs may be allowable under the FAR 31.201-4(c) criterion. However, the costs are unallowable when FAR 31.205-3, "Bad debts" and FAR 31.204(c), "Application of principles and procedures" are considered. As stated in the 14 October 1992 guidance, the uncollected amounts attributed to another PRP are "in their essential nature, bad debts." Allocability in accordance with FAR 31.201-4(c) is only one factor to be considered in determining whether a cost is allowable. FAR 31.201-2 requires other factors to be considered including reasonableness, CAS, GAAP, contractor terms, and any limitations set forth in Subpart 31.2. Like the cleanup costs in the above example, Federal income taxes are required by law and failure to pay could lead to the failure of the business; however, these costs, although allocable, are not allowable under FAR 31.205-4 and thus are not reimbursable in Government Contracts.

*Question 3:* Does the 14 October 1992 guidance misinterpret the cost principle on bad debts, FAR 31.205-3? The contribution amount which a contractor seeks from other PRPs is in the nature of a claim and not an accounts receivable or a liquidated debt which is the subject matter of the bad debt costs principle.

*Guidance*

It should be noted that the guidance does not state the uncollected amounts are bad debts. It states these amounts are "in their essential nature, bad debts." The guidance cites both FAR 31.205-3 and FAR 31.204(c) (Application of principles and procedures). FAR 31.204(c) states "the determination of allowability shall be based on the guidance contained in the subsection that most specifically deals with, or best captures the essential nature of, the cost at issue." We believe that the essential nature of the cost at issue is best captured at FAR 31.205-3. In addition, FAR 31.205-3 refers not just to uncollectible "accounts receivable" but also broadly to uncollectible "other claims."

## Calculation of the Contractor's Share of the Allowable Cleanup Costs

*Question:* How should the costs associated with the actual percentage of the contamination attributable to the contractor be calculated? For example, both a prior property owner and the contractor caused the contamination. If the contamination was caused by practices which were legal and illegal, how should the costs associated with each practice be calculated. For example, the contractor dumped chemicals in the ground before as well as after the practice became illegal.

*Guidance*

The method used to determine the contractor's share of the allowable cleanup costs depends on the circumstances. Often, technical assistance will be required. If the relationship between the party/practice and the contamination is known (e.g., contamination was the result of a particular manufacturing process which was unique to the other responsible party), then the costs should be allocated to each party or practice based on this relationship (e.g., 50% of the cost of cleanup was associated with the cleanup of PCB contamination which was solely attributed to the other party; therefore 50% of the costs should be allocated to the other party). If such relationships cannot be established, then the cleanup responsibility would have to be determined on some other basis, such as time period occupied or space occupied. For example, the contamination occured over a 20 year period. The other potentially responsible party (PRP) occupied the site for 5 of the 20 years. The PRP's share based on time occupied would be 25%. If the PRPs occupied the site simultaneously during the period of contamination, then space occupied might be an appropriate basis for apportioning the costs.

## Allocation of Costs of Past Environmental Contamination

*Question:* The 14 October 1992 guidance states the costs are to be allocated to contracts as part of the G&A expense pool. Why aren't other allocation bases appropriate?

*Guidance*

The costs to clean up past environmental contamination may be allocated to contracts on bases other than G&A, if the allocation method complies with CAS 418. However, normally, these costs will be G&A as defined by CAS 410.30:

> Any management, financial, and other expense which is incurred by or allocated to a business unit and which is for the general management and administration of the business unit as a whole. G&A expense does not include those management expenses whose beneficial or causal relationship to cost objectives can be more directly measured by a base other than a cost input base representing the total activity of a business unit during a cost accounting period.

CAS 418.40(c) requires that pooled costs "be allocated to cost objectives in reasonable proportion to the beneficial or causal relationship of the pooled costs to cost objectives." However, in general, a causal or beneficial relationship would not exist between the costs of cleanup of past contamination and the final costs objectives (contracts) of the current period. The operating activities which caused the contamination in the past and generated the current period environmental cleanup expenses relate to the performance of contracts in prior cost accounting periods (in most cases, many years prior to the current period). Normally, there would be no clear, measurable relationship between the costs generated by these prior period activities and the contracts of the current period. Under this circumstance, no matter what allocation base the contractor selects, the costs will not be allocated to contracts in proportion to the amount of benefit the contract received from the incurrence of the expense or the amount of expense the contract caused to be incurred, as required by CAS 418.40(c).

When the cleanup costs cannot be related to any cost objective through the showing of a causal or beneficial relationship, then the costs should be allocated on the CAS 410 G&A base. The CAS 410 G&A base is representative of the year's business activity and will most equitably apportion the expenses among the current period's cost objectives.

## Allocation of Compliance Costs

*Question:* The guidance should address the allocation method for compliance costs. For example, under the Resource Conservation and Recovery Act (RCRA), permits are required for facilities that treat, store, or dispose of hazardous wastes. Should costs incurred to comply with these permits be allocated on the CAS 410 G&A base or on a CAS 418 causal or beneficial basis?

*Guidance*

The compliance costs in the above example should be allocated on a CAS 418 causal or beneficial basis. However, costs incurred to comply with a regulatory agency's order to clean up environmental contamination which occurred in prior periods should be allocated on a CAS 410 G&A base in most cases (see previous discussion under Allocation of Costs of Past Environmental Contamination).

## Environmental Wrongdoing

*Question 1:* The guidance needs to address when a violation of environmental law occurs; i.e., must there be a formal or informal violation, warning or other action identified or cited by an enforcement group? If the contractor cleans up the contamination on a site for which it is responsible and there was no intent to cause the contamination; (i.e., resulted from an inadvertent spill or leak and not negligence) and no action is taken by an enforcement group, should its actions be considered legal and the related costs be considered allowable and recoverable?

*Guidance*

A violation occurs when the contractor does not comply with the specific requirements imposed by laws, regulations, orders or permits. A violation can occur without a formal citation by a governmental agency.

It is not necessary for us to make a determination of what is or is not a legal act in the grey areas of the law. If the review of the available records and other information discloses that the environmental damage occurred because the contractor's practices were not consistent with the actions expected of an ordinary reasonable, prudent businessperson performing non-Government contracts in a competitive marketplace, then the costs would be unreasonable and thus, unallowable.

*Question 2:* The language concerning violations should be changed to "If environmental cleanup costs are the result of a finding or ruling by a competent authority of contractor violation of laws, . . ." The reason is that if competent administrative or judicial authorities do not find or rule on violation, then are we in a position to so find or rule?

*Guidance*

There may be instances where there is sufficient evidence to conclude the contractor violated laws, regulations, orders or permits or disregarded warnings, or did not act prudently in disposing of hazardous materials, even though there is no administrative or judicial ruling or even a citation. Environmental authorities often drop charges made against a company when the company consents to remediate the environmental damage. These consent agreements are not a finding of innocence. The company's agreement to pay for the corrective action, along with other facts of the circumstances, may be considered in determining whether violations occurred. Comments should be sought from the environmental authorities and from counsel.

*Question 3:* What is meant by "disregard of warnings for potential contamination"? Warnings from whom? The regulators are not in the business of warning.

*Guidance*

Warnings can be from any competent source. For example, the contractor's internal or external environmental or safety reviews may disclose that its practice will result in environmental damage; however, the contractor disregards the warning and continues the practice. Circumstances will vary and determinations will need to consider all verifiable facts and data.

## CHAPTER TWENTY-SIX

# *Fraud: Administrative and Contractual Remedies*

"Simply because a party is a defense contractor does not mean that all doubts automatically are to be resolved against it and those in any way associated with it." *John Doe Agency v. John Doe Corp.*, 493 U.S. 146, 158 (1989).

## I. INTRODUCTION.

### A. Objectives.
Following this instruction, the student will understand:
1. The Department of Defense and Army programs and policies to combat fraud, waste and abuse in government contracting.
2. The administrative and contractual remedies available to the government in cases of contract fraud.

### B. References
1. DOD Dir. 7050.5, Coordination of Remedies for Fraud Corruption Related to Procurement Activities (June 7, 1989).
2. AR 27-40, Litigation, Ch. 8.
3. DOD Inspector General's Handbook on Indicators of Fraud in DOD Procurement, No. 4075-1.H (June 1987).

## II. DEPARTMENT OF DEFENSE POLICY FOR COMBATTING PROCUREMENT FRAUD.
DOD Dir. 7050.5, Coordination of Remedies for Fraud and Corruption Related to Procurement Activities (June 7, 1989).

### A. Coordination of Remedies Approach.
1. DOD policy requires each department to establish a centralized organization to monitor all *significant* fraud and corruption cases.
   a. Definition of a "significant" case.
      (1) All fraud cases involving an alleged loss of $100,000 or more.
      (2) All corruption cases that involve bribery, gratuities, or conflicts of interest.
      (3) All investigations into defective products or product substitution in which a *serious hazard* to health, safety, or operational readiness is indicated (regardless of loss value).
   b. In the Army, the centralized organization is the Procurement Fraud Division, United States Army Legal Services Agency (USALSA).
      (1) DA Policy implementing DOD Dir. 7050.5 is found in AR 27-40, Litigation, Ch. 8.
      (2) Procurement fraud attorneys must coordinate remedies on all cases.
2. Each centralized organization monitors all significant cases to ensure that all proper and effective criminal, civil, administrative, and contractual remedies are considered and pursued in a timely manner.

### B. Documentation.
1. Agencies should identify and document any adverse impact on a DOD mission.

2. Agencies should use adverse impact information to develop a remedies plan and victim impact statements.

## C. Product Substitution Cases.

The following actions are required by the centralized organization in product substitution investigations which involve a serious hazard to health, safety, or operational readiness.

1. Notify all appropriate safety, procurement, and program officials of the case.

2. Obtain from safety, procurement, and program officials an assessment of the adverse impact of the fraud.

3. Ensure that the affected procurement organization provides funding for the testing of defective products for criminal investigations.

4. Issue appropriate safety alerts.

## D. DOD Voluntary Disclosure Program.

1. DOD IG Pamphlet IGDPH 5505.50, Voluntary Disclosure Program—A Description of the Process (Sept. 1988), describes the process used by DOD and the Department of Justice in the administration of the DOD Voluntary Disclosure Program.

2. Contractors should adopt a policy of voluntary disclosure as a central part of their corporate self-governance and to enhance contractor responsibility.

3. Disclosures are made with no advance agreements or promises regarding resolution of matters by DOD or lack of criminal or civil prosecution by DOJ.

4. Prompt voluntary disclosure, full cooperation, complete access to necessary records, restitution, and adequate corrective actions are key indicators of contractor integrity.

5. Disclosure must not be triggered by the contractor's recognition that potential fraud is about to be discovered by the government.

6. For a matter to be accepted into the program, the disclosure must contain "sufficient information," i.e., meaningful disclosure.

7. Regulatory guidance on voluntary disclosure program. DFARS Subpart 203.70, Contractor Standards of Conduct, encourages contractors to establish a voluntary code of conduct program that facilitates timely discovery and disclosure of improper conduct.

8. The designated point of contact is the Assistant Inspector General for Investigations (AIG-I).

## III. AGENCIES INVOLVED IN FRAUD ABATEMENT.

### A. DOD Inspector General.

Inspector General Act of 1978, Pub. L. 95-452, as amended by Pub. L. No. 97-252; DOD Dir. 5106.1, Inspector General of Department of Defense (Mar. 14, 1983).

1. DOD IG has responsibility to initiate, conduct, supervise, and monitor investigations of fraud within DOD.

2. Investigative responsibility is carried out by Defense Criminal Investigative Service (DCIS).

### B. Military Criminal Investigative Organizations.

### C. Department of Justice.

DOD Dir. 5525.7, Memorandum of Understanding Between Department of Defense and Department of Justice Relating to the Investigation and Prosecution of Certain Crimes (Jan. 22, 1985).

1. Defense criminal investigative organizations have full jurisdiction over all fraud matters, except "significant" bribery, gratuity, and conflict of interest cases involving present, retired or former general or flag officers, and civilian executive-level employees.

2. Defense criminal investigative organizations may conduct complete investigation and refer case directly to DOJ.

3. FBI - investigative agency.

4. Defense Procurement Fraud Unit (DPFU) - specialized unit within DOJ to review and coordinate significant procurement fraud cases.

5. U.S. Attorneys - supervise and/or conduct

the prosecution of major procurement fraud cases.

### D. Procurement Fraud Division (PFD)

USALSA. AR 27-40, Litigation, ch. 8.

1. PFD monitors and coordinates disposition of Army procurement fraud and corruption cases.
2. PFD coordinates with DOJ and U.S. Attorneys in civil and criminal cases.
3. Procurement Fraud and Irregularities Coordinator (PFI) (MACOMs) - responsible for the MACOM procurement fraud program.
4. Procurement Fraud Advisors (PFA) (subordinate commands) - ensure that commanders and contracting officers pursue, in a timely manner, all applicable criminal, civil, contractual, and administrative remedies.
5. Key reporting requirements.
   a. Procurement flash reports. AR 27-40, para. 8-5(b).
   b. Comprehensive remedies plan. AR 27-40, para. 8-8.

### E. Defense Contract Audit Agency (DCAA).

## IV. CONTRACTING OFFICER AUTHORITY IN PROCUREMENT FRAUD CASES.

### A. Actions Clearly Exceeding Contracting Officer (KO) Authority.

41 U.S.C § 605, FAR 33.210.

1. KO authority does not extend to the settlement, compromise, payment, or adjustment of any claim involving fraud.
2. The KO may not administer, settle, or determine any claim or dispute for penalties or forfeitures prescribed by statute or regulation for which another federal agency is specifically authorized.
3. Termination for convenience.

### B. Actions Clearly Within KO Authority.

1. Refuse payment. FAR 49.106. *To the Secretary of the Army*, B-154766, 44 Comp. Gen. 110 (1964).
2. Suspend progress payments. 10 U.S.C. §

2307; *Brown v. United States*, 524 F.2d 693 (Ct. Cl. 1975); *Fidelity Constr.*, DOT CAB No. 1113, 80-2 BCA ¶ 14,819.

3. Withhold payment.
   a. When a debarment/suspension report recommends debarment or suspension based on fraud or criminal conduct involving a current contract, all funds becoming due on that contract shall be withheld unless directed otherwise by the head of the contracting activity or the Commander, USALSA. AFARS 9.406-3.
   b. Labor standards statutes provide for withholding for labor standards violations.
   c. Specific contract provisions may provide for withholding (service contract deductions for deficiencies in performance).
4. Terminate negotiations. FAR 49.106; *K & R Eng'g Co. v. United States*, 616 F.2d 469 (Ct. Cl. 1980) (ending settlement discussions of a terminated contract upon suspicion of fraud is proper).
5. Determine contractor to be nonresponsible. FAR Subpart 9.4; *see* section V. D., *infra*.

## V. ADMINISTRATIVE REMEDIES.

### A. Debarment and Suspension of Contractors.

10 U.S.C. § 2393; FAR Subpart 9.4.

1. Government policy is to solicit offers from, award contracts to, and consent to subcontracts with *responsible contractors* only.
2. Debarment and suspension are discretionary administrative actions to effectuate this policy and shall not be used for *punishment*. FAR 9.103(a); FAR 9.402.
3. Debarring and suspending officials. DFARS 209.403.
   a. Army: Commander, U.S. Army Legal Services Agency, or The Assistant Judge Advocate General when the Commander, U.S. Army Legal Services Agency, is unable to do so because of conflicts, disqualification, or unavailability.
   b. Navy: the General Counsel of the Navy.

c. Air Force: the Assistant General Counsel for Responsibility.

d. Defense Logistics Agency: the Special Assistant for Contracting Integrity.

4. Causes for debarment. FAR 9.406-2. DFARS 209.406-2.

a. Debarring official may debar a contractor for a CONVICTION of or CIVIL JUDGMENT for:

(1) Commission of fraud or a criminal offense in connection with (i) obtaining, (ii) attempting to obtain, or (iii) performing a public contract or subcontract.

(2) Violation of federal or state antitrust statutes relating to the submission of offers.

(3) Commission of embezzlement, theft, forgery, bribery, falsification or destruction of records, making false statements, or receiving stolen property.

(4) Commission of any other offense indicating a lack of business integrity or business honesty that seriously and directly affects the present responsibility of a government contractor or subcontractor.

(5) Criminal conviction for affixing "Made in America" labels to non-American goods.

(6) Unfair trade practices.

b. Debarring official may debar a contractor, based upon a PREPONDERANCE OF THE EVIDENCE for:

(1) Violation of the terms of a government contract or subcontract so serious as to justify debarment, such as —

(a) Willful failure to perform in accordance with the terms of one or more contracts.

(b) A history of failure to perform, or unsatisfactory performance of, one or more contracts.

(2) Violation of the Drug-Free Workplace Act of 1988, Pub. L. No. 100-690, 102 Stat. 4181.

(3) Any other cause of so serious or com-

pelling a nature that it affects the present responsibility of a government contractor or subcontractor.

c. "Preponderance" means proof by information that, compared with that opposing it, leads to the conclusion that the fact at issue is more probably true than not. FAR 9.403.

5. Causes for suspension. FAR 9.407-2.

a. Upon ADEQUATE EVIDENCE of:

(1) Commission of fraud or a criminal offense in connection with (i) obtaining, (ii) attempting to obtain, or (iii) performing a public contract or subcontract.

(2) Violation of federal or state antitrust statutes relating to the submission of offers.

(3) Commission of embezzlement, theft, forgery, bribery, falsification or destruction of records, making false statements, or receiving stolen property.

(4) Violation of the Drug-Free Workplace Act of 1988, Pub. L. No. 100-690, 102 Stat. 4181.

(5) Intentionally affixing a "Made in America" label to non-American goods.

(6) Unfair trade practices.

(7) Commission of any other offense indicating a lack of business integrity or business honesty that seriously and directly affects the present responsibility of a Government contractor or subcontractor.

b. "Adequate evidence" means information sufficient to support the reasonable belief that a particular act or omission has occurred. FAR 9.403.

c. Indictment for any of the causes in paragraph a above constitutes "adequate evidence" for suspension. FAR 9.407-2.

d. "Adequate evidence" may include allegations in a civil complaint filed by another federal agency. *See SDA, Inc.*, B-253355, Aug. 24, 1993, 93-2 CPD ¶ 132.

e. Upon adequate evidence, contractor may also be suspended for any other cause of so serious or compelling a nature that it affects the present responsibility of a government contractor or subcontractor. FAR 9.407-2.

6. Reporting requirements. DFARS 209.406-3.
   a. Burden is on contracting officer to make a report to debarment/suspension authority.
   b. Report required when:
      (1) Contractor has committed, or is suspected of having committed, any of the acts in FAR 9.406-2 (causes for debarment) and FAR 9.407-2 (causes for suspension). DFARS 209.406-3(a).
      (2) Other reasons listed in DFARS 209.406-3(a).
   c. Contents of the report. *See* DFARS 209.406-3 for complete listing.
   d. A good report develops the facts. Army Procurement Fraud Advisor's Update No. 2, Procurement Fraud Division, Office of The Judge Advocate General, Army, Dec. 21, 1989.

7. Procedures for debarment and suspension. FAR 9.406-3; FAR 9.407-3; DFARS Appendix H.

8. Effect of debarment or suspension. FAR 9.405; DFARS 209.405.
   a. Contractors proposed for debarment, suspended, or debarred may not receive government contracts, and agencies may not solicit offers from, award contracts to, or consent to subcontracts with these contractors, unless acquiring agency's head or designee determines that there is a *compelling reason* for such action.
   b. Bids received from any listed contractor are opened, entered on abstract of bids, and rejected unless there is a compelling reason for an exception.
   c. Proposals, quotations, or offers from listed contractors shall not be evaluated, included in the competitive range, or discussions held unless there is a compelling reason for an exception.
   d. Section 2455 of the Federal Acquisition Streamlining Act of 1994, Pub. L. No. 103-355, 108 Stat. 3243 (1994), directs the

issuance of regulations giving government-wide effect to the debarment, proposed debarment, suspension, or any other exclusion of an entity from procurement OR nonprocurement activities.

9. Fraudulent conduct may be imputed. FAR 9.406-5 (debarment); FAR 9.407-5 (suspension); *TS Generalbau Gmbh*, B-246034, Feb. 14, 1992, 92-1 CPD ¶ 189 (suspended contractor's misconduct imputed to an authorized signatory).

10. Period of debarment. FAR 9.406-4; DFARS 209.406-4.
    a. Commensurate with the seriousness of the cause(s). Generally, debarment should not exceed three years except that debarment for violations of the Drug-Free Workplace Act of 1988, Pub. L. No. 100-690, 102 Stat. 1481, may be for five years. FAR 23.506.
    b. Administrative record must include relevant findings as to the appropriateness of the length of the debarment. *Coccia v. Defense Logistics Agency*, C.A. No. 89-6544, 1990 U.S. Dist. LEXIS 6079, (E.D. Pa. May 15, 1990). (Upholding 15-year debarment of former government employee convicted of taking bribes and kickbacks from contractors in exchange for contracts.)
    c. The period of the proposed debarment, or any prior suspension, is considered in determining period of debarment.
    d. Debarment period may be extended, but not solely on the original basis; if extension necessary, normal procedures apply.
    e. Period may be reduced (new evidence, reversal of conviction or judgment, elimination of causes, bona fide change in management).
    f. Inconsistent treatment of corporate officials justifies overturning debarment decision. *Kisser v. Kemp*, 786 F. Supp. 38 (D.D.C. 1992).

11. Period of suspension. FAR 9.407-4.
    a. Suspension is temporary, pending completion of investigation or any ensuing legal proceedings.
    b. If legal proceedings are not initiated with-

in 12 months after the date of the suspension notice, terminate the suspension unless an Assistant Attorney General requests extension.

   c. Extension upon request by an Assistant Attorney General shall not exceed 6 months.

   d. Suspension may not exceed 18 months unless legal proceedings are initiated within that period.

12. Certification requirements for contracts expected to exceed the simplified acquisition threshold. FAR 9.409; FAR 52.209-5.

   a. Offerors must certify whether they or their principals are presently debarred, suspended or proposed for debarment.

   b. Offerors also must certify whether they have been convicted of a crime or had a civil judgment rendered against them for commission of fraud or other criminal offense related to efforts to obtain or perform a federal, state or local government contract (certification also extends to violations of federal or state antitrust statutes and commission of certain theft offenses).

   c. Offerors must certify whether they are currently under indictment or have been civilly charged by a government entity with violation of above offenses.

   d. Contractors must obtain a disclosure from subcontractors as to whether the subcontractor is, at the time of subcontract award, debarred or suspended by the Federal government. 10 U.S.C. § 2393(d).
—Prohibits the employment and other activities of individuals convicted of defense-contract related felonies at the first tier subcontractors level. 10 U.S.C. § 2408(a).

13. Factors to consider in making debarment decision. FAR 9.406-1.

## B. Actions to Preserve the Integrity of the Competitive Process.

FAR 1.602-2.

1. Contracting officers are ". . . responsible for ensuring performance of all necessary actions for effective contracting . . . and safeguarding the interests of the United States in its contractual relationships. . . . Contracting officers shall. . . [e]nsure that contractors receive impartial, fair, and equitable treatment . . . ." FAR 1.602-2.

2. The appearance of an unfair competitive advantage justifies the exclusion of an offeror from receiving the award of a contract. *Compliance Corp.*, 22 Ct. Cl. 193 (1990), *aff'd* 960 F.2d. 157 (Fed. Cir. 1992) (party disqualified from the competitive process for engaging in industrial espionage).

   a. An agency may exclude an offeror from the competition because of an apparent conflict of interest to protect the integrity of the procurement process so long as the determination is based on facts and not mere innuendo or suspicion. *Holmes and Narver Serv., Inc.*, B-239469.3, Sept. 14, 1990, 90-2 CPD ¶ 210; *see also CACI, Inc. - Federal v. United States*, 719 F.2d 1567 (Fed. Cir. 1983).

   b. A contracting agency may not disqualify a firm from competition because of an appearance of impropriety or apparent conflict of interest where the agency has conducted an internal investigation that established that no wrongdoing actually occurred. *FHC Options, Inc.*, B-246793.3, Apr. 14, 1992, 92-1 CPD ¶ 366; *Joseph L. DeClerk & Assocs., Inc. v. United States*, 26 Cl. Ct. 35 (1992).

   c. The mere employment of a former government employee who is familiar with the type of work required but not privy to the contents of proposals or to other inside information does not confer an unfair competitive advantage. *Textron Marine Sys., Inc.*, B-255580.3, Aug. 2, 1994, 94-2 CPD ¶ 63; *Regional Envt'l Consultants*, B-223555.2, Apr. 21, 1987, 66 Comp. Gen. 388, 87-1 CPD ¶ 428. *But see Childers Serv. Center*, B-246210, June 17, 1992, 92-1 CPD ¶ 524.

3. Conduct that compromises the integrity of the competitive process is sufficient to sus-

tain the termination of a contract. *Huynh Servs. Co.*, B-242297.2, June 12, 1991, 91-1 CPD ¶ 562.

4. Contracting officer's responsibility to safeguard the interests of the government is sufficient authority for procurement officials (and a contractor who is acting as the government's procuring agent) to disaffirm contracts tainted by actual or apparent conflicts of interests. *See* FAR 1.602-2; *Naddaf Int'l Trading Co.*, B-238768.2, Oct. 19, 1990, 90-2 CPD ¶ 316; *United Tel. Co. of the Northwest*, GSBCA Nos. 10031-P, 89-3 BCA ¶ 22,108; *see also TRW Env't'l Safety Sys., Inc. v. United States*, 18 Cl. Ct. 33 (1989) (contract tainted by a violation of a conflict of interest statute, which exists for the protection of the integrity of the procurement process, may be disaffirmed without any showing of prejudice).

## C. Cancellation of the Contract.

1. Statutory. 18 U.S.C. § 218; FAR Subpart 3.7.
   a. Requires conviction of 18 U.S.C. §§ 201-224 (bribery, gratuities, graft, improper business practices, conflict of interest).
   b. Procedures:
      (1) Written notice.
      (2) Contractor has 30 days, after receipt of notice, to respond.
      (3) Hearing held if requested; however, no inquiry requiring validity of conviction.
      (4) Written decision at secretarial level.
   c. Written demand for recovery of amounts expended under affected contracts is not a claim within CDA.
2. Common Law.
   a. Default clause reserves common law rights and remedies. FAR 52.249-8(h).
   b. No requirement for conviction. *K & R Eng'g Co. v. United States*, 616 F.2d 469 (Ct. Cl. 1980); *J.E.T.S., Inc.*, ASBCA No. 28642, 87-1 BCA ¶ 19,569.
   c. Cancellation may be partial or total. *Four-Phase Sys., Inc.*, ASBCA No. 26794, 86-2 BCA ¶ 18,924.

## D. Nonresponsibility Determinations.

1. Contracting officer must make an affirmative determination of responsibility prior to award. FAR 9.103(b).
2. Protester must show bad faith on part of the agency or that the nonresponsibility determination lacks any *reasonable basis. EPD Enter., Inc.*, B-234193, Feb. 21, 1989, 89-1 CPD ¶ 182; *Oertzen & Co. GmbH*, B-228537, Feb. 17, 1988, 88-1 CPD ¶ 158.
3. *De facto* debarment.
   a. Contracting officer's determination of nonresponsibility based upon contractor's prospective lack of integrity infringes a liberty interest. Contractor has a Constitutional right under the 5th Amendment to notice and opportunity to respond prior to contracting officer's decision. *Old Dominion Dairy Prods., Inc. v. United States*, 631 F.2d 953 (D.C. Cir. 1980); *Viktoria-Schaeffer Int'l. v. Dep't. of Army*, 659 F. Supp. 85 (D.D.C. 1987); *but see Coleman Am. Moving Servs., Inc. v. Weinberger*, 716 F. Supp. 1405 (M.D. Ala. 1989) (suspension action based on antitrust indictment did not entitle contractor to a hearing).
   b. Nonresponsibility determinations do not constitute *de facto* debarments because they do not prevent a firm from competing for other contracts and receiving an award if it is otherwise qualified and convinces the agency that it has corrected its past problems. *Energy Mgmt. Corp.*, B-234727, July 12, 1989, 89-2 CPD ¶ 38; *but see Related Indus., Inc. v. United States*, 2 Cl. Ct. 517 (1983) (*de facto* debarment found where contracting officer stated that under no circumstances would he award a contract to the company); *Leslie & Elliott Co. v. Garrett*, 732 F. Supp. 191 (D.D.C. 1990) (*de facto* debarment found where contracting officer, in a letter to the Small Business Administration, characterized the contractor as an administrative burden).
   c. Reliance in district court upon wiretap

evidence in support of its administrative nonresponsibility determination entitles the wiretapped party the right to challenge the lawfulness of the interception. *Cubic Corp. v. Cheney*, 914 F.2d 1501 (D.C. Cir. 1990).

4. Offeror who is subject of a fraud investigation need not be found nonresponsible for new contracts. *Krug Int'l*, B-232291.2, Feb. 6, 1989, 89-1 CPD ¶ 116.

5. Practical options.
   a. Determine whether fraudulent conduct related to or impacted on performance.
   b. Do not base nonresponsibility determination solely on lack of integrity.

## VI. CONTRACTUAL REMEDIES.

### A. Default Terminations Based on Fraud.

1. A contractor engaging in fraud commits a material breach which justifies terminating the entire contract for default. *Joseph Morton Co. v. United States*, 3 Cl. Ct. 120 (1983), *aff'd* 757 F.2d 1273 (Fed. Cir. 1985) (contractor convicted for conspiring to defraud the government and for submitting false cost statements).

2. Conviction for submitting false test reports is a proper basis for default termination. *Michael C. Avino, Inc.*, ASBCA No. 31752, 89-3 BCA ¶ 22,156; *see also Dry Roof Corp.*, ASBCA No. 29061, 88-3 BCA ¶ 21,096 (conviction for submission of forged performance and payment bonds support default termination).

3. The government's remedies for a contract tainted by bribery include refusal to honor the contract and pay claims, as well as forfeiture of the contact claim under the forfeiture statute, 28 U.S.C. § 2514. *Brown Constr. Trades, Inc. v. United States*, 23 Cl. Ct. 214 (1991).

4. U.S. Court of Federal Claims has jurisdiction over fraud claims. *Martin J. Simko Constr. Inc. v. United States*, 11 Cl. Ct. 257 (1986), *rev'd on other grounds*, 852 F.2d 540 (Fed. Cir. 1988).

   a. Contract terminated for default.
   b. Government asserted counterclaims alleging fraud, invoking Court of Federal Claims counterclaim jurisdiction under 28 U.S.C. §§ 1503 and 2508.
   c. Government counterclaims were based on the False Claims Act, 31 U.S.C. §§ 3729-3731, and the antifraud provision of the Contract Disputes Act, 41 U.S.C. § 604.

5. Basic problems with terminating for default for fraud.
   a. No grounds in clause.
   b. Not a basis for action against surety—must show that performance was deficient. *United States v. Seaboard Surety Co.*, 622 F. Supp. 882 (S.D.N.Y. 1985) (surety issued a performance bond, not a fidelity bond).

6. Practical options.
   a. Base default termination on substantive grounds (performance deficiencies).
   b. Plead fraudulent conduct as an affirmative defense.
   c. Terminate for default based on fraudulent conduct.
   d. Cancel the contract. 10 U.S.C. § 218; FAR Subpart 3.7.

### B. Denial of Claims Submitted By Contractor.

The Contract Disputes Act, 41 U.S.C. § 605(a), prohibits an agency head from settling, compromising or otherwise adjusting any claim involving fraud. FAR 33.210 reflects limitation in CDA—contracting officer must deny any claims involving fraud.

### C. Forfeiture of Claims under the Contract Disputes Act (CDA).

41 U.S.C. § 604.

1. If contractor is unable to support any part of its claim because of fraud, it is liable for the amount equal to *such part* and all costs of reviewing its claim.

2. Boards of contract appeals have no jurisdiction to entertain claims founded on 41 U.S.C. § 604 (CDA antifraud provision). *Comada Corp.*, ASBCA No. 26599, 83-2 BCA ¶ 16,681.

3. U.S. Court of Federal Claims has jurisdiction over claims founded on 41 U.S.C. § 604. *Martin J. Simko Constr. Inc. v. United States*, 11 Cl. Ct. 257 (1986), *rev'd on other grounds*, 852 F.2d 540 (Fed. Cir. 1988).

### D. Other remedies.

1. Use of inspection clause rights.
   a. Rejection of non-conforming goods.
   b. Correction of defects or replacement of goods.
   c. Unilateral price reduction by Contracting Officer.
2. Rejection of acceptance based on fraud or on gross mistake amounting to fraud.
3. Exercise of contract warranty rights.
4. Price reduction for defective pricing.

## VII. CONTRACTING OFFICER'S ACTION IN THE FACE OF FRAUD.

A. Report the Suspected Fraud.
   1. Datafax Procurement Flash Report to Procurement Fraud Division (PFD), USALSA. AR 27-40, para. 8-5(b).
   2. Submit Debarment/Suspension Report. DFARS 209.406-3.
B. Withhold Payments or Suspend Progress Payments.
C. Safeguard Documents.
D. Investigate the Allegations.
E. Consider All Potential Remedies.
F. Coordinate Action To Be Taken.
G. Prepare and Submit Comprehensive Remedies Plan. AR 27-40, para. 8-8.

## VIII. CONCLUSION.

A. Combatting procurement fraud involves a "team approach" by contracting officers, attorneys, and other support staff.
B. The contracting officer has a variety of available options to deal with procurement fraud without resorting to litigation.

## CHAPTER TWENTY-SEVEN

# *Introduction to Defective Pricing*

## I. INTRODUCTION—THE TRUTH IN NEGOTIATIONS ACT (TINA).

Pub. L. No. 87-653; 10 U.S.C. § 2306a, 41 U.S.C. § 254(d).

### A. Background and History.

1. 1950—GAO discovered overpricing.
2. 1959—DOD regulation required contractors to provide a Certificate of Current Pricing Data during negotiations.
3. 1961—DOD regulation added price reduction clause.
4. 1962—TINA passed.
5. 1994—Federal Acquisition Streamlining Act (FASA) passed.

### B. Defective Pricing Not Synonymous with Criminal Conduct.

## II. REQUIREMENT TO SUBMIT COST OR PRICING DATA.

10 U.S.C. § 2306a(f); FAR 15.804-2.

### A. Mandatory.

Pub. L. No. 101-501, § 803; Pub. L. No. 102-25; FAR 15.804-2(a)(1).

1. Award of a *negotiated contract* expected to exceed $500,000.
2. Pricing of any *prime contract change* involving a price adjustment expected to exceed $500,000 of a prime contract entered into after December 5, 1990.
3. Award of any *subcontract* expected to exceed $500,000.
4. Pricing of any *subcontract change* involving a price adjustment expected to exceed $500,000 of a prime contract entered into after December 5, 1990.

### B. Nonmandatory.

Pub. L. No. 101-501, § 803; FAR 15.804-2(a)(2).

1. A contracting officer may *not* require the submission of cost or pricing data for pricing actions over $25,000 but less than $500,000 unless the head of the agency personally determines that cost or pricing data are necessary. FASA § 1203.
2. DOD policy is that a contracting officer consider the submission of cost or pricing data if the offeror, contractor, or subcontractor:
   a. Has been the subject of recent or recurring, and significant findings of defective pricing.
   b. Has significant deficiencies in its current cost estimating systems; or
   c. Has been indicted recently for, convicted of, or the subject of an administrative or judicial finding of fraud regarding its cost estimating systems or cost accounting practices.
3. The data required shall be limited to that necessary to determine the reasonableness of the price. Contractors need not certify cost breakdowns provided for this purpose.

### C. Prohibition.

When awarding a contract for less than $25,000, the contracting officer shall not require certified cost or pricing data. FAR 15.804-2(a)(4).

**D. Certified Cost or Pricing Data.**

When required, certified cost or pricing data are comprised of two elements (FAR 15.804-2(b)):

1. Cost or pricing data; and

2. A Certificate of Current Cost or Pricing Data certifying that to the best of the contractor's knowledge and belief, the cost or pricing data were accurate, complete, and current *as of the date of final agreement on price.*

## III. EXEMPTIONS FROM THE REQUIREMENT TO SUBMIT COST OR PRICING DATA.

10 U.S.C. § 2306a(b)(1); FAR 15.804-3. A contracting officer *shall not* require cost or pricing data when the price agreed upon is founded on the following conditions.

**A. Adequate Price Competition.**

FAR 15.804-3(b)(1); DFARS 215.804-3; *Ramal Indus., Inc.*, B-224375, Oct. 6, 1986, 86-2 CPD ¶ 397.

1. Price competition exists if:

   a. The government solicits offers.

   b. Two or more responsible offerors submit responsive offers.

   c. Offerors compete independently for a contract to be awarded to the responsible offeror submitting the lowest evaluated price.

2. A price is "based on" adequate price competition if:

   a. It results directly from price competition; or

   b. If price analysis alone clearly shows the price is reasonable in comparison with current or recent prices for similar items in comparable quantities, terms, and conditions under contracts that resulted from adequate price competition.

3. Where there is a reasonable expectation of adequate price competition, a contracting officer rarely should need to require the submission or certification of cost or pricing data. DFARS 215.804-3. *See* DOD Memorandum dated 29 May 1992, SUBJECT: Certified Cost or Pricing Data ("Contracting officers shall not require the submission or certification").

4. Adequate price competition may exist for any contract, even though price is not the primary evaluation factor, provided that price is a substantial factor in the source selection criteria. DFARS 215.804-3; *accord Cubic Defense Sys.*, B-229884, Apr. 22, 1988, 88-1 CPD ¶ 395 (contracting officer has broad discretion to determine if adequate competition exists.)

5. If price competition exists, the contracting officer presumes it is adequate unless:

   a. One or more known and qualified offerors unreasonably denied opportunity to compete;

   b. Low offeror practically immune from competition; or

   c. There is a finding, supported by a statement of the facts and approved at a level above the contracting officer, that the lowest price is unreasonable. FAR 15.804-3(b)(2).

**B. Established Catalog or Market Price.**

FAR 15.804-3(c).

1. Prices are, or are based on, established catalog prices or established market prices of commercial items sold in substantial quantities to the general public.

2. Prices must be based on similar items.

3. Even though there is an established catalog or market price, the contracting officer may require cost or pricing data if:

   a. The contracting officer makes a written finding that the price is not reasonable.

   b. This finding is approved at a level above the contracting officer. FAR 15.804-3(c)(8).

**C. Prices Set by Law or Regulation.**

FAR 15.804-3(d) (utilities or commissions).

**D. Agency Waiver.**

In an exceptional case, the agency head may waive the requirement for the submission of certified cost or pricing data by written justification. FAR 15.804-3(i); DFARS 215.804-3(i).

## E. Commercial Items.

Agencies should acquire commercial items competitively. Accordingly, if there is adequate price competition on an acquisition of a commercial item, the contracting officer may not require cost or pricing data. FASA § 1204.

1. If there is inadequate price competition, the contracting officer may rely on commercial pricing information on the same or similar items sold in the marketplace. The contracting officer may obtain the information from the offeror/contractor or a third party. FASA § 1204.

2. If no pricing information is available, the contracting officer may require cost or pricing data and certification. FASA § 1204.

## F. Procedure for Claiming an Exemption for Established Catalog or Market Price and for Prices Set by Law or Regulation.

FAR 15.804-3(e), (f).

1. The contractor's request is submitted to the contracting officer on Standard Form 1412, Claim for Exemption from Submission of Certified Cost or Pricing Data.

2. The contracting officer must verify that requirements for an exemption are met. FAR 15.804(f).

3. The chief of a contracting office may authorize individual or class exemptions in exceptional cases. FAR 15.804-3(g).

4. The contracting officer must conduct a price analysis to determine the reasonableness of the price. FAR 15.804(h).

## G. Improperly Granted Exemptions Are Void.

Procurement officials may not waive the statutory requirement to furnish cost or pricing data. *M-R-S Mfg. Co. v. United States*, 203 Ct. Cl. 551, 492 F.2d 835 (1974). Significantly, however, the exercise of the contracting officer's discretion is binding on the government. *Honeywell Fed. Sys., Inc.*, ASBCA No. 39974, 92-2 BCA ¶ 24,966.

## IV. COST OR PRICING DATA.

### A. Definition of Cost or Pricing Data.

1. Statutory definition. "Cost or pricing data" means "all *facts* that, as of the date of agreement on the price of a contract (or the price of a contract modification), a prudent buyer or seller would reasonably expect to affect price negotiations significantly. Such term does not include information that is judgmental, but does include the factual information from which a judgement is derived." (emphasis added) 10 U.S.C. § 2306a(g).

2. Regulatory definition. "Cost or pricing data" means "all *facts* as of the date of price agreement that prudent buyers or sellers would reasonably expect to affect price negotiations significantly. Cost or pricing data are factual, not judgmental, and are therefore verifiable. While they do not indicate the accuracy of the prospective contractor's judgment about estimated future costs or projections, they do include the data forming the basis for that judgment. Cost or pricing data are more than historical accounting data; they are all the facts that can be reasonably expected to contribute to the soundness of estimates of future costs and to the validity of determinations of costs already incurred." (emphasis added) FAR 15.801.

3. Board definition. Factual information is discrete and quantifiable; it can be verified and audited. *Litton Sys., Inc., Amecom Div.*, ASBCA No. 36509, 92-2 BCA ¶ 24,842.

4. Examples of cost or pricing data. FAR 15.801.
   a. Vendor quotations.
   b. Nonrecurring costs.
   c. Information on changes in production methods and in production or purchasing volume.
   d. Data supporting projections of business prospects and objectives and related operations costs.
   e. Unit-cost trends such as those associated with labor efficiency.
   f. Make-or-buy decisions.

g. Estimated resources to attain business goals.

h. Information on management decisions that could have a significant bearing on costs.

## B. Fact Versus Judgment.

1. Fact versus judgment distinctions are often difficult to make. *Millipore Corp.*, GSBCA No. 9453, 91-1 BCA ¶ 23,345; *Texas Instruments, Inc.*, ASBCA No. 30836, 89-1 BCA ¶ 21,489; *Texas Instruments, Inc.*, ASBCA No. 23678, 87-3 BCA ¶ 20,195; *Boeing Military Airplane Co.*, ASBCA No. 33168, 87-2 BCA ¶ 19,714; *Grumman Aerospace Corp.*, ASBCA No. 27476, 86-3 BCA ¶ 19,091; *Bell & Howell Co.*, ASBCA No. 11999, 68-1 BCA ¶ 6993.

   a. Contractors need not certify judgmental information but the government may require them to disclose it.

   b. Information that is mixed fact and judgment presents special problems—and may be disclosable because of the underlying factual information. *See Litton Sys., Inc., Amecom Div.*, ASBCA No. 36509, 92-2 BCA ¶ 24,842 (applicable report was pure judgment, and *not* mixed fact and judgment).

2. Historical subcontractor and vendor pricing information are cost or pricing data. *Grumman Aerospace Corp.*, ASBCA No. 35188, 90-2 BCA ¶ 22,842 (data referring to labor and materials in a passive detections subcontract were disclosable); *see also* Memorandum from E. R. Spector, Deputy Assistant Secretary of Defense for Procurement, "Contractor Cost Estimating Systems," (Apr. 6, 1989).

   a. This type of information is often called decrement history/factors: it is the historical percentage reduction obtained by a prime contractor from its subcontractors' initial prices.

   b. The contracting officer should insist on receiving such information.

   c. The contracting officer should reduce the contract price if the contractor fails to submit decrement history, or submits defective decrement history.

## C. Cost or Pricing Data Must Be Significant Data.

1. The contractor must disclose the data if a reasonable person (a prudent buyer and seller) would expect it to be significant to the price negotiations. *Plessey Indus., Inc.*, ASBCA No. 16720, 74-1 BCA ¶ 10,603 (reasonable buyer or seller would not have expected this contractor to use two unsolicited quotations).

2. Prior purchases of similar items may be "significant data." *Hardie-Tynes Mfg., Co.*, ASBCA No. 20717, 76-2 BCA ¶ 12,121 (non-identical, previously purchased "bushings" - disclosable); *Kisco Co.*, ASBCA No. 18432, 76-2 ¶ 12,147.

3. The duty to disclose extends not only to data which a contractor knows it will use, but also to data that the contractor may use. If a reasonable person would consider the data in determining cost or price, the data is significant and must be disclosed. *Hardie-Tynes Mfg., Co.*, ASBCA No. 20717, 76-2 BCA ¶ 12,121; *See also*, *P.A.L. Sys. Co.*, GSBCA No. 10858, 91-3 BCA ¶ 24,259 (must disclose price list even if government does not qualify for the prices.)

4. The amount of the overpricing is not determinative of whether the information is significant. *Kaiser Aerospace & Elecs. Corp.*, ASBCA No. 32098, 90-1 BCA ¶ 22,489 (overpricing constituted two-tenths of one percent of total price); *Conrac Corp. v. United States*, 214 Ct. Cl. 561, 558 F.2d 994 (1977) (overpricing constituted one-tenth of one percent of the total price). *But see Boeing Co.*, ASBCA No. 33881, 92-1 BCA ¶ 24,414 ($268 overstatement on a $1.7 billion contract was "de minimis").

## V. THE SUBMISSION OF COST OR PRICING DATA.

### A. Procedural Requirements for the Submission of Data.

1. Contractors normally submit cost or pricing data on Standard Form (SF) 1411, Contract

Pricing Proposal Cover Sheet. FAR 15.804-6(b); FAR Table 15-2.

2. Contractors submit the SF 1411 to the contracting officer or his/her authorized representative. *The Singer Co., Librascope Div. v. United States*, 217 Ct. Cl. 225, 576 F.2d 905 (1978)(failure to submit to contracting officer); *Texas Instruments, Inc.*, ASBCA No. 30836, 89-1 BCA ¶ 21,489 (submission to administrative contracting officer sufficed).

3. Contractors may submit cost or pricing data actually or by specific identification in writing. FAR 15.804-1(a).

4. If data is "identified," the submission should answer the following questions (Armed Services Pricing Manual, para. 3-35):
   a. What is it?
   b. Where is it?
   c. How was it used?
   d. What does it represent?

## B. Adequate Disclosure of Cost or Pricing Data.

1. Before agreement on price, the contractor must provide or identify all cost or pricing data as of the latest dates for which information is reasonably available. FAR 15.804-4(c).
   a. The contractor must update previous submissions.
   b. The contractor's duty to provide updated data is not limited to the personal knowledge of its negotiators if the undisclosed facts are known to its management.
   c. Data within the contractor's or subcontractor's organization on matters significant to contractor management and to the government are considered to be readily available. FAR 15.804-4(c).

2. Merely making records available does not suffice; the contractor must advise the government of the kind and content of the cost or pricing data and its bearing on the contractor's proposal. FAR 15.804-6(d); *M-R-S Mfg. Co. v. United States*, 203 Ct. Cl. 551, 492 F.2d 835 (1974).

3. The contractor must provide a reasonable explanation of the data, unless its significance is self-evident. Knowledge by the other party of the data's existence is no defense if a reasonable explanation is necessary to appreciate the data's significance to the negotiations. *Grumman Aerospace Corp.*, ASBCA No. 35188, 90-2 BCA ¶ 22,842; *Boeing Co.*, ASBCA No. 32753, 90-1 BCA ¶ 22,270, *mot. for recon. denied*, 90-1 BCA ¶ 22,426.

## VI. CERTIFICATION OF DATA.

### A. Failure to Submit Certificate.
A contractor's failure to certify its cost data does not relieve it of liability. 10 U.S.C. § 2306a(e)(2); *S.T. Research Corp.*, ASBCA No. 29070, 84-3 BCA ¶ 17,568. However, a contractor need not certify the government's data. *United States v. Clayton Johnson*, 937 F.2d 392 (8th Cir. 1991).

### B. Due Date for Certification.
Certification is due as soon as practicable after price agreement is reached. FAR 15.804-4(a); *S.T. Research Corp.*, *supra*.

### C. Waiver of Certification Requirement.
The certification requirement may be waived if award is based on adequate price competition, established catalog or market prices, or prices set by law or regulation. FAR 15.804-4(e).

### D. Submission of Additional Cost or Pricing Data.
Action to take upon submission of additional cost or pricing data. Memorandum from E. R. Spector, Deputy Assistant Secretary of Defense for Procurement, "Contractor Delays in Submitting Certificates of Current Cost or Pricing Data" (June 7, 1989).

1. Obtain a statement from the contractor summarizing the impact of the additional data.

2. Reduce the price if the data indicates that the negotiated price was increased by any significant amount.

3. Price negotiation memorandum should list the data and identify the extent to which

such data was relied upon to establish a fair and reasonable price.

## VII. GOVERNMENT RIGHT TO EXAMINE CONTRACTORS' BOOKS AND RECORDS.

### A. Contracting Agency's Right.

1. Statutory basis. 10 U.S.C. § 2306a(f); 10 U.S.C. § 2313a.

    a. Section 2306a(f) permits any authorized representative of the head of an agency who is a government employee or a member of the armed forces to examine all records of a contractor or subcontractor related to:

    (1) The proposal for the contract or subcontract.

    (2) The discussions conducted on the proposal.

    (3) The pricing of the contract or subcontract.

    (4) The performance of the contract or subcontract.

    b. The Section 2306a(f) audit right enables the government to evaluate the accuracy, completeness, and currency of a contractor's cost or pricing data.

    c. Section 2313a permits DOD, NASA, and the Coast Guard, acting through authorized representatives, to inspect the plant and records of a contractor or subcontractor in connection with cost or cost-plus-fixed-fee contracts.

2. Contract audit clauses. FAR 52.214-26 (Sealed Bidding); FAR 52.215-2 (Negotiation).

    a. The Audit-Sealed Bidding clause permits the contracting officer or a representative who is an employee of the government to audit "cost or pricing data" submitted in connection with the modification of a contract.

    b. The Audit-Sealed Bidding clause gives the agency the right to examine and audit all books, records, documents and other data (including computations and projections) relating to negotiating, pricing, or performing a modification.

    c. The Audit-Negotiation clause gives the contracting officer or a representative who is an employee of the government the right to examine and audit all books, records, documents and other data (including computations and projections) relating to proposing, negotiating, pricing, or performing a contract or a modification to ensure compliance with TINA.

    d. The Audit-Negotiation clause also gives the contracting officer or representatives of the contracting officer the right to examine and audit books, records, documents, and other evidence and accounting practices and procedures with respect to cost-based contracts for verification of a contractor's claimed costs.

3. Subpoena power. 10 U.S.C. § 2313(d).

    a. The Director, Defense Contract Audit Agency (DCAA), may require, by subpoena, the production of books, documents, papers, or records of a contractor, access to which is granted the Secretary of Defense by section 2306a(f) or by section 2313a of Title 10.

    b. DCAA acts as a representative of the contracting officer under the FAR audit clauses.

    c. The subpoena power extends to the production of books, documents, papers, and records of a contractor or subcontractor that directly pertains to and involves transactions relating to the contract or subcontract.

4. Scope of agency's right.

    a. DCAA's subpoena power does not extend to a contractor's internal audit reports. *United States v. Newport News Shipbldg. and Dry Dock Co.*, 837 F.2d 162 (4th Cir. 1988) (Newport News I).

    (1) Internal audits are not related to a particular contract.

    (2) Internal audits contain a contractor's audit staff's subjective evaluations.

    (3) DCAA's subpoena is aimed at obtaining

objective data upon which a contractor's specific costs charged to government can be evaluated.

b. DCAA's subpoena power extends to a contractor's federal income tax returns and other financial data. *United States v. Newport News Shipbldg. and Dry Dock Co.*, 862 F.2d 464 (4th Cir. 1988) (Newport News II).

(1) DCAA's subpoena power is not limited to records relating to a contractor's pricing practices.

(2) DCAA's subpoena power also extends to objective factual records relating to overhead costs which may be passed to the government.

c. DCAA's subpoena power does extend to a company's estimates and projections of future labor rates and expenditures. *United States v. Newport News Shipbldg. and Dry Dock Co.*, 737 F. Supp. 897 (E.D. Va. 1989) (Newport News III), *aff'd* 900 F.2d 257 (4th Cir. 1990) (unpublished opinion affirming district court decision).

(1) The Audit-Negotiation clause (FAR 52.215-2) expressly includes computations and projections in the list of materials to which DCAA has access.

(2) The contractor acknowledged that it had routinely disclosed information in the form of estimates and projections to allow DCAA to evaluate cost or pricing data.

## B. General Accounting Office's Right.

1. Statutory basis. 10 U.S.C. § 2313(b); 41 U.S.C. § 254.

a. Both statutes give the Comptroller General and his representatives the right to examine a contractor's or subcontractor's books and records related to any contract awarded using other than sealed bidding procedures.

b. The Comptroller General's right applies to any books, documents, papers or other records that directly pertain (Title 10 provision) to and involve transactions related

to the contract. The Title 41 provision states that this right applies to records that are directly pertinent.

2. Audit clauses. FAR 52.215-1.

a. This clause applies to all negotiated contracts exceeding the simplified acquisition threshold in Part 13 of the FAR.

b. This clause gives the Comptroller General the right to examine and audit any directly pertinent books, documents, papers, or other records involving transactions related to the contract.

c. A prime contractor must include a clause in first-tier subcontracts granting GAO similar audit rights.

3. Subpoena power. 31 U.S.C. § 716.

a. Section 716 gives the Comptroller General the power to subpoena records of a person to which the Comptroller General has access by law or by agreement.

b. The Comptroller General may enforce his subpoena through action in a U.S. district court. *United States v. McDonnell-Douglas Corp.*, 751 F.2d 220 (8th Cir. 1984).

4. Scope of the General Accounting Office's right.

a. The term "contract" as used in the statute embraces not only the specific terms and conditions of a contract, but also the general subject matter. *Hewlett-Packard Co. v. United States*, 385 F.2d 1013 (9th Cir. 1967), *cert. denied*, 390 U.S. 988 (1968).

b. The Comptroller General's audit right is very broad with respect to cost-based contracts. With respect to fixed-price contracts, the books or records must bear directly on the question of whether the government paid a fair price for the goods or services. *See generally Bowsher v. Merck & Co.*, 460 U.S. 824 (1983).

## C. Inspector General's Right.

1. Statutory basis. 5 U.S.C. App. § 6(a)(1) & (4).

a. The Inspector General of an agency may examine all records, reports, audits, reviews, documents, papers and recommendations or other material that relate to programs and operations over which that agency has responsibility.

   b. This statutory right has no contractual implementation.

2. Subpoena power. 5 U.S.C. App. § 6(a)(1) & (4).

   a. An Inspector General may subpoena all data and documentary evidence necessary in the performance of its function.

   b. The subpoena may be enforced through action in a U.S. district court.

3. Scope of Inspector General's audit right. The scope of the Inspector General's audit right is extremely broad and includes internal audit reports. *United States v. Westinghouse Elec. Corp.*, 788 F.2d 164 (3d Cir. 1986).

### D. Time Limitation on Government Right to Examine Contractor's Books and Records.

The government's audit rights generally exist for three years after final payment.

### E. Obstruction of a Federal Audit.

18 U.S.C. § 1516.

1. The statute does not increase or enhance the government's audit rights.

2. The statute makes it a crime for anyone to influence, obstruct, or impede a Federal auditor (full or part-time government or contractual employee) with the intent to deceive or defraud the government.

## VIII. FRAUD INDICATORS.

DOD IG'S HANDBOOK ON INDICATORS OF FRAUD IN DOD PROCUREMENT, NO. 4075-1H, JUNE 1987.

A. High Incidence of Persistent Defective Pricing.

B. Continued Failure to Correct Known System Deficiencies.

C. Consistent Failure to Update Cost or Pricing Data with Knowledge That Past Activity Showed That Prices Have Decreased.

D. Failure to Make Complete Disclosure of Data Known to Responsible Personnel.

E. Protracted Delay in Updating Cost or Pricing

Data to Preclude Possible Price Reduction.

F. Repeated Denial by Responsible Contractor Employees of the Existence of Historical Records That Are Later Found to Exist.

G. Repeated Utilization of Unqualified Personnel to Develop Cost or Pricing Data Used in Estimating Process.

## IX. CONTRACTUAL REMEDIES.

### A. Contract Price Reduction.

FAR 15.804-7; FAR 52.215-22; FAR 52.215-23.

1. The government is entitled to a reduction in the contract price (including profit or fee) for any significant amount by which the price was increased because of defective cost or pricing data. 10 U.S.C. § 2306a(d)(1)(A).

2. The government's defective pricing claim is not subject to the normal six-year statute of limitations. *Radiation Sys., Inc.*, ASBCA No. 41065, 91-2 BCA ¶ 23,971. Nor is it an affirmative defense to a price adjustment claim. *Computer Network Sys., Inc.*, GSBCA No. 11368, 93-1 BCA ¶ 25,260.

3. Amount of reduction: any significant amount by which the price was increased. FAR 15.804-7(b); *Unisys Corp. v. United States*, 888 F.2d 841 (Fed. Cir. 1989); *Kaiser Aerospace & Elec. Corp.*, ASBCA No. 32098, 90-1 BCA ¶ 22,489; *Etowah Mfg. Co.*, ASBCA No. 27267, 88-3 BCA ¶ 21,054]; *see also Boeing Co.*, ASBCA No. 33881, 92-1 BCA ¶ 24414 ($268.39 defective pricing on a $1.7 billion contract was "de minimis").

### B. Government's Burden of Proof.

1. The government bears the burden of proof in a defective pricing case. *General Dynamics Corp.*, ASBCA No. 32660, 93-1 BCA ¶ 25,378. To meet its burden, the government must prove:

   a. The information meets the definition of cost or pricing data and existed before the agreement on price.

   b. The data was reasonably available before agreement on price.

c. The data submitted by the contractor was not accurate, complete, or current.

d. The government relied on the defective data.

e. The government's reliance on the defective data caused an increase in the contract price.

2. The judges at the ASBCA often view defective pricing cases as "too complicated" to resolve by summary judgment. *Grumman Aerospace Corp.*, ASBCA No. 35185, 92-3 BCA ¶ 25,059; *McDonnell Douglas Helicopter Co.*, ASBCA 41378, 92-1 BCA ¶ 24,655.

## C. Defenses to a Price Reduction.

1. The information at issue was not cost or pricing data.

2. The government did not rely on the defective data.

3. The price offered by the contractor was a "floor" below which the contractor would not have gone.

## D. Unsuccessful Defenses to a Price Reduction.

1. The contractor is a sole source. 10 U.S.C. § 2306a(d)(3)(A)(i).

2. The contractor was in a superior bargaining position. 10 U.S.C. § 2306a(d)(3)(A)(ii).

3. The contracting officer should have known that the data was defective. 10 U.S.C. § 2306a(d)(3)(B); *FMC Corp.*, ASBCA No. 30069, 87-1 BCA ¶ 19,544.

4. The contract price was based on total cost. 10 U.S.C. § 2306a(d)(3)(C).

5. The contractor or subcontractor did not submit a certificate of current cost or pricing data. 10 U.S.C. § 2306a(d)(3)(D).

## E. Offsets.

10 U.S.C. § 2306a(d)(4)(A) & (B); FAR 15.804-7(b)(4), (b)(5), (b)(6).

1. The contractor is entitled to a credit for any understated cost or pricing data *up to the amount of the government claim* for over-stated cost or pricing data arising out of the same transaction.

2. The offsets do not need to be in the same cost grouping (e.g. material, direct labor, or indirect costs).

3. The contractor must prove that the higher cost or pricing data existed prior to the date of agreement on price and that the data were not submitted.

4. The contractor is not entitled to an offset if:
   a. The contractor knew that its cost or pricing data were understated at the time it executed its certificate.
   b. The government proves that submission of such data would not have resulted in an increase in the price in the amount to be offset.

## X. JUDICIAL REMEDIES.

### A. Criminal.

1. False Claims. 18 U.S.C. § 287. *See Communication Equip. and Contracting Co., Inc. v. United States*, No. 72-88C, Claims Court, August 23, 1991 (unpublished), which held that TINA does not preempt the False Claims Act so as to limit the government's remedies.

2. False Statements. 18 U.S.C. § 1001.

3. The Major Fraud Act. 18 U.S.C. § 1031.

### B. Civil.

1. False Claims. 10 U.S.C. §§ 3729-33.

2. The Program Fraud Civil Remedies Act of 1986. 31 U.S.C. §§ 3801-3812; DOD Dir. No. 5505.5 (Aug. 30, 1988).

## XI. ADMINISTRATIVE REMEDIES.

A. Suspension and Debarment. FAR Subpart 9.4; DFARS Subpart 209.4.

B. Cancellation of the Contract. 10 U.S.C. § 218; FAR Subpart 3.7.

C. Termination of the Contract. *Joseph Morton Co. v. United States*, 3 Cl. Ct. 120 (1983), *aff'd*, 757 F.2d 1273 (Fed. Cir. 1985.

## CHAPTER TWENTY-EIGHT

# Contracting for Services

## I. INTRODUCTION.

### A. Objectives.

Following this block of instruction, students will understand:

1. The types of services commonly procured through federal contracts.
2. The policies and procedures applicable to service contracts.
3. The references and general policies applicable to the commercial activities program (CAP).

### B. Types of Service Contracts.

1. Research and development.
2. Engineering and field technician services.
3. Maintenance and repair of equipment.
4. ADPE and systems integration services.
5. Training.
6. Commercial activities program (CAP).
7. Management and advisory services, also known as contracted advisory and assistance services (CAAS).
8. Operation of government facility services (e.g., government-owned, contractor-operated (GOCO) plants).
9. Architect-engineer services.
10. Transportation and travel services.

## II. SERVICE CONTRACTING—GENERALLY.

### A. Definition of Service Contract.

"[A] contract that directly engages the time and effort of a contractor whose primary purpose is to perform an identifiable task rather than to furnish an end item of supply." FAR 37.101.

1. Nonpersonal Services. Services performed by contractor personnel who are not under the supervision and control of government employees.
2. Personal Services. Services performed under a contract that, by its terms or as administered, makes its personnel appear to be government employees. Agencies shall not award personal services contracts unless specifically authorized by statute. FAR 37.104(b).
3. Advisory and Assistance Services. Services other than those specifically exempted which support agency policy development, decision-making, management, or administration. FAR Subpart 37.2.

### B. Policy.

FAR 37.102.

1. Agencies shall generally rely on the private sector for commercial services.
2. In no event may an agency contract for the performance of an inherently governmental function.
3. The relative costs of government and contract performance require appropriate consideration where government performance is practicable.
4. Nonpersonal service contracts are proper under general contracting authority.

### C. Office of Federal Procurement Policy (OFPP) Policy Letter 91-2, "Policy Letter on Service Contracting"

56 Fed. Reg. 15110 (1991). It is the policy of the federal government that:

1. Agencies use performance-based contracting methods to the maximum extent practicable when acquiring services.

a. Statement of work. *See* MIL-HDBK-245B (1 June 1983). Agencies shall, to the maximum extent practicable, describe the work in terms of "what" is to be the required output rather than "how" the work is to be accomplished.

b. Quality assurance.

   (1) Contractors shall, to the maximum extent practicable, be responsible for quality performance.

   (2) Agencies shall develop formal, measurable performance standards and surveillance plans.

   (3) Agencies shall avoid relying on process-oriented inspection and oversight programs to assess contractor performance.

c. Source selection procedures.

   (1) Use competitive negotiations for acquisitions where the quality of performance over and above the minimum acceptable level will enhance agency mission accomplishment and be worth the corresponding increase in cost.

   (2) Agencies award most technical and professional services contracts using negotiations procedures.

d. Contract type. Select contract types most likely to motivate contractors to optimal performance.

e. Repetitive requirements. Rely on experience gained in prior contracts to improve current contractor performance. When appropriate, convert cost-plus to fixed-price arrangements.

f. Multiyear contracting. When appropriate, improve competition by soliciting for a stable, long-term contracting environment.

2. Agencies carefully select acquisition and contract administration strategies, methods, and techniques that best accommodate the requirements.

3. Agencies shall justify the use of other than performance-based contracting methods when acquiring services, and document affected contract files.

## D. OFPP Policy Letter 93-1, "Management Oversight of Service Contracts"

59 Fed. Reg. 26,818 (1994). This policy letter provides guidance using the "best practices" concept to help agencies improve contract management and administration. Examples of the kinds of "best practices" agencies should use include:

1. Review of the corporate experience section of an offeror's proposal to detect conflicts of interest; and

2. Review of monthly progress reports to detect whether the contractor is performing inherently governmental functions.

## E. Contracting Officer Responsibilities.

FAR 37.103.

1. Determine whether the proposed service is for a personal or nonpersonal services contract.

2. Verify the contract file contains the certifications required of contractor employees serving as government procurement officials.

## III. COMMERCIAL ACTIVITIES PROGRAM.

### A. Statement of Policy.

Rely on private enterprise for services and goods to the maximum extent possible, consistent with effective and efficient implementation of agency's mission, taking into account the relative costs of performance. FAR 7.301; AR 5-20, Commercial Activities Program, para. 1-5 (20 Oct. 1986).

### B. Definition of Commercial Activity.

Activity of a federal executive agency providing a product or service that could be obtained from a commercial source, is separable from other functions, and is a regularly needed (not one-time) activity. AR 5-20, para. 1-3.

### C. Magnitude of These Activities.

### D. Congressional Interest.

**E. References.**

1. 10 U.S.C. §§ 2461-69.
2. OMB Cir. A-76 (4 Aug. 1983); Supplement, OMB Cir. A-76 (Policy Implementation, Writing and Administering Performance Work Statements, Management Study Guide, and Cost Comparison Handbook).
3. FAR Subpart 7.3.
4. DOD Dir. 4100.15, Commercial Activities Program (10 Mar. 1989).
5. DOD Instr. 4100.33, Commercial Activities Program Procedures (9 Sept. 1985).
6. AR 5-20, Commercial Activities Program (20 Oct. 1986). A new version of the AR has been completed and is awaiting publication.
7. DA Pam 5-20, Commercial Activities Study Guide (17 Nov. 1992).

**F. Current Implementation of Executive Policy as Reflected in OMB Cir. A-76.**

*See* FAR 7.302.

1. Rely on the commercial sector to provide commercial products and services.
2. Retain governmental functions in-house.
3. Achieve economy and enhance productivity through the use of cost comparisons.
4. OMB Cir. A-76 and its supplement do *not* apply to everything.
    a. Governmental functions. *See* OFPP Policy Letter 92-1, 57 Fed. Reg. 45100 (1992) for definition of inherently governmental functions.
        (1) The act of governing.
        (2) Monetary transactions and entitlements.
    b. DOD in times of declared war or military mobilization.
    c. Conduct of research and development. *See Energy Compression Research Corp.*, B-243650.2, Nov. 18, 1991, 91-2 CPD ¶ 466.
5. Other activities. Activities not excluded are governed by the policies and procedures of OMB Cir. A-76 and are subject to review procedures.

**G. Moratorium on the Award of New Commercial Activities Contracts.**

The National Defense Authorization Act for Fis-cal Year 1994, Pub. L. No. 103-160, § 313, 107 Stat. 1547, 1618 (1993), extended the moratorium on the award of new CAP contracts through April 1, 1994. Since the Congress has not further extended this moratorium, agencies may now continue CAP studies and award new contracts.

## IV. EXCEPTIONS TO THE GENERAL POLICY OF RELYING ON THE PRIVATE SECTOR.

**A. No Satisfactory Commercial Source Available.**

OMB Cir. A-76, para. 8a; FAR 7.303; AR 5-20, paras. 2-3, 4-29b.

1. No satisfactory source is capable of providing the needed product or service.
    a. Must document this determination with at least three notices in the Commerce Business Daily over a 90-day period (with a minimum of 30 days between each notice).
    b. In an emergency, agencies may reduce this to two notices over 30 days, with a minimum of 15 days between them. FAR 7.303(b)(1), AR 5-20, para. 4-29b.
2. A commercial source would cause an unacceptable delay or disruption of an agency program.

**B. Patient Care.**

Patient care performed at a government operated hospital can be retained in-house, if an agency determines that in-house performance would be in the best interest of direct patient care. OMB Cir. A-76, para. 8c; AR 5-20, para. 2-3a.

**C. National Defense.**

National defense interests may justify performing the activity in-house. OMB Cir. A-76, para. 8b; AR 5-20, para. 2-3b. This exception includes selected military training in military skills, deployable activities, and rotation base.

**D. Cost Comparison.**

When a cost comparison demonstrates that in-house performance would be cheaper than contractor performance, the government may retain an activity in-house. OMB Cir. A-76, para. 8d.

## V. SPECIAL CONSIDERATIONS.

### A. Personal Services Contracts.

1. Defined. A contract that, by its express terms or as administered, makes the contractor personnel appear, in effect, to be government employees. FAR 37.101.
2. Prohibited unless authorized by statute (*see* 5 U.S.C. § 3109).
3. Each contract arrangement must be judged in light of its own facts and circumstances. The key question is: Will the government exercise relatively continuous supervision and control over the contractor personnel performing the contract? FAR 37.104(c)(2).
4. Descriptive elements to be used in assessing whether or not a proposed contract is personal in nature.
   a. Performance on site.
   b. Principal tools and equipment furnished by the government.
   c. Services are applied directly to the integral effort of agencies in furtherance of assigned function or mission.
   d. Similar agencies perform comparable services using civil service personnel.
   e. The need for the type of service provided can reasonably be expected to last beyond one year.
   f. The nature of the service, or the manner in which it is provided, reasonably requires, directly or indirectly, government direction or supervision of contractor employees to:
      (1) Adequately protect the government's interest;
      (2) Retain control of the function involved; or
      (3) Retain full personal responsibility for the function supported in a duly authorized federal officer or employee.
   g. If a specific statutory exemption applies, agencies should ensure a legal review sup-

ports procurement of the required personal services by contract.
   h. The Classification Act, 5 U.S.C. § 3109, limits payments under personal services contracts for the services of individual experts or consultants.
5. DFARS 237.104(b)(i) requires a D&F when acquiring personal services of an expert or consultant.
6. Private sector temporary services.
   a. Contracting officers may enter into contracts with temporary help service firms for the brief or intermittent use of the skills of private sector temporaries.
   b. These are *not* personal services.
   c. Comply with 5 C.F.R. Part 300, Subpart E, Use of Private Sector Temporaries, and any other agency procedures.

### B. Inherently Governmental Functions.

1. When contracting for services, agencies are prohibited from contracting for inherently governmental functions. FAR 37.102(b).
2. A governmental function is one which is so intimately related to the public interest as to mandate performance by government employees. OMB Cir. A-76.
   a. Will the contract require the contractor to exercise substantial discretion in applying governmental authority, or use substantial value judgments in making decisions for the government?
   b. Will the contract require contractor involvement in monetary transactions and entitlements, such as tax collection and revenue disbursements, control of treasury accounts, or administration of public trusts?
3. Totality of the circumstances. OFPP Policy Letter 92-1, "Policy Letter on Inherently Governmental Functions," para. 6, 57 Fed. Reg. 45101 (1992).

### C. Conflicts of Interest.

FAR Subpart 9.5.
1. Agencies should not award service contracts to any individual or organization which may

have an unfair competitive advantage over competing contractors *unless* every effort is taken to mitigate such conflict. OFPP Policy Letter 93-1, "Policy Letter on Management Oversight of Service Contracting," 58 Fed. Reg. 63596 (1993).

2. Performance of advisory and assistance services for an agency does not automatically disqualify that contractor from competing for other work with the agency based on a conflict of interest. *Abt Assocs., Inc.*, B-253220.2, Oct. 6, 1993, 93-2 CPD ¶ 269 (awardee did not have information providing it a competitive advantage).

3. If the response to any of the following questions is "yes," there may be a potential for a conflict of interest.
   a. Will the work under this contract create a significant conflict of interest on a future acquisition?
   b. Is the requirement for support services such that the potential offerors may have developed the system design specifications or aided in the production of the system?
   c. Have potential offerors participated in work involving the same program or activity?
   d. Will the contractor be evaluating a competitor's work?
   e. Will the services require the contractor to evaluate its own products or activities? *See KPMG Peat Marwick*, B-255224, Feb. 15, 1994, 94-1 CPD ¶ 111 (award would have required protester to review the results of its own audits).
   f. Will the work place the contractor in a position to influence broad government decision-making that will affect the contractor's current or future business?
   g. Will the work under this contract affect the interests of the contractor's other clients?
   h. Are any of the potential offerors former agency officials that were substantially involved in developing the requirement for these services within the past two years?

## D. Contracted Advisory and Assistance Services (CAAS).

*See* DOD Dir. 4205.2, Acquisition and Management of Contracted Advisory and Assistance Services (10 Feb. 1992); AR 5-14, Management of Contracted Advisory and Assistance Services (15 Jan. 1993).

1. Defined. Services to support or improve agency policy development, decision-making, management, and administration, or to support or improve the operation of management systems. FAR 37.201.

2. Policy. Agencies may contract for advisory and assistance services, when essential to the agency's mission, to:
   a. Obtain outside points of view concerning critical issues;
   b. Obtain advice regarding developments in industry, university, or foundation research;
   c. Obtain the opinions, special knowledge, or skills of noted experts;
   d. Enhance the understanding of, and develop alternative solutions to, complex issues;
   e. Support and improve the operation of organizations;
   f. Ensure the more efficient or effective operation of managerial or hardware systems.

3. The government shall not use advisory and assistance services to:
   a. Perform work of a policy, decision-making, or managerial nature which is the direct responsibility of agency officials;
   b. Bypass or undermine personnel ceilings, pay limitations, or competitive employment procedures;
   c. Contract on a preferential basis to former government employees;
   d. Aid in influencing pending legislation; or
   e. Obtain professional or technical advice which is readily available within the agency or another Federal agency.

4. Procedures:
   a. The requesting activity must certify, in writing, the requirement for the services

and that such services do not unnecessarily duplicate any previously performed work or services. FAR 37.206(a) & (b). This certification is included in a Management Decision Document prepared in accordance with AR 5-14, para. 4-3f.

b. The activity must obtain written approval by an official no lower than one level above the requesting office. FAR 37.206(c); AR 5-14, para. 4-3f(6).

c. The contracting officer must determine whether the requested services constitute advisory and assistance services and that all other requirements are met. FAR 37.207.

d. Section 6002 of the Federal Acquisition Streamlining Act of 1994, Pub. L. No. 103-355, 108 Stat. 3243 (1994), added a further limitation on the use of CAAS. Agencies may not contract for services to conduct evaluations or analyses of a proposal submitted for an acquisition unless the agency can certify that federal employees are not "readily available" to perform such functions. OFPP is to issue guidance for agencies to use in determining whether federal employees are readily available.

e. Congress has added the additional requirement that DOD conduct a standardized cost comparison analysis before contracting out for CAAS in excess of $100,000. National Defense Authorization Act for Fiscal Year 1995, Pub. L. No. 103-337, § 363, 108 Stat. 2663, 2733-34 (to be codified at 10 U.S.C. § 2410).

5. Master Agreements.

a. Agencies may, until September 30, 1994, award master agreements under which orders may be issued for CAAS. 10 U.S.C. § 2304; DFARS 237.270.

b. Agencies must establish agreements using

competitive procedures.

c. Agencies use basic ordering agreement procedures to enter master agreements.

## VI. CONTRACTING CONSIDERATIONS.

### A. Contract Type.
1. Firm-fixed-price.
2. Cost reimbursement.
   a. Completion.
   b. Level-of-effort.
   c. Incentive and award fee considerations.
3. Time and materials.

### B. Negotiations as an Acquisition Method.
Due to the need to evaluate more than price in every services contract, negotiations is the preferred acquisition method for all service contracts exceeding the small purchase threshold.

1. Uncomepensated overtime. Solicitations for contracts exceeding $100,000 must require offerors to identify uncompensated overtime to be worked by service employees. DFARS 252.237-7019. The *Christian* doctrine will not operate to correct an agency's failure to include the proper DFARS clause, however. *QuesTech, Inc.*, B-255095, Feb. 7, 1994, 94-1 CPD ¶ 82.

2. Unbalanced rates. *See Stanley Assocs., Inc.*, B-232361, Dec. 23, 1988, 88-2 CPD ¶ 617 (contractor "gaming" of its rate structure may present unacceptable performance risk to the government regarding the price the government ultimately will pay for contracted services).

### C. Contract Administration.
1. Personal services issues.
2. Training for technical managers.
3. Quality assurance/invoicing issues.

## CHAPTER TWENTY-NINE

# *Fraud: Criminal and Civil Remedies*

## I. INTRODUCTION.

## II. REFERENCES.

A. Regulations.

   1. Air Force Regulation (AFR) 123-2, Air Force Fraud, Waste, and Abuse Prevention, Detection, and Remedies. Section B, Procurement Fraud Remedies. Section C, Procurement Fraud Civil Remedies Act. *See also*, AFR 110-24, Air Force in Litigation.

   2. Army Regulation (AR) 27-40, Litigation, Chapter 8, Remedies in Procurement Fraud and Corruption. Appendix F, Sample Installation PFA Program SOP. Appendix H, Format for the Remedies Plan.

   3. Secretary of the Navy Instruction (SECNAVINST) 5430.92A, Assignment of Responsibility to Counteract Fraud, Waste, and Related Improprieties within the Department of the Navy. SECNAVINST 5430.102, Implementation of Program Fraud Civil Remedies Act; SECNAVINST 5520.3, Criminal and Security Investigations and Related Activities within Department of the Navy; SECNAVINST 5430.25D, General Counsel of the Navy: Assignment of Responsibilities.

B. DOD Directive 7050.5: Coordination of Remedies for Fraud and Corruption Related to Procurement Activities (7 June 1989).

C. DODIG Handbook 4075.1-H, *Indicators of Fraud in DOD Procurement* (The Red Book), June 1987.

D. John T. Boese, *Civil False Claims and Qui Tam Actions*, (1993).

## III. BACKGROUND.

### A. Definitions.

1. Fraud has been defined variously as "an assertion that is not in accord with the facts," RESTATEMENT (2D) CONTRACTS, §§ 159, 164, as "any cunning, deception, or artifice used to circumvent, cheat, or deceive another," 1 J. Story, EQUITY JURISPRUDENCE § 186, pp. 189-190 (1870), or as conscious wrongdoing with an intention to cheat or be dishonest. *United States v. Wunderlich*, 342 U.S. 98, 100 (1951).

2. A comprehensive definition of fraud encompasses elements of all those elements discussed above: "[Fraud is] [a]n intentional perversion of truth for the purpose of inducing someone to rely upon it and part with something of value or surrender a legal right. The three necessary elements of a cause of action for fraud are (1) false representation of past or present fact on the part of the defendant, (2) a plaintiff's action in reliance on that misrepresentation, and (3) damage resulting to the plaintiff from the action that was based on the misrepresentation. A fraudulent representation is a false statement as to a material fact that another party believes and relies upon, and that induces that other party to act to his or her injury. The speaker must know the statement to be false or must make the statement with utter disregard for

its truth or falsity and must intend that the other party will rely upon the statement." Nash and Schooner, THE GOVERNMENT CONTRACT REFERENCE BOOK at 196 (1992).

## B. Various Scenarios.

1. *Defective Products*: Defective products are those which do not conform to the contract specifications. In its most pernicious form, this category includes product substitution. The safety implications of product substitution or substandard items are especially pronounced in the military environment.

   a. *United States v. Aerodex*, 469 F.2d 1003 (5th Cir. 1972). Defendants contracted to provide 300 new master rod bearings, at $90 each. Defendants supplied reworked bearings which had been relabeled to appear to satisfy contract requirements. Failure of the bearing could cause complete engine failure. Navy removed and replaced the bearings at a cost of $161,000.

   b. *United States v. Rule Indus., Inc.*, 878 F.2d 535 (1st Cir. 1989). This case involved the "Buy American Act" where GSA contracted for hacksaw blades which required a "Buy American Act" certification, and Rule certified that its hacksaw blades would be "domestic end products." Rule used foreign-made hacksaw blanks, and the government brought an action under the FCA. The jury concluded that Rule knowingly made false claims on 302 separate invoices. The court assessed a penalty of $604,000.

2. *Defective Testing*: This arguable subset of defective products cases results from the failure of a contractor to perform contractually required tests, or its failure to perform such testing in the required manner. The crucial damages issue is the reliability of the product once the deficiency is known. An important element in such an analysis is the residual value of the untested or inadequately tested product. Civil penalties may function as a liquidated damages provision in the event that actual damages are difficult or impossible to calculate.

3. *Bid-Rigging*: The absence of competition deprives the government of its most reliable measure of what the price should have been. Measure of damages is "the difference between what the government actually paid on the fraudulent claim and what it would have paid had there been fair, open and competitive bidding." *United States v. Killough*, 848 F.2d 1523, 1532 (11th Cir. 1988); *see also Brown v. United States*, 524 F.2d 693, 706 (1975).

4. *Bribery and Public Corruption* (e.g. "Ill Wind"): The breach of an employee's duty of loyalty. *See, e.g., United States v. Carter*, 217 U.S. 286 (1910). If a contract is tainted by a conflict of interest, bribery, or corruption, the government may void or rescind the contract. *See, e.g., United States v. Mississippi Valley Generating Co.*, 364 U.S. 520 (1961) (violation of 18 U.S.C. § 434); *United States v. Medico Indus., Inc.*, 784 F.2d 840, 845 (7th Cir. 1986) (voiding contract due to conflict of interest); *K & R Eng'g v. United States*, 616 F.2d 469 (Ct. Cl. 1980) (cancellation based on conflicts of interest).

5. *Defective Pricing*: The Truth in Negotiations Act ("TINA"), 10 U.S.C. § 2306a, together with its implementing regulations, 48 C.F.R. § 15.8 *et seq.* ("Price Negotiation"), requires contractors in certain negotiated procurements to disclose and certify that disclosed details concerning expected costs ("cost or pricing data") are accurate, current and complete. TINA also provides sanctions for "defective pricing," *i.e.*, a failure to meet these requirements which causes an increase of the contract price. A perceived or actual violation of TINA may serve as the predicate for a fraud investigation and civil or criminal prosecution by the Government.

## IV. INITIAL COORDINATION.

### A. DOD Directive.

7050.5. 7 June 1989: Responded to lack of coordination and instituted a policy of coordinating all available and appropriate remedies.

## B. Army Implementation: Procurement Fraud Division (PFD).

AR 27-40, chap. 8 (with Interim Change 1). Coordination required at installation, MACOM, and DA levels. 5 key elements of Army approach: (1) centralized policy making and program direction through PFD; (2) fraud remedies coordination which assures that commanders and contracting officers pursue all remedies; (3) decentralized responsibility for operational matters such as reporting and remedial action; (4) continuous monitoring by PFD through final disposition; (5) command-wide fraud awareness training.

1. Procurement Fraud Advisors (PFA). AR 27-40, chap. 8. Focal point for remedies coordination in installation procurement fraud cases. Features of successful installation procurement fraud programs include:
   a. Effective working relationship among installation personnel;
   b. Proactive approach including fraud awareness and informational activity by PFA;
   c. Effective working relationship between local U.S. Attorney's office and installation command/staff judge advocate;
   d. "Procurement Flash Reports" transmitted by DATAFAX directly to PFD whenever a PFA receives notice of a procurement fraud indicator involving the Army.
2. The Comprehensive Remedies Plan. [Para. 8-8, AR 27-40.] Developed for each "significant investigation." Contents of the plan include:
   a. A summary of allegations and investigative results;
   b. Description of adverse impact on mission, combat readiness, and safety;
   c. Criminal, civil, contract, and administrative remedies considerations;

## C. Air Force Implementation.

Since 1 July 1991, the Air Force General Counsel has been responsible for procurement fraud program. POC: Mr. Rick Castiglia, SAF-GC, (703) 697-3900; DSN 227-3900. AFR 123-2 (IG series) details new SAF-GC responsibility.

## D. Navy and Marine Corps Implementation.

The procurement fraud program is under the Navy General Counsel and the Navy Inspector General. Suspension, debarment and PFCRA is under the Navy General Counsel. POC: Mr. John Farenish, Counsel, Procurement Integrity Office, SECNAV-GC, (703) 602-2703. Coordination of remedies (criminal, civil, administrative, contractual) is under Navy Inspector General. POC: Mr. Larry Lippolis, Counsel to Navy IG, (202) 433-2222. Marine Corps: coordinate first with Mr. George N. Brezna, Associate Counsel to the Commandant, (703) 614-2150.

## V. INVESTIGATIONS AND REMEDIES.

### A. Investigators.

Know the acronyms and who they represent: CID, FBI, DCAA, DCIS, OSI, NIS, AAA.

1. Case strategy: Does your installation have a judge advocate Special Assistant United States Attorney (SAUSA) who is a felony prosecutor? If not, you must "sell" prosecution to Assistant U.S. Attorney. Consider that person's point of view:
   a. Resources? Time to investigate, time to try; what will it cost? Jury appeal. Complexities of the government contracting process. Was the government at fault? Other problems: Declination guidance? Low dollar amount or low-level employees involved.
   b. Possible selling points: important local priority; product substitution (threat to personal safety and mission); persuasive victim impact statement (cost to inspect, test, identify, and replace).
2. An early and important decision: Grand Jury Subpoena or DOD Inspector General Subpoena? Be aware of the impact of Fed. R. Crim. P. 6(e), and the possible use of the Inspector General Act, 5 U.S.C. § 6(a)(4), and so-called "IG Subpoenas" which grant subpoena power over all information, docu-

ments, reports, records, accounts and other data needed (but no subpoena power over witnesses to obtain oral testimony).

3. Other investigative options. Search warrants (Fed.R. Crim. Pro. 41). Contract clauses. (*e.g.*, FAR 52.246-1 *et seq.*)

### B. Coordination of Remedies.

The ideal is the "global settlement." Such a settlement could include, for example:

1. Criminal Remedies, *e.g.*, indictment and guilty plea or conviction resulting in imprisonment and fines.

2. Administrative Remedies, *e.g.*, suspension or debarment of the contractor to prevent the award of additional or follow-on contracts.

3. Civil Remedies, *e.g.*, multiple damages and penalties awarded pursuant to the Civil False Claims Act.

4. Possible future consideration, *e.g.*, contractor agrees to changes in cost accounting and quality assurance procedures.

5. Possible employment actions, *e.g.*, dismissal of employees and managers engaged in fraud to assure government that a repeat of fraud is unlikely.

## VI. CRIMINAL STATUTES.

### A. Conspiracy to Defraud.

18 U.S.C. § 286 (with claims) and 18 U.S.C. § 371 (in general).

1. Conspiracy is one of the most frequently charged federal crimes and, for a number of reasons, a favorite charge among prosecutors.

   a. First, conspiracy is ill-defined and therefore difficult to defend; second, venue for a prosecution lies in the jurisdiction where the agreement occurred or where any overt act in furtherance of the conspiracy took place; third, courts liberally admit circumstantial evidence in conspiracy cases; fourth, there is a specific exception to the rule against hearsay for statements by coconspirators when offered against other members of the conspiracy; and finally, the fact that coconspirators may be jointly tried may allow juries to infer guilt by association.

   b. The Supreme Court has stated that Section 371 reaches "'any conspiracy for the purpose of impairing, obstructing or defeating the lawful function of any department of the Government.'" *Dennis v. United States*, 384 U.S. 855, 861 (1966).

2. The second applicable conspiracy statute, Section 286, prohibits conspiracy to defraud in connection with false claims. The vast majority of cases involve Section 371.

3. The general elements of a conspiracy under either statute include:

   a. knowing agreement by two or more persons which has as its object the commission of a criminal offense, or to defraud the United States;

   b. intentional and actual participation in the conspiracy;

   c. and performance by one or more of the conspirators of an overt act in furtherance of the unlawful goal. *United States v. Falcone*, 311 U.S. 205, 210-211 (1940); *United States v. Richmond*, 700 U.S. 1183, 1190 (8th Cir. 1983).

4. Some commentators believe that Section 286 requires proof of an overt act. The statute, however, does not contain such a requirement. As a practical matter, the difference is probably illusory since "convincing the merits of any case to a jury probably will require a showing of some acts having been done in furtherance of the conspiracy to affect the objects of it." Borch and Dworschak, "The Criminal Liability of Corporations: A Primer for Procurement Fraud Prosecutions," *The Army Lawyer*, August 1991, at 12.

### B. False Claims.

18 U.S.C. § 287.

1. The elements required for a conviction under Section 287 include:

   a. Proof of a claim for money or property, which is false, fictitious, or fraudulent and material.

—The claim need not be false, fictitious, and fraudulent; the language of the statute is to be considered in the disjunctive. *United States v. Blecker*, 657 F. 2d 629 (4th Cir. 1981), *cert. denied*, 454 U.S. 1150 (1982).

b. Made or presented against a department or agency of the United States;

c. Submitted with a specific intent to violate the law or with a consciousness of wrongdoing, i.e., the person must know at the time that the claim is false, fictitious, or fraudulent. *See generally United States v. Slocum*, 708 F.2d 587, 596 (11th Cir. 1983)(citing *United States v. Computer Sciences Corp.*, 511 F. Supp. 1125, 1134 (E.D. Va. 1981), *rev'd on other grounds*, 689 F.2d 1181 (4th Cir. 1981))(false indemnity claims made to USDA).

—The Government may establish the requisite knowledge by showing that the defendant deliberately closed his or her eyes to what would otherwise have been obvious to him or her. *See United States v. Gullett*, 713 F.2d 1203, 1212 (6th Cir. 1983)(usually actual guilty knowledge is required for false claims.)

d. It is of no significance to a prosecution under section 287 that the claim was not paid. *United States v. Coachman*, 727 F.2d 1293, 1302 (D.C. Cir.), *cert. denied*, 419 U.S. 1047 (1984).

## C. False Statements.

18 U.S.C. § 1001.

1. The elements include proof that:

a. The defendant made a statement or submitted a false entry. "Statement" has been interpreted to include oral, and unsworn statements. *United States v. Massey*, 550 F.2d 300 (5th Cir.), *on remand*, 437 F. Supp. 843 (M.D. Fla. 1977), but the definition is not without limits, as demonstrated in *Williams v. United States*, 458 U.S. 279 (1982), where the Supreme Court stated that a criminal false statement requires a factual assertion which may be characterized as true or false.

b. The statement was false. The fact that a statement may be unauthorized, misleading or even misrepresentative is not, without more, a sufficient basis for a prosecution under Section 1001.

(1) In some circuits, the Government is required to negate any reasonable interpretation that would make the defendant's otherwise ambiguous statement factually correct. *See, e.g., United States v. Anderson*, 579 F.2d 455, 460 (8th Cir. 1978), *cert. denied*, 439 U.S. 980 (1978).

(2) In other circuits, however, the statement's falsity needs to be evident as the statement is "fairly read." *See, e.g., United States v. Rodgers*, 624 F.2d 1303 (5th Cir. 1980)(defendants were convicted of making false statements in an alleged bid-rigging scheme. The Fifth Circuit rejected the contention that the literal meaning of the statement was true and held that a conviction will be valid where statements are false when fairly read), *cert. denied*, 450 U.S. 917 (1981).

c. The statement concerned a matter within the jurisdiction of a federal department or agency.

(1) In general, a department or agency has "jurisdiction" when it has the power to exercise authority in a particular situation. *United States v. Rogers*, 466 U.S. 475, 479 (1984) (The word "jurisdiction" as used in the statute must mean simply the power to act upon information when it is received).

(2) Where federal jurisdiction exists, there is no requirement that the person submitting the false statement be aware of it. *United States v. Yermian*, 468 U.S. 63 (1984).

d. The Government also must prove that a statement was "material."

(1) The test of materiality is whether the

natural and probable tendency of the statement would be to affect or influence governmental action. *United States v. Lichenstein*, 610 F.2d 1272, 1278 (5th Cir.) (capacity of a false statement to impair functions of a federal agency is the hallmark of materiality), *cert. denied*, 447 U.S. 907 (1980).

(2) The Government is not required to show actual reliance on the alleged deception. See, e.g., *Blake v. United States*, 323 F.2d 245, 247 (8th Cir. 1963)(Actual reliance of the governmental department on the false statement is not an essential element of the offense charged).

e. Intent.

(1) A conviction for making a false statement does not require the Government to prove intent to defraud. The statement must be made with intent to deceive, however, or be designed to induce a belief in the false statement. This required scienter has been defined as "the intent to deprive someone of something by means of deceit." *United States v. Lichenstein*, 610 F.2d 1272, 1277 (5th Cir.), *cert. denied*, 447 U.S. 907 (1980)).

(2) A false statement must be knowingly made and willfully submitted. *United States v. Guzman*, 781 F.2d 428, 431 (5th Cir. 1986). To commit an act "knowingly" means "[a]n act is done knowingly if the defendant realized what he or she was doing, and did not act through ignorance, mistake, or accident." *United States v. Ibarra-Alvarez*, 830 F.2d 968, 974 (9th Cir. 1987). However, intentional ignorance has been deemed to constitute constructive knowledge sufficient to satisfy this element. *United States v. Petullo*, 709 F.2d 1178 (7th Cir. 1983).

**D. Mail Fraud and Wire Fraud.**

18 U.S.C. §§ 1341-43.

1. The essence of the mail fraud and wire fraud statutes is the use of mails or wire communications to execute a scheme to defraud the United States. Both statutes are broadly worded to prohibit the use of the mails or interstate telecommunications systems to further such schemes.

2. The elements of the two offenses are similar. Because the elements are similar, the cases interpreting the more recent wire fraud statute rely on the precedents interpreting mail fraud. *See, e.g., United States v. Cusino*, 694 F.2d 185 (9th Cir. 1982), *cert. denied*, 461 U.S. 932 (1983). They include:

a. Formation of a scheme and artifice to defraud.

(1) "The scheme need not be fraudulent upon its face or misrepresent any material fact. All that is necessary is that it be a scheme reasonably calculated to deceive persons of ordinary prudence and comprehension." *United States v. Bruce*, 488 F.2d 1224, 1229 (5th Cir. 1973), *cert. denied*, 419 U.S. 825 (1974).

(2) The Government is not required to prove that fraudulent scheme caused actual economic loss. It is the scheme to defraud, and not the actual fraud, that will sustain a conviction. *United States v. Reid*, 533 F.2d 1255, 1261 (D.C. Cir. 1976)

b. Use either of the mails, or interstate wire transmissions in furtherance of the scheme. *See United States v. Pintar*, 630 F.2d 1270, 1280 (8th Cir. 1980)(mail fraud); *United States v. Wise*, 553 F.2d 1173 (8th Cir. 1977)(wire fraud).

**E. The Major Fraud Act.**

18 U.S.C. § 1031.

1. The act created a new criminal offense of "major fraud" against the United States. Designed to deter major defense contractors from committing procurement fraud by

imposing stiffer penalties and significantly higher fines.

2. Maximum punishments: ten years confinement; fines are determined on a sliding scale based on certain aggravating factors. Basic offense: $1,000,000 per count. Government loss or contractor gain of $500,000 or more: $5,000,000. Conscious or reckless risk of serious personal injury: $5,000,000. Multiple counts: $10,000,000 per prosecution.

3. Elements: *Fraud*—knowingly executing any scheme with intent to defraud the U.S. or to obtain money by false or fraudulent pretenses; *On a United States contract*—including "any procurement of property or services as a prime contractor or as a subcontractor or supplier"; *Valued at $1,000,000 or more*—"if the value of the contract, subcontract, or any constituent part thereof . . . is $1,000,000 or more." *See, e.g., United States v. Nadi*, 996 F.2d 548 (2d Cir. 1993): Statute is not unconstitutionally vague on its face as applied because it fails to define the term "value of the contract." The value of the contract subject to the fraud determines the value of the contract. § 1031 does not apply to fraud on a subcontract worth less than $1 million even though the prime contract's value is in excess of $1 million.

4. Statute of limitations: 7 years, to provide time for long and difficult investigations involving very complex facts.

5. Whistleblower protection: contractors may not discharge, demote, threaten, or harass employees who participate in prosecutions against them, or employees may sue in federal court for double back pay plus interest, special damages, attorneys fees, and same seniority status.

6. In *United States v. Broderson*, CR 93-177 (E.D. NY), a former vice-president of Grumman Data Systems Corp. was convicted on 22 felony counts including 11 counts violating the Major Fraud Act. The allegations were that he fraudulently certified that GDS had obtained 13.77% financing for a supercomputer, but had actually obtained 10.5% financing.

**F. Title 10 (UCMJ) Violations.**
1. Article 92, Dereliction of Duty, or Violating a General Regulation (e.g., DOD Joint Ethics Regulation).
2. Article 132, Fraud Against the United States.
3. Article 107, False Official Statement.
4. Article 108, Wrongful Disposition of Government Property.
5. Article 134, Bribery, Graft, or Solicitation.

## VII. VARIOUS CIVIL REMEDIES.

Statutory Civil Remedies to Combat Procurement Fraud:

1. *The Anti-Kickback Act of 1986*, Pub. L. No. 99-634, 100 Stat. 3523, 41 U.S.C. §§ 51-58 (1988) (payments by a subcontractor to a prime contractor to affect a government contract).

2. *Section 5 of the Contracts Disputes Act of 1978*, 41 U.S.C. § 604 (1988) (contractor liability for submission of a false or unsupported claim to a contracting officer under the contract's Disputes clause);

3. *The Program Fraud Civil Remedies Act of 1986*, 31 U.S.C. §§ 3801-3812 (1988) (provides an administrative alternative to litigation in civil false statements and smaller false claims cases);

4. *Federal Property and Administrative Services Act*, 40 U.S.C. § 489 (1988) (fraud in the disposal of surplus government property);

5. *Forfeiture of Claims*, 28 U.S.C. § 2514 (1988) (allows a so-called "special plea" in fraud for fraudulent claims asserted against the United States in the United States Court of Federal Claims (Federal Claims Court); provides for forfeiture of an entire claim if any part of it is fraudulent or supported by fraudulent evidence).

6. Congress did not intend for the False Claims Act to be the government's exclusive remedy for fraud. *United States v. Krietemeyer*, 506 F. Supp. 289, 291 (S.D. Ill. 1980). Moreover, in light of the FCA's breadth, there is a strong presumption against preemption of the FCA

by other statutes, such as the Anti-Kickback Act. *United States v. General Dynamics Corp*, 19 F. 3d 770 (2d Cir. 1994).

## VIII. THE CIVIL FALSE CLAIMS ACT.

### A. The Primary Litigative Weapon for Combatting Fraud is the Civil False Claims Act.

31 U.S.C. §§ 3729-3733 (1988).

1. Background: Congress enacted the original False Claims Act in 1863 in response to flagrant cases of contractor fraud perpetrated on the Union Army during the Civil War. The original Act provided a $2000 penalty for the submission of each false claim, and qui tam provisions authorizing individuals to bring suit in the name of the government against those seeking to defraud it.

2. The U.S. Supreme Court has held that the False Claims Act "was intended to reach all types of fraud, without qualification, that might result in financial loss to the government." *United States v. Neifert-White Co.*, 390 U.S. 228 (1968). Congress has "strongly endorse[d] this interpretation of the act". S. Rep. No. 99-345 at 19. The Report states that "[t]he False Claims Act is intended to reach all fraudulent attempts to cause the government to pay out sums of money or to deliver property or services." *Id*. at 7.

### B. The Amended False Claims Act. False Claims Amendments Act of 1986

Pub. L. No. 99-562, 100 Stat. 3153 (1986). Reasons for the amendments: (1) fraud in government programs and procurement was on a steady rise; estimates from the General Accounting Office (GAO) and the Department of Justice (DOJ) suggested that the monetary loss from program fraud could be *from one to ten percent* of the federal budget; (2) lack of deterrence and effective enforcement. The major changes in the legislation included:

1. An increased civil penalty to between $5000 and $10,000 per false claim. 31 U.S.C. § 3729(a). The imposition of the forfeiture pro-

vision is automatic and mandatory for each false claim. Proof of damages is not required. *Fleming v. United States*, 336 F.2d 475, 480 (10th Cir. 1964), *cert. denied*, 380 U.S. 907 (1965).

2. Establishing the preponderance of the evidence standard as the burden of proof needed to prove False Claims Act liability. 31 U.S.C. § 3731(c). Some courts of appeal had required proof by "clear, unequivocal evidence", *see, e.g., United States v. Ekelman & Assoc., Inc.*, 532 F.2d 545, 548 (6th Cir. 1976), based on a misconception that the civil False Claims Act is penal in nature.

3. Making *treble* damages the substantive measure of liability. 31 U.S.C. 3729(a). An exception to the treble damages "multiplier" exists where the "person" committing the violation provides all the information known to that person before the commencement of an investigation by the United States, and cooperates fully with any government investigation. This practice is known as a "voluntary disclosure."

4. Expanding the application of collateral estoppel principles to include pleas of nolo contendre. 31 U.S.C. § 3731(d). But for this amendment, Fed. R. Evid. 410 and Rule 11(e)(6), Fed. R. Crim. Pro., would have prohibited the collateral estoppel use of a plea of nolo contendre in a subsequent civil action.

5. Creating "tolling" provisions for the civil statute of limitations, potentially allowing as much as ten years to pursue civil remedies. Pursuant to 31 U.S.C. § 3731(b), the United States may bring an action under the False Claims Act either within six years of the date of the violation, or up to three years from the date when an official of the United States "charged with responsibility to act" is made aware of facts material to the government's right of action. In no case will the statute of limitations exceed ten years.

6. Expanding the qui tam provisions of the Act. 31 U.S.C. § 3730(c) and (d). The amendments increased the percentage of the rela-

tor's potential recovery, permitted the relator to remain a party to the lawsuit even if the government intervenes, and gave the relator a greater possible role in the prosecution and settlement of the lawsuit.

7. Defining the term "claim," 31 U.S.C. § 3729(c), to include: "[A]ny request or demand, whether under a contract or otherwise, for money or property which is made to a contractor, grantee, or other recipient if the United States government provides any portion of the money or property which is requested or demanded, or if the government will reimburse such contractor, grantee, or other recipient for any portion of the money or property which is requested or demanded."

8. Providing the Attorney General with authority to issue "civil investigative demands," enforceable by judicial order, on persons with knowledge of false claims. 31 U.S.C. § 3733. The authority to issue civil investigative demands ("CIDs") under the False Claims Act conforms with the legislative history and caselaw of the CID authority granted to DOJ's Antitrust Division under 15 U.S.C. §§ 1311-1314.

9. Lowering the requisite standard of knowledge necessary to prove a knowing violation of the Act. 31 U.S.C. § 3729(b).

## IX. LIABILITY UNDER THE FALSE CLAIMS ACT.

### A. In General.

31 U.S.C. § 3729(a), imposes liability on any person (defined comprehensively in 1 U.S.C. § 1 (1988) to include "corporations, companies, associations, partnerships, ... as well as individuals;....") who:

1. Knowingly presents, or causes to be presented, to an officer or employee of the United States government or a member of the Armed Forces of the United States, a false or fraudulent claim for payment or approval.
   a. Under this provision, the United States must prove that the person made, or

caused to be made, a "claim" for payment or approval by the government, that the claim was false or fraudulent, and that the person acted knowing that the claim was false. *Blusal Meats, Inc. v. United States*, 638 F.Supp. 824,827 (S.D.N.Y. 1986), *aff'd*, 817 F.2d 1007 (2d Cir. 1987).

   b. The "causes to be presented" language covers the situation where a fraudulent claim is presented to a third-party, who then submits it to the United States. For example, fraud by a subcontractor is violative of the False Claims Act if the claim subsequently is submitted by (or through) the prime contractor to the United States. *United States v. Bornstein*, 423 U.S. 303 (1976).

   c. Knowingly makes, uses, or causes to be made or used, a false record or statement to get a false or fraudulent claim paid or approved by the government. Under 31 U.S.C. § 3729(a)(2), the United States may seek treble damages and forfeitures if a defendant knowingly makes, uses, or causes to be made or used, a false record or statement to get a false or fraudulent claim paid or approved by the government. A common basis for asserting liability under this provision is a false certification by a contractor.

2. Conspires to defraud the government by getting a false or fraudulent claim allowed or paid. Under the conspiracy provision, the government must prove the knowing submission of a false claim, that an agreement existed among the conspirators, and the occurrence of at least one act in furtherance of the conspiracy. Upon such proof, joint and several liability will attach to all the conspirators. *See Kelsoe v. Fed. Crop Ins. Corp.*, 724 F. Supp. 448, 454 (E.D. Tex. 1988).

3. Knowingly makes, uses, or causes to be made or used, a false record or statement to conceal, avoid, or decrease an obligation to pay or transmit money or property to the United States. This provision covers the so-called "reverse false claim." S. Rep. 99-345 at 18. The

conduct proscribed is using a false statement *to avoid* paying the government. Prior to the 1986 amendments, there was some disagreement whether such conduct was subject to the False Claims Act. *See Id.* (citing cases).

**B. The Scienter Requirement.**

1. Except for the conspiracy provision, the False Claims Act specifically requires some sort of "knowledge" by the false claimant.

   a. The terms "knowing" and "knowingly" mean that a person, with respect to certain information-

      (1) has actual knowledge of the information;

      (2) acts in deliberate ignorance of the truth or falsity of the information; or

      (3) acts in reckless disregard of the truth or falsity of the information.

   b. No proof of specific intent to defraud is required. 31 U.S.C. § 3729(b).

   c. Scienter involves actual and constructive knowledge. Constructive knowledge includes "deliberate ignorance" and "reckless disregard" of the truth or falsity of information.

      (1) It is intended that persons who ignore "red flags" that the information may not be accurate, or who deliberately choose to remain ignorant of the process through which their company handles a claim, should be held liable under the Act. H.R. Rep. No. 660, 99th Cong., 2d Sess. 21 (1986).

      (2) Reckless disregard and gross negligence define essentially the same conduct. 132 Cong. Rec. 20535-36 (Aug. 11, 1986) (statement of Senator Grassley). *Contra, see* Joseph, Ackerman, and Nied, "Update: Defective Pricing —When Is It Defective? When Is It Fraud?", 54 Fed. Cont. Rep. 136 (July 30, 1990).

**C. Defenses.**

1. The courts have entertained assertion of affirmative defenses to actions brought under the FCA with mixed results. For example, in *Toepelman v. United States*, 263 F. 2d 697 (4th Cir. 1959), the court held the Government was under no duty to mitigate damages caused by a defrauding contractor. By contrast, under the unique facts of *United States v. Fox Lake State Bank*, 366 F.2d 962 (7th Cir. 1966), the Government was estopped from bringing an action under the FCA against the defendant.

2. The "government knowledge defense," also has met with mixed success, but it may serve to negate culpability or the imposition of damages. *See generally* Neal J. Wilson, "The Government Knowledge 'Defense' to Civil False Claims Actions," 24 Pub. Con. L. J. 43 (1994).

   a. The essence of the defense is that a claim cannot be "false" within the meaning of the FCA where it can be shown that the Government has been told the "truth" about the basis of the claim. *See Boisjoly v. Morton Thiokol*, 706 F. Supp. 795 (D. Utah 1988); *X Corp. v. Doe*, 816 F. Supp. 1086, 1093-94 (E.D. Va. 1993)(In *dicta*, the court observed that "there is no knowing presentation of a false claim where, as here, X Corp. advised the government about the true nature of the equipment provided.") *But see United States ex rel. Hagood v. Sonoma County Water Authority*, 929 F. 2d 1416, 1421 (9th Cir. 1991)("That the relevant government officials knew of the falsity is not in itself a defense."). *Accord Tyger Constr. Co. v. United States*, 28 Fed. Cl. 35, 59-60 (1993)(Government knowledge alone does not serve as a basis for dismissing a counterclaim under the Contract Disputes Act, 41 U.S,C, § 604), *reconsid. granted in part*, 32 Fed. Cl. 177 (1994).

   b. More recently, a district court relied on *Hagood* to reject the government knowledge defense, as well as affirmative defenses based on unclean hands, estoppel, and mitigation of damages. *United States ex rel. Ferguson v. General Dynamics Corp.*,

No. CV 90-4073 (C.D. Cal. Apr. 28, 1994) 1994 U.S. LEXIS 7666 (discussed at 61 Fed. Cont. Rep. (BNA) 680 (May 23, 1994).

3. A different kind of estoppel may result when there are parallel proceedings concerning the same operative set of facts. In *United States v. TDC Management Corp. Inc.*, 24 F.3d 292 (D.C. Cir. 1994), the Government was collaterally estopped from relitigating (in district court) the accuracy of progress payments DOTBCA implicitly had upheld

## X. DAMAGES.

### A. Impact of the 1986 Amendments.

In FY 1994, DOJ obtained $1.09 billion in civil fraud settlements and judgments. Defense procurement fraud was the largest category of civil recoveries accounting for $578 million. Health care fraud accounted for $411, doubling the $180 million recovered in FY 1993. "DOJ Recovers $1B in Civil Fraud in FY '94; Defense Fraud Tops List, Health Care Next," 62 Fed. Cont. Rep. (BNA) 373 (Oct. 17, 1994).

### B. Actual Damages.

1. Supreme Court Precedents.
   a. *United States ex rel. Marcus v. Hess*, 317 U.S. 537 (1943). The FCA is *remedial*, and "the device of double damages plus a specific sum was chosen to make sure that the government would be made *completely whole* (emphasis added)." The formula for damages is the amount that the government paid, less the amount that it would have paid had it been aware of the true facts.
   b. *United States v. Bornstein*, 423 U.S. 303 (1976). The FCA requires a focus on the conduct of the person from whom the government seeks to collect the forfeitures. In *Bornstein*, the subcontractor had submitted three invoiced shipments to the prime. These three shipments "caused" the prime contractor to submit false claims. Thus, the subcontractor was liable for three statutory forfeitures.

(1) The "make-whole purpose of the Act" is best-served by multiplying the government's damages *before* any compensatory payments were deducted.

(2) Damages are equal to the difference between the market value of tubes received and market value the tubes would have had *if* they had been of the specified quality. *Accord United States v. Ben Grunstein & Sons Packing Corp.*, 137 F. Supp. 197 (D. N.J. 1956) (applies "benefit of the bargain" rule to FCA).

### C. Different Scenarios.

1. *Defective Products*: Defective products are those which do not conform to the contract specifications. In its most familiar and pernicious form, this category includes product substitution.
   a. *United States v. Aerodex*, 469 F.2d 1003 (5th Cir. 1972). Defendants contracted to provide 300 *new* master rod bearings, at $90 each. Defendants supplied reworked bearings which had been relabeled to appear to satisfy contract requirements. Failure of the bearing could cause complete engine failure. Navy removed and replaced the bearings at a cost of $161,000.
   b. The Fifth Circuit concluded that the "retrofit" costs were "consequential damages" which resulted from the delivery and installation of the bearings, not from the submission of the false claims by Aerodex. The government had paid $27,000 for bearings which never were delivered, and that was the proper measure of the damages. The court of appeals did allow recovery of the so-called consequential damages under a breach of express warranty theory.
   c. Where the defendant, by his own wrong, prevents a more precise computation, recall the Supreme Court's decision in *Bigelow v. RKO Radio Pictures, Inc.*, 327 U.S. 251 (1946), that "the jury may make a

just and reasonable estimate based on relevant data, and render its verdict accordingly." Public policy requires that the wrongdoer bear the risk of the uncertainty which his own wrong has created.

2. *Defective Testing*: The crucial damages issue is the reliability of the product once the deficiency is known. An important element in such an analysis is the residual value of the untested or inadequately tested product. Civil penalties may function as a liquidated damages provision in the event that actual damages are difficult or impossible to calculate.

3. *Bid-Rigging*: Measure of damages is "the difference between what the government actually paid on the fraudulent claim and what it would have paid had there been fair, open and competitive bidding." *United States v. Killough*, 848 F.2d 1523, 1532 (11th Cir. 1988); *see also Brown v. United States*, 524 F.2d 693, 706 (1975).

   a. The absence of competition deprives the government of its most reliable measure of what the price should have been.

   b. Every claim submitted pursuant to a fraudulently acquired contract should be considered a "false or fraudulent" claim within the meaning of the FCA, and each false claim will mandate a civil penalty. *See* S. Rep. No. 345, 8-10 (1986) *reprinted in* 1986 U.S. Code Cong. & Admin. News 5266.

4. *Bribery and Public Corruption*: The government may bring common law counts against an employee who has breached his or her duty of loyalty. *See e.g. United States v. Carter*, 217 U.S. 286 (1910). In such a case, the remedy for the government is the amount of the bribe, whether or not substantive damages were suffered. In an action for inducing a breach of a fiduciary duty against the person who paid the bribe, the government may recover the amount of the bribe, because "the amount of the bribe provides a reasonable measure of damage, in the absence of a more precise yardstick." *Conti-*

*nental Management, Inc. v. United States*, 527 F.2d 613, 619 (Ct. Cl. 1975).

5. *Defective Pricing*: Under TINA caselaw and in DFARS 215.804-7(b)(2), there is a rebuttable presumption that the natural and probable consequence of defective data is to increase the contract price in the amount of the cost overstatement plus related burdens. Thus, for defective pricing, a defense contractor may be liable for a dollar-for-dollar reduction of the contract price based on cost discrepancy between overstated cost data submitted to the government, and undisclosed actual costs. *Aerojet-General Corp.*, ASBCA No. 12,264, 69-1 BCA ¶ 7664 (1969), *aff'd on reconsid.* 70-1 BCA ¶ 8140 (1970).

   —In *United States ex rel. Taxpayers Against Fraud v. Link Flight Simulation Corp.*, 722 F. Supp. 1248 (D. Md.), *aff'd*, 889 F.2d 1327 (4th Cir. 1989), the court applied that reasoning in a false claims act case, holding that the government is damaged dollar-for-dollar by nondisclosure. *See also United States v. Educational Development Network Inc.*, No. 89-7780 (E.D. Pa., Dec. 20, 1993)(in the absence of contrary evidence by defendant's, court relied on *Singer* and accepted the Government's use of 22% proposed profit to compute damages).

**D. Civil Penalties.**

1. Imposition is "automatic and mandatory for each false claim. S. Rep No. 345 at 8-10. *See also United States v. Hughes*, 585 F.2d 284, 286 (7th Cir. 1978) ("This forfeiture provision is mandatory; it leaves the trial court without discretion to alter the statutory amount.")

2. There is no requirement for the United States to prove that it suffered any damages. S. Rep. No. 345 at 8 (citing *Fleming v. United States*, 336 F.2d 475, 480 (10th Cir. 1964), *cert. denied*, 380 U.S. 907 (1965)). The government also does not have to show that it made any payments pursuant to false claims. *United States v. American Precision Products Corp.*, 115 F. Supp. 823 (D.N.J. 1953).

3. Each separate bill, voucher or other false payment demand constitutes a separate claim for which a forfeiture shall be imposed. This is true although many such claims may be submitted to the government at one time. S. Rep. No. 345 at 8-10.

4. *United States v. Halper*, 490 U.S. 435 (1989): defendant faced aggregated penalties $130,000 for fraud which had damaged the government in the amount of $585. A civil sanction, in application, may be so divorced from any remedial goal as to constitute punishment under some circumstances. The scope of the holding is a narrow one, addressed to "the rare case . . . where a fixed-penalty provision subjects a small-gauge offender to a sanction overwhelmingly disproportionate to the damages he has caused."

## XI. THE QUI TAM PROVISIONS OF THE FALSE CLAIMS ACT.

### A. Background.
1. "Qui tam pro domino rege quam pro se ipso in hac parte sequitur." ("Who as well for the King as for himself sues in this matter.")
2. Since 1986 False Claims Act Amendments, approximately 840 qui tam cases have been filed, rising from 12 in FY 1987 to 220 in FY 1994. DOJ has intervened in approximately 127, declined involvement in 455, and is investigating the remainder. 320 of the 455 cases thus declined were dismissed or abandoned by the plaintiff, while 21 resulted in damage awards.
3. The Government has recovered approximately $800 million in qui tam cases since the 1986 amendments, including $378 million in FY 1994. Plaintiffs have received $123 million of that amount, or 18% of the total recovery. Where DOJ has not intervened, plaintiff shares of recoveries have averaged 29%. *See* 62 Fed. Cont. Rep. (BNA) 505 (Nov. 14, 1994). Some recent examples:
   a. $325 million settlement from National Medical Enterprises for overcharging federal health programs for psychiatric care.
   b. The largest defense case involved a $150 million settlement by United Technologies based on improper progress payments.
4. Profile of potential plaintiffs: *See* "Contractors Can Identify Potential Qui Tam Plaintiffs In Advance, ABA Panelist Says." 54 Fed. Cont. Rep. (BNA) 726 (Nov. 12, 1990) (views expressed by Mr. Richard Sauber; profile is of an employee who consistently complains about a contractor's practice or procedure without getting any satisfaction; ignoring complaints makes qui tam lawsuit—at least arguably—a failure of management).

### B. Procedures.
1. 31 U.S.C. § 3730(b)(2) requires service of a complaint on the government pursuant to Rule 4(d)(4) of the Federal Rules of Civil Procedure (i.e. copy to U.S. Attorney for the district in which the action is brought and copy by registered mail to Attorney General).
2. The complaint must be filed *in camera* and remain under seal for at least 60 days. It is not served on the defendant without a court order. At the time of service the defendant has 20 days to respond. 31 U.S.C. § 3730(b)(3). The seal requirement allows the government to evaluate the suit, determine whether the government already is investigating, or whether the government's interests are served by intervening and taking over the suit.
3. The seal requirement protects both the government and the defendant, and is mandatory (i.e., "[it] shall remain under seal. . . .") Possibly, failure to abide by this requirement could result in loss of some or all rights by the relator. *See* "Judge Dismisses Qui Tam Case Due To Breach Of Statutory Seal Requirements," 62 Fed. Cont. Rep. (BNA) 239 (Sept. 12, 1994)(defendant's motion to dismiss granted after disclosure of qui tam action in related wrongful discharge case).
4. Written disclosure of substantially all material evidence *should* accompany complaint. *See* 31 U.S.C. § 3730(b)(2). The statute does

not require that this information be filed with the court. The initial 60 day time period for the Government's election of whether or not to intervene does not begin to run until the statutory requirements have been met fully.

5. The government may, *for good cause shown*, move the court for an extension of the time during which the complaint remains under seal. "Good cause" is not established by showing that the government was overburdened. The motion for an extension of time should be under seal, and may be supported by *in camera* affidavits or other submissions.

6. The Justice Department's Civil Division secures agency recommendations concerning intervention or declination, and prepares a memorandum containing summary of facts and recommendations. The final authority to intervene, or to decline intervention, rests with DOJ.

7. If the government intervenes, it is primarily (not solely) responsible for prosecuting the action. 31 U.S.C. § 3730(c)(1). The relator is still a party, but limitations may be imposed if unrestricted participation by the relator would interfere with or unduly delay the government's prosecution of the case. 31 U.S.C. § 3730(c)(2)(C).

8. Government may dismiss action over relator's objections, provided relator has opportunity to be heard. 31 U.S.C. § 3730(c)(2)(A). Government may settle case over relator's objections if court determines settlement to be fair, adequate and reasonable under the circumstances. 31 U.S.C. § 3730(c)(2)(B).

9. Initial declination does not preclude late entry in the case by the government upon a showing of "good cause." 31 U.S.C. § 3730(c)(2)(C). *United States ex rel. Siller v. Becton Dickinson & Co.*, 21 F. 3d 1339 (4th Cir. 1994)(filing requirements of 31 U.S.C. § 3730(b)(4) are not jurisdictional and therefore do not bar government's further prosecution of qui tam action despite its having missed court deadlines), *cert. denied*, 115 S. Ct. 316 (1994).

—If, the Government does not intervene and the relator settles the case with the defendant, the Government may ask for a hearing and submit a briefing on the fairness of the settlement, but there is no absolute right for the Government to veto settlements. *United States ex rel. Killingsworth v. Northrop Corp.*, 25 F. 3d 715 (9th Cir. 1994), *United States ex rel. Gibeaut v. Texas Instruments Corp.*, 25 F. 3d 725 (9th Cir. 1994).

10. Where the government intervenes, the relator shares between 15 and 25% of the government's recovery. If the government does not intervene, the relator's share may be as much as 30%.

11. Other Effects Of A Qui Tam Case. Profound impact on limited Government resources— may cause a change of investigative priorities, and thus limit executive prerogatives.

## XII. CURRENT ISSUES.

### A. Constitutionality.

1. *United States ex rel. Kelly v. Boeing*, 9 F.3d 743 (9th Cir. 1993), *cert. denied*, 114 S.Ct. 1125 (1994): upheld qui tam provisions as constitutional against challenges based on the appointments clause, separation of powers doctrine, and case or controversy (standing). *See also United States ex rel. Kreindler & Kreindler v. United Technologies Corp.*, 985 F.2d 1148 (2d Cir. 1993)(qui tam provisions of FCA did not violate Article III and did vest relator with standing), *cert. denied*, 113 S. Ct. 2962 (1993).

2. The major arguments:

   a. Separation of powers: Violated by the qui tam relator's power to continue a suit in the name of the United States despite a DOJ declination to intervene. In other words, Congress seems to have granted a prosecutorial (executive) function to qui tam relators.

   b. Appointments clause: Qui tam relator exercises civil law enforcement authority without having been appointed an "officer of the United States" within the meaning of the Constitution (Art. II, Sec. 2).

    c. Standing: Qui tam relators lack standing because they have not been injured by the actions of which they complain. In other words, there is no "case or controversy" involving the relator which can be remedied in the suit he or she brings.

    d. Due Process: Qui tam relator is, in essence, a contingency-fee prosecutor, with a vested interest in the outcome.

3. DOJ has not taken an "official" or public position on the constitutionality of the qui tam statute, but district courts unanimously have refused to dismiss qui tam suits as unconstitutional.

## B. Public Disclosure and the "Original Source" Rule.

1. The 1943 amendments created a so-called "jurisdictional bar" to "parasitical lawsuits." The amendments limited the information on which the qui tam plaintiff could base a suit, and the recovery available from a successful prosecution of the action. Courts lost jurisdiction over actions based on information the government had when action was brought, even if the "original source" of the government's information was the person filing suit. *See Safir v. Blackwell*, 579 F.2d 742 (2d Cir. 1978), *cert. denied*, 441 U.S. 943 (1979).

2. 31 U.S.C. § 3730(e)(4)(A) now permits a qui tam case to go forward *unless* it is based on public disclosure "of allegations or transactions in a criminal, civil, or administrative hearing, in a congressional, administrative, or Government Accounting Office report, hearing, audit, or investigation, or from the news media, unless the action is brought by the Attorney General or the person bringing the action is an original source of the information."

    a. A qui tam action is "based upon" a public disclosure when it is supported by or even "partly based upon" such information. *United States ex rel. The Precision Co. v.*

*Koch Indus., Inc.*, 971 F.2d 548 (10th Cir. 1992) (holding that a business which filed a qui tam suit based upon information disclosed in previous lawsuit filed by its majority shareholder was not an "original source" of the information), *cert. denied*, 113 S. Ct. 1364 (1993).

    b. Public disclosure of a corporate subsidiary's pension fund problems in newspapers and creditor meetings did not suggest intent to defraud the government by deliberate understatement of pension liability, and qui tam suit alleging such fraud was not barred as being based on public disclosure. *United States ex rel. Rabushka v. Crane Co.*, 1994 U.S. App. LEXIS 32274 (8th Cir., Nov. 16, 1994).

3. Who is an "original source"? *See* 31 U.S.C. § 3730(e)(4)(b) ("original source" means an individual who has direct and independent knowledge of the information on which the allegations are based and has voluntarily provided the information to the government before bringing action).

—*United States ex rel. Dick v. Long Island Lighting Co.*, 912 F. 2d 13 (2d Cir. 1990)(to be an original source a plaintiff must not only have direct and independent knowledge of the information on which his allegation is based, and have provided that information to the government, but must also have been a source to the entity that publicly disclosed the allegations on which the suit is based), *cert. denied*, 110 S. Ct. 1471 (1990).

## C. Government Relators.

1. Can a government employee be a relator? DOJ position. *See generally*, "Justice To Seek Legislative Bar On Govt. Employee Qui Tam Suits," 56 Fed. Cont. Rep. (BNA) 267 (Aug. 19, 1991). The DOJ position in a nutshell was provided in testimony before the House Judiciary Subcommittee on Civil and Constitutional Rights in April 1992, by then-Assistant Attorney General Stuart M. Gerson, who stated: "Unlike private persons, [federal employees] are already required by law to

report fraud and are paid by the taxpayers to do so; by giving these employees qui tam rewards, the taxpayers are essentially paying them for information that the government rightfully possesses."

2. Decisions allowing suit by government employees. *United States ex rel. Williams v. NEC Corp.*, 931 F.2d 1493 (11th Cir. 1991). *United States ex rel. Hagood v. Sonoma County Water Agency*, 929 F. 2d 1416 (9th Cir. 1991); *United States ex rel. Erickson v. American Inst. of Biological Sciences*, 716 F. Supp. 908 (E.D. Va. 1989).

3. *Contra*, at least where employee's job includes the investigation and disclosure of fraud. *United States ex rel. Leblanc v. Raytheon Co., Inc.*, 913 F.2d 17 (1st Cir. 1990), *cert. denied*, 111 S.Ct. 1312 (1991). *United States ex rel. Fine v. Univ. of California*, 821 F. Supp 1356 (N.D. Cal. 1993) (IG auditor cannot be an original source because he cannot have direct and independent knowledge of information he acquires as a result of audits).

4. Legislation. Sen. Grassley introduced S. 841 which would explicitly recognize the right of government employees to bring qui tam suits under the FCA. In the face of industry efforts to change the legislation, Justice Department support (as opposed to "hostile neutrality") is considered necessary before committee markup. The House version is HR 2915, was introduced by Rep. Berman. 1994 Daily Report for Executives (BNA) 123 (June 29, 1994).

## D. Other Matters.

1. Fighting Back: Legal fees for "frivolous" suit: Hughes Aircraft Co. was awarded $147 thousand to reimburse attorney fees incurred in defense of *United States ex rel. Haycock v. Hughes Aircraft Co.*, No. CV 90-1977 (C.D. Cal., May 9, 1994), a demonstrably "frivolous" qui tam action. *See* 61 Fed. Cont. Rep. (BNA) 678 (23 May 1994). The result differed from that in *United States ex rel. Schumer v. Hughes Aircraft Co.*, No. CV89-390 (C.D. Cal. June 25, 1992), *see* 58 Fed. Cont. Rep. 106 (BNA) (July 27, 1992), because in the latter case there was a significant dispute concerning the allocation of radar development costs.

2. DCAA guidance states that legal costs associated with defending against qui tam suits are not allowable under FAR 31.205-47(b) unless the government elects to intervene. If the government intervenes, the suit becomes a government suit and legal cost incurred by the contractor before and after intervention would be subject to FAR 31.205-47(b).

3. A contractor who is the defendant in a qui tam lawsuit may pursue counterclaims against the plaintiff whistleblower for breach of employment contract, breach of loyalty and fiduciary duty, and defamation. *United States ex rel. Burch v. Piqua Eng'g, Inc.*, 145 F.R.D. 452 (S.D. Ohio, 1992). To avoid a "chilling effect" on the filing of qui tam lawsuits, however, separate trial is ordered for the counterclaims. Other courts have dismissed counterclaims asserted by qui tam defendants.

4. *Neal v. Honeywell Inc.*, 33 F.3d 860 (7th Cir. 1994) holds that employees of contractors who report wrongdoing to their employer are protected by the civil False Claims Act anti-retaliation provision even if they do not file a qui tam action. They are not limited to state remedies as asserted by the defendant. Moreover, the FCA's statute of limitations is applicable to retaliatory discharge claims under 31 U.S.C. § 3730(h).
   —The whistleblower must show that the employer had knowledge that the employee engaged in protected activity. *Robertson v. Bell Helicopter Textron Inc.*, 32 F. 3d 948 (5th Cir. 1994).

# *Alphabetical Listing of Contract Abbreviations*

## A

AAA ...........U.S. Army Audit Agency
ACAB.........Army Contract Adjustment Board
ACO...........Administrative Contracting Officer
ADA...........Anti-Deficiency Act
ADPE.........Automatic Data Processing Equipment
AFARS........Army Federal Acquisition Regulation Supplement
AFFARS......Air Force Federal Acquisition Regulation Supplement
AGBCA ......Department of Agriculture Board of Contract Appeals
AL..............Acquisition Letter
APF...........Appropriated Funds
AP Plan......Advance Procurement Plan
AR .............Army Regulation
ASA(RDA)..Assistant Secretary of the Army for Research, Development, and Acquisition (formerly SARDA)
ASBCA .......Armed Services Board of Contract Appeals
ASPM.........Armed Services Pricing Manual
ASPR..........Armed Services Procurement Regulation, replaced by the DAR

## B

BAA ...........Buy American Act *or* Broad Agency Announcement
BCA ...........Board of Contract Appeals
BCM ..........Business Clearance Memorandum
BOA...........Basic Ordering Agreement
BPA............Blanket Purchase Agreement
BPD ...........Board of Contract Appeals Bid Protest Decisions

## C

CAP ..........Commercial Activities Program
CAFC.........U.S. Court of Appeals for the Federal Circuit
CAS............Cost Accounting Standards
CFR ...........Code of Federal Regulations
CO.............Contracting Officer
COC .........Certificate of Competency
COFC ........U.S. Court of Federal Claims (formerly U.S. Claims Court)
CPD...........Comptroller General's Procurement Decisions
CPAF..........Cost-Plus-Award-Fee
CPFF..........Cost-Plus-Fixed-Fee
CPIF ..........Cost-Plus-Incentive-Fee
CPPC.........Cost-Plus-A-Percentage-of-Cost
CWAS ........Contractor Weighted Average Share
CWAS-NA...Contractor Weighted Average Share—Not Applicable

## D

DA .............Department of the Army
DAC...........Defense Acquisition Circular
DA Form....Department of the Army Form
DAR...........Defense Acquisition Regulation (replaced by the FAR)
DARC ........Defense Acquisition Regulatory Council
DCA...........Defense Communications Agency
DCAA ........Defense Contract Audit Agency
DCMAO.....Defense Contract Management Office
DCMC .......Defense Contract Management Command
DCMCR .....Defense Contract Management Command Region
DEAR.........Department of Energy Acquisition Regulation
DFARS .......Defense Federal Acquisition Regulation Supplement
DFAS..........Defense Finance and Accounting Service
D&F...........Determinations and Findings
DLA ...........Defense Logistics Agency

DLAR .........Defense Logistics Agency Regulation
DOE...........Department of Energy
DOL...........Department of Labor
DOT ..........Department of Transportation
DOT CAB ..Department of Transportation Contract Appeals Board
DPA...........Delegation of Procurement Authority
DPC...........Defense Procurement Circular, replaced by DAC
DPRO ........Defense Plant Representative's Office

## E

EBCA .........Department of Energy Board of Contract Appeals
EEO ...........Equal Employment Opportunity
ENG BCA...U.S. Army Corps of Engineers Board of Contract Appeals
E.O ............Executive Order
8(a)............Section 8(a) of the Small Business Act

## F

FAR............Federal Acquisition Regulation
FASA ..........The Federal Acquisition Streamlining Act of 1994
FCAA ........The Federal Courts Administration Act of 1992
FCIA ..........The Federal Courts Improvement Act of 1982
FFP ............Firm-Fixed-Price
FIPR...........Federal Information Processing Resources
FIRMR .......Federal Information Resource Management Regulation
FMS ..........Foreign Military Sales
FP/EPA.......Fixed Price Contract with Economic Price Adjustment
FPD ..........Federal Court Procurement Decisions
FPR............Federal Procurement Regulation, replaced by the FAR
FY.............Fiscal Year

## G

GAO ..........General Accounting Office
GBL ...........Government Bill of Lading

G&A ..........General and Administrative Costs
GFE ...........Government Furnished Equipment
GFM ..........Government Furnished Material
GFP ...........Government Furnished Property
GOCO .......Government-Owned, Contractor-Operated
GOGO .......Government-Owned, Government-Operated
GPO ..........Government Printing Office
GSA ...........General Services Administration
GSAR ........General Services Administration Acquisition Regulation
GSBCA.......General Services Board of Contract Appeals

## H

HCA...........Head of Contracting Activity
HUD BCA ..Department of Housing and Urban Development Board of Contract Appeals

## I

IBCA ..........Department of Interior Board of Contract Appeals
IFB.............Invitation for Bids
IL&FM .......Installation, Logistics and Financial Management

## J

J&A............Justification and Approval
JAG ...........Judge Advocate General
JAGC.........Judge Advocate General's Corps

## K

K ..............Contract
KO.............Contracting Officer

## L

LBCA .........Department of Labor Board of Contract Appeals

## M

MIPR .........Military Interdepartmental Purchase Request
MCA ..........Military Construction Appropriation Act

# N

NAF ...........Nonappropriated Fund
NAFI .........Nonappropriated Fund Instrumentality
NAPS .........Navy Acquisition Procedures Supplement
NASA .........National Aeronautics and Space Administration
NASA BCA .National Aeronautics and Space Administration Board of Contracts Appeals (dissolved in 1993 and merged with ASBCA)
NCD ..........Navy Contract Directives
NSN ...........National Stock Number

# O

OASD.........Office of the Assistant Secretary of Defense
OFCC ........Office of Federal Contract Compliance
OFPP .........Office of Federal Procurement Policy
O&M .........Operation & Maintenance
OMA..........Operation & Maintenance, Army
OPA ...........Other Procurement, Army
OSD...........Office of the Secretary of Defense

# P

PARC .........Principal Assistant Responsible for Contracting
PCO...........Procuring Contracting Officer
PIL.............Procurement Information Letter (replaced by AL)
PR&C.........Purchase Request and Commitment
PSBCA .......U.S. Postal Service Boards of Contract Appeals
PWD..........Procurement Work Directive

# Q

QPL ...........Qualified Products List

# R

R&D ..........Research and Development
RD&A ........Research, Development and Acquisition
RDTE.........Research, Development, Test and Evaluation

RFP............Request for Proposals
RFQ ...........Request for Quotations
R.S .............Revised Statutes
Rule 4 File..Administrative Record Required by Rule Four of the Procedures of the Armed Services Board ofContract Appeals. See DFARS, App. A.

# S

SADBU ......Small and Disadvantaged Business Utilization
SARDA.......Assistant Secretary of the Army for Research, Development and Acquisition (now ASA(RDA))
SBA............Small Business Administration
SSA ...........Source Selection Authority
SSAC .........Source Selection Advisory Council
SSEB .........Source Selection Evaluation Board

# T

TALF ..........Trial Attorney Litigation File
TAR ..........Department of Transportation Acquisition Regulation
TCO...........Termination Contracting Officer
T for C.......Termination for Convenience (sometimes written T4C or T/C)
T for D ......Termination for Default (sometimes written T4D or T/D)
TINA..........Truth in Negotiations Act

# U

UMMIPS ....Uniform Material Movement and Issue Priority System

# V

VABCA.......Veterans Administration Board of Contract Appeals
VACAB.......Veterans Administration Contract Appeals Board

# Contract Law
# Research Materials

## I. STARTING POINT.

### A. Solicitation Provisions and Contract Clauses.

1. Definitions:

   a. "Solicitation provision" or "provision" means a term or condition used only in solicitations and applying only before contract award. FAR 52.101(a).

   b. "Contract clause" or "clause" means a term or condition used in contracts or in both solicitations and contracts, and applying after contract award or both before and after award. FAR 52.101(a).

2. Read the solicitation/contract.

3. For provisions/clauses incorporated by reference, see FAR Part 52 and Part 52 of the appropriate supplements. *See* FAR 52.102-1.

### B. TJAGSA Contract Law Deskbook.

## II. STATUTES.

A. The Federal Acquisition Streamlining Act of 1994 (FASA) Pub. L. No. 103-355, 108 Stat. 3243 (1994). It amended or repealed many sections of the statutes described below.

B. The Armed Services Procurement Act of 1947 (ASPA). 10 U.S.C. §§ 2301-2331.

   1. Basic procurement statute.

   2. Covers DOD, NASA, and Coast Guard.

C. The Federal Property and Administrative Service Act (FPASA). 41 U.S.C. §§ 251-260.

   1. Basic procurement statute.

   2. Covers GSA and other federal agencies not covered by ASPA.

D. Competition in Contracting Act (CICA). Pub. L. No. 98-369 (1983). Current statutes: 10 U.S.C. §§ 2301-2306; 41 U.S.C. § 403.

   1. Amended ASPA and FPASA to make both statutes identical.

2. Congress has changed both the ASPA and the FPASA since the enactment of CICA, so there now are differences between the statutes.

E. Contract Disputes Act of 1978 (CDA). 41 U.S.C. §§ 601-613.

   1. Waives sovereign immunity for contract appeals to agency boards of contract appeals (BCAs) and direct access suits to the United States Court of Federal Claims.

   2. Covers claim process, certification, litigation, establishment of boards of contract appeals, etc.

F. Tucker Act. 28 U.S.C. § 1491.

   1. Basic jurisdictional statute for the United States Court of Federal Claims.

   2. Creates "exclusive" judicial forum for resolution of pre-award protests. 28 U.S.C. § 1491(a)(3).

G. Brooks Automatic Data Processing Act. 40 U.S.C. § 759.

   1. Covers procurement of automatic data processing equipment (ADPE), currently referred to as federal information processing (FIP) resources by the FIRMR (discussed below).

   2. Jurisdictional statute permits the General Services Administration Board of Contract Appeals (GSBCA) to resolve protests involving ADP procurements.

H. Equal Access To Justice Act. 5 U.S.C. § 504, 28 U.S.C. § 2412(d).

   1. Requires the government to pay attorney's fees if the prevailing party is a small business and the government's position was not substantially justified.

   2. Title 5 applies to the BCAs. Title 28 applies to the U.S. Court of Federal Claims.

I. Annual Authorization and Appropriation Acts.

## III. REGULATIONS.

### A. Federal Acquisition Regulation (FAR).

1. Effective 1 April 1984.
2. General Services Administration operates the FAR Secretariat to print, publish, and distribute the FAR through the Code of Federal Regulations and a loose-leaf edition with periodic updates.
3. The FAR is located at:
   a. 48 C.F.R. Chapter 1.
   b. The loose-leaf edition of the FAR issued by GSA and published by the Government Printing Office (GPO), which is updated periodically by Federal Acquisition Circulars (FACs).
   c. Government Contract Reporter, published by Commerce Clearing House (CCH), Volume 5.
4. Proposed and final changes to the FAR are published in the *Federal Register* and published independently as Federal Acquisition Circulars (FACs). Final changes are incorporated into the C.F.R. and the loose-leaf version of the FAR by GPO. CCH updates the Government Contract Law Reporter.
5. Superseded the Defense Acquisition Regulation (DAR), the Federal Procurement Regulation (FPR), and the NASA Procurement Regulation (NASAPR). [Note that the DAR previously replaced the Armed Services Procurement Regulation (ASPR).]

### B. Departmental and Agency Regulations are located at various chapters of title 48 of the C.F.R. (*See* page 447.)

### C. The FAR System.

1. The FAR is divided into eight (8) subchapters and fifty-three (53) parts.
2. The FAR organizational system applies to the FAR and all agency supplements to the FAR. *See* FAR 1.104-2. (*See* page 448.)

### D. Federal Information Resources Management Regulation (FIRMR).

1. Regulates Federal Information Processing (FIP) Resource (formerly called Automatic Data Processing Equipment (ADPE)) and Telecommunication Systems and Facilities procurements.
2. Published by GSA.
3. Updated periodically by FIRMR amendments.
4. Located at 41 C.F.R. Part 201. *See also* FAR Part 39, Appendix A.

## IV. CASES.

### A. General.

Most court cases concerning government contracts were or are decided in the former Court of Claims, the former U.S. Claims Court, the current U.S. Court of Federal Claims, the U.S. Court of Appeals for the Federal Circuit, and the U.S. Supreme Court. A few contract cases have been decided in the federal District Courts and numbered U.S. Courts of Appeals.

### B. United States Supreme Court.

1. Decisions are reported in the official Supreme Court Reporter (U.S.) and unofficial reporters (S. Ct. and L. Ed. 2d).
2. United States Claims Court Reporter (Cl. Ct.) and United States Federal Claims Reporter (Fed. Cl.) contain procurement-related decisions of the U.S. Supreme Court resulting from appeals from the U.S. Court of Federal Claims and the U.S. Court of Appeals for the Federal Circuit.
3. Federal Court Procurement Decisions (FPD) contains procurement-related decisions of the U.S. Supreme Court resulting from appeals from the U.S. Court of Federal Claims and the U.S. Court of Appeals for the Federal Circuit.
4. New decisions are reported and summarized in United States Law Week (U.S.L.W.).

### C. United States Courts of Appeals.

Cases are reported in West's Federal Reporter (F., F.2d, F.3d). Of primary interest are the decisions of the Court of Appeals for the Federal Circuit upon appeals from the U.S. Court of Federal Claims and the boards of contract

## Agency Supplements to the FAR Found In Title 48, C.F.R.

**Chapter:**

2.　Defense FAR Supplement (DFARS). The DFARS was completely revised in 1991. *See also*: CCH's Government Contract Law Reporter, Volume 6.

3.　Health and Human Services.

4.　Department of Agriculture.

5.　General Services Administration Regulation (GSAR). *See also*: CCH's Government Contract Law Reporter, Volume 7.

6.　Department of State.

7.　Agency For International Development.

8.　Veterans Affairs.

9.　Department of Energy Acquisition Regulation (DEAR). *See also*: CCH's Government Contract Law Reporter, Volume 7.

10.　Treasury.

12.　Department of Transportation Acquisition Regulation (TAR). *See also*: CCH's Government Contract Law Reporter, Volume 7.

13.　Commerce.

14.　Interior.

15.　Environmental Protection Agency.

16, 17. Office of Personnel Management.

18.　NASA FAR Supplement (NFS). *See also*: CCH's Government Contract Law Reporter, Volume 7.

19.　United States Information Agency.

22.　Small Business Administration.

24.　Housing And Urban Development.

25.　National Science Foundation.

28.　Department of Justice.

29.　Department of Labor.

35.　Panama Canal Commission.

44.　Federal Emergency Management Agency.

51.　Department of the Army (AFARS). *See also*: CCH's Government Contract Law Reporter, Volume 6.

52.　Navy Acquisition Procedures Supplement (NAPS). *See also*: CCH's Government Contract Law Reporter, Volume 6.

53.　Department of the Air Force (AFFARS or AF FAR Supplement). *See also*: CCH's Government Contract Law Reporter, Volume 6.

* Defense Logistics Acquisition Regulation Supplement 4105.1 (DLAR). *See also*: CCH'S Government Contract Law Reporter, Volume 6.

---

appeals. The court's contract decisions are reprinted in the FPD, Cl. Ct., Fed. Cl., and CCF.

### D. United States District Courts.

Cases are reported in West Publishing Company's (West) Federal Supplement (F. Supp.).

### E. United States Court of Claims.

Decisions of the old Court of Claims appear in the official United States Court of Claims Reports (Ct. Cl.) and in West's Federal Reporter (before 1960 in West's Federal Supplement). The Federal Courts Improvement Act (FCIA) of

## Subchapter A: General

Part 1: Federal Acquisition Regulations System
Part 2: Definitions of Words and Terms
Part 3: Improper Business Practices and Personal Conflicts of Interest
Part 4: Administrative Matters

## Subchapter B: Acquisition Planning

Part 5: Publicizing Contract Actions
Part 6: Competition Requirements
Part 7: Acquisition Planning
Part 8: Required Sources of Supplies and Services
Part 9: Contractor Qualifications
Part 10: Specifications, Standards, and other Purchase Descriptions
Part 11: Acquisition and Distribution of Commercial Products
Part 12: Contract Delivery or Performance

## Subchapter C: Contracting Methods and Contract Types

Part 13: Small Purchase and Other Simplified Purchase Procedures
Part 14: Sealed Bidding
Part 15: Contracting by Negotiation
Part 16: Types of Contracts
Part 17: Special Contracting Methods
Part 18: [Reserved]

## Subchapter D: Socioeconomic Programs

Part 19: Small Business and Small Disadvantaged Business Concerns
Part 20: Labor Surplus Area Concerns
Part 21: [Reserved]
Part 22: Application of Labor Law to Government Acquisitions
Part 23: Environment, Conservation, Occupational Safety, and Drug-Free Workplace
Part 24: Protection of Privacy and Freedom of Information
Part 25: Foreign Acquisition
Part 26: Other Socioeconomic Programs

## Subchapter E: General Contracting Requirements

Part 27: Patents, Data, and Copyrights
Part 28: Bonds and Insurance
Part 29: Taxes
Part 30: Cost Accounting Standards Administration
Part 31: Contract Cost Principles and Procedures
Part 32: Contract Financing
Part 33: Protests, Disputes, and Appeals

## Subchapter F: Special Categories of Contracting

Part 34: Major System Acquisition
Part 35: Research and Development Contracting
Part 36: Construction and Architect-Engineer Contracts
Part 37: Service Contracting
Part 38: Federal Supply Schedule Contracting
Part 39: Acquisition of Information Resources
Part 40: [Reserved]
Part 41: [Reserved]

## Subchapter G: Contract Management

Part 42: Contract Administration
Part 43: Contract Modifications
Part 44: Subcontracting Policies and Procedures
Part 45: Government Property
Part 46: Quality Assurance
Part 47: Transportation
Part 48: Value Engineering
Part 49: Termination of Contracts
Part 50: Extraordinary Contractual Actions
Part 51: Use of Government Sources by Contractors

## Subchapter H: Clauses and Forms

Part 52: Solicitation Provisions and Contract Clauses
Part 53: Forms

1982 bifurcated the Court of Claims and created the United States Claims Court and the United States Court of Appeals for the Federal Circuit. 28 U.S.C. §§ 171 *et seq.*, 1494-1497, 1499-1503.

## F. United States Claims Court/Court of Federal Claims.

1. Decisions since the court's inception in October 1982 are published in West's Claims Court Reporter (Cl. Ct.). In 1992 (Vol. 27), the publication was renamed the Federal Claims Reporter (Fed. Cl.) with the change in the court's name.
2. The Claims Court/Federal Claims Reporter also contains:
   a. Decisions by the Court of Appeals for Federal Circuit (Fed. Cir.).
   b. U.S. Supreme Court reviews of Claims Court/Court of Federal Claims and Federal Circuit decisions.
3. Published in bi-weekly advance sheets and bound volumes.
4. Features:
   a. Each volume has tables of cases reported, statutes, and rules cited, and a words and phrases index.
   b. West's Key Number Digest.
   c. The Federal Claims Digest, published three times a year, provides cumulative tables of cases, tables of statutes and rules cited, words and phrases, and a Key Number Digest.

## G. Federal Court Procurement Decisions (FPD).

1. The FPDs report government contract decisions issued since 1 October 1982 by the U.S. Claims Court, the U.S. Court of Federal Claims, the U.S. Court of Appeals for the Federal Circuit, and the U.S. Supreme Court.
2. FPDs also include cases that are not officially published; they are printed as "public records" and are not citable as legal precedent.
3. Published monthly by Federal Publications, Inc. (Fed. Pubs., Inc.) in loose-leaf format.
4. Features:

   a. Case name index.
   b. Subject matter index.
   c. Full text of Contract Disputes Act.
   d. Court rules.
   e. Judges' pictures and biographies.

## H. Contract Cases Federal (CCF).

CCF is part of the loose-leaf service published by CCH in the Government Contract Reporter system. CCF contains decisions by the U.S. Court of Federal Claims and other federal courts concerning government contracts.

## V. COMPTROLLER GENERAL'S DECISIONS.

## A. Decisions of the Comptroller General of the United States (Comp. Gen.).

This is the official reporter of Comptroller General's Decisions.

1. Contains decisions rendered to heads of departments and establishments, to disbursing and certifying officers, and to interested parties.
2. Published by Government Printing Office in one volume per fiscal year.
   a. Decisions are presented in full text and represent about ten percent of total decisions rendered annually.
   b. For unpublished decisions and General Accounting Office (GAO) Reports, call the GAO at (202) 512-6000 (see also FLITE).
3. Features:
   a. Table of Decision Numbers - pre-1939 numbers begin with "A" prefix; post-1939 numbers begin with "B" prefix.
   b. Alphabetical list of claimants.
   c. Subject matter index.
   d. List of statutes, court cases, and Comptroller decisions cited.
4. GAO telephone research services.

## B. Comptroller General's Procurement Decisions (CPD).

1. Covers published and unpublished decisions issued by the Comptroller General since 1974.

2. Published by Federal Publications, Inc. in one or two volumes per calendar year.
3. Features:
   a. B- number index.
   b. Subject matter index.
   c. Index cross referencing the CPD's to official reporter.

### C. Comptroller General Decisions (CGEN).

1. CGEN is part of the loose-leaf service published by CCH in the Government Contract Reporter system. CGEN covers published and unpublished decisions by the Comptroller General issued since November 1986.
2. Select current Comptroller General decisions are published in the Government Contract Reporter, Volume 10. Periodically, they are transferred to "CGEN" binders.
3. Features:
   a. Subject matter index.
   b. B- number index.

## VI. DECISIONS OF BOARDS OF CONTRACT APPEALS.

### A. Board of Contract Appeals Decisions (BCA).

1. Includes most decisions and orders of the various boards of contract appeals.
2. Published by CCH in bound case books dating from 1956 (first volume is 56-2). One or more volumes are published annually depending on the number of decisions issued (three volumes per year since 1984).
3. Features:
   a. Alphabetical list of appellants.
   b. Docket number by title of board.
   c. Topical index.
   d. Board rules.
   e. Judges' biographies.
4. BCA decisions are initially published in the Government Contract Reporter loose-leaf system published by CCH. These decisions are published with the BCA volume and paragraph citation that will be designated in the bound BCA volume, so the loose-leaf issue is cited the same as the bound volume.

5. New BCA decisions are published bi-weekly in the Government Contract Reporter, Volume 9. They are superseded by the bound volumes of the BCAs.

## VII. COMMERCIAL TOPICAL SERVICES.

### A. Government Contracts Reporter.

1. Comprehensive procurement legal research tool.
2. Published in loose-leaf form and very timely.
3. Published by CCH in ten volumes:
   a. Volume 1 describes how to use the reporter, and it includes a topical index, case table, finding lists, and text coverage with annotation of the following subjects: Authority, Policy, Socioeconomic Programs, Methods of Procurement, Types of Contracts, Solicitations, Bids, Offers, Responsiveness, Mistakes.
   b. Volume 2 contains textual discussion with annotation on the following subjects: Selection, Price and Cost, Responsibility, Interpretation, Performance, Quality, Defaults, Delays, Patents, Bonds, Cost Principles.
   c. Volumes 3 and 4 contain textual discussion with annotation on the following subjects: Contract Performance; Quality Assurance; Defaults; Intellectual Property; Bonds; Cost Principles; Contract Management, Modifications, Terminations; Government Furnished Property; Disputes and Remedies; Government Financing and Payments. They also includes important procurement statutes and executive orders.
   d. Volume 5 contains the FAR.
   e. Volume 6 contains the Defense, military service, and defense agency FAR Supplements.
   f. Volume 7 contains FAR supplements for the civilian agencies; the Cost Accounting Standards; and the Federal Information Resources Management Regulation (FIRMR).
   g. Volume 8 contains a cumulative index that coordinates new developments back to the topical discussion in the first three volumes.

It also includes a current topical index and the Contract Cases Federal (CCF).

h. Volume 9 contains the BCA decisions and a section on new developments that contains items of interest in government contracting, such as proposals by the Defense Acquisition Regulatory Council and the Civilian Agency Acquisition Council to amend the FAR.

i. Volume 10 contains the Comptroller General Decisions (CGEN).

## VIII. CITATORS.

### A. Shepard's Federal Citations.

### B. Government Contracts Citator.

1. Published by Federal Publications, Inc.
2. Produced in two volumes in loose-leaf format.
   a. Basic Cumulation: 1956 through 1976.
   b. Supplementary Cumulation: 1977 through 1987.
3. Updated quarterly on various colored pages.
4. Arranged in two major divisions.
5. Court and agency opinions division.
   a. Opinions listed alphabetically by name of contractor.
   b. Name of each court or agency taking action on the case.
   c. Primary volume in which case is reported.
   d. Government Contracts citation.
   e. Names of decisions which have cited the decision.
6. Comptroller General's decisions division.
   a. Government volume section - officially published decisions listed by Comp. Gen. citation, B- number, and CPD citation.
   b. B- number section - not officially published decisions listed by B- number and CPD citation.
   c. Government Contracts citation.
   d. Other decisions citing the opinion.

### C. Commerce Clearing House (CCH) Citator Service.

1. The bound CCH Board of Contract Appeals Decisions and the loose-leaf CCH Contract Appeals Decisions include a citator for all board decisions in the CCH service.
2. The Main Citator Table is in one volume and includes BCA decisions from 56-2 through 86-1.
3. List of more recent decisions is contained in the current Citator Table of Contract Appeals Decisions Reports.

## IX. COMPUTER-ASSISTED LEGAL RESEARCH.

### A. LEXIS (Mead Data Central).

### B. WESTLAW (West Publishing Company).

### C. Federal Legal Information Through Electronics (FLITE).

1. Managed by the US Air Force, Legal Services and Research Division; Maxwell AFB, Alabama.
2. Covers BCA decisions; Comptroller General opinions; federal court decisions, and Army and Air Force regulations.
3. Also has access to LEXIS and WESTLAW.
4. Free to Air Force Attorneys. Army attorneys can access FLITE through the Corps of Engineers Automated Legal System (CEALS). Other federal agencies must pay a fee (amount varies with size of search). However, the Legal Research Division will perform research for all DOD attorneys free of charge.
5. Phone number: (334) 953-3008, DSN 493-3008. You can FAX your questions to the Research Division at: (334) 953-3008, DSN 453-7159.

### D. LAAWS Bulletin Board Service.

1. Operated by the Department of the Army, Office of the Judge Advocate General.
2. This electronic bulletin board serves as a clearinghouse for information and questions on government contract and fiscal law; environmental law; ethics and standards of conduct; and procurement integrity.
3. Free to Department of Defense attorneys.
4. TJAGSA Contract Law Deskbooks are regular-

ly uploaded to bulletin board and may be downloaded by authorized users.

5. Call (703) 806-5772 to sign onto the bulletin board.

## X. SPECIALIZED SOURCES.

### A. Extraordinary Contractual Relief Reporter (ECR).

1. Decisions under Public Law 85-804. *See* FAR Part 50.

2. Published by Federal Publications, Inc. in loose-leaf form.

3. Three volumes (Vol. 1, 1958-1965; Vol. 2, 1966-1973; Vol. 3, 1974-1980; loose-leaf binder covers to current date).

4. Updated periodically.

### B. Commerce Clearing House Labor Law Reporter.

1. Covers government labor standards.

2. Published by Commerce Clearing House in loose-leaf form.

3. Updated periodically.

### C. Cost Accounting Standards Guide.

1. Covers actions of Cost Accounting Board, federal agencies, and Congress concerning cost accounting practices.

2. Published by CCH in loose-leaf form.

3. Updated periodically.

## XI. JOURNALS AND PERIODICALS.

### A. The Government Contractor (GC).

1. Published by Federal Publications, Inc.

2. Produced weekly in loose-leaf format.

3. Contains reports and analyses of all *significant* government contract decisions and rulings by the courts, boards, and Comptroller General. It also gives notice of proposed and final statutory and regulatory changes.

4. Dates from January 1959. The bi-weekly issues of the publication are consolidated into bound volumes every three years.

5. Material is indexed by name, decision number, and subject matter.

### B. Federal Contracts Reports (Fed. Cont. Rep.).

1. Published by the Bureau of National Affairs, Inc. (BNA).

2. Produced weekly since 1964 in a newsletter format.

3. Reports on all major developments in government contracts.

4. Provides commentary and "history" leading up to changes in law and regulation.

5. Indexed by subject matter and contains a table of cases reported.

6. Cumulative indices are issued each quarter and each six months.

### C. Public Contract Law Journal (Pub. Cont. L.J.).

1. Specializes in contract law articles.

2. Published by Section on Public Contract Law of the American Bar Association.

3. Members also receive the Public Contract Newsletter (Pub. Cont. Newsl.) four times each year.

### D. The Nash & Cibinic Report (N&CR).

1. Published monthly by Federal Publications, Inc. beginning January 1987.

2. Provides government contract analysis by Professors Ralph C. Nash and John Cibinic.

3. Publishes monthly articles on varying areas of government contract law.

4. A N&C Roundtable held in early December of each year is complimentary to subscribers. The Round-table offers a discussion by guest experts of several major areas of current interest.

### E. Briefing Papers.

1. Monthly issue deals with a specific area of contract law - emphasis is practical.

2. Published by Federal Publications, Inc.

### F. National Contract Management Association.

1. National Contract Management Journal. Two volumes per year.

2. Contract Management magazine. Monthly.

3. Both publications contain typically non-legal discussion of broad range of procurement and contract administration issues.

## G. Government Contracts Costs, Pricing & Accounting Report.
1. Monthly issues include feature articles, comments, and discussion of financial issues.
2. Published by Federal Publications, Inc.
3. Cumulative indexes published periodically.

## H. The Army Lawyer.
1. Monthly Contract Law Notes.
2. Recent Developments in Contract Law - 19XX (Year) in Review, published in February of each year.

## I. Military Law Review.

## J. Air Force Law Review.

## XII. TEXTS/BOOKS.

A. Frank M. Alston, Margaret M. Worthington & Lewis P. Goldsman, *Contracting with the Federal Government*, published by John Wiley & Sons, Inc., 3d edition, 1992. Written primarily for accounting audience. Incorporates numerous FAR forms.

B. Donald P. Arnavas and William J. Ruberry, *Government Contract Guidebook*, published by Federal Publications, Inc., 1st edition, 1986, 1990 supplement. Broad overview of formation and administration issues.

C. James P. Bedingfield and Louis I. Rosen, *Government Contract Accounting*, published by Federal Publications, Inc., 2d edition, 1985.

D. Richard J. Bednar, John Cibinic, Jr., Ralph C. Nash, Jr., *et al.*, *Construction Contracting*, published by the George Washington University Government Contracts Program, 1991.

E. John Cibinic, Jr. and Ralph C. Nash, Jr., *Formation of Government Contracts*, published by the George Washington University Government Contracts Program, 2d edition, 1986. Replaces Volume I, *Federal Procurement Law*.

F. John Cibinic, Jr. and Ralph C. Nash, Jr., *Administration of Government Contracts*, published by the George Washington University Government Contracts Program, 3d edition, 1995. Replaces Volume II, *Federal Procurement Law*.

G. John Cibinic, Jr. and Ralph C. Nash, Jr., *Cost Reimbursement Contracting*, published by the George Washington University Government Contracts Program, 2d edition, 1993.

H. John Cibinic, Jr. and Ralph C. Nash, Jr., *Competitive Negotiation: The Source Selection Process*, published by the George Washington University Governmetn Contracts Program, 1993.

I. Department of Defense, *Armed Services Pricing Manual* (ASPM), published by the Government Printing Office in 2 volumes in 1986, 1987.

J. DOD Defense Contract Audit Agency, *DCAA Contract Audit Manual*, DCAAM 7640.1, published by the Government Printing Office in 2 volumes, updated regularly.

K. Brian C. Elmer, Jean-Pierre Swennen and Richard L. Beizer, *Government Contract Fraud*, published by Federal Publications, Inc., 1985.

L. General Accounting Office, *Principles of Federal Appropriations Law: Volumes I & II*, published by the Government Printing Office, July 1991 and December 1992.

M. Andrew K. Gallagher, *Negotiated Procurement*, published by GCA Publications, Inc. in hardback with looseleaf supplements through 1984. Outdated, but still useful.

N. Noel Keyes, *Government Contracts Under The FAR*, published by West Publishing, 1986, and pocket part. Organized to coincide with the FAR's 53 parts.

O. Peter S. Latham, *Government Contract Disputes*, published by Federal Publications, Inc., 2d edition, 1988, 1991 supplement.

P. James F. Nagle, *How to Review a Federal Contract & Research Federal Contract Law*, published by the American Bar Association, 1990.

Q. James F. Nagle, *History of Government Con-*

*tracting*, published by The George Washington University Government Contracts Program, 1992.

R. Ralph C. Nash, Jr., *Government Contract Changes*, published by Federal Publications, Inc., 2d edition, 1989.

S. Ralph C. Nash, Jr. and Leonard Rawicz, *Patents and Technical Data*, published by the George Washington University Government Contracts Program, 1983, with 1992 supplement.

T. Ralph C. Nash, Jr. and Steven L. Schooner, *The Government Contracts Reference Book: A Comprehensive Guide to the Language of Procurement*, published by The George Washington University Government Contracts Program, 1992.

U. Walter Pettit, Carl Vacketta, and David Anthony, *Government Contract Default Terminations*, published by Federal Publications, Inc., 1991.

V. Melvin Rishe, *Contract Costs*, published by Federal Publications, Inc., 1984.

W. William Rudland, *Defective Pricing*, published by Federal Contracting Press, 1990.

X. Seyfarth, Shaw, Fairweather & Geraldson, *The Government Contract Compliance Handbook*, published by Federal Publications, Inc., 2d edition, 1991. Good appendices.

Y. Paul Shnitzer, *Government Contract Bidding*, published by Federal Publications, Inc., 3d edition, 1987, 1991 supplement.

Z. John W. Whelan, *Federal Government Contracts: Cases and Materials*, published by Foundation Press in 1985, with supplements.

## XIII. REFERENCES.

A. "Techniques for Researching Public Contract Law," by Holmes and Holmes, 10 Public Contract Law Journal 58 (1978).

B. Army Law Library Service: (804) 972-6394.

# *Solicitation/Contract Award Checklist*

**NOTE:** *The following checklist is a "broad brush" tool designed to assist you GENERALLY in conducting solicitation and contract award reviews. Many agencies and commands have adopted more detailed procedures for solicitation and contract award reviews. If your agency has adopted additional policies and procedures, you should use that guidance. DO NOT use this as a substitute for examining the relevant statutes and regulations involved as needed.*

## SECTION I— SOLICITATION DOCUMENTATION

**1. Purchase request.**

a. Is it in the file?

b. Is the desired delivery date consistent with that stated in the IFB/RFP?

c. Does the description of the desired supplies or services correspond to that of the IFB/RFP?

d. Are funds properly certified as available for obligation?

e. Are the funds proper as to purpose and period of availability, and are they of sufficient amount?

**2. Method of acquisition.**

a. What is the proposed method of acquisition?

b. Is the "sealed bidding" method required? FAR 6.401(a).

c. Has the activity excluded sources? If so, have applicable competition requirements been met? FAR Subpart 6.2.

d. Has the activity proposed meeting its requirement without obtaining full and open competition? FAR Subpart 6.3.

e. Does a statutory exception permit other than full and open competition? FAR 6.302.

f. If other than full and open competition is proposed, has the contracting officer prepared the required justification and is all required information included? FAR 6.303. Does it make sense?

g. Have the appropriate officials reviewed and approved the justification? FAR 6.304.

**3. Publicizing the solicitation.**

a. Has the contracting officer published the solicitation as required by FAR 5.101 and FAR Subpart 5.2?

b. Has the activity allowed adequate time for publication? FAR 5.203.

c. Is there a proposed bidders list? FAR 14.203, FAR 14.205, and FAR 15.403. Is it adequate? If less than the entire list is being solicited, has the contracting officer properly limited potential offerors? FAR 14.205-4.

**4. Solicitation instructions.**

a. Are the date, time, and place for submission of offers indicated? Is the notation on the cover sheet consistent with the SF 30?

b. Is the time for submission of offers adequate? FAR 14.202-1.

c. Are required clauses listed in FAR 14.201 (for IFBs) or FAR 15.406 (for RFPs) included in the solicitation?

d. If a construction contract, have the special requirements and procedures of FAR Part 36 been followed?

**5. Evaluation factors.**

a. Does the solicitation state the evaluation factors that will be used to determine award? For sealed bids, *see* FAR 14.101(e) and FAR 14.201-8. For competitive proposals or negotiation, *see* FAR 15.605.

b. Are the evaluation factors clear, reasonable, and not unduly restrictive?

c. In competitive proposals or negotiations, are all factors identified, including cost or price and any significant subfactors that will be considered? Is the relative importance of each disclosed? FAR 15.406-5(c) and FAR 15.605.

**6. Pricing.**
a. Is the method of pricing clear?
b. If there are deliverables that are priced in another line item, is this clearly stated?
c. Does the solicitation clearly state how the price will be determined if the unit price and the extended price are ambiguous?
d. Are appropriate audit clauses included in the solicitation? FAR 14.201-7 and FAR 15.106.
e. Does the Truth in Negotiations Act apply to this solicitation or request? FAR Subpart 15.8.
f. If the Truth in Negotiations Act applies, does the solicitation contain the required clauses? FAR 15.804-8.
g. Are the clauses required by FAR 15.904 applicable, and have they been included in the solicitation?

**7. Contract Type.**
a. Is the proposed type of contract appropriate? FAR 14.104 and FAR 16.102.
b. If the proposed contract is a service contract, has the determination concerning personal or nonpersonal services been executed? FAR 37.103.
c. If the proposed contract is a requirements contract, is the estimated total quantity stated? Is the estimate reasonable? If feasible, does the solicitation also state the maximum quantity? FAR 16.503. Is appropriate ordering and delivery information set out? FAR 16.506. Are required clauses included in the solicitation? FAR 16.505.
d. If the proposed contract is an indefinite quantity type contract, are the minimum and maximum quantities stated and reasonable? FAR 16.504. Is appropriate ordering and delivery information set out? FAR 16.506. Are required clauses included in the solicitation? FAR 16.505.
e. Are special clauses required by the proposed

type of contract included in the solicitation? *See* FAR Part 16.
f. Does the selected contract type reflect sound business judgment?

**8. Purchase description or specifications.**
a. Are the purchase descriptions or specifications adequate and unambiguous? FAR 10.002; FAR 14.201-2(b) and (c); FAR 15.406-2(c).
b. If a brand name or equal specification is used, is it used properly? FAR 10.004(b)(3). Does the solicitation include DFARS 252.210-7000, Brand Name or Equal?
c. Are the provisions required by FAR 10.011 included in the solicitation?

**9. Descriptive data and samples.**
a. Will bidders be required to submit descriptive data or bid samples with their bids?
b. If so, have the requirements of FAR 14.202-4 and FAR 14.202-5 been met?

**10. Packing, inspection, and delivery.**
a. Is there an F.O.B. point? FAR 46.505.
b. Are appropriate quality control requirements identified? FAR 46.202.
c. Is there a point of preliminary inspection and acceptance? FAR 46.402.
d. Is there a point of final inspection? FAR 46.403.
e. Have the place of acceptance and the activity or individual to make acceptance been specified? FAR 46.502; FAR 46.503.
f. Are preservation, packaging, and packing requirements set forth? FAR 10.004(e).
g. Is the delivery schedule reasonable? FAR Part 12.

**11. Bonds and liquidated damages.**
a. Are bonds required? FAR Part 28.
b. If so, are the requirements clearly stated in the specification?
c. Is there a liquidated damages clause? Does it conform to the requirements of FAR 12.202? Is the amount reasonable? Are required clauses incorporated? FAR 12.204.

## 12. Government-furnished property.

a. Will the government furnish any type of property, real or personal, in the performance of the contract?

b. If so, is the property clearly identified in the schedule or specifications? Is the date of delivery clearly specified?

c. Has the contractor's property accountability system been reviewed and found adequate? FAR 45.104.

d. Are the contractor's and the government's responsibilities and liabilities stated clearly? FAR 52.245-2; FAR 52.245-5.

e. Have applicable requirements of FAR Part 45 been met? Are required clauses present?

## 13. Environmental issues.

a. Do the contract specifications require use of an ozone-depleting substance? DFARS 207.109; DFARS 210.002-71. If so, has the appropriate official granted a waiver? DFARS 210.002-71.

b. Has the government considered procurement of items containing recycled or recovered materials? FAR 23.401.

c. Has the government attempted to eliminate hazardous materials from the solicitation's requirements? DOD Dir. 4210.5(D).

d. Has the government considered energy efficiency and conservation in drafting its specifications and statement of work? FAR 23.203.

## 14. Labor standards.

a. Does the Davis-Bacon Act or Service Contract Act apply to this acquisition? *See* FAR Subparts 22.4 and 22.10.

b. If so, have the proper clauses and wage rate determinations been incorporated into the solicitation?

## 15. Clarity and completeness.

a. Have you read the entire solicitation?

b. Do you understand it?

c. Are there any ambiguities?

d. Is it complete?

e. Are the provisions, requirements, clauses, etc. consistent?

f. Are there any unusual provisions or clauses in the solicitation? Do you understand them? Do they apply?

## SECTION II— CONTRACT AWARD CHECKLIST

### 1. Sealed Bid Contracts.

a. Review the previous legal review of the solicitation. Has the contracting activity made all required or recommended corrections?

b. Did the contracting officer amend the solicitation? If so, did the contracting officer distribute amendments properly? FAR 14.208.

c. Has a bid abstract been prepared? FAR 14.403. Is it complete? Does it disclose any problems?

d. Is the lowest bid responsive? FAR 14.404-2; FAR 14.404-5; FAR 14.405. Are there any apparent irregularities?

e. Is there reason to believe that the low bidder made a mistake? FAR 14.406. Has the contracting officer verified the bid?

f. Has the contracting officer properly determined the low bidder? FAR 14.407; FAR 14.201-8.

g. Is the price fair and reasonable? FAR 14.407-2.

h. Has the contracting officer properly determined the low bidder to be responsible? FAR 14.407-2; FAR Subpart 9.1.

i. Did the contracting officer address any late or improperly submitted bids? FAR Subpart 14.3.

j. Are sufficient and proper funds cited?

k. Has the activity incorporated all required clauses and any applicable special clauses?

l. Is the proposed contract clear and unambiguous? Does it accurately reflect the requiring activity's needs?

m. Does the activity still need the item or service?

n. Has the contracting officer obtained all required approvals? FAR 14.407-1.

o. If a construction contract, have FAR Part 36 requirements been satisfied?

p. If the acquisition required a synopsis in the *Commerce Business Daily*, is there evidence of that synopsis in the file? Was the synopsis proper?

**2. Negotiated Contracts.**

a. Review the previous legal review of the request for proposals. Have all required or recommended corrections been made?

b. Were any amendments to the request for proposals made? If so, were they properly made and distributed? FAR 15.410.

c. Was any pre-proposal conference properly conducted? FAR 15.409.

d. Did the contracting officer address any late or improperly submitted proposals? FAR 15.412.

e. Has an abstract of proposals been prepared? Is it complete? Does it reveal any problems?

f. Is a pre-negotiation Business Clearance Memorandum (BCM) required? Is it complete? Does it reveal any problems? FAR 15.807; AFARS 15.890.

g. Were discussions conducted? FAR 15.610; FAR 15.607.

h. If the answer to *g* is no, did the solicitation contain a clause notifying offerors that the government intended to award without discussions? FAR 15.610(a).

i. If the answer to *g* is yes, were discussions held with all offerors in the properly determined competitive range? FAR 15.609; FAR 15.610; FAR 15.610(b).

j. Were proposals evaluated in accordance with the factors set forth in the request for proposals? FAR 15.608.

k. Were any changes to the government's requirements addressed properly by the contracting officer? FAR 15.606.

l. Were offerors properly notified of the request for best and final offers? FAR 15.611.

m. Were applicable source selection procedures followed and documented? FAR 15.612.

n. If applicable, did the contracting officer address make or buy proposals? FAR Subpart 15.7.

o. If the Truth in Negotiations Act applies, has the contractor submitted a proper certification? Is it complete and signed? FAR 15.804.

p. Is a post-negotiation Business Clearance Memorandum required? Is it complete? Does it reveal any problems? FAR 15.808; AFARS 15.890.

q. Has the activity resolved any audit exceptions? AFARS 15.891.

r. Are all negotiated prices set forth in the contract?

s. Does the proposed contract reflect all agreements reached during negotiation?

t. Has the contracting officer incorporated required and special clauses in the proposed contract?

u. Is the activity using the most appropriate type of contract?

v. Does the proposed profit or fee exceed that permitted by law? FAR 15.903(d).

w. Is the proposed price fair and reasonable?

x. Are sufficient and proper funds cited?

y. Is the proposed contract clear and unambiguous? Does it make sense? Does it reflect the requiring activity's needs?

z. If a construction contract, has the contracting officer satisfied the requirements of FAR Part 36 (and supplements)?

# Section of Public Contract Law

The mission of the Section of Public Contract Law is to improve public procurement and grant law at the federal, state, and local levels and promote the professional development of attorney and associate members in public procurement law. The Section pursues this mission through a structured committee system and educational and training programs that welcome and encourage member involvement.

The Section's goal is simple, yet ambitious: to be the most reliable, most respected nationwide source of balanced, unbiased, positive recommendations for improving the law relating to procurement at all levels of government. Because of its unique position as a national organization composed of lawyers and associates from government, corporations, and law firms, the Section has an extraordinary opportunity and a duty to work for improvements to the procurement process. To meet this opportunity, the Section is trying continuously to create an atmosphere in which the interests of all participants in the procurement process are heard, understood, and incorporated in Section proposals and activities.

## Application for Membership

Yes, enroll me in the Section of Public Contract Law. My ABA ID # is: ___ ___ ___ ___ ___ ___ ___ ___/___ ___

   ___ $35 for ABA members or associates.

   ___ $25 for lawyers or judges in government service.

   ___ $5 for ABA Law Student Division members.

*Note:* Membership or affiliation in the American Bar Association is a prerequisite to enrollment in the Section.

   ___ Please send an application to join the American Bar Association.

      ___ I am an attorney.

      ___ I am not an attorney.

   ___ I am a judge or lawyer in government or public service. Please send me information about the Joint Dues Program with the Government and Public Sector Lawyers Division.

CARD NUMBER _____

EXP. DATE _____ SIGNATURE _____ DATE _____

NAME _____

FIRM/ORGANIZATION _____

SUITE NUMBER/FLOOR _____ ADDRESS _____

CITY _____ STATE _____ ZIP _____

BUSINESS TELEPHONE _____ HOME TELEPHONE _____

$_____ Section Annual Dues

$_____ Publications Order Amount

$_____ TOTAL

_____ Payment enclosed (Make check payable to: American Bar Association)

_____ Visa _____ MasterCard

Dues include a $10.00 basic subscription to *Public Contract Law Journal* for one year. Membership dues in the American Bar Association and ABA Sections are not deductible as charitable contributions for Federal income tax purposes. However, such dues may be deductible as a business expense.

### Complete and return to:

ABA Section of Public Contract Law
750 North Lake Shore Drive
Chicago, Illinois 60611-4497

**312/988-5596**